Countries and Concepts

is in reader.

19 in reader
pg 86.

COUNTRIES AND CONCEPTS

POLITICS, GEOGRAPHY, CULTURE

TENTH EDITION

Michael G. Roskin

LYCOMING COLLEGE

PEARSON
Longman

New York San Francisco Boston
London Toronto Sydney Tokyo Singapore Madrid
Mexico City Munich Paris Cape Town Hong Kong Montreal

Acquisitions Editor: Vikram Mukhija
Executive Marketing Manager: Ann Stypuloski
Supplements Editor: Brian Belardi
Senior Media Editor: Regina Vertiz
Production Manager: Savoula Amanatidis
Project Coordination, Text Design, and Electronic Page Makeup: Big Sky Composition
Cover Design Manager: John Callahan
Cover Designer: Base Art Co.
Cover Photos: *Top left:* voting begins in Iranian elections (Majid/Stringer/Getty Images News); *top right:* Deng Pufang
talks with governor of Guangdong Province Lu Ruihua (Andrew Wong/Corbis/Reuters America LLC); *bottom left:*
Nigerian President Umaru Yar'Adua greets Indian Prime Minister Manmohan Singh (AFP/Getty Images);
bottom right: German Chancellor Angela Merkel and French President Nicolas Sarkozy (Axel Schmidt/AFP/
Getty Images)
Photo Researcher: IRC
Senior Manufacturing Buyer: Alfred C. Dorsey
Printer and Binder: R. R. Donnelley and Sons Company–Owensville
Cover Printer: Phoenix Color Corporation

Library of Congress Cataloging-in-Publication Data

Roskin, Michael
    Countries and concepts: politics, geography, culture/Michael G. Roskin.—10th ed.
      p. cm.
    Includes bibliographical references and index.
    ISBN 978-0-13-602653-2
    1. Comparative government.   I. Title.
JF51.R54 2008
320.3—dc22

                                        2008024579

Please visit us at www.pearsonhighered.com

ISBN-13: 978-0-13-602653-2
ISBN-10: 0-13-602653-2

2 3 4 5 6 7 8 9 10—ROO—11 10 09

Brief Contents

PART II   THE DEVELOPING AREAS   368

CONTENTS

CHAPTER 11   WHAT THE FRENCH QUARREL ABOUT   146

CHAPTER 12   GERMANY: THE IMPACT OF THE PAST   160

CHAPTER 13   GERMANY: THE KEY INSTITUTIONS   178

CHAPTER 14   GERMAN Political Culture   194

Chapter 6   What Britons Quarrel About   72

Chapter 7   France: The Impact of the Past   86

Chapter 8   France: The Key Institutions   102

Chapter 9   French Political Culture   118

CHAPTER 10   FRANCE: PATTERNS OF INTERACTION   132

CHAPTER 15   GERMANY: PATTERNS OF INTERACTION   208

CHAPTER 16   WHAT GERMANS QUARREL ABOUT   224

CHAPTER 17   THE EUROPEAN UNION   238

CHAPTER 18   JAPAN   258

CHAPTER 19   RUSSIA: THE IMPACT OF THE PAST   294

CHAPTER 20   RUSSIA: THE KEY INSTITUTIONS   310

CHAPTER 21   RUSSIAN POLITICAL CULTURE   326

CHAPTER 22   RUSSIA: PATTERNS OF INTERACTION   340

CHAPTER 23   WHAT RUSSIANS QUARREL ABOUT   354

PART II   THE DEVELOPING AREAS   368

CHAPTER 24   CHINA: THE IMPACT OF THE PAST   370

CHAPTER 25   CHINA: THE KEY INSTITUTIONS   386

Chapter 26   Chinese Political Culture   400

Chapter 27   China: Patterns of Interaction   414

CHAPTER 30   MEXICO   476

Chapter 31   Nigeria   510

CHAPTER 32   IRAN   540

Preface

Countries and Concepts does not attempt to create young scholars out of college students. Rather, it sees comparative politics as an important but usually neglected grounding in citizenship that we should be making available to our young people. I agree with the late Morris Janowitz (in his 1983 *The Reconstruction of Patriotism: Education for Civic Consciousness*) that civic education has declined in the United States and that this poses dangers for democracy. Our students are often uninformed about the historical, political, economic, geographical, and moral aspects of democracy, and to expose them to professional-level abstractions in political science ignores their civic education and offers material that is largely meaningless to them. An undergraduate is not a miniature graduate student.

Accordingly, *Countries and Concepts* includes a good deal of fundamental vocabulary and concepts, buttressed by many examples. It is readable. Many students neglect assigned readings; with *Countries and Concepts*, they can't make the excuse that the reading is long or boring.

Some reviewers have noted that *Countries and Concepts* contains values and criticisms. This is part of my purpose. The two go together; if you have no values, then you have no basis from which to criticize. Value-free instruction is probably impossible. If successful, it would produce value-free students, and that, I think, should not be the aim of the educational enterprise. If one knows something with the head but not with the heart, then one really does not know it at all.

Is *Countries and Concepts* too critical? It treats politics as a series of ongoing quarrels for which no very good solutions can be found. It casts a skeptical eye on all political systems and all solutions proposed for political problems. As such, the book is not out to "get" any one country. All political systems are flawed; none approach perfection. Let us simply say so. *Countries and Concepts* rejects absurd theories of smoothly functioning systems or rational calculators that never break down or make mistakes. Put it this way: If we are critical of the workings of our own country's politics—and many, perhaps most, of us are—why should we abandon that critical spirit in looking at other lands?

FEATURES

The tenth edition continues the loose theoretical approach of the previous editions with the simple observation that politics, on the surface at least, is composed of a number of human conflicts or quarrels. These quarrels, if observed over time, usually form patterns of some durability beyond the specific issues involved. What I call patterns of interaction are the relationships among politically relevant groups and individuals, what they call in Russian *kto-kovo*, who does what to whom. There are two general types of such patterns: (1) between elites and masses, and (2) among and within elites.

Before we can appreciate these patterns, however, we must first study the political culture of a particular country, which leads us to its political institutions and ultimately to its political history. Thus we have a five-fold division in the study of each country. We could start with a country's contemporary political quarrels and work backward, but it is probably better to begin with the underlying factors as a foundation from which to understand their impact on modern social conflict. This book goes from history to institutions to political culture to patterns of interaction to quarrels. This arrangement need not supplant other approaches. Instructors have had no trouble utilizing this book in connection with their preferred theoretical insights.

Also, political geography gets much deserved attention. Instructors agree that ignorance of geography is widespread; the subject seems to have been dropped from most school curricula. *Countries and Concepts* tries to fill this gap by combining political with geographical material, and the two fields overlap.

The structure and purpose of *Countries and Concepts* continue as before. The book analyzes four European nations plus China at some length (with five chapters devoted to each nation) and five other nations plus the European Union more briefly (with one long chapter for each nation and one long chapter for the European Union). The first part of the book (Chapters 2 through 23) deals with countries in developed areas, while the second part (Chapters 24 through 32) deals with countries in developing areas.

Inclusion of the developing areas—or Third World or Global South, call it what you will—in a first comparative course is problematic. The nations of Asia, Latin America, and Africa are so complex and differentiated that many (myself included) think labeling them with a single term is impossible. The semester is only so long. But if students are going to take only one comparative course—all too often the case nowadays—then they should get some exposure to the majority of humankind. I include, therefore, full-length treatment of China and briefer treatment of four emerging systems: India, Mexico, Nigeria, and Iran. These countries are not "representative" systems—what developing-area countries are?—but are interesting in their five different relationships to democracy: (1) the suppression of democracy in a rapidly industrializing China; (2) a durable if imperfect democracy in India; (3) democracy struggling in Mexico after a long period of one-party rule; (4) the difficult founding of a stable democracy in coup-prone Nigeria; and (5) democracy smothered by an Islamic revolution in Iran. These five systems provide a counterpoise to the more settled systems of Europe and Japan. Instructors can and do omit some or all of these emerging systems—for lack of time or in order to focus more closely on other countries—without breaking the continuity of the text.

The order of studying these ten countries is not fixed. I teach my own course in four groups, each followed by an exam, to facilitate comparisons between countries with similar problems: (1) Britain and France, (2) Germany and Japan, (3) Russia and China, and (4) India, Mexico, Nigeria, and Iran. The book may lend itself to other groupings.

Also included are the chapter-opening questions, which prime students for the main points, and the running marginal glossaries, which help students build their vocabularies as they read. The definitions here are those of a political scientist; in other contexts one might find different definitions. The feature boxes still have poster-heads—Geography, Democracy, Personalities, Political Culture, Key Concepts, and Comparison—to give them greater focus and continuity.

New to This Edition

Instructor input has prompted some major changes in this tenth edition of *Countries and Concepts*. Due to rapid economic growth, the world is paying more attention to the world's largest democracy; therefore, I have added India to the book. India is covered in one long chapter, as are Mexico, Nigeria, and Iran. Also, to hold down the total number of book pages (after having doubled the China coverage in the ninth edition), I have consolidated the coverage of Japan from five short chapters into one long chapter. (I did this with a heavy heart because Japan is fascinating.) Still, instructors will find that all of the main points about Japan remain in this edition.

Supplements

Longman is pleased to offer several resources to qualified adopters of this book and their students that will make teaching and learning from *Countries and Concepts* even more effective and enjoyable. Several of the supplements for this book are available at the Instructor Resource Center (IRC), an online hub that allows instructors to quickly download book-specific supplements. Please visit the IRC welcome page at www.ablongman.com/irc to register for access.

For Instructors

MyPoliSciKit for *Countries and Concepts*   This premium online learning resource features multimedia and interactive activities to help students make connections between concepts and current events. The book-specific assessment, video case studies, comparative exercises, mapping exercises, ABC newsfeeds, and a politics blog encourage comprehension and critical thinking. With GradeTracker, instructors can easily follow students' work on the site and their progress on each activity. MyPoliSciKit is available at no additional charge when packaged with this book. To learn more, please visit www.mypoliscikit.com or contact your Pearson representative.

MyPoliSciKit Video Case Studies for International Relations and Comparative Politics   This DVD series contains video clips featured in the MyPoliSciKit case studies for this and other Longman political science titles. Featuring video from major news sources and providing reporting and insight on recent world affairs, this DVD helps instructors integrate current events into their courses by letting them use the clips as lecture launchers or discussion starters.

Instructor's Manual/Test Bank (0-13-602654-0)   Written by the author, this resource includes up-to-date chapter summaries, multiple-choice questions, true/false questions, and essay questions for classroom discussions. This is also available on the IRC.

Computerized Test Bank (0-13-602657-5)   The flexible, easy-to-master computerized test bank includes all of the items in the print test bank. The software allows instructors to edit existing questions and to add their own items. Tests can be printed in several different formats and can include features such as graphs and tables. This is also available on the IRC.

For Students

MyPoliSciKit for *Countries and Concepts*   This premium online learning resource features multimedia and interactive activities to help students make connections between concepts and current events. The book-specific assessment, video case studies, comparative exercises, mapping exercises, ABC newsfeeds, and a politics blog encourage comprehension and critical thinking. With GradeTracker, instructors can easily follow students' work on the site and their progress on each activity. MyPoliSciKit is available at no additional charge when packaged with this book. To learn more, please visit www.mypoliscikit.com or contact your Pearson representative.

Longman Atlas of World Issues (0-321-22465-5)   Introduced and selected by Robert J. Art of Brandeis University and excerpted from the acclaimed Penguin Atlas Series, the *Longman Atlas of World Issues* is designed to help students understand geography and the major issues facing the world today, such as terrorism, debt, and HIV/AIDS. These thematic, full-color maps examine forces shaping politics today at a global level. Explanatory information accompanies each map to help students better grasp the concepts being shown and how they affect our world today. This is available at no additional charge when packaged with this book.

New Signet World Atlas (0-451-19732-1)   From Penguin Putnam, this pocket-sized yet detailed reference features 96 pages of full-color maps plus statistics, key data, and much more, and is available at a discount when packaged with this book.

Careers in Political Science (0-321-11337-3)   Offering insider advice and practical tips on how to make the most of a political science degree, this booklet by Joel Clark of George Mason University shows students the tremendous potential such a degree offers and guides them through the following: deciding whether political science is right for them; the different career options available; job requirements and skill sets; how to apply, interview, and compete for jobs after graduation; and much more. This is available at a discount when packaged with this book.

Acknowledgments

I welcome your suggestions on any area of the book and its supplementary materials. Many have generously offered their comments, corrections, and criticism. Especially valuable were the comments of Stephen Chilton, University of Minnesota–Duluth; Danny Damron, Brigham Young University; Robert L. Youngblood, Arizona State University; Eleanor E. Zeff, Drake University; Christian Soe, California State University at Long Beach; Cheryl L. Brown, University of North Carolina at Charlotte; Karl W. Ryavec, University of Massachusetts at Amherst; Frank Myers, State University of New York at Stony Brook; Ronald F. Bunn, University of Missouri–Columbia; Said A. Arjomand, State University of New York at Stony Brook; Larry Elowitz, Georgia College; Arend Lijphart, University of California at San Diego; Thomas P. Wolf, Indiana University, Southeast; Susan Matarese, University of Louisville; Hanns-D. Jacobsen, Free University of Berlin (on Germany); Ko Shioya of *Bungei Shunju* (on Japan); Carol Nechemias, Penn State–Harrisburg; Yury Polsky, West Chester University; Marcia Weigle, Bowdoin College (on Russia); Morgan

Barr, Dan O'Connell, and Ryan Costella (on China); Jim Coyle, Chapman University, and Lycoming colleague Mehrdad Madresehee (on Iran); John Peeler, Bucknell University (on Mexico); Tony Phillips, USAF Retired (on the European Union); Robbins Burling, University of Michigan, and Sumit Ganguly, Indiana University (on India); and Ed Dew, Fairfield University, for his suggestion to include geography. And to a student in China—who must remain nameless—I say thanks and *Minzhu!* All errors, of course, are my own. Instructors may send professional comments and corrections to me at Lycoming College, Williamsport, PA 17701, or e-mail roskin@lycoming.edu. I am grateful for suggestions for subsequent editions.

Michael G. Roskin

Countries and Concepts

Chapter 1
The Concept of Country

What are we chiefly studying? **Nations**? The Latin root of nation means *birth*, but instead of blood ties, nation now means people with a sense of identity and often the same language, culture, or religion. The nation-building process is not always easy or natural. To build modern France, kings united several regions first by the sword and then by language and culture. The United States is a bizarre mix of peoples, processed over time into a set of common values. India and Nigeria, both mixes of languages and religions, are still engaged in nation-building.

Should we call these entities **states**? Obviously these are not *states* in the sense of the fifty U.S. states, which lack **sovereignty** because ultimately Washington's laws prevail. State means governmental institutions and laws. Historically, states preceded and often formed nations. Over the centuries, the French government, by decreeing use of a certain dialect and spelling and enforcing nationwide educational standards, molded a French consciousness. The French state invented the French nation. All states are to a certain degree **constructed**, somewhat artificial.

We might settle on *country*, which originally meant a rural area where people shared the same dialect and traditions but broadened in meaning until it became synonymous with nation or state. Some used *nation-state* to combine the psychological and structural elements, but the term did not catch on. Nation-states were often defined as having territory, population, independence, government, and other attributes, but none of them are clear-cut.

Territory would seem to be basic, but what about those who have a strong sense of being a people but lack real estate? For example, the Jews turned their sense of nationhood into Israel, and the Palestinians now define themselves as a nation that is ready for statehood. And what happens when territorial claims overlap? History is a poor guide, as typically many tribes and invaders have washed over the land over the centuries. France's Alsatians, on the west bank of the Rhine River, speak German and have Germanic family names. But they also speak French and think of themselves as French. Should Alsace belong to France or Germany? Wars are fought over such questions.

Population is obviously essential. But many countries are **multinational**, with populations divided by language or **ethnicity**. Sometimes the nationalities are angry and wish to break away. Like the ex-Soviet Union, ex-Yugoslavia was composed of several quarrelsome nationalities, most of whom (Slovenes, Croats, Macedonians, Bosnian Muslims) left the Yugoslav state, which, they

QUESTIONS TO CONSIDER

1. What is the difference between nation and state?
2. Why are standard definitions of nation-state inadequate?
3. What factors produced the modern state?
4. Where did nationalism originate?
5. What does the author mean by "quarrels"?
6. How do we define Europe's regions?
7. Does stable democracy need a certain level of economic development?
8. What is a political institution?
9. What is political culture?
10. How are generalizations and theories related?
11. What is "redistribution" and why is it never settled?

nation   Cultural element of country; people psychologically bound to one another. (See page 1.)

state   Institutional or governmental element of country. (See page 1.)

sovereignty   Last word in law in a given territory; boss on your own turf. (See page 1.)

constructed   Deliberately created but widely accepted as natural. (See page 1.)

multinational   Country composed of several peoples with distinct national feelings. (See page 1.)

ethnicity   Cultural characteristics differentiating one group from another. (See page 1.)

diplomatic recognition   State announcing official contact with other state.

failed state   Collapse of sovereignty, essentially no national governing power.

reification   Taking theory as reality; from Latin *res*, thing.

causality   Proving that one thing causes another.

believed, was unfairly dominated by the largest nationality, the Serbs. Yugoslavia is an example of a recent (1918) and artificial construct that did not jell as a nation-state. All countries, to be sure, are more or less artificial, but over time some, such as France, have psychologically inculcated a sense of common nationhood that overrides earlier regional or ethnic loyalties. Germany has done this more recently, and India is still working on it. In Nigeria the process has barely begun.

Independence means that the state governs itself as a sovereign entity. Colonies, such as India under the British, become nation-states when the imperial power departs, as the British did in 1947. **Diplomatic recognition** by other countries, especially by the major powers, confirms a country's independence and helps its economy. China got a boost with U.S. recognition in 1972. Some countries, however, are more sovereign and independent than others. East European lands during the Cold War were Soviet satellites; Moscow controlled their major decisions. Are Central American "banana republics" and Iraq, under U.S. supervision, truly sovereign and independent? Sovereign independence may be a convenient legal fiction.

Government is the crux of being a state. No government means anarchy, with the high probability that the country will fall apart or be conquered. Some call countries like Afghanistan, the Congo, and Somalia **failed states**. Sometimes government can precede states. The Continental Congress preceded and founded the United States. A government can be in exile, as was de Gaulle's Free French government during World War II. The mere existence of a government does not automatically mean that it effectively governs the whole country. In many of the developing lands, the government's writ falls off as one travels from the capital. In several Mexican states drug lords fight Wild West style while the government tries to bring the chaos under legal control.

In sum, nation-states are not as clear-cut as supposed; their realities are messy but interesting. This is one reason for using the admittedly vague term "country": It avoids **reification**, a constant temptation in the social sciences, but one we must guard against.

THE MODERN STATE

Whatever we call the modern state—country, state, or nation-state—we must recognize that its current form is relatively recent. To be sure, we find states at the dawn of written history. (Ancient kingdoms, in fact, invented writing in order to tax and control.) But the modern state is only about half a millennium old and traces back to the replacement of old European feudal monarchies by what were called "new monarchies" and subsequently the "strong state." There are many factors in this shift; it is impossible to pinpoint which were the causes and which the consequences. **Causality** is always difficult to demonstrate in the social sciences, but the box on page 3 discusses changes that ushered in the modern state. Notice how they happened about the same time and how each reinforced the others in a package of incredible change.

By the end of the Thirty Years' War in 1648, the feudal system had been displaced by the modern state. **Feudalism** balanced power between monarch and nobles; it was loose and did not tolerate strong national government. It was not oriented to change or expansion. The new monarchies were **absolutist**, concentrating all power in themselves, disdaining the old medieval constitution in which their powers balanced with nobles, and using new economic, administrative, and military tools to increase their power. Royalist philosophers extolled the strong monarch and coined the term *sovereignty*. In consolidating their powers, monarchs had the nation celebrated, giving rise to the concept of nationality, of belonging to a nation rather than merely being the subject of a hereditary ruler.

> **feudalism**   Political system of power dispersed and balanced between king and nobles.
>
> **absolutism**   Royal dictatorship that bypasses nobles.
>
> **secularization**   Diminishing role of religion in government and society.

The Rise of Nationalism

The French Revolution unleashed modern nationalism. As the armies of German princes closed in on the Revolution in 1792, the French people rallied *en masse* to repel the foe, believing they were defending both the Revolution and the *patrie* (fatherland), and the two concepts merged. France,

Geography

What Made the Modern State?

Europe began to stir in the eleventh century (late Middle Ages), but the Renaissance, starting in the fourteenth century, accelerated growth in art, philosophy, science, commerce, and population across Europe. The political system changed from feudalism to absolutism as monarchs increased and centralized their power over the nobles. By the middle of the fifteenth century, Europe was set for a revolution:

1453   The Turks used cannons to crack open the walls of Constantinople. European monarchs quickly acquired the new weapon to subdue nobles and consolidate their kingdoms.

1454   Gutenburg printed with moveable type. Printing increased the rate of diffusion of information, speeding up all other processes and displacing Latin with local tongues. Printed materials helped the national capital govern outlying provinces.

1488   The Portuguese rounded Africa, soon followed by . . .

1492   The New World opened. Countries with access to the sea (Spain, Portugal, England, France, the Netherlands) rushed to Asia, Africa, and the Americas for trade and colonies.

1494   Italian monk Luca Pacioli invented accounting, making it possible to control large businesses and thus encouraging growth.

1517   Luther nailed his ninety-five theses to the church door and founded Protestantism. Soon Protestant kings split from Rome and set up national churches, as in England and Sweden.

1545   This led to the wars of religion, first the Schmalkaldic War of 1545–1555 and then the devastating Thirty Years' War of 1618–1648. These conflicts increased state power and curtailed the church's temporal power, leading to **secularization**.

1618–1648   During the Thirty Years' War, state administration greatly improved. Warring monarchs, desperate for money, needed reliable tax bases and tax collectors. France's Richelieu and Sweden's Oxenstierna founded modern, rational administration to control and tax an entire country. The state got its own budget, separate from the royal household budget.

quarrels As used here, important, long-term political issues.

power Ability of A to get B to do what A wants.

the revolutionaries claimed, was destined to liberate and reform the rest of Europe. The concept of a nation embodying everything good was thus born and spread throughout Europe by Napoleon's enthusiastic legions.

By its very nature, nationalism could not stay confined to the French soldiers, who soon turned into brutal and arrogant occupiers. All over Europe, local patriots rose up against them with the same kind of nationalistic feelings the French had introduced. The spillover of French nationalism thus gave rise to Spanish, German, and Russian nationalism. By the late nineteenth century, with German and Italian unification, most Europeans had either formed nationalistic states or desired to (for example, Poland). Thinkers such as Germany's Hegel and Italy's Mazzini extolled the nation as the highest level of human (or possibly divine) development.

The modern state and its nationalism did not stay in West Europe. Driven to expand, the Europeans conquered Latin America, Asia, and Africa. Only Japan and Turkey kept the Europeans out; Meiji Japan carried out a brilliant "defensive modernization." The European imperialists introduced nationalism to their subject peoples. By their very integration and administration of previously fragmented territories, the British in India, the French in Indochina, and the Dutch in Indonesia taught "the natives" to think of themselves as a nation that, of right, deserved to be independent. Now virtually the entire globe is populated by national states, each jealous of their sovereign independence and many of them fired by nationalism.

Looking for Quarrels

One way to begin the study of a political system is to ask what its people fight about. There is no country without political **quarrels**. They range from calm discussions over whether to include dental care in nationalized health insurance to angry conflicts over language rights to murderous civil wars over who should rule the country.

You can get a fair idea of a country's quarrels by talking with its people, interviewing officials, following the local media, and attending election rallies. This is how journalists work. Political scientists, however, go further. They want to know the whys and wherefores of these controversies, whether they are long-standing issues or short-term problems. Our next step, then, is to observe the quarrels over time. If the basic quarrel lasts a long time, we are onto an important topic. To explain the quarrel, we must dig into the country's past, its institutions, and its culture.

In this book, we look at ten countries, considering each in five sections, each focusing on a subject area. We start with the underlying causes of current quarrels:

- The Impact of the Past
- The Key Institutions
- The Political Culture

We study the past, including the country's geography, in order to understand the present. We do not seek the fascinating details of history but the major patterns that have set up present institutions and culture. We ask, "What happened then that matters now?" We study institutions to see how **power** is structured, for that is what institutions are: structures of power. We study culture to see how people look at their social and political system, how deeply they support it, and how political views differ among groups.

Moving from underlying factors to current politics brings us to the next two areas:

- Patterns of Interaction
- What People Quarrel About

political geography   How territory and politics influence each other.

elites   Those few persons with great influence.

mass   Most people; those without influence.

Here we get more specific and more current. The previous sections are, respectively, about the traditions, rules, and spirit of the game; the patterns of interaction are how the game is actually played. We look here for recurring behavior. The last section, the specific quarrels, represents the stuff of politics, the kind of things you see in a country's newspaper.

THE IMPACT OF THE PAST

We look first at a country's geography. *Physical geography* concerns the natural features of the earth, whereas **political geography** studies what is largely human-made. There is, of course, a connection between the two, as physical limits set by nature influence the formation, consolidation, and governing mentality of political systems.

Next, moving on to history, was the country unified early or late? For the most part, countries are artificial—not natural—entities, created when one group or tribe conquered its neighbors and unified them by the sword. The founding of nations is usually a bloody business, and the longer ago it took place, the better. We look at Sweden and say, "What a nice, peaceful country." We look at Afghanistan and say, "What a horror of warlords battling each other." Long ago, however, Sweden resembled Afghanistan.

The unification and consolidation of a country leave behind regional memories of incredible staying power. People whose ancestors were conquered centuries ago still act out their resentments in political ways, in the voting booth, or in civil violence. This is one way history has an impact on the present.

Becoming "modern" is a wrenching experience. Industrialization, urbanization, and the growth of education and communications uproot people from their traditional villages and lifestyles and send them to work in factories in cities. In the process, previously passive people become aware of their condition and want to change it. Mobilized by new parties, they start to participate in politics and demand economic improvement. This is a delicate time in the life of nations. If traditional **elites** do not devise some way to take account of newly awakened **mass** demands, the system may be heading toward revolution.

No country has industrialized in a nice way; it is always a process marked by low wages, bad working conditions, and, usually, political repression. The longer in the past this stage has happened, the more peaceful and stable a country is likely to be. We must look for the stage of development a country is in. A country just undergoing industrialization can expect domestic tensions of the sort that existed earlier in Europe.

Religion is a crucial historical question. Does the country have its church-state relationship settled? If not, it is a lingering political sore. Protestant countries had an easier time secularizing; their churches cut their ties to Rome, the state became stronger than the church early on, and the church stayed out of politics. In Roman Catholic countries, where the church had power in its own right, there was a long church-state struggle called the "clerical-anticlerical split," which is still alive in France and Mexico: Conservatives are more religious, and liberals and leftists are indifferent or hostile to religion. Iran now has the Muslim equivalent of a clerical-anticlerical split.

democracy   Political system of mass participation, competitive elections, and human and civil rights.

per capita   GDP divided by population, giving approximate level of well-being.

GDP   Gross Domestic Product; sum total of goods and services produced in a country in one year.

electoral franchise   Right to vote.

At a certain point in their development, countries become ready for **democracy**. Very few poor countries can sustain democracy, which seems to require a good-sized middle class to work right. Attempts to implant democracy in countries with **per capita GDPs** below $5,000 generally fail, but democracy usually takes root in countries that have per capita GDPs above $8,000. India is a large, fascinating exception. Notice in the table below that several of our countries are in this borderline area. This is one way economics influences politics.

As we learned in Iraq, democracy implanted by foreigners may not always work. Countries have to be ready for it. Trying to start democracy too early often fails amid rigged elections, powerful warlords, and civil unrest. Democracy can also come too late. If the traditional elite waits too long, the masses may mobilize, turn radical, and fall into the hands of revolutionary demagogues. What happened in Russia in 1917 happened again in Iran in 1979. The gradual expansion of the **electoral franchise**, as in Britain, is probably best.

The widening of the franchise means the rise of political parties. On what was a party first based? Urban middle class, farmers, workers, or a denomination? When was it founded? What were

COMPARING SOME BASIC FIGURES

	Population		Per Capita GDP		Workforce	Infant Mortality
	in Millions 2008	Annual Growth Rate 2007	ppp* 2007	Growth 2007	in Agriculture	per 1,000 Live Births
Britain	61	0.28%	$35,300	2.9%	1.4%	5.0
France	61	0.59	33,800	1.8	4.1	3.4
Germany	82	−0.03	34,400	2.6	2.8	4.1
Japan	127	−0.09	33,800	2.0	4.6	2.8
Russia	141	−0.50	14,600	7.4	4.6	11.0
China	1,321	0.61	5,300	11.4	43.0	22.0
India	1,130	1.61	2,700	8.5	60.0	34.6
Mexico	109	1.15	12,500	3.0	18.0	19.6
Nigeria	135	2.38	2,200	6.1	70.0	95.5
Iran	65	0.66	12,300	4.3	25.0	38.1
United States	301	0.89	46,000	2.0	0.6	6.4

*Purchasing Power Parity; see page 433.

Source: World Bank, *CIA World Factbook*. Regard all such tables as approximate. The recent decline of the U.S. dollar made Europeans look richer. Data can change wildly from one year and from one source to another, especially figures from developing countries, which are often estimates. Statistical quirks throw off economic-growth figures. For example, Nigeria, with a low base, enjoyed a recent jump in oil revenues that registers as a big percent increase and makes Nigeria look like a fast-growing economy. Population growth includes immigration, important for the U.S. figure. Averages deceive: Chinese, Indian, and Mexican figures, for instance, do not show the major gaps between rich and poor in income, population growth, and infant mortality.

its initial aims, and how has it changed over the years? Was the party strongly ideological? Left-wing parties argued that government should provide jobs, welfare, and education. Other parties, on the political center or right, either rejected the welfarist ideas, compromised with them, or stole them. Gradually, the country becomes a welfare state with a heavy tax burden.

Finally, history establishes political symbols that can awaken powerful feelings. Flags, monarchs, religion, and national holidays and anthems often help cement a country together, giving citizens the feeling that they are part of a common enterprise. To fully know a country, one must know its symbols, their historical origins, and their current connotation.

symbol   Political artifact that stirs mass emotions.

institution   Established rules and relationships of power.

constitution   Written organization of a country's institutions.

authoritarian   Nondemocratic or dictatorial politics.

THE KEY INSTITUTIONS

A political **institution** is a web of relationships lasting over time, an established structure of power. An institution may or may not be housed in an impressive building. With institutions we look for durable sets of human relationships, not architecture.

A good way to begin is to ask, "Who has the power?" When A commands, do B and C follow? Or do they ignore or counterbalance A? A nation's **constitution**—itself an institution—may give us some clues, but it does not always pinpoint real power centers. Britain's monarch and Germany's and India's presidents are more for decoration than governing. The 1958 French constitution originally made the president extremely strong, but that has changed, allowing more power to prime ministers.

DEMOCRACY

WAVES OF DEMOCRACY

Harvard political scientist Samuel P. Huntington saw democracy advancing in three waves. The first wave, from the American and French Revolutions through World War I, gradually and unevenly spread democracy through most of West Europe. But between the two world wars, a "reverse wave" of communist and fascist **authoritarian** regimes pushed back democracy in Russia, Italy, Germany, Spain, Portugal, and Japan.

The second wave, a short one, from the end of World War II until the mid-1960s, brought democracy to most of West Europe plus the many Asian and African colonies that got their independence. Most of Asia, Africa, and Latin America, however, quickly turned authoritarian.

Huntington's third wave began in the mid-1970s with the return of democracy to Portugal, Spain, and Greece and thence to Latin America and East Asia. In 1989, as Communist regimes collapsed, it took over East Europe and, with the 1991 Soviet collapse, Russia. Even Mexico's long-dominant party relaxed its grip to let an opposition party win the 2000 presidential election. On paper, most of the world's 194 countries are approximately democratic. But, warned Huntington, get ready for another reverse wave as some shaky democratic regimes revert to authoritarianism. Russia did precisely that.

parliament National assembly that considers and enacts laws.

political culture Values and attitudes of citizens regarding politics and society.

cynical Untrusting; belief that political system is wrong and corrupt.

Is the system presidential or parliamentary? (See box on page 40.) Both systems have **parliaments**, but a presidential system has a president who is elected and serves separately from the legislature; the legislature cannot vote out the president. The United States and Mexico are presidential systems. In parliamentary systems, action focuses on the prime minister, who is a member of parliament delegated by it to form a government (another word for cabinet). The prime minister and his or her cabinet can be ousted by a vote of no-confidence in parliament. Americans used to assume presidential systems were better and more stable than parliamentary systems. Recent problems might make Americans aware of the advantages of a parliamentary system, which can easily oust a chief executive. Besides, parliamentary systems, with the proper refinements such as Germany's, can be quite stable.

How powerful is the legislature? In most cases it is less powerful than the executive, and its power is generally declining. Parliaments still pass laws, but most of them originate with the civil servants and cabinet and are passed according to party wishes. In most legislatures (but not in the U.S. Congress), party discipline is so strong that a member of parliament simply votes the way party whips instruct. Parliaments can be important without originating many laws. They represent citizens, educate the public, structure interests, and, most important, oversee and criticize executive-branch activities.

Does the parliament have two chambers (bicameral) or one (unicameral)? Two chambers are necessary in federal systems to represent the territorial divisions, but they are often extra baggage in unitary systems. Most of the countries studied in this book have bicameral legislatures.

How many parties are there? Is it a one-party system, such as China; a dominant-party system, such as Russia; two-party systems, such as Britain and the United States; or multiparty systems, such as France and Germany? Party system is partly determined by a country's electoral system, of which there are two basic types, majoritarian and proportional. A majoritarian system, as in the United States and Britain, enables one party to have a majority in parliament. This encourages two-party systems. Proportional systems, where parliamentarians are elected according to the percentage of the vote their party won, as in Germany and Israel, rarely give one party control of parliament, so coalitions are necessary. Proportional representation encourages multiparty systems, which in turn may contribute to cabinet instability as coalition members quarrel.

How powerful is the country's permanent civil service, its bureaucracy? The bureaucracy today has eclipsed both cabinet and parliament in expertise, information, outside contacts, and sheer numbers. Some lobbyists no longer bother with the legislature; they go where the action is, to the important decision makers in the bureaucracy.

Political Culture

After World War II, political scientists shifted their emphasis from institutions to attitudes. The institutional approach had become suspect. On paper, Germany's Weimar constitution was a magnificent achievement after World War I, but it did not work in practice because too few Germans supported democracy. By the late 1950s a newly prominent **political culture** approach to comparative politics sought to explain systems in terms of peoples' values. This is a two-way street, however, because attitudes determine government, and government determines attitudes. Americans became much more **cynical** in the wake of Vietnam and Watergate, while Germans became more committed democrats as their country achieved economic success and political stability.

Legitimacy is basic to political culture. It originally meant that the rightful king was on the throne, not a usurper. Now it means that most citizens think that the government's rule is valid and that it should generally be obeyed. Governments are not automatically legitimate; they have to earn the respect of their citizens. Legitimacy can be created over a long time as a government endures and governs well. Legitimacy can also erode as unstable and corrupt regimes come and go, never winning the people's respect. One quick test of legitimacy is how many police officers a country has. With high legitimacy, a country needs few police because people obey the law voluntarily. With low legitimacy, a country needs many police.

Regimes attempt to shore up their legitimacy by manipulating symbols. One symbol frequently manipulated is **ideology**. An ideology is a grand plan to save or improve the country (see box on page 10). Typically, leaders take their ideology with a grain of salt. But for mass consumption, the Soviets and Chinese cranked out reams of ideological propaganda (which, in fact, most of their people ignored).

Most of the other political systems explored in this book are not so ideologically explicit, but all espouse various ideologies to greater or lesser degrees: German Social Democrats are committed to the welfare state, British Conservatives to free-market economics, and Chinese Communists to "socialism with Chinese characteristics." Every system probably has some sort of ideology. A system run on purely **pragmatic** grounds—if it works, use it—would be nonideological, but such systems are rare. Even Americans, who pride themselves on being pragmatic, are usually convinced of the effectiveness of the free market (Republicans) or moderate government intervention (Democrats). How ideological or pragmatic is a particular system and its political parties?

> **legitimacy**   Mass perception that regime's rule is rightful.
>
> **ideology**   Belief system to improve society.
>
> **pragmatic**   Without ideological considerations; based on practicality.

Political Culture

The Civic Culture Study

In a massive 1959 study, political scientists Gabriel Almond and Sidney Verba led teams that asked approximately one thousand people in each of five countries—the United States, Britain, West Germany, Italy, and Mexico—identical questions about their political values and attitudes. The Civic Culture study, which was a benchmark in cross-national research, discerned three types of political culture:

1. *Participant*, in which people know a lot about politics and want to participate in politics.
2. *Subject*, in which people are aware of politics but cautious about participating; they are more conditioned to obeying.
3. *Parochial*, meaning narrow or focused only on people's immediate concerns, in which people are not even much aware of politics and do not participate.

Almond and Verba emphasized that each country is a mixture of these types of political culture, with perhaps one type dominating: participant in America, subject in West Germany and Italy, parochial in Mexico, for example. A good mixture, which Almond and Verba found in America and Britain, produces what they called "the civic culture." Question: If Americans are so participant, why do they vote so little?

Another contributor to political culture is a country's educational system. Nearly everywhere, education is the main path to elite status. Who gets educated and in what way helps structure who gets political power and what they do with it. No country has totally equal educational opportunity. Even where schooling is legally open to all, social-, economic-, and even political-screening devices work against some sectors of the population. Most countries have elite universities that produce a big share of their political leadership, at times a near monopoly. The elite views formed in such schools determine much of a country's politics.

PATTERNS OF INTERACTION

Here we come to what is conventionally called "politics": Who does what to whom? We look for the interactions of parties, interest groups, and bureaucracies. Elites play a major role. Even democratic politics is usually the work of a few. Most people, most of the time, do not participate in politics.

KEY CONCEPTS

WHAT IS "IDEOLOGY"?

Political ideologies can be an important part of political culture. They are belief systems—usually ending in *-ism*—that claim to aim at improving society. Believers in an ideology say: "If we move in this direction, things will be much better. People will be happier, catastrophe will be avoided, society will become perfected." An ideology usually contains four elements:

1. The *perception* that things are going wrong, that society is headed down the wrong path. Fanatic ideologies insist that catastrophe is just around the corner.

2. An *evaluation* or analysis of why things are going wrong. This means a criticism of all or part of the existing system.

3. A *prescription* or cure for the problem. Moderate ideologies advocate reforms; extremist ideologies urge revolution.

4. An effort to form a *movement* to carry out the cure. Without a party or movement, the above points are just talk without serious intent.

Marxism-Leninism is a perfect example of ideology. First, we have Marx's perception that capitalism is unjust and doomed. Second, we have Marx's theory that capitalism contains internal contradictions that bring about economic depressions. Third, we have a Marxist prescription: Abolish capitalism in favor of collective ownership of the means of production—i.e., socialism. And fourth, especially with Lenin, we have the determined movement to form a strong Communist party—the "organizational weapon"—to put the cure into effect by overthrowing the capitalist system. (How well does environmentalism fit this fourfold pattern?)

Ideologies are usually based on a serious thinker, often an important philosopher. Communism traces back to Hegel, classic liberalism to John Locke. But the philosopher's original ideas become popularized, vulgarized, and often distorted at the hands of ideologists who are trying to mass-market them. Deep thoughts are turned into cheap slogans.

Ideologies are always defective; they never deliver what they promise—perfect societies and happy humans. Classic liberalism produced an underclass, Marxism-Leninism produced brutal dictatorships, and Iran's Islamic fundamentalism produced rule by rigid and corrupt clerics.

But there are various kinds of elites, some more democratic than others. How much of these interactions are an elite game with little or no mass participation?

    Do groups come together to compete or strike deals? How do political parties persuade the public to support them? We look not for one-time events but for recurring things. Finding such patterns is the beginning of making **generalizations**, and generalizing is the beginning of **theory**. Once we have found a pattern, we ask why. The answer will be found partly from what we have learned

> **generalization**   Finding repeated examples and patterns.
>
> **theory**   Firm generalization supported by evidence.

KEY CONCEPTS

THE POLITICS OF SOCIAL CLEAVAGES

Most societies are split along one or more lines. Often these splits, or "cleavages," become the society's fault lines along which political views form. Here are some of the more politically relevant social cleavages.

Social Class   Karl Marx thought social class determined everything. Whether one was bourgeois or proletarian determined most political orientations. Marx held that middle- and upper-class people were conservative; working-class people were progressive or radical. This oversimplifies, as some poor people are extremely conservative, and some middle-class intellectuals are radical.

    Still, social class does matter in structuring attitudes. The working class does tend toward the left, but never 100 percent, and it tends to the moderate left of social democracy rather than the radical left of communism. Such is the case of the German Social Democratic party. Social class by itself seldom explains all political orientations. Other factors—such as religion and region—are usually present. The question, as Joseph LaPalombara put it, is, "Class plus what?"

Geographic Region   Most countries have regional differences that are often politically important. Once a region gets set in its politics it can stay that way for generations. Often the region remembers past conquests and injustices. Scotland still resents England, and likewise the south of France resents the north. The Muslim north and Christian south of Nigeria seriously dislike each other. We must study the regions of a nation, what their politics are, and how they got to be that way.

Religion   Religious struggles played major roles in most nations' histories and in some countries still do. You can predict with fair accuracy how a French person will vote by knowing how often he or she attends Mass. You can partly predict how a German will vote by knowing if he or she is Protestant or Catholic. In India, many Hindus and Muslims see each other in hostile terms. Religion accounts for the formation of more political parties than does social class.

Urban-Rural   Urban dwellers tend to be more aware of politics, more participatory, and more liberal or leftist. This is especially true in developing lands, where the countryside remains backward while the cities modernize. China, for example, has a major urban-rural split in terms of living conditions, education, and political orientation. The 2008 U.S. election graphically illustrates our urban-rural split.

    There are other politically relevant social cleavages. In some countries gender matters, as in the United States, where women vote more Democrat than men. Occupation, as distinct from social class, can also influence political attitudes. A miner and a farmer may have the same income, but the miner will likely be leftist and the farmer conservative. Age can be a political factor. Young people are usually more open to new ideas and more likely to embrace radical and even violent causes than older citizens. Germany's terrorists, China's Red Guards, and Iran's Pasdaran were all young. In India, caste is a political issue.

interest group   Association aimed at getting favorable policies.

about each country in preceding chapters and partly from the nature of political life where struggle and competition are normal and universal.

Some interactions are open and public; others are closed and secretive. The interactions of parties and citizenry are mostly open. Every party tries to convince the public that their party is the one fit to govern. This holds equally true for democratic and authoritarian systems. Do they succeed? Whom do the parties aim for, and how do they win them over? By ideology? Promises? Common interests? Or by convincing people the other party is worse?

The parties interact with each other, sometimes cooperatively but more often competitively. How do they denounce and discredit each other? Under what circumstances do they make deals? Is their competition murderous or moderate? Parties also interact with the government. In China, the Party nearly is the government. In more politically open countries, parties try to capture and retain governmental power. How do parties form coalitions? Who gets the top cabinet jobs? Once in power, is the party able to act, or is it immobilized by opposition forces?

Politics within the parties is important, as most parties have factions. In Japan, factions within the leading party battle each other as if they were separate parties. Does the party have left and right wings? How do its leaders hold it together? Do they pay off factions with ministerial positions? Do factional quarrels paralyze the party? Could it split?

Parties also interact with **interest groups**. Some groups enjoy "structured access" to like-minded parties. In Europe, labor unions are often linked formally to labor parties. Here we need to know: Does the party co-opt the interest group, or vice versa? How powerful are interest-group views in determining party policy?

Interest groups often decide it is not worth working on the electoral-legislative side and instead focus their attention on bureaucracies. One of the key areas of politics is where bureaucracies and

DEMOCRACY

CRISIS OF DEMOCRACY?

Worldwide, social scientists worry that the public opinion in firmly established democracies is becoming more cynical about government. If the trend deepens, it could undermine the basis of democracy. Observers focus on two trends: (1) A falloff of roughly 10 percent in voting turnout from the 1950s to the 1990s; (2) public-opinion polls that show Americans, Europeans, and Japanese all trust government and politicians less. Is democracy threatened?

Be careful of doomsters; their predictions are usually wrong. The voting falloff may be due in part to the lowering of the voting age in the early 1970s nearly everywhere from 21 to 18. Young people vote less. Cynical opinions may be due to increased expectations that government must provide jobs, health, and happiness—hyped by politicians—that government cannot possibly deliver. Viewed in this light, democracy may have been too successful.

Democracy may be entering a new phase in which better-educated citizens know more and criticize more: "critical citizens." Citizen efforts to fight corruption, curb the influence of powerful interest groups, and reform defective institutions are widespread. And how is the Internet affecting democracy?

businesses interface. Are interest groups controlled by government, or vice versa? What kind of relationships do businessmen and bureaucrats establish? Which groups are the most influential? These important interactions are generally out of the public sight and often corrupt. Does money change hands?

redistribution   Taxing the better off to help the worse off.

What People Quarrel About

Here we move to current issues, the political struggles of the day. We start with economics, the universal and permanent quarrel over who gets what. Politics and economics are closely connected; one can make or break the other. (Political scientists should have a grounding in economics; take an economics course.)

First, we inquire if the economy of the country is growing. Rapidly or slowly? Why? Are workers lazy or energetic? Are managers inept or clever? How much of the economy is supervised and planned by government? Does government help or hinder economic growth? If the economy is declining, will it lead to political upheaval (as in the Soviet Union)? Why are some countries economic success stories and others not? How big a role does politics play in economic growth?

Other issues: Have unions and management reached durable understandings, or are strikes frequent? Have unions won laws on wages, benefits, and layoffs? Has this led to "labor-force rigidities" that slow growth? Does government try to influence wage increases? Do workers have any say in running their companies? How much imported labor is there? How much unemployment?

Once we have a realistic picture of the economic pie, we inquire who gets what slice. How equal—or unequal—is the distribution of income and wealth? Does the government redistribute incomes to make people more equal or does it let inequality grow? Does unequal distribution lead to social and political resentment? **Redistribution** is another name for a welfare system, and all advanced democracies are to some extent welfare states. How high and how progressive are taxes?

Comparison

The Importance of Being Comparative

"You cannot be scientific if you are not comparing," UCLA's late, great James Coleman used to tell his students. Countries are not unique; they are comparable with other countries. When we say, for example, the parliament of country X has become a rubber stamp for the executive, this is not a meaningful statement until we note that it is also the tendency in countries Y and Z.

The "uniqueness trap" often catches commentators of the American scene off-guard. We hear statements such as: "The U.S. political system is breaking down." Compared to what? To France in 1958? To Russia in 1991? Or to the United States itself in 1861? Compared to these other cases, the United States today is in great shape. We hear statements like: "Taxes in this country are outrageous." But what percentage of GDP do Americans pay in taxes compared to Britons, French, and Germans? Our thinking on politics will be greatly clarified if we put ourselves into a comparative mood by frequently asking, "Compared to what?"

How many and how generous are welfare benefits? Do people want more welfare and higher taxes or less welfare and lower taxes? Which people? If stuck with an overgenerous welfare system, can the government trim it?

There are, to be sure, noneconomic quarrels as well. Regionalism is persistent and growing. Britain, France, Russia, India, and Nigeria have breakaway regional movements. East and West Germany resent each other. Mexico's regions vote differently from one another. What are a country's regions? Which of them are discontented? Why are they discontented and how do they show their discontent? Is there violence? Is there movement to decentralize or devolve power to the regions? One quarrel getting nastier throughout West Europe is what to do with the millions of immigrants, mostly from the developing lands: Let in more or keep them out? Integrate them or send them home?

KEY TERMS

absolutism (p. 3)

authoritarian (p. 7)

causality (p. 2)

constitution (p. 7)

constructed (p. 2)

cynical (p. 8)

democracy (p. 6)

diplomatic recognition
   (p. 2)

electoral franchise (p. 6)

elites (p. 5)

ethnicity (p. 2)

failed state (p. 2)

feudalism (p. 3)

GDP (p. 6)

generalization (p. 11)

ideology (p. 9)

institution (p. 7)

interest group (p. 12)

legitimacy (p. 9)

mass (p. 5)

multinational (p. 2)

nation (p. 2)

parliament (p. 8)

per capita (p. 6)

political culture (p. 8)

political geography (p. 5)

power (p. 4)

pragmatic (p. 9)

quarrels (p. 4)

redistribution (p. 13)

reification (p. 2)

secularization (p. 3)

sovereignty (p. 2)

state (p. 2)

symbol (p. 7)

theory (p. 11)

FURTHER REFERENCE

Dalton, Russell J. *Citizen Politics: Public Opinion and Political Parties in Advanced Industrial Democracies*, 5th ed. Washington, D.C.: CQ Press, 2008.

de Blij, Harm. *Why Geography Matters: Three Challenges Facing America: Climate Change, the Rise of China, and Global Terrorism*. New York: Oxford University Press, 2005.

Fukuyama, Francis. *State-Building: Governance and World Order in the 21st Century*. Ithaca, NY: Cornell University Press, 2004.

Judt, Tony. *Postwar: A History of Europe since 1945*. New York: Penguin, 2005.

Lane, Jan-Erik, and Svante Ersson. *Culture and Politics: A Comparative Approach*, 2nd ed. Williston, VT: Ashgate, 2005.

Lim, Timothy C. *Doing Comparative Politics: An Introduction to Approaches and Issues.* Boulder, CO: L. Rienner, 2006.

Munck, Gerardo L., and Richard Snyder, eds. *Passion, Craft, and Method in Comparative Politics.* Baltimore, MD: Johns Hopkins University Press, 2007.

Perry, Robert L., and John D. Robertson. *Comparative Analysis of Nations: Quantitative Approaches.* Boulder, CO: Westview, 2001.

Stepan, Alfred. *Arguing Comparative Politics.* New York: Oxford University Press, 2001.

Wiarda, Howard J. *Comparative Politics.* Lanham, MD: Rowman & Littlefield, 2006.

ARCTIC OCEAN

SWEDEN

FINLAND

RUSSIA

ESTONIA

LATVIA

LITHUANIA

RUS.

DENMARK

UNITED KINGDOM

NETHERLANDS

POLAND

IRELAND

GERMANY

BELGIUM

LUXEMBOURG

CZECH REP.

SLOVAKIA

AUSTRIA

HUNGARY

FRANCE

ATLANTIC OCEAN

SLOVENIA

CROATIA

ROMANIA

ITALY

BULGARIA

MACEDONIA

PORTUGAL

SPAIN

GREECE

TURKEY

MALTA

CYPRUS

Countries featured in Part I

EU-member countries featured in Part I

EU-member countries not featured in Part I

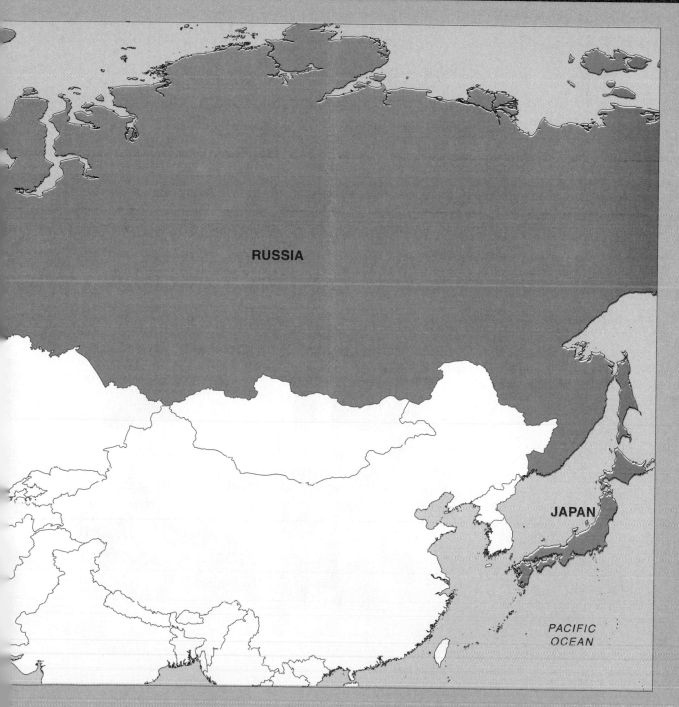

RUSSIA

JAPAN

PACIFIC
OCEAN

Chapter 2
Britain:
The Impact of the Past

A Polish student I once knew at UCLA had to write a paper for her English class on what she most wished for her native land. She took the question as a geographical one and wrote: "I wish Poland be island like England." She would like to fix Poland's problem, its location on a plain between large, hostile neighbors (Germany and Russia) that has given it a sad history of invasion and partition.

England long ago was invaded many times. For a millennium and a half, waves of **Celts**, Romans, Angles and Saxons, Danes, and finally **Normans** washed upon Britain. One tribe of Celts, the Britons, gave their name to the entire island. Britishers, like most peoples, are not of one stock but of many.

The fierce Germanic tribesmen who rowed across the North Sea during the third to fifth centuries A.D. brought over Anglisch, what we call Old English, the language of the Angles, close to the Frisian of the Netherlands and German coast. "England" was simply the land of the Angles. The Angles and Saxons slowly moved across England, destroying towns and massacring inhabitants. The Celts were pushed back to present-day Wales and Scotland, which became a "Celtic fringe" to England. Some Celts fled to France and gave their name to Brittany. Preserving their distinct identity and languages (Cymric in Wales, Gaelic in Scotland), Britain's Celts never quite forgot what the newer arrivals did to them.

Other invaders followed. In the ninth century, Danish Vikings held much of eastern England (the Danelaw), but they were eventually absorbed. Another group of Vikings had meanwhile settled in France; these Norsemen (Normans) gave their name to Normandy. In 1066, with the English throne in dispute, William of Normandy put forward his own dubious claim and invaded with a force gathered from all over France. He defeated the English King Harold at the famous battle of Hastings, and England changed dramatically.

William the Conqueror replaced the entire Saxon ruling class with Norman nobles, who earned their **fiefdoms** by military service. At first the Norman conquerors spoke only French, so vast numbers of French words soon enriched the English language. Backed by military power, administration was better and tighter. William ordered a complete inventory of all lands and population in his new domain; the resulting Domesday Book provided a detailed tool for governance. The **Exchequer**—the name derived from the French word for a checkered counting table—became the king's powerful treasury minister, a title and office that still exists. Furthermore, since William and his descendants ruled both England and parts of France, England was tied for centuries to the affairs of the Continent.

QUESTIONS TO CONSIDER

1. How has geography influenced British development?
2. What does the Union Jack stand for?
3. What did the Magna Carta preserve?
4. What is the Common Law?
5. When did Parliament eclipse the monarch?
6. How did Puritanism influence democracy?
7. How did democracy come to Britain?
8. What was the difference between Hobbes and Locke?
9. How are Britain and Sweden so comparable?

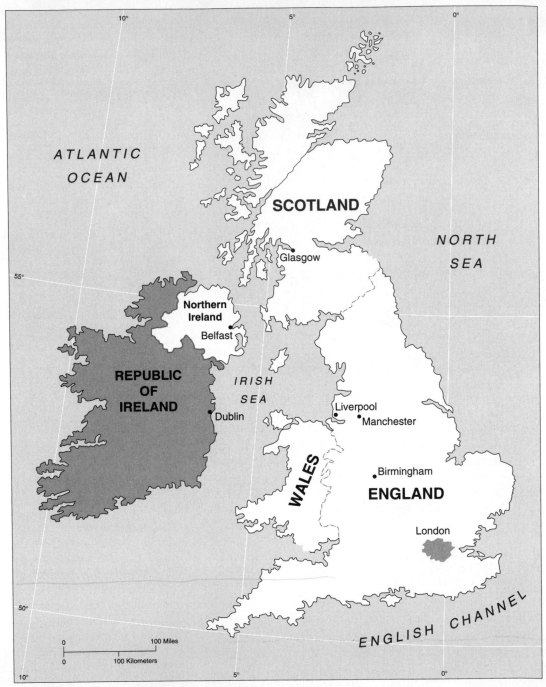

GREAT BRITAIN

MAGNA CARTA

The Normans brought to England a political system that had first emerged on **the Continent**—*feudalism*. The feudal system was a contractual agreement in which lords would grant vassals land and protection while the vassal would support the lord with military service. Feudalism appears when central authority breaks down and a money economy disappears, for then land and fighting ability take on tremendous importance. The collapse of the Roman Empire meant kings could survive and thrive only if they had enough lords and knights to fight for them. The lords and knights in turn got land. Power here was a two-way street: The king needed the nobles and vice versa.

The **mixed monarchy** of the Middle Ages was a balance between king and nobles. The nobles of Aragon expressed it bluntly in their oath to a new monarch: "We who are as good as you swear to you, who are no better than we, to accept you as our king and sovereign lord provided you observe all our statutes and laws; and if not, no."

Centuries of English history were dominated by the struggle to make sure the king did not exceed his feudal bounds and become an absolute monarch, which happened in most of Europe. This English struggle laid the foundation for limited, representative government, democracy, and civil rights, even though the participants at the time had no such intent.

The Great Charter the barons forced on King John at Runnymede in 1215 is not so far-reaching or idealistic; it never mentions liberty or democracy. The barons and top churchmen simply wanted to stop the king from encroaching on feudal customs, rights, and laws by which they held sway in their localities. In this sense the **Magna Carta**, one of the great documents of democracy, was feudal and reactionary. It did, however, limit the monarch's powers and make sure he stayed within the law.

The Magna Carta meant the king stayed in balance with the nobles, thus preventing either despotism or anarchy, the twin ills of the Continent, where countries either went to *absolutism*, as in France, or broke up into small principalities, as in Germany. British, and by extension, American democracy owes a lot to the stubborn English barons who stood up for their feudal rights.

Celts   Pre-Roman inhabitants of Europe. (See page 19.)

Normans   Vikings who settled in and gave their name to Normandy, France. (See page 19.)

fiefdom   Land granted by a king to a noble in exchange for support. (See page 19.)

Exchequer   Britain's treasury ministry. (See page 19.)

the Continent   British term for mainland Europe, implying they are not part of it.

mixed monarchy   King balanced by nobles.

Magna Carta   1215 agreement to preserve rights of English nobles.

GEOGRAPHY

INVADABILITY

Britain is very hard to invade. The last successful invasion of England (by the Normans) was in 1066. The barrier that is posed by the English Channel has kept Spaniards, French, and Germans from invading and conquering Britain. Politically, this has meant that England has been able to develop its own institutions without foreign interference, a luxury not enjoyed by most Continental lands.

Militarily, it has meant that England rarely has needed or had a large army, of great import in the seventeenth century when British kings were unable to tame Parliament because the monarch had few soldiers.

THE RISE OF PARLIAMENT

During the same century as the Magna Carta, English kings started calling to London, by now the capital, two to four knights from each shire (roughly a county) and a similar number of **burghers** from the towns to consult with the king on matters of the realm. These kings were not latent democrats but needed to raise taxes and get the support of those who had local power. The French holdings of English kings meant that they had to fight wars in France. These were expensive, and the only way to raise revenues to pay for them was by inviting local notables to participate, at least symbolically, in the affairs of state. Little did the kings know they were founding an institution in the thirteenth century that would overshadow the monarchy by the seventeenth century.

burghers   Originally, town dwellers; by extension, the middle class; French *bourgeoisie.*

Parliament   When capitalized, Britain's legislature, now usually meaning the House of Commons.

Commons   Lower house of Parliament; the elected, important chamber.

Lords   Upper house of Parliament; less important than *Commons.*

Parliament began as an extension of the king's court, but over the centuries took on a life of its own. Knights and burghers formed what we call a lower house, the House of **Commons**. Those of noble rank, along with the top churchmen, formed what we call an upper house, the House of **Lords**. In time, a leading member of the Commons, its Speaker, became its representative to the king. In order to conduct business unhampered, parliamentary privileges developed to prevent the arrest of members.

The House of Commons at this stage was not "representative," at least not in our sense. It represented only a few males who were locally wealthy or powerful. But more important than fair representation (which came in the nineteenth century), Parliament continued the blocking mechanism of the Magna Carta: It diffused power and prevented the king from getting too much.

GEOGRAPHY

THE UNITED KINGDOM

The full and official name of Britain is the United Kingdom of Great Britain and Northern Ireland. "Great Britain" refers to the whole island, which includes Wales and Scotland as well as England.

The British flag, the "Union Jack," stands for three saints representing different parts of the United Kingdom. The larger red cross is the Cross of St. George of England, the diagonal white cross is that of St. Andrew of Scotland, and the thinner, diagonal red cross is that of St. Patrick of Ireland. (Note this cross is off-center.) Now some English nationalists display just the English flag (red cross on a white field). In Edinburgh, capital of Scotland, most of the flags are now Scottish

(diagonal white cross on a blue field), an indication that the United Kingdom has grown less united. Symbols matter.

HENRY VIII

Parliament got a major boost during the reign of Henry VIII (1509–1547), when Henry declared a partnership with Parliament in his struggle against Rome. In addition to having to deal with growing tensions between the **Vatican** and London—the universal Church on the one hand and new religious ideas on the other—Henry needed the pope to grant him a divorce. His marriage to Catherine of Aragon had failed to produce the male heir Henry thought he needed to ensure stability after him. (Ironically, it was his daughter Elizabeth who went down in history as one of England's greatest monarchs.)

The pope refused to grant the divorce—Catherine's Spanish relatives controlled the papacy at that time—so Henry summoned a parliament in 1529 and kept it busy for seven years, passing law after law to get England out of the Catholic church and the Catholic church out of England. At the head of the new **Anglican** church was an Englishman, who granted Henry his divorce in 1533. Henry married a total of six wives (and had two of them beheaded) but was not lusting for young brides; he was desperate for a male heir.

The impact of Henry VIII's break with Rome was major. England was cut loose from Catholic guidance and direction. Countries that stayed Catholic—such as France, Spain, and Italy—experienced wrenching splits for centuries between pro-church and **anticlerical** forces. England (and Sweden) avoided this problematic division because from early on the state was stronger than the church and therefore controlled it. This meant that in England it was far easier to *secularize* society and politics than in Roman Catholic countries, where the church was still powerful.

Vatican   Headquarters of the Roman Catholic church.

Anglican   Church of England; Episcopalian in America.

anticlerical   Favoring getting the Roman Catholic church out of politics.

Common Law   System of judge-made law developed in England.

precedent   Legal reasoning based on previous cases.

COMPARISON

COMMON LAW

One of England's contributions to civilization is the **Common Law**, the legal system now also practiced in the United States (but not Louisiana), Canada, Australia, and many other countries once administered by Britain. Common Law grew out of the customary usage of the Germanic tribal laws of the Angles and Saxons, which stressed the rights of free men. It developed on the basis of **precedent** set by earlier decisions and thus has been called "judge-made law." After the Normans conquered England, they found the purely local nature of this law was too fragmented, so they set up central courts to systematize the local laws and produce a "common" law for all parts of England—hence the name.

Common Law is heavily case law and differs from code law, which is used by most of the Continent (and Scotland) and of the world, that emphasizes fixed legal codes rather than precedent and case-study. Code law is essentially Roman Law that was kept alive in the Canon Law of the Catholic Church, revived by modernizing Continental monarchs, and updated in 1804 into the *Code Napoléon*. Compared to code law, Common Law is flexible and adapts gradually with new cases.

---
landlocked   Country with no
seacoast.

Parliament became more important, as Henry needed it for his break with Rome. In 1543 Henry praised Parliament as an indispensable part of his government: "We be informed by our judges that we at no time stand so highly in our estate royal as in the time of parliament, wherein we as head and you as members are conjoined and knit together into one body politic." Henry unknowingly started an institutional shift from monarch to parliament. A century later Parliament beheaded an English king.

Parliament versus King

In the late fifteenth century several European monarchs expanded their powers and undermined the old feudal *mixed monarchy*. The weakened power of Rome in the sixteenth century gave kings more independence and introduced the notion that kings ruled by divine right, that is, that they received their authority directly from God without the pope as intermediary. Political theorists searched for the seat of *sovereignty* and concluded it must lie in one person, the monarch. This gave rise to absolutism. By 1660 absolute monarchs governed most lands of Europe—but not England.

The seventeenth century brought uninterrupted turmoil to England: religious splits, civil war, a royal beheading, and a military dictatorship. The net winner, when all of the dust had settled, was Parliament.

Trouble started when James I brought the Stuart dynasty from Scotland to take over the English throne after the death of Elizabeth I—the last Tudor—in 1603. James united the crowns of Scotland and England, but they remained separate countries until the 1707 Act of Union. James I held the absolutist notions then common throughout Europe; he did not like to share power and he thought that existing institutions should simply support the king. This brought him into conflict with Puritanism, an extreme Protestant movement that aimed to reform the "popish" elements out of the Anglican church. James preferred the church to stay just the way it was, for it was one of the pillars of his regime. Because of James's harassment, some Puritans ran away to Massachusetts.

Geography

Seacoast

A country with outlet to the sea has a major economic advantage over **landlocked** countries. Sea transport is cheap and does not require crossing neighboring countries. Usable natural harbors also help. Peter the Great battled for years to obtain Russian outlets on the Baltic and Black Seas. Atlantic Europe had an incredible advantage from the start. England's Atlantic orientation contributed to its empire, early industrialization, and prosperity.

By now Parliament had started to feel equal with the king and even, in the area of raising revenues, superior. Hard up for cash, James tried to impose taxes without the consent of Parliament, which grew angry over the move. James's son, Charles I, took over in 1625 and fared even worse. He took England into wars with Spain and France; both wars were unsuccessful and increased the king's desperation for money. Charles tried to play the role of a Continental absolute monarch, but the English people and Parliament would not let him.

When the **Royalists** fought the **Parliamentarians** in the English Civil War (1642–1648), the latter proved stronger, for the Parliamentarian cause was aided by Puritans and by the growing merchant class. The Parliamentarians created a "New Model Army," which trounced the Royalists. (As previously mentioned, the king had no standing army at his disposal.) Charles was captured, tried by Parliament, and beheaded in 1649.

> **Royalists** Supporters of the king in English Civil War.
> **Parliamentarians** Supporters of Parliament.
> **republic** Country not headed by a monarch.
> **Commonwealth** A republic.
> **republican** In its original sense, favoring getting rid of monarchy.
> **Levellers** Radicals during English Civil War who argued for equality and "one man, one vote."

CROMWELL'S COMMONWEALTH

From 1649 to 1660 England had no king. Who, then, was to rule? The only organized force left was the army, led by Oliver Cromwell. Briefly, England became a **republic** called the **Commonwealth**, led by Cromwell. Discord grew. To restore order, Cromwell in 1653 was designated Lord Protector, a sort of uncrowned king, and imposed a military dictatorship on England. When Cromwell died in 1658, most Englishmen had had enough of turbulent republicanism and longed for stability and order. In 1660, Parliament invited Charles II, son of the beheaded king, to return from Dutch exile and reclaim the throne. The English monarchy was restored, but now Parliament was much stronger and demanded respect.

DEMOCRACY

"ONE MAN, ONE VOTE"

Among the antiroyalists were **republicans**, called **Levellers**, who sought political equality. Soldiers in the New Model Army argued that people like themselves—tradesmen, artisans, and farmers—should have the vote. They were influenced by Puritanism, which taught that all men were equal before God and needed no spiritual or temporal superiors to guide them. (This Puritan influence also powerfully impacted American democracy.)

One group of Levellers, meeting in Putney in 1647, even went so far as to advocate "one man, one vote." This radical idea was a good two centuries ahead of its time, and the more conservative forces of England, including Cromwell, rejected it out of hand. Still, the Putney meeting had introduced the idea of the universal franchise—that is, giving everybody the right to vote.

THE "GLORIOUS REVOLUTION"

Charles II knew he could not be an absolute monarch; instead, he tried to manipulate Parliament discreetly, but religion tripped him up. Charles was pro-Catholic and secretly ready to proclaim allegiance to Rome. In 1673 he issued the Declaration of Indulgence, lifting laws against Catholics and non-Anglican Protestants. Parliament saw this act of tolerance toward minority religions as an illegal return to Catholicism and blocked it. Anti-Catholic hysteria swept England with fabricated stories of popish plots to take over the country.

prime minister Chief of government in parliamentary systems.

minister Head of a major department (ministry) of government.

When Charles II died in 1685, his openly Catholic brother James took the throne as James II. Again a Declaration of Indulgence was issued, and again Parliament took it as a return to both Catholicism and absolutism. Parliament dumped James II (but let him escape) and invited his Protestant daughter Mary and her Dutch husband William to be England's queen and king. This was the "Glorious Revolution" of 1688: A major shift of regime took place with scarcely a shot fired. (In 1690 William beat James in Ireland, but that was after the Revolution.) In 1689 a "Bill of Rights" (unlike its U.S. namesake) spelled out Parliament's relationship to the Crown: no laws or taxes without Parliament's assent.

The majority of Englishmen approved. If it was not clear before, it was now: Parliament was supreme and could invite and dismiss monarchs. In 1714 Parliament invited George I from Hanover in Germany to become king; the present royal family is descended from him. Since that time, the British monarch has been increasingly a figurehead, one who reigns but does not rule.

THE RISE OF THE PRIME MINISTER

One of the consequences of bringing George I to England was that he could not govern even if he wanted to. He spoke no English and preferred Hanover to London. So he turned to an institutional device that had been slowly developing and gave it executive power—the cabinet, composed of ministers and presided over by a first or prime minister. Headed by Sir Robert Walpole from 1721 to 1742, the cabinet developed nearly into its present form, but lacked two important present-day features: The **prime minister** could not pick his **ministers** (that was reserved for the

DEMOCRACY

"POWER CORRUPTS"

Nineteenth-century British historian and philosopher Lord Acton distilled the lessons of centuries of English political development in his famous remark: "Power tends to corrupt; absolute power corrupts absolutely."

Acton feared the human tendency to abuse power. His insight is absolutely accurate—check today's news— and underlies democratic thinking.

king), and the cabinet was not responsible—meaning, in its original sense, "answerable"—to Parliament.

Absolutism had one last gasp. George III packed Commons with his supporters and governed with the obedient Lord North as his prime minister. One unforeseen result was the U.S. Declaration of Independence, which sought to regain the traditional rights of Englishmen and spurred a revolution against the too-powerful king. Following this British defeat, William Pitt the Younger restored the

state of nature   Humans before civilization.

civil society   Humans after becoming civilized; modern usage: associations between family and government.

conservatism   Ideology of preserving existing institutions and usages.

PERSONALITIES

HOBBES, LOCKE, BURKE

Thomas Hobbes lived through the upheavals of the English Civil War in the seventeenth century and opposed them for making people insecure and frightened. Hobbes imagined that life in "the **state of nature**," before "**civil society**" was founded, must have been terrible. Every man would have been the enemy of every other man, a "war of each against all." Humans would live in savage squalor with "no arts; no letters; no society; and which is worst of all, continual fear, and danger of violent death; and the life of man, solitary, poor, nasty, brutish, and short." To escape this horror, people would—out of self-interest—rationally join together to form civil society. Society thus arises naturally out of fear. People would also gladly submit to a king, even a bad one, in order to prevent anarchy.

John Locke saw the same upheavals but came to less harsh conclusions. Locke theorized that the original state of nature was not so bad; people lived in equality and tolerance with one another. But they could not secure their property: There was no money, title deeds, or courts of law, so their property was uncertain. To remedy this, they contractually formed civil society and thus secured "life, liberty, and property." Locke is to property rights as Hobbes is to fear of violent death. Americans are the children of Locke; notice the American emphasis on "the natural right to property."

Edmund Burke, a Whig member of Parliament, was horrified at the French Revolution, warning it would end up a military dictatorship (it did). The French revolutionists had broken the historical continuity,

Thomas Hobbes

John Locke

Edmund Burke

institutions, and symbols that restrain people from bestial behavior, argued Burke. Old institutions, such as the monarchy and church, must be pretty good because they have evolved over centuries. If you scrap them, society breaks down and leads to tyranny. Burke understood that **conservatism** means constant, but never radical, change. Wrote Burke: "A state without the means of some change is without the means of its conservation." Progress comes not from chucking out the old but from gradually modifying the parts that need changing while preserving the overall structure, keeping the form but reforming the contents.

Whigs Faction of Parliament that became Liberal party.

Tories Faction of Parliament that became Conservative party.

cabinet and prime minister to power and made them responsible only to Commons, not to the king. This began the tradition—which has never been written into law—that the "government" consists of the leader of the largest party in the House of Commons along with other people he or she picks. As party chief, top member of Parliament, and head of government combined, the prime minister became the focus of political power in Britain.

The Democratization of Parliament

Parliament was supreme by the late eighteenth century, but it was not democratic or representative. In the eighteenth century, parties began to form. The labels **Whig** and **Tory** first appeared under Charles II, connoting his opposition and his supporters, respectively. Both were derisive names: The original Whigs were Scottish bandits, and the original Tories were Irish bandits. At first these proto-parties were simply parliamentary caucuses, Tories representing the landed aristocracy, Whigs the merchants and manufacturers. Only in the next century did they take root in the electorate.

Comparison

The Origins of Two Welfare States

Both Britain and Sweden are welfare states, Sweden more so than Britain. How did this come to be? In comparing their histories, we get some clues.

- Swedish King Gustav Vasa broke with Rome in the 1520s, a few years earlier than Henry VIII. In setting up churches that were dependent on their respective states—Lutheran in Sweden, Anglican in England—the two countries eliminated religion as a source of opposition to government.

- Because of this, politics in both lands avoided getting stuck in a clerical-anticlerical dispute over the role of the Church, as happened in France, Italy, and Spain. In Britain and Sweden, the main political split was along class lines, working class versus middle class.

- Britain and Sweden both developed efficient and uncorrupt civil services, which are an absolute essential for effective welfare programs.

- Workers in both countries organized strong, but not Marxist, labor unions, the TUC in Britain and LO in Sweden.

- These two labor movements gave rise to moderate, worker-oriented parties, Labour in Britain and the Social Democrats in Sweden, which over time got numerous welfare measures passed. One big difference between the labor movements is that the Social Democrats have been in power in Sweden for all but a few years since 1932 and have implemented a more thorough—and more expensive—welfare state.

During the nineteenth century, a two-party system emerged. The Whigs grew into the Liberal party and the Tories into the Conservative party (still nicknamed Tories). Parliamentarians were not ordinary people. The House of Lords was limited to hereditary peers. The House of Commons, despite its name, was the home of gentry, landowners, and better-off people, who often won by bribing the few voters. This has been termed **Whig democracy**, and it is standard in the opening decades of democratic development, as in the pre-Jackson United States. Mass participation usually comes later.

Whig democracy   Democracy with limited participation, typical of democracy's initial phases.

Reform Acts   Series of laws expanding the British electoral franchise.

welfare state   Political system that redistributes wealth from rich to poor, standard in West Europe.

By the time of the American and French revolutions in the late eighteenth century, however, Parliament noticed demands to expand the electorate. People talked about democracy and the right to vote. Under the impact of the industrial revolution and economic growth, two powerful new social classes arose— the middle class and the working class. Whigs and Tories, both elite in their makeup, at first fought demands for the mass vote.

Gradually, though, the Whigs saw that political stability required bringing some ordinary Britons into politics to give them a stake in the system. Furthermore, they realized that the party that supported broadening the franchise would most likely win the new voters. After much resistance by Tories in Commons and by the entire House of Lords, Parliament passed the **Reform Act** of 1832, which allowed more of the middle class to vote but still only expanded the electorate by about half, to about 7 percent of adults. The Reform Act established the principle, though, that Commons ought to be representative of, and responsive to, the broad mass of citizens, not just the notables. In 1867, it was the Conservatives' turn. Under Prime Minister Benjamin Disraeli, the Second Reform Act doubled the size of the electorate, giving about 16 percent of adult Britons the vote. In 1884, the Third Reform Act added farm workers to the electorate and thus achieved nearly complete male suffrage. Women finally got the vote in 1918.

The interesting point about the British electorate is that its growth was slow. New elements were added to the voting rolls only gradually, giving Parliament time to assimilate the forces of mass politics without going through an upheaval. The gradual tempo also meant citizens got the vote when they were ready for it. In some countries where the universal franchise—one person, one vote—was instituted early, the result was fake democracy, as crafty officials rigged the voting of people who did not understand electoral politics. Spain, for example, got universal suffrage in the 1870s, but election results were set in advance. By the time the British working class got the vote, they were ready to use it intelligently.

With the expansion of the voting franchise, political parties turned from parliamentary clubs into modern parties. They had to win elections involving thousands of voters. This meant organization, programs, promises, and continuity. The growth of the electorate forced parties to become vehicles for democracy.

The Rise of the Welfare State

By the beginning of the twentieth century, with working men having the right to vote, British parties had to pay attention to demands for welfare measures—public education, housing, jobs, and medical care—that the gentlemen of the Liberal and Conservative parties had ignored. Expansion of the electoral franchise led to the growth of the **welfare state**.

One force pushing for welfare measures was the new Labour party, founded in 1900. At first, Labour worked with the Liberals—the "Lib-Lab" coalition—but by the end of World War I, Labour pushed the Liberals into the weak third-party status they have languished in to this day. Unlike most Continental socialists, few British Labourites were Marxists. Instead, they combined militant trade unionism with intellectual social democracy to produce a pragmatic, gradualist ideology that sought to level class differences in Britain. As one observer put it, the British Labour party "owed more to Methodism than to Marx."

The British labor movement of the late nineteenth century was tough, a quality it long retained. Resentful of being treated like dirt, many working men went into politics with a militancy that still characterizes some of their heirs. In the 1926 General Strike, the trade unions attempted to bring the entire British economy to a halt to gain their wage demands. They failed.

Labour was briefly and weakly in power under Ramsay MacDonald in the 1920s, and then won resoundingly in 1945 and implemented an ambitious welfare program plus state takeover of utilities, railroads, coal mines, and much heavy manufacturing. Since then, the chief quarrel in British politics has been between people who like the welfare state and state ownership and people who do not.

KEY TERMS

Anglican (p. 23)
anticlerical (p. 23)
burghers (p. 22)
Celts (p. 21)
civil society (p. 27)
Common Law (p. 23)
Commons (p. 22)
Commonwealth (p. 25)
conservatism (p. 27)
Continent, the (p. 21)
Exchequer (p. 21)

fiefdom (p. 21)
landlocked (p. 24)
Levellers (p. 25)
Lords (p. 22)
Magna Carta (p. 21)
minister (p. 26)
mixed monarchy (p. 21)
Normans (p. 21)
Parliament (p. 22)
Parliamentarians (p. 25)
precedent (p. 23)

prime minister (p. 26)
Reform Acts (p. 29)
republic (p. 25)
republican (p. 25)
Royalists (p. 25)
state of nature (p. 27)
Tories (p. 28)
Vatican (p. 23)
welfare state (p. 29)
Whig democracy (p. 29)
Whigs (p. 28)

FURTHER REFERENCE

Callaghan, John. *Socialism in Britain Since 1884.* Cambridge, MA: Basil Blackwell, 1990.

Chrimes, S. B. *English Constitutional History.* London: Oxford University Press, 1967.

Clarke, Peter. *Hope and Glory: Britain 1900–1990.* New York: Penguin, 1996.

Colley, Linda. *Britons: Forging the Nation, 1707–1837.* New Haven, CT: Yale University Press, 1992.

Davies, Norman. *The Isles: A History.* New York: Oxford University Press, 1999.

Greenleaf, W. H. *The British Political Tradition,* 3 vols. London: Methuen, 1987.

Hattersley, Roy. *Borrowed Time: The Story of Britain between the Wars.* Boston: Little Brown, 2007.

Hibbert, Christopher. *Cavaliers & Roundheads: The English Civil War, 1642–1649.* New York: Scribner's, 1993.

Hilton, Boyd. *A Mad, Bad, and Dangerous People? England, 1783–1846.* New York: Oxford University Press, 2008.

Kishlansky, Mark. *A Monarchy Transformed: Britain, 1603–1714.* New York: Allen Lane/Penguin Press, 1997.

McKibben, Ross. *Classes and Cultures: England 1918–1951.* New York: Oxford University Press, 1998.

Pearce, Edward. *The Great Man—Sir Robert Walpole: Scoundrel, Genius, and Britain's First Prime Minister.* London: Jonathan Cape, 2007.

Thorpe, Andrew. *A History of the British Labour Party.* New York: St. Martin's, 1997.

CHAPTER 3
BRITAIN:
The Key Institutions

It is commonly said that Britain has no written constitution, but parts of the British constitution are written. It does not consist of a single document but is rather a centuries-old collection of Common Law, historic charters, **statutes** passed by Parliament, and, most important, established custom.

This **eclectic** quality gives the British constitution flexibility. With no single, written document to refer to, nothing can be declared "unconstitutional." Parliament—specifically the House of Commons—can pass any law it likes, letting the British political system change over time without a systemic crisis. The U.S. Supreme Court sometimes blocks changes as unconstitutional, rarely a problem in Britain.

The negative side to this was that Britain had little to guarantee human rights. In 1991, six men convicted as IRA bombers in 1975 were freed with the shameful admission that confessions had been beaten out of them and the police had rigged evidence. The European Court of Human Rights, located in Strasbourg, France, ruled against British justice in several such cases, a considerable embarrassment for Britain. In 2000, Britain adopted the European Convention on Human Rights as domestic law, finally giving Britons the equivalent of a U.S. Bill of Rights.

The British speak of "the **Crown**," an all-encompassing term meaning the powers of government in general. Originally, the Crown meant the king, but over the centuries it has broadened to include everyone helping the king or queen, such as Parliament, the cabinet, and civil servants. Let us consider some of these.

QUESTIONS TO CONSIDER

1. What did Bagehot mean by "dignified" as opposed to "efficient" offices? Examples?
2. How is Britain a "prime ministerial government"?
3. Does Britain have checks and balances?
4. What are Brown's political positions?
5. When does Britain hold general elections?
6. What are the differences between presidential and parliamentary systems?
7. What did Blair do with Lords?
8. How does the British electoral system work?
9. What are Britain's main parties?

THE MONARCH

In Britain there is a clear distinction between "head of state" and "chief of government." In America this distinction is ignored because the two are merged into one in the presidency. In most of the rest of the world, however, there is a top figure without much power who symbolizes the nation, receives foreign ambassadors, and gives speeches on patriotic occasions. This person—often a figurehead—can be either a hereditary monarch or an elected president, although not a U.S.-style president. Britain, Sweden, Norway, Denmark, the Netherlands, Belgium, and Spain are monarchies. This does not mean they are undemocratic; it just means the head of state is a carryover from old days.

statute Ordinary law, usually for a specific problem. (See page 33.)

eclectic Drawn from a variety of sources. (See page 33.)

Crown The powers of the British government. (See page 33.)

dignified In Bagehot's terms, symbolic or decorative offices.

efficient In Bagehot's terms, working, political offices.

A hereditary head of state can be useful. Above politics, a monarch can serve as psychological cement to hold a country together because he or she has no important role in government. Because the top position in the land—what royalist philosophers used to call the sovereign—is already occupied, there are no political battles over it. The nastiest struggles in the world are precisely over who is to be sovereign; in Britain, the issue has long been settled.

The great commentator on the British constitution, Sir Walter Bagehot, divided it into **dignified** and **efficient** parts. The monarch, as head of state, is a dignified office with much symbolic but no real political power. He or she "reigns but does not rule." The king or queen nominally appoints a cabinet of His or Her Majesty's servants (see box on page 36), but otherwise a monarch is more like an official greeter.

The "efficient" office in Britain is the chief of government, the prime minister—a working politician who fights elections, leads his or her party, and makes political deals. Despite the prestige of a prime minister, it does not have nearly the "dignity" that the monarch has. There is an advantage in the way Britain and other countries split the two positions. If the chief of government does something foolish or illegal, he or she will catch the public's ire, but the blame will fall on the individual prime minister, and respect will not diminish for the head of state, the "dignified" office. The system retains its legitimacy. Where the two offices are combined, as in the United States, and the president is involved in something crooked, the public gets disgusted at both the working politician and the nation's symbolic leader. "The British do not need to love their prime minister," said one diplomat. "They love their queen."

The 1997 death of Princess Di, ex-wife of Prince Charles, jolted Britain, including the royal family. Di was the only royal with the common touch; her charity work and love life upstaged the cold and remote House of Windsor. Amidst the outpouring of grief for Di came mutterings that the royal family really did not much care. Some even thought it might be time to dump the monarchy. But old dynasties know how to survive, and the Queen and Prince Charles quickly became more public and outgoing.

Although few would exchange the monarchy for a republic, some (including Queen Elizabeth herself) suggest reforms that would cut government funds for the royal house and make female heirs to the throne the equal of males. Look for a major decision point when Queen Elizabeth dies. Will Charles automatically accede to the throne? Even with his 2005 remarriage? To a commoner (herself divorced)? The last time this happened, in 1936, King Edward VIII abdicated, but a replay is unlikely;

Prince Charles, Britain's future king and head of the state, in happier days with his then-wife, the late Princess Diana, and their children, Prince William, also a future king, and Prince Henry. The divorce of Charles and Diana in 1996 did not affect Charles's succession to the throne.

times have changed. Britain will likely retain a monarchy, but it may be a monarch with reduced financial support and political roles.

THE CABINET

The British cabinet also differs from the U.S. cabinet. The former consists of members of Parliament (most in Commons, a few in Lords) who are high up in their parties and important political figures. Most have lots of experience, first as ordinary **MPs** (members of Parliament), then as **junior ministers**, and finally as cabinet ministers. In 2006 eight junior ministers resigned their positions (but not their seats in Parliament) to protest Blair's refusal to set a date for stepping down. It was one of the pressures on Blair to leave in 2007. Prime ministers are powerful, but only with the solid support of their parties.

MP Member of Parliament.

junior minister MP with executive responsibilities below cabinet rank.

portfolio Minister's assigned ministry.

fusion of powers Connection of executive and legislative branches in parliamentary systems; opposite of U.S. separation of powers.

Cortes Spain's parliament.

antithetical Ideas opposed to one another.

Originally, the British cabinet consisted of ministers to the king. Starting in the seventeenth century, the cabinet became more and more responsible to Parliament and less and less to the king. A British minister is not necessarily an expert in his or her **portfolio** but is carefully picked by the prime minister for political qualifications. Both major British parties contain several viewpoints and power centers, and prime ministers usually take care to see they are represented in the cabinet. When Prime Minister Thatcher ignored this principle by picking as ministers only Tories loyal to her and her philosophy, she was criticized as dictatorial and ultimately lost her job. Balancing party factions in the cabinet helps keep the party together in Parliament and in power. British cabinet government has been declining since World War I, which required speedy, centralized decisions. Now the prime minister develops policy with a small personal staff and then informs the cabinet of it. British commentators fear the rise of a "command premiership" in this development.

Notice the British cabinet straddles the gap between "executive" and "legislative." The elaborate American separation of powers (adopted by the Founding Fathers from an earlier misperception of British government by Montesquieu) does not hold in Britain or in most of the world. The United Kingdom has a combining or **fusion of powers**.

DEMOCRACY

THE LAST POLITICAL MONARCH

Unlike other European monarchs, King Juan Carlos of Spain retains some crucial political functions. Juan Carlos took over as head of state after Franco's death in 1975 and initiated and backstopped a process that turned Spain from dictatorship to democracy. He named a prime minister who dismantled the Franco structure, carried out Spain's first free elections in forty-one years, and drafted a new constitution—all with the open approval of the king.

Juan Carlos's real test as defender of democracy came in 1981 when some disgruntled officers attempted a coup; they held the entire **Cortes** at gunpoint. In military uniform, the king addressed the nation on television and ordered the troops back to their barracks. They complied, and democratic Spaniards of all parties thanked God for the king. Democracy and monarchy are not **antithetical**; one can support the other. ¡*Viva el rey!*

The British cabinet practices "collective responsibility," meaning they all stick together and, in public at least, support the prime minister. Occasionally, a minister resigns in protest over a major controversy. In recent years, the cabinet has consisted of some twenty ministers, although this number and portfolio titles change. Prime ministers design their own cabinet; they add, drop, rename, or combine ministries. Each cabinet is different. Most countries function that way (not, of course, the United States). The 2007 Brown cabinet consisted of the following "secretaries of state":

Chancellor of the Exchequer (treasury)	Communities and Local Government
Lord Chancellor (member of Lords, heads judiciary)	Business, Enterprise, and Regulatory Reform
Foreign and Commonwealth Affairs	Health
Home Department (internal governance, including police)	Northern Ireland
	Wales
Environment, Food, and Rural Affairs	Scotland
International Development	Defense
Work and Pensions	Trade and Industry
Children, Schools, and Families	Innovation, Universities, and Skills
Transport	Culture, Media, and Sport

The Secretary for Defense did double duty as Secretary for Scotland; the Secretary for Work and Pensions also served as Secretary for Wales. The leaders of both Commons and Lords are in the cabinet, along with a chief secretary for the cabinet as a whole. In addition, several junior ministers and "parliamentary private secretaries" held specialized offices in the cabinet. A British cabinet is almost a free-form exercise created by each prime minister.

Below cabinet rank are more than thirty noncabinet "departmental ministers" and a similar number of "junior ministers" assigned to help cabinet and departmental ministers. All totaled, at any given time about a hundred MPs are also serving in the executive branch. The hope of being named to one of these positions ensures the loyalty and obedience of most younger MPs.

DEMOCRACY

THE QUEEN CHOOSES A NEW PRIME MINISTER

In June 2007 an old ritual was repeated. Ostensibly Queen Elizabeth II chose a new prime minister, but of course she really had no choice at all. Events unrolled according to the fiction that the prime minister is still chief advisor to the monarch.

Labour Prime Minister Tony Blair, having served ten years, resigned to make way for his fellow Labourite Gordon Brown, who had ably served as Chancellor of the Exchequer. The two rivals inside the Labour party had made a deal: Blair would serve first, then Brown would step up. Brown was publicly impatient for his turn. It was an unusual transition, with neither a general election nor a party conference to make Brown party chief and PM. Instead, Blair simply designated Brown as his successor.

Blair called on the Queen and formally resigned as first minister to Her Majesty. (He also resigned his seat in Parliament and resigned as Labour's leader.) That same day the Queen called Gordon Brown, as leader of the largest party in the Commons, to Buckingham Palace and "asked" him to form a new government. He accepted.

For all intents and purposes, in Britain (and in most parliamentary systems) cabinet equals **government**; the two terms are used interchangeably. One speaks of the "Brown government." (Only the United States uses the word "administration.") When the "government falls" it simply means the cabinet has resigned. Britain is often referred to as "cabinet government," although some call it "prime ministerial government."

> **government**   A particular cabinet, what Americans call "the administration."
>
> **whip**   Parliamentary party leader who makes sure members obey the party in voting.
>
> **division**   Vote in the House of Commons.

The Prime Minister

The prime minister, PM for short (not to be confused with MP, which he or she also is), is the linchpin of the British system. In theory, the PM's powers could be dictatorial. Because the prime minister picks and controls the cabinet and heads the largest party in Parliament, he or she should be able to get nearly any measure passed. British parliamentarians are well-disciplined; party **whips** make sure their MPs turn out for **divisions** and vote the party line. Yet even with the reins of power held by one person, prime ministers do not turn into dictators, chiefly because general elections are never more than five years away.

Key Concepts

Prime Ministers into Presidents

Political scientists have for some time noted that prime ministers are becoming more and more presidential. Postwar British prime ministers increasingly concentrated and centralized power in their immediate office at the expense of the cabinet and Commons.

Brown, for example, no longer pretended to be "first among equals" in his cabinet, which met less often and decided issues less frequently. Like the U.S. cabinet secretaries, British ministers became more like top administrators. Instead, Brown presided over an enlarged staff at 10 Downing Street, headed with trusted advisors, and used them to make decisions, rather like the White House.

Continuing a trend, Brown spent less time in Commons. Prime Minister Churchill voted in 55 percent of Commons divisions in 1951. Prime Minister Wilson voted 43 percent of the time in 1974. Tony Blair voted 5 percent of the time in Commons in 1997.

Some called both Blair and Brown "control freaks" who broke with British tradition in order to amass personal power. Maybe, but personality alone does not explain the long-term trend for prime ministers

everywhere to become presidential. One key factor worldwide: television, which centralizes election campaigns, emphasizes the top candidates, creates massive need for fundraising, bypasses parties and parliaments, and enables leaders to reach people directly. Other factors include the decline of legislatures, the growth of interest groups, and the tendency of voters to concentrate in the center of the political spectrum.

Parliamentary systems cannot operate as before. Systems as different as Britain, France, Germany, and Japan have tended to "presidentialize" themselves as prime ministers gain power and start acting as if they have been directly elected. Everywhere, even in parliamentary systems, parties in elections showcase their leading personality as if he or she was a presidential candidate. Parliamentary systems will not turn completely into U.S.-type systems, but neither will any of them return to the pure parliamentary model, which was never completely realistic. Even in parliamentary systems, power long ago began shifting to prime ministers, and this has continued. A strong prime minister begins to resemble a U.S.-type president.

Prime ministers are usually cautious about introducing measures that might provoke public ire. When Tory PM John Major saw his popularity slipping, he knew he would lose if he "went to the country" with new elections, so he tried to stall, hoping his party's fortunes would rise before the five years were up. Typically, prime ministers introduce moderate, piecemeal measures to avoid offending key blocks of voters. Fear of losing the next election keeps most prime ministers (but not Thatcher) cautious.

PERSONALITIES

FROM BLAIR TO BROWN

Tony Blair   Gordon Brown

Two back-to-back Labour prime ministers—Tony Blair (1997–2007) and Gordon Brown (2007–)—show much continuity but also some interesting differences, mostly related to personality. Both were born in Scotland—Blair in Edinburgh in 1953, Brown in Glasgow in 1951—but Blair always considered himself English and Brown a Scot. Both are very bright but Brown probably brainier. Brown, physically rugged, lost an eye playing rugby. Blair studied law at Oxford; Brown went to the University of Edinburgh at age 16 to earn a doctorate on Scottish Labour party history. Blair joined Labour only after college; Brown was committed to it from youth. Both lost their first tries at election to Commons but won their second attempts, both in 1983. Brown still represents his constituency near Edinburgh in Parliament.

The two helped push the Labour party from its leftist positions—which cost it four elections in a row—to a reformist and centrist "New Labour" that won the 1997 elections in a landslide. Earlier, Blair and Brown vied for Labour leadership, but in a murky 1994 deal Brown agreed to let Blair lead the party and become PM first while Brown would do economic policy and become PM later.

In 1997 Blair became Britain's youngest prime minister since 1812; Brown became Chancellor of the Exchequer (treasury minister) and did an excellent job of keeping the British economy growing and scrutinizing the ministries' budgets. Brown is an energetic detail person. Blair and Brown continued a trend that some observers say has been underway since the 1960s: prime ministers acting more like presidents. They indeed centralized and concentrated power in the prime minister's office at the expense of the cabinet and Commons (see box on page 37).

Over time, Brown's impatience to step up to Number 10 grew more public, but Blair wanted a full ten years to push through his agenda—a settlement of the Northern Ireland conflict, devolution for Scotland and Wales, reform of Lords (see page 43), and adoption of the EU human rights charter. Neither Blair nor Brown wished to change Margaret Thatcher's free-market economic policies. Blair made himself unpopular by sending British forces to Iraq—he was called "Bush's poodle"—and under heavy party pressure agreed to step down in mid-2007. Brown likes America and knows it well—he often vacationed there and follows American scholarship—but never liked the Iraq War. He pulled British forces out of Iraq with an eye to the next general election, which he must call by mid-2010.

Personality made a difference in Blair's and Brown's tenures. Blair was nice, optimistic, chatty, and superficial. Brown, son of a Presbyterian minister, exudes the Protestant work ethic and demands it of others. Brown is the dour Scot and detail person who can blow up when angered. Some call Brown a rigid and domineering "control freak," and his popularity has plunged as the British economy has slowed. By-elections and public opinion surveys suggest Brown's tenure could be short.

Furthermore, a prime minister has to be careful of the major currents of opinion within party ranks. As in the United States, the two large British parties contain left, right, and center wings, as well as regional viewpoints, and a prime minister usually constructs the cabinet with top MPs representing several views within the majority party. In cabinet meetings the PM tries to fashion a consensus from the several stands.

Then the cabinet has to sell the policy to their MPs back in Commons. Party discipline is good but rarely total. The prime minister, through the chief whip, has a hold on the MPs, but never a perfect hold. Many leftist Labour MPs voted against Blair's centrist policies and the Iraq War. One who does not "take the whip" (follow the party line on a vote), however, risks losing his or her nomination for reelection—in effect, getting fired from Parliament, which happened to one especially anti-Blair Labourite. If a party policy really bothers an MP, the member can "cross the aisle" and join the other party in protest (as did the young Winston Churchill).

A prime minister can even be dumped by MPs. Labour and Conservative cabinets have had to withdraw or water down legislative proposals amid a backbenchers' revolt within their own party. A backbenchers' revolt helped oust Thatcher in 1990. In 2005 forty-nine backbenchers revolted against a bill Blair said was necessary to fight terrorism. The vote was over how long police could detain without charges, but the underlying issue was Blair's Iraq policy. Labour backbenchers shot down Blair's bill, in effect saying: "Blair, time for you to go." In 2007, he went.

Commons can oust a PM on a **vote of no-confidence**, but that is rare; it indicates the ruling party has split so badly its MPs are willing to give up power. Blair's 2005 loss was not a "motion of confidence" and so did not require him to resign. Loss of a big measure, such as the budget, would require the PM to resign.

The PM does have a potent political weapon: the power to call new elections whenever he or she wishes. By law, the Commons can go up to five years without a general election. **By-elections** when an MP dies or retires can come any time; they are closely watched as political barometers. Crafty prime ministers call for new general elections when they think the party will do best. A good

---

vote of no-confidence Parliamentary vote to oust cabinet.

by-election Special election for vacant seat in Parliament.

WHO WAS WHEN: BRITAIN'S POSTWAR PRIME MINISTERS

Clement Attlee	Labour	1945–1951
Winston Churchill	Conservative	1951–1955
Anthony Eden	Conservative	1955–1957
Harold Macmillan	Conservative	1957–1963
Alec Douglas-Home	Conservative	1963–1964
Harold Wilson	Labour	1964–1970
Edward Heath	Conservative	1970–1974
Harold Wilson	Labour	1974–1976
James Callaghan	Labour	1976–1979
Margaret Thatcher	Conservative	1979–1990
John Major	Conservative	1990–1997
Tony Blair	Labour	1997–2007
Gordon Brown	Labour	2007–

economy and sunny weather tend to produce a happy electorate, one that will increase the seats of the ruling party. In 1974 Britain held two general elections because Prime Minister Harold Wilson thought he could boost Labour's strength in the Commons (he did). In 2001 and 2005 Tony Blair called elections a year early to take advantage of good economic news and disarray in the Conservative party; he won handily. New elections must be held by 2010 but again will likely be called a year early. Public-opinion polls and by-elections help the prime minister decide when to ask the queen to dissolve Parliament and hold new elections.

DEMOCRACY

PARLIAMENTARY VERSUS PRESIDENTIAL SYSTEMS

In a parliamentary system, like Britain, voters choose only a parliament, which in turn chooses (and can oust) the executive branch, headed by a prime minister. The executive is a committee of the legislature. In a presidential system, such as the United States, voters choose both a legislature and a chief executive, and the two are expected to check and balance each other. In a parliamentary system, they are not.

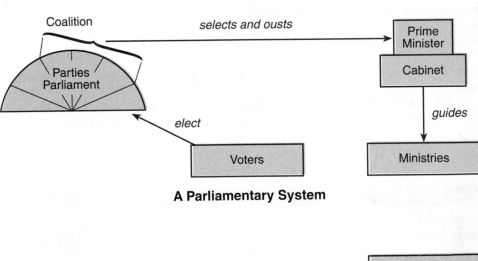

A Parliamentary System

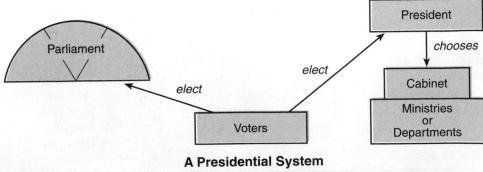

A Presidential System

Since 1735 British prime ministers have resided in an ordinary brick row house, No. 10 Downing Street. Except for London bobbies on guard outside, it looks like a private home. This is deceptive; behind the walls, Downing Street is the nerve center of **Whitehall**. Upstairs at No. 10, the prime minister has his or her apartment. On the ground floor, in the back, the cabinet meets in a long white room. No. 10 connects to No. 12 Downing Street, the residence of the chief whip, the prime minister's parliamentary enforcer. They can visit without being seen from the street. Also connecting out of sight is No. 11 Downing Street, residence of the important Chancellor of the Exchequer, head of the powerful Treasury Ministry. Next door is the Foreign Office. At the corner of Downing Street, also connecting to No. 10, is the cabinet secretariat, responsible for communication and coordination among the departments.

Whitehall	Main British government offices.
Westminster	Parliament building.

COMMONS

One can look at the cabinet as a committee of the House of Commons sent from **Westminster** to nearby Whitehall to keep administration under parliamentary control. Another way is to view Commons as an electoral college that stays in operation even after it has chosen the executive (the cabinet). In Lockean theory, legislative power has primacy, but in practice Commons has rarely been free and independent and is becoming less so. Prime ministers lead and control Commons.

House of Commons in session. Notice how small it is.

opposition   Parties in Parliament that are not in the cabinet.

backbencher   Ordinary MP with no executive responsibility.

The two main parties in Commons—Conservative and Labour—face each other on long, parallel benches. The largest party is automatically Her Majesty's Government and the other party is Her Majesty's Loyal **Opposition**. Commons is very small—only 45 by 68 feet (14 by 21 meters)—and was originally designed for only about 400 members. How then can it possibly hold the current membership of 646? Membership has increased over the years as Britain's population has grown in some areas more than in others. Parliament in 2005 cut thirteen seats by combining some smaller constituencies, but it is still crowded. Unlike most modern legislators, Parliament members have no individual desks. For important votes, MPs have to pack in like sardines and sit in the aisles.

The cramped setting ensures that members face each other in debate a few yards apart. The parallel benches go well with the two-party system; the half-circle floor plan of most Continental legislatures facilitates pie-like division into multiparty systems. The chamber was always small, ever since 1547 when Henry VIII first gave Commons the use of the St. Stephen's royal chapel. During World War II when Commons was damaged by German bombs, Prime Minister Winston Churchill ordered it rebuilt exactly the way it had been.

Each side of the oblong chamber has five rows of benches. The front row on either side is reserved for the leading team of each major party, the cabinet of the government party, and the "shadow cabinet" of the opposition. Behind them sit the **backbenchers**, the MP rank and file. A neutral Speaker, elected for life from the MPs, sits in a throne-like chair at one end. The Speaker, who never votes or takes sides, manages the floor debate and preserves order. In 1992, Commons elected its first woman Speaker, Labourite Betty Boothroyd.

A table in the center, between the party benches, is where legislation is placed (the origin of the verb "to table" a proposal). The Speaker calls the house to order at 11:30 A.M. and sessions can go on until 7:30 P.M. Unless "the whip is on"—meaning an MP had better be there because an important vote is expected—many MPs are busy elsewhere.

DEMOCRACY

THE DECLINE OF LEGISLATURES

Commons is less important than it used to be. As in most of the world, legislatures, the great avenues of democracy are declining in power. Fewer people—especially young people—bother voting and fewer follow debates in Commons, which gets less media attention. The debates matter little; thanks to Britain's (over)disciplined parties, the prime minister almost always gets his or her way. The only way to jump-start Commons back into life would be to let MPs ignore the whip and vote as they wish. A deliberate weakening of Britain's parties might make Commons exciting, unpredictable, and messy, like the U.S. Congress. A word of caution here: Capitol Hill has also been losing power to the White House. This may be an unstoppable world trend. Even so, legislatures are invaluable for scrutinizing executive power, holding it accountable, and occasionally ousting it. If they do this, they are still bulwarks of democracy.

How Commons Works

Each year Parliament opens in November with another tradition, a Speech from the Throne by the queen. The MPs are ritually summoned from Commons by Black Rod, the queen's messenger, and then they file into the nearby House of Lords. (Neither monarchs nor lords may enter Commons.) From a gold-paneled dais in Lords, Her Majesty reads a statement outlining the policies "her government" will pursue. The speech has been written by the prime minister, with the queen merely serving as the announcer. George VI, a conservative king, once read a Labour speech (in 1945) promising extensive nationalization of industry.

> **select committee** Specialized committee of Commons focusing on one ministry.
>
> **life peers** Distinguished Britons named lords for their lifetimes only; does not pass on to children.

Just as the queen takes her cues from the prime minister, so does Commons. Practically all legislation is introduced by the "government" (that is, the cabinet) and stands a high chance of passing nearly intact because of the party discipline discussed previously. What the PM wants, the PM usually gets. When a Labour government introduces bills into Commons, Labour MPs—unlike their American counterparts in Congress—rarely question them. Their job is to support the party, and individual conscience seldom gets in the way.

The task of challenging proposals falls to the opposition, seated on the Speaker's left. From the opposition benches come questions, denunciations, warnings of dire consequences, anything that might make the government look bad. There is no bipartisanship. Government MPs, particularly the cabinet and subcabinet ministers on the front bench, are duty-bound to defend the bills. In situations like these, the famous rhetorical ability of MPs produces debates matched by few other legislatures.

Although the rhetoric is brilliant and witty, the homework is somewhat lacking. Because they are expected simply to obey their party, few MPs specialize. Traditionally, British parliamentary committees were also unspecialized; they went over the precise wording of bills but called no witnesses and gathered no data. The structure of legislative committees is an important key to their power, and eventually some MPs recognized the need for a more American type of committee system. In 1979, fourteen **select committees** were established to scrutinize the workings of each ministry; these committees have the power to gather written and oral evidence. The select committees—with permanent, stable membership—resemble U.S. Congressional committees.

Peerless Lords

In 1999, Parliament drastically reformed the House of Lords by kicking out most of its hereditary peers, thus turning it over to **life peers**. Since 1958, distinguished Britons in the disciplines of science, politics, diplomacy, military service, business, literature, and the arts have been named as Lords or Ladies of the Realm, but for their lifetimes only. This change has done nothing to enhance Lords' weak powers. Lords now has some 740 peers (a number that changes with deaths and new appointments), most of them life peers, along with 92 hereditary peers and 26 top churchmen.

Law Lords Britain's top judges, members of Lords.

anachronism Something from the past that does not fit present times.

The British Parliament is nominally bicameral, but Commons has limited Lords' powers over the centuries, so that now when one says "Parliament," one really means Commons. Early on, Commons established supremacy in the key area of money: raising revenues and spending them. (An echo of this is the U.S. provision that money bills originate in the lower chamber, the House of Representatives.) Britain's seventeenth-century battles centered on the power of Commons, and it emerged the winner; Lords gradually took a back seat. By 1867 Bagehot considered Lords a "dignified" part of the constitution. Strictly speaking, a unitary system like Britain does not need an upper house; federal systems do, to represent the component parts (see page 188 in Chapter 13). New Zealand realized this and dropped its upper chamber in 1951.

Since Britain's unwritten constitution does not specify or make permanent the powers of the two chambers, it was legally possible for Commons to weaken Lords. The 1911 Parliament Act allows Lords to delay legislation not more than thirty days on financial bills and two years (since 1949, one year) on other bills. Lords can amend legislation and send it back to Commons, which in turn can (and usually does) delete the changes by a simple majority. Every few years, however, Lords jolts the government by forcing Commons to take another look at bills passed without sufficient scrutiny. Lords, then, is somewhat more important than a debating club. It is the only British institution in a position to check the powers of a prime minister who has a large and disciplined majority in Commons. It is thus a weak analog to the U.S. Supreme Court, a "conscience of the nation." Lords is also able to debate questions too hot for elected officials—for example, laws concerning abortion and homosexuality.

Usually, fewer than three hundred lords turn up in the House of Lords; a quorum is three. A few lords are named to the cabinet or to other high political or diplomatic positions. The chamber is also home to the five **Law Lords**, life peers who are the top judges in the British court system to whom cases may be appealed. Now that Britain has a Human Rights Act (see page 78), a sort of embryonic constitution, the law lords can declare something "unconstitutional." The law lords may thus turn into a U.S.-style Supreme Court.

Most Britons agree that Lords is an **anachronism** ripe for reform but cannot agree on what to do with it. Blair's 1999 step depriving most hereditary peers of their seats made Lords meritocratic but not democratic. In 2007 Commons proposed making Lords fully elected, like the U.S. Senate, but some feared that would dilute the legislative supremacy of Commons and turn Lords over to vote-seeking party politicians. Changing constitutions is tricky: When you change one thing, you change everything.

THE PARTIES

Commons works as it does because of the British party system. This is a fairly recent development; only since the time of the French Revolution (1789) has it been possible to speak of coherent parties in Britain. Parties are now the cornerstone of British government. If a party elects a majority of the MPs, that party controls Commons and forms the government.

British parties are more cohesive, centralized, and ideological than American parties. It is fair to say there are as many differences within the two big U.S. parties as between them. Now, however, like their U.S. counterparts, the two large British parties tend to converge to the center. Earlier, British Labourites, who sometimes called themselves Socialists, favored nationalization of industry, more welfare measures, and higher taxes. Conservatives urged less government involvement in society and the economy and lower taxes. Internal party differences arose from the degree to which party members supported these general points of view. Now, as we shall explore subsequently, differences between the two parties are muted.

In 1981, the moderate wing of the Labour party split off to form a centrist Social Democratic party. They argued that Labour had fallen under the control of leftist radicals. The Social Democrats faced the problem that besets Britain's third party, the struggling Liberal Democrats, namely, that single-member plurality districts penalize smaller parties.

"two-plus" party system   Two big parties and several small ones.

single-member district   Sends one representative to Parliament.

FPTP   "First past the post," short for "single-member districts with plurality win."

plurality   Largest quantity, even if less than a majority.

majoritarian   Electoral system that encourages dominance of one party in a parliament, as in Britain and the United States.

Key Concepts

Britain's Two-Party System

Britain is usually described as a two-party system, but some third parties are important. Britain, like many democracies, is more accurately a **"two-plus" party system**. In 1979, for example, the withdrawal of support by the eleven Scottish Nationalists in Commons brought down the Callaghan government in a rare *vote of no-confidence*. In general elections, the Liberal Democrats may win 20 percent, forcing the Labour and Conservative parties to change positions on some issues.

Britain's electoral system keeps two parties big and penalizes smaller parties. Britain, like the United States and Canada, uses **single-member districts** as the basis for elections. This old English system is simple: Each electoral district or constituency sends one person to the legislature, the candidate that gets the most votes even if less than a majority, sometimes called "first past the post," **FPTP**. In 1992, for example, a Lib Dem in Scotland won with just 26 percent of the vote. This system of single-member districts with **plurality** victors tends to produce two large political parties. The reason: There is a big premium to combine small parties into big ones in order to edge out competitors. If one

of the two large parties splits, which sometimes happens, the election is thrown to the other party, the one that hangs together. In countries with proportional representation there is not such a great premium on forming two large parties, and that contributes to multiparty systems.

Countries that inherited the British **majoritarian** system tend toward two large parties, one left, the other right, such as the U.S. Democrats and Republicans. India is an exception to this pattern, because its parties are territorially concentrated, so that India's parliament has dozens of parties (see pages 455–457). Canada has this to a lesser extent, permitting the separatist Bloc Québécois and socialistic New Democrats to win seats. New Zealand used to have the Anglo-American system, and it, too, yielded two large parties. It also left many New Zealanders discontent because other viewpoints got ignored, so its parliament in 1993 adopted a new electoral law, modeled on Germany's hybrid system of half single-member districts and half PR (see page 189). New Zealand soon developed a more complex party system.

proportional representation (PR),
electoral system of multimember
districts with seats awarded by
percentage parties win.

The Liberal party illustrates how smaller parties suffer under the British system of electing MPs. In the nineteenth century it was one of the two big parties, but by the 1920s it had been pushed into a weak third place by Labour. Now, although the Liberal Democrats often win nearly 20 percent of the vote, they rarely get more than a few dozen Commons seats because their vote is territorially dispersed, so in few constituencies does it top Tories or Labourites.

In 1983 and 1987, the Liberals and Social Democrats ran jointly as the "Alliance," and in 1988 they merged into the Liberal Democratic party. Because they are spread rather evenly, the "Lib Dems" still get shortchanged on parliamentary seats (see box on page 45). The Liberal Democrats would like to move away from the majoritarian system and toward **proportional representation** (PR). The leading proposal is to keep FPTP but "top off" seats to more accurately reflect nationwide party strengths. (The German system, by contrast, starts with PR but adds FPTP.)

Scottish and Welsh nationalist parties have had spurts of growth and decline. Their territorial concentration enables them to win a few seats in Westminster and many seats in the Scottish and Welsh assemblies instituted in 1999. We will explore patterns of interaction among the parties and the voters in Chapter 5.

Key Terms

anachronism (p. 44)

antithetical (p. 35)

backbencher (p. 42)

by-election (p. 39)

Cortes (p. 35)

Crown (p. 34)

dignified (p. 34)

division (p. 37)

eclectic (p. 34)

efficient (p. 34)

FPTP (p. 45)

fusion of powers (p. 35)

government (p. 37)

junior minister (p. 35)

Law Lords (p. 44)

life peers (p. 43)

majoritarian (p. 45)

MP (p. 35)

opposition (p. 42)

plurality (p. 45)

portfolio (p. 35)

proportional representation
  (p. 46)

select committee (p. 43)

single-member district
  (p. 45)

statute (p. 34)

"two-plus" party system
  (p. 45)

vote of no-confidence
  (p. 39)

Westminster (p. 41)

whip (p. 37)

Whitehall (p. 41)

Further Reference

Bogdanor, Vernon, ed. *The British Constitution in the Twentieth Century.* New York: Oxford University Press, 2003.

Bower, Tom. *Gordon Brown, Prime Minister.* London: Harper, 2007.

Foley, Michael. *The British Presidency: Tony Blair and the Politics of Public Leadership.* New York: St. Martin's, 2000.

Foster, Christopher. *British Government in Crisis.* Oxford: Hart, 2005.

Hennessey, Peter. *The Prime Minister: The Office and Its Holders since 1945*. New York: Palgrave, 2001.

Kavanagh, Dennis, and Anthony Selden. *The Powers behind the Prime Minister: The Hidden Influence of Number Ten*. New York: HarperCollins, 2000.

Lipsey, David. *The Secret Treasury*. New York: Viking, 2000.

Norton, Bruce F. *Politics in Britain*. Washington, D.C.: CQ Press, 2007.

Poguntke, Thomas, and Paul Webb, eds. *The Presidentialization of Politics: A Comparative Study of Modern Democracies*. New York: Oxford University Press, 2005.

Riddell, Peter. *Parliament under Blair*. London: Politico, 2000.

Selden, Anthony. *Blair*. New York: Free Press, 2004.

Chapter 4
British
Political Culture

"England is a snob country," one longtime American resident in London told me. She added: "And I'm a snob, so I like it here." Her candor touched one of the facets of British political life: the large and often invidious distinctions made between and by social classes.

Social class can be analyzed in two different ways, objectively and subjectively. The objective approach uses data such as income and neighborhood to place people into categories. The subjective approach asks people to place themselves into categories. There are often discrepancies between the results of the two approaches, as when, for example, a self-made businessman, thinking of his humble origins, describes himself as **working class**, or when a poorly paid schoolteacher, thinking of her university degrees, describes herself as **middle class**. In Britain and in most industrialized democracies, the main politically relevant distinction is between working class and middle class.

Objectively, class differences in Britain are no greater than in the rest of West Europe. The time has long passed when Disraeli could write that Britain was not one nation but two, the rich and the poor. Since then, the British working class has grown richer, the middle class bigger, and the small upper class poorer. But **subjectively** or psychologically, class differences remain. Working-class people live, dress, speak, and enjoy themselves differently than the middle class. Britons seem to like these differences and try to preserve them.

German sociologist Ralf Dahrendorf believed that the key word in Britain is not class but **solidarity**. Although there has been a leveling of objective class differences, Dahrendorf held, the idea of individual competition and improvement has not caught on in Britain as it has in other industrial countries. Rather than struggling to improve themselves individually, many Britons relish the feeling of solidarity that they get from sticking with their familiar jobs, neighborhoods, and pubs. "Britain is a society in which the values of solidarity are held in higher esteem than those of individual success at the expense of others," Dahrendorf wrote. Whether one refers to Britain's divisions as class or solidarity, the fact is that they influence British politics. They contribute to the way Britons vote, color the attitudes of labor unions and of the Labour party, and—very importantly—give birth to Britain's elites through the education system.

QUESTIONS TO CONSIDER

1. How does a wage differ from a salary? In class terms?
2. What is the difference between objective and subjective?
3. What is a British "public" school?
4. How does an "Oxbridge" education form an elite?
5. What is *class voting,* and has it declined?
6. What story does a map of the 2005 elections tell?
7. What center-periphery tensions does Britain have?
8. Have British parties always been pragmatic?
9. What do polls tell politicians about voters' ideology?
10. How did Northern Ireland become such a problem?

"Public" Schools

Although many claim that since World War II Britain has become a **meritocracy**, having the right parents still helps. No society, including the United States, is purely merit-based. One way the British upper and upper-middle classes pass on their advantages is the **"public" school**—actually private and expensive—so called after their original purpose of training boys for public life in the military, civil service, or politics. Eton, Harrow, Rugby, St. Paul's, Winchester, and other famous academies have for generations molded the sons of better-off Britons into a ruling elite.

What a small minority of young Britons learn from ages thirteen to eighteen is more than their demanding curriculum. It is the personal style inculcated in public schools: self-confident to the point of arrogance, self-disciplined, bred to rule. Spy novelist John Le Carré recalled with distaste how his public schoolmates during World War II felt nothing but contempt for lower-class "oiks." In terms of class relations, added Le Carré decades later, "nothing, but absolutely nothing, has changed" since the 1940s.

The British private-school system generates an **old boy** network that assists graduates later in life. The years of floggings, vile food, and bullying by upper-classmen forge bonds among old schoolmates, and they often help each other get positions in industry and government. Most of Britain's elite have gone to private boarding schools, including over half of Conservative MPs. Fewer Labour MPs went to such schools; Prime Minister Brown did not but Blair did. Most of Thatcher's and Major's ministers had been privately educated, but only a minority of Blair's and Brown's.

Until the 1970s, most young Britons took a frightening exam at age eleven (the "11-plus") that selected the best into state-funded *grammar* schools but left most in *secondary modern* schools. In all but

social class   Layer or section of population of similar income and status. (See page 49.)

working class   Those paid an hourly wage, typically less affluent and less educated. (See page 49.)

middle class   Professionals or those paid salaries, typically more affluent and more educated. (See page 49.)

objective   Judged by observable criteria. (See page 49.)

subjective   Judged by feeling or intuition. (See page 49.)

solidarity   Feeling of cohesion within a social class. (See page 49.)

meritocracy   Promotion by brains and ability rather than heredity.

public school   In Britain, a private, boarding school, equivalent to a U.S. prep school.

old boy   Someone you knew at public school.

DEMOCRACY

WHAT TO DO WITH "PUBLIC" SCHOOLS?

The British Labour party has long sought to do away with the country's private boarding schools. Labourites regard these schools as undemocratic, part of a class system that benefits a privileged few. Many Conservative politicians have attended "public" schools, but few Labour politicians have. Conservatives want to maintain the schools, arguing that they train the best people and imbue them with a sense of public service.

In practice, Labour governments essentially let the private boarding schools alone while they upgrade the quality of publicly supported "comprehensive" schools. Blair's and Brown's education policies, for example, left the public schools untouched. The problem may be solving itself: Boarding-school enrollment has slumped while day-school popularity has climbed. Changing lifestyles have convinced many British parents that sending their children away is cruel and unloving.

Northern Ireland, Labour governments phased out most of the selective grammar schools in favor of *comprehensive* schools for all, like U.S. high schools. This did not solve the twin problems of educational quality and equality. Now better-off children go to boarding schools, middle-class children go to private day schools, while working class children go to mediocre state-funded comprehensive and technical schools, from which many drop out. Until after World War II, there was no free high-school system in Britain. Only 65 percent of British seventeen-year-olds are still in school (including technical training), the lowest level of any industrial land. (Comparative figures: Germany, 97 percent; United States, 88 percent; Japan, 83 percent.) In spite of the efforts of the Labour party since World War II, British education is weak and still divided by class.

Oxbridge Informal, Oxford and Cambridge universities.

Rhodes scholarship Founded by South African millionaire; sends top foreign students to Oxford.

class voting Tendency of classes to vote for parties that represent them.

"Oxbridge"

The real path to position and power in Britain is through the elite universities of Oxford or Cambridge. Nearly half of Conservative MPs are Oxford or Cambridge graduates (usually after attending a public school, such as Eton), while a quarter of Labour MPs are **Oxbridge** products. In the cabinet, these percentages are higher. And most prime ministers are graduates of either Oxford or Cambridge; Thatcher and Blair were Oxonians. In recent years, only Labour Prime Minister James Callaghan (1976–1979) and Conservative John Major (1990–1997) never went to college. In few other industrialized countries are the political elite drawn so heavily from just two universities.

British university education used to be elitist, enrolling the products of private schools. Since World War II, education opened to the working and lower-middle classes by direct-grant secondary schools and scholarships for deserving youths. Oxford and Cambridge became less class-biased in their admissions, and many new institutions were founded or expanded. (They are now called euphemistically "mainstream" universities.) The percentage of British secondary (high-school) graduates going to some type of higher education shot up from 14 in 1985 to nearly 40 today, approaching U.S. levels.

Only a small percentage of Oxbridge students go into politics, but those who do start with advantages. An Oxford or Cambridge degree—which takes three years to earn—commands respect and hones political skills. One popular major for aspiring politicians is "PPE"—philosophy, politics, and economics—in effect, how to run a country. Debating in the Oxford or Cambridge Unions trains students to think on their feet and confound their opponents with rhetorical cleverness, a style that carries over into the House of Commons. Perhaps the main advantage of an Oxbridge education, however, is the "sense of effortless superiority" graduates carry all their lives. One U.S. president (Clinton), two Supreme Court justices, and several cabinet secretaries attended Oxford on **Rhodes scholarships**.

Class and Voting

Britain used to be a good example of **class voting**—a situation where most of the working class votes for the left party (in this case, Labour) while most of the middle class votes for the right (in this case, Conservative). Actually, class voting in Sweden is higher than in Britain, but nowhere is it

deferential Accepting leadership of social superiors.

the Establishment Half in jest, supposed monopoly of clubby social elite in British politics.

100 percent because some working-class people vote Conservative, and some middle-class people vote Labour. Class differences may be part of Britain's political culture, but they do not translate into class voting on a one-to-one basis.

What dilutes class voting? Some working-class people are simply convinced that Conservatives do a better job governing. Some workers have a sentimental attachment to the country's oldest party. Some issues have little to do with class. The Tories win a large part of the working class on the issues of economic growth, keeping taxes down, and keeping out immigrants.

Going the other way, many middle-class and educated people are intellectually convinced that the Labour party is the answer to what they see as an establishment-ruled, snobbish class system. Such intellectuals provide important leadership in the Labour party. The leader of the Labour left for a long time was an aristocrat, Anthony Wedgewood Benn, or, as he liked to be known, Tony Benn. Furthermore, some middle-class people grew up in working-class families and vote like their parents.

Class voting changes over time. The British generation that came of age during and after World War II, especially the working class, was quite loyal to the Labour party, which it swept to power in 1945. Since then, class voting has declined in Britain and other advanced, industrialized democracies, including the United States. Class is not what it used to be in any country's voting patterns.

It is, however, still a factor. Typically, political scientists find voting behavior is influenced by social class plus one or more other factors, such as region, ethnic group, religion, and urban-rural differences. The 2005 British general election partially bears this out (see box on page 53). Tories were strongest in England, especially the south of England, and in small towns and rural areas. They were weaker in Scotland and Wales and in the big industrial cities, places with a long-term Labour identification and unemployment. Class by itself explains only part of British voting patterns. Class plus region explains more.

The Deferential British?

One old image of the British was that they were **deferential**, that is, the average Briton deferred to the political judgment of the Oxbridge-educated **Establishment** and let it lead. The deferential model is now obsolete. Perhaps in earlier decades, when class differences were enormous, the working class deferred to its social betters, but they also built up resentment. As noted in Chapter 2, the labor movement came into British politics in the nineteenth century with a snarl. Some sectors of the British working class still show their resentment in the militant socialism within the Labour party and in indifferent work attitudes and a readiness to strike. The deferential model cannot explain such behavior.

The "working-class Tory" has been explained as a wage-earning voter who defers to the Conservatives and votes for them. But such voting may have little to do with deference. Many such voters think that the Conservatives have the right policies, the Labour party has swung too far left, and there are too many nonwhite immigrants. Furthermore, the 1997, 2001, and 2005 elections saw a return of the "middle-class Labour voter," a shift that has nothing to do with social deference.

Geography

The 2005 Elections: Region and Class

A country's electoral geography—rooted in the history, resentments, and culture of its regions—is long-lasting. Britain illustrates that how a region voted in the past likely predicts how it will vote next time. Labour won a third victory in 2005, but scored above its national average in Scotland, Wales, and the industrial areas of London, Liverpool, Yorkshire, and the Northeast, areas where it has long held sway. Social class is also a factor, as Labour scores well among people who feel disadvantaged: the Scots, the Welsh, and the working class. The areas where the Conservatives fare above average (the shaded portion) are mostly in England, especially in rural and suburban parts. In a nearly universal political pattern, large cities tend to vote left. Region plus class predicts the British vote.

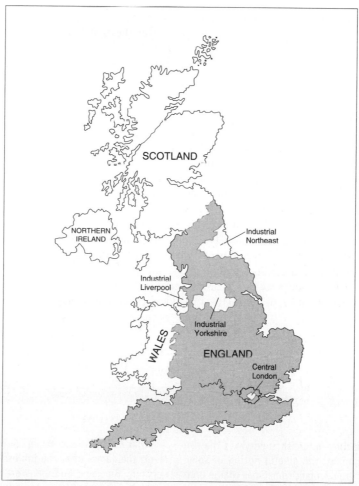

Shaded: Where Tories Won above Average in 2005

British Civility

In Britain, **civility** is based on a sense of limits: Do not let anything go too far. Thus, while Labourites and Conservatives have serious arguments, they keep them verbal. The British political game is not one of total annihilation, as it has sometimes been in France, Germany, and Russia. British politicians are fairly decent toward one another.

---

civility   Good manners in politics.

heckling   Interrupting a speaker.

hooliganism   Violent and destructive behavior.

But British civility allows **heckling**. In Parliament a cabinet minister presenting a difficult case sometimes faces cries of "Shame!" or "Treason!" from the opposition benches. Margaret Thatcher faced Labourites chanting "Ditch the bitch." Insults and heckling are a normal part of British debates and are not viewed as out of bounds but rather as tests of a debater's poise and verbal skills.

Civility is usually the case in public also, but not always. Amateur orators at the famous Speakers' Corner of Hyde Park in London can have their say on any subject they like, although they, too, face heckling. British politics turned uncivil on the question of race, which we will discuss later, and there have been demonstrations and riots that led to deaths. Murder rather than civility was the norm for years in Northern Ireland. British civility has been overstated; Swedes are more civil.

PRAGMATISM

As noted in Chapter 1, *pragmatic* has the same root as *practical* and means using what works regardless of theory or ideology. British political culture, like American or Swedish, is generally pragmatic. The Conservatives used to pride themselves on being the most pragmatic of all British parties. They were willing to adopt the policies of another party if they won votes. In the nineteenth century, Disraeli crowed he had "dished the Whigs" by stealing their drive to expand the voting franchise. In the 1950s, the returning Conservative government did not throw out Labour's welfare state; instead they boasted that Tories ran it more efficiently. This changed with the laissez-faire economic program of Prime Minister Thatcher in 1979. The fixity of her goals contributed to ideological debates within and between the two large and usually pragmatic parties. Pragmatism returned to the Tories after Thatcher.

The British Labour party historically offered little ideology beyond the welfare state. With the Callaghan government in the 1970s, however, ideological controversy engulfed Labour. Callaghan was

Political Culture

FOOTBALL HOOLIGANISM

Underscoring the decline in British civility was the rise of football **hooliganism**, the gleeful rioting of some British soccer fans. Drunken fans sometimes charge onto the field in the middle of a game. In 1985, Liverpool fans killed thirty-eight Italian spectators by causing their bleachers to collapse. All over Europe, the English fanatics were feared and sometimes barred from games.

What causes the violence? Some blame unemployment; the games offer the jobless one of their few diversions. But most hooligans are employed and some earn good livings. Others see hooliganism as the erosion of civilization itself. "The truth is," said one self-confessed Manchester hooligan, "we just like scrappin'."

a very moderate, pragmatic Labourite, hard to distinguish from moderate Conservatives. Many Labour personalities, including some union
heads, resented Callaghan's centrism and rammed through a socialist
party platform despite him. The moderate wing of the Labour party
split off in 1981 to form a centrist party, the Social Democrats. As we
shall consider in Chapter 5, a series of Labour party leaders pushed the
party back to the nonideological center, leading to its 1997, 2001, and 2005 electoral victories.

> **periphery**   Nation's outlying regions.
> **center-periphery tension**   Resentment in outlying areas of rule by nation's capital.

There is and always has been a certain amount of ideology in British politics, but it has usually been balanced with a shrewd practical appreciation that ideology neither wins elections nor effectively governs a country. The ideological flare-up of the 1980s in Britain made it perhaps the
most polarized land of West Europe. Ironically, at this same time, French parties, long said to be far
more ideological than British parties, moved to the center, where British parties used to cluster.

One aspect of British pragmatism is their "muddling-through" style of problem solving. The
British tend not to thoroughly analyze a problem and come up with detailed options or "game plans."
They try to "muddle through somehow," improvising as they go. This often works with small prob-
lems, but with a big problem, such as the situation in Northern Ireland, it amounts to a nonsolution.

TRADITIONS AND SYMBOLS

As noted, British politics keeps traditions. Political usages often follow well-worn paths, observed
even by left-wing Labourites, who, whether they recognize it or not, subscribe to Burke's idea of
keeping the forms but changing the contents. As Burke saw, traditions and symbols contribute to society's stability and continuity; people feel disoriented without them.

The typical British man or woman likes traditions and symbols. Although some Britons wince
at the tabloid lifestyle of the younger generation of "royals," only a minority would abolish the monarchy in favor of a republic with a president. Parades with golden coaches and horsemen in red tunics

GEOGRAPHY

CENTERS AND PERIPHERIES

A country's capital is often called its "center," even
though it may not be in the precise center of the land.
Closer to the boundaries of the state are the **peripheral**
areas. Often these are more recent additions to the territory of the state. Some of them still speak a different language and resent rule by the capital. This
center-periphery tension is nearly universal.

Over the centuries, England added Wales, Scotland,
and Ireland. Resentment was so high in Ireland that
Britain granted it independence in the last century. Now
Britain retains only Northern Ireland, long a source of
resentment and violence. Scotland and Wales also harbor grudges against rule by London and demand more

home rule. As we shall consider in Chapter 6, Tony Blair's
Labour government tried to calm these feelings by
granting Scotland and Wales their own legislatures.

The U.S. Civil War was an effort by the southern periphery to cast off rule by Washington. In terms of culture and economics, the North and South really were
two different countries, a gap that has been partly
closed since then. The center of U.S. population, politics, economics, communications, education, and culture
long remained in the northeast. This still fosters slight
center-periphery tension; some western politicians express irritation at rule by Washington.

center-peaked   Distribution with most people in the middle, a bell-shaped curve.

center-seeking   Tendency of political parties toward moderate politics calculated to win the center.

are not just for tourists—although they help Britain's economy—they also serve to deepen British feelings about the rightness of the system.

Traditions can also tame political radicals. Once they win seats in Commons, radicals find themselves playing according to established parliamentary usages. "Well, it simply isn't done, old boy," is the standard lesson taught to newcomers in Parliament. They may still have radical views, but they voice them within traditional bounds.

Political Culture

THE SHAPE OF THE BRITISH ELECTORATE

Virtually all modern democracies show a strong clustering in the ideological center with a tapering off toward the extremes: bell-shaped curves. Such a **center-peaked** distribution is probably necessary to sustain democracy, for it encourages **center-seeking** politics. A U-shaped distribution indicates extreme division, possibly heading toward civil war (example:

Spain, 1936). Pollsters and political consultants constantly remind their clients of the distribution of ideological opinion and warn them not to position themselves too far left or right. It took the Labour party several electoral defeats to get the message. Tony Blair finally pushed Labour into about the 5 position (exact center) with vague but upbeat party positions.

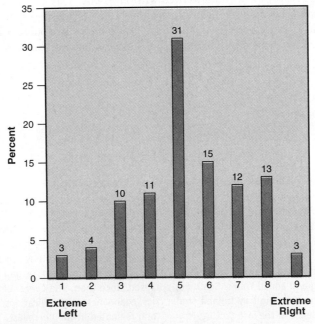

The Self-Placement of British Voters on a Left/Right Ideological Scale

Legitimacy and Authority

Legitimacy is a feeling of rightness about the political system. As we noted in Chapter 1, it originally meant the right king was on the throne, not a usurper. As used by political scientists, it refers to public perceptions that the government's rule is rightful. Legitimacy is a feeling among the people; it is not the same as "legal." When a political system enjoys high legitimacy, people generally obey it. They will even do things they do not want to, such as paying their income taxes.

> **authority**   Political leaders' ability to be obeyed.
>
> **Irish Republican Army**   (IRA), anti-British terrorists who seek unification of all Ireland.

Legitimacy is closely related to **authority**, obeying duly constituted officials. British legitimacy and authority were famous, but they were exaggerated and oversold. British policemen did not carry guns and had good relations with the people on their beat. Political scientists used to cite such points to illustrate Britain's nonviolent qualities. During the 1970s, however, Britain turned more violent. The **Irish Republican Army** (IRA) spread their murderous tactics from Ulster, planting bombs that killed dozens. In 1984, one bomb blew up near Prime Minister Thatcher. Criminals started using handguns. In Britain's inner cities, relations between police and youths, especially black youths, grew hateful and contributed to urban riots (which, nonetheless, cost very few lives). After the 2005 London subway bombings, police shot and killed an innocent passenger on the mistaken suspicion that he was a terrorist. Some critics decried the gunplay as the Americanization of their police. A few British policemen now carry guns and riot gear, a symbol of the erosion of legitimacy and authority in Britain.

The Ulster Ulcer

While Britons on the whole still value civility, pragmatism, legitimacy, respect for authority, and non-violence, Northern Ireland (sometimes called Ulster) is a massive exception. Northern Ireland illustrates how a system that works amid widespread legitimacy fails when it is lacking. Unlike the rest

Political Culture

THE IRA: BALLOTS AND BULLETS

The Irish Republican Army is illegal in both Eire and Northern Ireland, but its political arm, Sinn Féin (pronounced *shin fane,* "We Ourselves") is not. It still ultimately aims to get Britain out of Northern Ireland so it can unify with the Republic. Many Northern Irish Catholics vote for Sinn Féin candidates; in 2005 five were elected to Commons (where they do not vote). Sinn Féin leader Gerry Adams, an MP representing Belfast West, denies belonging to the IRA but never condemned its violence. Now voicing a moderate line, he urges peace and disarmament of all sides and only political means to unite Ireland. Ever disrespectful of the English Crown, he calls Queen Elizabeth "Mrs. Windsor."

In 1981 Ulster's Catholics elected Bobby Sands, an imprisoned IRA gunman, who starved himself to death in a hunger strike. The fact that so many men and women of Ulster are willing to vote for an extremist party indicates the depth of hatred and the difficulty of compromising on the basic question of which country to belong to, Britain or Ireland.

Malthusian View that population growth outstrips food supply.

home rule Giving region some autonomy to govern itself.

Eire Republic of Ireland.

Orangemen After King William of Orange (symbol of Netherlands royal house), Northern Irish Protestants.

anglophile Someone who loves England and the English.

francophobe Someone who dislikes France and the French.

of Britain, Ulster is a split society, more like those of Latin Europe—France, Spain, and Italy—where part of the population does not see the government as legitimate.

The Ulster problem has its roots in the eight centuries England ruled Ireland, at times treating the Irish as subhuman, seizing their land, deporting them, even outlawing the Catholic faith. In the 1846–1854 Potato Famine a million Irish starved to death while the English, with plentiful food stocks, watched. (An example of what happens when you make too many babies, admonished English **Malthusians**.) At that time about a million and a half Irish emigrated, most to the United States. The Irish problem was the great issue of nineteenth-century British politics, "the damnable question" of whether to keep it firmly under British control or grant it **home rule**.

In the spring of 1916, while the English were hard-pressed in World War I, the "Irish Volunteers" used guerrilla warfare in the Easter Rising in an attempt to win freedom for Ireland. (They renamed themselves the IRA in 1919.) By 1922, after brutally crushing the rising, the British had enough; Ireland became a *free state* of the British Commonwealth. In 1949, the bulk of Ireland ended this free-state status and became sovereign **Eire**.

But this did not solve the Ulster problem; a majority of the 1.5 million people in these six northern counties are Protestant (descended from seventeenth-century Scottish immigrants) and are determined to remain part of Britain. Fiercely Protestant, for years these **Orangemen** treated Northern Irish Catholics as a different race and feared "popish" plots to bring Northern Ireland into the Catholic-dominated Irish Republic to the south. In control of Ulster's local government, the Protestants shortchanged the Catholic minority in jobs, housing, and political power. For many years, most Catholics did not even have the right to vote for the Ulster legislature.

In 1968 Catholic protests started, modeled on U.S. civil-rights marches. But Catholic *nationalists* or *republicans*, who sought to join the Republic of Ireland, soon battled with Protestant *loyalists* or *unionists*, who insisted that Northern Ireland stay part of Britain. A *"provisional"* wing of the IRA enrolled Catholic gunmen, and Protestant counterparts reciprocated. Murder became nearly random. Over 3,600 were killed—including MPs, Earl Mountbatten, British soldiers, but mostly innocent civilians—and for some years the United Kingdom was the most violent nation in West Europe. Most Ulstermen welcomed a 1998 power-sharing agreement. Violence has largely ended, but mistrust remains (see Chapter 6).

A Changing Political Culture

We are trying to put British political culture into perspective. Britons are neither angels nor devils. Political scientists used to present Britain as a model of stability, moderation, calm, justice, and niceness. In contrast, France was often presented as a model of instability and immoderate political attitudes. The contrast was overdrawn; neither the British nor the French are as good or as bad as sometimes portrayed.

Observations of a country's political culture can err in two ways. First, if you are favorably disposed toward a country—and Americans are great **anglophiles** (while many are **francophobes**)—you may overlook some of the nasty things lurking under the surface or dismiss them as aberrations. For years U.S. textbooks on British politics ignored or played down the violence in Northern Ireland.

Such "incivility" seemed too un-British to mention. Riots in impoverished parts of British inner cities caught observers by surprise.

Second, studies of political culture are carried out during particular times, and things change. The data for Almond and Verba's *Civic Culture* (see box on page 9), were collected in 1959 and 1960. Their composite portrait of Britain as a "deferential civic culture" has not been valid for decades. Since World War II, Britain has undergone trying times, especially in the area of economics. This did not erase British culture wholesale; they simply made manifest what had been latent. Political attitudes change; they can get nastier or better.

KEY TERMS

anglophile (p. 58)
authority (p. 57)
center-peaked (p. 56)
center-periphery tension
   (p. 55)
center-seeking (p. 56)
civility (p. 54)
class voting (p. 51)
deferential (p. 52)
Eire (p. 58)
Establishment, the (p. 52)

francophobe (p. 58)
heckling (p. 54)
home rule (p. 58)
hooliganism (p. 54)
Irish Republican Army
   (p. 57)
Malthusian (p. 58)
meritocracy (p. 50)
middle class (p. 50)
objective (p. 50)
old boy (p. 50)

Orangemen (p. 58)
Oxbridge (p. 51)
periphery (p. 55)
public school (p. 50)
Rhodes scholarship (p. 51)
social class (p. 50)
solidarity (p. 50)
subjective (p. 50)
working class (p. 50)

FURTHER REFERENCE

Adams, Ian. *Ideology and Politics in Britain Today.* New York: St. Martin's, 1998.

Adonis, Andrew, and Stephen Pollard. *A Class Act: The Myth of Britain's Classless Society.* London: Hamish Hamilton, 1997.

Curtice, John, Katarina Thomson, Lindsey Jarvis, Catharine Bromley, and Nina Stratford. *British Social Attitudes: Public Policy, Social Ties.* Thousand Oaks, CA: Sage, 2002.

Dahrendorf, Ralf. *On Britain.* Chicago, IL: University of Chicago Press, 1982.

Field, William H. *Regional Dynamics: The Basis of Electoral Support in Britain.* Portland, OR: F. Cass, 1997.

McCormick, John. *Contemporary Britain,* 2nd ed. New York: Palgrave, 2007.

McKittrick, David, and David McVea. *Making Sense of the Troubles: The Story of the Conflict in Northern Ireland.* Chicago, IL: New Amsterdam Books, 2002.

Miller, William L., Annis May Timpson, and Michael Lessnoff. *Political Culture in Contemporary Britain: People and Politicians, Principles and Practice.* New York: Oxford University Press, 1996.

Rose, Richard, and Ian McAllister. *The Loyalties of Voters: A Lifetime Learning Model.* Newbury Park, CA: Sage, 1990.

Ruane, Joseph, and Jennifer Todd. *The Dynamics of Conflict in Northern Ireland.* New York: Cambridge University Press, 1996.

Chapter 5

Britain:
Patterns of Interaction

In Britain, as in most democratic countries, the relationship between people and political parties is complex, a two-way street in which each influences the other. The parties project something called **party image**, what people think of the party's policies, leaders, and ideology. Most voters, on the other hand, carry in their heads a **party identification**, a long-term tendency to think of themselves as "Tory" or "Democrat" or whatever. The strategy of intelligent party leadership is to project a party image that wins the loyalty of large numbers of voters and gets them to identify permanently with that party. If they can do this, the party prospers and wins many elections.

QUESTIONS TO CONSIDER

1. What is party image? Party identification?
2. What is a *safe seat* and how do you get one?
3. Who picks British candidates?
4. What did "New Labour" mean as a political party?
5. Why do the Liberal Democrats have such an uphill struggle?
6. How did Thatcher differ from a traditional Tory?
7. What is the big British labor confederation? How big?
8. Where and what is the Question Hour?
9. How democratic is Britain? As much as the United States?

Both party image and party identification are reasonably clear in Britain: Most Britons recognize what the main parties stand for, and most identify with a party. The situation is never static, however, for the parties constantly change the images they project, and some voters lose their party identification and shift their votes.

In every country, parents contribute heavily to their children's party identification. In Britain (and the United States), if both parents are of the same party, most of their children first identify with that party, although this may later erode as young people develop their own perspectives. By the same token, party images are rather clear, and most Britons are able to see differences between their two largest parties: Labour aiming at helping people through social and educational reforms, and Conservatives aiming at economic growth through hard work with little state intervention.

For confirmed Labour or Conservative voters there is little doubt about whom to vote for. Until recently, most British voters were reliably Labour or Conservative. The **swing** vote is those who move their votes among parties, either because their party identification is not strong, or their perceptions of the parties' images shift, or both. A swing of a few percentage points can determine who will form the next government, for if each constituency shifts a little one way, say, toward Labour, the Labour candidate will win in many constituencies. Single-member districts often exaggerate percentage trends and turn them into large majorities of **seats**.

The game of British electoral politics consists of the parties trying to mobilize all of their party identifiers—that is, making sure their people bother to vote—plus winning over the uncommitted swing vote. In 1970 the Labour government of Harold Wilson suffered a surprise defeat by the Conservatives under Edward Heath. Labour identifiers had not suddenly switched parties; rather, some were unhappy with Wilson's policies and did not vote.

National and Local Party

Political scientists used to describe the British national party—Conservative or Labour—as nearly all-powerful, able to dictate to local party organizations whom to nominate for Parliament. Actually, there is a bargaining relationship between the parties' London headquarters and the local **constituency** party. The local party might have a bright local person they want to run and ask the Labour or Tory **central office** in London for approval. More often, however, the central office suggests bright comers from elsewhere to the local party, who may or may not accept them. Britain has both national and local input into British candidate selection with a veto on both sides. The U.S. system is purely local; essentially candidates for Congress nominate themselves.

Some constituency organizations insist that a candidate actually live in the district. Americans expect all candidates to be from the district they represent; those who are not are called **carpetbaggers** and have an uphill battle. Most countries, however, including Britain, impose no such requirements, although being a local person can help. Some British constituencies like their people to establish a residence there once they have won, but many do not insist that their MP actually live there; after all, the MP's job is mainly in London, and periodic visits are sufficient for him or her to hear complaints and maintain ties with electors. In Britain, party is more important than personality. Probably a minority of MPs are natives of the constituency they represent.

The name of the game for parliamentary candidates is the **safe seat** and getting adopted by the local constituency organization to run for it. Party leaders are normally assigned very safe seats, for it is highly embarrassing if one of them loses his or her seat in the Commons. Prime Minister Brown, for example, represents Kirkcaldy and Cowdenbeath, a solid Labour constituency north of Edinburgh, Scotland. About 450 (of 646) seats are usually considered safe.

What about the unsafe seats, those where the other party usually wins? These are the testing grounds for energetic newcomers to politics. The Conservative or Labour central offices in London may send a promising beginner to a constituency organization that knows it cannot win. Again, the local unit must approve the candidate. Even if the candidate loses, his or her energy and ability are carefully watched—by measuring how much better the candidate did than the previous one—and promising comers are marked. For the next election, the London headquarters may offer the candidate a safer constituency, one where he or she stands a better chance. Finally, the candidate either wins an election in a contested constituency, is adopted by a safe constituency, or bows out of politics. Most of Britain's top politicians, including prime ministers (Blair and Brown among them), lost their first races and were transferred to other constituencies. There is no stigma attached; it is normal, part of the training and testing of a British politician.

Politics within the Parties

British political parties, like British cabinets, are balancing acts. A party leader must neither pay too much attention to his or her party's factions nor totally ignore them. In constructing their policies, leaders usually try to give various factions a say but keep the whole thing under moderate control

---

party image Electorate's perception of a given party. (See page 61.)

party identification Psychological attachment of voter to political party. (See page 61.)

swing Voters who change party from one election to the next. (See page 61.)

seat Membership in a legislature. (See page 61.)

constituency The district or population that elects a legislator.

central office London headquarters of British political party.

carpetbagger In U.S. usage, candidate from outside the *constituency*.

safe seat *Constituency* where voting has long favored a given party.

with an eye to winning the next election. The Labour party, portraying itself as more democratic, elects its leader at an annual party conference. Tories tried that for a time but in 2005 reverted to their old elite tradition of having only Conservative MPs elect their chief, not a party conference.

general election Nationwide vote for all MPs.

Party leaders must balance between sometimes extremist party militants and a generally moderate voting public. If a party takes too firm an ideological stand—too left in the case of Labour or too right in the Conservative case—it costs the party votes. Thus party leaders tend to hedge and moderate their positions, trying to please both the true believers within their party and the general electorate. If they slip in this balancing act, they can lose either party members or voters or both. When Labour veered left in the 1980s and the Conservatives followed their hard-right Thatcher course, the centrist Liberal Democratic Alliance (later turned into a party) won a quarter of the 1983 vote, a warning to both major parties.

Although long described as ideologically moderate, both the British Labour and Conservative parties have important ideological viewpoints within their ranks. The Labour party is divided into "left" and "right" wings. The Labour left, springing from a tradition of militant trade unionism and intellectual radicalism, wants nationalization of industry, the dismantling of "public" schools, higher taxes on the rich, leaving the European Union, and no nuclear weapons—British or U.S. Some

DEMOCRACY

2005: LABOUR SQUEAKS THROUGH

In the May 2005 **general election**, after eight years in office, Britain's Labour party won a third term, the first time Labour had done that. Its vote dropped from 41 percent in 2001 to 35 percent, but it still won a majority of Commons' 646 seats. Remember, Britain's electoral system overrepresents the winning party, just as in the United States. As usual for Britain, 2005 gave Labour only a plurality of the votes cast; since 1935 no British party has scored an actual majority. Turnout was a weak 61.3 percent (but higher than 59.4 percent in 2001).

The Conservatives gained a little in the popular vote and moved up from 25 percent of the seats to 30 percent. The Liberal Democrats gained, too, but were still underrepresented because their voters are territorially dispersed. The rest of the vote, 10.5 percent, was scattered among small, mostly regional parties. Scottish, Welsh, and Northern Irish parties won a few seats each.

Labour won again because the British economy was excellent; its unemployment rate was the lowest in thirty years. Many Labour supporters, however, detested Blair for following President Bush into the Iraq War and voted Lib Dem. The Tories could not use this issue because they also supported U.S. policy on Iraq. The third Tory chief in four years, Michael Howard, made anti-immigration the Conservatives' big issue, but it never caught fire. The Tories became known as the "nasty party" with little positive to offer. Howard resigned after the 2005 elections, leaving the Conservatives divided and unfocused.

	% Votes		Seats	
	2005	2001	2005	2001
Labour	35.2	40.7	356 (55%)	413 (63%)
Conservative	32.3	31.7	197 (30%)	166 (25%)
Liberal Democrat	22.0	18.3	62 (10%)	52 (8%)

Marxist   Follower of socialist theories of Karl Marx.

Trotskyist   Follower of Marxist but anti-Stalin theories of Leon Trotsky.

New Labour   Tony Blair's name for his very moderate Labour party.

traditional Tory   Moderate or centrist Conservative, not *Thatcherite*.

Thatcherite   Free-market, anti-welfarist ideology of former British Prime Minister Margaret Thatcher.

neoliberalism   Revival of free-market economics, exemplified by *Thatcherites*.

Marxists and **Trotskyists** have won Labour offices. The Labour right, on the other hand, is moderate and centrist. It favors some of the welfarist approach of Continental social-democratic parties, such as the German SPD, but now wants little government-owned industry or higher taxes. It is pro-NATO, pro-Europe, and pro-American in foreign policy. The rightists in Labour argue that the left wing's ideas are extremist and cost the party votes. With Tony Blair, the Labour right won and told the left to shut up. For the 1997 election, Blair called his party **New Labour**, friendly to business, growth, and political reform.

As an amorphous party proud of its pragmatism, Conservatives were long thought immune to ideological controversy or factional viewpoints. This is not completely true, for the Tories comprise two broad streams of thought, which we might label as traditional and Thatcherite tendencies. The former is not a U.S.-style conservative, advocating a totally free economy with no government intervention. Instead, the **traditional Tory** wants a party that takes everybody's interests into account, plus traditional ways of doing things, and under the guidance of people born and bred to lead. This has been called a "one-nation" Tory view because it rejects notions of class divisions.

The **Thatcherite** wing (which traces back to nineteenth-century *liberalism* and is called **neoliberalism** in Europe and Latin America) is like American conservativism: They want to roll back government and free the economy. After World War II this view crept into Conservative ranks and,

Democracy

The Struggle of the Liberal Democrats

Public-opinion polls at times suggest that the Liberal Democratic party could become Britain's second-largest party. In a few constituencies they already are. Widespread disillusionment with the two large parties gave the Liberal Democrats a boost in the 2005 elections, because they were the only ones opposed to the Iraq War. The Lib Dems, like the Liberals before them, used to be a center party between Labour and Tories, but now that Labour has taken over the center, the Lib Dems have taken up positions often to the left of the Labour party.

The Liberal Democrats were born of the 1988 merger of the old Liberal party and the small, new Social Democratic party that in 1981 had broken away from Labour. The two strands did not see eye-to-eye. On many questions—especially on the economy and defense matters—the Social Democrats were more conservative than the Liberals. The Liberals tended to be ultra-liberal on questions of gay rights and open immigration. They wanted Britain out of NATO and free of nuclear weapons. True to their origins in the right wing of the Labour party, the Social Democrats were not unilateral disarmers and felt that lifestyle questions cost the party votes. The new party is a parallel to the many and incoherent viewpoints of the U.S. Democratic party.

The British electoral system—single-member districts with plurality win—is brutal on third parties (just as it is in the United States), especially those like the Liberal Democrats that are territorially dispersed. This discourages potential voters, who do not want to waste their votes on a party they fear will never be in power. The Liberal Democrats' great hope is to bring to Britain some elements of a proportional-representation electoral system.

with the 1975 elevation of Margaret Thatcher to party chief, moved to the forefront. Thatcher dubbed the traditional Tories **wets**, the militant Thatcherites **dries**. (The terms were taken from boarding-school slang in which "wets" are frightened little boys who wet their pants, and "dries" are strong and brave lads who do not.)

The trouble here is that some old-style British Conservatives find total capitalism almost as threatening as socialism. As industries went bankrupt in record number, Thatcher faced a revolt of Tory "wets" against her "dry" policies. After John Major took over, Thatcherite MPs sought to dump him. Attitudes toward European unity still split the Tories. Thatcher favored the Common Market but opposed turning it into a European Union that infringed on British sovereignty. She and her followers were dubbed **Euroskeptics**. Major and his followers were enthusiastically pro-Europe—**Euroenthusiasts**—and were for the 1993 Maastricht Treaty, which took European unity a big step forward. Tory chief Michael Howard, a Euroskeptic, had trouble leading a party split between forward-looking "modernizers"

wets In Thatcher's usage, Tories too timid to apply her militant *neoliberalism*.

dries In Thatcher's usage, Tories who shared her *neoliberal* vision.

Euroskeptic Does not wish to strengthen the EU at the expense of national sovereignty.

Euroenthusiast Likes the EU and wishes to strengthen it.

charisma Pronounced "kar-isma"; Greek for gift; political drawing power.

Democracy

Saving Labour from the Unions

From its 1983 electoral disaster, the Labour party struggled to recover. Part of its problem was a too-left party image. Another part was its doddering and ineffective leader, Michael Foot. At its annual conference that fall, the Labour party tried to repair both areas by overwhelmingly choosing as its new leader Neil Kinnock, a silver-tongued Welshman as charming as Margaret Thatcher was aloof. At forty-one, Kinnock, son of a coal miner, was the youngest Labour leader ever. Kinnock first had to curb Labour extremists; he got the Trotskyist Militant Tendency faction expelled (it formed a miniparty). Kinnock did well, lifting Labour from 27.6 percent of the popular vote in 1983 to 35.2 percent in 1992. But he came across as too slick and was still hurt by the Tory charge that the unions dominated Labour. Labour indeed was founded by and heavily based on trade unions, some led by militant socialists who would rather lose elections than lose their principles.

Following Labour's fourth defeat in a row in 1992, Kinnock resigned, making way for John Smith, a fifty-three-year-old Scottish lawyer who was even more pragmatic than Kinnock. Smith, a wooden speaker with little **charisma**, set out to reorient Labour more to the middle than the working class. Higher taxes and public ownership were out; discipline in education was in. But Smith had to break the union hold on the Labour party. Many union leaders resisted; they liked controlling—through the proxy votes of millions of union members—90 percent of the vote at Labour's annual conferences. This union domination, often strongly leftist, rendered Labour unacceptable to most British voters. In 1993, Smith got a change in Labour's rules to return the candidate selection process back to local party organizations; unions now control less than half the conference votes. In 1994 Smith died of a heart attack.

Tony Blair then took on the unions and got the party to drop its Clause Four, part of its constitution since 1918, that called for the "common ownership of the means of production," in other words, socialism. With Blair's very moderate 1996 manifesto, Labour—now called "New Labour"—started looking a lot like the U.S. Democrats. Although union and leftist militants disliked Blair, Labour's membership and electoral support climbed until it won three elections in a row, 1997, 2001, and 2005. It was not just Blair's doing, though; the process of pushing Labour back to the center had been underway since Kinnock began it in 1983.

and backward-looking "traditionalists" and resigned after losing the 2005 elections. As Labour had done earlier, the Tories tried to rebrand themselves as a centrist party by naming a fresh, young person as their leader in 2005: David Cameron (then thirty-nine). Cameron—a product of Eton and Oxford—is an attractive modernizer and moderate who boosted Tory electoral fortunes.

Parties and Interest Groups

What politicians say and what they deliver are two different things. Politicians speak to different audiences. To party rank and file they affirm party gospel, championing either the welfare state or free enterprise, as the case may be. To the electorate as a whole they usually tone down their ideological statements and offer vague slogans, such as "Stability and prosperity," or "Time for a change." But quietly, usually behind the scenes, politicians are also striking important deals with influential interest groups representing industry, commerce, professions, and labor. A large fraction of the British electorate belong to at least one interest group.

Trades Union Congress (TUC), British labor federation, equivalent to the U.S. AFL-CIO.

interested member MP known to represent an interest group.

sleaze factor Public perception of politicians on the take.

Confederation of British Industry (CBI), leading British business association, equivalent to U.S. National Association of Manufacturers.

Some 25 percent of the British work force is unionized, down from 55 percent when Thatcher took office but still twice the level in the United States or France (but only half that of Sweden). Labor unions are constituent members of the Labour party and, until 1993, controlled a majority of votes at Labour's annual conference. Unions still contribute most of the party's budgets and campaign funds and provide grass-roots manpower and organization. Especially important are the views of the head of the **Trades Union Congress** (TUC). No Labour party leader can totally ignore the wishes of Britain's union leaders.

This opened up Labour to charges that it is run by and for the unions, which earned a reputation as too far left, too powerful, and too ready to strike. To counteract this, both Labour party and union leaders deny union dominance. Indeed, one Labour party campaign tactic is to claim that only the Labour party can control the unions, rather than the other way around. Tony Blair pointed out to union chiefs the folly of losing one election after another. Ironically, Blair's and Brown's Thatcherite economic policies pushed some British unions back into militancy. Blair partially broke the close association of labor federation to social-democratic party that had been the norm for the industrialized countries of Northern Europe, as we shall see when we study Germany.

Dozens of union members sit as Labour MPs in Parliament; dozens more MPs are beholden to local unions for their election. This union bloc inside the Labour party can force a Labour government to moderate measures that might harm unions. At times, however, Labour party chiefs have made union leaders back down, explaining to them that if the unions get too much, the Labour party will lose elections. To reiterate, to be a party leader means performing a balancing act among several forces.

MPs known to directly represent special interests—an **interested member**—are not limited to the Labour side. Numerous Tory MPs are interested members for various industries and do not hide it. When the connection is concealed or when money changes hands, an MP pushing for favors to a group becomes known as sleazy. The **sleaze factor** hurt the Tories under Major and Labour under Blair, some of whose aides sold peerages for cash. Politicians taking money on the side are found everywhere, in all parties and in relatively clean countries.

The Conservative counterpart of the TUC is the influential **Confederation of British Industry** (CBI), formed by an amalgamation of three smaller groups in 1965. The CBI speaks for most British employers but has no formal links to the Conservative party, even though their views are often parallel. The CBI was delighted at Thatcher's antinationalization policies, although British industrialists gulped when they found this meant withdrawal of **subsidies** to their own industries. Thatcher could not totally ignore them, for CBI members and money support the Tories, and dozens of CBI-affiliated company directors occupy Conservative seats in Commons.

---

subsidy   Government economic aid to individual or business.

Question Hour   Time reserved in Commons for MPs to query ministers.

permanent secretary   Highest civil servant who runs a ministry, nominally under a minister.

knighthood   Lowest rank of nobility, carries title "Sir."

The Parties Face Each Other

There are two ways of looking at British elections. The first is to see them as one-month campaigns coming once every few years, each a model of brevity and efficiency, especially compared to the long, expensive U.S. campaigns. Another way, however, is to see them as nearly permanent campaigns that begin the day a new Parliament reconvenes after the latest balloting. The formal campaign may be only a few weeks, but long in advance the opposition party is planning how to oust the current government.

The chief arena for this is the House of Commons. British parliamentarians are seldom animated by a spirit of bipartisanship. The duty of the opposition is to oppose, and this they do by accusing the government of everything from incompetence and corruption to sexual scandal. The great weapon here is embarrassment, making a cabinet minister look like a fool. The time for this is the **Question Hour**, held Monday through Thursday when Commons opens. By tradition, this hour is reserved for MPs to aim written questions at cabinet ministers, who are on the front bench on a rotating basis. Most Wednesdays at noon, for example, Prime Minister Brown personally countered Tory criticism in Commons. Other cabinet ministers face questions on other days of the week. Each written question can be followed up by supplementary oral questions. The opposition tries to push a minister into an awkward position where he or she has to tell a lie, fluff an answer, or break into anger. Then the opposition, in effect, smirks, "You see, they are not fit to govern."

The Cabinet and the Civil Servants

As we discussed earlier, British cabinet ministers are generalists, not specialists, and are chosen more for political reasons than for any special ability to run their departments. Who then does run them? The nominal head of each British department is the minister; he or she represents that ministry in cabinet discussions and defends it in Commons. But the minister does not run the department; civil servants do.

Ministers come and go every few years; the highest civil servants, known as **permanent secretaries** are there much longer. Permanent secretaries often have an edge on their ministers in social and economic terms as well. Most permanent secretaries are knighted later in life while few ministers are. Although **knighthood** is now purely honorific in Britain, it still conveys social superiority. Permanent secretaries earn more than ministers, in some cases nearly twice as much. Ministers find it nearly impossible to fire or transfer permanent secretaries, who have a say in determining who will replace them when they retire or leave for well-paid positions in private industry; they tend to be a self-selecting elite. Permanent secretaries always play the role of humble, obedient servants, but some ministers come to wonder just who the boss really is.

Treasury   British ministry that supervises economic policies and budgets of other ministries.

rule of anticipated reactions   Friedrich's theory that politicians plan their moves so as not to anger the public.

The permanent secretary is assisted by several deputy secretaries who in turn are supported by undersecretaries and assistant secretaries. These names look like those of an American department, but in America all or most of these people are political appointees, serving at the pleasure of the president and resigning when a new president takes office. In Britain, only the ministers assisted by some junior ministers—about a hundred persons in all—change with a new government. What in America are temporary political appointees are permanent officials in Britain.

This gives them power. They are not amateurs but know their ministry—its personnel, problems, interests, and budget. Knowledge is power, and over time top civil servants come to quietly exercise a lot of it. While permanent secretaries or their assistants never—well, hardly ever—go public with their viewpoints, they reveal them through the kinds of ideas, programs, bills, and budgets they submit to the minister, their nominal boss. The minister theoretically commands them, but in practice he or she simply does not know enough about the workings of the ministry. Instead, the minister relies on them. Accordingly, while most bills and budget proposals pass through the cabinet, they do not originate there. The permanent civil servants do the jobs that are the stuff of governance.

The real power among the several British ministries is the **Treasury**. Sometimes called the "department of departments," Treasury not only supervises the main lines of economic policy but has the last word on who gets what among the ministries. Anyone with a bright idea in British government—a new minister or an innovative civil servant—soon comes up against the stone wall of Treasury, "the ministry that says no."

DEMOCRACY

HOW DEMOCRATIC IS BRITAIN?

The power of bureaucrats brings us to a fine irony. We have seen how Britons marched toward democracy by first limiting the power of the monarch and then expanding participation. If we look closely, though, we notice that many important decisions are only partly democratically controlled. Civil servants make much policy with no democratic input. Does this mean there is no real democracy in Britain? No, it means we must understand that no country exercises perfect control over its bureaucracy and that parties and elections are only attempts to do so.

Indeed, most of the interactions we have talked about are not under any form of popular control. Ideological infighting, the influence of interest groups on parties and the bureaucracy, the relationship of top civil servants with ministers, the granting of titles—these and other interactions are removed from democratic control. The people do not even choose whom they get to vote for; that is a matter for party influentials. All the people get to do is vote every few years, and the choice is limited.

Again, does this mean there is no democracy in Britain? No, not at all. Some people have an exaggerated vision of democracy as a system in which everyone gets to decide on everything. Such a system never existed at the national level, nor could it. The most we can ask of a democracy is that the leading team—in Britain, the prime minister and cabinet—are held accountable periodically in elections. This keeps them on their toes and anxious to pay attention to the public good, holds down special favors and corruption, and makes sure the bureaucracy functions. It is in the fear of electoral punishment that Britain, or any other country, qualifies as a democracy. What the great Carl J. Friedrich called the **rule of anticipated reactions** keeps the governors attentive. We will learn not to expect much more of political systems.

Britain's treasury minister goes by the old name of Chancellor of the Exchequer—originally the king's checker of taxes—and is now the second most powerful figure in the cabinet, the first being the prime minister. Some Chancellors of the Exchequer later be-come prime ministers—as did Gordon Brown in 2007—so the person in that office is watched closely.

peerage A Lord or Lady, higher than knighthood.

Under the Chancellor are the usual secretaries and civil servants, but they are a breed unto them-selves, smarter and more powerful than other bureaucrats. Operating on a team-spirit basis, Treasury chaps trust only other Treasury chaps, for only Treasury can see the whole picture of the British gov-ernment and economy and how the many parts interrelate. The other departments see only their corner, hence they should not be heeded. This attitude gives Treasury and its people an image of cold, callous remoteness, "government by mandarins"—but no one has tried to replace them.

The Civil Service and Interest Groups

We mentioned earlier the relationship between interest groups and political parties. But this is only one way for interest groups to make their voices heard and is often not the most important way. Much interest-group impact is in their quiet, behind-the-scenes contact with the bureaucracy. In-deed, with Parliament's role curtailed as a result of powerful prime ministers and party discipline, and cabinet ministers themselves dependent on permanent civil servants, many interest groups ask them-selves, "Why bother with Parliament? Why not go straight to where the action is, the bureaucracy?"

This approach is especially true of business and industry; the major effort of the unions is still focused on the Labour party. The reason for this is partly in the nature of what trade unions want as opposed to what business groups want. Unions want general policies on employment, wages, welfare, and so on, that apply to tens of millions of people. Industry usually wants specific, narrow

Political Culture

The Utility of Dignity

Another British holdover from the past is the monarch's bestowal of an honor such as knighthood. More than quaint, it is a payoff system that serves a number of purposes. The granting of titles is a reward and an encouragement to retire, opening positions to fresh, energetic younger people. A person looking for-ward to a knighthood (Sir) or a **peerage** (Lord) is more likely to go quietly. These honors also civilize recipi-ents; even militant union leaders and rapacious busi-nessmen start talking philosophically about the common good once they have titles in front of their names.

The queen awards these and other distinctions only on the advice of the prime minister, who has a small staff that watches for meritorious civil servants, busi-ness people, unionists, soldiers, politicians, scholars, artists, and writers, and recommends who should get what. In addition to becoming knights and peers, dis-tinguished Britons may be named to the Order of the British Empire, Order of the Garter, Order of Merit, Order of the Bath, the Royal Victorian Order, and many oth-ers. The granting of honors is a part of British political culture, a way of bolstering loyalty to and cooperation with the system.

rulings on taxes, subsidies, regulations, and the like that apply to a few firms. Thus unions tend to battle in the more open environment of party policy while business groups may prefer to quietly take a government official to lunch.

In working closely with a branch of Britain's economic life, a given ministry comes to see itself not as an impartial administrator but as a concerned and attentive helper. After all, if that industry falters, it reflects on the government agency assigned to monitor it. In this manner civil servants come to see leaders of economic interest groups as their "clients" and to reflect their clients' views. When this happens—and it happens in every country—the industry is said to have "captured" or "colonized" the executive department.

Reinforcing this pattern is the interchange between civil service and private industry. A permanent secretary can make much more money in business than in Whitehall; every now and then one of them leaves government service for greener pastures. (We will also see this pattern in France and Japan.) By the same token, business executives are sometimes brought into high administrative positions on the dubious theory that if they can run a company well, they can run government. The point is that cozy relationships develop between civil servants and private business.

Key Terms

carpetbagger (p. 62)
central office (p. 62)
charisma (p. 65)
Confederation of British
   Industry (p. 66)
constituency (p. 62)
dries (p. 65)
Euroenthusiast (p. 65)
Euroskeptic (p. 65)
general election (p. 63)
interested member (p. 66)
knighthood (p. 67)

Marxist (p. 64)
neoliberalism (p. 64)
New Labour (p. 64)
party identification (p. 62)
party image (p. 62)
peerage (p. 69)
permanent secretary (p. 67)
Question Hour (p. 67)
rule of anticipated
   reactions (p. 68)
safe seat (p. 62)
seat (p. 62)

sleaze factor (p. 66)
subsidy (p. 67)
swing (p. 62)
Thatcherite (p. 64)
Trades Union Congress
   (p. 66)
traditional Tory (p. 64)
Treasury (p. 68)
Trotskyist (p. 64)
wets (p. 65)

Further Reference

Barberis, Peter. *The Elite of the Elite: Permanent Secretaries in the British Higher Civil Service.* Brookfield, VT: Ashgate, 1996.

Bartle, John, and Anthony King, eds. *Britain at the Polls, 2005.* Washington, D.C.: CQ Press, 2006.

Bevir, Mark, and R. A. W. Rhodes. *Interpreting British Governance.* New York: Routledge, 2003.

Dunleavy, Patrick, Andrew Gamble, Richard Heffernan, and Ian Holliday. *Developments in British Politics 6.* New York: Palgrave, 2002.

Geddes, Andrew, and Jonathan Tonge, eds. *Labour's Second Landslide: The British General Election 2001*. New York: Palgrave, 2002.

Hickson, Kevin, ed. *The Political Thought of the Conservative Party*. New York: Palgrave, 2005.

King, Anthony, and Iain McLean, eds. *Rational Choice and British Politics: An Analysis of Rhetoric and Manipulation from Peel to Blair*. New York: Oxford, 2001.

McKinstry, Leo. *Fit to Govern*. London: Bantam Press, 1996.

Norris, Pippa, and Christopher Wlezien, eds. *Britain Votes 2005*. New York: Oxford University Press, 2005.

Seyd, Patrick, and Paul Whiteley. *New Labour's Grassroots: The Transformation of the Labour Party Membership*. New York: Palgrave, 2002.

Chapter 6
What Britons Quarrel About

Britain was in economic decline for decades. At first it was only a **relative decline** as the economies of West Europe and Japan grew more rapidly than the British economy. By the 1970s, however, Britain was in an **absolute decline** that left people with lower living standards as inflation outstripped wage increases. The first industrial nation saw Italy overtake it in per capita GDP in the 1980s. Likewise, Britain's former colonies of Hong Kong and Singapore had higher per capita GDPs than Britain. In Britain, **deindustrialization** seemed to be taking place; in some years the British GDP shrank. They called it the "British disease," and some Americans feared it was contagious.

QUESTIONS TO CONSIDER

1. What is the difference between relative and absolute decline?
2. What was the Thatcher cure for Britain's economy? Did it work?
3. What is the Beer thesis on Britain's decline?
4. What is productivity and why is it so important?
5. In what areas could Britain undergo constitutional reform?
6. Does Britain's National Health Service work? Compared to U.S.?
7. What is devolution? Does it lead to quasi-federalism?
8. Did Northern Ireland return to peace? Why or why not?
9. What is Britain's stance on the European Union? On the euro?

The "British Disease"

Why did Britain decline? There are two basic approaches to such a complex problem. One begins with what happens in people's attitudes—a psychocultural approach. The other begins with what happens in the physical world—a politico-economic approach. We might summarize this as "head stuff versus hard stuff." The two are not mutually exclusive but have a chicken-egg relationship: One feeds into the other.

Some emphasize British nonwork attitudes as the root of the problem. The old aristocracy, which disdained work as tawdry moneymaking, was never thoroughly displaced in Britain. Rather, the rising entrepreneurs aped the old elite and became gentlemen of leisure and culture. In public schools and Oxbridge, young Britons learn to despise commercial and technical skills in favor of the humanities. The emphasis was on having wealth rather than creating it. Accordingly, Britain tended to lack daring and innovative capitalists. Many Britons prefer more leisure time to more money.

The British class system made matters worse. British managers—mostly middle class—were snobbish toward workers; they did not mix with them and provided inadequate guidance and incentives. British workers reacted by showing solidarity with their "mates" and more loyalty to their union than to their company. If the psycho-cultural approach is correct, the only way to save Britain was to change British culture, but deep-seated attitudes resist change.

The other approach, the politico-economic, argues that the bad attitudes reflect faulty government policy. Change the policy to create a new context, and attitudes will change. Thatcherites propounded this, blaming the growth of the welfare state that Labour introduced in 1945. This let many **consume** without **producing** and subsidized inefficient industries. Unions, given free rein by previous governments, raised wages and lowered **productivity**. The growing costs of the welfare state drained away funds that should have gone for investment. Insufficient investment meant insufficient production, which meant stagnating living standards. Cut both welfare benefits and industry subsidies and you will force—with some pain—a change in attitudes, argued Thatcherites.

THE THATCHER CURE

The Thatcher cure for Britain's economic problems is still debated. Thatcherites argue that her policies were not implemented thoroughly or long enough. Anti-Thatcherites in all the parties argue the policies were brutal and ineffective. The way Thatcherites see it, the permissive policies of both Labour and previous Conservative governments had expanded welfare programs beyond the country's ability to pay for them. Unions won wage increases out of line with productivity. Nationalized and subsidized industries lost money. The result: **inflation** and falling productivity that were making Britain the sick man of Europe. The cure, in part, came from the **monetarist** theory of American economist (and Nobel Prize winner) Milton Friedman, which posits too-rapid growth of the money supply as the cause of inflation. Thatcher cut bureaucracy, the growth of welfare, and subsidies to industry in an effort to control Britain's money supply and restore economic health.

relative decline   Failing to keep up economically with other nations. (See page 73.)

absolute decline   Growing weaker economically compared to one's own past. (See page 73.)

deindustrialization   Decline of heavy industry. (See page 73.)

consumption   Buying things.

production   Making things.

productivity   Efficiency with which things are made.

inflation   Increase in most prices.

monetarism   Friedman's theory that the rate of growth of money supply governs much economic development.

privatization   Selling state-owned industry to private interests.

Some Britons wondered if the cure was worse than the disease. Unemployment at one point reached 14 percent of the work force, thousands of firms went bankrupt, and Britain's GDP growth was still anemic. Even moderate Conservatives pleaded for her to relent, but Thatcher was not called the Iron Lady for nothing. "The lady's not for turning," she intoned. She saw the economic difficulties as a purge Britain needed to get well. One of her economists said: "I don't shed tears when I see inefficient factories shut down. I rejoice." Thatcher and her supporters repeated, "You cannot consume until you produce."

Gradually the argument began to take hold. Many Britons had to admit they had been consuming more than they were producing, that subsidized factories and mines were a drain on the economy, and that bitter medicine was necessary to correct matters. It was almost as if Britons had become guilty about their free rides and knew they now had to pay up. In the 1980s, more working-class Britons voted Tory than voted Labour.

But did Thatchernomics work? By the time the Tories left office in 1997 the picture was mixed but generally positive. Inflation was down and economic growth among the fastest in Europe. State-owned British Steel, British Leyland (motor vehicles), and other industries that had been nationalized since the war to prevent unemployment trimmed their bloated work forces and raised productivity. Many state-owned plants were sold off, a process called **privatization**.

Competition increased by **deregulation**. Renters of public housing got the chance to buy their homes at low cost, a move that made some of them Conservatives. Unions eased their wage and other demands, and union membership dropped sharply. Many weak firms went under, but thousands of new small and middle-sized firms sprang up. Capital and labor were channeled away from losing industries and into winners, exactly what a good economic system should do. A California-like computer industry produced a "silicon glen" in Scotland and a "software valley" around Cambridge University.

Thatchernomics jolted workers out of their trade-union complacency ("I'm all right, Jack"). When the government's National Coal Board closed hundreds of unprofitable pits and eliminated twenty thousand jobs, miners staged a long and bitter strike in 1984, which was supported by some other unionists. Thatcher would not back down; after a year, the miners did. (At about the same time, President Reagan faced down striking air-traffic controllers.) New legislation limited union chiefs' abilities to call strikes, and the number and length of strikes in Britain dropped drastically.

As in the United States in recent decades, income inequality grew in Britain. The number of Britons in families with less than half the average income increased under Thatcher and Major from 5 million in 1979 to 14 million in 1993. High youth unemployment led to urban riots. Major regional disparities appeared between a rich, resurgent South of England, with new high-tech industries, and a decaying, abandoned North, where unemployment hit hardest. Thatcher never did get a handle on government spending, much of which, like U.S. **entitlements**, must by law be paid. British welfare benefits actually climbed sharply during the Thatcher and Major years despite their best efforts to trim them. Cutting the welfare state is tempting but rarely successful; too many people have come to depend on it. Furthermore, in the late 1980s, a credit and spending

---

deregulation Cutting governmental rules regarding industry.

entitlement Spending programs citizens are automatically entitled to, such as Social Security.

pluralistic stagnation Theory that out-of-control interest groups produce policy logjams.

counterculture Rejection of conventional values, as in the 1960s.

pluralism Autonomous interaction of social groups with themselves and with government.

KEY CONCEPTS

"PLURALISTIC STAGNATION"

Harvard political scientist Samuel Beer advanced a provocative thesis on the cause of Britain's decline: too many interest groups making too many demands on parties who are too willing to promise everyone everything. The result was **pluralistic stagnation** as British groups scrambled for welfare benefits, pay hikes, and subsidies for industry. The two main parties bid against each other with promises of more benefits to more groups.

Furthermore, in the 1960s, a strong **counterculture** emerged in Britain, which repudiated traditional civility and deference and made groups' demands more strident. With every group demanding and getting more, no one saw any reason for self-restraint that would leave them behind. Government benefits fed union wage demands, which fed inflation, which fed government benefits . . .

The interesting point about the Beer thesis is that it blamed precisely what political scientists long celebrated as the foundation of freedom and democracy: **pluralism**. Beer demonstrated, though, that it can run amok; groups block each other and government, leading to what Beer called the "paralysis of public choice." Any comparison with your system?

recession   A shrinking economy, indicated by falling GDP.

boom kicked inflation back up to over 10 percent, and the economy slumped into **recession**. Competitively, British productivity was low and its wages high, so Britain continued to lose manufacturing jobs to other countries.

Thatcher's main legacy is the changed terms of Britain's political debate. In 1945 Labour had shifted the debate to the welfare state, and Tories had to compete with them on their own terms, never seriously challenging the underlying premise that redistribution is good. Thatcher changed this all around and made the debate one about productivity and economic growth; now Labour had to compete on *her* terms. It was a historic shift, and one that influenced the political debate in other lands, including the United States. Labour Prime Ministers Blair and Brown did not repudiate Thatcher's free-market economic policies; they stole them and possibly ran them better. In 2007 Britain's unemployment was a low 5 percent while France's and Germany's were around 9 percent. And Britain had virtually no public debt or inflation. Britain had indeed turned around.

The Trouble with National Health

The centerpiece of Britain's welfare state is the National Health Service (NHS), which went into operation in 1948 as part of Labour's longstanding commitment to helping working Britons. Before World War II, British medical care was spotty, and many Britons were too unhealthy and

COMPARISON

The Cost of the Welfare State

The other side of the welfare state is how expensive it is. In 2005, all types of taxes at all levels of government took the percentages of GDP shown in the table below.

Almost all advanced industrialized countries have been cutting taxes. Most of the percentages shown in the table are lower than a few years earlier, indicating growth in the overall economy and cuts in welfare funds.

Sweden	50
France	44
Italy	41
Euro area average	40
Britain	37
Germany	35
Canada	33
Australia	31
Japan	27
United States	27

Source: OECD.

scrawny for military service during the war. Conservatives and the British Medical Association fought the NHS, but the tide was against them.

Did the NHS work? The answer is both yes and no. The British population is much healthier than it used to be. Infant mortality, one key measure of overall health standards, dropped from 64 out of 1,000 live births in 1931 to 5 now. The British working class has especially benefited. Britons spend only 9 percent of their GDP on health care but are healthier than Americans, who spend 15 percent.

But NHS has been unable to keep up with skyrocketing costs, even though it eats nearly a fifth of total government spending. Britons have become more elderly, and old people consume

Comparison

The Productivity Race

No production, no goodies. Production is what gets turned out. Productivity is how efficiently it gets turned out. You can have a lot of production with low productivity, the Soviet problem that brought down the Communist regime. Among the major economies, Britain's productivity was a bit weak. Compared to Britain, in 2005 GDP per hour worked was 20 percent higher in France, 18 percent higher in the United States, and 3 percent higher in Germany, but Canada was 6 percent lower and Japan was 17 percent lower.

The growth of productivity—the additional amount a worker cranks out per hour from one year to the next—is the measure of future prosperity. Rapid growth in productivity means quickly rising standards of living; low growth means stagnation or even decline. The percent average annual growth in labor productivity from 2000 to 2005 is shown in the table below.

China's and India's rapid productivity growth was similar to Japan's in earlier decades. Newly industrializing countries, because they are starting from a low level, show the biggest percentage gains. After a while, when all of the easy gains have been made, a country becomes more "normal," like Japan. Earlier, U.S. productivity growth had been among the weakest of the industrialized countries. Its surge in the late 1990s reflected major investments in efficiency and information technology that made workers more productive.

Productivity does not tell the whole story of an economy, because it focuses on manufacturing. Advanced economies employ most people not in factories but in the service sector, where productivity gains are harder to make and to measure.

China	8.7
India	4.1
United States	2.5
Japan	2.3
France	2.1
Britain	1.8
Germany	1.3
Canada	1.1
Mexico	0.4

Source: OECD, The Conference Board

many times as much medical care as younger people. Technical advances in medicine are terribly expensive. The system requires many bureaucrats. With a staff of 1 million, the NHS is the largest employer in West Europe, but personnel and facilities have not kept pace with demand. The money simply is not there. If surgery is not for an emergency, patients may wait a year or more. The debate in Britain is over whether to keep funding the NHS by general tax revenues, which Labour favors, or to adopt European funding models, which include mandatory employee and employer contributions and a bigger role for private health care.

DEMOCRACY

WHICH BLAIR PROJECT?

Blair's chief project was not Britain's economy but its institutions. His bold constitutional reforms modernized Britain's political institutions, many of which had been little changed in centuries. Some of his projects were passed into law while others are debated by the Brown government. Blair will go down as Britain's modernizer.

1. *A written constitution.* With no fixed limits, power can be abused in Britain. PM Brown wants more written rules to make the powers of government more accountable.

2. *A bill of rights,* U.S.-style. Blair accomplished this by having Parliament adopt the European Convention on Human Rights as domestic law, bringing Britain into line with the rest of the EU, starting in 2000. For the first time Britons got legal guarantees of media freedom and protection from heavy-handed police methods. Brown may carry it further with a purely British charter of rights.

3. *Judicial review.* Any bill Parliament passes is automatically constitutional in Britain. As in most of the world, British courts cannot check executive excesses. Many Britons admire the role of the U.S. Supreme Court, which, among other things, guarantees . . .

4. *Freedom of information.* Britain has an Official Secrets Act that comes close to censorship. All manner of government wrongdoing is concealed. Many Britons admire the U.S. Freedom of Information Act.

5. *A meaningful upper house.* As we discussed in Chapter 3, in 1999 Blair modernized Lords by kicking out most hereditary peers and leaving it largely in the hands of life peers. This still left it with little power. Brown is considering giving it some powers to check Commons and the cabinet.

6. *Devolution,* which Blair carried out smartly in granting extensive home rule and elected assemblies to Northern Ireland, Scotland, and Wales. (See the subsequent discussions.)

7. *A new electoral system.* As we considered in Chapter 3, the traditional FPTP system over-rewards the two big parties and penalizes third parties. Adding some PR ("topping off"), as is done in elections for the new Scottish and Welsh parliaments, would be much fairer, especially to the Lib Dems. Brown may consider it.

8. *Public services* are hurting in Britain. Education, railways, and the National Health Service have lagged behind the rest of Europe. New management and money are needed to improve them, and Brown indicated he would work on this.

9. *Fox hunting* has become an angry symbol of "a crisis in the countryside." Rural dwellers protest declining farm incomes, outsiders driving up home prices, and the mishandling of a big hoof-and-mouth outbreak in 2001. "Now they want to take away our tradition of 'riding to hounds,'" they complain. Their real message: more money to improve rural services.

Is Northern Ireland Settled?

There is a sort of peace now in Ulster, but hatreds still run deep after thirty years of violence. One cannot tell if the power-sharing government formed in 2007 is stable. Previous understandings have broken down. Catholics and Protestants are more segregated than ever into two societies.

In 1998, on Good Friday, the two sides reached agreement, but it soon failed as it did not settle the fundamental question: Should the North unify with the Republic of Ireland? What most Catholics wanted, Protestants angrily rejected. The moderate parties on both sides shrank as the extremist parties grew. In 2005 the militant Democratic Unionist party of Rev. Ian Paisley won nine of Ulster's eighteen seats. Gerry Adams, the Sinn Féin chief who once advocated violence, announced in 2005 that the IRA—which has lost support for its indiscriminate killings—would give up its arms and pursue its goals by political means. Paisley called Adams a terrorist, and indeed Adams is on the IRA's seven-member council.

> **Good Friday agreement**   1998 pact to share power in Northern Ireland.
>
> **consociation**   Sharing of political power at the executive level, giving all major parties cabinet positions.
>
> **subject**   Originally, a subject of the Crown; now means British citizen.
>
> **Commonwealth**   Organization of countries that were once British colonies.

Prime Minister Blair pushed for the 1998 **Good Friday agreement**; his Conservative predecessors did little because they would not negotiate with Sinn Féin. The deal looked good on paper but took nine years to implement. The agreement reopened the Northern Ireland Assembly at Stormont, which had been closed since 1974. Previously dominated by Protestants, it was one of the reasons for Catholic protest. Stormont's powers and budget are substantial. It runs Northern Ireland's education, medical, social, housing, and agricultural services.

Stormont's 108 members are now elected by the type of proportional representation used in the Republic of Ireland. Ministries are awarded on a balanced basis; most of the parties in Stormont get at least one portfolio. Political scientists call such an arrangement **consociation**, sometimes useful to hold together fractured societies. First minister (in effect, governor) is Rev. Paisley, but his deputy is Martin McGuinness, a close associate of Gerry Adams of Sinn Féin. At the signing of the 2007 deal Paisely and Adams even smiled and shook hands. Mutual exhaustion and mass disgust at the "Troubles" may have finally persuaded the unlikely pair to cooperate.

Britain's Racial Problems

British society, like U.S. society, is split along racial and religious lines. Whites have little to do with nonwhites and Muslims, and there is animosity between them. Going back as far as 1958, race riots have flared in Britain every few years. Nonwhites, most born in Britain, are now about 7 percent (4 percent South Asian and 2 percent black) of Britain's population, many ghettoized in the declining industrial cities in the north of England.

The race/Muslim problem in Britain is a legacy of empire. Britain in 1948 legally made the natives of its many colonies British **subjects**, entitled to live and work in the United Kingdom. Although the colonies were granted independence from the late 1940s through the 1960s, as members of the British **Commonwealth** their people were still entitled to immigrate to Britain. In the 1950s, West Indians arrived from the Caribbean, then Indians and Pakistanis, taking lowly jobs that Britons did not want, then sending for relatives. For years they labored in Britain's textile industry, but it closed, leaving many Muslims unemployed. Britain now has some 1.6 million Muslims, mostly Pakistanis. (France has far more Muslims.) Meanwhile, white resentment builds,

jihadi   From *jihad* (holy war); Muslim holy warrior.

emigration   Moving out of your native country.

immigration   Resettling into a new country.

especially among the working class in areas of industrial decline and high unemployment. Some Britons refer to "Londonistan" in a non-joking way. In 1967 an openly racist National Front formed, advocating the expulsion of all "coloureds" back to their native lands. Skinheads, supporting the Front or its successor British National party (BNP), like "Paki bashing." With slogans such as "Rights for Whites," the anti-immigrant vote grew but never won a seat in Parliament. The BNP was much weaker than its Continental counterparts such as the French National Front.

Two forces keep Muslims segregated: discrimination by whites and wanting to preserve their original faith and culture. A special irritant: Muslim women in full-face veils. Caught between two cultures, some unemployed and alienated Muslim youths fall under the sway of fanatic *Islamist* preachers (see page 548). In 2005 four Muslim youths (three of Pakistani origin but born in England, one born in Jamaica) set off three bombs on London's Underground and one on a bus that killed fifty-six and injured 700. Other bombings followed. Said one bitter young Muslim social worker, "When they bomb London, the bigger the better. I know it's going to happen because Sheikh bin Laden said so. Like Bali, like Turkey, like Madrid—I pray for it, I look forward to the day." A minority of Britain's Muslims hate Britain.

Tories have long wooed voters with calls for a "clear end to immigration" before it "swamps" British culture, but both major parties have since 1962 tightened immigration to Britain until it is now very restrictive. Prime Ministers Blair and Brown have both denounced bombings and warned Muslim clerics who preach *jihad* to cease or face expulsion. Some worry about an erosion of civil rights in Britain, but many more applaud government vigilance.

Britain faces the same old problem: How does a tolerant society handle militant intolerance? Most Britons are prepared for less tolerance when it comes to situations like suicide bombings. Britain, like all Western countries, has thus found itself debating where civil rights end and homeland security begins. No Western country tolerates **jihadis** on its soil. Notice how France (pages 155–157) and Germany (page 234) face the identical problem, which is made worse by the fact that historically European lands have been countries of **emigration**, not countries of **immigration**. The United States handles immigration better because we are all immigrants or their descendants. Americans, too, however, expect new arrivals to become patriotic Americans and get angry if they do not.

A black Labour candidate campaigns in London. Several black MPs have won Labour seats in Parliament.

BRITAIN AND EUROPE

Until recent decades, Britons did not see themselves as Europeans; most looked down on anyone from across the English Channel. Rather than working toward a united Europe after World War II, as the Continental countries did, Britain emphasized its Commonwealth ties and "special relationship" with the United States. As the rest of Europe kept distant from U.S. policy on Iraq, Tony Blair supported it.

> **human capital** Education, skills, and enthusiasm of nation's work force.
>
> **underclass** Permanently disadvantaged people.

Britain stayed out of the 1957 Treaty of Rome, which set up the European Community (EC, since 1993 the EU, for European Union), but in 1960 built a much looser grouping, the European Free Trade Association (EFTA). While the EC Six (France, West Germany, Italy, Belgium, the Netherlands, Luxembourg) economies surged ahead, the EFTA Outer Seven (Britain, Austria, Denmark, Finland, Iceland, Norway, Portugal, Sweden, and Switzerland) were slowly cut off from the main European market. In 1963, Britain applied to join the EC, but French President Charles de Gaulle vetoed British entry, charging that Britain was still too tied to the Commonwealth and the United States to be a good European. He was right.

By the time de Gaulle resigned in 1969, Britain was ready to join the EC, but not all Britons liked the idea. For traditional Tories, it meant giving up some British sovereignty to the EC headquarters in Brussels and even treating Europeans as equals. For everyone it meant higher food prices. For manufacturers it meant British products had to compete with often better and cheaper Continental imports that now come in tariff-free. For fishermen it meant British fishing areas were open to all EC fishermen. For workers it meant loss of some jobs. Many Britons want to stay firmly British. The small UK Independence party (UKIP) aims to get Britain out of the EU.

The arguments in favor of the EU stress that Britain needs change and competition, the very forces that had invigorated European industries. Euroenthusiasts argue that geographically, strategically, economically, even spiritually, Britain really is part of Europe and should start acting like

COMPARISON

HOW TO IMPROVE BRITISH EDUCATION

One limit to British economic growth has been poor educational levels. Britain's **human capital** does not compare favorably with other countries. Many leave school at age 16 with weak math and verbal skills, forming a U.S.-style **underclass**. British parents who can afford it send their children to private schools.

As in the United States, the British debate an old question: quality versus equality in education. Tories opt for quality, returning to testing to select the best for elite high schools, some of them independent but with government subsidies. Northern Ireland kept these old "grammar schools" and shows better overall performance. Labour, still seeking equality in education, rejects selectivity but wants to improve funding, standards, and discipline for the comprehensive schools. By 2000, British 15-year-olds tested better than most of the Continent and much better than U.S. scores. Surprising: the drop in German scores to U.S. levels. Unsurprising: high Japanese math scores.

regional nationalism Particularist and separatist movements in some peripheral areas.

it. The Euro-debate cuts across party lines, sometimes producing a strange coalition of right-wing Tories and left-wing Labourites, each opposing Europe for their own reasons. In 1971, under a Tory government, the Commons voted 356 to 244 to join; 69 Labour MPs defied their party whip to vote in favor while 39 Conservatives, freed from party discipline, voted "no" along with Labour, demonstrating that British party discipline is not perfect. On January 1, 1973, Britain, along with Denmark and Ireland, made the Common Market Six, the Nine. (For more on the EU, see Chapter 17.)

When Labour returned to power, Prime Minister Harold Wilson offered the British public a first—a referendum, something common in France. But Britain, with its tradition of parliamentary supremacy, had never held one before. The 1975 referendum found that most Britons wanted to stay in Europe, but one-third voted no. If put to another referendum, British voters would

GEOGRAPHY

DEVOLUTION FOR SCOTLAND AND WALES

Britain, a centralized unitary state, has become a little less centralized. Northern Ireland, Scotland, and Wales show the center-periphery tensions that afflict many countries. In general, the farther from the nation's capital, the more regional resentment. Wales has been a part of England since the Middle Ages; the thrones of England and Scotland were united in 1603, but only in 1707 did both countries agree to a single Parliament in London. The old resentments never died. Wales and Scotland were always poorer than England, leaving Welsh and Scots feel they were economically ignored.

In the twentieth century the political beneficiary of these feelings was the Labour party, which still holds sway in Wales and Scotland. Voting Labour in Scotland and Wales became a form of regional nationalism, a way of repudiating rule by England, which goes Conservative. Center-periphery tensions reveal themselves in voting patterns. In the 1960s the small Plaid Cymru (pronounced *plyde kum-REE*, meaning "Party of Wales") and the Scottish Nationalist party grew, and both now win seats in Parliament.

Regional nationalism grew in many countries besides Wales and Scotland, starting in the 1970s: Corsican and Breton in France, Quebecker in Canada, Basque and Catalan in Spain. In the 1990s, the Soviet Union and Yugoslavia fell apart. There are several causes of local separatism. Economics plays a role; local nationalists claim their regions are shortchanged by central governments. Some emphasize their regions' distinct languages and cultures and demand that they be taught in schools. Some of the impulse behind local nationalism is the bigness and remoteness of the modern state, the feeling that important decisions are out of local control, made by distant bureaucrats. And often smoldering under the surface are historical resentments of a region that once was conquered, occupied, and deprived of its own identity. Whatever the mixture, local nationalism sometimes turns its adherents into fanatics willing to wreck the entire country to get their way. Happily, this did not happen in Britain. The Scots and Welsh never became as extreme as Basques in Spain or Corsicans in France.

In Scotland, the economic factor played a large part in its rising nationalism. When oil was discovered in the North Sea off Scotland in the 1960s, some Scots did not want to share the petroleum revenues with the United Kingdom as a whole: "It's Scotland's oil!" Petroleum offered Scotland the possibility of economic independence and self-government, of becoming something more than a poor, northerly part of Britain. (Alberta has much the same feeling about its oil.)

have rejected the new EU constitution, which French and Dutch voters did reject in 2005 (see pages 252–253).

Thatcher, a British nationalist and Euroskeptic, took a tough line on the EU. A common market was fine, she argued, but not turning it into a supranational entity that would infringe on Britain's sovereignty. Many Britons rejected joining the European Monetary Union (EMU) or its new euro currency. Their slogan: "Europe yes, euro no." The EMU indeed takes away an important part of sovereignty, the ability of each country to control its currency, and gives it to the European Central Bank in Frankfurt. Many Britons (and some other Europeans) feared that Europe's strongest economy—Germany—would dominate the EMU and that policy on money supply and interest rates would be set by the Bundesbank. Britain (along with Denmark and Sweden) stood aside as the euro was introduced. Blair and

---

devolution   Central government turns some powers over to regions.

referendum   Vote on an issue rather than for an office.

quasi-federal   Halfway federal.

The leading issue for Welsh nationalists has been language, the ancient Celtic tongue of Cymric (pronounced *kim-rick*). Some 13 percent of Welsh speak Cymric, a number that has been growing as it is required in Welsh schools. Cymric is now officially co-equal with English within Wales, which has a Cymric TV channel.

The Labour party has been more open to home rule or autonomy for Scotland and Wales, what is called **devolution**, the granting of certain governing powers by the center to the periphery. A 1977 devolution bill to set up Scottish and Welsh assemblies, however, failed in **referendums**. After the 1997 election, in which Scotland and Wales stayed overwhelmingly Labour, Tony Blair once again offered Scotland and Wales their own parliaments, and this time the referendums passed. In 1999, at about the same time that Ulster got home rule, Scots and Welsh elected regional parliaments with a new voting system that could eventually be adopted for Britain as a whole. The German-style system (see pages 189–192) gave each voter two votes, the first for FPTP single-member districts and the second for parties in multimember districts. The results of the second vote were used to "top off" the number of seats for each party until they were roughly proportional to its share of the votes.

The new assemblies have some powers in education, economic planning, and taxation, but some Scots dismiss their assembly as "a wee pretendy parliament" and want full independence. Prime Minister Brown, himself a Scot, is very much against it. In 2007 elections to the 129-member Scottish Parliament, the SNP edged Labour. Some predicted a loss of Labour seats in Scotland to the SNP in the next general election.

Britons do not use the word, but Britain now has **quasi-federalism**, and it could go further. Fewer call themselves "British"; increasingly they specify English, Scottish, or Welsh. Devolution may have started a logical sequence leading to federalism. Scots and Welsh get to vote on their own local affairs *plus*, in Westminster, vote on England's affairs, too. It is unfair, and two-thirds of the English now want their own *English* parliament. Logically, England—either as a whole or divided into regions—should have the right to govern its local affairs. (Or Scottish and Welsh MPs could refrain from voting on purely English matters, a clumsy way to run things.) England is divided into nine administrative regions, which some say could form the basis of federalism within England. A federal Britain, which is a long way off, could at last give the House of Lords a major function: representing the regions. Other unitary systems, such as France and Spain, have loosened up into quasi-federal systems (see pages 112–113).

---

unilinear   Progressing evenly and always upward.

Brown, cautious Euroenthusiasts, waited to see how the euro worked. Euroskeptics lead the Tories, and Britain is still split over Europe. Some Britons would like to drop out of the EU. Perhaps Britain really is an Atlantic country and not a European one. Britain's natural community may be the English-speaking lands across the oceans.

GREAT BRITAIN OR LITTLE ENGLAND?

This sums up the dilemma of modern Britain: the problem of scaling down its vision of itself. Britain, in the course of a century, has clearly declined, both internationally and domestically. When Britain was a mighty empire and the most industrialized country in the world in the second half of the nineteenth century, it had power, wealth, and a sense of mission. This in turn fostered order, discipline, and deference among the British people. Losing its empire and slipping behind the economies of West Europe, decay, violence, and resentment appeared.

Britain's trajectory refutes the idea that progress is **unilinear**. In the case of Britain we see that what goes up can eventually come down. But this process is never static. Now that Britain is adjusting to its new reality—as one European country among many—regeneration has already begun. To see how another country has turned around, how a society and economy can change from static to dynamic, let us now consider France.

KEY TERMS

absolute decline (p. 74)

Commonwealth (p. 79)

consociation (p. 79)

consumption (p. 74)

counterculture (p. 75)

deindustrialization (p. 74)

deregulation (p. 75)

devolution (p. 83)

emigration (p. 80)

entitlement (p. 75)

Good Friday agreement (p. 79)

human capital (p. 81)

immigration (p. 80)

inflation (p. 74)

jihadi (p. 80)

monetarism (p. 74)

pluralism (p. 75)

pluralistic stagnation (p. 75)

privatization (p. 74)

production (p. 74)

productivity (p. 74)

quasi-federal (p. 83)

recession (p. 76)

referendum (p. 83)

regional nationalism (p. 82)

relative decline (p. 74)

subject (p. 79)

underclass (p. 81)

unilinear (p. 84)

FURTHER REFERENCE

De Bréadún, Deaglán. *The Far Side of Revenge: Making Peace in Northern Ireland*. Wilton, Ireland: Collins, 2001.

Denver, David. *Scotland Decides: The Devolution Issue and the 1997 Referendum*. Portland, OR: F. Cass, 2000.

Green, E. H. H. *Thatcher*. New York: Oxford University Press, 2006.

Hansen, Randall. *Citizenship and Immigration in Post-War Britain: The Institutional Origins of a Multicultural Nation*. New York: Oxford University Press, 2000.

Hearn, Jonathan. *Claiming Scotland: National Identity and Liberal Culture*. New York: Columbia University Press, 2001.

MacGinty, Roger, and John Darby. *Guns and Government: The Management of the Northern Ireland Peace Process*. New York: Palgrave, 2002.

Owen, Geoffrey. *From Empire to Europe*. New York: HarperCollins, 1999.

Pierson, Paul. *Dismantling the Welfare State? Reagan, Thatcher, and the Politics of Retrenchment.* New York: Cambridge University Press, 1994.

Sawyer, Malcolm, ed. *The UK Economy*, 16th ed. New York: Oxford University Press, 2005.

Seldon, Anthony, ed. *The Blair Effect*. Boston, MA: Little, Brown, 2001.

Wall, Stephen. *A Stranger in Europe: Britain and the EU from Thatcher to Blair*. New York: Oxford University Press, 2008.

Chapter 7

France:
The Impact of the Past

"**F**rance has everything," many French rightly boast. Hexagon-shaped, with three sides on seas and three on land, France is simultaneously an Atlantic country, a Mediterranean country, and an Alpine country. It has lush farmland, navigable rivers, many minerals, and a moderate climate. It does not, however, have a moat like England; France is vulnerable to land attack from the north and the east. While England historically had a small army, France needed a large army, a point that helps explain the rise of French absolutism. French kings had troops to rely on.

Internally, France is divided into a North and a South. Culturally and temperamentally, the two regions differ and, until the late Middle Ages, even spoke different languages. The Germanic northerners spoke *langue d'oil*, "the tongue of *oil*," their word for yes, which grew into the modern French *oui*. The Mediterranean southerners spoke *langue d'oc*, after their word for yes, *oc*. It declined after the Paris kings conquered the South in the thirteenth century. To this day, southerners have a different accent and resent rule by Paris. The region is still called Languedoc.

QUESTIONS TO CONSIDER

1. How does the Roman influence in France compare to the Roman influence in Britain?
2. What is France's core area? How did it come to be?
3. Who epitomized French absolutism?
4. What was the theory of mercantilism?
5. What caused the French Revolution?
6. How did great French thinkers differ from the British?
7. What is Brinton's theory of revolution?
8. With what regime did France become a stable democracy?
9. What did the Dreyfus Affair show?
10. Who ran France during World War II?
11. How did de Gaulle come to power?

THE ROMAN INFLUENCE

Like most peoples, the French are a mixture of ethnic stocks. In the centuries before Christ, tribes of Celts pushed into France and merged with the native Ligurians. The Romans conquered the area and called it *Gallia* (Gaul). Roman influence in France was longer and deeper than in England, which the Anglo-Saxons obliterated, but the Germanic tribes that moved into Gaul became Romanized themselves. Thus, English is a Germanic language and French a Romance language.

By the time the Roman Empire collapsed, one Germanic tribe, the Franks, had managed to take over most of present-day France. Their chief, Clovis—from whom came the name Louis—was baptized in 496, and France has been mostly Catholic ever since, the "eldest daughter of the Church." The Franks under Charles Martel turned back the invading Moors in 732, possibly saving Europe. Charles Martel's grandson, Charlemagne, in 800 founded a huge empire—the Holy Roman Empire—that encompassed what someday would amount to most of the six original EU countries. Although the empire soon disintegrated, Charlemagne had planted the idea of European unity.

France

THE RISE OF FRENCH ABSOLUTISM

In the confusion after Charlemagne, France was reduced to several petty kingdoms and dukedoms, as was Germany. While Germany stayed divided until the nineteenth century, French kings pursued unification and centralization of their power with single-minded determination. Pushing outward from the Paris area, the *Ile de France* (Island of France), French kings added territory while retaining control in Paris.

Estates-General   Old, unused French parliament.

Huguenots   French Protestants.

intendants   French provincial administrators, answerable only to Paris; early version of *prefects*.

aristocrat   Person of inherited noble rank.

autonomy   Partial independence.

Feudalism in France began to give way to absolutism with the crafty Louis (pronounced *Lwie*) XI, who ruled from 1461 to 1483 and doubled the size of France until it was nearly its present shape. He also weakened the power of the feudal nobles, ignored the **Estates-General**, and developed a royal bureaucracy to increase taxation. This pattern was strengthened for at least three centuries, leaving the France of today still highly centralized. Louis XI also cultivated relations with Rome. There was never an English-style break with the Vatican; instead, the Catholic Church remained a pillar of the French monarchy. The **Huguenots** were controlled, massacred, and driven into exile. In 1589, however, the royal line of succession fell to a Huguenot, Henry of Navarre. The Catholic Church offered the throne to Henry only if he accepted Catholicism. Shrugged Henry: "Paris is well worth a Mass."

Under Louis XIII, Cardinal Richelieu became chief minister and virtual ruler from 1624 to 1642. Obsessed with French power and glory, Richelieu further weakened the nobles, recruited only middle-class bureaucrats, and sent out **intendants** to control the provinces for Paris. Richelieu was an organizational genius who put his bureaucratic stamp on France for all time.

French nobles fought centralization but lost. In 1648 and again in 1650 some French **aristocrats** staged an uncoordinated revolt called the *Fronde*. Recall that at this time English nobles and their commoner allies beheaded a king who tried to act like an absolute monarch. In France, the nobles were quickly broken and lost the **autonomy** enjoyed by English lords.

GEOGRAPHY

RIVERS

Navigable rivers are economic arteries, tying a country together and often boosting international trade. England's Thames also gives it an inland outlet to the sea. France's Seine, Rhine, Rhone, and Loire give it trade routes and outlets to the sea in all four points of the compass. French kings supplemented the rivers with an ambitious system of canals, some of which are still in use. The Rhine has for centuries served as a West European highway, connecting Switzerland, France, Germany, and the Netherlands. The Danube stitched together the Austro-Hungarian Empire, but for centuries its outlet in the Black Sea was controlled by the hostile Turks. Russia's rivers flow the wrong way, either to the Arctic Ocean or to the Black Sea, where the Ottomans held the vital Turkish Straits. China's economic and political life grew up around the Yellow and Yangzi Rivers, the early Indian kingdoms along the Indus and Ganges.

GEOGRAPHY

CORE AREAS

Most countries have an identifiable **core** area, a region where in most cases the state originated. Some countries contain more than one core area, and this may produce regional tension. Typically, the country's capital is in its core area. Farther out are the peripheral areas, often more recent additions where people may speak a different language and resent rule by the core area. At times the resentment can turn deadly, as when provinces such as Serbia's Kosovo, Turkey's Kurdish area, and China's Taiwan attempt to break away. Part of the tragedy of Kosovo is that it was the medieval Serbian core, but after Turkish conquest in 1389, Serbs were displaced northward, and Kosovo slowly became a majority Albanian. Looking to their history, Serbs refused to give up their ancient heartland.

France is an almost perfect example of a core area, centered on Paris, spreading its rule, language, and culture with an eye toward perfecting national integration. This has been a slow process and one that is still not complete. In the nineteenth century, some regions of France still spoke strange dialects. Under deliberate educational policy, corps of schoolteachers directed by Paris spread across France to turn "peasants into Frenchmen," in the words of historian Eugen Weber. Because of this some peripheral areas still harbor resentment against Paris. Brittany, Corsica, and Languedoc try to keep alive local dialects and regional culture. Extremists in Corsica practice occasional violence.

England is the core area of the United Kingdom, and the Valley of Mexico is Mexico's core area, established and reinforced by Toltecs, Aztecs, and Spaniards. The German core area is much less clear. The many German ministates of the Middle Ages kept their sovereignty and dialects for an unusually long time. Prussia led German unification in the nineteenth century, and so Berlin became the nation's capital. But many regions had little respect for Prussia; Catholic lands such as Bavaria and the Rhineland disliked Prussia's authoritarianism and Protestantism.

Germany remained riven by **particularism**, a factor that contributed to present-day federalism. Nazism was in part a contrived effort to bring all German regions under central control by means of lunatic nationalism. Nigeria, assembled by British imperialists, has no core area, which is the root of its breakaway tribalism.

The Soviet Union represented a huge gap between its Slavic core area and its non-Slavic peripheral areas. Russia's numerous nationalities are still distinct and discontent. Lacking the kind of cohesion that other nation-states have, the Soviet Union was a type of colonial empire. The Slavic core of Russia, Belarus, and Ukraine gradually beat back Tatars, Turks, and Swedes until it straddled the vast belt where Europe meets Asia. Then the tsars sent expeditions eastward to claim Siberia to the Pacific. During the mid-nineteenth century Russia acquired most of the Muslim-Turkic peoples of Central Asia. **Russification** proved impossible, however, and fostered nationalist hatred against Moscow. The breakaway of republics from the Soviet Union may be seen as decolonization. The remaining Russian Federation still contains lands like Chechnya that would like to break away.

China's core area was the Yellow River Valley, but before the time of Christ, China had consolidated a major empire. So numerous and united—despite occasional civil wars—were the **Han** Chinese that the addition to the kingdom of a few outer barbarians (Mongols, Tibetans, Turkic Muslims, and others) bothered the Han little. Recently, however, Central Asian dissidents have set off bombs to protest rule by Beijing.

Japan, with Tokyo-Yokohama as its core area, has some center-periphery tension between East and West Japan and from agricultural and fishing prefectures. Iran has non-Persian-speaking peripheral areas that resent rule by Tehran. The U.S. core area began with the thirteen colonies along the Atlantic seaboard, especially the northern ones, which are still somewhat resented by the rest of the union.

Louis XIV: The High Point of Absolutism

"L'état, c'est moi" ("The state—that's me"), Louis XIV is often quoted as saying. By the time Louis XIV became king in 1661, French absolutism was already well developed; he brought it to a high point. Louis's emblem was the sun, around which all things revolved. The Sun King further increased centralization and bureaucratization, all aimed at augmenting his own and France's power. Louis used his large army in almost continual warfare. He acted as his own prime minister and handled much administration personally. He never bothered convening the Estates-General. He constructed **Versailles** and made hundreds of nobles live there, diverting them from power seeking to game playing—games of intrigue, love, and flattery. While English lords ruled as small kings on their estates, French nobles were reduced to **courtiers**.

Louis's policies of "war and magnificence" were financial drains. In order to harness the French economy to serve the state, Louis's minister, Colbert, practiced **mercantilism**, the theory that a nation was as wealthy as the amount of gold it possessed and that the way to amass gold was for the government to supervise the economy with plans, subsidies, monopolies, and tariffs. This set a pattern

core Region where the state originated. (See page 90.)

particularism Region's sense of its difference. (See page 90.)

Russification Making non-Russian nationalities learn Russian. (See page 90.)

Han Original and main people of China. (See page 90.)

Versailles Palaces and park on outskirts of Paris begun by Louis XIV.

courtier Person who hangs around a royal court.

mercantilism Theory that a nation's wealth is its gold and silver, to be amassed by government controls on the economy.

bound To name bordering countries.

Geography

Bound France

There is an old technique for teaching geography that has been forgotten; we are going to revive it here. The technique requires the student to recite, from forced recall, the boundaries of a given country in the following form:

France is bounded on the north by Belgium and Luxembourg;

on the east by Germany, Switzerland, and Italy;

on the south by the Mediterranean Sea and Spain;

and on the west by the Atlantic Ocean.

The four directions need be only approximate. Germany is also on France's northern border but is mainly to the east of France. Bounding is a more effective learning tool than labeling a blank map, as a map gives several clues. **Bounding** forces students to reconstruct the map in their minds without clues. To reinforce your knowledge, based on the map on page 89, sketch out and label France and its neighbors. Next do it again from memory. Once you can bound each of our ten countries, you will be able to label much of all the continents except Africa, which is extremely fragmented and complex. To fill in the blank spots, we also include other countries in our bounding exercises. Bounding has only limited utility for Britain, as the United Kingdom has only one land boundary. What is it?

Personalities

Three French Geniuses: Voltaire, Montesquieu, Rousseau

Voltaire

Montesquieu

Rousseau

Each in his own way, three eighteenth-century thinkers—Voltaire, Montesquieu, and Rousseau—helped persuade many French—especially middle-class intellectuals—that the *ancien régime* was rotten and that it was possible to construct a better system. Their weapon was reason—abstract, **Cartesian**, logical—in contrast to English thinkers, who relied more on empirical reality. The French dislike reality for failing to live up to their logical constructs, an approach that lends itself to radicalism.

Voltaire (1694–1778) was the epitome of the **Enlightenment**, doubting and ridiculing everything stupid he saw around him. His chief target: the Catholic Church, which he saw as intolerant, irrational, and hypocritical. Voltaire's phrase, *"Ecrasez l'infâme"* ("crush the infamous thing," meaning the Church), became the founding cry of anticlericalism and spread through most Catholic countries, including Mexico. (But not Ireland or Poland. Any idea why?) As we shall see, France still has some remnants of the old clerical-anticlerical split.

The Baron de Montesquieu (1689–1755) traveled all over Europe to gather material for one of the first books of comparative politics, *The Spirit of the Laws*. Montesquieu was especially impressed with English liberties, which he thought resulted from the "checks and balances" of the different parts of their government. Montesquieu wrote about an idealized model of an English system that had already passed into history, but the American Founding Fathers read him literally. Montesquieu suggested that countries could more or less rationally choose their governmental institutions. The French have been choosing and discarding them ever since.

Jean-Jacques Rousseau (1712–1778), who was born in Geneva but lived in France, was the most complex and dangerous of these three thinkers. Rousseau hypothesized man in the state of nature as free, happy, and morally good. (Note the contrast to Hobbes's and Locke's states of nature.) He believed it was society that corrupted humans, chiefly with private property, which leads to inequality and jealousy. Rousseau, in a famous phrase at the beginning of his book *The Social Contract*, wrote: "Man is born free but everywhere is in chains." How can humans be saved? Rousseau further hypothesized that beneath all the individual, petty viewpoints in society there is a **general will** for the common good. This general will could be discovered and implemented even though some people might object; they would be "forced to be free." Critics of Rousseau charge that he laid the intellectual basis for both nazism and communism because his theory lets dictators crush dissent and claim that they "really know" what the people want and need.

The French political thinkers tended to call for major, sweeping change; English thinkers, for slow, cautious change that preserved the overall system. The French thinkers fundamentally hated their government; the English did not.

found in most European countries and in Japan: Instead of there being a totally free market, the government supervises the economy.

Louis XIV was an able monarch who impressed all of Europe; other kings tried to imitate him. French cuisine, architecture, dress, and language dominated the Continent. From the outside, the France of Louis XIV looked more impressive than England. Without "checks and balances" to get in the way, the centralized monarchy of France accomplished great things. But the English, by developing political participation, devised a more stable system.

Why the French Revolution?

For all its splendor, France in the eighteenth century was in difficulty. Its treasury was often near bankruptcy. Especially costly was French support for the American colonists against Britain; the French did it more for revenge than for love of liberty. The bureaucracy was corrupt and inefficient. Recognizing too late that mercantilism was bad economics, the regime tried to move to a free market, but by then French industry and agriculture were used to state protection and wanted to keep it. Also important was the spread of new ideas on "liberty," "consent of the governed," and "the general will." Ideas can be dynamite and undermined the **ancien régime**.

As Alexis de Tocqueville pointed out, revolutions seldom start when things are bad but, rather, when they are getting better. France enjoyed improving economic conditions for most of the eighteenth century, but that increased expectations and awakened jealousies

Cartesian   After French philosopher René Descartes, philosophical analysis based on pure reason without empirical reference. (See page 92.)

Enlightenment   Eighteenth-century philosophical movement advocating reason and tolerance. (See page 92.)

general will   Rousseau's theory of what the whole community wants. (See page 92.)

ancien régime   French for old regime, the monarchy that preceded the Revolution.

DEMOCRACY

LEFT, RIGHT, AND CENTER

The way delegates were seated in the National Assembly during and after the French Revolution gives us our terms for radical, conservative, and moderate. In a half-circle chamber, the most radical delegates, those representing the common people, were seated to the left of the speaker's rostrum, and the most conservative, those representing the aristocracy, were seated to the right. This allowed like-minded legislators to caucus and separated delegates who might start fist fights.

The precise meanings of left, right, and center have varied through the ages and from country to country. In general, however, the left favors greater equality of incomes, welfare measures, and government intervention in the economy. The right, now that it has shed its aristocratic origins, favors individual achievement and private industry. The center tries to synthesize the moderate elements in both viewpoints. Those just a little to one side or the other are called center-left or center-right.

Third Estate Largest chamber of Estates-General, representing commoners.

alienated Psychologically distant and hostile.

Thermidor Month when Robespierre fell, a calming down after a revolutionary high.

toward people who were getting richer faster. As we shall see in Iran under the Shah, economic growth can be highly destabilizing. Furthermore, Louis XVI had decided to reform the political system and provide for some kind of representation. But as we shall see in Russia and Iran, the reforming of an unjust and unpopular system is extraordinarily difficult, often leading to revolution.

In the spring of 1789, Louis XVI convened the Estates-General for the first time since 1614. Its three estates—the clergy, the nobility, and the commoners—were elected by nearly universal male suffrage. The **Third Estate**, the commoners, demanded that all three houses meet together, meaning that the more numerous Third Estate could override the conservative First and Second Estates. The Third Estate argued that it represented the popular will, but Louis

KEY CONCEPTS

BRINTON'S THEORY OF REVOLUTION

The great Harvard historian Crane Brinton in his 1938 *The Anatomy of Revolution* argued that all revolutions pass through similar stages. He compared several revolutions, but his main model was the French. Brinton's stages are as follows:

- The old regime loses its governing effectiveness and legitimacy. It becomes inept and indecisive. Intellectuals especially become **alienated** from it. An improving economy provokes discontent and jealousy.

- The first stage of revolution comes with the growth of antiregime groups. Triggering the revolution is a political problem—such as whether the three estates should meet separately or together—that the old regime cannot solve. Rioting breaks out, but troops sent to crush it desert to the rioters. The antiregime people easily take over power amid popular rejoicing.

- Moderates initially seize power. They opposed the old regime, but as critics rather than as revolutionaries. They want major reform rather than total revolution. Extremists call them weak and cowardly, and indeed they are not ruthless enough to crush the extremists.

- Extremists take over because they are more ruthless, purposeful, and organized than the moderates. In what Brinton likened to a high fever during an illness, the extremists whip up a revolutionary frenzy, throwing out everything old, forcing people to be good, and punishing real or imagined enemies in a reign of terror. In France, this stage came with Robespierre; in Iran, it came with Khomeini.

- A **Thermidor**, or calming-down period, ends the reign of terror. Every revolution has a Thermidor, which Brinton likened to a convalescence after a fever, because human nature cannot take the extremists and their revolutionary purity for too long. Power may then fall into the hands of a dictator who restores order but not liberty—a Napoleon or a Stalin.

Brinton's theory became a classic and has largely stood the test of time. Revolutions do seem to pass through stages, although their timing cannot be predicted with accuracy. Russia and Iran, as we shall see, followed the Brinton pattern.

resisted. By the time he gave in, many parliamentarians were angry and radicalized and voted themselves into a **National Assembly**, its name today.

Shortly afterward, the common people of Paris, furious over rising bread prices, stormed the **Bastille** on July 14, 1789. Bastille Day became the French national day. Upon hearing of the Bastille incident the king exclaimed, *"C'est une révolte,"* meaning something that could be put down. A duke corrected him: *"Non, Sire, c'est une révolution."* It was the first modern usage of the word **revolution**.

One reason Louis XVI was unpopular was his frivolous and extravagant Austrian-born queen, Marie Antoinette. She was said to have once inquired why there had been riots and was told it was because the people had no bread. "No bread?" she tittered. "Then let them eat cake." The masses hated her. She was guillotined in 1793 a few months after Louis XVI.

National Assembly France's parliament.

Bastille Old and nearly unused Paris jail, the storming of which heralded the French Revolution in 1789.

revolution Sudden and complete overthrow of a regime.

constitutional monarchy King with limited powers.

French Revolution 1789 popular ouster of monarch.

Reign of Terror Robespierre's 1793–1794 rule by guillotine.

coup d'état Military takeover of a government.

From Freedom to Tyranny

In 1791 the National Assembly constructed a **constitutional monarchy**, and if it had stopped there the **French Revolution** might have resembled the English Revolution of a century earlier. But the French constitutional monarchy was undermined from two sides: from the king and some aristocrats who wanted to restore absolute power, and from a militant faction called the Jacobins, who wanted a radical revolution. Their cry: *"Liberté, Egalité, Fraternité!"* The king was caught conspiring with foreign princes to invade France and restore him to power. The attempted invasion of 1792 helped the Jacobins take over. With a makeshift but enthusiastic citizen army—"the nation in arms"—they repelled the invaders at Valmy.

Power fell into the hands of the misnamed Committee of Public Safety under Maximilien Robespierre, a provincial lawyer and fanatic follower of Rousseau who was determined to "force men to be free." Instituting the **Reign of Terror**, Robespierre and his followers guillotined more than twenty thousand people, starting with the king, queen, and nobles but soon spreading to anyone who doubted Robespierre. Finally, in 1794, during the revolutionary calendar's month of Thermidor, Robespierre's comrades, afraid they might be next, guillotined *him*, and the Terror ended.

During all this turmoil, the army became the only coherent institution, especially one young artillery officer, the Corsican Napoléon Bonaparte, who had won fame leading French armies in Italy and Egypt. In 1799 a **coup d'état** overthrew the weak civilian Directory and set up a Consulate with Bonaparte as First Consul. Brilliant in both battle and civil reform, Napoleon crowned himself emperor in 1804.

Above all, Napoleon loved war. As Henry Kissinger pointed out, a revolutionary power, like France in the midst of hostile conservative monarchies, can feel secure only by conquering all potential threats. Napoleon made France master of all Europe, using dashing tactics and a large, enthusiastic army to crush one foe after another until at last they went too far. Facing a British-led coalition, harassed by guerrilla warfare in Spain, and frozen in the Russian winter, Napoleon was defeated and exiled to the Mediterranean island of Elba in 1814. The next year he tried a comeback and thousands of his old soldiers rallied around him to fight at Waterloo and lose.

tyrannical   Coercive rule, usually by one person.

plebiscite   Referendum; mass vote for issue rather than for candidates.

chauvinism   After Napoleonic soldier named Chauvin; fervent, prideful nationalism.

Bourbon   French dynasty before the Revolution.

Napoleon left behind an ambiguous legacy. Although he claimed to be consolidating the Revolution, he actually set up a **tyrannical** police state. Trying to embody Rousseau's elusive general will, Napoleon held several **plebiscites**, which he always won. He unleashed **chauvinism** by proclaiming France to be Europe's liberator. Napoleon was not just a historic accident, though, for we shall see similar figures emerge in French politics. When a society is badly split, as France was over the Revolution, power tends to gravitate into the hands of a savior, and democracy does not have a chance.

THE BOURBON RESTORATION

Europe breathed a sigh of relief once Napoleon was packed off to a remote island in the South Atlantic and the brother of Louis XVI was restored to the French throne as Louis XVIII. In the **Bourbon** Restoration, exiles from all over Europe returned to France to claim their old rights. Many French disliked the returning Bourbons and sighed, "They learned nothing and they forgot nothing."

GEOGRAPHY

A TALE OF TWO FLAGS

The Bourbon flag had been blue and white with a fleur-de-lis (iris). (Today's Quebec flag is blue and white with four irises.) The Revolution introduced the tricolor of red, white, and blue. The post-Napoleon restoration brought back the old flag, for the tricolor symbolized everything the Bourbons hated. In 1830, the Orleanist monarchy, to mollify revolutionary sentiment, brought back the tricolor, France's flag ever since.

Blue

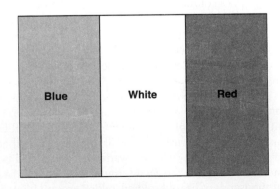

Blue   White   Red

France was badly split. Most aristocrats hated the Revolution, while most commoners supported at least a version of it. The Catholic Church was reactionary, for the Revolution had confiscated church lands and ended its tax privileges. French Catholics for generations opposed the anticlericalist republicans, who in turn mistrusted the church. Residuals of the clerical-anticlerical split persist in France. But France had also changed in the quarter-century since the Revolution. Parliaments now counted for something; kings could no longer rule without them. The civil reforms of Napoleon were preserved. People insisted on equality before the law.

At first the French, tired from upheaval and warfare, accepted the Bourbons. But by 1830 they proved to be as pig-headed as ever, and rioting broke out. In a semilegal switch, the liberal Duc d'Orleans, Louis-Phillipe, replaced the last Bourbon, Charles X. He, too, proved inept, and a small uprising in that revolutionary year of 1848 brought the Second Republic. This did not last long either.

The French have historically turned from tumultuous democracy to authoritarian rule. In 1848 they overwhelmingly elected Napoleon's self-proclaimed nephew, Louis Napoleon, as president. Using plebiscites, in 1852 he turned the Second Republic into the Second Empire with himself as Emperor Napoleon III. This brought two decades of peace and progress until Louis Napoleon, in 1870, allowed himself to be goaded into war with Prussia. Bursting with overconfidence, the French were quickly trounced. The Germans surrounded Paris and shelled it daily, but there was no French government left to surrender. In Paris itself, a revolutionary takeover by common citizens brought the short-lived **Paris Commune**, which conservative French troops crushed, killing some twenty thousand Parisians. Karl Marx mistakenly saw the Commune as the first proletarian uprising, and among leftists the Commune grew into a legend of worker power.

> **Paris Commune**   Takeover of Paris government by citizens during German siege of 1870–1871.
>
> **belle époque**   "Beautiful epoch," France around 1900.
>
> **Zionism**   Jewish nationalist movement that founded Israel.

Political Culture

THE DREYFUS AFFAIR

Nothing better reveals the deep division of French society in the late nineteenth century than the trial of Captain Alfred Dreyfus, an officer on the French general staff. In 1894, Dreyfus was accused of selling secrets to the Germans; he was given a rigged military trial with fake evidence and sent to Devil's Island for life. It soon became clear that Dreyfus was not the culprit and had been convicted by bigoted officers simply because he was a Jew, a handy scapegoat.

France split in two. Those defending Dreyfus—the *Dreyfusards*—supported the republican traditions of equality. These tended to be people on the left. Novelist Emile Zola published his famous letter *J'accuse!* (I accuse!), charging the government with covering up for the military. The *Anti-Dreyfusards*—reactionary aristocrats, army officers, fanatic Catholics, and anti-Semites—were equally passionate in defense of pre-revolutionary values. Most French took one side or the other; there was even street fighting.

The French Supreme Court finally exonerated Dreyfus in 1906, but the episode left scars. It showed how the beautiful, civilized veneer of **belle époque** France concealed reaction and anti-Semitism. A Viennese journalist covering the trial, Theodore Herzl, was so shocked by the anti-Semitism unleashed by the trial that he immediately organized a world **Zionist** movement to save Jews from what he (correctly) feared would be worse outbursts.

The Third Republic

Amidst near anarchy, the **Third Republic**, France's first stable democracy, was born. Its first task was a humiliating peace with Germany that cost France the province of Alsace (which has many German-speaking people) plus a billion dollars in gold. The enraged French ached for revenge and transferred their traditional hatred of Britain to Germany.

Third Republic France's democratic regime from 1871 to 1940.

bourgeois Middle-class.

reactionary Seeking to go back to old ways; extremely conservative.

The accidental Third Republic turned out to be the longest-lasting French regime since the ancien régime. The Third Republic was basically fairly conservative and **bourgeois**. France was not healed during its long tenure; indeed, social tensions mounted. A **reactionary** Catholic right dreamed of an authoritarian system, while the left organized Socialist and later Communist parties. Economic and population growth was slow, and France slipped further behind the rapidly growing Germany. Still, the Third Republic staggered through the ordeal of World War I. At first the French were delighted with a chance for revenge against Germany, but soon the appalling losses—a million and a half French lives—turned France bitter and defeatist even though it was on the winning side. France regained Alsace but had no stomach to fight again.

Political Culture

FRANCE'S POLITICAL ERAS

The political history of France is rich and complex. Notice how conservative and radical eras approximately alternate. It is more difficult to construct such a table for British political development because it has had no drastic regime changes since the Commonwealth in the seventeenth century.

Name	Years	Remembered for
Old Regime	–1789	Absolutist monarchy; centralized administration; supervised economy.
Revolution	1789–1799	Tumultuous; repel invaders; Reign of Terror; Thermidor.
Napoleon	1799–1814	Redoes civil code; conquers most of Europe; crowns self emperor.
Bourbon Restoration	1815–1830	Try to restore monarchy in badly split France.
Orleanist	1830–1848	Liberal monarchy.
Second Republic	1848–1852	Attempted liberal republic.
Second Empire	1852–1870	Louis Napoleon's conservative stability.
Third Republic	1871–1940	Bourgeois liberal democracy.
Vichy	1940–1944	German puppet government.
Provisional Government	1944–1946	De Gaulle-led coalition.
Fourth Republic	1946–1958	Unstable, fractious, immobilized; Indochina and Algeria.
Fifth Republic	1958–	De Gaulle strong president; state-led modernization.

French defeatism played into the hands of Nazi Germany, which swept easily through France in May–June 1940. Only one French unit fought well, a tank column commanded by an obscure colonel named de Gaulle, who had been warning for years of the need to develop better French armored forces. The French thought they could prevent a repetition of the World War I bloodshed by hiding behind the **Maginot Line**, but fixed defenses cannot move; the Germans simply went around them on the north.

Vichy: France Splits Again

The Germans largely let the French run occupied France. Named after the town of Vichy in central France where it was set up, the **Vichy** government was staffed by the same sort of reactionaries who earlier had reviled Dreyfus, people who hated democracy and admired the authoritarian Germans. The aged Marshal Pétain, hero of World War I, became chief of state, and an opportunistic politician, Pierre Laval, became premier without elections. Some French thought Vichy was an improvement over the Third Republic, which had voted the **Popular Front** into power in 1936. "Better the Nazis than the Communists," muttered Vichy supporters. French SS units fought in Russia. French police rounded up Jews for deportation to death camps. French workers volunteered to work in Germany. Although most French hated to admit it, many collaborated with the Germans and even liked them.

Other French, however, hated the Germans and Vichy. Some joined the **Résistance**, an underground network that sabotaged and spied on the Germans, rescued British and American airmen, and occasionally killed collaborators. Again, France split. The Vichy period was, in the words of Stanley Hoffmann, "a Franco-French war." The Resistance attracted French people of many political persuasions, but the left predominated. The Communists, who refused to attack Germans until the 1941 invasion of Russia, became the most effective underground fighters and emerged from the war with prestige and a good organization.

The rallying point of the Resistance was Charles de Gaulle (promoted to general in the last days of the Third Republic), who broadcast from London: "France has lost a battle, but France has not lost the war!" Organizing French-speaking people around the world—France had sizable colonies and thousands of able-bodied men who fled from France—de Gaulle declared a provisional government comprised of **Free French** expatriates. Participating in military actions in North Africa, the Normandy landings, and the liberation of Paris in 1944, the Free French Army was of considerable help to the **Allies**. During the war de Gaulle came to think of himself as the savior of France, a modern Joan of Arc.

The Fourth Republic

From 1944 to early 1946, de Gaulle headed a provisional government. A newly elected constituent assembly, dominated by parties of the left, drafted a constitution for the **Fourth Republic** that gave great power to the legislative branch. De Gaulle opposed the new constitution and resigned with the warning that the Fourth Republic would have the same institutional weaknesses as the Third. He retired to the small town of Colombey-les-Deux-Eglises, not to return to power until the people called him back to save France again twelve years later.

Maginot Line Supposedly unbreachable French defenses facing Germany before World War II.

Vichy Nazi puppet regime that ran France during World War II.

Popular Front Coalition government of all leftist and liberal parties in France and Spain in the 1930s.

Résistance World War II French underground anti-German movement.

Free French De Gaulle's World War II government in exile.

Allies World War II anti-Axis military coalition.

Fourth Republic 1946–1958 French regime.

immobilisme   Government inability to solve big problems.

decolonization   Granting of independence to colonies.

Indochina War   First Vietnam war, 1946–1954, between French and Communist Viet Minh.

He was right about the Fourth Republic resembling the Third: From its inception the Fourth was plagued by a weak executive, a National Assembly paralyzed by small, squabbling parties, and frequent changes of cabinet. The result was, as before, **immobilisme**. Politicians played games with each other; they were good at wrecking but not at building.

Still, like the Third Republic, the Fourth might have endured if not for the terrible problems of **decolonization**, problems the fractious parliamentarians could not solve. The first problem was Indochina, a French colony since the 1880s, occupied by the Japanese in World War II and then reclaimed by France. The **Indochina War** broke out in 1946 and dragged on until the fall of the French fortress of Dienbienphu in 1954. (The United States came close to jumping into the Vietnam conflict that year but backed off.)

Algeria was even worse. The French had been there since 1830, at first to suppress piracy but later to settle. Close to a million Europeans dominated Algerian economic, social, and political life; Algeria was even declared part of France. Algerian nationalists started their revolt in 1954 with urban terrorism. This time the French army, determined to win, hunted down nationalists and tortured them. When civilian politicians in Paris opposed the Algerian War, the French army in Algeria began a *coup d'état* in 1958. Paratroopers were ready to drop on their own country; France tottered on the brink of civil war. At the last minute both sides agreed to call back General de Gaulle. The army assumed he would keep Algeria French (he did not). De Gaulle, acting as if he had known all along that history would recall him to lead France, demanded as his price a totally new constitution, one that would cure the ills of the Fourth Republic. He got it. In the next chapter, we explore the institutions of the Fifth Republic.

KEY TERMS

FURTHER REFERENCE

Bernier, Olivier. *Louis XIV: A Royal Life*. New York: Doubleday, 1987.

Blanning, Timothy C. W. *The Culture of Power and the Power of Culture: Old Regime Europe, 1660–1789*. New York: Oxford University Press, 2002.

Gildea, Robert. *Marianne in Chains: Daily Life in the Heart of France during the German Occupation*. New York: Metropolitan Books, 2003.

Hazareesingh, Sudhir. *Political Traditions in France*. New York: Oxford University Press, 1994.

Jackson, Julian. *France: The Dark Years, 1940–1944*. New York: Oxford University Press, 2001.

Johnson, Paul. *Napoleon*. New York: Viking, 2002.

Kedward, Rod. *La Vie en Bleu: France and the French since 1900*. New York: Overlook, 2006.

Nossiter, Adam. *The Algeria Hotel: France, Memory, and the Second World War*. Boston, MA: Houghton Mifflin, 2001.

Robb, Graham. *The Discovery of France: A Historical Geography from the Revolution to the First World War*. New York: Norton, 2007.

Schama, Simon. *Citizens: A Chronicle of the French Revolution*. New York: Knopf, 1989.

Scurr, Ruth. *Fatal Purity: Robespierre and the French Revolution*. New York: Metropolitan, 2007.

Vinen, Richard. *The Unfree French: Life under the Occupation*. New Haven, CT: Yale University Press, 2006.

Williams, Charles. *The Last Great Frenchman: A Life of General De Gaulle*. New York: Wiley, 1995.

Chapter 8
France:
The Key Institutions

The British constitution grew piecemeal and has not yet been formalized into one document. French constitutions—fifteen of them since the Revolution—are all written but often altered in practice. Americans regard their Constitution with religious awe, but the French and most other Europeans have seen constitutions come and go and see the need to rewrite them every few decades.

By 1958 many French agreed that the Fourth Republic was inherently flawed and unable to settle the ghastly Algerian War. The chief problem, as defined by de Gaulle, lay in the weakness of the executive, the **premier**. The **president** was simply a figurehead, typical of European republics. The premier depended on unstable **coalitions**. Faced with controversial issues, one or more coalition parties could drop out, vote against the government in a vote of no-confidence, and thereby bring it down. In all, there were twenty cabinets ("governments") in less than twelve years. Politicians sometimes voted against effective premiers out of personal resentment. Pierre Mendès-France, for example, settled the Indochina War in 1954, but that made him too popular and effective, so the National Assembly voted him out.

The Fourth Republic embodied all the weaknesses of a multiparty parliamentary system that still plague Israel. Such a system can work well and with stability, as in Sweden, but it depends on the party system and the national political style. Given French parties and political style, a pure parliamentary system may never work well.

Questions to Consider

1. What are the weaknesses of multiparty parliamentary systems?
2. How has the French *semipresidential* system evolved?
3. What problem did *cohabitation* solve?
4. How does the French electoral system work?
5. How do the two big French parties resemble their U.S. counterparts?
6. What is a *technocrat?* Does the United States have any?
7. How has the French parliament been weakened?
8. What good is the French Senate? How does it compare to the U.S. Senate?
9. Why are the French and British party systems different?
10. Is France still a highly centralized unitary system?

A Semipresidential System

De Gaulle hated the executive weakness of the Fourth Republic, but neither did he like the American-style presidential system with its checks and balances that might hamper his style. So he devised a **semipresidential** system, a hybrid with both an executive president and a premier (see box on page 105). For over a quarter-century, however, instead of some kind of balance between the powers of the president and those of the premier, the president held sway by virtue of

premier　French for prime minister. (See page 103.)

president　Elected head of state, not necessarily powerful. (See page 103.)

coalition　Multiparty alliance to form government. (See page 103.)

semipresidential　System with features of both presidential and parliamentary systems. (See page 103.)

Fifth Republic　*Semipresidential* regime devised by de Gaulle, 1958 to present.

referendum　Mass vote on an issue rather than on candidates; same as *plebiscite*.

Elysée　Presidential palace in Paris, equivalent to U.S. White House.

commanding the largest bloc of votes in the National Assembly. Thus, for the first twenty-eight years of the **Fifth Republic**, the system functioned as a presidential or even "superpresidential" system. Only with the parliamentary elections of 1986—which produced a conservative National Assembly while a Socialist president was still in office—did we finally see semipresidentialism in action.

Let us first examine the original setup of the Fifth Republic, the one de Gaulle devised and commanded from 1958 to 1969. The general structure of it continues, but the powers of the president have weakened. The French president was originally elected for seven years and could be reelected without limit. Realizing that a seven-year term is too long, a 2000 **referendum** shortened it to five years. Originally, the president was selected by an electoral college of parliamentarians and local office holders. De Gaulle soon discovered he wanted nothing—certainly no politicians—to stand between him and the people, so he led a referendum in 1962 to provide for direct election of the president. It has been that way ever since.

The constitution specifies some powers for the president and some for the premier, but the practice was unclear. On paper, the president appoints a premier (but cannot fire him) who then selects his own cabinet. No parliamentary approval is required for this. Until 1986 the president was so assured of an obedient National Assembly that he handpicked both premier and cabinet ministers as mere helpers to carry out the president's program. The president presided at cabinet meetings. Virtually all foreign and defense affairs were in his hands (still mostly the case). The **Elysée** originated most legislation, often with the advice of ministers, and could even force the National Assembly to vote simply yes or no on executive proposals. The president, however, does not have the power to veto legislation. De Gaulle saw the role of president in almost mystical terms, as a "guide" and "arbiter" of the nation.

One important—and perhaps overused—power de Gaulle liked is the calling of referendums. Such mass votes on issues are alien to British tradition but very much a part of French usage, especially by leaders who believe they embody the general will and communicate directly with the people, bypassing the politicians. De Gaulle called five such plebiscites (see Chapter 10) and won each except the last. Feeling repudiated, he resigned, perhaps establishing another constitutional tradition.

Who Was When: The Fifth Republic's Presidents		
Charles de Gaulle		1959–1969—reelected in 1965, resigned in 1969
Georges Pompidou	Gaullist	1969–1974—died in office
Valéry Giscard d'Estaing	UDF	1974–1981—served one term
François Mitterrand	Socialist	1981–1995—reelected in 1988
Jacques Chirac	neo-Gaullist	1995–2007—reelected in 2002
Nicolas Sarkozy	neo-Gaullist	2007–

Another potentially major power at the disposal of the French president is the ability to invoke *emergency powers* in time of danger to the nation. While many democracies have such an emergency provision, it can be abused, as Hitler used Article 48 of the Weimar constitution to snuff out freedom. Article 16 of the French constitution seems to place no limits on what a president can do during an emergency, a

deadlock U.S. tendency for executive and legislature, especially when of opposing parties, to block each other.

censure Legislative condemnation of executive.

Key Concepts

The French Semipresidential System

Most European governments are parliamentary; that is, they depend on votes in parliament to put a cabinet into executive power and keep it there (see page 40). The cabinet, usually composed of members of parliament, is a sort of parliamentary steering committee that also guides the ministries or departments. If no party in parliament has a majority, a coalition of parties is necessary, and this may be unstable. In policy splits, a *vote of no-confidence* may oust the cabinet. Where a single party dominates the parliament—mostly the case in Britain—the system can be very stable.

In a presidential system (see page 40), such as the United States and Mexico, the executive does not depend on parliamentary support, for here the chief executive is elected more or less directly for a fixed term. The parliament can do what it wants, but it cannot oust the president in a vote of no-confidence. (It may impeach the president.) The advantage of a presidential system is its stability and certainty: There will always be a president to lead. The disadvantage is that the president and the legislature may **deadlock**, producing something similar to the *immobilisme* that plagues parliamentary systems.

The French system is *semipresidential*, for the cabinet still has a certain parliamentary connection. The premier is named by the president but can be **censured** and forced to resign by the National Assembly. If that happens—and it has occurred only once, in 1962—the president can dissolve the legislature and hold new elections. Influenced by the French model, Russia and China also adopted semipresidential systems.

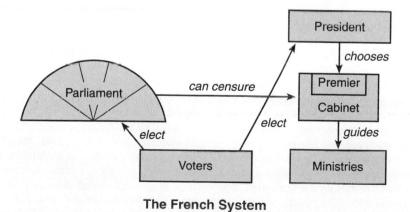

The French System

turnout   Percentage of those eligible who vote in a given election.

situation that is up to the president to define. During such an emergency the National Assembly must meet, but it has no power to block presidential decisions. The emergency clause has been invoked only once—in 1961, when the same generals who put de Gaulle into power tried to overthrow him for pulling out of Algeria—and many agreed it was a genuine emergency.

The presidential paradise came to an end with the National Assembly elections of 1986, which produced, as expected, a legislature dominated by conservative parties. The problem was that President François Mitterrand, a Socialist, had two years remaining in his seven-year term. For the first time the Fifth Republic had a president who did not control the National Assembly. No one knew how to handle it; the constitution was unclear. Some feared a hostile deadlock and paralysis of government. Others thought that Mitterrand would have to resign in order to make way for the election of a conservative president. Instead, Mitterrand played a waiting game that preserved him as president but reduced the powers of the presidency. Mitterrand thus clarified the French constitution and set a precedent for when the same situation occurred in 1993 and 1997.

DEMOCRACY

FRANCE'S PRESIDENTIAL ELECTION OF 2007

"Sarko et Ségo" were the nicknames the French gave to their two leading candidates for president in 2007, neo-Gaullist Nicolas Sarkozy, 52, and Socialist Ségolène Royal, 53. Both were energetic achievers who held high positions while still young. Both were first elected to the National Assembly in 1988. Sarkozy sparkled with plans for change and economic reinvigoration; Royal was vague about a "just order" of welfare and equality, standard Socialist themes. It was a hot contest; both rounds drew huge 84 percent **turnouts**.

French elections are held in two rounds. The first round on Sunday (most European elections are on Sundays), April 22, had twelve candidates. The results are shown in the large table on page 107. Only the two top vote-winners then went on to the decisive second round two weeks later, which Sarkozy won 53 to 47 percent. As might be expected, Sarkozy won big among those over 60, the self-employed, and farmers.

Ten minor candidates took 43 percent of the first-round vote. Many French protest against the system by voting for no-chance parties on the first round, figuring that only the second round counts, and everyone knew it would be between Sarko and Ségo. In 2002, frivolous voting for several left parties dropped Premier

Ségolène Royal

Lionel Jospin, a serious contender for the Socialists, into third place on the first round and out of the contest. The French left was more careful in 2007, concentrating on Royal to make sure she would be in the second round two weeks later.

Both Sarko and Ségo were unusual candidates. Sarkozy (see box on page 108), the son of an immigrant, portrayed himself as an outsider. Royal, the first major-party woman candidate, was one of eight children of an authoritarian army colonel, against whom she rebelled and whom she sued. Brilliant, she studied at both the Political Studies Institute and the ENA (see page 125 in Chapter 9), the typical path for the French

In 1986 Mitterrand called on the leader of the largest conservative party (sometimes called **neo-Gaullist**), Jacques Chirac, to become premier and went along with most of Chirac's cabinet choices. Mitterrand also did not block most of Chirac's legislative program, which rolled back many of Mitterrand's socialist experiments in the economy. The two struck an informal bargain—called **cohabitation**, living together but not married—in which Chirac concentrated on domestic affairs and Mitterrand on foreign and defense policy plus the symbolic functions of the presidency. In 1993, faced with another conservative victory in parliamentary elections, Mitterrand named another neo-Gaullist, Edouard Balladur, as his premier. In 1997, faced with a Socialist victory in the early parliamentary elections he had called, President Chirac named Socialist chief Lionel Jospin as premier, an arrangement that lasted until 2002. As of this writing, France does not have cohabitation because both president and premier are of the same party. Should the split occur again, Paris knows how to handle it: cohabitation again. During cohabitation, French presidents are not as strong as de Gaulle was, and premiers are stronger than he intended. Institutions evolve.

neo-Gaullist   Chirac's revival of Gaullist party, now called Union for a Popular Movement (UMP).

cohabitation   French president forced to name premier of opposing party.

elite. She held several ministerial positions under President Mitterrand. Royal had four children with her civil-union partner (they never married), Socialist leader François Hollande. Such private matters rarely bother Continental voters. (But they do American and British. Why the difference?)

First Round

Nicolas Sarkozy	Union for a Popular Movement	31.2%
Ségolène Royal	Socialist	25.9
François Bayrou	Union for French Democracy	18.6
Jean-Marie Le Pen	National Front	10.4
Olivier Besancenot	Communist Revolutionary League	4.1
Phillipe de Villiers	Movement for France	2.2
Marie-George Buffet	Communist	1.9
Dominique Voynet	Greens	1.6
Arlette Laguiller	Workers Struggle	1.3
José Bové	Independent anti-globalization activist	1.3
Frédéric Nihous	Hunting, Fishing, Nature, Tradition	1.2
Gérard Schivardi	Workers party	0.3

Second Round

Sarkozy	53%
Royal	47

If the French want to avoid cohabitation and restrengthen the presidency, they could cut the last link between legislative and executive branches (the "can-censure" arrow) and become a straight presidential system, U.S.-style. True, the U.S. system often deadlocks between the White House and Capitol Hill, but the president still has plenty of power to govern without permission from Congress.

PERSONALITIES

SARKOZY: BRASH, ENERGETIC OUTSIDER

French President Nicolas Sarkozy, elected in 2007, is different from most previous French presidents. There is nothing elite about him. He is the son of an immigrant, a Hungarian aristocrat who left his family when Nicolas was five and who married twice more. Nicolas rarely saw his father and said he felt abandoned and humiliated. He grew up in the Paris home of his maternal grandfather, a physician and Greek Jew who converted to Catholicism. There was not much money; his mother worked as a lawyer and Nicolas worked while going to college.

Nicolas Sarkozy

Most French leaders have been brilliant intellectuals and graduates of an elite Great School (see page 125), but Sarkozy was a mediocre student. He graduated from a Catholic high school and the overcrowded Nanterre University in business law. He divorced his second wife and married his third—both former models—shortly after taking office. He is short (five feet five, 1.65 meters) but trim and fit. What he lacked in size and pedigree he made up for in energy and brashness.

A Gaullist since childhood (learned from his Gaullist grandfather), Sarkozy ran for and won a seat on the city council of a wealthy Paris suburb at age 22. At 28 he was elected mayor and at 33 a deputy in the National Assembly. In 1993, at age 38, he became budget minister in the *cohabitation* (see page 107) cabinet of Premier Edouard Balladur, a neo-Gaullist.

In 1976, Jacques Chirac had taken over and reorganized the moribund Gaullists, turning them into the biggest right-wing party, now the Union for a Popular Movement (UMP), often known as "neo-Gaullist." (De Gaulle left office in 1969 never having bothered to build a strong Gaullist party.) Sarkozy immediately became a Chirac protégé but in 1995 backed Balladur for president. Chirac won and the two have disliked each other ever since, even though Chirac subsequently named him finance and interior minister. A consistent pattern: Sarkozy served and then turned against powerful politicians in his climb to the top.

In 2004 Sarkozy was elected leader of the UMP and became their presidential candidate in 2007. When Muslim youth rioted in 2005, Interior Minister Sarkozy called them "scum" and ordered the police to crack down. Most French approved, and Sarkozy won the presidency in 2007 on a platform of law and order, equal opportunity, and economic rejuvenation. The French left hates him and calls him an authoritarian demagogue who, with brilliant speaking skills, manipulates populist themes.

Hard to pigeonhole, Sarkozy sounds both conservative and liberal themes. He appointed four Socialists—including Bernard Kouchner, founder of Doctors Without Borders—and seven women ministers, including a woman of North African origin. Another big difference: Only one minister is an ENA graduate (see page 125), but half are lawyers, unusual for France. Sarkozy pledged to invigorate the economy but, in keeping with French tradition, used state supervision and funds to do it. He did not mind running hefty budget deficits, which clashed with EU policy. He claimed to be pro-American, but as an equal partner, not an obedient follower. Initial French enthusiasm for him soon soured into irritation at his blunt ways and sparse results, but the media feasted on his marriages, divorces, and outbursts.

PREMIER AND CABINET

Until cohabitation, French ministers, including the prime minister, served as little more than messenger boys for the president. The premier's main function was to push presidential measures through parliament. Under cohabitation, however, Premiers Chirac, Balladur, and Jospin brought much power to that office by pursuing their own legislative agendas. Even with no cohabitation since 1997–2002, the premiership did not return completely to the subservient model designed by de Gaulle. French presidents like to appear above ordinary politics, so they let their premiers do the heavy work, especially on the economy. The precise balance of powers between president and premier in France has not been settled and is likely to change with new personalities and situations. Just after Nicolas Sarkozy won the 2007 presidential election, he named a fellow neo-Gaullist, François Fillon, as his premier.

deputy   Member of French and many other parliaments.

interior ministry   In Europe, department in charge of homeland security and national police.

Premiers name ministers, who do not have to be approved by the National Assembly but usually are. A cabinet not to the liking of parliament could be censured and ousted. Accordingly, Socialist Mitterrand felt he had to name neo-Gaullists Chirac and Balladur, because they had majority support in parliament. This is the general basis for selecting prime ministers throughout Europe (compare with Britain, page 36, and Germany, pages 181–183).

The president cannot directly fire a premier, but, if they are of the same party, the president may persuade the premier to resign. In 2002 Chirac named as premier Jean-Pierre Raffarin, a rumpled provincial senator, but got him to resign in 2005 after the EU constitution fiasco. Socialist President Mitterrand had earlier named and dropped several Socialist premiers; two of them served less than a year. Cohabitation actually improves a premier's tenure in office, because the president cannot use party pressure to get premiers to resign. During the first two cohabitation periods, Mitterrand had no party leverage over his neo-Gaullist premiers, Chirac and Balladur, who lasted two years until new elections. Curiously, Socialist Lionel Jospin, in cohabitation with Gaullist Chirac, was one of France's longest-serving premiers (1997–2002). Divided government may be good for France.

Another difference from parliamentary systems is that a French **deputy** chosen to be a minister must resign his or her seat. (A replacement is elected along with each deputy, so there is no need for by-elections, as in Britain.) In parliamentary systems, such as Britain, ministers keep their seats in parliament. De Gaulle wanted to make sure ministers could not run back to parliament to protest

COMPARISON

WASHINGTON GETS AN INTERIOR MINISTRY

In 2002, the United States finally got something like a European **interior ministry**, the Department of Homeland Security. America, fearing centralized police powers, had never accepted the European view that national government exists to supervise the nation. The terror attacks of 9/11 made Americans a little more European. By combining and centralizing portions of existing departments to safeguard Americans in their own country, the new DHS does many of the same things as a European interior ministry, although there is still no national U.S. police. The new U.S. department also demonstrated that from time to time governments must add departments to meet new situations. European governments do this frequently, whenever the prime minister wishes. The American process requires elaborate Congressional approval.

technocrat Official, usually unelected, who governs by virtue of economic skills.

his policies. By the same token, unlike Britain, French ministers do not have to be members of parliament; many are experienced administrators and nonparty **technocrats** who have never been elected to anything. De Gaulle picked as one of his premiers Georges Pompidou, who had never run in an election (but who went on to become an effective president in his own right).

Like most European cabinets, the French cabinet can be easily remade to suit the premier. Ministries are not quite the same as U.S. departments, which are firmly fixed by statute and change only after great deliberation. Paris ministries, often renamed, are almost ad hoc combinations of existing French agencies and bureaus and change according to the policy goals of the executive. In 2007 Premier Fillon named a rather trim cabinet of fourteen ministers (seven of them women) for these ministries:

Foreign Affairs

Defense

Finances

Interior

Justice

Social Affairs and Housing

National Education

Environment

Health and Solidarity

Agriculture

Transportation, Public Works, Tourism, and Sea

Culture

Overseas France

Youth and Sports

Additional *ministers delegate* filled more specialized offices within the ministries and were also considered part of the government. In general, left-wing governments have larger cabinets since they propose major changes under state supervision. Conservative governments, on the other hand, usually like smaller cabinets, as they do not plan to supervise society. Repeated changes in ministries sounds chaotic to Americans, but the same career civil servants still run the various bureaus; the changes are only at the top, at the ministerial level. In France we see bureaucrats actually running the country, a pattern developed even more fully in Japan.

THE NATIONAL ASSEMBLY

During the Third and Fourth Republics the National Assembly was dominant. Making and unmaking cabinets, the parliament controlled the executive. Some say this sort of parliamentary system has a weak executive and strong legislature, but that is not quite accurate. In this case the legislature was not strong either. Divided into several quarrelsome parties that were unable to form stable coalitions, the French National Assembly was no more able to govern than were the cabinets. The government "fell" every few months on average.

This is not quite as chaotic as it sounds. When a government in a parliamentary system "falls," it does not mean the entire structure of government collapses; indeed, little changes. It just means there has been a policy quarrel among the parties so that the cabinet coalition no longer commands a majority in parliament. The cabinet then either resigns, is ousted in a vote of no-confidence, or limps along as a minority government. After several days or weeks of negotiations, another cabinet is put together that wins majority approval. Often this cabinet is composed of the same ministers in the same jobs as the previous cabinet. Instead of too much change, parliamentary systems often suffer from too little. As the French have said for decades: *"Plus ça change, plus c'est la même chose."* (The more it changes, the more it stays the same.) Some premiers have their hands so full just keeping the coalition together that they are often unwilling to risk doing anything that might make it come apart. The result is *immobilisme*.

Palais Bourbon   Paris house of French National Assembly.

Meeting in the windowless **Palais Bourbon**, deputies prior to 1958 tended to play politics with each other and ignore what was happening outside. In a massive avoidance of responsibility, deputies concentrated on either getting into the cabinet or bringing it down. Things changed with the Fifth Republic; the legislators' paradise came to an abrupt end.

The National Assembly no longer makes cabinets; today that power belongs to the premier, in consultation with the president. Indeed, the relationship between the cabinet and the legislature has been deliberately weakened; as noted earlier, a deputy named to the cabinet must resign his or her seat. One link does remain: The National Assembly can censure a cabinet, indicating its extreme displeasure. The president on the other hand, can dissolve the National Assembly for new elections before the end of its normal five-year term, which is what Chirac did in 1997. The president is limited to one dissolution per year.

The premier and president, not the legislature, now hold key powers of legislation. Most bills originate with the government. The government sets the agenda. If the government specifies, its proposals must be considered without amendments on a take-it-or-leave-it basis called a *blocked vote*,

COMPARISON

ISRAEL'S EXPERIMENT

Israel, to some extent, followed in France's footsteps. Both had a weak executive dependent on a shaky coalition of several parties. Both modified their systems. De Gaulle ended the Fourth Republic's parliamentary system and founded the Fifth's semipresidential one. Israel stayed parliamentary but also tried to strengthen the executive.

Israel's single house, the 120-member Knesset, is elected by proportional representation and permits any party that wins at least 2 percent of the national vote to have at least a few seats in parliament. (It used to be only 1 percent.) Israel has a dozen or more parties—some based on a single personality—none of them having a majority in parliament. Thus every Israeli government has been a coalition, prone to breakup when the parties in it quarreled. Israel, too, suffered immobilism in the face of major problems.

Taking a turn to semipresidentialism, in 1996 Israel tried directly and separately electing its prime minister by popular vote. Each Israeli voter had two votes, one for a party in the Knesset, the other for prime minister. Designed to bring greater stability to Israel's chief executive, the experiment failed because the prime minister could still be ousted on a vote of no-confidence and coalition cabinets were as hard to form as ever. Israeli voters, figuring they had selected a strong prime minister, then scattered their votes among a dozen small parties, fractionating the Knesset even more. After two elections under the unique, hybrid system, Israel repealed it in 2001 and went back to the regular parliamentary system. The moral: Be careful when mixing components of different systems (presidential and parliamentary).

unitary   System that centralizes power in the capital with little autonomy for component areas.

first-order civil division   Main territorial units within countries, such as departments in France.

prefect   French *préfet*; administrator of department.

Midi   French for "noon"; the South of France.

which prevents parliamentary dilution of legislation. The National Assembly no longer has the time or structure to consider legislation closely: Its sessions are limited to five-and-a-half months a year; it has only six committees; and a bill cannot be bottled up in committee but must be reported out.

The government is able to pass many laws by simple decree, provided the premier and the president agree (with cohabitation they may not). The 1958 constitution specifies the types of laws that must go through parliament; presumably no other laws need to. While most decrees concern details, the power of government decree also extends to the budget. Here, the legislature has lost its original, most fundamental, power—the power of the purse. Any parliamentary motion to either decrease revenues (a tax cut) or increase spending (a new program) are automatically out of order. And if the parliament cannot settle on the budget within seventy days, the government may make it law by simple decree.

Geography

Decentralizing Unitary Systems

A state's territorial organization—its "civil divisions" and their relationship to the capital—can heighten or dampen center-periphery tensions, although no sure-fire formula has been found. There are two approaches, **unitary** and federal. More than Britain, France is a unitary system, a carry-over from monarchical times, whereby the **first-order civil divisions**—counties in Britain, departments in France, prefectures in Japan—have little autonomy and serve mostly as administrative conveniences for the national capital.

These units can be changed and their boundaries redrawn with little ado. The leading executives in these civil divisions are appointed and supervised by the national government. France's **prefects** are perhaps the best examples of how the unitary state rules. There are, to be sure, elected county, departmental, and municipal councils, but their powers to tax and spend are limited. Any major project must be cleared with and usually funded by the national authorities. Most countries in the world are unitary systems. (U.S. states, although they look like federal systems, are actually unitary.)

The advantage of a unitary system is that it gives greater control to the center for rational administration and modernization. Standards can be enforced nationally. Central administration can knead disparate groups into a single nationality, as France has done over the centuries. The unitary system best suits a country like Japan that is not too large or does not contain different cultures and languages.

There are several difficulties with unitary systems. One is that they may ignore the wishes of local people, especially those at the periphery. Crushing the **Midi** caused centuries of resentment. Many of today's *méridionaux* (southerners) see themselves as a race separate from the northerners. Thus a unitary system may foster center-periphery tensions (see page 55). Corsican and Breton violence shows the incomplete integration of France's regional subcultures into a French whole.

Further, a unitary system, because it is so uniform, can be overly rigid and make big, nationwide mistakes that in a federal system would be implemented and corrected piecemeal, as the components tried various policies. Often there is too much national control over purely local issues. Even trivial matters such as a new traffic light might have to be approved by Paris or Tokyo.

A Senate That Fights Back

Most parliaments are composed of two chambers, and most do not know what to do with the upper chamber. Sweden simply abolished its upper house. The greatest value of an upper house is in representing territorial subunits, as the U.S. Senate represents the states. Where the system is unitary (Britain, France, China) rather than federal (the United States, Germany, Russia, India, Mexico, Nigeria) an upper chamber does not have much use.

département   Department; French first-order civil division, equivalent to British county.

France's main legislative body, comparable to the British House of Commons, is also the lower house, the 577-member National Assembly elected every five years (or sooner if the president wishes it). The upper house, the *Sénat*, has 326 members elected for nine years each—with elections for about a third every three years—by a gigantic electoral college made up of National Assembly deputies plus more than 100,000 regional and municipal councilors. De Gaulle thought that these councilors, because they would overrepresent rural and small-town France, would produce a conservative Senate amenable to his direction.

Britain, France, and Spain in recent years loosened their unitary systems by instituting regional autonomy. Britain devolved some home rule to Scotland, Wales, and Northern Ireland. France's twenty-two regions and Spain's seventeen *autonomías* now have elected councils with considerable decision-making powers on economic growth, education, housing, and other regional concerns. Although not nearly federalism, these unitary systems have moved in a quasi-federal direction.

The change in France under Mitterrand is particularly striking, for it rolled back a tradition that started with Louis XI. French monarchs tried to erase regional differences but sometimes only worsened local resentments. Napoleon perfected this centralizing and homogenizing pattern. He abolished the historic provinces and replaced them with smaller, artificial units called **départements** named after rivers. The departments were administrative conveniences to facilitate control by Paris.

Each department—there are now ninety-six (plus four for overseas territories)—is administered by a prefect, a lineal descendant of Richelieu's old *intendant*, now an official of the Interior Ministry.

Prefects, very bright and highly trained (often at the ENA—see page 125) monitored laws, funds, and mayors with Olympian detachment.

In 1982, Mitterrand got a law that reduced the domain of prefects and increased local autonomy. Elected councils in the departments and regions got policy-setting and taxation powers in education, urban and regional planning and development, job training, and housing. Soon French local and regional government became more important, and elections to their councils were hotly contested. Competition set in as cities, departments, and regions sought to attract new industries. Local taxes increased, but the ways of assessing them became widely divergent and innovative.

The subnational units of French government started acting somewhat like American states, developing their own strategies for prosperity. France in no sense became a federal system—indeed, its decentralization did not go as far as Spain's during this same period—but decentralization was Mitterrand's most important and lasting contribution to the French political system.

National Front   French
anti-immigrant party.

Rural France is not necessarily conservative; it looks out for farming. Above all, the Sénat represents farmers' viewpoints; indeed, 8.5 percent of senators are farmers. The French Senate criticizes and amends numerous government bills. Sénateurs are not under pressure like lower-house assembly members to pass what the government wants. The French Senate—sometimes called the "agricultural chamber"—is listened to by the government on farm matters, for angry French farmers can create havoc. Still, when the government wants a measure passed, it can override Senate objections by a simple majority in the National Assembly.

The French Senate, although not equal in power to the National Assembly, cannot be dissolved by the government. De Gaulle came to regret the Senate's autonomy and in 1969 tried to dilute its power by a plebiscite. The French people, annoyed by de Gaulle, supported their Senate, the last arena of French parliamentary freedom, and rejected the referendum. The UMP held a majority in the National Assembly but lost its majority in the Senate in 2004.

THE FRENCH MULTIPARTY SYSTEM

Parties can make or break a political system. Britain's stability and efficiency would diminish if instead of one party with a majority in Commons there were half a dozen parties of about equal size. Much of what was wrong with the Third and Fourth Republics was not government institutions but the parties that tried to operate them.

We must avoid evaluating all two-party systems as good and all multiparty systems as bad. Americans especially disdain multiparty systems and often cite Italy and the Fourth Republic as examples of the ills they create. But several multiparty parliamentary democracies are stable and effective, for example, Sweden, Switzerland, Holland, and Belgium. At least as much depends on the way the parties behave as on how many parties there are.

By the same token, the Fifth French Republic would not have worked the way it did had not the Gaullist party ballooned into the largest party. Indeed, if the Fourth Republic had been preserved but with Gaullists occupying the largest slice of the National Assembly, the most troublesome problem of that system—*immobilisme*—would have disappeared, for de Gaulle would have had a stable majority at his disposal.

France has at present two large parties, three small ones, plus a sprinkling of minor parties. The largest and currently ruling party is the center-right Union for a Popular Movement (*Union pour une Movement Populaire*, UMP), commonly referred to as "neo-Gaullists." The smaller Socialist party (PS) occupies the center-left. In between, the centrist Union for French Democracy (UDF) ran a respectable third in the 2007 presidential race but has been largely absorbed by the UMP in parliamentary races. On the right, the racist **National Front** gets a protest vote for president but no parliamentary seats. The once-mighty French Communist party has drastically shrunk. (For more on French parties, see Chapter 10.)

FRANCE'S ELECTORAL SYSTEM

French presidential and legislative elections normally come every five years. The two were originally intended to be out of kilter, but starting in 2002 presidential elections come shortly before legislative elections. The five-year presidential term was intended in part to end the need for presidents to either cohabit or to dissolve the National Assembly for new elections.

The traditional electoral system of the Fifth Republic—single-member districts with runoff—is actually taken from the Third Republic. Like Britain and America, France uses single-member districts but instead of a simple plurality to win (FPTP) requires a majority (more than 50 percent). If the candidate does not get it on the first ballot—and that is usually the case—the contest goes to a runoff a week later, this time with either the top two candidates or those with at least 12.5 percent of the eligible voters of that district. Now only a simple plurality is needed to win. The second round, then, is the decisive one; the first round is a bit like U.S. primaries.

Presidential elections run under similar rules. All but the top two candidates for president are eliminated in the first round; a second round two weeks later decides between the top two. In 2002, the unexpected first-round win of the National Front's Le Pen humiliated France. To prevent a recurrence, France might consider dropping the two-round system and go to simple plurality win (FPTP) in one round. That would force small parties to coalesce into larger parties before the election. No electoral system works perfectly, as Americans learned in 2000, when Gore outpolled Bush by half a million votes but still lost in the electoral college.

The French system permits or encourages several parties to exist but not necessarily to win; the Anglo-American systems discourage third parties. Proportional-representation systems, on the other hand, permit small parties to exist and even win. In Germany, for example, a Green vote of over 5 percent wins them dozens of seats. But the French party system is rooted in French society, and this

DEMOCRACY

FRANCE'S PARLIAMENTARY ELECTIONS OF 2007

France's parliamentary elections followed the presidential victory of Nicolas Sarkozy and gave 313 of the National Assembly's 577 seats to the center-right Union for a Popular Movement (UMP). Sarkozy—who still had a safe majority, especially with help from small kindred parties—had been hoping for a coattails effect, but the rival Socialists actually gained on the UMP, winning 186 seats. There were several smaller parties and some independents.

A few candidates won actual majorities in their districts, and they were declared winners immediately. In most districts, however, voters had to go to a runoff a week later. Candidates who had polled less than one eligible voter in eight in the first round were dropped. In most districts weaker candidates also withdrew and endorsed the candidate who most matched their preferences. For example, a New Center candidate who scored lower would withdraw and urge his supporters to vote for the UMP candidate in the second round. As with the presidential contest, the second round is the decisive one.

	1st Round	2nd Round	Total Seats
Union for a Popular Majority (UMP)	40%	47%	313 seats
New Center	2	2	22
Socialists	25	42	186
National Front	4	0	0
Communists	4	2	15
Greens		3	3

is a more complex and fragmented society than the British or American. In any case, the French party system seems to be coalescing into two large blocs, one left and one right. Over the decades, there have been fewer and fewer relevant parties in France.

THE CONSTITUTIONAL COUNCIL

In the 1980s, a little-noticed branch of the French government started drawing attention: the Constitutional Council. Although it was part of the 1958 constitution, it came into its own as a buffer between Mitterrand and the conservative-dominated parliament during his two cohabitation periods. Some started comparing it to the U.S. Supreme Court. The comparison is shaky.

- Both have nine members, but the French serve for nine years, not for life. Three members of the French court are appointed each by the president, the speaker of the National Assembly, and the speaker of the Senate.
- The French Council members are rarely lawyers and see their role as political rather than legal. The U.S. Supreme Court sees its role the other way around.
- The scope of the French Council is much more limited. It can review the constitutionality of laws only after they are passed by parliament but before they have been signed by the president. It considers cases not from lower courts but on demand by the executive or any sixty members of either chamber of parliament.
- Rather than establishing legal precedents as the U.S. Supreme Court does, the French Constitutional Council has acted as a brake against hasty and ill-considered legislation. As such, the ruling parties in France tend to dislike its decisions while the opposition parties often like them.
- In 1999 the head of the Constitutional Court had to step down over allegations that he had siphoned off vast sums from a giant state-owned oil company he had earlier headed. This did the Court's reputation no good.

The role and powers of the U.S. Supreme Court are unique. Some French thinkers would like to see their council become more like the U.S. Supreme Court. The German Federal Constitutional Court is one of the few that approach the Supreme Court in importance.

KEY TERMS

censure (p. 105)

coalition (p. 104)

cohabitation (p. 107)

deadlock (p. 105)

département (p. 113)

deputy (p. 109)

Elysée (p. 104)

Fifth Republic (p. 104)

first-order civil division (p. 112)

interior ministry (p. 109)

Midi (p. 112)

National Front (p. 114)

neo-Gaullist (p. 107)

Palais Bourbon (p. 111)

prefect (p. 112)

premier (p. 104)

president (p. 104)

referendum (p. 104)

semipresidential (p. 104)

technocrat (p. 110)

turnout (p. 106)

unitary system (p. 112)

FurtHer Reference

Bell, David S. *Presidential Power in Fifth Republic France*. New York: Berg, 2001.

———. *François Mitterrand: A Political Biography*. Cambridge, UK: Polity Press, 2005.

Cole, Alistair, and Peter Campbell. *French Electoral Systems*, 3rd ed. Brookfield, VT: Gower, 1989.

Elgie, Robert, ed. *The Changing French Political System*. Portland, OR: F. Cass, 2000.

Gaffney, John, and Lorna Milne, eds. *French Presidentialism and the Election of 1995*. Brookfield, VT: Ashgate, 1997.

Knapp, Andrew, and Vincent Wright. *The Government and Politics of France*, 5th ed. New York: Routledge, 2006.

Lewis-Beck, Michael, ed. *How France Votes*. New York: Chatham House, 2000.

Raymond, Gino G., ed. *Structures of Power in Modern France*. New York: St. Martin's, 2000.

Safran, William. *The French Polity*, 6th ed. White Plains, NY: Longman, 2002.

Schmidt, Vivien A. *Democratizing France: The Political and Administrative History of Decentralization*. New York: Cambridge University Press, 1991.

Stone, Alec. *The Birth of Judicial Review in France: The Constitutional Council in Comparative Perspective*. New York: Oxford University Press, 1992.

Thody, Philip. *The Fifth French Republic: Presidents, Politics, and Personalities*. New York: Routledge, 1998.

Chapter 9
French
Political Culture

Two Parisian families I knew during the Bicentennial of the French Revolution in 1989 illustrate the deeply divided nature of French society. One couple, although not university-educated, were bright and hard-working and had turned their small suburban house into a tidy and pleasant home. They read the conservative daily *Le Figaro* and a Catholic weekly and did not like the Socialist government. When they entered a church, they crossed themselves. They showed little interest in celebrating the Bicentennial July 14 and cautioned me about the crowds in Paris. They suggested a picnic in the countryside instead.

The other family was typical Parisian intellectuals, both university-educated, inhabiting a charming, book-strewn older apartment not far from one of Paris's great boulevards. They read the leftish *Le Monde* and were irreligious. They liked the current Socialist government. They urged me to join the street festivities the night before July 14 and then catch the spectacular parade. They thought the French Revolution was really worth celebrating.

There, in miniature, was conservative France and radical France, the former Catholic and indifferent or even a little hostile to the French Revolution, the latter secular and enthusiastically in favor of it. The split created by the French Revolution continues to this day, although in subdued form. Conservative France no longer battles radical France; rather, the two preserve a chilly distance.

Both families deeply love France, but they love different facets of France. France has a mystique, a drawing power that can equally attract conservatives such as de Gaulle and Socialists such as Mitterrand. The conservatives are drawn to French civilization, its Catholic roots, and its *grandeur* (greatness). Liberals and leftists, on the other hand, are drawn to the ideals of the French Revolution—liberty, equality, fraternity—and see France as guarding these ideals. Some French envision their land as a person, a princess, or even a Madonna. They have a reverence for their country that few Americans or Britons can match. The dramatic and stirring **"La Marseillaise"** (see box on page 120) shows the depth of French patriotism.

French patriotism in the abstract, however, does not carry over into the real, grubby, daily life of French politics. The French are more cynical about politics than Britons or Americans. The French may be the world's greatest complainers: Nothing works right; reforms do not work; all governments are crooked. France in the abstract is glorious; France in the here and now is shabby. De Gaulle said France needs national greatness, for only with such a vision can the French rise above the sordid reality and pursue the mythical ideal.

QUESTIONS TO CONSIDER

1. What is the split nature of French political culture?
2. What is statism? Is it still found in Europe?
3. What was the slogan of the French Revolution?
4. What is anticlericalism? Where else is it found?
5. What is the typical education path into the French elite?
6. What is the ENA and why is it important?
7. How do presidential press conferences show differences of political culture?
8. What happened to Marxism in France?

Sarkozy was elected in 2007 in part because of his ability to project an idealistic vision of rein-vigorated France with a neo-liberal twist. The French initially liked the notion, but once Sarkozy was in power they grew quickly disillusioned with the reality.

Historical Roots of French Attitudes

Where did this French political schizophrenia come from? Part of the problem is historical, trace-able to the centralization of French kings, who implanted an **omnipotent** state, a state that tried to supervise everything. In theory, a centralized system should plan and build rationally; in practice, it often fails. The French, educated to expect a powerful government to help them (the ideal), are always disappointed when it does not (the real). This is reinforced by the promise of every new French govern-ment to cut France's high unemployment rate. They fail, leaving French citizens bitter. The solution: Either stop promising or disman-tle the impediments to a free economy that would hire more people. Few French politicians are willing to do either.

"La Marseillaise"   French national anthem. (See page 119.)

omnipotent   All-powerful.

statism   Idea that a strong government should run things, especially major industries.

bureaucratized   Heavily controlled by civil servants.

French **statism** also stunted the development of a voluntary, do-it-ourselves attitude, something taken for granted in the United States. France simply has no tradition of voluntary groups of neighbors un-dertaking local governance. When local groups take responsibility and something goes wrong, you can only blame yourselves. In France, with all responsibility, until recently, in the hands of the central government, people blame Paris.

Centuries of **bureaucratized** administration also left the French used to living by uniform, im-personal rules—and lots of them. This creates hatred, the hatred of the little citizen on one side of

Political Culture

"La Marseillaise"

Possibly the world's greatest national anthem is the French "La Marseillaise." Dashed off in a single night in 1792 by a 32-year-old army officer, Rouget de Lisle, to accompany volunteers from Marseille marching north to defend the Revolution, "La Marseillaise" soon became the Revolution's, and then France's, anthem.

Extremely stirring and bloodthirsty, it is the perfect anthem for fighting for a nation. The refrain goes as follows:

Aux armes, citoyens, formez vos bataillons!
Marchons! Marchons!
Qu'un sang impur abreuve nos sillons!

(To arms, citizens, form your battalions!
We march! We march!
Until [the enemy's] impure blood overflows our furrows!)

If you have never heard it sung, catch the movie *Casablanca* on late-night television. Like the French flag, "La Marseillaise" became a controversial political symbol. Part of the Revolution, it was banned by Napoleon and the Bourbons, accepted by the liberal Or-leans monarch in 1830, banned again by Napoleon III, and made permanently the national anthem in 1879. In a split society, nothing is simple.

the counter facing the cold, indifferent bureaucrat on the other. Centralization and bureaucratization are the products of the "order and reason" approach to governance that has been practiced in France for centuries. Order and reason, unfortunately, are mere ideals. Since they are always deficient in practice, the French become unhappy with a reality that always falls short of ideals.

culmination   Logical outcome or end.

A Climate of Mistrust

In personal relations, the French are sometimes distant and mistrustful to people outside their family. Indeed, attitudes of mistrust are widespread throughout Latin Europe—they are extremely pronounced in Italy—while trustful attitudes are more common in North Europe. American scholar Laurence Wylie found villagers in the Vaucluse, in the south of France, constantly suspicious of *les autres*, "the others," those outsiders who talk behind your back, blacken your name, and meddle in your affairs. The best way to live, people there agreed, was not to get involved with other people and to maintain only correct but distant relations with neighbors. With modernization, such extreme mistrust has receded.

French philosopher and playwright Jean-Paul Sartre voiced a very French feeling about interpersonal relationships when he wrote, *"L'enfer, c'est les autres"* (Hell is other people). He meant, in his play *No Exit*, that having to get along with other people was his idea of hell.

Political Culture

How to Celebrate a 200-Year-Old Revolution

The French Revolution was still a divisive political issue in 1989. Even choosing the official historian for the Bicentennial was a political problem. Conservative historians called the Revolution a giant mistake, the root of France's subsequent troubles. Such views anger the left and were hardly a way to celebrate the Bicentennial. Radical or leftist historians, on the other hand, read into the Revolution the harbinger of all things good and of the Bolshevik Revolution in Russia. This was hardly acceptable to conservative France.

In François Furet the Mitterrand government found their historian: a former Marxist who had turned away from radicalism to produce a moderate and sober synthesis with something for everyone. Furet found nothing wrong with the revolutionary ideals of *liberté, egalité, fraternité,* but he argued that with the collapse of the monarchy and takeover of the revolution by extremists, the revolution had to "skid out of control"

(*dérapage*). It was not just evil or foolish people that caused the revolution to skid out of control, Furet argued, but the logic of revolutions themselves. Furet's thinking parallels that of Crane Brinton, discussed in Chapter 7.

A change in the political context enabled Furet and other French intellectuals to accept this troubling analysis of the French Revolution. For decades, many French intellectuals naively celebrated the 1917 Russian Revolution as a continuation of the French Revolution. With the erosion of French leftism and decay of Soviet communism, French intellectuals saw that the Bolshevik Revolution had been a mistake. But if 1917 was the **culmination** of 1789, then logically the French Revolution itself must have been badly flawed. The new attitude about communism forced the French to reevaluate their own revolution.

patrie   French for fatherland.

Foreigners notice how shut off the French family is. Typical French houses are surrounded by high walls often topped by broken glass set in concrete. Shutters are not just for decoration; they bang shut as if to tell the world to mind its own business. Traditionally, French people rarely entertained at home—they would go to a restaurant instead; inviting outsiders to your table was an invasion of family privacy. This has changed, however; I have been invited into several French homes for superb meals.

Special mistrust is reserved for the government. In Wylie's village it was taken for granted that all government is bad, a necessary evil at best. The duties of a good citizen, which schoolchildren memorize in their civics course, are mere ideals, but in the real world, government is corrupt, intrusive, and ineffective. French children learn to love **la patrie** in the abstract but to disdain politics in the here and now. Politics are also best kept private and personal; discussing politics with others only leads to arguments. Besides, it is none of their business.

The Nasty Split

Catholic countries have a serious problem that Protestant (and Eastern Orthodox) countries do not have to worry about: the role of the church. When Britain and Sweden broke with Rome and established national churches, they also subordinated churchmen to the state. The Anglican church

COMPARISON

THE INSTABILITY OF SPLIT SOCIETIES

Unlike the stable and settled countries of North Europe, such as Britain and Sweden, the countries of Latin Europe continued to experience political upheavals well into the twentieth century. In France, Italy, and Spain, regimes have tended to be personal creations (for example, those of de Gaulle, Mussolini, and Franco) that end or change with the demise of their creator.

The underlying factor in this instability seems to be the split quality of French, Italian, and Spanish political culture that is rooted in their histories. Roughly half the population of each country is Catholic and conservative and favors strong executive leadership; the other half is anticlerical and liberal or radical and favors a strong parliament. The center is small; people in Latin Europe historically tended to identify with either the left or right camp, each severely mistrusting the other.

When the right was in power—historically, most of the time—the left denounced the government with shrill Marxist rhetoric as the tool of capitalists. When

the left was in power, the right denounced them as dangerous incompetents, possibly serving Moscow's interests. At any given time, roughly half the country regarded the government as illegitimate, and this stunted feelings of legitimacy about government in general. In Latin Europe, few take pride in their nation's governmental institutions.

In the absence of shared values and underlying consensus, political difficulties can lead to violence, coups, and even civil war, which in turn lead to authoritarian rule. In the 1930s, Spain split into left and right camps and exploded into a vicious civil war won by the Catholic and conservative forces of General Franco. Disgruntled rightists in the Spanish military attempted a coup as recently as 1981. Portugal had a coup in 1974. In 1958 France nearly had a military coup. In opposition, François Mitterrand referred to the Gaullist constitution as a "permanent coup." (In office, he found that the presidential powers it gave him really were not so bad.)

in Britain and the Lutheran church in Sweden depended strictly on London and Stockholm, respectively, for support; they could not turn to Rome. As a result, in these societies the church no longer played an independent political role.

In Latin European countries—France, Italy, Spain—the Roman Catholic faith retained its political power, supporting conservative regimes and retaining special privileges, such as control of education, tax exemption for church lands, and a considerable say in government policy. Because of this temporal power, many people in Latin Europe developed anticlerical attitudes. Their most brilliant spokesman was Voltaire (see page 92). Anticlericalism was not necessarily atheism; it rather sought to get the church out of government, what Americans call the separation of church and state.

Anticlericalism spread in Latin Europe, especially among intellectuals. After the French Revolution and Italian unification (in mid-nineteenth century), many people wanted a purely secular state, that is, one with no church influence in government. That was easy to do in America, where there was no single established church, but it was hard in France, Italy, and Spain, where church and state were intertwined. To separate them required drastic surgery: sale of church lands, banning of some Catholic orders (such as the Jesuits), and state rather than church control of schools. The reaction to this was predictable. Just as the Republic was anticlerical, the church turned anti-Republic. Church sentiment went from conservative to reactionary, and the Roman Catholic faith became a pillar of monarchical restoration because that meant a return of church privileges.

In this way conservative France retained its Catholicism, while revolutionary France became strongly anticlerical. The battle raged for more than a century. At one point the Vatican instructed faithful Catholics to steer clear of any political involvement with the "Jacobin" Republic. During the Dreyfus affair, French clericalists and anticlericalists took opposing sides. Finally, in 1905, the National Assembly completed the separation of church and state; France no longer had an established church. Until the twentieth century, to be in favor of the Republic meant to be anticlerical. France's great premier of World War I, Georges Clemenceau—*le tigre*—was a passionate republican and supporter of Dreyfus. He recalled how his father used to tell him, "There's only one thing worse than a bad priest—and that's a good one."

The French left—chiefly the Socialists—still draw their supporters most heavily from the anticlerical tradition. The right—chiefly the Gaullists—attract mostly people from the pro-church tradition. Indeed, in all of Latin Europe—Italy, Spain, and Portugal as well as France—if you know how often a person goes to Mass you can usually predict his or her vote; strongly Catholic almost automatically means politically conservative.

Most French babies are baptized Catholic, but only 13 percent of French Catholics attend Mass weekly. (Europeans in general are much less religious than Americans.) Although the great battles between clericalists and anticlericalists have subsided, some issues reawaken the old quarrel. The abortion controversy and question of state control of Church schools can still bring protest demonstrations in the streets of Paris. Once established, social and political cleavages have tremendous staying power.

School for Grinds

Schooling also contributes to French political culture. The curriculum was set generations ago and is changed only slowly. Heavy on memorization, French education tends to produce diligent grinds rather than lively intellects. Even small children lug home briefcases bulging with books. A "good" child is one who puts in long homework hours.

privatistic   Tending to purely private and family concerns.

lycée   French academic high school.

baccalauréat   French high-school exam and diploma.

Until recently, everywhere in the country French children learned the same thing, as established by the Ministry of Education in Paris, with no local input. Generations ago an education minister looked at his watch and told an interviewer what Latin verb was being conjugated all over France. (Starting in the late nineteenth century, Paris used uniform education to replace local dialects and subcultures with common Frenchness.) Since then, French school curricula have become less centralized and less classical.

The curious thing about the standardized, memorized French education, however, is its deeply humanistic and individualistic content. Outwardly, French schoolchildren appear to be mechanically digesting an inflexible, unimaginative curriculum; inwardly, they are exposed to ideas that would be banned in American schools (such as the ideas in the novel *The Immoralist*). This tension between outward conformity and inward freedom can give rise to **privatistic** attitudes, along with occasional eruptions of rebellion. It encourages young French people to keep their thoughts to themselves. In this way, a set, rigid educational pattern may actually contribute to French individualism.

The French pride themselves on the equality of educational opportunity that their system offers. France has few English-style boarding schools for the rich, but, as everywhere, opportunities are still skewed. While the French school system is open to all, the lofty content of French education is tilted toward the children of middle- and upper-class homes. Working-class and peasant children, not necessarily exposed to correct speech—and the French are maniacs about their language—or to abstract, intellectual thoughts, begin school at a disadvantage and have lesser chances at higher education. (Is educational stratification in the United States the same?)

The great gateway to social, economic, and political power in France is the **lycée**. Napoleon developed them to train army officers. Most lycées are state-run. Admission is competitive, and the curriculum is demanding. Not all communities have lycées, which are concentrated in cities. Students complete the lycée with an examination at age 18 and get a **baccalauréat**, which entitles

Political Culture

How Would You Do on the "Bac"?

In about twelve hours of nationwide essay exams spread over a week, France's seventeen- or eighteen-year old lycéens face questions like the following, taken from the philosophy section of a recent baccalauréat exam. How would you do? Choose one. Spend no more than two hours.

- Why defend the weak?
- Comment on Rousseau's declaration that "one must have societies where inequality is not too great, where the tyranny of opinion is moderated and where voluptuousness reigns more than vanity."
- What is it to judge?
- Is it reasonable to love?

French students now get their choice of bac exams. Some are scientific or technical; the most prestigious is math (because you cannot bluff). The French government is trying to move students from the humanities to technology.

them to university admission. Now, as the result of government policy to upgrade French educational levels, over 60 percent of French young people earn the "*bac*," but they still tend to be from middle-class families.

THE "GREAT SCHOOLS"

Just as Oxford and Cambridge tower over other English universities, the **grandes écoles** dominate French higher education. French universities, which stress the "impractical" liberal arts, are nearly free, unselective, and unimportant. Anyone with a bac can get into a French university—now 1.5 million students crowd France's eighty-two universities—but many drop out. Altogether, some 45 percent of French twenty- to twenty-four-year-olds are in full-time education, the highest percentage in Europe and comparable to the United States. Suggestions to let universities select students competitively and charge tuition are shouted down. Result: Not one French university makes the global top forty.

> **grande école**   French for "great school"; an elite, specialized college.
>
> **Ecole Nationale d'Administration** (ENA), France's School for top bureaucrats.

In contrast, the "Great Schools" are highly selective. Skimming off the brightest and most motivated 4 percent by means of rigorous entrance exams, the schools train (rather than "educate") French youths in the practical matters of running a country and then place them in top civil-service and managerial positions. The Great Schools form the people who run France. No other country has anything quite like them. It would be as if West Point produced not army officers but leading administrators. Some denounce the *grandes écoles* as elitist and undemocratic, but few suggest abolishing them.

Although there are several Great Schools, three are politically the most important. The *Ecole Polytechnique* was used by Napoleon to train military engineers. Called X for short, *xiens* have their pick of technology and management jobs when they graduate. The *Ecole Normale Supérieure*, founded by Napoleon to create loyal lycée instructors, still produces many of France's leading intellectuals—among its graduates have been Jean-Paul Sartre, Raymond Aron, and President Georges Pompidou. The newest Great School, founded by de Gaulle in 1945, is the **Ecole Nationale d'Administration** (ENA), which quickly became the most important. Many of the country's top civil servants are "enarchs," as they call themselves.

Like all Great Schools, the ENA is extremely selective. Many of its students are already graduates of the *Institut d'Etudes Politiques* in Paris, itself a *grande école* (and still known as "Sciences-Po," a birthplace of modern political science). Getting into the ENA is even harder; typically, fewer than one in ten pass the legendary written and oral exams to join the entering class of 100 or so. ENA students get monthly stipends and spend half of their twenty-seven months interning in government ministries. Most ENA graduates get high positions in the civil service. About one-third of France's prefects and ambassadors are ENA graduates. Until recently, cabinets were dominated by enarchs. President Chirac (class of 1959) and Premier de Villepin ('80, along with his sister, Véronique) graduated ENA, as did 2007 Socialist presidential candidate Ségolène Royal ('80) and Socialist leader François Hollande (also '80). Royal, of course, lost to Sarkozy, a law graduate of an ordinary university.

A break with "enarchy," as French critics call it, came with Sarkozy's 2007 cabinet, which had only one enarch. French voters may be tired of their arrogance, and some think ENA has passed its peak of influence. Extensive privatization has shrunk the number of positions running state-owned industries, and many bright young people now prefer MBAs and private industry. France's most prestigious MBA is from the HEC (*Ecole des Hautes Etudes Commerciales*), another Great School.

hegemony   Being top or commanding power.

Training in a Great School epitomizes the best and worst of French education. You have to be very smart and hard-working. But you also have to be cold, logical, and removed from ordinary people. Products of the *grandes écoles* may be brilliant, but they often lack common sense and humanity. Some critics call them, pejoratively, *technocrats* (see page 110), people who rule by technical criteria. In line with their training by the state, they also tend to propose the same old statist solutions. A perfect example is Alain Juppé, a brilliant ENA graduate (1972) and Chirac's first premier, whose cold, technocratic leadership made him the most unpopular premier of the Fifth Republic and the biggest single cause of his party's setback in the 1997 parliamentary elections.

The Fear of "Face to Face"

Whatever the educational institution—lycée, university, or Great School—the teaching style is similar: cold, distant, uninvolved. Class discussion is rare. Questions are from the instructor, not the students. When I taught long ago at the University of Toulouse, I was determined to break this

Political Culture

The French-U.S. Love-Hate Relationship

The French have contradictory attitudes toward America. At times, anti-Americanism seems to be part of French political culture. Many French, especially intellectual and political elites, dislike the United States, its compassionless capitalism, its lack of culture, and its global **hegemony**, all symbolized by McDonald's. Sarkozy did not share this view; he praised America.

French critics call the United States a "*hyperpuissance*" (hyperpower) that tries to remake the world in its own image. But France, they say, will go its own way, based on its own traditions and culture. Millions of ordinary French people, however, like America and flock to U.S.-made movies and eat "McDos." McDonald's has grown rapidly to close to a thousand restaurants in France, all French-owned and French-run.

What is eating the French elites? First, they look back to the time when French power, language, and culture (and cuisine) dominated Europe and much of the world. They resent being replaced by U.S. power and English language. De Gaulle, angered at not being treated as an equal by Roosevelt and Churchill during the

war, led France on nationalistic and anti-U.S. paths. France, not the United States, was to lead Europe. Many French, especially in the Foreign Ministry, still follow this design.

French elites do all they can to hold back the tide of Americanization. They outlaw English words ("*franglais*"). They limit the number of U.S. movies and TV shows. They reject a totally free market and cling to state ownership and supervision.

The French try to retain their Frenchness, much as the Japanese try to retain their Japaneseness. Neither are completely successful. Little by little, French ways resemble American ways, "*le business à l'américaine*" (an example of franglais). The international economy requires it; much business is now global and conducted in English. French firms buy American firms and vice-versa. Some French Great Schools now offer English-language MBAs. Some French think they are fighting American cultural domination, but they are really fighting modernization.

pattern; I urged and demanded student participation. The result was stony silence; my request was outside their experience.

By the time they are teenagers, French adolescents have picked up one of the basic characteristics of French culture, what sociologist Michel Crozier called *"l'horreur du face-à-face."* Aside from family and intimate friends, French people feel uncomfortable with warm, cozy, face-to-face relationships. Some tourists find the French unfriendly. They really are not; they are simply reserved and formal to everyone, including other French people. The French style is opposite that of the American, which emphasizes informality and friendliness. In the United States everyone is supposed to be outgoing, use first names, smile, and say, "Have a nice day." Such behavior—much of it shallow—boggles the French mind.

To avoid face-to-face relationships, the French prefer a structured system with clear but limited areas of competence and set, impersonal rules. That way people know where they stand and nobody butts into another's private domain. British-style pragmatism and "muddling through" are not the French style.

COMPARISON

FRENCH AND AMERICAN PRESS CONFERENCES

A French presidential press conference offers a quick insight into French political style. A rare event—maybe once or twice a year—the press conference takes place in an imposing salon of the Elysée Palace, the French White House. The president is seated. On the wall behind him is either a brocade or tapestry. In keeping with the elegant setting, the president is attired in a conservative suit and plain tie.

The journalists sit quietly taking notes. The president expounds abstractly on progress, national greatness, reason, and order, like a professor giving a lecture. He speaks beautiful French, slowly and clearly, with utter confidence and literate, witty phrases, for he is the product of an elite education. Then, if there is time, the president takes a few questions from the reporters. The questions are polite, even timid, for no one dares to trip up or embarrass the president. The president in return treats the journalists like small children who do not understand the logic and clarity of his policies. The president is, in keeping with French political style, magisterial and rational.

The American presidential press conference takes place against a plain blue backdrop. The president stands at a lectern. He is wearing an indifferent suit and striped tie. The president is nervous and ill-at-ease, for he knows that the newspeople are out to get him, just as they have been out to get every president. As they see it, that is their job. He offers a few opening remarks in an almost defensive tone to explain his recent actions. Then, with a forced smile, he throws the conference open to questions from the floor. The journalists descend like a wolf pack, clawing at the air with their upraised hands, each one demanding attention.

The newsperson called upon—often by name, as the president wants to show he likes them personally—gives a little lecture setting the background for his or her question. The question itself—implying a scandal or how the president's policies are failing—is hostile, trying to catch the president in an uncomfortable situation. The president replies in stammering, ungrammatical English, for he is the product of an American college. The president, in keeping with the democratic American style, tries to treat the journalists as friends and equals, but his smile and handshakes as he leaves can scarcely conceal his adversarial relationship with the media.

FREEDOM OR AUTHORITY?

compartmentalization Mentally separating and isolating problems.

ideal-typical Distilling social characteristics into one example.

The points discussed so far—the lack of trust, fear of face-to-face relationships, rigid and rote education—all contribute to a French political personality that cannot quite make up its mind whether it wants freedom or authority. Actually, it wants both, the abstract *liberté* extolled by philosophers and the controlled hierarchies built for centuries by French bureaucrats. What happens is **compartmentalization**: The private French person loves freedom, while the public French person—in school, on the job, facing the bureaucracy—knows he or she needs reason, order, and formal, impersonal rules. A typical French person has been described as an anarchist who secretly admires the police but could equally be a policeman who secretly admires the anarchists.

The result of this mental split is a continual longing for freedom and a perfect society but an equal tendency to surrender to authority and a highly imperfect society. The balance is unstable; from time to time the quest for liberty bursts out, as in 1789, 1830, 1848, the Paris Commune of 1871, the Events of May of 1968, and the 2005 youth riots. We will explore this pattern more fully in the next chapter, but it is interesting to note that most of these outbursts ended with a surrender to authority. French political culture has been described as limited authoritarianism accompanied by potential insurrection. When they vote, some French say half in jest, "The heart is on the left, but the billfold is on the right."

Legitimacy in France is weaker than in Britain. Rather than a strong feeling of the rightness of institutions and authority, some French accord their system only half-hearted support. A few, on the extreme left and right, hate it.

Social Class

As is Britain, France is a class society. The gap between French working and middle class is one of the biggest in Europe and—with the educational system slanted in favor of middle-class children—social mobility is not what it could be. In France, as in Britain, few born working class or Muslim climb the income ladder. Distribution of income in France is more unequal than in Britain or even Spain. The rich live superbly in France; the poor scrape by.

Class differences tend to reinforce other cleavages in French society—clerical-anticlerical, urban-rural, radical-conservative, even to a certain extent North-South. That is, these factors tend to line up on one side—never perfectly, of course—but enough to produce a left-right split in French voting. Very broadly, the **ideal-typical** French voters of the left and the right are depicted in the table below.

Left Voter	Right Voter
Working class	Middle class
Anticlerical	Pro-church
Urban	Rural or small town

THE GREAT CALMING DOWN

French intellectuals, some of them from the same *grandes écoles* as the governing elite, were for a long generation attracted to Marxism. Observing the huge gap between the ideal of equality and the reality of gross inequality, many educated and middle-class French turned to Marxist explanations

DEMOCRACY

THE CENTRIST FRENCH

The real winner of recent French elections has been neither the left nor the right but the center. Observers referred to the "normalization" of French political life and a healing of the great split in French society. Politicians of the left and right tended to move to the center. Gone are the old ideological visions; moderation and pragmatism are now fashionable. Underscoring this was a 1992 poll that asked Frenchmen to place themselves on a nine-point ideological scale, ranging from extreme left to extreme right. The results are not too different from Britain (page 56) and Germany (page 210): Most people are centrist. French politicians are thus on notice: Any party or candidate perceived as too far left or right will lose. This helps explain the decline of the Communists. As this lesson sinks in, France turns into a "two-plus"-party system, like many other industrialized democracies.

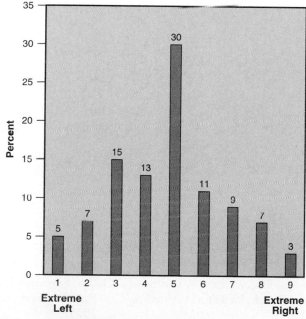

THE SELF-PLACEMENT OF FRENCH VOTERS ON A LEFT/RIGHT IDEOLOGICAL SCALE

and sometimes to membership in the Communist party. Philosopher Jean-Paul Sartre backed every leftist cause and urged other intellectuals to become likewise *engagé*. Another *normalien*, his conservative adversary Raymond Aron, disparaged Marxism as "the opium of the intellectuals," a play on Marx's famous statement that "religion is the opium of the masses."

Under Mitterrand, if not before, this changed. French intellectuals became disillusioned with Marxism, communism, and traditional leftist positions. The French Communist party declined to irrelevance. There seem to be several reasons for this major shift, which has long-term implications for French political life. In the 1970s, a new generation of French intellectuals criticized the Soviet Union and communism. The Soviet-approved coup in Poland by a Polish general in late 1981 reminded many French of Marshal Pétain in the service of Germany during World War II.

But most important, with the election of a Socialist government in 1981, the left was in power. It was one thing to criticize a conservative government but quite another to run a government yourself. French intellectuals and leftists saw how difficult it was to improve the economy, assume a role in world affairs, and transform French society. Clever slogans do not translate into effective policy, and many French intellectuals became moderates. Some celebrated free-market capitalism, a strange position for French intellectuals. The Mitterrand presidency contributed a lot by freeing French society from the allure of leftist ideology and guiding it to a middle-of-the-road pragmatism, one that most governments continued. French politics became centrist, like politics in most of Europe. (Curiously, at this same time, U.S. politics polarized, and the middle ground shrank. Any idea why?) With the onset of the Bicentennial, much of the passion that earlier surrounded the French Revolution went out of it. French politics entered into what might be termed "the great calming down" of de-ideologized pragmatism. As François Furet put it, "The Revolution is over." Most French agreed.

Key Terms

baccalauréat (p. 124)

bureaucratized (p. 120)

compartmentalization (p. 128)

culmination (p. 121)

Ecole Nationale
    d'Administration (ENA)
    (p. 125)

grande école (p. 125)

hegemony (p. 126)

ideal-typical (p. 128)

"La Marseillaise" (p. 120)

lycée (p. 124)

omnipotent (p. 120)

patrie (p. 122)

privatistic (p. 124)

statism (p. 120)

Further Reference

Bernstein, Richard. *Fragile Glory: A Portrait of France and the French.* New York: Alfred A. Knopf, 1990.

Ehrmann, Henry W., and Martin Schain. *Politics in France,* 5th ed. New York: HarperCollins, 1997.

Godin, Emmanuel, and Tony Chafer, eds. *The French Exception.* New York: Berghan, 2005.

Judt, Tony. *Past Imperfect: French Intellectuals, 1944–1956.* Berkeley, CA: University of California Press, 1993.

Khilnani, Sunil. *Arguing Revolution: The Intellectual Left in Post-War France*. New Haven, CT: Yale University Press, 1994.

Mahoney, Daniel J. *De Gaulle: Statesmanship, Grandeur, and Modern Democracy*. Westport, CT: Praeger, 1996.

Reader, Keith A. *Intellectuals and the Left in France since 1968*. New York: St. Martin's, 1986.

Roger, Philippe. *The American Enemy: The History of French Anti-Americanism*. Chicago, IL: University of Chicago Press, 2005.

Sa'adah, Anne. *Contemporary France: A Democratic Education*. Lanham, MD: Rowman & Littlefield, 2003.

Scriven, Michael. *Jean-Paul Sartre: Politics and Culture in Postwar France*. New York: St. Martin's, 1999.

Singer, Daniel. *Is Socialism Doomed? The Meaning of Mitterrand*. New York: Oxford University Press, 1988.

Weber, Eugen. *My France: Politics, Culture, Myth*. Cambridge, MA: Harvard University Press, 1991.

Chapter 10
France:
Patterns of Interaction

Party image and voter identification with parties are less developed in France than in Britain. Many French voters do not have long-term party preferences, and French parties tend to come and go and change their names, blurring their images. One result is that many voters are not attached to one party and shift their votes as a form of protest. In 2002, this inadvertently led to a top contender, Socialist Premier Jospin, getting knocked out of the presidential race by a right-wing extremist. In most of West Europe, elections show only small swings of a few points from the previous contest, but not in France, where new parties can rise and fall within a few years. French parties may gain or lose ten to twenty percentage points from their previous showing. French voting can be **volatile**.

QUESTIONS TO CONSIDER

1. What does *volatility* do to French voting?
2. Why is the French party system more complex than Britain's party system?
3. How does the French electoral system force parties together?
4. What is *Gaullism*? Is it an ideology or a mood?
5. Why is the French right split into three?
6. Could something like the *Events of May* happen again?
7. How can referendums be misused?
8. How do French labor unions differ from British and U.S. labor unions?
9. How do statism, *dirigisme*, and *tutelle* relate to each other?

Few French parties have not changed their names at one time or another. The Gaullists especially have changed their name often. From 1947 to 1952 they called themselves the Rally of the French People (RPF). With de Gaulle's coming to power in 1958, they became the Union for the New Republic (UNR), then in 1967 the Democratic Union for the Fifth Republic (UDV^e), in 1968 the Union for the Defense of the Republic (UDR), in 1971 the Union of Democrats for the Republic (with the same initials, UDR), in 1976 the Rally for the Republic (RPR), and in 2002 the Union for a Presidential Majority (UMP), quickly renamed the Union for a Popular Movement (still UMP).

An American would exclaim: "But how can you build party identification with so many changes?" The Gaullists—since 1976 known as the "neo-Gaullists"—saw themselves less as a structured political party than as a mass rally of patriotism. What makes sense in one political culture does not in another. The name changes showed the Gaullists were always starting fresh. Neo-Gaullist Nicolas Sarkozy was elected president in 2007.

The Socialists, founded in 1905, originally called themselves the French Section of the Workers International, or SFIO. In 1969, merging with some smaller left groups, they changed the name to the *Parti Socialiste* (PS). In 1981, the PS under Mitterrand won both the presidency and the National Assembly. It again became the largest party in parliament in 1997 but shrank to second-largest in the 2002 and 2007 elections.

The French center is unusually messy, possibly because many figures strive for prominence and do not like to merge into one party. The Union for French Democracy (*Union pour la Démocratie*

volatile   Rises and falls quickly. (See page 133.)

Française, UDF) began as a parliamentary grouping in 1962 and first ran in elections in 1966 as the Republicans. In 1974 its leader, Valéry Giscard d'Estaing, was elected president and later merged several small centrist parties with the Republicans to form the UDF, a loose federation of five center-right parties. By 2007, the UDF had split into the New Center (NC) and Democratic Movement (MoDem). The French center, where small parties continually rise, fall, and change names, has been aptly called "the eternal swamp."

One French party does not play around with name changes, the Communists (PCF), although they, too, have trouble with their party's image. The Communists plunged from 25 percent of the parliamentary French vote in 1972 to only 2 percent in 2007. On the other side of the spectrum, the National Front emerged in 1986 as the anti-immigrant party but wins no parliamentary seats. To make things even more confusing, left parties often run jointly as the United Left or Common Program

GEOGRAPHY

THE PERSISTENCE OF REGION

In 1936 the leftist Popular Front won in the shaded départements (map, left). In 1981, Socialist François Mitterrand won the presidency with a very similar pattern (map, right). Maps of recent elections look much the same. Region, as well as social class and religion, often produces distinct and durable voting patterns.

1936: POPULAR FRONT VOTE

1981: MITTERAND VOTE

(Socialist and Communist), and right parties as the Presidential Majority or Alliance (Gaullists and New Center).

bloc   Grouping or alliance of parties.

The Emerging Party System

The French party system is not as complex as it used to be; it is down from ten parties in 1958 to perhaps four relevant ones today. France's parties have been consolidating and forming into two **blocs**—one left and one right—seemingly headed for a "two-plus" party system. Much depends on whether the Union for a Popular Movement (UMP) can unite the French right. Schematically it looks like this:

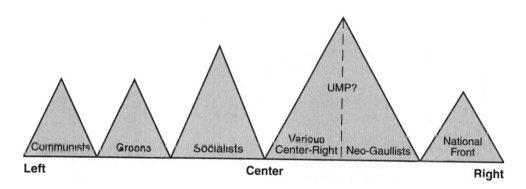

The two blocs are divided internally. As we shall see, the Communists and other far-left parties are always feuding with the Socialists, and the small centrist parties are constantly trying to eat into the neo-Gaullists. If they can help it, none of the other parties wants anything to do with the racist National Front. In terms of voter appeal, however, the two blocs fit into two great French tendencies of which we spoke earlier. The left favors ways to make people more equal, by taxing the rich, controlling the economy, and providing more welfare benefits. The right also favors change, but based on economic growth and modest reforms. Both look to a strong state, but the left dislikes free-market solutions while Sarkozy claimed to favor some of them. Sarkozy is unlikely to implement a really competitive economy, which the UMP never supported. The National Front wants expulsion of most immigrants and France out of the EU.

The Demise of the French Communists

In most countries, Socialist and Communist parties were natural enemies ever since the Communists followed Lenin's command and broke from the Socialists shortly after World War I. Typically, where one was strong the other was weak. Britain, Sweden, Germany, and Spain all had large socialist-type parties and small Communist parties. In Italy, on the other hand, a large Communist party—now renamed the Democratic Party of the Left—overshadowed the Socialists. In France it used to be that way, but during the 1970s and 1980s the Socialists grew and the Communists shrank, so that now the PS is by far the largest left party in France.

Eurocommunism   1970s move by Italian Communists away from Stalinism and toward democracy.

Stalinist   Brutal central control over Communist parties.

protest vote   Ballot cast against existing regime.

The two parties have common roots. The PCF in 1920 broke away from the Socialists. In a battle that raged over the twentieth century, the Communists claimed that the Socialists were not militant enough, that they abandoned revolutionary Marxism for gradual, pragmatic reformism. The PCF echoed the Soviet line. As was the case worldwide, the Communists did not join in the Resistance until Germany attacked the Soviet Union in 1941. Since Stalin's death, however, the PCF gradually became more moderate. It denounced the 1968 Soviet invasion of Czechoslovakia and claimed to favor Eurocommunism. French voters could not trust the Communists, though, for old **Stalinist** tendencies reappeared—as when the party expelled dissenting intellectuals, laid down dogmatic lines, or stabbed fellow leftists in the back.

The result was an unstable alliance of Socialists and Communists. The two parties hated each other but knew they needed each other. The second round, or runoff, of a French election places a great premium on combining parties, for in the French runoff a simple plurality wins. If the Communists and Socialists ran separately on the second ballot they would always lose to the combined Gaullists and other center-right parties. Accordingly, the left parties—the PS, PCF, and now many small leftist parties—generally support the strongest left candidate, regardless of party, on the second ballot. It is the French electoral system that drives rivals on the French left together.

When François Mitterrand took over the shrunken and demoralized Socialist party in 1971, it was overshadowed on the French left by the Communists, who regularly won a fifth of the vote. Given France's peculiar electoral system—single-member districts with runoff—Mitterrand knew the PS could not grow on its own. He also knew that a good third of the Communist vote was not from committed Communists; it was a **protest vote** that could be won over by an attractive Socialist party. He cleverly embraced the Communists, used them, won away their lukewarm supporters, and then discarded the PCF. In 1984 a shrunken, demoralized PCF left the cabinet and has done worse and worse in elections ever since.

The decline of the French Communist party, however, did not solve the problem of the fragmented French left. It may have made it worse, as it spawned several far-left parties trying to grab its militant tradition and worker and intellectual electorate. In the 2007 presidential election, four far-leftist candidates fragmented the left vote. Two Trotskyist parties (Workers Struggle and Revolutionary Communists) together took 5.4 percent of the first-round vote. In France, as in most of Europe, at least a third of the electorate vote for one leftist party or another—ranging from the Socialists at center-left to the Communists at medium-left to far-left Trotskyists—because the issues that inspire the left remain: poverty, inequality, unemployment, and U.S. hegemony. The demise of the French Communists meant the rise of other left parties.

The Fractured Right

As the French left is fragmented, so is the right. France has one large party on the right, but two smaller ones speak to other parts of the electorate. Some trace the division of the French right back to the Revolution, which produced (1) an ultraconservative monarchist right, (2) a moderate Orleanist right, and (3) a populist Napoleonic right. Today, these three strands are represented by the (1) National Front (FN), (2) New Center (NC), and (3) neo-Gaullists. As noted, the NC descended from the old UDF. Further right, outside of the mainstream, the National Front and other small groups spit venom at immigrants and the European Union.

For the right, ideology and doctrine are less important than personality. Gaullists traditionally have been skeptical of European unity and the free market, while most small centrist parties have been for them. But in speaking to the same middle-class electorate, some of these small parties and the Gaullists often cooperate and agree on a single parliamentary candidate on the first ballot. In 2007 the neo-Gaullists attempted a grand merger of parties into the Union for a Popular Movement (UMP), but that is difficult because on the right—and this is true of many countries—personality becomes the dominant issue.

Here, the shadow of de Gaulle still looms. The French right is torn between those who want to keep his image alive and those who favor more traditional center-right politics. De Gaulle, a Napoleonic figure above parties, never aimed at founding a political party. Like Franco, Mussolini, and Latin American military dictators, de Gaulle hated parties, blaming their incessant squabbles for all the troubles of the Third and Fourth Republics. De Gaulle did not even much care for the Gaullist party; he never formally headed or endorsed it. His attitude seemed to be: "Alright, if you must, go ahead and worship me." During his long reign (1958–1969), the Gaullist party was simply a tool for his control of the National Assembly. In the legislative elections of 1968, the Gaullists won 46 percent of the popular vote and an outright majority of National Assembly seats.

A single charismatic figure leading a national movement is a tough act to follow. Such a leader does not tolerate other important personalities around him; he prefers obedient servants and yes-men. As a result, when de Gaulle departed in 1969, he left a vacuum that no one in the Gaullist party could fill. His former premier, Georges Pompidou, won the presidency that year, but by the time Pompidou died in 1974, the Republican candidate, Valéry Giscard d'Estaing (who later formed the UDF),

COMPARISON

THE RISE OF EUROPE'S ANGRY RIGHT

For some years most European lands have seen the growth of angry rightist parties led by charismatic speakers, such as Le Pen's National Front in France, Jörg Haider's Freedom party in Austria, Pim Fortuyn (assassinated in 2002) in the Netherlands, Germany's National Republicans and Law and Order Offensive, the Flemish Bloc in Belgium, the Danish People's party, and Italy's Northern League and National Alliance. While they differ in many respects, all are anti-immigrant, anti-crime, and anti-EU and can draw one voter in five. Even Japan has an angry, anti-immigrant nationalist as Tokyo's governor.

Some call them fascist, but they deny it and are probably not. Rather, they voice voter concerns that conventional politicians ignored for years. Many Europeans really do not like Muslim immigrants and crime. Nobody ever asked them if they wanted their neighborhoods taken over by foreign cultures. Mainstream politicians have been too politically correct to talk about this. Likewise, European elites have almost reflexively favored the EU even though many ordinary citizens fear the loss of their countries' sovereignty, culture, and jobs in a united Europe (see Chapter 17). Anti-immigrant politicians simply filled the gap left by the conventional politicians. This is also happening inside the U.S. Republican party.

Is this a threat to European democracy, or is it democracy in action? If one party does not give voters what they want, another party will. In any country a certain percentage of disgruntled citizens is receptive to the simplified arguments of populist demagogues. America has its George Wallaces and Ross Perots but also has some advantages: (1) Americans are used to immigrants from all continents; and (2) many of the alienated Americans do not vote. (Perhaps we should be grateful for our low electoral turnout.)

passé Outmoded; receded into the past.

stalemate Politically stuck among competing groups.

was more attractive than the Gaullist candidate. Because de Gaulle disdained parties, he never bothered institutionalizing his movement into a durable party. The real genius in politics is the one who builds lastingly; de Gaulle did not.

Trying to fill the vacuum, Jacques Chirac in 1976 reorganized the moribund Gaullists into the Rally for the Republic, commonly called "neo-Gaullist." A slick performer who alienated many French people by his high-handedness, Chirac alternately quarreled and made up with the UDF. Pushed into a less-active role when he was forced to cohabit with a Socialist cabinet after the 1997 election, Chirac gave up party leadership. Chirac and his party won in 2002 by default because Socialist Jospin was knocked out in the first round by frivolous left voting. The problem for the Gaullists parallels that of the Socialists: What do we stand for now? Most French now consider Gaullism **passé**, a vaguely conservative mood rather than a party.

The Neo-Gaullists show that there are several types of conservatism. When Nicolas Sarkozy was interior minister under President Chirac, he fought with Premier Dominique de Villepin. Both were UMP and conservatives, but Sarkozy was pro-market and pro-United States, while de Villepin wanted to preserve the French welfare state and oppose U.S. power. Sarkozy is a modern, Thatcher-type conservative, de Villepin a traditional French big-government conservative. Conservatism means different things in different countries.

The relationships among the French right parties are similar to those among the French left parties: The electoral system has them compete with each other on the first round but ally on the second round. The difference on the right is that the hatred is largely personal, a struggle between bright, ambitious party leaders who want to be president. If parties merge, it means the leaders of one party become second fiddles, something most politicians dislike. Before you condemn French politicians as unusually petty and jealous, ask yourself if American politicians are much different.

In France, everything fragments. One way to cure electoral fragmentation: Drop the first round of elections and go to straight FPTP, U.S.- and British-style, which would force like-minded parties together. The first round, a kind of primary, may not be necessary. Already the large UMP and Socialists practice a kind of primary election by having on-line votes for nominees.

The Stalemate Cycle

French politics seems to run in a roughly cyclical pattern. "Normal" politics in France usually leads to a **stalemate** in which political groups, constantly feuding among themselves, block major change. This produces crises the stuck system cannot handle, which in turn lead to an explosion every generation or two. To get out of the stalemate, the French have repeatedly turned to a hero, a charismatic figure who has not been sullied by "status quo" politics. French politics seems to require a Napoleon from time to time.

After a dozen years of revolutionary turmoil, France welcomed the first Napoleon as a hero to end the chaos. Half a century later, they turned to Louis Napoleon for the same reason. In 1940 the French parliament actually voted dictatorial powers for the aged Marshal Pétain. Pierre Mendès-France was the thinking-person's hero in 1954 when he got France out of Indochina, but he lacked the charisma of the outsider who is above ordinary politics. That figure arrived in 1958 with de Gaulle, who saved France from civil war over Algeria.

De Gaulle believed he had ended France's recurrent stalemates by constructing a Fifth Republic with a strong president. But did the Fifth Republic really transcend French history? At first it appeared to. France withdrew from the Algerian horror, streamlined its party system, and surged ahead economically. In 1968, however, all hell broke loose (see box on page 139), and people began to wonder if the Fifth Republic was suffering from some of the same ills that had plagued predecessors.

Mitterrand also discovered that the transformation of French politics was not as complete as de Gaulle believed. De Gaulle's personal popularity ensured not only his election as president but a large Gaullist party in the National Assembly. This made it easy to govern; any law or budget de Gaulle wanted was rubberstamped in the Palais Bourbon. The Fifth Republic did not depend on the unstable coalitions of the Third and Fourth in order to govern. But how much did it depend on the same party maintaining control of both the executive and legislative branches?

France found out in 1986. With the election of a National Assembly dominated by the Republicans and Gaullists, Mitterrand named a conservative as premier but stayed on as president. Cohabitation (see Chapter 8) kept the government functioning, but only because Mitterrand consented to letting Premier Chirac pretty much have his way in naming ministers and pursuing conservative policies. Mitterrand played a waiting game, letting Chirac take the blame for unpopular policies. After some time, when Mitterrand's popularity eclipsed Chirac's, Mitterrand began to oppose some of Chirac's policies. A U.S.-style deadlock emerged as neither the president nor the premier could get his way. Chirac controlled parliament, but Mitterrand could denounce his legislative program and criticize him personally. The second cohabitation period was somewhat more relaxed as Mitterrand, probably aware he was dying, attempted little. In the third cohabitation period, 1997–2002, Chirac named Jospin premier. It worked fairly well, but underneath was a smoldering discontent that gave Le Pen the edge on Jospin in the first round of the 2002 presidential election.

Events of May Euphemism for riots and upheaval of May 1968.

CRS Republican Security Companies, French paramilitary police.

Political Culture

THE EVENTS OF MAY 1968

Just ten years after the near civil war over Algeria that brought de Gaulle to power, his regime suffered another explosion, the **Events of May**. A month of student and worker strikes and battles with police revealed that under the law-and-order surface of Gaullist France throbbed the old revolutionary tradition. The great split that had plagued France for generations had not completely healed; the cleavage still ran through French society like a California earthquake fault line, ready to crack open without warning.

Trouble began at the University of Nanterre in a suburb of Paris. Students—fed up with bad facilities and curricula—staged a strike that quickly spread to most universities and many factories. France split again, this time largely on age lines; the young were tired of obeying the old. The **CRS** (*Compagnies Républicains de Sécurité*) waded into protesters with tear gas and truncheons. De Gaulle placed troops and tanks around Paris.

But then the revolution—if that is what it was—burned out, like many previous uprisings in French history. De Gaulle promised more participation and held parliamentary elections in which Gaullists won an actual majority of seats in the National Assembly. "When the French are fearful," noted one French political scientist, "they swing to the right," the tendency in many countries.

Some see recent riots as resurgences of French revolutionary feeling. But 2005 rioting was confined to young Muslim males who were alienated from French society and who had no goals or purposes; some called it simple vandalism. In 2006 students protested against a new employment law. After the 2007 election of Sarkozy, young people rioted and shouted "Sarko fascist!" The commonality of all these: angry young people marginalized by the system.

Referendum Madness

French presidents often use plebiscites or referendums to pose major questions directly to the people without going through elected representatives in parliament. The referendum, almost unknown in Britain, has been used twenty times since 1793 in France. It fits neatly into a very French tradition: Rousseau's idea of the general will. On the surface, nothing could be more democratic than consulting the people directly on their wishes.

In reality, plebiscites can be very tricky, an authoritarian tool that manipulates the citizenry. The key power in a referendum belongs to the one who writes the question. The question can be posed in such a simplified way that one almost has to vote yes. Furthermore, a referendum usually comes after the decision has already been made and the leader just wants popular endorsement.

De Gaulle played the plebiscite game to the hilt. For him, a referendum was not merely to gain mass approval for a given policy but to reinforce his personal rule. After every plebiscite he could turn to his old enemies, the traditional politicians, and say, "You see, the people understand and support me. Who needs you?" In French political theory, again derived from Rousseau, a nation run by a leader who communicates directly with the people—without parties, parliaments, politicians, or interest groups getting in the way—is the ideal democracy. Some, however, see in this model the seeds of dictatorship.

De Gaulle attached his personal prestige to each referendum. "If the nation rejects the measure," he in effect told France, "it also rejects me, and I shall resign." This blunt approach worked every time until the last. In 1958 people were glad to get a new constitution. In 1961 and 1962 they were delighted to see Algeria become independent and French troops come home. But de Gaulle's second referendum of 1962 raised some questions. De Gaulle had made a mistake in the 1958 constitution in having the president chosen by a gigantic electoral college composed of local office holders, whom he assumed would be conservative and pro-de Gaulle; they were not. So in October 1962, bypassing the National Assembly, he asked the voters to amend the constitution to allow direct election of the president. The referendum passed with a 62 percent yes vote, but this represented only 46 percent of the total electorate, far less than de Gaulle expected.

The hint was clear—the French were happy to get out of Algeria but not so happy about tinkering with the constitution—but de Gaulle ignored it. In 1969, after riding out the 1968 Events of May with resounding electoral success, de Gaulle once again sought to demonstrate that the people were behind him. He picked a rather technical issue that did not require a plebiscite: the reform (that is, weakening) of the Senate and the setting up of regional subunits. The French people said no, and true to his word, de Gaulle resigned. He went back to Colombey-les-Deux-Eglises, where he died the following year.

Geography

Sailing the Mediterranean

On your luxury yacht, you are sailing in a great, clockwise circle around the Mediterranean Sea, always keeping the shore a few kilometers to port (left, for you landlubbers). You enter through the Strait of Gibraltar. Which countries do you pass one after another on your left?

Spain, France, Italy, Slovenia, Croatia, Bosnia (minute shoreline), Croatia again, Montenegro, Albania, Greece, Turkey, Syria, Lebanon, Israel, Egypt, Libya, Tunisia, Algeria, and Morocco.

Since then, there have been five referendums. In 1972 Pompidou proposed enlarging the Common Market to include Britain, Ireland, and Denmark. Mitterrand's 1988 referendum on granting the Pacific territory of New Caledonia greater independence passed but with only a 37 percent turnout. In 1992, Mitterrand brought the Europe-unifying Maastricht Treaty before the French electorate, which narrowly endorsed it. The 2000 referendum to cut the presidential term to five years had only a 31 percent turnout. The 2005 French referendum to ratify a new EU constitution failed (see Chapter 17), humiliating Chirac. In none of these cases were referendums needed to solve a constitutional problem. Rather, presidents tried to use a referendum to bolster mass support and deflect attention away from more serious matters. Voter apathy and negativity suggest that the French have tired of referendums. (Have Californians?)

Fragmented Labor Unions

In Britain we saw how interest groups were well-organized and powerful, especially big labor and big business. This pattern is true of North Europe in general, as we shall see in Germany. In France, and in Latin Europe in general, there are plenty of interest groups, but they are usually splintered along party lines.

In Britain (and Germany and Sweden), for example, there is one big labor federation. In France (and Italy and Spain) there are several labor unions—Communist, Socialist, Catholic, and independent unions—competing against each other. The Communist-led CGT (*Confédération Generale du Travail*) is considered powerful in France, but on a comparative basis it is weak. Indeed, only 9 percent of the French workforce, mostly in the public sector, is organized into unions; even U.S. unions are proportionally bigger (12 percent of the workforce).

French unions also quarrel among themselves. The CGT has collided angrily with the smaller, Socialist-oriented CFDT (Confédération Française Démocratique du Travail) and nonparty Force Ouvrière. Labor's voice in France is weak and divided. Accordingly, French unions are strong neither in bargaining with management nor in making an impact on government. There are many strikes in France, but they tend to be short because unions lack strike funds. Transportation workers disrupt rail and subway service every few years.

Part of the problem with French unions is their political slant. Since the largest union, the CGT, is led by Communists, the other parties, especially those who control the government, ignore their demands. French unions engage in political strikes, actions aimed at government policy rather than bread-and-butter demands. In the 1980s and 1990s French unions often protested closures or layoffs at state-owned industries, much as in Thatcher's Britain. Few French unions take the American view that a union is a device to negotiate better terms with management, not a political tool.

Latin Europe's Divided Unions

	France	Italy	Spain
Communist	CGT	CGIL	CO
Socialist	CFDT	—	UGT
Catholic	CFTC	CISL	—
Other	FO (centrist)	UIL (soc. dem.)	CNT (anarchist)

Medef	French business association.

The relative weakness of French unions has an important side effect: It makes them more, rather than less, militant and ideological. Feeling that the government has turned its back on them, French workers are more bitter than the workers of Germany and Sweden, where strong unions have an important voice in government. In those two countries, large and well-organized unions have become moderate and pragmatic.

BUSINESS AND THE BUREAUCRACY

French business is perhaps no more influential than labor. The French Enterprise Movement (*Mouvement des Enterprises de France*, **Medef**) seeks reforms to cut taxes, privatize pensions, and free up labor laws. Only business creates jobs, it argues, not government. This Thatcherite view is just catching on in France, but Medef does not have much political access. Unlike Americans, most French people see business as callous, exploitive, and inhumane. Few French politicians are openly pro-business the way American politicians are. It would be bad politics in France.

Mitterrand ignored business interests to pursue a leftist economic program. This worried businesses; they cut investment in France and increased it in the United States. Mitterrand backed off and tried to make peace with French business. Premier and later President Chirac privatized large sections of France's nationalized industries, including a state-owned television network, but never endorsed a free-market society. Socialist Jospin continued privatization but talked about worker rights. Sarkozy talked about "economic patriotism" rather than a free economy.

Medef is not as influential as the CBI in Britain because of the French tendency of individualism. A French firm may belong to Medef but rely only on its own resources for discreet contacts with the bureaucracy. The big advantage business has over labor is that the French business executive and civil servant are the same kind of people, often graduates of the same *grande école*, who move back and forth between top jobs in government and industry. Such connections give France's

GEOGRAPHY

"EVERY COUNTRY HAS A SOUTH"

This old saw contains much truth. Except for very small countries, the south of most lands in the northern hemisphere is poorer and less developed than the north. Industry has tended to cluster in the north of France, Germany, Italy, Spain, and the United States. People in the south of these countries are often described as fun-loving but slow and lazy. The northern people are often described as efficient and hardworking. The south usually votes differently from the north. People of the *Midi* describe themselves as a different, Mediterranean race that does not like the cold, germanic northern French.

The picture changes when you go too far north; development in the Scandinavian countries and Russia generally centers on the temperate areas and avoids the frozen north. In the southern hemisphere it is reversed, for there the southerly areas are more temperate. Centuries ago, Montesquieu held that climate produces culture. Why should political and economic growth be closely associated with temperate or even slightly chilly zones?

major firms **structured access** to the machinery of administration, something small-business people, farmers, and labor unionists do not enjoy. This builds up bitterness and frustration in the latter groups that explode from time to time in flash parties such as the National Front, in produce dumping by farmers, and in wildcat strikes. The political-bureaucratic systems of North Europe, by providing access for all major groups, generally avoid such outbursts.

But neither do French businesspeople dominate government decision making. French political tradition is stacked against it. In the Anglo-American tradition, pluralism—the open interplay of interest groups with government—is respected, sometimes even celebrated. Lobbying by farmers, businesspeople, trade unionists, and ethnic groups in Washington is perfectly normal. In Britain's Commons, "interested members" make no secret that they represent certain industries. French political theory, however, still devoted to Rousseau's notion that interest groups are immoral—because they represent partial wills rather than the general will—tends to view such groups as illegitimate. The French tradition is **dirigiste**, from the top down, ignoring interest-group demands, and doing what civil servants deem best for French power and prestige. This gives great power to bureaucrats.

> **structured access**   Permanent openness of bureaucracy to interest-group demands.
>
> **dirigiste**   Bureaucrats directing industry; closely connected to French statism.
>
> **Grands Corps**   Top bureaucrats of France.

The Eternal Bureaucracy

France has been developing its bureaucracy for five centuries. Almost every change of regime has led to growth in the number (now 5 million) and functions of French bureaucrats. During the revolving-door cabinets of the Fourth Republic, people used to say that the fall of governments did not really matter that much because the bureaucracy ran the country anyway. Tocqueville recognized the problem in 1856, when he complained about France's "regulating, restrictive administration, which seeks to anticipate everything, take charge of everything."

In France, civil servants oversee almost everything in the French economy, all leading to lack of competition. The closest parallel to French bureaucrats are Japanese bureaucrats, who have similar powers and frames of mind. France has several nationalized industries—aircraft, automobiles, coal mines, banks, steel, gas, and electricity—in addition to the areas that are state-run throughout Europe, such as the "PTT" (post, telephone, and telegraph) and the railroads. Workers in these industries are not considered civil servants, but top management people are. Every French teacher, from kindergarten to university, is a civil servant.

The civil servants we are concerned with, however, are the several thousand who staff the Paris ministries, the **Grands Corps**, most of whom are graduates of one of the Great Schools. Even more powerful than their British counterparts, French civil servants of the administrative class (about the top 20 percent) run France. If anything, bureaucratic power grew with the coming of the Fifth Republic, for de Gaulle so hamstrung the National Assembly that it could no longer provide a policy counterweight to, or check on, the actions of the top civil servants. Furthermore, by long French tradition, many top politicians were themselves civil servants, often graduates of the ENA or of another *grande école*. Typically, three-fourths of ministers and two-fifths of National Assembly deputies are civil servants. This close connection leads to government of the bureaucrats, by the bureaucrats, and for the bureaucrats.

This is not to say that French bureaucrats run things badly; often they do their jobs very well. It is the bureaucratic attitude that alienates their countrymen: aloof, arrogant, cold, logical, and

tutelle French for tutelage; bureaucratic guidance.

Inspection Short for General Finance Inspection; very top of French bureaucracy, with powers to investigate all branches.

rigid. It is not that they do not meet and interact with other Frenchmen; civil servants sit on thousands of committees and councils all over the country with representatives of business, labor, and farming. The highest of these is the national Social and Economic Council, but even it has a purely advisory capacity, and often advice is ignored as "unobjective." Its composition is increasingly bureaucratic; some 30 percent of its members are named by the government. The French bureaucratic approach is expressed in their term **tutelle**, for they act more as tutors than as servants of the public.

Many say the real elite running France is the *Inspection Générale de Finance*. Selected from among the top ten ENA graduates (see page 125) each year, the superbright *inspecteurs de finances* snoop all around France to see how public funds are spent. All levels of French government are afraid of them. Few countries have the precise equivalent of the **Inspection**. It would be as if the U.S. Government Accountability Office (formerly the General Accounting Office), a branch of Congress, had the enforcement powers of the FBI. *Inspecteurs* of all ranks and ages agree to always see each other. Inspectors who "put on the slippers" (see box below) still have clout, as they offer each other the best public and private jobs. And if they tire of these, they can return to the IGF at a top salary.

GOVERNMENT by BUREAUCRACY

More than in Britain, the civil service in France constitutes a powerful governing body uncontrolled by elected officials, who sometimes denounce the bureaucracy as an "administrative labyrinth" or even as "administrative totalitarianism." But they can do little about it.

We should not think France is unique in this regard, for no country has devised a way to keep its bureaucracy under control. France, with a longer history of bureaucratization and the Great Schools' monopoly over the top civil service, merely reveals the pattern more fully. In Japan, it reaches a high point. In trying to reform, trim, or democratize a bureaucracy we run into a problem: Almost any solution we can think of requires adding *more* bureaucrats. In France, for example, Mitterrand once tried a ministry for the reform of administration—still more bureaucracy.

COMPARISON

"PUTTING ON THE SLIPPERS"

The movement of top French civil servants to the executive suites of industries is called *pantouflage*, or "putting on the slippers." Japan has the exact same pattern, called "descent from heaven." In France, a graduate of the *Ecole Polytechnique* or the ENA, after a few years in a Paris ministry, can slip into a cushy, high-paying management job, often in a firm he or she used to deal with as an official. Over half the chief executives of France's largest firms are former high civil servants, and two-thirds are graduates of the ENA or X. *Pantouflage* is an important connecting link between French business and bureaucracy. It also invites corruption, which seems endemic in France. One top French administrator after another gets caught using business connections to supplement their income.

We can see here why the French people, faced with an unresponsive, undemocratic bureaucratic maze, turn frustrated and bitter. Where bureaucracy thrives, democracy shrivels. In trying to fix this, France's top politicians step into a contradiction. Statism needs lots of bureaucracy—to run welfare programs, supervise industry, and plan the economy. But privatization means loosening bureaucratic controls and letting market forces guide society. Most mainstream French politicians oppose this, for that would mean turning away from what they regard as the humane French model of the welfare state and to a savage "Anglo-Saxon" market system (exception: Sarkozy). Again, France is stuck.

KEY TERMS

bloc (p. 135)	Grands Corps (p. 143)	stalemate (p. 138)
CRS (p. 139)	Inspection (p. 144)	Stalinist (p. 136)
dirigiste (p. 143)	Medef (p. 142)	structured access (p. 143)
Eurocommunism (p. 136)	passé (p. 138)	tutelle (p. 144)
Events of May (p. 139)	protest vote (p. 136)	volatile (p. 134)

FURTHER REFERENCE

Bell, David S. *French Politics Today*. Manchester, UK: Manchester University Press, 2002.

DeClair, Edward G. *Politics on the Fringe: The People, Policies, and Organization of the French National Front*. Durham, NC: Duke University Press, 1999.

Friend, Julius W. *The Long Presidency: France in the Mitterrand Years*. Boulder, CO: Westview, 1998.

Hauss, Charles. *Politics in France*. Washington, D.C.: CQ Press, 2007.

Hewlett, Nick. *Modern French Politics: Analysing Conflict and Consensus since 1945*. Malden, MA: Blackwell, 1998.

Levy, Jonah D. *Tocqueville's Revenge: State, Society, and Economy in Contemporary France*. Cambridge, MA: Harvard University Press, 1999.

Marcus, Jonathan. *The National Front and French Politics: The Resistible Rise of Jean-Marie Le Pen*. New York: New York University Press, 1996.

Pierce, Roy. *Choosing the Chief: Presidential Elections in France and the United States*. Ann Arbor, MI: University of Michigan Press, 1995.

Shields, James. *The Extreme Right in France: From Pétain to Le Pen*. New York: Routledge, 2007.

Wilson, Frank L. *Interest-Group Politics in France*. New York: Cambridge University Press, 1988.

Chapter 11
What the French Quarrel About

The French economy was almost the opposite of the British, which declined after World War II, dropping Britain back among the industrialized countries. The French economy, which had grown only slowly in the nineteenth and early twentieth centuries, awoke as if from a slumber after World War II with growth rates reaching 6 percent a year. The French still remember the period of 1945 to 1975 as *les trentes glorieuses* (the thirty glorious years). After that, however, French growth slowed and unemployment climbed. Most French feel their country is in economic decline. The growth policies of one epoch often fail in the next, and politicians are reluctant to inflict the pain of change on voters.

What invigorated France after World War II? The typical French business firm prior to the war was a small family affair. Growth was not emphasized; keeping it in the family and earning enough for a good living was all that mattered. This meant lots of little companies and stores rather than a few big ones. Rather than compete by lower prices or better goods, the French, with a **petit bourgeois** mentality, sought to hide behind a protective government that would set prices and keep out foreign competition by high tariffs. It was a cozy arrangement for French business families, but it held France's economy back.

World War II jolted the French elite, which, smarting from German conquest and eager to restore France to world leadership, planned a growth economy. A Planning Commission set "indicative plans" to encourage—but not force—French businesses to expand in certain sectors and regions. Quite distinct from Communist-style centralized planning, **indicative planning** in effect said to various industries, "Look, everything is favorable for a new widget factory in the southwest. If you build one you will make a lot of money." With the warm connections between top French bureaucrats and business, businesspeople soon got the hint. The French Planning Commission provided economic research and incentives to nudge businesses along designated paths. (Japan's MITI did this even more; see Chapter 18.)

Foreign competition was another jolt. First, the European Coal and Steel Community (ECSC) in 1952, then the Common Market in 1957, dismantled France's **protective tariffs** (see Chapter 17). At first French businesspeople were terrified, sure that more aggressive German industry would swamp them. But gradually they learned that French firms could compete and gain major sales in the Common Market. French business firms changed, becoming bigger, more modern, and expansion-oriented. But success brought its own problems.

QUESTIONS TO CONSIDER

1. Why did the French economy improve after World War II?
2. Why are too many small farmers and shopkeepers a problem?
3. Why is the state sector of the French economy still large?
4. How do French and U.S. conservatism differ?
5. Why is European unemployment so high?
6. How do U.S. and European views on welfare compare?
7. How does France's racial problem resemble America's?
8. Can sports ease racial tensions?
9. How do France's education problems differ from America's?

Big Guys versus Little Guys

On a street where I lived in Toulouse, in the space of a few blocks, there were at least three different pharmacies, bakeries, butchers, cafés, and houseware, furniture, vegetable, and tobacco shops. Perhaps two miles distant, in a suburb, a one-stop **hypermarché** (fittingly named Mammouth) under one roof combined supermarket (offering perhaps a hundred cheeses), discount house (everything from clothes to auto parts), and cafeteria. Selection and prices were better at Mammouth than among the myriad neighborhood stores. Such developments have been going on throughout France for years. Some call it the Americanization of France, but it is really just the modernization of an old-fashioned economy. The impact on the small shopkeepers is predictable: They are squeezed out, screaming all the way. What they regarded as their birthright—the small, family-owned, uncompetitive shops—are closing. As Marx put it: "One capitalist kills many."

A parallel problem hits French farmers. There are too many small farms; half are run part-time. France remained a nation of peasants an unusually long time. A third of the French workforce

petit bourgeois   Small shopkeeper. (See page 147.)

indicative planning   Government suggestions to industry to expand in certain areas. (See page 147.)

protective tariff   Tax on imported goods to prevent them from competing with domestic products. (See page 147.)

hypermarché   French for "hypermarket," a huge store that sells everything.

COMPARISON

NUCLEAR POWER À LA FRANÇAISE

The French complain and quarrel about many things, but nuclear energy is not one of them. Most French accept nuclear energy, and none of the major parties is against it. The anti-atom Greens won just four seats in the 2007 legislative elections. The French, short of other energy sources, have gone all-out for nuclear-generated electricity and have made a success of it. France has fifty-nine nuclear power stations that produce 79 percent of its electricity, compared to 34 percent in Japan, 31 percent in Germany, 20 percent in Britain, 19 percent in the United States, and 3 percent in India. French nuclear-generated electricity costs less than half of America's. New Hampshire's problem-plagued Seabrook reactor could have been built by the French for one-sixth its actual cost.

How do the French do what Americans cannot? Here we see some of the occasional advantages of centralized, technocratic rule. Electricité de France,

the state-owned utility, developed a single type of reactor and stuck with it. Competing U.S. manufacturers proffered a variety of designs, some not well-tested. When Paris gives the word to build a reactor, the political, financial, regulatory, and managerial sectors mesh under central direction, and the project gets done on time. In the United States, those sectors quarrel and have no central guidance, and the project takes years longer than it should. Environmentalist groups in France—not very big or powerful groups anyway—have no legal power to block or delay projects. The centralized French system is also better able to train personnel; there have been no Three Mile Islands in France. Nuclear power plants are an important part of France's export trade. The very strengths of the American system—decentralization, competition, light regulation, and pluralist interplay—have tripped up the U.S. nuclear industry.

was still on the land at the end of World War II. With postwar industrialization this changed so that now only 4 percent of the labor force works in agriculture. Since 1950, three-fourths of France's farms, mostly small, have disappeared. Still, French agriculture, like

---

entrepreneurial Starting your own business.

---

its U.S. counterpart, overproduces, and French farmers often dump produce on highways to protest what they regard as inadequate prices. France is the world's second largest food exporter (first place: the United States) and the EU's largest food producer. One French idea: Instead of subsidizing farmers to produce more than is needed, pay them to look after the environment.

The small shopkeepers and farmers who are squeezed out contribute to France's electoral volatility. They shift allegiances rapidly, to whoever promises their survival. The Gaullists have been a major beneficiary, but the frightened shopkeepers have also contributed to extremist parties. There is no nice solution to the problem of too many small shops and farms; they must go, and it hurts. Attempts to retain them are hopeless and reactionary, the stuff demagoguery is made of. (Think this is a French problem? How do U.S. communities react to a proposed Wal-Mart?)

In 1953, for example, Pierre Poujade founded the Union for the Defense of Shopkeepers and Artisans (UDCA) to protect small-business people from the bigger, more efficient department stores and supermarkets that were driving many of them out of business. Tinged with reaction and anti-Semitism, Poujadism caught fire, and in the parliamentary elections of 1956

COMPARISON

WHO HAS THE MOST RED TAPE?

Enterprise and **entrepreneurial** are French words but not French practice. French laws and regulations make France one of the hardest places to start your own business. The OECD rates government burdens and regulations on entrepreneurship, with 6 as the most restrictive. The figures for 1999 are shown in the table below.

Starting a business is easier in Britain than in the United States and much easier than in France. President Sarkozy vowed to trim regulations, but that goes against France's statist tradition.

France	2.75
Italy	2.75
Japan	2.30
Germany	2.10
Sweden	1.80
Netherlands	1.40
United States	1.25
Britain	0.50

won 12 percent of the popular vote; some thought it was the coming party. It turned out to be a **flash party**, however; Poujadism disappeared in 1958 when de Gaulle took over the French right. Le Pen was a Poujadist and, some say, continues its views in his National Front.

The Privatization Question

For much of the postwar period, one-fourth of French business and industry was state-owned, more than any other West European country. Now, after major privatization programs, one-quarter of the French work force (including police, military, and school teachers) is still in the public sector, among the highest in Europe. In addition, the French government has majority ownership of some 1,500 private-sector businesses. Some industries such as telecoms and railways were state-owned in Europe from the start. Some, such as cars and steel, were taken over because without government subsidies they would close, creating unemployment. High-tech areas such as aircraft, nuclear power, and computers are state-owned prestige industries that boost France's world standing but often lose money.

flash party   One that quickly rises and falls.

protectionism   Keeping out imports via tariffs and regulations in order to help domestic producers.

Traditionally, the French left demanded more nationalization, including all big banks and industries. They argued that under state control big industries would pay workers fairly, hire more people, and produce what French people really need rather than capitalist luxuries that only a few can afford. Traditionally, much of the French right also liked state-owned industries, believing that they contributed to national power and greatness and were best run by brilliant *xiens* and *énarques* (see page 125). De Gaulle, for example, supported a major state sector in heavy and high-tech industry.

Political Culture

The French and Statism

Starting far back in the Old Regime, *étatisme* (statism) became part of French political culture. Also early, some French thinkers recognized that it was bad economics. France coined the term *laissez-faire* ("leave us be"). The French Physiocrats in the eighteenth century invented the free-market argument and profoundly influenced Adam Smith. In the mid-nineteenth century, French economist Frédéric Bastiat ridiculed trade **protectionism** by suggesting Paris protect French candlemakers from "the ruinous competition of a foreign rival"—the sun.

For many French, state ownership and protectionism just seem right, and it is not only a question of culture. Many employees owe their jobs and retirement at age 55 to state supervision of the economy. The political elite is trained in the statist mold of the ENA. Virtually all French politicians oppose full capitalism. Gaullist former President Chirac swore "France will never let Europe become a mere free-trade area." His premier, Dominique de Villepin, called protectionism "economic patriotism." Earlier Socialist Premier Jospin (1997–2002) said firms should not be free to let workers go. In France, welfare, statism, and protectionism are entwined in French identity and worked to defeat the new European constitution in 2005 (see Chapter 17).

Remember, **conservatism** in Europe is not the same as conservatism in America. In the 2007 elections, no party ran as free-marketeers.

Waves of privatization and deregulation by both left and right governments roll in about every two decades but then roll back, leaving France still with a great deal of state ownership, controls, and rules that always need to be pruned. French leaders flinch at thorough privatization because they fear making unemployment, already high, any worse. French public-sector unions demonstrate against privatization, which would end their high pay and early retirements.

The center-right UDF had perhaps the strongest commitment to privatization, but the pain of change led to the Socialist victory of 1981. Good economics is sometimes bad politics. But, as Mitterrand discovered, good politics is sometimes bad economics. Generous policies on welfare, wages, and benefits brought inflation, stagnation, and higher unemployment. The Socialists nationalized several large firms and banks and then discovered that they were money-losers. In 1983, Mitterrand reversed course in favor of private business and a market economy. "You do not want more state?" asked Mitterrand. "Me neither." (Compare with Clinton: "The era of big

conservatism   Desire to preserve or return to old ways.

COMPARISON

THE CONCORDE: TECHNOLOGICAL NATIONALISM

The United States has private firms such as Boeing to build jetliners. Europe uses state-owned firms. The Concorde supersonic aircraft illustrates what goes wrong with nationalized industries: They can build the wrong product for the wrong reason and cost taxpayers a fortune. The Concorde's development began in 1962 as a joint Anglo-French enterprise to give their lagging aircraft industries a technological jump on the Americans. They thought it would be purchased by airlines all over the world.

But huge overruns boosted development costs to $4.28 billion and the price per plane to $92 million, close to ten times what had been estimated. The Concorde consumed three times the fuel per passenger mile of a Boeing 747. Only British and French airlines purchased Concordes and then only because their nationalized air carriers were required to by law. Because they seldom filled their one hundred seats, the airlines lost money on Concorde runs. Only fourteen Concordes were ever finished before production shut down in 1978.

Why did Britain and France do it? A nationalized industry often has different priorities than a normal commercial venture. In this case "technological nationalism"

was a factor; that is, they felt they had to boost their high-tech industries or lose to U.S. dominance. Employment was another factor; Britain and France created thousands of jobs with the Concorde. Once the project was underway and the cost overruns mounting, neither country wanted to admit it had made a mistake. Because the Concorde's makers had access to their national treasuries, they did not have to undergo the discipline of raising capital in the marketplace.

This is not to say that nationalized industries always do things wrong. Aerospatiale of France finally dropped Concorde to form the Airbus consortium, whose shares are owned by both private investors and several European governments. Airbus competes with Boeing and is used by some U.S. airlines. In 2004 Airbus flew its A380 super-jumbo, a challenge to the Boeing 747. Airbus, however, still gets government subsidies. Boeing charged unfairness, but Airbus points out that Boeing was also subsidized through defense contracts to develop bombers, then used the technology for passenger planes. (Boeing's 707 jetliner was a lot like its B-52 bomber; prototypes of both first flew in 1954.)

labor-force rigidities   Unwillingness of workers to take or change jobs.

social costs   Taxes for medical, unemployment, and pension benefits.

informal economy   Off-the-books transactions to avoid taxes and regulations.

government is over.") Believers in socialism had received a real slap in the face and some abandoned their leftism. Chirac, first as premier and later as president, reoriented the Gaullists toward privatization of state-owned industry. Much was sold, but unemployment was so huge it led to the Socialists' 1997 parliamentary election victory. Jospin promised to slow or reverse privatization, but in practice he sold more French state-owned enterprises than all five of his immediate predecessors put together. He never, however, used the word "privatization," for that would be following an Anglo-Saxon policy. Even reformist President Sarkozy, who favors vigorous free markets, was cautious about using the word privatization.

UNEMPLOYMENT: THE GIANT PROBLEM

Unemployment in France (and West Europe generally) has long been high and seemingly incurable, at times twice the U.S. level. And Europe's high unemployment has occurred when, for the most part, its economies were growing. Many believe the key problem is European **labor-force rigidities**. These are related to West Europe's generous welfare and unemployment benefits, which discourage many unemployed Europeans from seeking new jobs. Wages and **social costs** are so high that European firms are reluctant to hire new workers. A French employer pays almost half as much in taxes as in wages, a German employer even more. And there are some forty deductions that must be enumerated on French pay stubs, drastically increasing paperwork. Laws in most of Europe prevent easy layoffs; when a firm lets a worker go it must give hefty severance pay.

Hence, the reluctance of French (and German) firms to hire: It is too expensive, involves much red tape, and you may not be able to let workers go in a downturn. The solution for business people: Either (1) do not hire anyone, or (2) hire on the **informal economy**, or (3) set up shop

COMPARISON

EUROPEAN AND U.S. ATTITUDES TOWARD WELFARE

France, like most of Europe, approves of a more extensive, and expensive, welfare state than Americans do. The French constitution, for example, promises a "decent means of existence." French welfare recipients get about 50 percent more than their U.S. counterparts. Most Americans are delighted to cut welfare benefits and drop recipients off welfare rolls.

There is clearly a major cultural difference here. Many European politicians, especially but not exclusively leftists, attack the "savage" unrestrained capitalism of America and point to its large underclass. "We

will not become like the cruel U.S. economy," they say (not noticing France's large Muslim underclass). Not many Americans see their economy as savage or cruel; most see it as flexible and competitive with opportunities for all. Making something of that opportunity is up to individuals. Sociologist Seymour Martin Lipset defined the American ethos as "competitive individualism." Europeans tend to solidarity, to the view that society as a whole should look out for its weakest members. Like any element of culture, this view does not change easily.

in another country. French businesses do all three. Europe's high off-the-books workforce indicates an economy choked with taxes and controls. In France, as in all of Europe, the working class generally votes left to protect jobs and wages—never mind if protection creates inefficiencies and unemployment—while managers press to roll back restrictions and free up the labor market. The U.S. labor force is much more flexible; wages and social costs are low; and hiring and layoffs are easy. Result: The U.S. economy creates far more new jobs a year, something West Europeans envy.

austerity Drastically holding down government expenses.

High French unemployment also puts a brake on further privatization. As we noted, one-fourth of French workers are employed in the public sector, compared to one-seventh in the United States and Britain, and one-sixth in Germany. Those figures are not just "bureaucrats" but anyone who works for any form or level of government, including military personnel, police, and schoolteachers. French public-sector workers enjoy job security plus good pay, benefits, and retirement plans. Their unions stage strikes over any efforts to trim these bounties, and Paris usually backs down, a pattern shared by other statist systems. President Sarkozy's soon faced strikes by public-sector unions over their lush retirement benefits that permitted railway, metro, and electricity workers to retire young on full pensions. Public opinion favored Sarkozy.

Another contributor to high unemployment: the euro (see page 241). In order to join Europe's single-currency club, France had to bring France's budget deficit down to 3 percent of GDP and maintain a *franc fort* (strong franc). Britain said to hell with the euro and dropped out of the European Monetary Union, but Chirac was determined, partly for reasons of prestige, to stay in, whatever the domestic economic costs. Many considered Chirac's **austerity** policy foolishly rigid and the chief cause of high unemployment and his loss in the snap parliamentary elections of

KEY CONCEPTS

EUROPEAN AND U.S.-STYLE CONSERVATISM

American students have difficulty understanding that conservatism in Europe is not the same as in the United States. For Europeans, U.S.-style conservatism is not conservatism at all; it is the classic *liberalism* of Adam Smith: little government and a free market. European conservatism hearkens back to a time when monarchs and aristocrats ruled and a strong state supervised the economy for the sake of national power. In the twentieth century, European conservatives transferred their loyalties to strong leaders and saw nothing wrong with statism and the welfare state. Prime examples: de Gaulle and the Gaullists.

Gradually, however, U.S.-style conservatism took hold in European conservative parties, spurred on by intellectuals who saw that defending old class privileges and uncompetitive, state-owned industries retards growth and job creation. They called the movement "neo-liberalism," a revival and updating of Adam Smith. Prime examples: Margaret Thatcher and the Tory "dries." The movement appeared in France with Premier Raymond Barre's efforts in the late 1970s to liberalize the French economy. Even the Socialists realized in the early 1980s that state ownership of industry was a problem. Now Sarkozy is attempting neo-liberal economic policies. France has privatized much industry but is unlikely to go all the way to a U.S.-style free market because the French have a cultural block against what they call "savage liberalism." A 2006 poll found that 71 percent of Americans said a free-market economy is best, compared to 66 percent of Britons, 65 percent of Germans, but only 36 percent of French.

value-added taxes   (VAT), large, hidden national sales taxes used throughout Europe.

1997. In the 2000s, both France and Germany routinely exceeded the 3 percent deficit limit to bring down unemployment. Sarkozy bluntly told the EU he would do the same.

How to cure unemployment? All incoming French governments swear it is their top priority, but most are voted out in part because they fail to make a dent in the problem. The Jospin government's bright idea came from Germany: France cut its work week from thirty-nine to thirty-five hours without cuts in pay on the theory that this would force firms to hire more workers. Results were mixed but not all bad, because it forces firms to become more efficient, so labor productivity increased to among the world's highest.

In 1997 Jospin said that he would create 350,000 jobs, mostly for young people, in health services, schools, welfare, transportation, and construction. Almost reflexively, Paris turns to statist remedies. Recipients got five-year contracts at minimum wage ($1,100 a month), most of it from government. Little came of the program. Hiring for public projects at taxpayers' expense seldom yields long-term solutions. For that, France will have to end laws that keep firms from easily hiring and firing. France made a step in that direction with a 2006 law allowing workers under age 26 to be fired with no delay or reason within their first two years on a job. Most French opposed the move and young people protested in the streets, so the government dropped the plan. The French, like many Europeans, have difficulty understanding that making it hard to let workers go means firms hire few new workers even in good times; they fear getting stuck with them in slack times. America's easy-hire, easy-fire policy contributes to labor-force flexibility and low U.S. unemployment rates.

The latest attempt to free up the French economy came with President Sarkozy, who sought new laws to overcome the thirty-five-hour work week by taxing overtime pay more lightly: "Work more to earn more." He also proposed later retirement, less bureaucracy, and ending unemployment benefits if recipients rejected two valid job offers. No one has come up with a legislative cure

COMPARISON

IS THERE A VAT IN OUR FUTURE?

Throughout Europe, governments raise close to 30 percent of their revenues through hefty (10 to 20 percent) **value-added taxes** (VAT). In contrast, U.S. sales taxes, mostly at the state level, average around 6 percent and altogether make up only 15 percent of all U.S. taxes (federal, state, and local). But European VATs are invisible; they are calculated at every stage that value is added to a product (for example, after pieces of cloth are sewn together to make a shirt), not added to the purchase price at the cash register, as in America. Accordingly, European governments reason that it is not so painful as other kinds of taxes.

Under the Bush 43 administration, Republicans, having run up massive budget deficits, floated the idea of a "consumption tax" or "national sales tax," in effect a VAT. They had cut income taxes and swore they would never raise them again. A tax on consumption would encourage Americans to save more and make more money available for loans to expand the economy. Because people would be less eager to spend, a VAT slows inflationary tendencies. A VAT, however, is a regressive tax, hitting the poor, working class, and retirees harder than the rich. Few gave an American VAT much chance of becoming law.

for unemployment. It will take a change in French psychology from valuing leisure to valuing work. Thatcher was partly successful in this in Britain. Can Sarkozy do it in France?

Muslim Follower of Islam; also adjective of *Islam*.

FRANCE'S RACIAL PROBLEMS

France has a worse problem with immigrants than Britain and Germany (and the United States). There are some 9 million foreigners living in France (if one counts naturalized citizens and the second generation), about 16 percent of the French population. France has long assimilated European immigrants. From 1880 to 1960 some 7 million Italians, Spaniards, Portuguese, Poles, and Russians were integrated into French society.

But starting in the 1960s, many **Muslims** arrived and fueled major racial tensions. Now numbering between 5 and 6 million, perhaps 9 percent of France's population, most are from former French colonies in West and North Africa—such as Algeria, Morocco, Tunisia, Senegal, and Mali. They flee misery and unemployment to take the hardest, dirtiest, lowest-paid work in France, but many are still unemployed, especially young people. They live in shabby high-rise public housing. When I stayed in the suburb of Aulnay-sous-Bois northeast of Paris in 1989, I reckoned that one-third of my fellow rail commuters were African or Arab. One French homeowner there ruefully wisecracked that it had become "Aulnay-sous-Cameroun." (In 2005, rioting hit Aulnay.)

Most French say there are too many Muslims in France, and some want them sent home, which the National Front advocates. All of France's main parties are against any more newcomers, so that now (legal) immigration is as tight as in Britain, and France turns away hundreds of

GEOGRAPHY

THE GEOGRAPHY OF MIGRATION

Everywhere the Third World is trying to sneak into the First. The reason: economic opportunities. Pakistanis in Britain, Algerians in France, Turks in Germany, and Mexicans in the United States are all expressions of the same problem: not enough jobs in the home country. Japan tries to block foreign job-seekers, but even there one finds Filipino, Thai, Sri Lankan, and other workers. There is one place on earth where you can walk from the Third World into the First: the Mexico-U.S. border. In a kind of osmosis, migrants are drawn through a membrane (border) by the pressure of unemployment and low living standards.

But is this a problem? From a purely economic standpoint, no. The immigrants take jobs local people shun in favor of welfare. And, as we shall consider in Chapter 16, the rich countries have few babies and rapidly growing numbers of retirees. Without immigrants, there would be too few workers to pay for the oldsters' pensions. Part of the problem is that immigrants preserve their old cultures in the new country. In France, discrimination and limited schooling mean immigrants and their children do not master French, gain no job skills, and become ghettoized into crime, drugs, and even extremist Muslim organizations. This in turn fuels resentment against immigrants and has led to the British and French National Fronts and the German National Democrats. Closely parallel: the U.S. movement against illegal immigrants.

thousands of desperate refugees each year. Said Sarkozy (whose father fled Hungary): "France needs immigrants, but France cannot and should not welcome *all* immigrants."

The French republican ideal posits a single French identity without subgroups. France has no affirmative action and does not even collect official data on racial, religious, and ethnic groups, the way the U.S. Census does. Increasingly, critics say such statistics are needed to overcome the very obvious racial gaps. France now has millions of citizens of color who are treated as permanent foreigners. Said one West African who was educated in France: "The French don't think I'm French."

COMPARISON

MEDICAL CARE AND COSTS

France delivers some of the world's best medical care at moderate cost, the World Health Organization concluded. Medical care is tricky to measure, and the 2000 WHO study, the first to compare medical delivery worldwide, was so controversial it has not been updated. Japanese are the healthiest people in the world (probably related to diet) and spend less, but those are indications of health, not of medical care. The two are not the same. Health is what God gives you, plus diet and exercise. Medical care is what doctors and hospitals give you. Spending more on the latter does little to improve the former. Some figures are shown in the table below.

Worldwide, medical costs are increasing, from 3 percent of gross world product in 1948 to 7.9 percent half a century later. Americans spend by far the most on medical care but are less healthy than many who spend less (again, diet). The U.S. government does little to hold down costs, so insurance (some Medicare, mostly private) struggles to keep up with high-tech care and new, costlier drugs. Some 45 million uninsured Americans hope they do not get sick. Most of Europe has nationwide insurance (some public, some private) that covers everyone and caps costs. But Europeans pay in other ways, by long waits and not-so-high-tech treatment: de facto rationing. Will the United States have to do something similar to hold down its soaring medical costs?

	WHO Ranking	Medical Costs per Person/Yr.	Percent of GDP
France	1	$3,300	10.5
Japan	10	2,580	7.8
Britain	18	2,570	8.1
Germany	25	3,380	10.6
United States	37	6,770	15.4
Mexico	61	690	6.5
Iran	93	570	6.6
India	112	190	5.0
Russia	130	732	6.0
China	144	360	4.7
Nigeria	187	69	4.6

Source: World Health Organization

France now has angry Muslim youths who look a lot like the black underclass of U.S. ghettoes. Although most of these Muslim youths were born in France, they are still called "immigrants" and are largely outside French society. Often from broken homes, they slide into gangs, drugs, and petty crime. A few are drawn to Islamic extremism. The police harass them, and they hate the police. "No one will give you a job," said one youth. "How long can we stand here before we blow a fuse?" In 2005, the fuse blew as young males, mostly Muslim, rioted for three weeks across France and burned more than 8,000 cars. Tough police methods and a curfew finally quelled the riots. Then-Interior Minister Sarkozy, in charge of France's police, called the rioters "scum" and vowed to "clean out" their neighborhoods. Most French agreed, but few said so openly. Smaller rioting broke out in 2007. The problem is far from solved.

> **social mobility** Movement of individuals from one class to another, usually upward.

A running issue was *l'affaire du foulard* ("the question of the headscarf"), Muslim girls wearing the traditional *hijab*, required by their religion, in school. France, intent of keeping religion out of schools, outlawed it in 2004. Thundered one *imam* (Muslim cleric): "Allah's law takes precedence over French law." The French deported him, as they do any Muslim preacher who advocates *jihad*. A 1996 French law lets judges detain people for "association with wrongdoers involved in a terrorist enterprise." Faced with terrorism, the French are not as fastidious on human rights as the British or Germans. After 9/11 and the London bombings, the United States and Britain both moved closer to the French zero-tolerance position.

Most French politicians agree that the immigrants should be better integrated into French economic and cultural life, but they disagree on how. Improving the immigrants' housing, schooling, and jobs all cost money. The tax burden falls most heavily on the municipalities where there are the most immigrants, one reason the National Front vote is the strongest where there are more Muslims. The Socialist and other parties on the left are more willing to spend additional funds. Trying to curb radical tendencies and encourage dialogue, Paris in 2003 created the French Council of the Muslim Faith. In 2005, some 5,000 French Muslim delegates elected a moderate Council board.

Racial amity gets brief boosts when the French soccer team wins major matches, because many players are black or brown. France erupts with pride. France's (and possibly Europe's) top footballer was Zinedine Zidane, born in Marseilles of Algerian parents (he retired in 2006). Sports may be more important than government programs in fostering racial integration. (Is that true in the United States?)

FRANCE'S EDUCATION PROBLEMS

France has expanded educational opportunity in order to improve **social mobility** and integrate all, even immigrants, into French society. This effort is praiseworthy, reminiscent of U.S. efforts to solve social problems by increased school integration. But, as in the United States, it leads to new problems.

Paris decided that a much larger portion of French young people should achieve the "bac," discussed in Chapter 9. The Socialist government in 1985 began an ambitious plan to send 80 percent of all young people to *lycées* by 2000, a goal largely achieved. The bac has been expanded to include technical and vocational options in order to form the literate and qualified labor force needed by a modern economy. But even with a major upsurge in education spending, the public *lycée* system became severely overburdened, as evidenced by dilapidated buildings, crowded classrooms (some with over 40 students per teacher), and crime in the hallways and restrooms. (Sound

---

Common Agricultural Program (CAP), EU farm subsidies, the biggest part of the EU budget.

---

familiar?) Middle-class French parents, afraid of school decay, increasingly send their children to private *lycées*. French student street protests from time to time shake the Paris government, reminders of the 1968 Events of May.

FRANCE AND EUROPE

Unlike Britain, France did not hang back in building a united Europe. Indeed, the idea originated with two French officials, Jean Monnet and Robert Schuman, after World War II (see Chapter 17). France was one of the original six of the ECSC and then of the Common Market. Members cut tariffs with each other and let in workers from member countries. The invigorating effects of this boosted French economic growth. The EU's **Common Agricultural Program** (CAP) eats 40 percent of the EU budget, and French farmers are the biggest beneficiaries. French farmers like this; German and Dutch taxpayers do not.

French voters rejected a new EU constitution 55 to 45 percent in 2005. Most still favor the EU in general but used the referendum to show their displeasure with the elites who run France and the EU. Most French leaders favor European unification, partly because they see France leading a united Europe, but they disagree on what kind of a Europe they want. Not all want a full federation, for that would blot out French sovereignty. Charles de Gaulle voiced this in the 1960s when he spoke of a *Europe des patries* ("Europe of fatherlands," later the view of Britain's Margaret Thatcher). This is especially true if newly unified Germany is Europe's leader, not France. And how big should the EU be? Should it include Turkey? Sarkozy says no way. The further eastward the EU expands, the more it makes Germany its natural hub. Many French oppose that privately but rarely say so publicly. Since German unification in 1871—after it beat France in a war—France has always worried about its large, powerful neighbor to the east, to which we now turn.

KEY TERMS

austerity (p. 153)
Common Agricultural
  Program (p. 158)
conservatism (p. 151)
entrepreneurial (p. 149)
flash party (p. 150)

hypermarché (p. 148)
indicative planning (p. 148)
informal economy (p. 152)
labor-force rigidities (p. 152)
Muslim (p. 155)
petit bourgeois (p. 148)

protectionism (p. 150)
protective tariff (p. 148)
social costs (p. 152)
social mobility (p. 157)
value-added tax (p. 154)

FURTHER REFERENCE

Culpepper, Pepper D., Peter A. Hall, and Bruno Palier, eds. *Changing France: The Politics That Markets Make*. New York: Palgrave, 2006.

Favell, Adrian. *Philosophies of Integration: Immigration and the Idea of Citizenship in France and Britain*. New York: St. Martin's, 1998.

Fenby, Jonathan. *France on the Brink*. New York: Arcade, 1999.

Fysh, Peter, and Jim Wolfreys. *The Politics of Racism in France*. New York: St. Martin's, 1998.

Gildea, Robert. *France since 1945*. New York: Oxford University Press, 1996.

Laurence, Jonathan, and Justin Vaïsse. *Integrating Islam: Political and Religious Challenges in Contemporary France*. Washington, D.C.: Brookings, 2006.

Schmidt, Vivien A. *From State to Market? The Transformation of French Business and Government*. New York: Cambridge University Press, 1996.

Simmons, Harvey G. *The French National Front: The Extremist Challenge to Democracy*. Boulder, CO: Westview, 1996.

Smith, Timothy B. *France in Crisis: Welfare, Inequality, and Globalization since 1980*. New York: Cambridge University Press, 2005.

Chapter 12

Germany:
The Impact of the Past

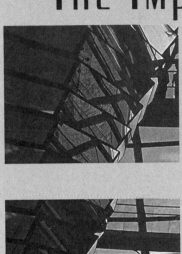

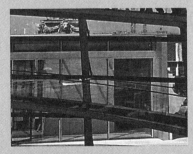
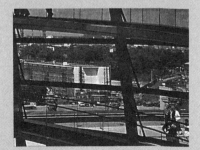

Britain has natural borders. France claims to have natural borders, but one of its six sides (the east) has been disputed. Germany, however, has natural borders only on its north and south (the Baltic Sea and Alps), and this fact has contributed to its tumultuous history. Germany has expanded and contracted over the centuries, at times stretching from Alsace (now French) to East Prussia (now Polish and Russian). After World War II its eastern wing was chopped off, and the country was divided into eastern and western occupation zones, which in 1949 became East and West Germany. The Federal Republic of Germany that reunified in 1990 is considerably smaller than the mighty Second Reich at the turn of the century.

Germany's location in the center of Europe and the flat, defenseless North European Plain imposed two unhappy options on it. When Germany was divided and militarily weak—its condition throughout most of history—it was Europe's battleground. On the other hand, when Germany united and became militarily strong enough to deter any combination of potential attackers, it was also strong enough to beat them all one at a time. When Germany unified in the nineteenth century, it automatically became a threat to the rest of Europe; it was big, populous, and strategically located. Some Europeans still fear a united Germany.

QUESTIONS TO CONSIDER

1. What are Germany's geographic problems?
2. How was Germany the opposite of French centralization?
3. What did *cuius regio* attempt to solve? How?
4. What did Prussia contribute to Germany?
5. How did nationalism combine with racism in Germany?
6. What were the First, Second, and Third Reichs?
7. How did Bismarck retard Germany's democratic development?
8. Why was the Weimar Republic doomed?
9. What were the main elements of Nazism?

WHO ARE THE GERMANS?

Contrary to Nazi race theory, the Germans are an ethnic mixture. The original Germans identified by the Romans were a collection of several barbarian tribes, some of which became Romanized. The invasion of the Huns in the fourth century set off vast migrations throughout Europe. Many Germans sought refuge in Roman territory, and Rome hired some as mercenaries. Soon Germanic tribes were roaming through and destroying the Roman Empire and settling in various parts of it.

Since that time Germans have presented one face to the West and another to the East. To the West—to France and Italy—the heirs of Rome, they were respectful of their older high culture, which they tried to copy. To the East, however, they saw barbarians—first Huns, then Slavs—whom they either Germanized, exterminated, or pushed back. Whole Slavic- or Baltic-speaking areas were

Germany

Germanized, and many of today's Germans are of East European descent. The Nazis hated to admit it, but Germans are a combination of Celts, Romans, Jews, several Germanic tribes, Slavs, and Balts. When the Nazis introduced their model of the perfect Nordic specimen, some quietly chuckled, for very few of the Nazi leaders matched the tall, athletic, blond, blue-eyed image.

THE FRAGMENTED NATION

The Germanic tribes were so impressed by Rome—whose empire they were destroying—that they pretended to continue the empire. When in 800 the Frankish king Charlemagne (German: Karl der Grosse) was crowned in Rome, he called his gigantic realm the Holy Roman Empire (which, Voltaire later quipped, was "neither holy, nor Roman, nor an empire"). Although it soon fell apart, the German wing continued calling itself that until Napoleon ended the fiction in 1806.

Habsburg   Leading Catholic dynasty that once held Austria-Hungary, Spain, Latin America, and the Netherlands.

Thirty Years War   1618–1648 Habsburg attempt to conquer and Catholicize Europe.

Westphalia   Treaty ending Thirty Years War.

In England, power between king and nobles was kept in balance, resulting in a constitutional monarchy that moved in spurts toward civil liberty, limited government, and rule by Parliament. In France, absolutism upset the balance as the French kings amassed power leading to a centralized, bureaucratic state. Germany went the other way: The nobles gained more power until, by the thirteenth century, the emperor was a mere figurehead while princes and leading churchmen ran ministates as they saw fit. Germany was not one country but a crazy quilt of hundreds of independent principalities and cities.

The split between Roman Catholics and Protestants accentuated Germany's fragmentation. Protestant reformer Martin Luther in the early sixteenth century reflected the feeling of much of northern Germany that the Roman church was corrupt and ungodly. The North German princes especially did not like paying taxes to Rome and found Lutheranism a good excuse to stop. South Germany and the Rhineland stayed mostly Catholic, the north and east predominantly Protestant, a pattern that still characterizes modern Germany.

Two wars resulted from the religious question. In the first, the Schmalkaldic War (named after the town of Schmalkalden where Protestant princes formed a coalition) of 1545–1555, the **Habsburg** Emperor Charles V nearly succeeded in crushing Lutheranism. The Protestants, however, allied with Catholic France to beat Charles. Trying to decide which parts of Germany should be Catholic and which Protestant, the Religious Peace of Augsburg in 1555 came up with the formula *cuius regio eius religio*—"whoever reigns, his religion." Thus the religion of the local prince decided an area's religion, a point that deepened the disunity of Germany and the power of local princes.

The peace proved shaky, though, and in 1618, as the Habsburgs again tried to consolidate their power, a much worse war broke out, the **Thirty Years War**. Again, at first the Catholic Habsburgs won. By 1631, help from other countries arrived. Cardinal Richelieu feared Habsburg power would encircle France, so he aided the Protestants. In international relations, power and national interests are more important than religious or ideological affinity. A strong Swedish army under Gustavus Adolphus battled in Germany for the Protestants. Germany suffered terribly, losing perhaps 30 percent of its population, most by starvation. Until World War I, the Thirty Years War was the worst in human history. The Treaty of **Westphalia** in 1648 confirmed *cuius regio* and left Germany atomized into 360 separate political entities.

The Changing Shape of Germany

800: Charlemagne's Holy Roman Empire

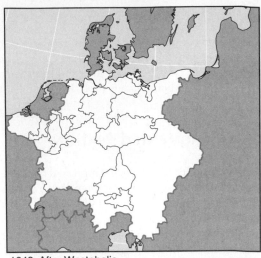

1648: After Westphalia

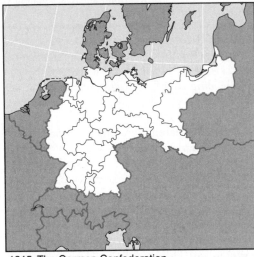

1815: The German Confederation

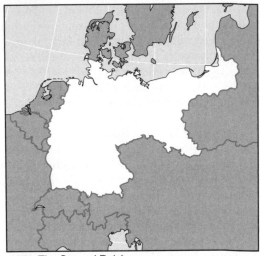

1871: The Second Reich

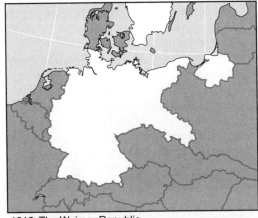

1919: The Weimar Republic

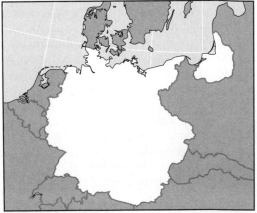

1939: Hitler's Third Reich

1945: Occupied Germany (Four Zones)

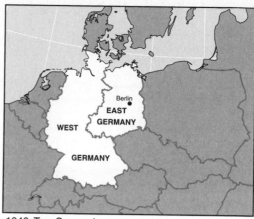

1949: Two Germanies

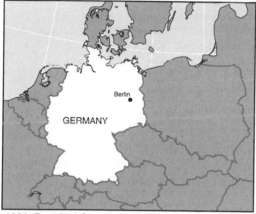

1990: Reunited Germany

Consider the political impact of religion on the three countries we have studied so far. England broke with Rome; the return of Catholic kings merely confirmed the power of Parliament. In France, the Catholic Church and *ancien régime* stayed loyal to one another while many French turned anticlerical, dividing French society into conservative Catholics and anticlerical radicals. Germany did not split into clerical and anticlerical but into Catholic and Protestant. The result was ghastly: a long and ruinous war, further breakup of an already fragmented country, and centuries of ill will between Germans of different faiths.

Prussia Powerful North German state; capital Berlin.

The Rise of Prussia

One German state eventually came to dominate the others. Brandenburg, later known as **Prussia**, expanded greatly during the eighteenth century, taking over the eastern German conquests of the Middle Ages along the Baltic and adding Silesia and parts of the Rhineland. In the eastern Baltic regions, a type of nobility had developed, descended from the old Teutonic knights, which

Junker From *junge Herren,* young gentlemen, pronounced YOON care; Prussian nobility.

had a major impact on German history. The **Junkers** held great estates worked by obedient serfs. Unlike the English lords, however, they did not retain their independence and act as a counterweight to the king but became a state nobility, dependent on the government

GEOGRAPHY

BOUNDARIES: LINES ON A MAP

Precisely where one state leaves off and another begins is often unsettled. Looking at maps, you might think that boundary lines are real, perhaps decreed by nature or hallowed by time. In point of fact, almost all boundaries are artificial, some more artificial than others.

Germany's boundaries, for example, consolidated, expanded, and contracted with great fluidity. Consider the maps of Germany (on pages 164–165) over the centuries. Germany's boundaries were drawn widest under Bismarck in 1871 and under Hitler before and during World War II. The Second Reich included much of present-day Poland and a large sweep of Prussia to the east. With defeat in World War I, Germany lost part of Prussia and Pomerania to make a "Polish corridor" to the Baltic. Alsace returned to France. Hitler expanded the map of Germany by adding Austria, Bohemia (now the Czech Republic), Alsace, and parts of Poland. These lands were immediately stripped away with Germany's defeat in World War II. Germany was also two countries from 1949 to 1990.

Which are the "correct" boundaries for Germany? It is impossible to apply historical, moral, or even demographic standards to determine with certainty Germany's boundaries. One might attempt, as Hitler did, to draw Germany's borders so as to include all Germans. But the peoples of Europe—as in most of the world—are not neatly arrayed in demographic ranks, with, say, Germans on one side of a river and Poles on the other. Instead, they are often "interdigitized," with some German villages in Polish territory and Poles living in some German cities. Whatever border you draw will leave some Germans in Poland and some Poles in Germany.

Poland's boundaries are a perplexing example of border questions. As the empires that had partitioned Poland since the 1790s (German, Austrian, and Russian empires) collapsed in World War I, Polish patriots under

Pilsudski reestablished Poland, but it included many Lithuanians, Belorussians, and Ukrainians. Stalin never liked that boundary and during World War II pushed Soviet borders westward. In compensation, Poland got former German territories, so that now its western border is formed by the Oder and Neisse Rivers. Millions of Germans were expelled. In effect, Poland was picked up and moved over 100 miles westward! After much hesitation (because of German interest groups from the Oder-Neisse territories), Germany confirmed the new boundary.

Only boundaries that have been set up and observed over the centuries are without controversy. To be legal, a border must be agreed upon in a boundary treaty and demarcated with physical indicators, such as concrete pylons. Few borders in the world are like that.

Control of borders is a chief attribute of sovereignty, and nations go to great lengths to demonstrate that they alone are in charge of who and what goes in and goes out across their borders. One of the first points of violence in Lithuania and Slovenia were their passport and customs houses. In forcibly taking over these border checkpoints, Soviet and Yugoslav federal forces in 1991 respectively attempted to show that they, rather than the breakaway republics, were in charge of the entire national territory. They did not succeed, and their countries fragmented.

Boundary questions abound, such as India's border with Pakistan (especially over Kashmir), China's borders with India and with Russia, Venezuela with Guyana, Argentina with Chile (over Tierra del Fuego) and with Britain (over the Falklands), Syria with Lebanon (over the Bekaa Valley), Morocco with Algeria (over the former Spanish Sahara), and Iraq with Iran (over the Shatt al-Arab waterway). Such questions cause wars.

and controlling all the higher civil-service and military positions. Famous for their discipline and attention to detail, the Junkers contributed to modern Germany a passion for control in both military and civil administration.

> **nationalism**   Belief in greatness and unity of one's country and hatred of rule by foreigners.

Prussian kings, with potential enemies on all sides, became obsessed with military power, leading to Voltaire's wisecrack that "Prussia is not a country with an army but an army with a country." In the early eighteenth century, King Frederick William acted as drillmaster to his entire people, demanding military obedience and Prussian efficiency, not only on the parade ground—where he personally marched his handpicked corps of oversize soldiers—but in civilian life as well. Especially in Prussia, obedience to authority became a German character trait.

His son, Frederick the Great, who ruled from 1740 to 1786, inherited the Prussian army, which he kept in such a high state of readiness that it frightened the monarchs of larger states. Administering his kingdom personally, Frederick became known as the "enlightened despot" who brought art and culture (Voltaire stayed at his court for a while), as well as military triumphs and territorial expansion, to Prussia. A brilliant commander and daring strategist, Frederick served as a model for expansion-minded German nationalists. Trying to identify himself with Frederick the Great, Adolf Hitler in 1933 announced the founding of the Third Reich from Frederick's tomb in Berlin.

GERMAN NATIONALISM

At the time of the French Revolution, there were still over three hundred German states. Prussia and Austria were the strongest of them, but they, too, were pushovers for Napoleon's legions. German liberals, fed up with the backwardness and fragmentation of their country, at first welcomed the French as liberators and modernizers. Napoleon consolidated the many German ministates—but not Prussia or Austria—into about thirty, calling them the Confederation of the Rhine, and introduced new laws to free the economy and society from archaic laws.

The French brought with them more than liberalism, however; everywhere they went they infected conquered lands with the new idea of **nationalism**, the most contagious *-ism* of all; when one country catches it, so do neighboring lands. Soon Germans, Russians, and Spaniards were

GEOGRAPHY

MOUNTAINS

Mountains can serve as defensive barriers, making a country hard to invade. The Alps help guard Germany's southern flank; the Pyrenees do the same for France. Russia, with no mountains until the Urals rise up to form Europe's border with Asia, lay nearly defenseless before the horsemen of the east (who passed south of the Urals), the Swedes of the north, and the Germans of the west. Mountains can also slow political and economic development. Very mountainous countries, such as Spain and Mexico, may be harder to unify, as the nation's capital cannot easily penetrate regions shielded by mountains. As the West Virginia motto says, *Montani Semper Liberi* (Mountaineers are always free). Because much of Japan is too mountainous for farms or factories, most Japanese live in narrow and crowded coastal strips.

Volksgeist German for "spirit of the people"; has racist connotations. (Note: All German nouns are capitalized.)

Lebensraum German for "living space" for an entire nation.

Metternichian system Contrived conservative system that tried to restore pre-Napoleon European monarchy and stability.

fired with anti-French nationalism. Napoleon, without realizing it, had let an imp out of the bottle; the push he gave to German nationalism indirectly led to three German invasions of France. Great historical events have unpredictable long-term consequences.

As we saw in the case of France's borrowing English and American notions of freedom, ideas conceived in one country often become warped when applied to another. This happened with German nationalism, which became romantic, angry, and racist and hearkened back to a mythical past. German nationalist intellectuals of the nineteenth century spoke of a **Volksgeist**, a combination of *Volk* (people) and *Geist* (spirit), that implied a Germanic tribal spirit that was superior to other peoples. German geographers coined the term **Lebensraum** and argued that Germany was entitled to more territory. (Japanese militarists argued precisely the same.) Long before Hitler, many Germans favored expansionist nationalism.

Germany looked to Prussia for leadership in throwing off the French yoke, and Prussian troops did contribute to Napoleon's downfall. Like France, Germany after Napoleon was not the same. Caught up in nationalism and liberalism—more of the former than the latter—German thinkers wanted a unified and modernized nation. The reactionary Austrian Prince Metternich, who hated both nationalism and liberalism, helped create a German Confederation of thirty-nine states, which he thought would contribute to European stability after Napoleon.

In 1848 revolution broke out all over Europe as discontented liberals and nationalists sought to overthrow the **Metternichian system**. Amid urban uprisings, German liberals met in Frankfurt to set up a unified, democratic Germany. They sent a delegation to Berlin to offer the king of Prussia leadership of a German constitutional monarchy, but he contemptuously refused it with the remark that he "would not accept a crown from the gutter." The army cleared out the National Assembly in Frankfurt, and German liberals either converted to pure nationalism or immigrated to the United States.

The Second Reich

In contrast to the attempts of liberal nationalists in 1848, German unification came not from the people but from above, from the growth of Prussia. Neither was it the work of liberals but rather of a staunch conservative, Otto von Bismarck, who had seen the liberals in action in 1848 and thought

GEOGRAPHY

BOUND GERMANY

Germany is bounded on the north by the Atlantic, Denmark, and the Baltic Sea;
on the east by Poland and the Czech Republic;
on the south by Austria and Switzerland;
and on the west by France, Luxembourg, Belgium, and the Netherlands.

To reinforce your knowledge, sketch out and label Germany and its neighbors. Note also the old border between East and West Germany that disappeared with unification in 1990.

they were fools. Bismarck, who became Prussia's prime minister in 1862, was not really a German nationalist; he was first and foremost a loyal Junker servant of his king who saw German unification under Prussian leadership as the only way to preserve and defend Prussia. As such, Bismarck's goals were quite limited; he had no intention of turning a united Germany into a military, expansionist state.

GEOGRAPHY

BOUND POLAND

Poland is bounded on the north by the Baltic Sea, Russia (Kaliningrad Oblast), and Lithuania;

on the east by Belarus and Ukraine;

on the south by Slovakia and the Czech Republic;

and on the west by Germany.

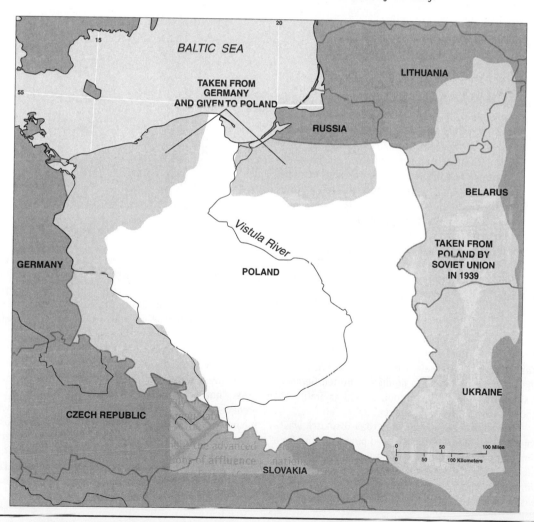

Reich   German for empire.

Kulturkampf   Culture struggle, specifically Bismarck's with the Catholic Church.

Machtpolitik   Power politics (cognate to "might").

Realpolitik   Politics of realism.

For Bismarck, armies and warfare were just tools. In 1862, when the Prussian parliament was deadlocked over the military budget, Bismarck simply decreed new taxes and spent the money without parliamentary approval, declaring, "Not by speeches and majority decisions will the great questions of the time be decided—that was the fault of 1848 and 1849—but by iron and blood."

Bismarck used his military tools to solve the great question of his day: Who was to lead a unified Germany, Prussia or Austria? In a series of three limited wars—in 1864 against Denmark, in 1866 against Austria, and in 1870 against France—Bismarck first consolidated the many German states behind Prussia, then got rid of Austria, then firmed up German unity. The new Second **Reich** (Charlemagne's was the first) was actually proclaimed in France, at Versailles Palace, in 1871.

PERSONALITIES

BISMARCK'S DUBIOUS LEGACY

Otto von Bismarck

Otto von Bismarck, Germany's chancellor from 1871 to 1890, was a Prussian Junker to the bone, and the stamp he put on a unified Germany retarded its democratic development for decades. Bismarck and Disraeli knew and liked each other, and many compared them as dynamic conservatives. English and German conservatism, however, are two different things. Disraeli's Tories widened the electorate and welcomed a fair fight in Parliament. Bismarck hated parties, parliaments, and anyone who opposed him. Bismarck left Germany an authoritarian and one-man style of governance that was overcome only by Allied occupation following World War II. Bismarck's **Kulturkampf** with the Catholic Church, which he wished to subordinate to the German state, sharpened Catholic resentment against the Protestant north, a feeling that lingers.

Bismarck's most dangerous legacy to Germany was in his foreign policy. He practiced both **Machtpolitik** and **Realpolitik** to manipulate first his own Prussia and then the rest of Europe to produce a unified Germany. War for Bismarck was just a tool. Cynical amorality was another pattern Bismarck bequeathed to Germany.

Germany's real problem was that Bismarck was a tough act to follow. Bismarck used power politics for a limited end, the unification of Germany. His successors picked up his amoral *Machtpolitik* but forgot about the limits, the *Realpolitik*. Bismarck, for example, could have easily conquered all of Denmark, Austria, and France,

but he did not because he knew that would bring dangerous consequences. Bismarck used war in a controlled way, to unify Germany rather than to conquer Europe. Once he got his Second Reich, Bismarck concentrated on making sure potential enemies would not form coalitions against it.

Bismarck cautioned that an alliance with Austria, supporting Austrian ambitions in the Balkans, could eventually lead to war. "The entire Balkans," he said, were "not worth the bones of one Pomeranian grenadier." His fear came true, for that was precisely the way World War I came about. Bismarck's successors, men of far less ability and great ambition, let Austria pull them into war over the Balkans. The tragedy of Bismarck is that he constructed a delicate balance of European power that could not be maintained without himself as the master juggler.

The Second Reich, lasting from 1871 to 1918, was not a democracy. The legislature, the **Reichstag**, had only limited power, namely, to approve or reject the budget. The chancellor (prime minister) was not "responsible" to the parliament—that is, he could not be voted out—and handpicked his own ministers. The German **Kaiser** was not a figurehead but actually set policy. The individual states that had been enrolled into a united Germany retained their autonomy, a forerunner of the present federal system.

Germany, which had been industrially backward, surged ahead, especially in iron and steel. The once-pastoral Ruhr became a smoky workshop. With the growth of industry came a militant and well-organized German labor movement. In 1863 Ferdinand Lassalle formed the General German Workers' Association, partly a union and partly a party. In 1875 the group became the Sozialdemokratische Partei Deutschlands (**SPD**), now the oldest and one of the most successful social-democratic parties in the world.

Bismarck hated the SPD and suppressed it in 1878. He tried to take the wind out of the Socialists' sails by promoting numerous welfare measures himself in the Reichstag. In the 1880s Germany became the first country with medical and accident insurance, a pension plan, and state employment offices. Germany has been a welfare state ever since.

> **Reichstag**   Pre-Hitler German parliament; its building now houses *Bundestag*.
>
> **Kaiser**   German for Caesar; emperor.
>
> **SPD**   German Social Democratic party.
>
> **revisionism**   Rethinking an ideology or reinterpreting history.

THE CATASTROPHE: WORLD WAR I

The Second Reich might have evolved into a democracy. Political parties became more important. After Bismarck was fired in 1890, the SPD came into the open to become, before World War I, Germany's largest party, with almost one-third of the Reichstag's seats. Gaining responsibility in elected offices, the German Socialists grew moderate, turning away from their Marxist roots and toward **revisionism**, the idea that socialism can grow gradually through democratic means rather than by radical revolution. So domesticated had the SPD become that in 1914, when the emergency war budget was placed before the Reichstag, SPD deputies forgot about the "international solidarity of all workers" and voted—for it.

After Bismarck, Germany's foreign policy turned expansionist. Kaiser Wilhelm II saw Germany as a great imperial power, dominant in Europe and competing with Britain overseas. A program of naval armament, begun by Germany in 1889, touched off a race with Britain to build more battleships. Wilhelm supported the Boers against the British in South Africa and the Austrians who were coming into conflict with the Russians over the Balkans. By the time the shots were fired in Sarajevo in 1914, Germany had managed to surround itself with enemies, exactly what Bismarck had worked to prevent.

GEOGRAPHY

BOUND HUNGARY

Hungary is bounded on the north by Slovakia; on the east by Ukraine and Romania; on the south by Serbia and Croatia; and on the west by Slovenia and Austria.

Dolchstoss   German for "stab in the back."

Versailles Treaty   1919 treaty ending World War I.

Weimar Republic   1919–1933 democratic German republic.

hyperinflation   Very rapid inflation, more than 50 percent a month.

The Germans, with their quick victory of 1870 in mind, marched joyously off to war. In early August of 1914 the Kaiser told his troops: "You will be home before the leaves have fallen from the trees." All of Europe thought the war would be short, but it took four years and 10 million lives until Germany surrendered.

Many Germans could not believe they had lost militarily. Right-wing Germans swallowed the **Dolchstoss** myth that Germany had been betrayed on the home front by democrats, socialists, Bolsheviks, and Jews. Fed nothing but war propaganda, Germans did not understand that the army and the economy could give no more. The war ended before there was any fighting on German soil, so Germans did not see their troops beaten. Worse was the **Versailles Treaty**, which blamed the war on Germany and demanded an impossible $33 billion in reparations. Germany was stripped of its few colonies (in Africa and the South Pacific) and lost Alsace and the Polish corridor. Many Germans wanted revenge. The Versailles Treaty was a catastrophe, leading straight to Hitler and World War II.

Republic without Democrats

Looking back, we can see how the **Weimar Republic**—which got its name from the town of Weimar, where its federal constitution was drawn up—started with three strikes against it. First, Germans had no experience with a republic or a democracy, yet suddenly Germany became a democratic republic when the Kaiser fled to Holland at the war's end. Second, for many Germans, the Weimar Republic lacked legitimacy; it had been forced upon Germany by the victorious allies and "back stabbers" who had betrayed the Reich. Third, the Versailles Treaty was so punitive and its demands for payment so high that Germany was humiliated and economically hobbled.

It has been estimated that only about one German in four was a wholehearted democrat. Another quarter hated democracy. The rest went along with the new republic until the economy collapsed and then shifted their sympathies to authoritarian movements of the left or right. Weimar Germany, it has been said, was a republic without republicans and a democracy without democrats.

The German government, in a crisis with France over reparations, printed money without limit, bringing a **hyperinflation** so insane that by 1923 it took a wheelbarrowful of marks to buy a loaf of bread. Especially hard hit were middle-class families whose businesses and savings were wiped out; many of them became eager recruits for the Nazis. The period left an indelible mark on Germans, and to this day the German government emphasizes preventing inflation.

By the mid-1920s the economy stabilized and things looked better. Cabinets changed frequently: twenty-six in fourteen years. The Social Democrat, Catholic Center, and Conservative parties were the largest; the Nazis were tiny and considered something of a joke. Hitler did resemble Charlie Chaplin. Then the world Depression started in 1929, and German democracy went down the drain. Moderate parties declined, and extremist parties—the Nazis and the Communists—grew (see box on page 173). Unemployment was the key: The more people out of work, the higher the Nazi vote.

One combination might have blocked the Nazis' rise to power. If the Social Democrats and Communists had formed a united front, the Weimar system might have been saved. But the German Communists, who split off from the SPD after World War I, reviled the Social Democrats as "social fascists." Under Stalin's orders, the German Communists rejected a joint program with the Socialists on the theory that the Hitler regime would soon collapse and, the Communists would take over. This was one of Stalin's greatest blunders, and Communists and Socialists alike paid for it.

By late 1932, the Nazis had won a third of the German vote, and the aged President Hindenburg, a conservative general, named Hitler as chancellor in January 1933. The Weimar Republic, Germany's first try at democracy, died after a short, unstable life of fourteen years.

---

polarized pluralism   A multiparty system that produces two extremist blocs with little in the center.

Key Concepts

The Horrors of Polarized Pluralism

Columbia University political scientist Giovanni Sartori described what happens when a multiparty democracy such as Weimar's or Spain's in the 1930s gets terribly sick. The leading parties in the center face nasty opposition on both their right and left. In competing for votes in a highly ideological atmosphere, parties engage in a "politics of outbidding" by offering more radical solutions.

Voters flee from the center to the extremes, to parties dedicated to overthrowing democracy. Sartori called this syndrome **polarized pluralism**, and the last years of Weimar are a good example of it.

Compare the percentage of votes parties got in 1928 with what they got in 1933, and the "center-fleeing" tendency is clear.

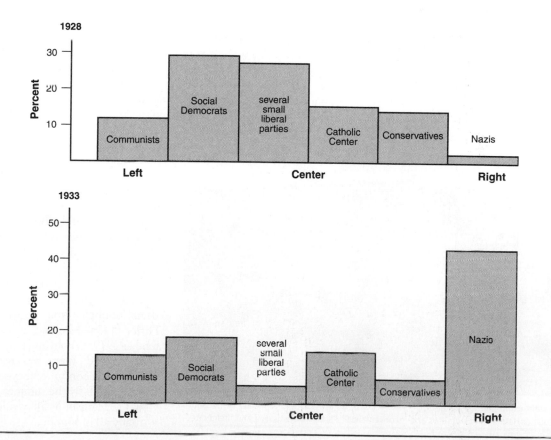

The Third Reich

Nazi was the German nickname for the National Socialist German Workers party. Nazism, like other forms of fascism, had a fake socialist component that promised jobs and welfare. The Nazis did not put industries under state ownership like the Communists in the Soviet Union; instead they practiced **Gleichschaltung** (coordination) of the economy under party supervision. Many Germans got work on government projects, such as building the new **Autobahn**. Although the Nazis never won a majority in a fair election, by the late 1930s a majority of Germans supported Hitler, whom they saw as restoring prosperity.

Gleichschaltung Nazi control of Germany's economy.

Autobahn Express highway, like U.S. interstate.

opportunist Unprincipled person out for himself or herself.

Most Germans had not been enthusiastic about democracy, and few protested the growth of tyranny. Some Communists and Socialists went underground, to prison, or into exile, and some old-style conservatives disliked Hitler, who, in their eyes, was nothing but an Austrian guttersnipe. But most Germans got along by going along. Centuries of being taught to obey authority led them to accept Nazi rule.

For some, membership in the Nazi party offered better jobs and snappy uniforms. Many ex-Nazis claimed they joined only to further their careers, and most were probably telling the truth. You do not need true believers to staff a tyranny; **opportunists** will do just as well. The frightening thing about Nazi Germany was how it could turn normal humans into coldblooded mass murderers.

Among the first and worst to suffer were the Jews, who formed less than 1 percent of the German population. Exploiting widely held racist feelings, Hitler depicted the Jews as a poisonous, foreign element who aimed to enslave Germany in the service of international capitalism, international communism, or both. Logical consistency was never the Nazis' strong point. Jews were deprived, one step at a time, of their civil rights, their jobs, their property, their citizenship, and finally their lives.

Few Germans were aware of it, but Hitler ached for war. At first he seemed to just be consolidating Germany's boundaries, absorbing the Saar in 1935, Austria and the Sudetenland in 1938, and Czech lands in 1939. Germany's enemies from World War I, still war weary, did nothing to stop the growth of German power and territory. Hitler's generals, it is now known, were ready to overthrow him if the British said no to his demands at Munich in 1938. But it looked as though Hitler could amass victories without even fighting, so the German generals suppressed their doubts. Finally, when Hitler invaded Poland in September 1939, Britain and France declared war. France was overrun, Britain contained beyond the Channel. By the summer of 1940 Germany or its allies ruled virtually all of Europe.

The main extermination camp of the Nazi regime was at Auschwitz-Birkenau in the south of Poland. Here millions of Jews and inconvenient Christians were gassed and incinerated.

In 1941 Hitler ordered his **Final Solution** to the Jewish question to begin. Death camps killed some six million Jews and a similar number of inconvenient Christians (Poles, gypsies, and others). A new word was added to mankind's vocabulary: **genocide**. The Nazis kept their death camps secret, and many Germans claimed they did not know what was going on.

Hitler—just a week before he attacked Poland in 1939—had completed a **nonaggression pact** with Stalin. In the summer of 1941, however, Hitler assembled the biggest army in history and gave the order for "Barbarossa," the conquest and enslavement of the Soviet Union. Here, at last, Hitler's dream departed from reality. The Russian winter and surprising resistance of the Red Army devoured whole German divisions. From late 1942 on it was all downhill for Germany.

Final Solution   Nazi program to exterminate Jews.

genocide   Murder of an entire people.

nonaggression pact   Treaty to not attack each other, specifically the 1939 treaty between Hitler and Stalin.

Cold War   Period of armed tension and competition between the United States and the Soviet Union, approximately from 1947 to 1989.

THE OCCUPATION

This time there could be no Dolchstoss myth; Germans watched Russians, Americans, British, and French fight their way through Germany. German government ceased to exist, and the country was run by foreign occupiers. At Yalta in February 1945, the Allied leaders agreed to divide Germany into four zones for temporary occupation; Berlin, deep inside the Soviet zone, was similarly divided.

Initially, the Allies, shocked by the Nazi concentration camps, treated Germans harshly, but that reversed with the coming of the **Cold War**, which grew in large part out of the way the Soviets handled Germany. The Soviets, having lost some twenty-seven million people in the war, were intent on looting the conquered nation. They dismantled whole factories, shipped them home, and flooded the country with inflated military currency. The British and Americans, on the

Political Culture

GERMANY'S POLITICAL ERAS

Name	Years	Remembered for
Holy Roman Empire	800–1806	Charlemagne, fragmentation, religious wars.
Nineteenth century	1806–1871	Consolidation, modernization stir.
Second Reich	1871–1918	Bismarck unites Germany; industry and war.
Weimar Republic	1919–1933	Weak democracy; culture flourishes.
Nazis	1933–1945	Brutal dictatorship; war; mass murder.
Occupation	1945–1949	Allies divide and run Germany.
Federal Republic	1949–	Democracy; economic miracle; unification; from Bonn to Berlin.

Marshall Plan Massive U.S. financial aid for European recovery.

deutsche Mark German currency from 1948 to 2002.

Berlin airlift U.S.-British supply to West Berlin by air in 1948–1949.

other hand, distressed at the brutal Soviet takeover of East Europe, decided to revive German economic and political life in their zones. The U.S. **Marshall Plan** and other aid programs pumped billions of dollars into German recovery. In 1948 the British and Americans introduced a currency reform with a new **deutsche Mark** (DM), which effectively ended Soviet looting of the western zones. In retaliation, the Russians blockaded Berlin, which was supplied for nearly a year by an incredible British-American **Berlin airlift**. The Cold War was on, centered in Germany.

In 1949, the Western allies gave governing power back to West Germans in order to ensure their cooperation against Soviet power. A few months later, the Soviets set up East Germany. Both German regimes were children of the Cold War, with the Americans and the Soviets as the parents. When the Cold War ended—often dated to the fall of the Berlin Wall in late 1989—prosperous and democratic West Germany swallowed weak and dependent East Germany. To examine how West Germany succeeded, let us turn to Germany's institutions.

Geography

Another Tale of Two Flags

Like France, Germany's divided loyalties have been symbolized by its flags' colors. The German nationalist movement flag was black, red, and gold, colors of a Prussian regiment that fought Napoleon. By 1848 it symbolized a democratic, united Germany. Bismarck rejected it and for the Second Reich's flag chose Prussia's black and white, plus the white and red of the medieval Hansa commercial league.

The Reich's collapse in 1918 and the founding of the Weimar Republic brought back the democratic black, red, and gold German flag. Hitler, a fanatic for symbols, insisted on authoritarian black, red, and white colors. The Bonn republic designed the present German flag with the original democratic colors.

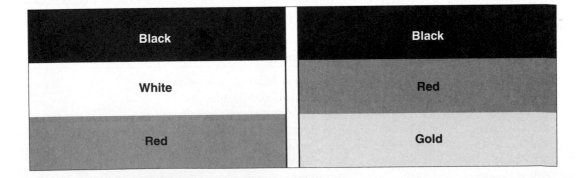

KEY TERMS

Autobahn (p. 174)

Berlin airlift (p. 176)

Cold War (p. 175)

deutsche Mark (p. 176)

Dolchstoss (p. 172)

Final Solution (p. 175)

genocide (p. 175)

Gleichschaltung (p. 174)

Habsburg (p. 163)

hyperinflation (p. 172)

Junker (p. 166)

Kaiser (p. 171)

Kulturkampf (p. 170)

Lebensraum (p. 168)

Machtpolitik (p. 170)

Marshall Plan (p. 176)

Metternichian system
(p. 168)

nationalism (p. 167)

nonaggression pact (p. 175)

opportunist (p. 174)

polarized pluralism (p. 173)

Prussia (p. 165)

Realpolitik (p. 170)

Reich (p. 170)

Reichstag (p. 171)

revisionism (p. 171)

SPD (p. 171)

Thirty Years War (p. 163)

Versailles Treaty (p. 172)

Volksgeist (p. 168)

Weimar Republic (p. 172)

Westphalia (p. 163)

FURTHER REFERENCE

Berghahn, Volker R. *Imperial Germany, 1871–1914: Economy, Society, Culture, and Politics.* Providence, RI: Berghahn Books, 1994.

Carr, William. *A History of Germany, 1815–1990,* 4th ed. New York: Oxford University Press, 1995.

Craig, Gordon A. *Germany, 1866–1945.* New York: Oxford University Press, 1978.

Darmstaedter, Friedrich. *Bismarck and the Creation of the Second Reich.* Piscataway, NJ: Transaction, 2008.

Evans, Richard J. *The Coming of the Third Reich.* New York: Penguin, 2004.

———. *The Third Reich in Power, 1933–1939.* New York: Penguin, 2005.

Feldman, Gerald D. *The Great Disorder: Politics, Economics, and Society in the German Inflation, 1914–1924.* New York: Oxford University Press, 1993.

Fritzsche, Peter. *Life and Death in the Third Reich.* Cambridge, MA: Harvard University Press, 2008.

Kershaw, Ian. *Hitler, 1936–1945: Nemesis.* New York: Norton, 2000.

Kreuzer, Marcus. *Institutions and Innovation: Voters, Parties, and Interest Groups in the Consolidation of Democracy—France and Germany, 1870–1939.* Ann Arbor, MI: University of Michigan Press, 2001.

Merkl, Peter H. *The Origin of the West German Republic.* New York: Oxford University Press, 1963.

Ozment, Steven. *A Mighty Fortress: A New History of the German People.* New York: Harper, 2005.

Stern, Fritz. *Five Germanys I Have Known.* New York: Farrar, Straus & Giroux, 2006.

Weitz, Eric D. *Weimar Germany: Promise and Tragedy.* Princeton, NJ: Princeton University Press, 2007.

Chapter 13
Germany:
The Key Institutions

Read 13-14
- Then Comparative Pol
- II 16

In 1949, the founders of the **Federal Republic of Germany** were hopeful that the east and west sections of their country would reunify. Accordingly, in drafting their founding document—based in part on the 1848–1849 Frankfurt and 1919 Weimar constitutions—they called it the **Grundgesetz** (Basic Law) rather than *Verfassung* (constitution), which was to come only when Germany reunified. They meant to indicate that the Federal Republic was temporary and operating under temporary rules. Sixty years later, the question is a legal quibble; the Basic Law continues as unified Germany's constitution, and an excellent one at that.

QUESTIONS TO CONSIDER

1. How was the debate over Berlin as Germany's capital a question of core areas?
2. Is federalism the best route for Germany? Why?
3. How do the French and German presidencies differ?
4. How do the British and German prime ministries differ?
5. How does Germany's constitutional court differ from the U.S. Supreme Court?
6. What is the German lower house? How does it differ from the upper?
7. What are Germany's main parties?
8. How does the German electoral system work?

The new West Germany revived an old pattern in German history, **federalism**. Germany's **Länder** have at least as much power as American states, maybe more. Education, medical care, police, and many other functions are run by Land governments. Part of the reason for this strong federalism was to repudiate Nazi centralization and to make sure it could never happen again.

Berlin was a strange situation. Located 110 miles (180 kilometers) inside East Germany, Berlin was nominally governed by the four occupying powers. The Soviets, however, in 1949 turned East Berlin into the capital of East Germany, and the American, British, and French sectors became, to all intents and purposes, a part of West Germany. Bonn counted West Berlin as its eleventh Land, but the wartime Allies did not recognize it as such. So officially West Berlin was not part of the Federal Republic, but in practice it was. West German currency, laws, and passports applied in West Berlin, but the city sent only nonvoting representatives to the Bonn parliament. The anomaly was solved in 1990 with the unification of the two Germanys. With the Berlin Wall down, Greater Berlin became a Land and in 1999 the official capital of united Germany, although six ministries (including defense) remained in Bonn.

East Germany, set up by the Communists in 1949, continued the Nazi pattern of centralized rule with fourteen administrative districts, each named after its leading city, without autonomy. Unification in 1990 brought back to life East Germany's five Länder, so now the Federal Republic has sixteen Länder, ten from West Germany, five from East Germany, plus Greater Berlin.

The President

Germany's federal president (*Bundespräsident*) is the classic European president, a figurehead with few political but many symbolic duties. Like the monarchs of Britain and Scandinavia, the German president is an official greeter and ambassador of good will rather than a working executive. The French president of the Third and Fourth Republics and today's Israeli president are other examples of weak presidencies. De Gaulle, of course, greatly strengthened the French presidency.

The president is the "head of state" rather than "chief of government" (for the distinction, see pages 33–34), and as such receives new foreign ambassadors who present their credentials to him rather than to the people they will actually be working with, the chancellor and foreign minister. The president proclaims laws (after they have been passed by parliament), dissolves the **Bundestag** (upon the chancellor's request), and appoints and dismisses the chancellor (after the leading party has told him to). In short, the German president is, to use Bagehot's terms, a "dignified" rather than "efficient" part of government.

The president is elected by a special Federal Assembly composed of all Bundestag members plus an equal number from the state legislatures. The president serves five years and may be reelected once. A sort of semi-retirement job, it is usually given as a reward to distinguished

---

Federal Republic of Germany Previously West Germany, now all of Germany. (See page 179.)

Grundgesetz Basic Law; Germany's constitution. (See page 179.)

federalism System in which component areas have considerable autonomy. (See page 179.)

Land Germany's first-order civil division, equivalent to U.S. state; plural *Länder*. (See page 179.)

Bundestag Lower house of German parliament.

Mitteleuropa Central Europe.

Geography

From Bonn to Berlin

The 1991 debate that led to restoring Berlin as the capital of united Germany was essentially a conflict over core areas. Bonn, a small town in the Catholic Rhine area well to the west, had served as West Germany's capital since 1949. It shifted Germans' attention westward in values, economics, and alliances. Berlin, a major city near the eastern border of Germany, had earlier been the capital of Protestant Prussia but served as Germany's capital from 1871 to 1945. Moving back to Berlin shifted Germans' attention to the problems of the poorer, former-Communist, eastern part of their country. Some critics feared that in the long run it would turn Germany from the West and toward the old concept of a German-dominated **Mitteleuropa**.

Billions in subsidies poured in to reconstruct ministries, parliamentary offices, embassies, museums, and hotels. Even the old Reichstag building, now housing the Bundestag, was redone with a new glass dome that visitors can climb via spiral ramps. Berlin's economic base, however, is weak. Little industry grows

The Reichstag Dome, the work of British architect Lord Norman Foster, has become Berlin's top tourist attraction. Inside the redone building below the dome, the Bundestag meets.

while unemployment and poverty are high. In 2006 the Constitutional Court rejected Berlin's claim for funds to bail out its $79 billion debt. Germans got tired of vast subsidies for Berlin. Some fear that Berlin will be a city of government and museums.

senior politicians. In 2005, economist Horst Köhler, former head of the International Monetary Fund, was elected president with the support of the CDU and FDP. Urging the parties to stop feuding and pass reforms needed to cut Germany's high unemployment, he quickly became the most popular political figure in the country. Unfortunately, the president is not in charge of economic policy or much else.

---

chancellor   German prime minister.

center   In federal systems, the powers of the nation's capital.

The Chancellor

Germany has a weak president but a strong **chancellor**. Unlike the changing chancellors of the Weimar Republic, the FRG chancellorship has been stable and durable. Part of the reason for this is that the Basic Law requires the Bundestag to simultaneously vote in a new chancellor if it wants

GEOGRAPHY

FEDERATIONS

Diversity is the advantage of federalism, a system that yields major autonomy to the components, be they U.S., Indian, Mexican, or Nigerian states, German Länder, or Canadian provinces. The components cannot be legally erased or split or have their boundaries easily changed; such matters are grave constitutional questions. Typically, certain powers are reserved for the federal government (defense, money supply, interstate commerce, and so on) while other powers are reserved for the components (education, police, highways, and so on). Large countries or those with particularistic languages or traditions lend themselves to federalism.

The advantages of a federal system are its flexibility and accommodation to particularism. Texans feel Texas is different and special; Bavarians feel Bavaria is different and special; Québécois feel Quebec is different and special; and so on. If one state or province wishes to try a new formula for funding health care, it may do so without upsetting the state-federal balance. If the new way works, it may be gradually copied. If it fails, little harm is done before it is phased out. U.S. states in this regard have been called "laboratories of democracy": You can try something in one state without committing the entire nation to it. Governments at the Land or state level also serve as training grounds for politicians before they try the national level. Examples: Texas Governor George Bush, Lower Saxony Premier Gerhard Schröder, and Guanajuato (Mexico) Governor Vicente Fox.

The disadvantage is inconsistent and sometimes sloppy administration among components. Many federal systems cannot achieve nationwide standards in education, environment, welfare, or health care. One state wants something and can afford it; another state cannot. One state says certain types of persons are eligible for a program; another says they are not. Federal systems are less coherent than unitary systems. To correct such problems, many federal systems have granted more power to the **center** at the expense of the states. The United States is a prime example of this; compare the relative powers of the states and of Washington over the course of a century.

One might say that in unitary systems there is a tugging in the direction of federalism, whereas in federal systems there is a tugging in the direction of unitary systems. This does not necessarily mean that the two will eventually meet in some middle ground; it merely means that neither unitary nor federal systems are finished products and that both are still evolving.

A federal system may also achieve a stable balance between local and national loyalties, leading gradually to a psychologically integrated country, like the United States, Germany, and Switzerland. But this does not always work. Soviet, Yugoslav, and Czechoslovak federalism actually fostered resentments of the republics against the center. When their Communist parties weakened, local nationalists took over and declared independence.

constructive no-confidence
Parliament must vote in new cabinet when it ousts current one.

to vote out the present one. This reform ended one of the worst problems of parliamentary (as opposed to presidential) governments, namely, their dependence on an often-fickle legislative majority.

The German reform is called **constructive no-confidence** because Bundestag has to offer something constructive—a new cabinet—rather than a mere negative majority to get rid of the old one. This has happened only once, in 1982, when the small Free Democratic party abandoned its coalition with the Social Democrats in midterm and

PERSONALITIES

ANGELA MERKEL: A GERMAN THATCHER?

Her supporters hoped that Angela Merkel, who became chancellor in 2005 at age fifty-one, would be a German Margaret Thatcher and give a free-market jolt to the German economy. But the 2005 election that brought Merkel to office produced a *grand coalition* (see page 187) that hamstrung Merkel's ability to push through needed reforms. The German MMP (see page 192) electoral system did not give Merkel a majority in parliament the way the British FPTP system gave Thatcher a Tory majority.

Merkel is unusual in several ways. She is Germany's first woman chancellor and the first from East Germany. Her English and Russian are nearly perfect. A Protestant, she heads a heavily Catholic party. She wants free-market economics; much of the CDU/CSU still seeks "social justice" and opposes her on some measures. She is now in her second marriage and has no children. Merkel was born in West Germany but went as a baby to East Germany, where her pastor father was assigned a church. She grew up entirely in East Germany but kept her critical views of the Communist regime to herself. Instead of the usual law studies, she took a doctorate in physics at Leipzig University and did research in quantum chemistry. (Thatcher graduated Oxford in chemistry.)

When the Berlin Wall fell in late 1989, Merkel helped organize a conservative party that merged with the Christian Democratic Union. Elected to the Bundestag, she still represents a constituency in the northern *Land* of Mecklenburg-Pomerania. Chancellor Helmut Kohl appointed Merkel to his cabinet, first as minister of women and youth and then environment. After Kohl's defeat in 1998, Merkel became CDU chair in 2000. After the CSU's Edmund Stoiber lost to SPD Chancellor Gerhard Schröder in 2002, Merkel became the leading opposition figure.

Angela Merkel

By this time, Schröder was stalled and losing popularity. He proposed reforming Germany's slow-growth and high-unemployment economy but got little support from his own SPD, which fights any reforms that cut welfare benefits. Unable to govern, a frustrated Schröder arranged a Bundestag defeat to call elections a year early. Schröder, an outgoing personality and good speaker, was more popular than his party. "Angie," as her supporters call her, was a bland and poor speaker, less popular than her party. Personality matters in German politics, and the CDU saw its early 20-point lead over the SPD narrow to a maddening tie (see box on page 190). After two months of negotiations, the CDU and SPD agreed to a grand coalition with Merkel as chancellor. Merkel wanted go farther with reforms to free the economy and trim the welfare state, but the SPD half of her cabinet limited her to what she calls "small steps," such as a watered-down reform of Germany's creaky health-care system. Merkel could not even get reform of Germany's rigid labor market on the agenda. Merkel, thanks to Germany's very different political structure, could not remotely become a Thatcher.

WHO WAS WHEN: GERMANY'S CHANCELLORS		
Konrad Adenauer	CDU	1949–1963
Ludwig Erhard	CDU	1963–1966
Kurt Georg Kiesinger	CDU	1966–1969
Willy Brandt	SPD	1969–1974
Helmut Schmidt	SPD	1974–1982
Helmut Kohl	CDU	1982–1998
Gerhard Schröder	SPD	1998–2005
Angela Merkel	CDU	2005–

voted in a new Christian Democratic chancellor. Constructive no-confidence makes ousting a chancellor between elections a rarity.

Another reason the chancellor is strong stems from the first occupant of that office: Konrad Adenauer, a tough, shrewd politician who helped found the Federal Republic and served as chancellor during its first fourteen years. First occupants, such as Washington in the American presidency, can put a stamp on the position, defining its powers and setting its style for generations. Adenauer—who was seventy-three when he first became chancellor—showed strong leadership and made numerous decisions without bothering parliament or his cabinet too much. A Catholic Rhinelander, he formed the CDU, set up a "two-plus" party system, pointed Germany decisively westward into NATO and the EU, and established a special relationship with France. Chancellors ever since Adenauer have been measured against him. His successor, for example, the amiable and intelligent Ludwig Erhard, was found wanting because he could not exercise firm leadership.

Partly thanks to the style Adenauer set, the German chancellor is approximately as powerful as the British prime minister, which is to say quite powerful. The chancellor picks his or her own cabinet—with political considerations in mind—like the British PM. He or she is responsible for the main lines of government policy and has to defend them before the Bundestag and the public. As such, he or she is implicitly held responsible for what ministers say and do.

The Cabinet

The typical German cabinet is usually smaller than its British counterpart and is now even smaller than the fifteen-department U.S. cabinet. In 2005, Chancellor Merkel, after extensive negotiations between the two coalition parties, named a cabinet with fourteen ministries, eight headed by Social Democrats and six by Christian Democrats:

Foreign Affairs	Health
Interior	Families
Justice	Labor
Finance	Education
Economy and Technology	Development (foreign aid)
Defense	Environment
Agriculture	Transport

As usual in Europe, ministries are added, deleted, combined, split, and reshuffled from one cabinet to another. For example, Schröder combined the economy and labor ministries into a "super-ministry" to fight unemployment (it didn't work). Merkel's cabinet separated them again. Redefinitions of ministries are no big deal in Europe; what prime ministers want, they get. The chief job of the interior ministry is protection of the constitution (*Verfassungsschutz*), which includes monitoring extremist parties and movements. Unlike the French unitary system, though, the only police they have at their disposal are the Federal Border Police; all other police are at the *Land* or municipal level.

As in Britain (but not in France), practically all German cabinet ministers are also working politicians with seats in the Bundestag. Like their British counterparts, they are rarely specialists in their assigned portfolio. Most are trained as lawyers and have served in a variety of party and legislative positions. The job of parliamentary state secretary serves as a training ground for potential cabinet ministers. Below cabinet rank, a parliamentary state secretary is assigned to each minister to assist in relations with the Bundestag, in effect a bridge between executive and legislative branches, as in Britain.

THE BUNDESTAG

Konrad Adenauer, the authoritarian democrat, did not place great faith in the Bundestag. Germany never had a strong parliamentary tradition. Bismarck all but ignored the Reichstag (whose building the Bundestag now occupies). During the Weimar Republic, the Reichstag, unprepared for the governing responsibilities thrust upon it, could not exercise power. Then in 1949 came Adenauer who, like most Germans, had never seen an efficient, stable, responsible parliament, and so tended to disdain the new one. Since Adenauer's time, the Bundestag has been trying to establish itself as a pillar of democracy and as an important branch of government. Success has been gradual and incomplete. Many Germans still do not respect the Bundestag very much.

DEMOCRACY

PREFIX TO DEMOCRACY

In Germany today almost everything associated with the federal government bears the prefix *Bundes-*, meaning "federal." Thus:

- *Bundesrepublik Deutschland* is the Federal Republic of German, FRG.
- *Bundestag* is the lower house of the federal parliament.
- *Bundesrat* is the upper house.
- *Bundeskanzler* is the federal chancellor (prime minister).

- *Bundeswehr* is the army.
- *Bundesministerium* is a federal ministry.
- *Bundesregierung* is the federal government.

The prefix *Bundes-* is relatively new, stemming only from the founding of West Germany in 1949, and as such it has a modern, democratic ring to it. The old prefix of many of the same words, *Reichs-* (imperial), has a slightly sinister, discarded connotation. In Germany, "federal" has become synonymous with "democratic."

The Bundestag has at least 598 members but usually gets additional deputies and now totals 614. Deputies are elected for four years, but elections can be called early, as they were in 2005. Under a parliamentary (as opposed to presidential) system, the legislature can never be a severe critic of the administration in the manner of the U.S. Congress. After all, the Bundestag's majority parties produce the government; they cannot very well criticize it too harshly. Neither is the Bundestag the tumultuous assembly of the French Third and Fourth Republics; the FRG legislature can unmake a government only when it makes a new one. Nor is the Bundestag the docile rubber stamp that de Gaulle made of the French National Assembly. Still less is it the colorful debating chamber of the House of Commons, where clever orators try to sway the public for the next election. On balance, the Bundestag has less independent power than the U.S. Congress but more than the French National Assembly and possibly even the British House of Commons.

One interesting point about the Bundestag is its many women members, close to a third, typical of North European systems that use proportional representation, which allows parties to place women candidates on party lists. Over 40 percent of Sweden's Riksdag are women. The number of women in most parliaments has grown in recent years: 18 percent of British, 16 percent of Mexican, 14 percent of U.S., and 11 percent of French national legislators. These lower numbers are partly the result of single-member electoral districts. PR is fairer to women. Japan has only 7 percent female legislators.

The Bundestag's strong point is its committee work. Here, behind closed doors (most sessions are secret), Bundestag deputies, including opposition members, can make their voices heard. German legislative committees are more important and more specialized than their British counterparts. German party discipline is not as tight as the British so that deputies from the ruling party can criticize a government bill while opposition deputies sometimes agree with it. In the give and take of committee work, the opposition is often able to get changes made in legislation. Once back on the Bundestag floor—and all bills must be reported out; they cannot be killed in committee—voting is on party lines with occasional defections on matters of conscience.

The Bundestag standing committees generally correspond to the cabinet ministries listed earlier in this chapter. The system is designed that way: Each cabinet minister can deal directly with a parallel, relevant Bundestag committee. The ministers, themselves Bundestag members, sometimes come over from their executive offices to explain to committee sessions a proposed piece of legislation.

In a parallel with French deputies, Bundestag membership is heavy with civil servants. German law permits bureaucrats to take leaves of absence to run

A symbol of reunified Germany is the refurbished Brandenburg Gate at the heart of Berlin near the Federal parliament, the Bundestag.

for and serve in the Bundestag. Another important category is people from interest groups: business associations and labor unions. Together, these two groups usually form a majority of the Bundestag membership, contributing to a public feeling that parliament is dominated by powerful interests. Making this worse, a series of scandals revealed that many Bundestag members get "secret money" from private firms for no work, a parallel with British MPs' "sleaze factor."

THE CONSTITUTIONAL COURT

Very few countries have a judiciary equal in power to the legislative or executive branches. The United States and Germany are two; both allow the highest court in the land to review the constitutionality of laws. The **Federal Constitutional Court** (*Bundesverfassungsgericht*, BVerfG), located in Karlsruhe, was set up in 1951 partly on American insistence. The American occupiers reasoned that something like the Supreme Court would help prevent another Hitler, and many Germans agreed with what was for Germany (and indeed all of Europe) a new concept.

Federal Constitutional Court
Germany's top court, equivalent to U.S. Supreme Court.

extreme multipartism Too many parties in parliament.

"two-plus" party system Two big parties and several small ones.

monocolor In parliamentary systems, cabinet composed of just one party.

The Karlsruhe court is composed of sixteen judges, eight elected by each house of parliament, who serve for nonrenewable, twelve-year terms. The BVerfG operates as two courts, or "senates," of eight judges each to speed up the work. Completely independent of other branches of German government, the court decides cases between Länder, protects civil liberties, outlaws dangerous political parties, and otherwise makes sure that statutes conform to the Basic Law.

The Constitutional Court's decisions have been important. It has declared illegal some right and left extremist parties on the grounds that they sought to overthrow the constitutional order. It found that abortion bills collided with the strong right-to-life provisions of the Basic Law and thus ruled them unconstitutional. (In 1993, however, it decided not to prosecute women who had first-trimester abortions.) In 1979 it ruled that "worker codetermination" in the running of factories was constitutional. In 1983 and 2005 it found that chancellors had acted within the constitution when they arranged to lose a Bundestag vote of confidence in order to hold elections early. In 1994 it ruled Germany can send troops overseas for peacekeeping operations. In 1995 it overrode a Bavarian law requiring a crucifix in every classroom. Judicial review has worked well in Germany, although the Constitutional Court, because it operates in the context of the more rigid code law, does not have the impact of the U.S. Supreme Court, whose decisions serve as precedents within the U.S. Common Law system.

FROM "TWO-PLUS" TO MULTIPARTY SYSTEM?

Much of the reason the FRG government worked rather well is the party system that evolved since 1949, but that may have ended in 2005. The Weimar Reichstag suffered from **extreme multipartism**; a dozen parties, some of them extremist, made it impossible to form stable coalitions. The Federal Republic seemed to have fixed that, and Germany turned into a **"two-plus" party system**, because German governments almost always consisted of one large party in coalition with one small party. Britain, with its majoritarian system, almost always gives one party a majority in parliament. Germany, with its proportional system, seldom produces **monocolor** governments. A two-plus party system is somewhere between a two-party system and a multiparty system. Recent elections, alas, turned Germany back into a multiparty system, with all the threats to stability that implies. (For a discussion of coalition formation in Germany, see page 211.)

> **grand coalition** A government composed of the largest parties, leaving only minor parties in opposition.

For most of the FRG's history the largest party has been the Christian Democratic Union (*Christlich Demokratische Union*, CDU). The CDU is now chaired by Angela Merkel, who became chancellor in 2005. Its Bavarian affiliate is the Christian Social Union (CSU), chaired by Edmund Stoiber, Bavaria's governor and 2002 chancellor candidate. Together, the two are designated CDU/CSU as if they are one party. The original core of the CDU was the old Catholic Center party, one of the few parties that held its own against the growth of Nazism in the early 1930s. After World War II, Center politicians like Adenauer decided to go for a broader-based center-right party, one in which Protestants would feel welcome. Like France's Gaullists, the CDU never embraced totally free-market capitalism (and still does not); instead it went for a "social market" economy (see Chapter 16). The CDU/CSU has been the largest party in every election except 1972 and 1998, when the SPD pulled ahead. In 2002 it tied the SPD with 38.5 percent of the national vote and in 2005 edged it out with 35.2 percent.

The Social Democratic party (*Sozialdemokratische Partei Deutschlands*, SPD) is the grand old party of European socialism and the only German party that antedates the Federal Republic. Starting out Marxist in the late nineteenth century, the SPD gradually revised its positions until, in 1959, it dropped Marxism altogether. It was then that its electoral fortunes grew as it expanded beyond its traditional working-class base and into the middle class, especially intellectuals. Now a center-left party, the SPD's socialism is basically support for the welfare state. The SPD's lingering problem: Its leadership is generally centrist, but it still contains many leftists who try to gain control of the party. From 1998 to 2005 the SPD governed in coalition with the Greens. In 2005 it won 34.2 percent of the vote, just behind the CDU/CSU, which it joined in a grand coalition. The SPD's current chief is a Land minister-president (governor), Kurt Beck, one of several possible SPD chancellor candidates.

KEY CONCEPTS

GRAND COALITION

In 2005 Germany revived the **grand coalition** of Christian Democrats and Social Democrats that had governed from 1966 to 1969, which functioned adequately but hurt German democracy because it left only small parties to oppose and criticize. The advantage of a grand coalition: It has such an overwhelming majority in parliament that it cannot be ousted and can pass any laws it likes. The 2005 grand coalition had to happen because no other combination of parties was able to form a coalition (see page 211), but its two parties, the CDU and SPD, were at odds on economic reform and stalemate over important policies.

The 1966–1969 grand coalition made citizens feel that no one could seriously criticize the government, that politics was a game rigged by the powerful, and that democracy was a sham. In the late 1960s a leftist "extraparliamentary opposition" grew and criticized the government in radical terms. Some of West Germany's terrorists first became active in disgust at the wall-to-wall grand coalition, which is probably useful only for emergencies; if it stays in office too long it starts undermining faith in democracy. A good democracy requires a lively interaction between "ins" and "outs" rather than collusion between the two.

Greens   Environmentalist parties.

regierungsfähig   Literally, "able to form a government"; a party that has matured and is able to rule.

Bundesrat   Literally, federal council; upper chamber of German parliament, represents states.

Landtag   German state legislature.

The small Free Democratic party (*Freie Demokratische Partei*, FDP) is a classic liberal party seeking a free society, free market, more individual responsibility, and less government. It used to be placed in the center of the political spectrum between the CDU and SPD but now is often placed to the right of the CDU, rather like U.S. Libertarians. (Note again that liberalism in Europe means about the opposite of U.S. liberalism.) The FDP had trouble defining itself and dropped to 7.4 percent of the vote in 2002 but rebounded to 9.8 percent in 2005. The FDP, now Germany's third-largest party, is an alternative for voters mistrustful of the two big parties.

In 1983, a new ecology-pacifist party, the **Greens**, made it into the Bundestag. In 2005 it won 8.1 percent and shrank from third-largest to fifth-largest party. In the 1998–2005 coalition with the SPD, the leader of the Greens, Joseph (better known as Joschka, "Little Joe") Fischer, was foreign minister, the usual portfolio for the head of the second party in a coalition. The Greens, once radical, turned pragmatic and **regierungsfähig** during the 1990s. They want to phase out Germany's nuclear power plants and to put hefty "eco-taxes" on gasoline. Fischer, a slightly impish speaker and Germany's most popular politician, stepped down as Green leader in 2005.

As soon as the Wall came down in 1989, West Germany's parties simply moved in and took over East Germany. The small, new East German parties that had spearheaded the ouster of the Communists were elbowed aside by the CDU and SPD, who had the money and organization. One regional East German party survived, the Party of Democratic Socialism (PDS), composed of ex-Communists and those who feel ignored by the new system. In 2002 it fell below 5 percent but still won two districts (in East Berlin) outright, and it was entitled to keep those two seats in the Bundestag. With East Germany still poor, the PDS scored well there in Land elections. In 2005 the PDS joined with disgruntled SPD leftists to form a new Left party (*Linkspartei*), which ran well in the east and gained 8.7 percent of votes overall, making it the Bundestag's fourth-largest party. None of the other parties, however, considered it a fit coalition partner. Some small rightist parties, including neo-Nazis, win seats in local and Land elections but have never won seats in the Bundestag.

The Bundesrat

Neither Britain nor France really needs an upper house because they are unitary systems. The German federal system needs an upper house, the **Bundesrat**. Not as powerful as the U.S. Senate—an upper house that powerful is a world rarity—the Bundesrat represents the sixteen Länder and has equal power with the Bundestag on taxes, finances, and laws that effect the federal-state balance. The Bundesrat can veto bills, but the Bundestag can override it. On more serious bills, the matter goes to a mediation committee with sixteen members from each house, but compromise often eludes them. An SPD-dominated Bundesrat blocked the reform measures of CDU Chancellor Kohl in the 1990s. With things reversed in the early 2000s, a CDU-dominated Bundesrat blocked the reform measures of SPD Chancellor Schröder. When the Bundesrat is in the hands of the opposition party, Germany has the divided legislature found in the United States when one party controls the House and another the Senate. To try to remedy this, a 2006 reform trimmed the powers of the Bundesrat but gave more powers to Land governments.

The Bundesrat has sixty-eight members. Every German Land, no matter how small, gets at least three. More populous Länder get four; the most populous get six. Each Land appoints its delegates and usually sends the top officials elected to the **Landtag**, who are also cabinet members in the Land government. They may be from different parties (if the Land government is a coalition), but each Bundesrat delegation must vote as a bloc, not as individuals or as parties. The theory here is that they represent states, not parties.

mixed-member (MM), electoral system that combines single-member districts with proportional representation.

A Split Electoral System

Britain and the United States use single-member districts with plurality win (FPTP) in their parliamentary elections. This system anchors a deputy to a district, giving representatives an abiding interest in their constituents, but it does not accurately reflect votes for parties nationwide; seats are not proportional to votes. (It also gives U.S. Representatives too much interest in looking after the folks back home and too little interest in the good of the country as a whole.)

The alternative, proportional representation (PR), makes the party's percentage of seats nearly proportional to its votes. Weimar Germany had a PR system, which was part of its undoing. PR systems are theoretically the fairest but in practice often lead to difficulties. They permit many small parties in parliament, including antidemocratic parties. They make coalitions hard to form and unstable because usually several parties must combine. Israel, with over a dozen parties in parliament, suffers these consequences of pure proportional representation.

Comparison

Germany's Electoral System: An Export Product

Germany's hybrid **mixed-member** (MM) electoral system—sometimes called a *parallel system*—was much talked about for decades. In the early 1990s, several countries paid Germany the highest compliment by adopting mixed-member systems, with national variations. The aim in all cases was to combine the simplicity of single-member districts with the fairness of PR. Some of the German-inspired hybrids:

■ Russian elections from 1993 to 2003 filled half of the 450-seat lower house by single-member districts and half by PR with a 5 percent threshold. Putin returned to straight PR in 2005.

■ In 1993, Italy dropped its traditional PR system for one in which 75 percent of the seats of both chambers are filled from single-member districts and 25 percent by PR.

■ In 1994, Japan turned from its unique electoral system of multimember districts with plurality victors to an MM system in which more than half the members of each house are elected from single-member districts and the remainder by PR in eleven regions (see pages 271–272).

■ New Zealand in 1993 turned from single-member districts to an MM system for its unicameral legislature of sixty such districts plus sixty elected by PR at the national level with a 5 percent threshold.

■ The 1999 elections for Scottish and Welsh parliaments had single-member FPTP districts but "topped off" the parties' seats by PR so that they are roughly proportional to their vote share.

■ Mexico in 1986 adopted an MM system in which most lower and upper house seats are filled from single-member districts and the rest by PR (see page 489).

DEMOCRACY

2005: A SPLIT ELECTORAL SYSTEM IN ACTION

Chancellor Gerhard Schröder's SPD-led government found itself blocked in 2005. It proposed reforms to trim the welfare state and reinvigorate Germany's economy, but many SPD voters protested any cuts in their benefits. Even when Schröder got a bill through the Bundestag, the CDU-controlled Bundesrat would veto it. In May of 2005 the SPD lost elections in the large, industrialized Land of North Rhine-Westphalia, where it had held sway for twenty-nine years. Schröder felt trapped in a declining situation, so he arranged to lose a Bundestag vote, allowing him to dissolve the Bundestag and hold elections a year early.

The SPD was supposed to lose big in the September 2005 elections; polls favored the CDU/CSU by as much as 20 percentage points. But personality counts in German elections. Schröder was an outgoing personality who kept his points general while CDU leader Angela Merkel was stiff and detail-oriented. The SPD warned that the CDU/CSU would dismantle the welfare state many Germans depend on. Schröder also won votes with criticism of President Bush's Iraq war. Schröder steadily narrowed the gap with Merkel. Election posters featured portraits of Schröder and Merkel, almost as if it were a presidential election.

A turnout of 78 percent barely made the CDU/CSU the largest party in the Bundestag, with 226 seats to the SPD's 222. With neither having a majority, after two weeks of negotiations, they formed a grand coalition (see box on page 187) with each other. Germany's MM electoral system (see box on page 189) is based on PR, but about half the seats are filled from single-member districts with plurality win (as in Britain). First, notice the percent of vote (on the right-hand, PR ballot) is close to the percent of Bundestag seats

But notice also that the parties got more seats than their percentage of the votes. This is partly because some small parties (the neo-Nazi National Democrats, for example) won less than 5 percent and got no seats. Further, ticket-splitting—voting, as many did in 2005, for the individual CDU candidate on the left-hand half of the ballot but for the FDP on the PR right-hand side—won the CDU more seats than did the percentage of their party votes. The Greens and FDP win seats almost entirely on the second ballot, the party list; they are rarely big enough to win a single-member district.

Those who win a single-member constituency (the left half of the ballot) keep the seat even if it exceeds the percentage that their party is entitled to from the PR (right half of the ballot) vote. These "bonus seats" (in 2005 most of them went to the CDU) make the Bundestag larger than its nominal size of 598 seats; it now has 614 members. Is the German electoral system now clear to you? Not to worry. Many Germans do not fully understand it. Basically, just remember that it is a split system: roughly half single-member districts and half PR, but PR sets the overall share of seats. It is proportional but not perfectly proportional.

	% of Vote	Seats
CDU/CSU	35.2	226 (36.8%)
Social Democrats	34.2	222 (36.2%)
Free Democrats	9.8	61 (9.9%)
Left	8.7	54 (8.8%)
Greens	8.1	51 (8.3%)

Stimmzettel

für die Wahl zum Deutschen Bunderstag im Wahlkreis 63 Bonn
am 27. September 1998

Sie haben 2 Stimmen

hier 1 Stimme
für die Wahl

eines/einer Wahlkreis-
abgeordneten

hier 1 Stimme
für die Wahl

einer Landesliste (Partei)
- maßgebende Stimme für die Verteilung der Sitze
insgesamt auf die einzelnen Parteien -

Erststimme

Zweitstimme

	Erststimme					Zweitstimme	
1	**Kelber,** Ulrich **SPD** Dipl. Informatiker Bonn-Beuel Neustraße 37	Sozialdemokratische Partei Deutschlands	( )	( )	**SPD**	Sozialdemokratische Partei Deutschlands — Franz Müntefering, Anke Fuchs, Rudolf Dreßler, Wolf-Michael Catenhusen, Ingrid Matthäus-Maier	1
2	**Hauser,** Norbert **CDU** Rechtsanwalt Bonn-Bad Godesberg Elfstraße 26	Christlich Demokratische Union Deutschlands	( )	( )	**CDU**	Christlich Demokratische Union Deutschlands — Dr. Norbert Blüm, Peter Hintze, Irmgard Karwatzki, Dr. Norbert Lammert, Dr. Jürgen Rüttgers	2
3	**Dr. Westerwelle,** Guido **F.D.P.** Rechtsanwalt Bonn Heerstraße 85	Free Demokratische Partei	( )	( )	**F.D.P.**	Freie Demokratische Partei — Dr. Guido Westerwelle, Jürgen W. Möllemann, Ulrike Flach, Paul Friedhoff, Dr. Werner H. Hoyer	3
4	**Manemann,** Coletta **GRÜNE** Dipl. Pädagogin Bonn Humboldtstraße 2	BÜNDNIS 90/ DIE GRÜNEN	( )	( )	**GRÜNE**	BÜNDNIS 90/DIE GRÜNEN — Kerstin Müller, Ludger Volmer, Christa Nickels, Dr. Reinhard Loske, Simone Probst	4
				( )	**PDS**	Partei des Demokratischen Sozialismus — Ulla Jelpke, Ursula Lötzer, Knud Vöcking, Ernst Dmytrowski, Astrid Keller	5
				( )	**Deutschland**	Ab jetzt ... Bündnis für Deutschland — Horst Zaborowski, Dr. -Ing. Helmut Fleck, Dietmar-Lothar Dander, Ricardo Pielsticker, Uwe Karg	6
				( )	**APPD**	Anarchistische Pogo- Partei Deutschlands — Rainer Kaufmann, Matthias Bender, Daniel-Lars Kroll, Markus Bittmann, Markus Rykalski	7
8	**Müchler,** Frank **BüSo** Buchhändler Düsseldorf Ohligserstraße 45	Bürgerrechts- bewegung Solidarität	( )	( )	**BüSo**	Bürgerrechtsbewegung Solidarität — Helga Zepp-LaRouche, Karl-Michael Vitt, Andreas Schumacher, Hildegard Reynen-Kaiser, Walter vom Stein	8

"You Have Two Votes": A German Ballot

party list Party's ranking of its candidates in PR elections; voters pick one list as their ballot.

threshold clause Minimum percent party must win to get any seats.

The German system combines both approaches, single-member districts and proportional representation. The voter has two votes, one for a single representative in one of 299 districts, the other for a party. The party vote is the crucial one because it determines the total number of seats a party gets in a given Land. Some of these seats are occupied by the party's district winners; additional seats are taken from the party's *Landesliste* to reach the percentage won on the second ballot. This Landesliste (the right-hand column on the sample ballot on page 191) is a list of persons whom the party proposes as deputies, starting with the names at the top of the list. The **party list** is the standard technique for a PR system. Leading party figures are assigned high positions on the list to ensure that they get elected; people at the bottom of the party list do not have a chance.

The German system works like proportional representation—percentage of votes (nearly) equals percentage of Bundestag seats—but with the advantage of single-member districts. It is technically known as *mixed-member proportional* (MMP), as it preserves overall proportionality. (The systems discussed in the box on page 189 are just *mixed-member*, as their parliaments do not have overall proportionality of parties.) As in Britain and the United States, German voters get a district representative. More than in straight PR systems, personality counts in German elections; a politician cannot be just a good party worker but has to go out and talk with voters to earn their confidence on a personal basis. It is a matter of considerable pride among FRG politicians to be elected from a single-member district with a higher percentage of votes than their party won on the second ballot. It suggests that voters split their tickets because they liked the candidate better than his or her party.

For most of the postwar years, the German system slowly cut down the number of parties compared to Weimar days until it was a two-plus system (a big CDU and SPD, plus a small FDP). One reason: A party must win at least 5 percent nationwide to get its PR share of Bundestag seats. The **threshold clause** was designed to keep out splinter and extremist parties. More recently, however, some new small parties have made it into parliament, the Greens, the PDS, and now the Left party. Even if below 5 percent, a party gets whatever single-member constituency seats it wins, the reason the PDS got two seats in the 2002 Bundestag. Variations on the German hybrid electoral system were adopted by several countries (see box on page 189).

German parties get government help for campaign funds, but after the election. Every party that makes it into the Bundestag gets several euros for each vote. Furthermore, parties' contributions and membership fees are matched 50 percent by federal funds. Typically, a German national election costs taxpayers $150 million or more (cheap by U.S. standards).

KEY TERMS

FurtHer Reference

Beyme, Klaus von. *The Legislator: German Parliament as a Centre of Political Decision-Making.* Brookfield, VT: Ashgate, 1998.

Conradt, David, Gerald R. Kleinfled, George K. Romoser, and Christain Soe. *Power Shift in Germany: The 1998 Election and the End of the Kohl Era.* Providence, RI: Berghan, 1999.

Eberle, Edward J. *Dignity and Liberty: Constitutional Visions in Germany and the United States.* Westport, CT: Praeger, 2002.

Glaessner, Gert-Joachim. *German Democracy: From Post–World War II to the Present Day.* New York: Berg, 2005.

Green, Simon, and William E. Paterson, eds. *Governance in Contemporary Germany: The Semisovereign State Revisited.* New York: Cambridge University Press, 2005.

Helms, Ludger, ed. *Institutions and Institutional Change in the Federal Republic of Germany.* New York: St. Martin's, 2000.

Jacoby, Wade. *Imitation and Politics: Redesigning Modern Germany.* Ithaca, NY: Cornell University Press, 2000.

Klein, Hans, ed. *The German Chancellors.* Carol Stream, IL: Edition Q, 1996.

Moeller, Robert G., ed. *West Germany under Construction: Politics, Society, and Culture in the Adenauer Era.* Ann Arbor, MI: University of Michigan Press, 1997.

Nicholls, A. J. *The Bonn Republic: West German Democracy, 1945–1990.* New York: Longman, 1997.

Quint, Peter E. *The Imperfect Union: Constitutional Structures of German Unification.* Princeton, NJ: Princeton University Press, 1997.

CHAPTER 14
GERMAN
Political Culture

A German woman once recounted to me how the Americans, in the last days of World War II, had bombed her hometown, a charming North Bavarian place with a splendid church and no military value. The town was a mess: Bodies lay unburied, water and electricity were out, food supplies were unmoved. What did the towns people do? She shrugged, "We waited for the Americans to come and tell us what to do."

Such were the beginnings of democracy in West Germany: a foreign implant grafted onto a people who were used to being told what to do. Can democracy be transplanted? (Even in Iraq?) Has it in fact taken root in Germany? This is the bothersome question. Germany's institutions are fine; in several ways the Federal Republic's Basic Law is a model constitution. But, as we saw with Weimar, good institutions are not worth much if people do not support them. Are democratic values sufficiently strong and deep in Germany to withstand economic and political hard times?

QUESTIONS TO CONSIDER

1. What is *liberal democracy?* Why was it weak in Germany?
2. How have Germans handled the Nazi period and the Holocaust?
3. How are German and American multiculturalism alike?
4. What is *postmaterialism?* Is it nearly everywhere?
5. What are Germany's *political generations?*
6. Why do Wessis and Ossis resent each other?
7. Is German democracy as solid as any? How can you tell?
8. How did Willy Brandt represent a turning point?

Historically, there has long been a liberal tradition, but a losing one. It grew out of the Enlightenment, as in France. In Britain, democracy gradually triumphed. In France, democracy and reaction seesawed back and forth, finally reaching an uneasy balance. In Germany, on the other hand, democracy was overwhelmed by authoritarian forces. In 1849 the German liberals were driven out of the Frankfurt cathedral. In Bismarck's Second Reich they were treated with contempt. In the Weimar Republic they were a minority, a pushover for authoritarians.

East Germany attempted to develop "people's democracy" (communism) rather than **liberal democracy** in the Western sense. Although communism and fascism are supposed to be opposites, both made individuals obedient and powerless. Many East Germans were confused and skeptical at the onrush of democracy from West Germany in 1990; they had known nothing but authoritarian rule since 1933. It is taking some time and education for East German democratic attitudes to reach the levels of West Germany.

THE MORAL VACUUM

In addition to a weak democratic tradition, Germany faced a more subtle problem after World War II. A liberal democracy requires certain moral foundations. If you are entrusting ultimate authority to the people through their representatives, you have to believe that they are generally moral,

liberal democracy Combines tolerance and freedoms (liberalism) with mass participation (democracy). (See page 195.)

denazification Purging Nazi officials from public life.

Holocaust Nazi genocide of Europe's Jews during World War II.

multiculturalism Preservation of diverse languages and traditions within one country; in German *Multikulti*. (See page 197.)

reparations Paying back for war damages. (See page 197.)

perhaps even a bit idealistic. When this belief vanishes, a democracy loses legitimacy. People may go along with it but with doubts. Such was the Weimar period.

The Nazis left a moral vacuum in Germany, and filling it has been a long, slow process. One problem that hindered German democracy was the persistence of ex-Nazis in high places. Every time one was discovered, it undermined the moral authority of the regime. People, especially young people, thought, "Why should we respect democracy if the same old Nazis are running it?"

Immediately after the war, the Allied occupiers tried to "denazify" their zones. Party members, especially officials and the Gestapo (secret police), lost their jobs and sometimes went to prison. Henry Kissinger, then a U.S. Army sergeant, rounded up Gestapo agents in the town he was running by advertising in the newspaper for experienced policemen; when they showed up he jailed them. Still, aside from the 177 war criminals tried at Nuremberg (twenty-five sentenced to death), **denazification** was spotty, and many Nazis got away, to Latin America or to new lives within Germany. Many made themselves useful to the occupation authorities and worked their way into business, politics, the civil service, and even the judicial system.

It was the judicial system that kept mass murderers from coming to trial. There are German laws against such people, but Nazi criminals were rarely brought to trial until the 1960s. By then younger people had worked their way up the judicial ladder and were willing to prosecute cases their elders let pass. This helps explain why Nazi war criminals were still being tried in the 1990s.

The Cold War also delayed a thorough look at the Nazi past. By 1947 the Western Allies decided they needed Germany to block Soviet power, so they stopped rubbing Germans' noses in the past. Tough questions about the wartime behavior of German civilian and military officials were not asked; now they were on our side. (U.S. occupation policy shifted at the same time and for the same reason in Japan.) With the founding of the Federal Republic in 1949, such matters were placed in the hands of West German authorities, and many preferred not to "open old wounds."

Two presidents of the Federal Republic, Walter Scheel of the FDP and Karl Carstens of the CDU, and one chancellor, Kurt Kiesinger of the CDU, had once been Nazi party members. All asserted they were nominal rather than active members, "just opportunists" out to further their careers during a time when the Nazis controlled paths to success. While none were accused of any crime, what kind of moral authority did "just an opportunist" lend to the highest offices of a country trying to become a democracy?

The Remembrance of Things Past

Can a society experience collective guilt? Was it realistic to expect Germans as a whole to feel remorse for what the Nazis did? The West German response was initially to flush the Nazi era down the memory hole: "Past, go away!" German fathers were reluctant to say much about what they had done. For some decades, German history textbooks stopped at 1933 and picked up again in 1945. The result was ignorance among young Germans in the 1950s and 1960s about the Nazis and the **Holocaust**. Then, in 1979, the American-made TV miniseries "Holocaust" riveted Germans' attention and triggered German books, movies, documentaries, and discussion. In the 1980s, curricula and textbooks began to treat the Nazi period more fully. This belated Holocaust flood, however, made some Germans feel resentful and picked-upon.

Political Culture

HOW TO HANDLE THE HOLOCAUST

Keep it front and center, or retire it as an overworked issue from a bygone era? This was the dilemma Germany faced as it restored Berlin as the capital in the 1990s. The problem was more subtle than nazism and anti-Semitism, which are not serious threats. Some Germans felt that leftists had turned guilt for the Holocaust into an all-purpose tool to promote **multiculturalism** and political correctness. Many tired of hearing about the Holocaust, which only the oldest Germans have personally lived through.

Germany has paid some $60 billion in **reparations** for the Holocaust, and many Germans felt this was enough. A more recent question was whether and what kind of Holocaust memorial should be built in the heart of Berlin. CDU Chancellor Kohl had urged it; SPD Chancellor Schröder and his party had some doubts. Some argued that there were already enough such memorials. A new Jewish Museum opened in Berlin in early 1999 (designed and directed by **Americans**). Some argued that no memorial could possibly do justice to the magnitude of the horror. Some suggested that a death camp was the proper site. Some wanted a big memorial, others small. Some wanted a traditional monument, others abstract. In 1999, the Bundestag finally authorized a large memorial by a U.S. architect in the heart of Berlin; it opened in 2005.

German businesses had a rough time with the Holocaust issue as well. Under the Nazis, they had benefited from the money and property seized from Jews and from Jewish (and other) slave labor. For decades, German businesses, banks, and insurance companies rejected survivors' demands for compensation with the claim that private firms, like everyone else, had to follow Nazi orders. They belatedly made efforts to settle when faced with U.S. lawsuits. In 1999, Chancellor Schröder, backed by twelve major German firms, set up a $5 billion compensation fund "to counter lawsuits, particularly class-action suits, and to remove the basis of the campaign being led against German industry and our country." The controversy reminded some of the old Nazi line that an international Jewish conspiracy was keeping Germany down.

Busy Berlin square features the reminder, "Places of Horror That We Must Never Forget," a list of World War II concentration camps. At the top: Auschwitz.

Vergangenheitsbewältigung   Literally, "mastery of the past"; coming to grips with Germany's Nazi past.

Can a society simply forget its past, blot it out? West Germans tried. Climbing out of the ruins of World War II, they threw themselves with single-minded devotion into work, making money, and spending it conspicuously. The results were spectacular; the economy soared, and many Germans became affluent. The West German archetype became the *Wunderkind* (wonder child), the businessman who rose from rubble to riches in the postwar boom with a fat body, a fat cigar, and a fat Mercedes. But material prosperity could not fill the moral and historical void. Many young Germans in the 1960s were profoundly dissatisfied with the emphasis on materialism that seemed to be a cover-up for a lack of deeper values. Some of them turned to far-left and later "green" politics.

This factor contributed to the radical and sometimes violent politics among young Germans in the 1970s and 1980s. They were not poor; often they were from wealthy families. Prosperity and materialism, in fact, rubbed them the wrong way. Said one rich girl: "I'm sick of all this caviar gobbling." She joined the terrorists and helped murder an old family friend, a banker. (She and other gang members were arrested in 1990 in East Germany, where the secret police, the Stasi, had protected them.) The Baader-Meinhof gang committed murder and bank robbery in the name of revolution, and some young Germans sympathized with them. The terrorists, in their warped, sick way, put their finger on the German malaise: German society, avoiding its past, had developed a moral void with nothing to believe in but "caviar gobbling." The past does not stay buried; it comes back to haunt the society trying to forget it. As William Faulkner said: "The past isn't dead; it isn't even past."

German Catholic writer Heinrich Böll coined the term **Vergangenheitsbewältigung** in the 1950s to direct Germans' attention to the moral vacuum. He meant that Germans must face the past squarely and admit some collective guilt. Many German intellectuals take this as the necessary foundation of German democracy. If Germans cannot come to grips with their own past, if they try to cover it up, German democracy could again be taken over by mindless nationalists, cautioned former President Richard von Weizsäcker and leftist writer Günter Grass.

Memories of war are preserved in the Kaiser Wilhelm Church, which was deliberately left half-ruined in Berlin.

Under Communist rule, the East Germans used a different approach to avoid coming to grips with the past: deny it was their past. "We were not Nazis," taught the Communist regime, "We fought the Nazis. So we have nothing to be ashamed of or to regret. The Nazis are over there in West Germany." East Germany avoided moral responsibility by trying to portray the Nazis as a foreign power, like Austria has done. In this area, as in many others, East German attitudes lagged behind West German attitudes.

The Generation Gap

As a guest in a German home long ago, I saw how the family reacted when one of the daughters found, in the back of a china closet, an old poem, *"Die Hitlerblume"* (the Hitler flower), comparing the *Führer* to a blossom. The three college-age children howled with laughter and derision. "Daddy, how could you go along with this garbage?" they asked. The father, an old-fashioned authoritarian type, grew red in the face and stammered, "You don't know what it was like. They had everybody whipped up. The times were different." He was quite embarrassed.

> **output affect** Attachment to a system based on its providing material abundance.
>
> **system affect** Attachment to a system for its own sake.

The incident underscores the rapid generational changes in German political attitudes; simply put, the younger the generation, the more open, free-spirited, democratic, and European it is. Most younger Germans give unqualified allegiance to democracy and European unity. Only a handful of personality problems hanker for an authoritarian system. Feeling no personal responsibility for what the Nazis did, they are also less inclined to ponder Germany's past.

The younger generation has also freed up German society. No longer are German women confined to *Kinder, Küche, Kirche* (children, kitchen, and church); most now work outside the home and participate in politics. German youngsters are not so obedient, and German fathers no longer beat them as in the old days. If democracy starts in the home, Germany now has a much better foundation for democracy.

The typical German of today is far more democratic in attitudes than in 1949, when the Federal Republic was founded. Those who would support another Hitler, trade civil rights for "security," or think a one-party system is best have steadily dwindled, while those who think democracy and civil rights are important in their own right have steadily increased. West German attitudes are now at least as democratic as any of their European neighbors, and the East Germans are likely to become so.

Is the change permanent? Political scientist Sidney Verba drew a distinction between **output affect** and **system affect** in his discussion of German political culture. The former means liking the system for what it produces (jobs, security, and material goods), the latter, liking the system because it is perceived as good. Verba thought Germans showed more of the first than the second; that is, they liked the system while the going was good—they were "fair-weather democrats"—but had not yet become "rain-or-shine democrats" the way Britons or Americans are. Verba's point was made in the early 1960s. Since then, system affect among Germans has increased as the younger generation has come of age. Some East Germans, however, are still caught up in the output affect, judging democracy by the cars and jobs it provides them.

A Normal Germany?

Many Germans now argue that Germany has become a "normal" country and no longer bears any special guilt about the past. Most Germans were born after the Nazis, they note, and German democracy is as solid as any. As good Europeans, Germans should help prevent massacres in Bosnia and Kosovo, a majority of Germans felt, thus breaking the FRG taboo against using German forces outside of Germany. Until recently, most Germans hid their nationalism, but now many politicians say they are patriotic and proud to be German.

Ostpolitik Literally "east policy"; Brandt's building of relations with East Europe, including East Germany.

Is Germany now strictly a normal country? The question flared up in 2002 when the deputy leader of the small Free Democratic party, Jürgen Möllemann, sharply criticized Israel and sided with the Palestinians, as many Europeans do. In Germany, however, this is awkward; some say it is neo-Nazi. Others argue that in a "normal" country criticism of Israel is no longer taboo. Foreign Minister Fischer noted: "Whenever Israel is discussed in Germany, the fundamental debate about German identity is never far behind. Can we criticize Israel? The very question raises suspicion." Germany may never be a completely normal country.

PERSONALITIES

WILLY BRANDT AS TURNING POINT

Willy Brandt

One of the signs that democracy had taken root in Germany was the 1969 election that made Willy Brandt chancellor. It would not have been possible even a few years earlier, for Brandt represented a repudiation of German history and society that few Germans could have tolerated earlier. First, Brandt was an illegitimate child, a black mark that Adenauer used in election campaigns. Second, Brandt was a Socialist, and in his youth in the North German seaport of Lübeck had been pretty far left (although never Communist). No Socialist had been in power in Germany for decades; the CDU kept smearing the SPD as a dangerous party, and many Germans believed it. Third, and most damaging, was that Brandt had fled to Norway in 1933, became a Norwegian citizen, and had not reclaimed his German nationality until 1947. Some even falsely accused him of fighting Germans as a Norwegian soldier.

With a record like that, it seemed Brandt was starting into German politics with three strikes against him. But many Germans, especially younger ones, admired Brandt. He was "Mr. Clean," a German who had battled the Nazis—literally, in Lübeck street fights—and who had never been "just an opportunist" who survived by going along. Brandt seemed to represent a newer, better Germany as opposed to the conservative, traditional values of Adenauer and the CDU.

As mayor of West Berlin from 1957 to 1966, Brandt showed how tough and anti-Communist he was by standing up to Soviet and East German efforts at encroachment. A leading figure in the SPD, Brandt supported its 1959 move away from Marxism. In 1964 he became the SPD's chairman, and this boosted the party's electoral fortunes.

In 1966 the SPD joined the cabinet in a grand coalition with the CDU. As is usual in coalitions, the head of the second largest party is foreign minister. Here, Brandt showed himself to be a forceful and innovative statesman with his **Ostpolitik**. By 1969 the SPD had enough Bundestag seats to form a small coalition with the FDP, and Brandt became the FRG's first Socialist chancellor. The event was a symbolic breakthrough: Germany looked more democratic under an anti-Nazi than an ex-Nazi (Brandt's predecessor, Kiesinger).

In 1974 it was discovered that a Brandt assistant was an East German spy. (West Germany was riddled with East German spies.) Brandt, regretting his security slip, resigned the chancellorship to become the grand old man of not only German but also West European social democracy. By the time he died in 1992 he could see the fruits of his Ostpolitik.

The younger generation of Germans brings with them new concerns about jobs and the environment that the older generation did not worry about. A distance developed between many young Germans and the mainstream political parties. In the German party system, newcomers must slowly work their way up the ranks of the major parties, starting at the local and state levels, before they can have a say at the national level. By the time they can, few are young. (One interesting exception: In 1998, a twenty-two-year-old SPD candidate from East Germany won a seat in the Bundestag, the youngest German deputy ever.) In the meantime, they are expected to obey party dictates and not have much input. Some youth organizations of both the Social Democrats and Free Democrats became so rambunctious that they had to be disowned by their parent parties. For many young Germans, both the Christian Democrats and Social Democrats, who alternated in power, looked staid and elderly, and neither was responsive to young people.

Belatedly, some German politicians recognized the problem. Former President Richard von Weizsäcker worried about "the failure of my generation to bring younger people into politics." Young Germans, he noted, "do not admire the moral substance of the older generation. Our economic achievement went along with a very materialistic and very selfish view of all problems."

Young Germans also turned away from the United States. In the 1950s and early 1960s, young Germans nearly worshiped the United States; it was their model in politics, lifestyles, and values. Events over forty years reversed this. The assassination of President Kennedy—who had recently proclaimed "Ich bin ein Berliner" at the Berlin Wall—horrified Germans and made them wonder about the United States. The Vietnam War was worse; some young Germans compared it to Hitler's aggression. Rising tensions between East and West and the war-like posture of President Reagan convinced many young Germans that the United States was willing to incinerate Germany. With the 2003 Iraq war most Germans saw Americans as violent and arrogant. It was ironic that the United

> **postmaterialism**   Theory that modern culture has moved beyond getting and spending.
>
> **affluence**   Having plenty of money.

KEY CONCEPTS

THE RISE OF "POSTMATERIALISM"

One of the trends among rich nations—especially pronounced in West Germany—is the feeling of some young people that modern society is too focused on material goods. Starting in the late 1960s, "countercultures" sprang up in every advanced country. Young people rejected the work-and-buy ethic of their parents and turned instead to beards, blue jeans, and "quality of life" questions. This caught on strongly in the Federal Republic as young Germans sought to repudiate the hypermaterialism of their parents.

Postmaterialism is found throughout the advanced industrialized world. Raised in conditions of **affluence** with no depression or war, young Britons, French, Germans, Japanese, and Americans tend to ignore their parents' values and embrace few causes. The postmaterial generation is tolerant, introspective, fun-loving, and not drawn to conventional political parties or religions or marriage and family. Said young German writer Judith Hermann: "The older generation has been more interested in the past, the war, politics. My generation looks at itself."

Postmaterialism underlies the Federal Republic's leftist, antinuclear, ecology, and pacifist movements, much of which came together in the Greens. Postmaterialism also plugged into German romanticism and nationalism. Will postmaterialism last or decline? If it has created a vacuum of values, what might eventually fill the vacuum?

Wessi   Informal name for West German.

Ossi   Informal name for East German.

political generation   Theory that age groups are marked by the great events of their young adulthood.

States—which had tutored Germans to repudiate militarism—became the object of German antiwar feeling.

The preceding attitudes fed the Green and later the Left parties. In elections, these two parties do best among young voters. Their attitudes also contribute to a new German nationalism that no longer follows in America's footsteps. Instead of automatically looking west, some young Germans look to a reunified Germany taking its rightful place as the natural leader of Central Europe. Some turned anti-United States and anti-NATO. The entirely new situation created by German unification, the end of the Cold War, fighting in Bosnia and Kosovo, and the 2003 Iraq War changed German attitudes, especially those of young people. Schröder boosted the 2002 SPD vote by criticizing U.S. policy on Iraq. Germans no longer look to the United States for guidance or solidarity.

The Disorienting Unification

There is still a big cultural gap between East and West Germans. When the Wall came down in late 1989, there was much celebration and good will. **Wessis** were generous to the **Ossis**, but soon the relationship soured. The Ossis kept demanding the bounties of the prosperous West as a right; after all, they were all Germans, and the Wessis had so much. The Wessis did not see things that way. "We've worked hard for more than forty years for this," they argued, "Now you Ossis must do the

Key Concepts

Political Generations in Germany

German sociologist Karl Mannheim coined the term **political generations** to describe how great events put a lasting stamp on young people. We can see this in Germany. Today's young Germans were formed by the fall of the Berlin Wall in 1989. Sometimes called "89ers," they stand in marked contrast with previous German generations: the 45ers, who climbed out of the rubble and rebuilt a new Germany, and the 68ers, who rebelled against complacent materialism.

Many 68ers changed over time. Chancellor Schröder had been a Marxist Juso who turned quite centrist. Green leader Joschka Fischer dropped out of high school and fought police in the streets but became a popular and effective foreign minister. Otto Schily had been a far-left lawyer who defended terrorists but joined the SPD and became interior minister, which includes internal security. Most Germans were unbothered by their pasts.

The 89ers were relatively few in number (because of the strong trend to one-child couples) and worry about unemployment, destruction of the environment, and having to pay off the staggering burden of German unification and the lavish pensions of older Germans. Generally liberal and tolerant, *postmodern* Germans are also fun-loving, individualistic, irreligious, and apolitical; they do not much care for hard work, marriage, having children, or politics. Many do not vote, and few like the main political parties, but some are open to the Greens or Left. Few join formal groups or associations.

Now some younger Germans repudiate the rebellion of the 68ers and playfulness of the 89ers by returning to the *bourgeois* values of earlier times (*die Neue Bürgerlichkeit*). Relying on the welfare state is less fashionable; self-reliance and volunteering is back in. Hippie clothing is out; nicely dressed is in. Such people could boost CDU electoral fortunes.

(elem
Haupi
collar
bac) fo
some
on. So
Kurt F

T
Germa
than t
than t
usually
mon L
flexibl
ate an
orient

M
makin
Germa
laws. E

Be
In few
One G
Econo
mut Sc
inflatic
cession

The (

The Fr
belling
and rea

Ge

Back
clockv
with L
the Sk

same." With newly acquired D-Marks from West German taxpayers, Ossis snatched up modern products while their own economy collapsed. West Germans quickly developed negative stereotypes of East Germans living well at Wessi expense—like poor relatives who had come to sponge off them.

As the costs of bringing East Germany up to West German levels started to sink in, some Germans grew angry. The East German economy was found to be in far worse shape than foreseen and needed huge bailouts. Much industry simply had to be closed; unemployment shot up. West German business executives talk down to their East German counterparts. Wessis think Ossis have been trained into inefficiency by the Communists. Ossis feel belittled by and alienated from the West German system that was quickly imposed on them. This has led to an increase in East German consciousness, which is now greater than before unification. There is nothing like togetherness to separate people.

Politically, Ossis have weak party identification (see pages 61 and 133) and easily shift their votes from one election to the next, first to the CDU, then to the SPD, and recently to the Left party, the party of East German resentment and nostalgia (*Ostalgie*). The Left is supported by ex-Communists, people worried about their pensions, and Ossis who feel the other parties ignore them. The collapse of East Germany left citizens disoriented and lacking something to believe in. "Freedom" is not clear enough; some are still ideologically socialist and crave order and a system that guarantees their livelihood. One of the lessons of Germany's unification: You have to pay as much attention to psychological and social transitions as to economic ones.

The economy, too, was a problem. Since unification, German economic growth has been slow, making many Germans frightened of unemployment (more than twice as high in East Germany as in West) and resentful at the massive transfer of funds to the east. Some Germans wonder if unification has been worthwhile. Some are disoriented and ask which is the right way for unified Germany in a vastly different Europe. Some left-wing intellectuals warn of the return of a racist Germany. Neo-Nazi and skinhead youths (found throughout Europe) lent weight to the warnings: Over a decade more than a hundred Africans and Turks were killed and Jewish sites desecrated. Predicting a stable future for a united Germany is more difficult than it was for West Germany alone.

bounce-back effect   Tendency of trends and values to reverse.

skinheads   Racist youth, begun in England, with shaved heads and quasi-military attire.

Democracy

A Bounce-Back Effect?

Germans, especially young Germans, are looser, freer, and more open than ever. Some observers think this is the way things are going worldwide, the generational shift to *postmodernism* (see box on page 202). Historically, however, there have been **bounce-back effects** that have abruptly reversed values. American journalist William Shirer recalled how young Germans in the 1920s pursued fun and freedom, but this reversed under the Nazis. Young Germans in the 1950s and early 1960s were hard-working, moderate, and pro-American; by the late 1960s many were dropout anti-American multicultural radicals. In 2005, a fair fraction of Germans voted left, green, and pacifist.

Many young Germans now face long-term unemployment. Some resent foreigners who, they think, take their jobs. German **skinheads** rob and beat foreigners. Some young Germans reject *Multikulti* and Holocaust guilt. They did not do it, so why should it concern them? Young Germans will likely continue to seek fun and freedom, but that can sometimes turn destructive. What comes is highly unpredictable, but it will probably be to a rock beat.

Tl

M;
age
pre
Ge
ity
Th
ma
fro
be
era
th

as
ip;
sy:
lo
er,
wo
po
an

S

G
is
in

KEY

These th
ly spread
lustrate:
(see pag
lot with
sence of
massive
to keep

CHAPTER 15

GERMANY:
PATTERNS OF INTERACTION

We saw how the Weimar Republic collapsed with the shrinking of the moderate parties and growth of extremist parties—"polarized pluralism." Could this happen in the Federal Republic? For most of the history of West Germany, the answer was no. With only two-plus parties, they, for good political reasons, stuck close to the center of the political spectrum. Political competition in West Germany tended to be **center-seeking**. Voters had their choice of three moderate parties (there were several tiny parties on the ballot, but they were largely ignored), and these three parties could combine in only three different coalitions (CDU and FDP, CDU and SPD, SPD and FDP). This made West German politics stable compared to more tumultuous multiparty systems.

QUESTIONS TO CONSIDER

1. Why has German coalition formation become more difficult?
2. Why is a unimodal distribution of opinion necessary for democracy?
3. How do German political views resemble British and French?
4. What is the difference between *Weltanschauung* and catchall parties?
5. How have German elections come to resemble presidential ones?
6. Are fund-raising scandals part of democracy?
7. What is the union-party linkup in North European countries?
8. In what ways does voting follow geography?

With unification—and even a little before—German politics became less stable and more complex. The party system is no longer "two-plus," but with the arrival of the Greens and Left is now more accurately described as multiparty. The two large parties lost some of their votes to smaller parties. This made coalition formation more difficult, for now a German coalition may require three partners instead of the previous two. Now there are nine possible coalition combinations (see box on page 211). This in turn makes German government less stable and predictable.

PARTIES AND THE ELECTORATE

Social scientists repeatedly find that political opinion in most modern democracies resembles a bell-shaped curve: A lot of people are in the center, with fewer and fewer as one moves to the left or right. If you want to sound scientific you call this a **unimodal** distribution of opinion. (A **bimodal** distribution indicates extreme division, what happened during Weimar.) Routinely, Europeans are asked to place themselves on a one-to-nine ideological scale, one for the most left and nine for the most right. Germany comes out, like most West European countries, as a bell-shaped curve (see graph at the top of page 210).

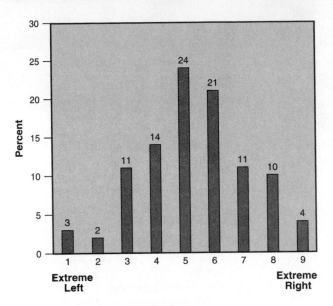

The Shape of the German Electorate: The Self-Placement of German Voters on a Left/Right Ideological Scale

How does this affect political parties? When party leaders come to understand the shape of the electorate, either through modern polling techniques or by losing elections, they usually try to modify their party image so that it appeals to the middle of the opinion spectrum. If the Social Democrats position themselves too far left—say, at two on the nine-point scale—by advocating nationalizing private industry and dropping out of NATO, they may please left-wing ideologues in the party but do poorly in elections because few Germans are at the two position. So the Social Democrats tone down their socialism and emphasize their commitment to democracy plus welfare measures, moving to perhaps the four position.

Now they do much better in elections, but the left wing of the SPD is unhappy with the dilution of socialist gospel. Finally, sniffing the possibility of becoming Germany's governing party, the SPD throws out socialism and tells the electorate that they will do a better job running the capitalist, market economy. Now they are in roughly the five position, but the party's left wingers are angry, accusing the SPD leadership of selling out to capitalism; some left-wing socialists even quit the SPD. But the SPD does well in elections. By emphasizing democracy and minimizing socialism, they gain many centrist Germans. But now there is some vacant ideological space on the left, which the Greens and Left party fill.

The preceding, in a nutshell, is the history of the SPD. A century ago the Social Democrats started to shed their Marxism, in practice if not yet in theory. In the 1950s, seeing the CDU triumphantly win the center, they decided to break out of their left-wing stronghold. Meeting in Bad Godesberg (just outside Bonn) in 1959, they drew up a Basic Program so moderate one can hardly find any socialism in it. Marxism was *kaputt*; the SPD proclaimed itself "rooted in Christian ethics, humanism and classical philosophy."

While the Social Democrats moved rightward, the Christian Democrats had in the meantime already taken a broad swath of the ideological spectrum, claiming to stand for everything—a party of all Germans—just as the British Conservatives used to claim to represent all Britons. The CDU downplayed its conservatism, for it, too, understood that if the party image were too rightist it would lose the big prize in the center. The result is two large parties that have generally tried to be centrist but in so doing have rubbed their respective left and right wings the wrong way (see boxes on pages 212 and 213). They also make politics boring.

center-seeking Parties trying to win a big centrist vote with moderate programs. (See page 209.)

unimodal Single-peaked distribution. (See page 209.)

bimodal Two-peaked distribution. (See page 209.)

KEY CONCEPTS

GERMANY'S COALITIONS

Two-party coalitions have been the norm for Germany, usually consisting of one large party and one small party. When either of the two large parties (CDU or SPD) gets around 40 percent of the vote (and of Bundestag seats), formerly the case, it forms a coalition with a small party that won around 10 percent and thus controls a (bare) majority of the Bundestag. This relatively happy situation gives rise to coalition possibilities 1 through 4, which have governed the FRG thus far:

1. Christian-Liberal Coalition: The CDU/CSU wins about 40 percent of Bundestag seats and the FDP wins about 10 percent, allowing for the same coalition that sustained Kohl and earlier cabinets in power.

2. Social-Liberal Coalition: The SPD edges out the CDU with about 40 percent of Bundestag seats and turns to the FDP with, say, 10 percent in order to rebuild the coalition that supported Brandt and Schmidt in the 1970s.

3. Grand Coalition: If the two big parties, the CDU and SPD, shrink to around 35 percent, and the small parties get about 10 percent each, then coalition possibilities 1 and 2 are in fact impossible. The two big parties could make a coalition with each other; they did in the late 1960s and again in 2005 (see page 187).

4. Red-Green Coalition: If the SPD (red) gets 40 percent and the Greens get 10 percent, they build a social-ecological coalition, which Schröder did from 1998 to 2005.

Five other coalitions are possible but difficult:

5. "Traffic Light" (*Ampel*) Coalition: Red, green, and yellow (for the FDP). If the SPD won under 40 percent, it might need two small coalition partners, each with 6 to 10 percent of Bundestag seats, in order to build a majority. The Greens and Liberals, however, are ideologically incompatible and oppose each other.

6. "Jamaica" Coalition (named after the colors of the Jamaican flag): This coalition would be the rightwing counterpart of the above *Ampel*—black (CDU), yellow (FDP), and green. The FDP and Greens, however, are ideologically incompatible and oppose each other.

7. An SPD-Left coalition: The new Left party is too far left for most other parties but in a pinch the SPD could turn to it. A complicating factor: Left leader Oskar Lafontaine had earlier led the SPD but split angrily with centrist Chancellor Schröder; they still hate each other.

8. An all-left coalition: If the SPD gets about 40 percent and the Greens and Left both get 5 percent, all three could form a leftist coalition.

9. A "government of national unity" of all parties: These can be useful for emergency situations such as war, but not for much else. According to the theory of coalitions, you stop adding partners once you have topped 50 percent; there is no point to adding more. And an all-party coalition would not stay together for long.

The fragmentation of the German party system into five parties makes one long for the old and relatively simple "two-plus" system in which the only alternatives were, with two exceptions, coalition possibilities 1 and 2.

The game is never finished, though. While they had transformed themselves into a center-left party, the SPD allowed the area on their left to be taken over by newer, more radical parties, the Greens and Left. (In one study Green voters placed themselves at 3.4 on the scale.) Partly to try to win over these leftist voters, partly in response to Juso (see box below) influence within the SPD, and partly out of irritation at the hawkishness of the Reagan administration, the SPD moved leftward in the late 1980s, much like the British Labour party had done earlier. The SPD came out against both U.S. nuclear missiles in Germany and nuclear power plants, two key Green demands. But the shift hurt the SPD in elections; they dropped from 42.9 percent of the vote in 1980 to 33.5 in 1990, their poorest showing since 1957.

The SPD is still pulled in two directions. Tugging leftward is the traditional socialist wing once headed by former party chairman Oskar Lafontaine. This wing, based heavily on workers and older people, wants to help those in need and to preserve the welfare state. Tugging rightward is the Blairite wing of Chancellor Gerhard Schröder, which wants reforms to cut taxes, pensions, subsidies, bureaucracy, unemployment, and regulations that slow economic growth. The two men had such serious differences that Lafontaine resigned from the cabinet and as party chair in 1999 and in 2005 joined the new Left party. His departure drew sighs of relief from the business community. But Schröder could not turn the SPD into a genuine New Middle on the model of Blair's New Labour. By his second term, many Germans were fed up with Schröder's incoherence and indecisiveness.

The Chancellor and the Electorate

Two factors especially hurt the SPD in the 1990s. The CDU's embrace of rapid unification made the SPD look narrow and carping in its warnings about the expense and economic impact of quick merger. Go slow and think it through, was the SPD message, not a popular one in 1990, although

Political Culture

UNHAPPY ON THE LEFT: THE JUSOS

In his youth, Chancellor Gerhard Schröder (1998–2005) was a Juso hothead, but he calmed as he aged. The youth branch of the SPD—the *Jungsozialisten*, or Jusos for short—has been a continual thorn in the left side of the party. Limited to people under thirty-five, the Jusos attract (and create) young radicals and Marxists. Impatient and idealistic, many Jusos find the mainstream SPD too moderate and gradualist. One favorite Juso target became, ironically, Schröder, their leader long ago.

Periodically, the SPD has to disown its offspring. If it does not, it costs the party votes. Some Jusos cannot understand that Germans as a whole are moderate in their political views, and there is little support for pulling out of NATO, nationalization of industry, "cultural revolution," and massive taxes on the rich. When the Jusos helped move the SPD toward such positions in the early 1980s, the party lost four national elections in a row, just like the British Labour party. Some Jusos defected to the Greens or Left. The SPD faces the question of whether to try to retain young radicals by moving leftward.

their "I told you so" won them some votes in 1994. SPD chancellor-candidate Oskar Lafontaine in 1990 was also part of the problem. He was too clever and radical for most German voters. The SPD's next candidate, the bearded young intellectual Rudolf Scharping came across in 1994 much the same way. In 1998, the SPD took a leaf from Tony Blair's 1997 success in Britain: Assume vague, centrist positions; emphasize that the conservatives have been in office too long; and offer a younger, outgoing personality for prime minister. The SPD, in effect, learned the unimodal shape of the German electorate in the 1950s and 1960s, forgot it in the 1980s, and remembered it in the late 1990s.

> **Weltanschauung** Literally "world view"; parties offering firm, narrow ideologies.
>
> **catchall** Nonideological parties that welcome all.

Chancellor Schröder cleverly positioned himself slightly leftward in the 2002 election. By denouncing Washington's Iraq policy, Schröder won over some leftists who might otherwise have voted PDS (explaining why it slumped below the 5 percent threshold) and some pacifists who might not have voted at all. It angered President Bush but narrowly won the election for Schröder. Typically, that is all politicians care about.

In Germany, as in most advanced countries, personality has become more important than ideology in the mind of many voters. With the decline of **Weltanschauung** parties (see box on page 214) and the move of large parties to the center of the political spectrum, the personality of candidates is often what persuades voters. This has long been the case in the United States and is now becoming the European norm as well. Some call it the Americanization of European politics, but it is less a matter of copying than it is of reflecting the rise of **catchall** parties. Throughout Europe, election posters now feature the face of the top party leader, the person who would become prime minister. Although voting may be by party list, citizens know that in choosing a party they are actually electing a prime minister. In 2005 Schröder was more popular than the SPD while Angela Merkel was less popular than the CDU.

German (and British) campaigns are conducted almost as if they were for the direct election of a president—as in the United States and France. Officially there is no "candidate for chancellor," but in practice the leading figures of the two big parties are clearly identified as

Political Culture

THUNDER ON THE RIGHT: CSU

Bavaria is the Texas of Germany, a land with its own raucous brand of politics. On principle, the Christian Social Union (CSU) never let itself be absorbed into the CDU; instead it calls itself an allied party and sometimes threatens to burst out of Bavaria—where it often wins a majority of the vote—and set itself up in nationwide competition with the CDU.

The CSU is to the right of the CDU, demanding a tougher anti-immigrant stance, a firmer crackdown on radicals, and a rollback of welfare. The CSU's kingpin was the late Franz Josef Strauss, Germany's right-wing tough guy who tried to minimize the Nazi past and used to say, "I do not care who is chancellor under me." Edmund Stoiber, Bavaria's minister-president (governor) and 2002 chancellor candidate, hurt the CDU in the 2005 election when he called East Germans welfare-dependent.

dealignment Voters losing identification with any party.

such—in the media, on billboards, and in the public mind—so that much of the campaign revolves around the personalities of the two leading candidates.

A German candidate for chancellor must project strength and levelheadedness. In a country that still fears inflation, the candidate's economic background plays a bigger role than in most nations. Two of Germany's postwar chancellors have been economists. The candidate's adherence to democratic rules also matters, and Franz Josef Strauss's authoritarian streak contributed to his defeat in the 1980 race.

Personality contributed to the results of the 1990s elections, too. The CDU/CSU had the steady, optimistic image of Helmut Kohl. SPD candidates of the 1990s came across as radical intellectuals until Gerhard Schröder ran in 1998. By that point, many Germans were tired of Kohl, who had been in office sixteen years and was showing his age. Much of postwar German politics can be described as parties groping for the right leader to bring them to power in the Bundestag and chancellor's office. When they find the right ones—such as Adenauer and Kohl of the CDU—they stick with them.

GERMAN DEALIGNMENT?

For many years political scientists have worried that American voters have shown an increasing **dealignment** with the main parties. Some decades ago, U.S. parties used to present a fairly clear "party image," and most voters carried around in their heads a fairly clear "party ID."

KEY CONCEPTS

THE "CATCHALL" PARTY

In prewar Europe, many political parties used to imbue their supporters with a "view of the world" (*Weltanschauung*) corresponding to the party's ideology and philosophy. This was especially true of parties on the left, and it came to a high point in Weimar Germany. After World War II most Weltanschauung parties disappeared as they broadened their appeal or merged into bigger parties.

Noting their demise, German political scientist Otto Kirchheimer coined the term "catchall party" to describe what was taking their place: big, loose, pluralist parties that have diluted their ideologies so they can accommodate many diverse groups of supporters. His model of a catchall party was the CDU, a political vacuum cleaner that draws in all manner of groups:

farmers, businesspeople, labor, women, Catholics, Protestants, white-collar workers, blue collar, you name it.

For a while, under crusty Kurt Schumacher, the SPD tried to stay a Weltanschauung party, defining itself in rigid and ideological terms that turned away many middle-of-the-road voters. Since 1959, the SPD, too, has become a catchall party, appealing to Germans of all classes and backgrounds. Indeed, by now the catchall party is the norm in modern democracies. Almost axiomatically, any large party is bound to be a catchall party, for example, the French neo-Gaullists, Canadian Liberals, British Conservatives, Japanese Liberal Democrats, and, of course, both major U.S. parties.

Where the two connected (for example, U.S. Democrats and blue-collar workers), you had reliable party-voter "alignments." These could change every few decades in what were called "realignments," new matches of voters to parties. But some think U.S. voters are dealigning: Their preferences, often unfocused, connect with no party on a long-term basis. Their votes easily shift from one party to another in response to candidate personality and clever advertising.

> **transparency** Making public political and economic information.

Is electoral dealignment spreading to West Europe? There is evidence of it in Britain, France, and Germany. Increasingly, Germans dislike both major parties and doubt that either does any better in office than the other. German turnout in elections, as in most of Europe, is falling, from a high of 91 percent in 1972 to a low of 78 percent in 2005. More citizens now scatter their votes among a variety of small parties all over the political spectrum, from left to right. One center-right group that enjoyed brief notice called itself the *Statt* (instead of) party.

Where does dealignment come from? It is the normal and natural maturation process that most advanced democracies go through. One step in this process is the formation of the catchall party (see box on page 214). If two catchall parties face each other, as in the United States and Germany, their positions become so moderate and similar that they become boring. Neither offers much in the way of exciting new choices, programs, or personalities. Joschka Fischer was popular because he was not boring. (After his fourth divorce he got a young girlfriend. Imagine that in U.S. politics.)

Meanwhile, the society is being hit by problems scarcely anyone could imagine a generation ago: immigration, environmental degradation, the movement of jobs to low-wage countries,

DEMOCRACY

GERMANY'S FUND-RAISING SCANDALS

At the start of the new millennium, former Chancellor Helmut Kohl almost single-handedly wrecked his CDU party. As chancellor during the 1990s, Kohl got millions in secret donations for the CDU. Ironically, Kohl himself had demanded a new strict **transparency** law, which requires declaring the source and amounts of big contributions. Then Kohl's successor, Wolfgang Schäuble, admitted to illegal contributions. The CDU declined against the SPD in polls.

The trouble is, soon Land SPD branches stood accused of corruption along with their CDU and CSU counterparts. Bribes, tax evasions, false invoices, and kickbacks on waste-disposal and construction contracts are rife in Germany, involving both major parties. The SPD defense minister was fired for taking money on the side, and the PDS party chief and several other Bundestag members were ousted for personal use of government frequent-flier miles. Peter Eigen, founder of Transparency International in Berlin (see page 535), said Germany "is much more corrupt than previously thought."

Notice how in all advanced democracies—the United States, Britain, France, Germany, and Japan—there are party fund-raising scandals. They seem to come with democracy. Parties need big money to conduct elections, and economic interests always need friends in high places. The good news is that all over the world citizens are getting fed up with "money politics" and demanding reforms. For more on these scandals, see Chapter 18 on Japan, where they are especially pronounced.

Rechtsstaat   Literally, state of laws; government based on written rules and rights.

and crushing tax and debt burdens. None of the catchall parties has any convincing solution; all waffle in some middle ground. Also, suddenly gone is the cement that helped hold the system together: the Soviet threat and the Cold War. It is a disorienting time, and none of the great catchall parties provides much in the way of guidance. The public response is lower voter turnouts and small and less-stable shares of the vote for the catchall parties; in a word, dealignment.

The Bundestag and the Citizen

One reason German elections have become almost presidential elections for chancellor is the murky status of the Bundestag in the mind of many voters. They know what the chancellor does but are not too clear on what the Bundestag does. Part of the blame for this rests on the concept Bundestag deputies have of their role. The **Rechtsstaat** tradition is focused on laws. The Bundestag, now housed in the old Reichstag building in Berlin, is staffed heavily by lawyers and civil servants and has become a law factory.

But is it not a legislature's purpose to legislate? Well, not entirely. By confining their activities to law books and committee meetings, the Bundestag deputies have failed to grasp the less obvious functions of a legislature. Actually, the most important role of a legislature is in overseeing the activities of the national government, catching corruption and inefficiency, uncovering scandals, threatening budget cuts, and keeping the bureaucrats on their toes.

The harsh glare of publicity cures much governmental wrongdoing. Too-cozy relationships between ministers and business thrive in the dark. It is in this area that the Bundestag has been weak. Although there are commissions of inquiry and a question hour, the former are not pursued as thoroughly as on Washington's Capitol Hill—where televised committee hearings are a major preoccupation—and the latter is not carried out with as much polish as in Commons. (Bundestag deputies can be quite insulting, but it sounds crude rather than clever.) In functioning as little but lawmakers, German legislators have contributed to the boredom problem.

One function the Bundestag has failed to develop is that of education. The way a legislature operates, the arguments that are presented, the manner in which members of parliament conduct themselves, these are great teachers of democracy. Instead, Bundestag activity makes a weak impression. The Bundestag does not generate good press because it is a dull story. U.S. senators and representatives get more attention because they do interesting and unpredictable things, like disobeying their own party, something that rarely happens in Germany.

Another function of an effective parliament is to represent people. Voters must feel that someone speaking for them really understands their needs. In this the Bundestag suffers from a problem common to all elected legislatures: It is not representative of the voters. The average Bundestag deputy is close to fifty years old, male, trained as a lawyer, and employed as a civil servant, party leader, or interest-group official.

The strong German party system means that people must slowly work their way up in party ranks before they will be put on a ballot. Accordingly, candidates tend to be older, seasoned, party loyalists rather than bright, fresh, new faces. Unlike the American system, a German candidate cannot "come from out of nowhere" and win an election on his or her own. You are either a piece of the party machine, or you are nothing. The result is unrepresentative representatives. Said one German newspaper: "This gap between electorate and elected has become too wide." Many Germans do not feel represented; they feel that the Bundestag is the arena where the powerful interests of society work out deals with little reference to the common citizen, the little guy. Such feelings contributed to the Green and Left vote.

THE UNION-PARTY LINKUP

Unions in Germany are still strong but they are not what they used to be, another sign of the fraying of Germany's "consensus model" (discussed in the next chapter). One historical characteristic of North European political systems—and here we include Britain and Sweden along with Germany—has been the close relationship between labor unions and social-democratic parties. In these countries unions are large and cohesive; blue-collar workers are heavily organized, and their unions form a single, large labor federation. Such federations support the social democratic parties with money, manpower, and votes. Often union leaders actually run for office on the party ticket.

Compare this pattern with the Latin European systems. Labor is weakly organized and fragmented into several federations—Communist, Socialist, Christian, and other. The fragmentation dilutes the working-class voice. American unions are also fragmented into several federations and historically did not tie themselves to one party. U.S. labor no longer has the same kind of political input as North European labor. In North Europe, labor unions founded the welfare state.

In Britain, TUC unions are actual constituent members of the Labour Party. In Sweden, the gigantic LO is so close to the Social Democrats that some of their top personnel are the same. The German Basic Law forbids a formal union-party tie, but here, too, everyone knows that labor support is an important pillar of the SPD.

In the United States, 12 percent of the labor force is unionized; in Germany 20 percent is (in Sweden, some 50 percent). Eleven German industrial unions—the largest being the metalworkers (*IG Metall*, with 2.3 million members)—are federated into an umbrella organization, the *Deutscher Gewerkschaftsbund* (DGB) with 6.6 million members, down from 11.8 million in 1990. (Notice how U.S., British, French, and German unions have all declined. Is this permanent or reversible?)

The DGB's voice is still heeded by the Social Democrats; its leaders are regularly consulted by SPD chiefs and get some of what they want: an elaborate welfare system, a short work week, and even directors' seats on the boards of large companies (more on this in the next chapter). Many of the SPD's Bundestag deputies have union ties. The labor minister in Schröder's cabinet was deputy chairman of IG Metall.

Union-Party Links in Four Countries		
Country	Union	Party Linkage
Britain	TUC	Labour
Sweden	LO	Social Democrat
Germany	DGB	SPD
United States	AFL-CIO	Democrat

There is a new force on the labor front: In 2001 five service unions formed the 3-million-member Verdi (*Vereinte Dienstleistungsgewerkschaft*) to organize everything from clerks to nurses to civil servants. Service unions like Verdi have different demands than those of the industrial unions in the DGB. As the industrial sector shrinks in favor of services (see page 467), unions shift, too. In modern societies, unions grow most noticeably among government employees and teachers.

The catchall nature of the SPD prevents any one group dominating it. The more the SPD seeks votes in the center of the political spectrum, the more it has to turn away from close cooperation with unions. (The British Labourites faced the same problem with the TUC; when they let the unions dominate, they lost.) Starting in the 1970s, the SPD and unions diverged. Chancellor Helmut Schmidt (1974–1982), representing the SPD right, was a better democrat and economist than he was a socialist. Union relations with the SPD grew cool. Still, most German unions support the Social Democrats. The Schröder government had to tell unions that raising wages and benefits works against adding new jobs. Instead, it told them that cutting benefits and flexible work rules were necessary. The unions did not want to hear it and grew angry at Schröder. A few unionists went to the Left party.

On the management side, there is a similar pattern. The powerful *Bundesverband der Deutschen Industrie* (Federation of German Industries, BDI) has warm connections with the CDU, but not as close as those of unions with the SPD. The BDI wants flexible labor contracts and tax cuts, points the CDU also likes. One point of conflict: German business wants select immigration (such as computer specialists) to fill high-tech vacancies, but the CDU/CSU says no to all immigration. When the Social Democrats are in power, the BDI finds it can get along with them, too. As in Britain and France, big business does not need to get close to one party; it is to their advantage to work with all parties. The major focus of business is the bureaucracy, not the parties. Providing information to the relevant ministry, explaining to civil servants why regulations should be modified, going along with government economic plans—in these and other ways business quietly cements ties with government.

The Länder and Berlin

Britain and France are unitary systems that have moved, respectively, to devolution and decentralization. Germany is a federal system that some would like to make a little more centralized. The interesting thing here is that in both unitary and federal systems there are pressures to move toward a middle ground. Centralization in France was rigid, inefficient, and ignored local wishes and regional pride. Federalism in Germany is often uncoordinated, powerless, and deadlocked and encourages federal-state squabbles. In some ways the distinctions between unitary and federal systems are overdrawn; some see the emergence of a new "regional" pattern midway between the unitary and federal.

Germany is probably more federal than the United States; that is, its Länder run more of their own affairs and get a bigger portion of taxes than do American states. For example, individual and corporate income taxes are split between Berlin and the Länder with equal 42.5 percent shares; local governments get 15 percent. The Länder also get 45.9 percent of the value-added tax, the large but hidden sales tax used throughout Europe (see page 154). The poorer Länder—the new eastern ones—get additional funds. German Länder are directly plugged into the federal tax system, an idea Americans might do well to consider.

Germany's federalism has some drawbacks. For example, there is really no nationwide police force, so law enforcement is a Land affair. Terrorists who commit their crimes in one Land can flee to another, counting on communication and coordination foul-ups to delay police. Cleaning the seriously polluted Rhine River took decades because such matters are controlled by the states, and each sees its environmental responsibilities differently. In 1986 the Bundestag set up a fed-

"Friendly to the environment" is the German phrase for using bikes and recycling glass (three, in the center) and paper. The ecology movement is big in Germany.

eral environment ministry, but it could not override Land environment ministries. And decentralized education made it impossible for federal authorities to insist on the study of the Nazis and their crimes in schools.

Many Germans would like Berlin to have more control over things. But the German Länder, like American states, resist moves that would erode the powers of Land officials, and they have the perfect means to do so: the Bundesrat, which is often in the hands of the opposition party. Not directly elected, Bundesrat delegations are designated by Land governments, which usually means the state's political chiefs. The Bundesrat must concur on any move that would alter the balance of powers between federation and state, and they usually reject such moves. The Bundesrat, like the U.S. Senate, acts as a check on both the cabinet and the lower house. A 2006 reform trimmed the Bundesrat's blocking powers in exchange for allowing the Länder to have control of education, civil-service pay, and other areas, which made Germany more federal.

German Voting Patterns

In Britain, as we saw, the vote is structured at least in part along lines of social class and region. Labour usually wins much of the working class, plus Scotland, Wales, and large industrial cities. French voting is similar, with the added factor of religious attitude, clerical or anticlerical. West German voting patterns also tended to follow class, region, and religion, but the addition of East Germany in 1990 muddied some of these generalizations. The general dealignment muddied them further.

GEOGRAPHY

ELECTIONS AND MAPS

Virtually all elections show geographical voting patterns and regional variations in party strength. The map of Britain showing where parties scored above average seldom needs to be changed; major parties tend to preserve their regional strength. Once rooted, regional voting patterns can persist for decades. Here are some of the patterns.

1. *Cities vote liberal.* Urban areas are almost always to the left of rural areas. Cities are places of education, intellectuals, and critical thinking calling for change and reform. Workers tend to be urban, and they are often discontent over wages and benefits. The countryside tends to be calmer, more accepting of the status quo, and often still controlled by political bosses or old traditions. Rural and farming people often resent urban intellectuals for having more experimental notions than common sense. Accordingly, in most countries, big cities vote liberal or left while the countryside and small towns vote conservative or right.

England outside of the big cities votes Conservative; central London votes Labour. Catholic Bavaria votes Christian Social, but Munich votes Social Democrat. Paris needs some qualification, for in Paris the better-off people live in the city while the working class lives in the suburbs. This tends to give Paris a conservative core but a "red belt" around the city, now eroding as the old working-class suburbs gentrify. In Russian elections the big cities, led by Moscow and St. Petersburg, more strongly support relatively liberal parties than the countryside, which likes Putin and fears economic disruption. Iranian city dwellers are more moderate or liberal, rural people more religious and traditional. U.S. elections show strong urban-rural splits.

2. *Every country has regional voting.* Regions vote according to their resentments. Typically, the periphery votes against the core area. If the core votes for party X, the periphery votes for party Y. Much depends on how the core area acquired the peripheral region. If by conquest, the periphery long remembers this fact, as has the U.S. South. Scotland and Wales show their resentments toward England by voting Labour, but England stays Tory. France south of the Loire River and Spain south of the Tagus River tend to go Socialist, acting out their resentments toward, respectively, Paris and Madrid. The south of Italy, on the other hand, was long a bastion of conservatism. More recently, the north of Italy spawned a breakaway movement over resentment at paying for the impoverished south. As the Soviet Union's republics held free and fair elections, many strongly nationalistic republic governments took office and proclaimed their independence. Lithuanians and Georgians' hatred of Moscow led them to support nationalistic parties.

3. *Voting follows religion.* Religious attitudes tend to be distributed regionally. Indeed, the religion factor is one explanation for points 1 and 2, previously discussed. Big cities tend to be less religious than small towns, inclining the cities to vote liberal or left. Some regions have different religions than the core area. Scottish Presbyterians show their difference from the Anglicans by not voting Tory. German Protestants are still rather inclined to see the Christian Democratic Union as a Catholic party and therefore to vote against it, a tendency muddied by other factors. Immediately after unification, largely Protestant East Germany went CDU, but it has since swung to leftist parties—the SPD and Left. Religion helped to pull the Soviet Union apart, as Muslim republics installed Islamic regimes that were implicitly anti-Christian. In the Caucasus, persons of Christian origin, even if irreligious, feel threatened. Surrounded by hostile Islamic peoples, they elect implicitly anti-Muslim Christian governments, as in Armenia and Georgia.

Compare Percent of Catholics per Land (top) to Percent of CDU/CSU Vote per Land (bottom)

Close match: The percent of Catholics in each Land (see top map) predicts the percent of CDU/CSU vote in each Land (see bottom map).

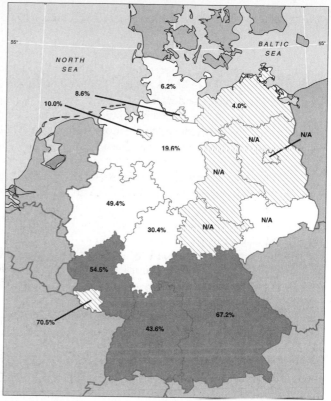

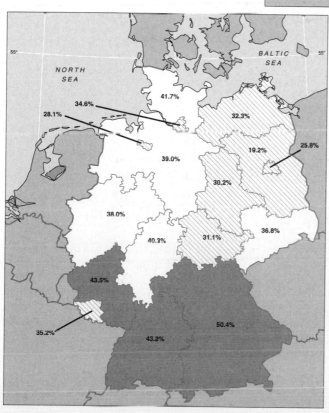

In Germany, religion means either Catholic or Protestant. German Catholics are more likely to vote CDU; therefore, heavily Catholic Länder such as Baden-Wurttemberg generally go with the CDU. The CSU has long had Catholic Bavaria sewn up. Further north, in the largely Protestant Länder, the SPD tends to do better, as they do in large cities. In Germany, the rural and small-town vote tends to go to the CDU. German workers, especially those who belong to a labor union, are generally more loyal to the SPD than British workers are to the Labour party. Thus, an *ideal-typical* (see page 128) SPD voter in Germany is a Protestant worker in a large northern city. His or her CDU counterpart is a middle-class Catholic in a small southern town. The Free Democrats appeal to some of the Protestant middle class, the Greens generally attract the young people, and the Left attracts East Germans and those who feel left out of the overall prosperity.

East Germany—although it is almost completely Protestant, and it followed a pre-1933 SPD voting tradition—went heavily Christian Democrat in 1990. As the costs and disappointments of unification became clear, some East Germans moved to the SPD, confirming the SPD as a party that is more attractive to Protestants and to urban workers. But a good number of Ossis lent their votes to the Greens (who had merged with the East German Alternative/90 in early 1993), then to the ex-Communist Party of Democratic Socialism, and then in 2005 to the Left party. German voting, like the German party system, has become more complex and less predictable.

KEY TERMS

bimodal (p. 210)

catchall (p. 213)

center-seeking (p. 210)

dealignment (p. 214)

Rechtsstaat (p. 216)

transparency (p. 215)

unimodal (p. 210)

Weltanschauung (p. 213)

FURTHER REFERENCE

Alan, Christopher S., ed. *Transformation of the German Political Party System: Institutional Crisis or Democratic Renewal?* Providence, RI: Berghahn, 1999.

Braunthal, Gerard. *Parties and Politics in Modern Germany.* Boulder, CO: Westview Press, 1996.

Dalton, Russell J., ed. *The New Germany Votes: Reunification and the Creation of a German Party System.* Providence, RI: Berg, 1993.

Glees, Anthony. *Reinventing Germany: German Political Development since 1945.* Providence, RI: Berg, 1996.

Hancock, M. Donald, and Henry Krisch. *Politics in Germany.* Washington, D.C.: CQ Press, 2007.

Huelshoff, Michael G., Andrei Markovits, and Simon Reich, eds. *From Bundesrepublic to Deutschland: German Politics after Unification.* Ann Arbor, MI: University of Michigan Press, 1993.

Karapin, Roger. *Protest Politics in Germany: Movements on the Left and Right since the 1960s.* State College, PA: Pennsylvania State University Press, 2007.

Lafontaine, Oskar. *The Heart Beats on the Left.* Malden, MA: Blackwell, 2000.

Mayer, Margit, and John Ely, eds. *The German Greens: Paradox between Movement and Party.* Philadelphia, PA: Temple University Press, 1998.

Padgett, Stephen, ed. *Parties and Party Systems in the New Germany.* Brookfield, VT: Dartmouth, 1993.

Pulzer, Peter. *German Politics, 1945–1995.* New York: Oxford University Press, 1996.

Chapter 16
What Germans Quarrel About

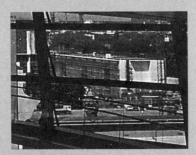

The great quarrel in Germany—indeed, in most of Europe—is over the generous welfare state and its taxes and rules that keep unemployment high and economic growth low. Keep them or cut them? Once a welfare state has been built, it is terribly difficult to cut, because people expect the state to provide job and income security and fear the uncertainties of a free economy. (Notice how U.S. politicians of both parties do not cut Social Security or Medicare.) German welfare benefits grew during the **Wirtschaftswunder** of the postwar years, when it seemed like the economy could afford almost anything. But now the miracle is over. Business leaders warn that Germany is no longer competitive, but many Germans are so comfortable with the welfare state that they resist any trims in it.

QUESTIONS TO CONSIDER

1. What made the German *Wirtschaftswunder?* Can there be a second one?
2. What did the German Model consist of? Is it over?
3. What do high labor costs do to a country's economy?
4. How were the major "left" governments of West Europe different? Who did the best job?
5. Could East and West Germany have merged gradually?
6. Why are immigrants necessary for a country like Germany?
7. How does the new Berlin Republic differ from the Bonn Republic?
8. What difficulties came with the euro?

Nothing produces economic miracles, it has been said, like losing a war. This is surely the case in West Germany and Japan following World War II. There was simply nothing to do but work. Some German factories were destroyed by Allied bombing. The Red Army ripped out machine tools and shipped them back to the Soviet Union. The British and Americans patched up their old industries, but the Germans were forced to rebuild theirs with new and more efficient equipment.

The aftermath of war had some psychological benefits. Almost everybody was poor; food and fuel were barely sufficient for survival. This produced greater material equality among Germans; income distribution was more equitable in Germany (and Japan) than in the victorious countries. Consequently, the bitter class antagonisms found in Britain and France did not develop in Germany. Everyone started from a similar low level, and most West Germans felt that everyone got a share of economic growth. Furthermore, defeat in the war and empty stomachs following it left Germans with more modest expectations than Britons or Americans, who expected some kind of postwar paradise. For West Germans after Hitler, hard work to foster economic growth was their only outlet for national pride.

Under the leadership of the CDU and Economics Minister (later Chancellor) Ludwig Erhard, Bonn pursued a largely laissez-faire policy. While Britain turned to Labour's welfare state and France to *planification* after World War II, West Germany relied mainly on market forces. During the 1950s, the West German economy recovered almost miraculously. It was built on the

Wirtschaftswunder German for "economic miracle." (See page 225.)

Sozialmarkt "Social market"; Germany's postwar capitalism aimed at reconstruction and welfare.

Modell Deutschland German economic model.

consensus Agreement among all constituent groups.

Mitbestimmung "Codetermination"; unions participating in company decisions.

wage restraint Unions holding back on compensation demands.

Sozialmarkt of Ludwig Erhard, which was basically a free market but aimed by bank loans to socially needed ends, such as rebuilding Germany's bombed-out cities. It continued and expanded the welfare state begun by Bismarck. Some called it "capitalism with a conscience."

During the 1970s the **Modell Deutschland** that stressed **consensus** among all social groups was successful and admired. In it, no one's views were ignored. Workers, for example, have **Mitbestimmung**, which gives unions a role in overall company policy. Each large firm has a supervisory board with half its directors chosen by labor and half by top management and big shareholders. For example, in 1999, when BMW ousted its chiefs, the ten worker representatives on the board vetoed a proposed executive they did not like and got one they did. Codetermination is one reason Germany has few strikes; workers feel they are part of the system. With slow economic growth and massive unemployment, however, critics now blame codetermination for stifling economic innovation and expansion.

The End of the Miracle

By the time of unification in 1990, the miracle had worn off. German wages and welfare benefits had climbed during the 1970s and 1980s, making Germany less of an economic dynamo. Basically, rapid economic growth comes from wages that lag behind productivity, as in Germany and Japan. After the war, German workers' skills were still high, and much of Germany's infrastructure was intact. At first, labor unions practiced **wage restraint**; they did not demand every DM they could

COMPARISON

EUROPE'S DIFFERENT "LEFTS"

Most of West Europe has recently had center-left governments, but notice—comparing Blair (Britain's prime minister 1997–2007), Jospin (France's premier 1997–2002), and Schröder (Germany's chancellor 1998–2005)—how they were quite different. Blair accepted the Thatcherite notion that business, not government, creates jobs. Instead of trying to undo her promarket reforms, he tackled important noneconomic issues—Northern Ireland, devolution, human rights, reform of Lords—that the Tories had neglected. In Blair's "Third Way," there was little left left.

Jospin, on the other hand, proclaimed "democratic socialism" and was a still-traditional *dirigiste* who never

publicly accepted the primacy of markets (few French do); he still saw a major role for the French state. For example, to cut unemployment he proposed publicly funded jobs and training. In France, the left was still left.

Schröder's "New Center" accepted the free market but turned almost reflexively to Germany's consensus model—his Alliance for Jobs, an attempt to bring down unemployment that did not work. In a parallel to Jospin's plan, Schröder aimed to place 100,000 German youths in jobs or training programs. In each country "left" meant something different, something rooted in each land's political culture.

get but let capital grow until it provided jobs and good wages for all. This period—from the 1950s through the 1970s—was the time of Germany's rapid growth (as well as France's and Japan's). In contrast, British and U.S. productivity lagged behind wage increases.

unit labor costs   What it costs to manufacture the same item in different countries.

By the 1980s, however, German wages surpassed U.S. wages, German social taxes were much higher, and German productivity was no longer growing quickly. In the meantime, America was getting more and more competitive; wages had been essentially stagnant (by the time you account for inflation) since the early 1970s, but productivity grew. The U.S. welfare floor, always much lower than the German, was less of a tax burden. U.S. labor costs were much lower than German labor costs and U.S. productivity was higher, making it cheaper to produce things in the United States (see box below). Until recently, individual and corporate taxes were more steeply progressive in Germany than in America, and Germany still has far more regulations. Under such economic pressures, German capital flees abroad. German investment in the United States, for example, created some two-thirds of a million jobs for Americans while unemployment in Germany climbed.

Comparison

WHO WINS THE MANUFACTURING RACE?

It is not necessarily those with the lowest wages who win the global manufacturing race. What you need to win the race is lower wages combined with higher productivity. The table below shows how the situation looks among five industrialized democracies.

Hourly labor costs, here for 2005, include bonuses, benefits, and social security and other taxes (such as health insurance), which in Germany add 80 percent to regular wages. These "social taxes" are low in the United States and Japan. **Unit labor costs** combine total labor costs with productivity. The clear winner: the United States, which benefits from the cheaper dollar. Productivity figures change constantly and are closely monitored as signs of a nation's economic vitality. China beats them all by several miles, but standardized, accurate Chinese data are hard to come by.

	Average Hourly Labor Costs	Unit Labor Costs
Britain	$26	165
France	25	145
Germany	33	140
Japan	22	125
United States	22	100

Source: U.S. Department of Labor, Swedish Employers Federation

By the 1990s, Germans enjoyed short work weeks (35 hours), long vacations (six to eight weeks!), the world's highest pay, lush unemployment benefits, male retirement at sixty-three (women at sixty) with fat pensions, and almost no strikes. With these *labor-force rigidities* (see page 152), however, firms hired few new workers. In 2005 German unemployment hit a postwar record of 12.6 percent overall (twice as high in the east as in the west) even as the German economy

GEOGRAPHY

COULD GERMANY HAVE UNIFIED GRADUALLY?

Germany probably could not have unified gradually. The real problem behind the difficulties and costs of merging the two Germanys is the speed with which it occurred. Some Social Democrats and economists urged a gradual unification over several years. But that really could not happen, for once the ball started rolling, it could not be slowed. Events took on a fast-paced life of their own.

1. The hardline Honecker regime in East Berlin refuses all thought of reform for most of 1989. But East Germans, seeing reforms taking place elsewhere in the Soviet bloc, become more restless.

2. Hungary lets East Germans exit into Austria. The Communist regime in Budapest had pledged not to let East German tourists flee to the West, but in the summer of 1989 they stop enforcing this pledge. Why? My hunch is that debt-burdened Hungary, by then under reform-minded Communists, got some nice financing from Bonn. Economic carrots had long been part of West German policy in East Europe. At an accelerating rate, thousands of East Germans "vacation" in Hungary but proceed to West Germany. East Berlin screams in protest, and Budapest shrugs. By September, more than 18,000 East Germans flee via Hungary, another 17,000 via Czechoslovakia. East Germany closes its border with Czechoslovakia to staunch the flow.

3. Massive demonstrations break out in East Germany in September, centered in Leipzig. In October Gorbachev (see page 346 in Chapter 22) visits to urge reform and warn Honecker, "Life punishes those who delay." Clearly, Gorbachev wishes to be rid of the problems and expenses of maintaining a Soviet empire in East Europe. By now some 100,000 protesters march in Leipzig chanting "Gorby! Gorby!"

4. Honecker orders a "Chinese solution" like the massacre at Tiananmen Square that June (see page 424) and tells police to get ready to fire on the Leipzig demonstrators. But security chief Egon Krenz fears catastrophe and countermands the order. On October 18, Honecker is out and Krenz becomes party chief and president. By now a million East Germans, led by intellectuals in the New Forum movement, protest for democracy.

5. On November 9, 1989, Krenz orders the Berlin Wall opened to gain some good will and time for reform. The Wall has kept East Germans locked in since 1961, and now tens of thousands pour into the West with no intention of returning. At this point, the days of a separate East Germany are numbered. Krenz resigns; much has happened because he countermanded the order to fire on protesters. Liberal and reform-minded Communists take over the party and government and pledge free elections.

6. Too many East Germans pour into the West because they are not sure that their own system is going to change. They want the good life of West Germany. Some half a million come across in the four months after the Wall opens, overburdening West Germany's job and apartment market, financial resources, and patience. Stay home, Chancellor Kohl urges; we will merge and rescue you soon enough.

7. Free East German elections in March 1990 put Christian Democrats in power. They see things Kohl's way and want speedy unification; this is why East Germans voted for them. Impatiently, East Germans want West Germany's economic prosperity.

8. Bonn gives East Germans a favorable exchange rate. East German marks are not worth much, but East Germans argue that they have worked for and saved

grew and again became the world's biggest exporter (in dollar amounts), ahead of the United States or China. GDP growth does not guarantee low unemployment. Those with the right education and skills do well; those without lose jobs and form an American-style underclass. By 2007 the German economy had improved, with unemployment below 10 percent and growth over 3 percent a year.

Ostmarks for decades. They demand a one-to-one exchange. Bonn argues that Ostmarks are essentially funny money and should be exchanged at a much lower rate. They compromise on one-to-one for each Ossi's first 2,000 marks (about $1,000) and one Westmark for two East above 2,000. It is a generous deal for East Germans, but if Bonn had not agreed to it, Ossis would have continued to pour into West Germany. In a sense, the one-to-one rate is a bribe to get them to stay put. On July 2, 1990, the Westmark becomes the official currency for both Germanys.

9. East Germans buy everything Western, nothing Eastern. With Westmarks in their pockets and Western products on store shelves, they turn their backs on their own products, now seen as junk. Suddenly, competing in a free market with the West, the East German economy collapses; it never had a chance to adjust.

Could anything have been done to prevent or slow the preceding sequence? We would have to go back to step one and get the Honecker regime committed to reforms that would gradually turn the East German economy into a market system that could compete with Western products. Then the two economies could merge without one of them collapsing. But Honecker was a devoted Communist to whom marketization meant abandoning communism, something he would not consider. And once East Germans started pouring across, what could Bonn do? Rebuild the border fence between the two Germanys to make East Germans wait at home? The critics of too-rapid unification are right: It would have been better if it had been slower. But that was not in the cards.

Top: Brandenburg Gate in East Berlin behind the Wall. Bottom: Party time as the Wall comes down in November 1989.

blocked society   One in which interest groups prevent major, necessary change.

Can Germany's consensus model still work in a very different world from the 1950s when it was created? Some urged abandoning the cozy consensus model for a more competitive "Anglo-Saxon" model, which the German left (like the French) denounced as savage "neo-liberalism." Many Germans did not understand that competitive capitalism is precisely what made Germany prosperous.

In a 1996 austerity package, the Bundestag cut Germans' health, unemployment, and welfare benefits and gradually raised the retirement age to sixty-five for men and sixty-three for women (now being slowly raised to sixty-seven, already the U.S. norm). Kohl's CDU government defended the cuts as moderate, necessary, and supported by most Germans, who were fed up with high taxes. Opponents of the cuts, including the SPD, called them "socially obscene" and the "destruction of the welfare state." The cuts helped the SPD win the 1998 elections, but Schröder had to deliver similar austerity budgets, tightening of welfare benefits, and greater work and wage flexibility. The left wing of his SPD howled—some deserted to the new Left party—but the economy allowed him no choice.

Merkel campaigned on going further than Schröder. She pledged to stand up to Germany's powerful unions, drop job-protection laws, and cut the very high payroll taxes that fund the welfare state. The SPD rejected this Thatcher-type program, and they were half of her coalition. Unable to move on economic reforms, Merkel simply presided over the status quo, which suited most Germans, who like their welfare state. Ironically, Social Democrat Schröder accomplished more economic liberalization than Christian Democrat Merkel.

And here we see the trouble with the consensus model. With all major groups having a say—and German lobbies are powerful—any one group can veto change. Try telling unions they will have to accept lower pay and work longer hours. Try telling health-care providers that major funding reforms are overdue. Try telling the jobless that their unemployment benefits must be cut. Try telling retirees that their pensions must be trimmed. All fight like hell to keep their cushy deals. Earlier, France had been called a **blocked society**; now the title may be passing to Germany. Reforms tend to get stuck by the veto powerful groups. (Does this happen in the United States?)

Schröder promoted an "Alliance for Jobs"—labor, capital, and government together coming up with ideas to create jobs. It was an attempt to refurbish the old consensus model when there was no more consensus. It produced few jobs. Schröder then had to carry out—against much opposition inside his own SPD—what he called Agenda 2010, conservative-type reforms in taxation, welfare, and workforce flexibility. Schröder's policies were not much different from Kohl's.

How to Merge Two Economies

The sudden merging of two very different systems added to Germany's economic difficulties. Over forty-five years, the largely free-market West German economy had become a world giant, in some years exporting more (in dollar value) than the United States. The centrally controlled and planned East German economy, although it was the envy of the East bloc, had a per capita GDP half that of West Germany. West German products were desired throughout the world; East German products were sold mostly to the Soviet bloc plus some Third World lands too poor to afford better. Two very different German economies existed side-by-side but with little trade between them, so they did not directly compete.

In 1990, the physical and political barriers between the two Germanys suddenly disappeared. West German currency and products flooded into East Germany, and the East German economy collapsed with a speed and thoroughness no one had foreseen. It was thought to have been a working economy that just needed West German capital and know-how. This scenario was much too rosy. East Germans simply ceased buying East German products as soon as they could buy nicer West German goods. As gigantic state subsidies ended, East German factory and farm production plummeted. East German unemployment shot from essentially zero into the millions, and both East and West Germans turned angry. Few East German enterprises survived the transition to a market economy.

Saving the East German economy required tons of money, far more than anticipated—€1.5 trillion (over $2 trillion) so far—from the federal government. Ultimately, of course, it comes from West German taxpayers. Some 4 percent of Germany's GDP flows to the east every year in subsidies. Thus, the first great quarrel of united Germany grew out of how to merge the two economies and who was going to pay for it. Chancellor Kohl said the bailout of the East German economy could be done without higher taxes. The opposition Social Democrats scoffed—their chief, Oskar Lafontaine, chided, "read my lips" (in English) in the 1990 election—and sure enough, the Kohl government next year put on a 7.5 percent "solidarity surcharge" on income taxes. Nobody liked the tax, which lasted for years, but Germany needed it to try to get its budget deficit below 3 percent of GDP, as required for the new European currency. (Both France and Germany now continually run deficits higher than 3 percent, and the *European Central Bank* does not know what to do about it.)

East Germany before and after the arrival of West German money: a Street in Stalsund (Stralsund) in 1990 (top) and in 1995 (bottom).

fertility rate   How many children an average woman bears.

demography   Study of population growth.

Can West Germany's earlier economic miracle apply to the East German economy? The desperate postwar feelings that made West Germans work so hard are not found in post-Wall East Germany. Under the Communists' centrally planned economic system, East Germans did not develop attitudes of hard work and entrepreneurial risk-taking. They got used to a vast welfare system that offered security for all but few incentives for individual exertion. Ossis say, "It's not our fault that the Communists saddled us with an inferior economic system. Besides, you Wessis got billions of dollars in U.S. Marshall Plan aid; we got ripped off by the Soviets. So it's only fair that you boost us up to your standard of living, and quickly."

West Germans are appalled at such attitudes, which seem like excuses to avoid work. Why set up factories in East Germany when you can get good productivity out of Poles and Czechs, whose labor costs are a fraction of German levels? Resentment flared in each half of Germany against the other half. From this resentment, especially in the East, grew some of the extremist groups that targeted foreign workers.

How Much Welfare?

As we considered with Britain, European countries are welfare states, and all are under pressure to cut welfare. One-third of Germany's GDP goes for social spending, a heavy tax burden on Germany's manufacturing competitiveness. Germany's welfare system is Europe's oldest and has grown

Geography

THE GEOGRAPHY OF DEMOGRAPHY

Almost all industrialized countries produce few babies. In Germany, for example, despite hefty children's allowances, an average German woman bears only 1.4 children, one of the world's lowest **fertility rates** (which is not the same as the "birth rate," a different measure). In comparison, 2007 estimates show a U.S. rate of 2.1, British 1.9, Japanese 1.2, and a Russian 1.4. Poor countries generally have higher rates: Nigeria at 5.5, India at 2.8, Mexico at 2.4, but China at only 1.75 and Iran at 1.7.

Replacement fertility rate is 2.1—one for each parent and a little to spare—the level at which a population will hold steady, and it is found in few advanced industrialized countries. Large families are not prized, and women now have increased educational and career options. These rates take no account of immigration and are one reason why some countries need immigrants

to do the work that supports the increasing portion of the population that is retired.

By 2025, an estimated 24 percent of Germans and Japanese will be sixty-five or over; some 20 percent of Britons, French, and Americans will be in that age bracket. By 2050, Germany's population is projected to drop to 60 million from 83 million, with one German in three over 65. All of West Europe faces the problem of soon having too few people in the work force supporting too many people in retirement. Germany already has the heaviest burden, with two working persons supporting one retiree, one reason German taxes are high. By 2035, the ratio could become an impossible 1:1. The solution: either more babies, more immigrants, or (what is already happening) later retirements. **Demography** leads to tough political choices.

and become accepted by just about everyone, even conservatives. The CDU, for example, has a tradition of Catholic trade-unionism.

But now one of the great questions of European politics has become, "How much welfare can we afford?" Even previously committed social democrats worry that their generous welfare provisions are pricing them out of the market. Both CDU and SPD governments had to cut unemployment and welfare benefits.

German pensions are generous, but to pay for them German workers must contribute 20 percent of their wages, and this will soon rise to an impossible 30 percent if present trends continue. Without further drastic reforms, the German welfare system will impose an impossible burden on the younger generation (see box on page 232).

Gastarbeiter   "Guest workers"; temporary labor allowed into Germany.

The Flood of Foreigners

Like Britain and France, Germany gets immigrants from poor countries seeking jobs while citizen resentment of them builds. There are 7 million foreigners in Germany (8.5 percent of Germany's population), mostly from Mediterranean nations (Turkey, ex-Yugoslavia, Greece, Italy, and Spain). Over 2 million are workers; the rest are spouses and children.

The trend started in 1955 when the economic miracle had absorbed all working Germans and was still short of labor. Italian and later Spanish **Gastarbeiter** were invited to West Germany and they came, eager for the plentiful jobs. Soon Germans began abandoning dirty, dangerous, and unskilled work for better positions, leaving their old jobs to foreigners. At first the impact seemed temporary: The migrant workers were supposed to stay three years and rotate back home. But the "guest workers," faced with unemployment at home, often remained and sent for their families. Large numbers began arriving from Turkey, where unemployment is especially high. There are now some 3.3 million Muslims in Germany, 2.7 million of them Turks. Whole neighborhoods have turned Turkish, and the Turkish *döner* (lamb slices and salad in a pita) has become Germany's fast food (highly recommended). The "guests" had come to stay.

By the 1980s, poor people worldwide had discovered Germany's very liberal asylum law. Simply upon arriving, foreigners had only to claim they were politically persecuted back home. Although motivation was usually economic, legal tangles let asylum-seekers stay in Germany for years, all the while on welfare. The FRG, along with Austria, strengthened border controls and expelled many undocumented visitors. Amid

Turkish women in the Kreuzberg district of Berlin, a center for Turkish immigrants, of whom there are 2.3 million in Germany.

xenophobia   Fear and hatred of foreigners.

jus sanguinis   Latin for "right of blood"; citizenship based on descent.

jus soli   Latin for "right of soil"; citizenship given to those born in the country.

great political controversy (with the SPD fighting it), the asylum law was tightened to exclude most claimants. Britain, which also had a liberal asylum policy, had to do the same.

As in Britain and France, antiforeign feeling grows; many Germans believe foreigners bring crime and terrorism. The 9/11 plot was hatched by Arab students in Hamburg. As in Britain and France, some Muslims want Islamic family law to govern such traditional practices as wife-beating, instant divorce, and "honor killings" of unchaste women. Most Germans demand that Muslims learn German culture and obey German law or leave Germany. As in the United States, *multiculturalism* (see page 196) came under criticism. "Multiculturalism has failed, big time," said CDU leader Angela Merkel, who became chancellor in 2005.

Two-thirds of Germans oppose more immigration, and the CDU/CSU strongly agrees. Immigration to Germany, as in all of Europe, has been tightened. Germany issues limited numbers of "green cards" (they borrow the U.S. word for work visas) to skilled immigrants, such as 20,000 computer specialists from India. Conservative politicians huffed: *"Kinder statt Inder"* (Children instead of Indians), but the German fertility rate would have to shoot up to an impossible 3.8 (from the current 1.4) to fill the need. As more Germans retire, Germany will need some quarter of a million new workers a year. How can there be both 4 million unemployed and a need for new workers? Few of the unemployed have the skills for the job openings, and many will not take low-wage work.

FRG law allows a person of German descent arriving from Russia or Romania, whose ancestors had left Germany centuries ago, to get instant FRG citizenship. A Turk, on the other hand, born and raised in Germany could not, until recently, become a German citizen. The law was reformed, and now a third of Turks in Germany are citizens. Many immigrants are integrating into German society, much like the U.S. melting pot. There are SPD and Green Bundestag members of Turkish origin.

Like the British and French National Front parties, small anti-immigrant parties sprang up in Germany that would expel foreigners and get tough on crime, issues the CDU/CSU used to its advantage. Turks and Africans who had been working in Germany for many years were murdered. In some cases, police and neighbors did nothing to stop the violence. On the other side, hundreds of thousands of Germans attended rallies and protests against **xenophobia** and violence.

GEOGRAPHY

CITIZENSHIP: BLOOD OR SOIL?

Europe traditionally used **jus sanguinis** to determine citizenship: If your parents were German, you are German. The United States from its beginning used **jus soli**: If you were born here, you are American. Other countries of immigration, such as Australia and Brazil, also use *jus soli*. Slowly and grudgingly, Germany is introducing *jus soli*. Under SPD sponsorship, a 2000 law allows German citizenship for those who have resided eight years (down from fifteen) in the FRG and makes it automatic for children born in Germany, provided one parent lived there eight years. This is a major switch in Germany's definition of who is a German, and it provoked conservative opposition. Elections went against the SPD over the citizenship issue. (Notice the parallel with U.S. Democrats and Republicans on immigration.)

Is Berlin Weimar?

By most measures the Federal Republic of Germany is an unqualified success story. Its constitution, leading parties, and economy deserve to be studied by other countries. But some observers have wondered if, under the glittering surface, democracy has taken firm root. How will German institutions function with a multiparty system instead of a two-plus party system? Could the present democracy go the way of Weimar's?

European Central Bank   Supervises interest rates, money supply, and inflation in the euro area, like the U.S. Fed.

All survey data have said no. Germans have grown more democratic in their values. By now they are at least as committed to a pluralist, free, democratic society as the British and French. They weathered terrorism and economic downturns as well as any of their democratic neighbors. Now, with much pain and complaint, East Germans are slowly turning into free-market democrats.

Things have changed in both the domestic and international contexts of German democracy, however. Germany's consensus and welfare state has become rigid and costly. Like most of West Europe, Germany's wages, taxes, welfare benefits, and overregulation have led to chronic high

Geography

Euro or DM?

Germans were among the most enthusiastic supporters of European union, but many did not like the euro replacing the DM, symbol of a solid and hard-working German economy since it was introduced in 1948. If it had been brought to a vote, it would have failed in Germany. The euro debuted in 1999 with electronic transactions (such as credit-card purchases). Over the first few months of 2002, the euro replaced paper money and coins in most EU countries (Britain not among them). No more DM, francs, or lire.

The euro brought terrific advantages. No more changing money (with a fee of several percent) at borders. Trade and transactions moved even more freely across West Europe. American tourists were delighted with the simplicity of a uniform currency that initially was close to $1. Psychologically, the euro made Europeans feel equal to Americans and no longer dependent on the dollar.

But many Germans saw disadvantages. Merchants used the switch to boost prices. German currency was no longer under German control. Would the euro mean inflation? The Bundesbank, remembering the worthless Weimar and Nazi currencies, had been tough on

inflation. At German insistence, euro members had to limit their budget deficits to 3 percent to block inflation. The **European Central Bank** located in Frankfurt would supervise and fine any government that went over. But Germany was one of several countries that topped the limit in order to fund generous welfare benefits while cutting taxes. The ECB did not punish limit-breakers, and its credibility took a beating. If Germany and France cheat, why not everyone? That could bring inflation.

Some economists had warned of difficulties from locking most member countries into one currency and predicted that euroland could break up. Some countries need to expand money in circulation to promote growth; others need to freeze it to halt inflation. Ireland, on an economic roll, expanded currency over the limit and did not apologize. Some countries may cheat and print more euros than they are entitled to. (Each member country prints its own, with a standard pattern on one side and a national one on the other, all equally good.) If Europe's largest economy ever abandons or alters the terms of the euro, the EU would be drastically set back. In monetary policy, one size does not fit all.

Warsaw Pact Soviet-led alliance of Communist countries, now defunct.

Comecon Trading organization of Communist countries, now defunct.

Bonn Republic West Germany, 1949–1990, with capital in Bonn.

Berlin Republic Reunified Germany, since 1990, with capital in Berlin.

unemployment. Competition from low-wage, low-tax countries is fierce, and many German firms have moved production to Poland, the Czech Republic, or Slovakia. Berlin hotels send their laundry to Poland.

Both Germanys were children of the Cold War. At times, a third of a million U.S. soldiers were camped in West Germany, over half a million Soviet soldiers in East Germany. This situation was tense but stable. The FRG was firmly anchored to NATO and the European Union, the GDR to the **Warsaw Pact** and **Comecon**. Suddenly the international context changed. The Cold War is over and Germany is unified. The Soviet troops left and only a few U.S. troops remain. The **Bonn Republic** was anchored to the West. Will the new **Berlin Republic** stay cemented to Western ideals and institutions, or could it someday go off on its own, with a nationalistic and expansionist foreign policy?

Unlikely. German democracy is solid. The new institutions of a uniting Europe are making Germans good Europeans, and most major politicians are committed to Europe. The German army is small (250,000) and has no ABC (atomic, biological, or chemical) weapons. Three of Germany's European neighbors have nuclear weapons, which by itself means that Germany will never go on the warpath. Germans have no taste for militarism, for they have seen what it leads to. Germany sent nearly 9,000 troops for peacekeeping in Afghanistan, Kosovo, Lebanon, and Bosnia but is not eager for more assignments. Germany has accomplished so much more by peaceful economic means than it could ever obtain by war-like means. The Weimar analogy is misplaced on present-day Germany.

KEY TERMS

Berlin Republic (p. 236)
blocked society (p. 230)
Bonn Republic (p. 236)
Comecon (p. 236)
consensus (p. 226)
demography (p. 232)
European Central Bank (p. 235)

fertility rate (p. 232)
Gastarbeiter (p. 233)
jus sanguinis (p. 234)
jus soli (p. 234)
Mitbestimmung (p. 226)
Modell Deutschland (p. 226)

Sozialmarkt (p. 226)
unit labor costs (p. 227)
wage restraint (p. 226)
Warsaw Pact (p. 236)
Wirtschaftswunder (p. 226)
xenophobia (p. 234)

FURTHER REFERENCE

Brady, John S., Beverly Crawford, and Sarah Elise Wiliarty, eds. *The Postwar Transformation of Germany: Democracy, Prosperity, and Nationhood.* Ann Arbor, MI: University of Michigan Press, 2000.

Clasen, Jochen. *Reforming European Welfare States: Germany and the United Kingdom Compared.* New York: Oxford University Press, 2005.

Dettke, Dieter, ed. *The Spirit of the Berlin Republic.* New York: Berghahn, 2003.

Edinger, Lewis, and Brigitte Nacos. *From Bonn to Berlin.* New York: Columbia University Press, 1998.

Hampton, Mary, and Christian Soe, eds. *Between Bonn and Berlin: German Politics Adrift?* Lanham, MD: Rowman & Littlefield, 1998.

Heneghan, Tom. *Unchained Eagle: Germany after the Wall*. London: Pearson, 2000.

Markovits, Andrei S., and Simon Reich. *The German Predicament: Memory and Power in the New Europe*. Ithaca, NY: Cornell University Press, 1997.

Merkl, Peter H., ed. *The Federal Republic of Germany at Forty-Five: Union Without Unity*. New York: New York University Press, 1995.

Posen, Adam S. *Reform in a Rich Country: Germany*. Washington, D.C.: Institute for International Economics, 2006.

Sinn, Hans-Werner. *Can Germany Be Saved? The Malaise of the World's First Welfare State*. Cambridge, MA: MIT Press, 2007.

Starkman, Ruth A., ed. *Transformations of the New Germany*. New York: Palgrave, 2006.

Chapter 17
The European Union

What is the European Union? A big nation? No, not nearly. A trade bloc? It is more than that. A confederation? It is stronger than that. A federation? Well, it is trying to become one. There is no good name for this emerging entity. Instead of calling it a "nation-state," some suggest calling it a "market-state." At what point should the EU be treated as sovereign? Perhaps when it demonstrates that the powers of the EU headquarters in Brussels override the sovereignty of member states. In the United States, this began only after the Civil War.

QUESTIONS TO CONSIDER

1. How does the EU compare to the United States under the Articles of Confederation?
2. What would make the EU institutional structure effective?
3. What is a "qualified majority vote"? What is the U.S. solution to this problem?
4. Will the many nationalities of Europe ever think of themselves as "Europeans"?
5. What is the quarrel between "liberal" and "social" Europe?
6. Should the EU attempt to be a counterweight to U.S. power?
7. Why did ratification of the EU constitution fail in 2005 and 2008?
8. Should the EU go "wider" or "deeper"? Or neither?
9. Does complexity limit popular acceptance of laws and constitutions?

Europe has a long way to go to reach the U.S. level of federation, but it took a big step in that direction with the institution of the **euro** currency. Some people argue that it doesn't make much sense to consider the nations of West Europe separately, because increasingly it is the **European Union** (EU) that determines Europe's laws and economy. Those people may have a point. A third to a half of Europe's new legislation comes out of the EU headquarters in Brussels, not from national capitals. In standardizing currency, taxes, and regulations, increasingly the EU calls the tune.

The EU is not yet a union in the way that the United States is, however. EU members may opt out of some of the provisions that they don't like. Of the EU's twenty-seven members, only fifteen currently use the euro. Sovereignty still resides in London, Paris, Berlin, and other national capitals rather than in Brussels. Institutionally, the EU structure is still undemocratic. A new constitution drafted in 2004 that reformed and consolidated the EU's several institutions failed to win ratification in 2005 and 2008. The EU's inability to do anything about the Bosnia situation in the 1990s illustrates the EU's lack of concerted foreign and security policies, weaknesses that the EU is trying to overcome. European unity is gradually growing, but it will be some time before the EU becomes the United States of Europe. As the United States of Europe, the EU would be able to declare and wage war as a sovereign entity.

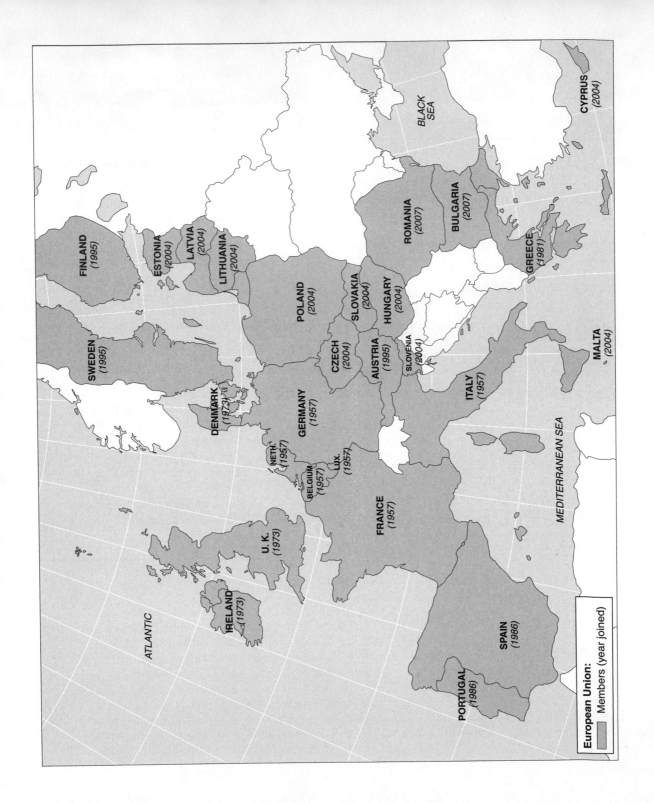

FINLAND
(1995)

ESTONIA
(2004)

LATVIA
(2004)

LITHUANIA
(2004)

SWEDEN
(1995)

POLAND
(2004)

CZECH
(2004)

SLOVAKIA
(2004)

HUNGARY
(2004)

AUSTRIA
(1995)

SLOVENIA
(2004)

DENMARK
(1973)

GERMANY
(1957)

NETH.
(1957)

BELGIUM
(1957)

LUX.
(1957)

FRANCE
(1957)

ITALY
(1957)

ROMANIA
(2007)

BULGARIA
(2007)

GREECE
(1981)

CYPRUS
(2004)

MALTA
(2004)

U. K.
(1973)

IRELAND
(1973)

SPAIN
(1986)

PORTUGAL
(1986)

BLACK
SEA

MEDITERRANEAN SEA

ATLANTIC

European Union:
Members (year joined)

THE IMPACT OF THE PAST

A History of Wishful Thinking

Rome planted the seed of European unification with an empire that at its height in the first century A.D. covered most of West Europe, including the western portion of what is now Germany. Weakened from overextension and overrun by barbarians, the western half of the Empire collapsed in A.D. 476. (The eastern half lingered for another millennium.)

When Charlemagne—himself of Frankish, that is to say barbarian, descent—formed his giant realm in 800 he called it the Holy Roman Empire. This grandson of Charles Martel, who beat back the invading Moors in 732, thought he could unite much of Western Christendom. His empire included all of what later became France (except Brittany), Belgium, and the Netherlands, most of Germany, and the northern half of Italy. These are precisely the same six countries that founded the Common Market in 1957, the core of the present European Union. Charlemagne fathered European union, although his own empire was brief.

The Holy Roman Empire splintered among Charlemagne's grandsons, but the Roman Catholic Church kept alive a dream of European unity under the banner of "Christendom," led by Rome. Kings were supposed to be crowned by the pope or his representative to emphasize that they owed their first allegiance to the Church. Europe's kings, however, intent on expanding their kingdoms by war, often disobeyed the pope. The notion of Christendom reached a high point with a papal call for the

euro (symbol: €) Currency for most of West Europe since 2002; value around $1.55 in 2008. (See page 239.)

European Union (EU), quasifederation of most European states; began in 1957 as Common Market. (See page 239.)

GEOGRAPHY

WHO'S IN THE EU?

Grouping EU members into six groups of three plus one group of five and two groups of two will help you remember them. (And yes, they will be on the examination.)

The Big Three: Britain, France, Germany

The "Benelux" Countries: Belgium, Netherlands, Luxembourg

Latin Europe: Portugal, Spain, Italy

The Nordics: Denmark, Sweden, Finland

The Periphery: Ireland, Austria, Greece

Ten joined in 2004:

The Baltics: Lithuania, Latvia, Estonia (former Soviet republics)

The Central Europeans: Czech Republic, Hungary, Poland, Slovakia, Slovenia (first four were Soviet satellites; Slovenia was part of Yugoslavia)

The Mediterraneans: Cyprus (just the Greek part) and Malta

The Balkans: Romania and Bulgaria, joined in 2007

Notice that Iceland, Norway, and Switzerland are *not* members. They could easily join but do not wish to.

GEOGRAPHY

EUROPE'S REGIONS

There are no binding definitions of Europe's regions, but the end of the Cold War made the old division into eastern and western obsolete. There is still, to be sure, a West Europe, which may be defined as those states that touch the Atlantic, plus Italy and Switzerland. The ex-Communist countries in what used to be called East Europe, though, should be separated into Central Europe (a pre–World War II term now revived) and the Balkans.

Central Europe is the region between West Europe and Russia that used to be, in whole or in part, the Habsburgs' Austro-Hungarian Empire. It includes Austria, Hungary, the Czech Republic, Slovakia, Slovenia (do not confuse the two), Croatia, and Poland (southern Poland was Austrian-ruled before World War I, as was part of northern Italy). These countries are predominantly Catholic and (with the exception of Austria, which was never Communist) poorer than West Europe.

Freed from Communist rule, most turned quickly to democracy and market economies.

The Balkans (Turkish for a mountain chain), for centuries part of the Ottoman Turkish Empire, are largely Eastern Orthodox and a more backward area that includes Romania, Bulgaria, Albania, Greece (which was never Communist), and half of Yugoslavia. These countries lag behind Central Europe in setting up democracies and market economies. Yugoslavia was a special problem, because half of it (Slovenia and Croatia) was under the Habsburgs while the other half (Serbia, Bosnia, and Macedonia) was under the Turks. And it is precisely on this fault line that Yugoslavia violently split apart in the early 1990s, with half Central European in character and the other half Balkan. Russia, because it reaches clear to the Pacific is, along with other ex-Soviet republics, sometimes called "Eurasia."

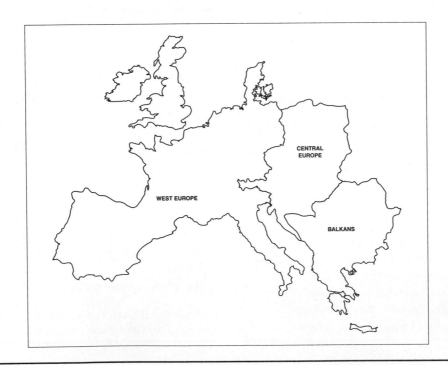

First Crusade (1096–1099), which knights from much of Europe battled Islam for control of the Holy Land. Meanwhile, a loose grouping of princely states called the "Holy Roman Empire" lingered for centuries, mostly in Germany. French writer Voltaire wisecracked that it was "neither holy, nor Roman, nor an empire."

The Habsburg Empire reached its height of power and wealth in the sixteenth and seventeenth centuries when it attempted to unite Europe by the sword and return Protestant lands to the Catholic Church. With gold and silver freshly looted from Latin America and large armies from Spain and Central Europe, the Habsburgs might have done it, but Protestant countries and France fought them to a draw, formalized in the 1648 Treaty of Westphalia.

The **Enlightenment** revived the dream of a united Europe. Prussian philosopher Immanuel Kant suggested a "League for Perpetual Peace" in which Europe's monarchs would conciliate their differences. Napoleon briefly united most of Europe by conquering it, but his dreams died in the snows of Russia from 1812 to 1813. Actually, occupation by Napoleon's arrogant legions created Spanish, German,

Enlightenment Eighteenth-century philosophical movement advocating reason and tolerance.

supranational Literally "above national"; organizations that group together several countries.

Maastricht 1992 treaty setting up the EU.

Schengen 1990 treaty ending passport controls in most of West Europe.

NAFTA 1994 North American Free Trade Agreement among the United States, Canada, and Mexico.

Mercosur "Southern market"; free-trade area covering southern part of South America.

GEOGRApHY

BEYOND THE NATION-STATE?

Many thinkers suggest that the nation-state has outlived its usefulness. By jealously guarding its sovereignty, the modern state whips up destructive nationalism, spends too much on arms, engages in unnecessary wars, impedes the free flow of trade and travel, and is unable to tackle global problems such as hunger, overpopulation, and environmental degradation. The fact that the modern state is only about five centuries old suggests that it is not the last or highest form of human organization. Humanity may be headed toward **supranational** forms of organization.

At **Maastricht** in the Netherlands, in 1992 EC members concluded the Single European Act that turned the EC into the present European Union, its name since 1993. (The British Parliament debated long and hard before ratifying it.) Since 1994 the **Schengen** agreement has lifted passport controls among most EU members (but not Britain). Once you have gone through customs at the Paris airport, for example, you do not have to show your passport to enter Germany or Italy.

(Britain stayed out of "Schengenland," but aloof Switzerland joined it.)

With such measures, the EU is our best example of a supranational political entity. It uses economic means to a political end: European integration. Is this a glimpse of the future? The EU's parallel—not a close one—is **NAFTA**, which links Canada, the United States, and Mexico in a common market that may expand southward, eventually combining with **Mercosur**. NAFTA, however, has no supranational aims or structures; it is just a trade area.

Supranationalism has some good and some bad points. The economic growth is good, but if the blocs erect trade barriers to keep out the products of other blocs, world trade will shrink and international tensions will climb. Already the EU feuds with the United States on trade in everything from beef to jetliners. One of the great international questions today is whether to build regional trade blocs or skip the blocs and open the entire world to unrestricted trade.

Russian, and other brands of nationalism, making Europe harder to unify than ever. After Napoleon, Europe's leading monarchs set up a vague "Concert of Europe" to suppress liberalism and nationalism. In 1849, a time of revolutionary hopes throughout Europe, French writer Victor Hugo appealed for a unified Europe that even included Russia. The point is that until recently a unified Europe had either been a cover for conquest or wishful thinking.

"Ever Closer Union"

Hitler, too, dreamed of a unified Europe, unified under Germany, that is. World War II convinced many Europeans that nationalism must never be permitted to run amok again, that Europe had to create a supranational entity. The path to unity, charted by two French officials, Jean Monnet and Robert Schuman (see box below), was to use economics to pull Europe together and gradually add political institutions.

PERSONALITIES

MONNET AND SCHUMAN

The Common Market was invented by two Frenchmen, a high civil servant, Jean Monnet, and a politician, Robert Schuman. Their ultimate aim: to prevent further war. Said Schuman, "Because Europe was not united, we have had war." They used economic means for a political end, and it worked, eventually becoming today's European Union.

Jean Monnet

Robert Schuman

Monnet (1888–1979) was a brilliant young French economist who very early realized that purely national economies were outmoded and ineffectual. During World War I he worked on meshing the Allies' economies and then as an economist at the Versailles Peace Conference, which set up the League of Nations. Monnet was the League's deputy secretary general from 1919 to 1923. In 1925 a New York investment bank made him its Paris partner. With the start of World War II in 1939, he was named chair of the Franco-British Economic Coordination Committee and urged a Franco-British economic union.

After the fall of France in 1940, Monnet worked in Washington as part of the British Supply Council. He concluded that a key to American prosperity was its continent-sized market wherein goods and labor moved without barriers. In 1943 Monnet went to newly liberated Algeria to become a top economic administrator of de Gaulle's Free French government. With France liberated, Monnet headed a committee to plan France's economic recovery, the 1947 Monnet Plan. De Gaulle appreciated Monnet's talents but never shared his interest in what de Gaulle called "supranational monstrosities."

Schuman (1886–1963), first elected to the French National Assembly in 1919, was arrested by the Gestapo after the Germans occupied France in 1940. He escaped and worked underground in the Resistance until Liberation in 1944 and then helped found the centrist Popular Republican Movement party. Schuman served as France's premier (1947–1948) and foreign minister (1948–1952), in which capacity he pushed for the European Coal and Steel Community, the first step toward today's EU.

It started with the six-nation European Coal and Steel Community in 1952 but really got serious with the 1957 Treaty of Rome, which set up what was colloquially known as the "Common Market." (The official name was the European Economic Community, EEC.) By cutting 10 percent off their tariffs with each other every year, after a decade goods, capital, and labor flowed freely from one member country to another. It was never intended to be just a trade bloc but was to move to "ever closer union," in the famous words of the 1957 treaty. With the Treaty of Maastricht coming into effect at the beginning of 1993, the EU took its present name and became one economy, which meant that it was also becoming one political entity.

By the early 1960s the Common Market was such an economic success that other European countries decided they had to join. Free trade and the movement of workers among countries invigorated the economies of all six members. Nonmembers, who in 1960 organized the loose and ineffective European Free Trade Area (EFTA, dubbed the *Outer Seven*), fell behind. By the early 1960s, even Britain, which had originally rejected the Common Market, saw its economic advantage was in membership and applied. President de Gaulle of France, however, convinced that Britons were not wholehearted Europeans (he was correct), in 1963 vetoed British entry with his famous *Non!* Britain reapplied later and with Denmark and Ireland joined the EEC in 1973, making the Six into the Nine. (Ireland was the first non-NATO member to join the EEC, but several other non-NATO countries have since done the same.) Norway considered joining the EEC in 1973, but Norwegians rejected membership in a referendum.

The Nine became the Ten with Greece's entry in 1981, and then the Twelve with Spain and Portugal in 1986. Finland, Sweden, and Austria (nonmembers of NATO) made it the Fifteen when they joined in 1995. (Norwegians voted to stay out for the second time; they think they can go it alone with their oil.) The eastern part of Germany automatically became a member when it unified with West Germany in 1990. Freed from communism, Poland, Hungary, Czech Republic, Slovakia, Slovenia, Lithuania, Latvia, and Estonia immediately applied and, after six years of complex negotiations, joined in 2004, along with the Mediterranean islands of Malta and Cyprus. Romania and Bulgaria joined in 2007. West Europe is their natural market, source of investment capital, and outlet for surplus labor. To stand outside the EU risks economic stagnation. Now even some Swiss would like to join.

The EU now has twenty-seven member nations with a combined population of 494 million and a combined $13.9 trillion GDP. The United States has the same GDP but a population of only 301 million, making it richer per cap; both the U.S. economy and population grow faster than the EU's.

COMPARISON

"THAT'S HISTORY"

The EU's top foreign-policy official, Javier Solana of Spain, noted that when Americans say, "That's history," they mean something is over and irrelevant. When European say it, "they usually mean the opposite." History is still very much alive in Europe. Old grudges are keenly remembered and hard to overcome. Borders, languages, wars, and symbols loom large. In 2007, for example, Poland argued that it deserved more weight in EU voting because, if the Germans had not murdered millions of Poles in World War II, Poland would now have a bigger population. The past does not stay buried. We should bear this in mind when wondering why Europe does not integrate more fully and faster.

subsidiary Letting smaller government units decide most questions; equivalent to the U.S. Tenth Amendment, "reserved to the states."

qualified majority voting (QMV), complex voting procedure in EU Council of Ministers that weighs votes by member countries' populations.

The growth of the EU, both in members and economic integration, led to the gradual and cautious transfer of certain aspects of sovereignty from national capitals to Brussels, home of the EU Commission. With this developed some supranational political power. The EU introduced a common currency, the euro, in 2002, and as it forges a combined foreign policy, it will become more than a trade bloc and start taking on the characteristics of a nation, except that it will be composed of many states that will never fully surrender their sovereignty. It will be a new entity, one for which we do not yet have a good name.

THE KEY INSTITUTIONS

The EU's governing institutions are not those of an ordinary country. Most were initially set up by treaties in the 1950s when the Common Market had only six members and did not undertake nearly as many tasks. It was more like a meeting of ambassadors. Laws and regulations were supposed to be based on the principle of **subsidiarity**, of not concentrating power in Brussels. Now, with twenty-seven members and Brussels handling major laws and responsibilities, the structure is unworkable. The 2004 constitution would have modernized and streamlined it but was voted down in France and the Netherlands (see below). The EU's main bodies are as follows:

The European Commission is a sort of twenty-seven member collective presidency. Located in Brussels, which is in effect the EU's capital, the powerful but unelected Commission both initiates and executes laws and policies. Each EU member state names one commissioner with a five-year term, chaired by a Commission President, also with a five-year term. President José Manuel Barroso of Portugal (2004–2009) does not have nearly the powers of a U.S. president. The Commission also oversees some 24,000 EU civil servants, most of them selected by competitive examinations.

The European Council (formerly Council of Ministers) is a sort of upper house of twenty-seven ministers but in a unique way. Ministers are sent from their home-country cabinets to Brussels to represent their country. Which minister attends depends on the subject area under consideration. Each country's foreign minister, for example, participates when the Council discusses external relations. When the Council takes up farm issues (a very big and expensive item), twenty-seven agricultural ministers attend.

The Council now has a six-month rotating presidency, really little more than a temporary chairperson who also changes along with subject areas. The first half of 2008 was Slovenia's turn, so meetings on the environment were chaired by Slovenia's environment minister. Reformers are trying to lengthen the presidency to two-and-a-half years. The Council, often jointly with the European Parliament, decides on Commission initiatives and budgets and can veto them.

Until 1987 the Council required unanimity, which meant even one small country could veto something. Now voting in the Council is weighted according to population, but with much compression. The four biggest members—Britain, France, Germany, and Italy—get twenty-nine votes each. Little Malta gets three votes; the total is 345. The Council mostly uses **qualified majority voting** (QMV). First, a majority of the twenty-seven member countries (in some cases, two-thirds) must approve. Second, 255 votes out of the total of 345 must be for it. Third, if a member state requests, states representing 62 percent of the EU population must be for it. Some sensitive areas, such as taxes and immigration policy, still require unanimity. This complicated system (everything about the EU is complicated) is designed to prevent either the big countries deciding everything or little countries blocking everything. (Notice how the U.S. bicameral system is designed to do the same. Should the EU go bicameral?)

The European Parliament, which has offices in both Brussels and Strasbourg, France (near the German border), is a bit like a lower house. It can censure the Commission and ask it to resign, but this has never happened. The 785 Members of the European Parliament (MEPs) are elected directly in their home countries for five years. As in the Council, with whom the European Parliament shares legislative and budgetary powers, seats are somewhat proportional to population, ranging from ninety-nine for Germany to five for Malta. MEPs are organized along EU-wide party lines, ranging from Socialists to Christian Democrats. The 2007 Reform Treaty would have made the European Parliament more important and would have helped solve the EU's "democratic deficit."

The European Court of Justice, located in Luxembourg, is a sort of EU supreme court. Its twenty-seven judges adjudicate the growing body of EU law, including claims by and against the Commission and disputes among member states.

DEMOCRATIC DEFICIT

The student of comparative politics notices at least two things about EU institutions: (1) They lack a clear locus of power, and (2) they are not very democratic. The EU structure has no strong executive like the presidents or prime ministers we have studied. This is understandable, as the EU is not a sovereign entity and was not set up as one. The EU executive is the twenty-seven member Commission. The Council and Parliament have only weak checks on the Commission. Only the Parliament is democratically elected, but turnouts for MEP elections are weaker than for national elections, as Europeans recognize that the Europarliament is far less important than their own parliaments.

The EU draft constitution of 2004 was meant to remedy some of these defects, but it failed to win ratification. The 2007 Lisbon Treaty, shorter and simpler than the constitution, aimed to do the same. The Common Market, later the EU, has never had a constitution. It was started and built in a series of treaties between member countries. Its structure, at first very loose, was better suited to just the original six members. By the time it got to fifteen, it was clumsy. Long before it reached the current twenty-seven, many realized that EU institutions had to be codified and streamlined.

Drafting a constitution began in 2003 with 105 delegates from all member countries under the chairmanship of former French President (from 1974 to 1981) Valéry Giscard d'Estaing. Self-consciously modeling themselves on the United States of the late 1780s, they called the meeting their "Convention," capitalized Constitution, and likened pro-ratification arguments to the *Federalist Papers*. It was a poor analogy, as European countries with diverse languages and histories are a lot harder to unite than thirteen colonies that were culturally very close and had not (yet) warred among themselves.

The 2004 EU constitution and 2007 Lisbon Treaty were not total revisions of current usages but more of a consolidation that included the following:

- A Council president elected for two-and-a-half years instead of the rotating six-month presidencies staffed by member-country top leaders. This would strengthen the Council presidency.

- A new European foreign minister to help the EU speak with one voice on the world scene, implicitly to stand up to the United States. Many Europeans like this idea but do not like giving up their countries' ability to stake out separate foreign policies.
- Qualified majority voting in the European Parliament that requires approval by fifteen of the twenty-seven member states representing at least 65 percent of the EU's total population.

The 2004 constitution and 2007 treaty, which both failed, were only modest changes to the existing setup, but both were elitist, far too detailed, and written in legal jargon. When subject to referendums in France and the Netherlands in 2004, the constitution was rejected for those reasons. The 2007 Lisbon Treaty had basically the same provisions but was shorter (only 287 pages) and simpler. Only Ireland put it to a referendum, which failed 53–47 percent in June 2008. The rest of Europe was furious at the Irish for setting back the constitution. The EU limped along as before.

EU POLITICAL CULTURE

One of Italy's nineteenth century unifiers famously proclaimed, "Having made Italy, we must now make Italians." He meant that his countrymen continued to think of themselves as Tuscans, Sicilians, Venetians, and so on, not as Italians. The same problem now applies to citizens of the EU: Few think of themselves as Europeans, and most still think of themselves as French, German, Italian, and so on. Making them psychologically European will take a long effort.

COMPARISON

U.S. FOUNDING DRAMAS

It was easy for the United States to form an American consciousness. A nation of immigrants crossing the seas to enter a new land where all started equal and fresh—and had to learn English—was quite different from the centuries of historical, linguistic, and religious baggage the Europeans still carry. The founding American dramas—the Revolutionary War with England and the framing of the Constitution—stirred mass enthusiasm. George Washington was a charismatic figure. Americans read and discussed the eighty-five *Federalist* essays by Alexander Hamilton, James Madison, and John Jay and after two years of debate made an informed decision to adopt the Constitution. All this planted a political culture taught and accepted by generations of Americans.

Europe was quite different. It had no distinct founding drama, just a sense of weariness and futility following World War II, in which the enemy had been fellow Europeans. During the long Cold War, America took over the defense of Europe as the leading power in NATO. There were no great historical incidents or charismatic figures to rally Europeans. Instead of dramas that stirred the heart, Europe was founded and is still constructed by bureaucrats who produce thousands of pages of mind-numbing rules no one can love or even understand. The 2004 proposed constitution was not seriously debated before ratification failed. A constitution is more than a big law; to be effective, it must have an emotional or psychological component.

Euroenthusiasm comes in spurts or waves. A few years of enthusiasm and adding new members is followed by a decade or two of indifference as the EU adjusts to its enlarged size. In the early 1960s, not long after the Common Market began its tariff cutting, Europeans were proud of what they were building. Some put EEC flag decals (a circle of gold stars on a blue field) on their cars. By the late 1960s, however, the enthusiasm had faded. New members in the 1970s and 1980s brought other spurts of Euroenthusiasm. The massive addition of ten new members in 2004 followed by another two in 2007, most of them in the east, brought doubts that the EU was trying to swallow too many poor countries at once. Recent polls show Europeans now skeptical and indifferent.

> **utilitarian**   Promotes material payoffs; "useful."

A basic problem is that the EU was founded on an economic or **utilitarian** basis: "The Common Market is good because it makes my country more prosperous." This approach to building Europe was perfectly rational, even a necessity. Millions of Europeans understand that integration into a Continent-size market has enhanced their prosperity and security. Missing, however, is a sense of European patriotism, a love of country, and the sense that it is good and legitimate. Political scientist (and Carter advisor) Zbigniew Brzezinski claimed that "no 'European' is willing to die for 'Europe.'" (Actually, dozens of West European soldiers—with Spain in the lead—died in Bosnia for Europe.)

Some European nationalities, such as the Italians, are Euroenthusiastic; others, such as the British, are Euroskeptical. In response to a 2006 survey statement, "Our country's membership in the EU is a good thing," only half of Europeans overall agreed. The highest in the affirmative,

Political Culture

Anti-Americanism

Europeans have little that positively unites them but have one major negative point that many agree on: their growing dislike of the United States. Actually, European attitudes are more complex than simple dislike. After World War II America, which had just liberated West Europe and then stabilized it against Stalin's designs, was greatly admired, although some leftists criticized the United States for alleged brutal capitalism, exaggerated material consumption, racism, and militarism. Some elites criticized America for lack of a refined and classic culture. (They likely resented the attractiveness of U.S. popular culture to young Europeans, who love rock and rap.)

As Europe gained strength and the threat of Soviet invasion receded, Europeans picked up different perspectives. The Vietnam War was a watershed. Washington asked for European help or at least political support, but no European government contributed, and many Europeans thought the U.S. war was foolish and mistaken. De Gaulle publicly warned against war in Vietnam, where France had been beaten in 1954. West Europe did support the United States in the 1991 Gulf War and contributed small military units. Support for the 2003 Iraq War was much weaker—only Britain sent major forces—and some 80 percent of Europeans opposed the war. Dislike of President Bush 43 was especially strong.

One of the selling points for the 2004 EU constitution, especially pushed by French President Chirac, was that only a united Europe could stand up to the United States and form a counterweight to excessive U.S. power. Few Europeans really cared. Europeans admire what America has accomplished in building a free and prosperous continental democracy but fear giving up any more national sovereignty to Brussels.

Helsinki Final Act 1975 agreement to make Europe's borders permanent.

around 75 percent, were Italy and the Benelux countries. The lowest, under 40 percent, were Britain, Austria, and Finland. (No European nationality identifies more with Europe than with their own country, whereas virtually all Americans identify with their country more than with their state.)

If European integration had to rely solely on mass support, it would have made little headway. The absence of mass participation and discussion throughout the history of the EU has led to public distrust of the EU. Said the Dutch economy minister, as his countrymen voted down the new EU constitution in 2005: "The non-debate of the past twenty years cannot be overcome in three weeks."

PATTERNS OF INTERACTION

Instead of mass support, European integration is very much an elite thing. Its founders, Monnet and Schuman, were high French officials, who were trained to "guide" their society from an elite perspective. Indeed, most of Europe (and Japan) has a bureaucratic governing mentality, the English-speaking lands less so.

GEOGRAPHY

PERMANENT BORDERS FOR EUROPE

In Helsinki in 1975, thirty-five nations agreed to the Final Act of the Conference on Security and Cooperation in Europe (CSCE). Among its provisions to calm and stabilize Europe was Principle III of Basket I: "The participating States regard as inviolable all one another's frontiers as well as the frontiers of all States in Europe." Europe's boundaries can be changed only by peaceful means. Europe's boundary problems are over, especially the very touchy German-Polish border (see pages 166 and 169).

But other problems loom. First, the **Helsinki Final Act** is not a treaty, although it is treated virtually like one. It lacks the legally binding quality of treaties. Second, some of the CSCE's other provisions conflict with Principle III. For example, Principle VIII guarantees "self-determination of peoples," used to justify German unification and the dissolution of the Soviet Union, which left behind several potential boundary conflicts.

Third, Serbia attempted to enlarge its boundaries by taking portions of Croatia and Bosnia, with great bloodshed and "ethnic cleansing" that tore a great hole in the CSCE agreement. Serbs were eventually pushed back but still hold part of Bosnia. Later, Albanians in Kosovo broke away from Serbia. Which governs: permanent borders or self-determination?

Still, the CSCE Final Act was a praiseworthy attempt to settle Europe's boundaries, especially the German-Polish border. Conflicts may arise, as between Albania and Greece, Hungary and Romania, and Romania and Russia (over the Romanian-speaking republic of Moldova, annexed by Stalin in 1940). But the conflicts are likely to be peripheral and containable. Now called the OSCE (for Organization), the body shows a Europe trying to overcome centuries of warfare, much of it concerning boundaries.

This is not to say the Eurocrats did a poor job. The march to European unification is a great success, no matter how much EU citizens grumble. It lifted the confidence and economies of its members, made war unthinkable, and, among its new members, implanted democracy. Actually, new members are admitted only after they demonstrate they are democracies, but the inducement of EU membership persuaded several East European lands to get democratic faster. Now Turkey, hoping to join the EU, emphasizes human rights and moderate politics like never before. No democracy, no membership.

aggregate Items or persons taken together.

The big EU problem now is whether it attempted to grow too big too quickly. The EU has a built-in and very positive impulse to include all or most of Europe. The payoffs are peace and prosperity. The new members in Central Europe are growing much faster than the earlier members. Much of this is the result of the statistical quirk that poorer countries, starting with a smaller denominator, register bigger percentage gains than richer countries. (If you give $1 to a man with $10, he enjoys a 10 percent gain. If you give it to a man with $100, he gains only 1 percent.) Technology does not need to be developed; it is simply transferred eastward. Much lower wages and taxes in Central Europe pull West European investments eastward. Central Europe and the Baltics are now cemented into the EU and NATO with little to fear from Russia. All of Europe relaxes.

But there are losers in this process: West European workers fear for their jobs. Notice how this parallels American workers who worry about their jobs going to China, India, and other low-cost producers. Such fears underlay the failure of the proposed EU constitution.

KEY CONCEPTS

THE LIMITS OF COMPLEXITY

One reason the EU constitution failed in 2005 and 2008 was that it was just too long and complicated to understand, a problem not limited to Europe. President Clinton's health plan and Bush's Social Security changes and Medicare drug benefits earned public opposition because few could make sense of them. Americans hate the Internal Revenue Service in part because of its 10,000 pages of rules. Only specialists understand portions of it, and only because the clauses benefit their interest groups.

Why do legislators add complexity without limit? They do not mean to; they mean to add only small items that benefit the groups they represent or receive money from. They argue that their minor insertions are rational and fair. In the example mentioned, Maltese claim that foreigners would soon buy up much of their island. Accordingly, the EU convention inserted the comically specialized protocol to keep Malta for the Maltese. But when every group inserts its special demands, the document becomes incoherent. What is individually rational, in the **aggregate** can be insane.

Another factor contributes to the complexity problem: These documents are drafted by lawyers and other specialists. They are trained to and enjoy delving into every possibility and detail. Their general argument: "Look, we live in a complex society and economy, so you cannot expect simple solutions." That may be true, but the payback they get from the public is often anger, rejection, and indifference. The complexity factor may set limits to the amount and level of legislation that citizens in a democracy can support. Both European and American drafters of laws should remember the acronym KISS (Keep It Simple, Stupid).

ATTACK OF THE POLISH PLUMBERS

As France and the Netherlands rejected the new EU constitution there was much talk of soon having to compete with low-wage "Polish plumbers." The term caught on, half in jest, as a threat to West Europe's jobs in general. EU membership includes the free movement of labor, although there was a delay of several years before workers from the new member states in the east could move freely into West Europe. Such movement is natural but angers those who feel their livelihoods are threatened.

In mid-2005 the French voted *non* and Dutch *nee* to the new EU constitution, which was actually in the form of a 2004 treaty among EU member states. Indeed, European unification is nothing but a series of treaties, always one of its problems. Treaties seldom grab public enthusiasm. Polls had predicted both rejections, but they still shocked the Eurocratic elite who drafted the constitution and thought they did a great job.

Each EU member country ratifies treaties its own way. Most simply have their parliaments approve a treaty, like the U.S. Senate does. Several EU countries earlier had their parliaments ratify the new constitution without much fuss: Lithuania, Hungary, Slovenia, Italy, Greece, Slovakia, Germany, and Austria. But eleven EU states decided to refer the question to the entire electorate. Spain did this, and it passed. France especially has a long tradition of *referendums,* a mass vote on an issue rather than for candidates (see pages 140–141). This tradition, a dubious one, doomed the EU constitution in 2005. The French voted it down 55–45 percent with a 69 percent turnout. Then the Dutch, who have no tradition of referendums, voted it down 62–38 percent with a 63 percent turnout. Since the constitution had to be approved by all members to take effect, it died.

France and the Netherlands, both founding members of the original Common Market, were actually expressing negative opinions found throughout West Europe. (East Europeans are still somewhat Euroenthusiastic.) If they had a chance, many EU electorates would have voted against the constitution on a variety of grounds:

- Increasing power in Brussels infringes on national sovereignty (true, precisely the point of the EU).
- The constitution promotes competition in a free-market economy. (True, but this is what made Europe prosperous.)
- We were not consulted on the EU suddenly adding ten new, poor members to the east in 2004 (true). Now we're saying what we think about that.
- Unemployment here is terrible, around 10 percent (true at the time) and made worse by shipping our jobs to the new, low-wage members in the east (likely untrue). Even worse, "Polish plumbers" will come here and take our jobs. We'll lose our 35-hour workweek.
- The new constitution is too long, detailed, and complex to understand. (This is absolutely correct.)
- No one consulted us on Turkey joining the EU, and by voting "no" we reject it.
- The new constitution will let in even more non-European immigrants, who bring crime, unemployment, and Islam with them. (This is not part of the constitution but is happening anyway.)
- The introduction of the euro currency in early 2002 did not bring the promised economic growth, just inflation (true, but we cannot be sure the euro caused it).

- A narrow political elite, out of touch with ordinary citizens, has been telling us what to do and think for too long, and now we repudiate them (valid).
- For the French: Chirac is a crook and mismanaged the economy; we do not trust him. For the Dutch: Prime Minister Jan Peter Balkenende is ineffective. (Who elected them?)

---

direct democracy   One in which citizens vote on many issues, bypassing elected representatives.

representative democracy   One in which citizens do not rule directly but through elected and accountable representatives.

Note that several of the items have little or nothing to do with the new constitution; they were a way of showing mass resentments on a variety of issues, blowing off steam. And this is why it is often a mistake to submit complex issues to the electorate: They may vote against the question for unrelated reasons. Almost by definition, any government-sponsored referendum that fails was a mistake. The French and Dutch governments misunderstood mass opinion. **Direct democracy** can be dangerous; all modern countries are **representative democracies**, which calm and guide mass passions. Ireland repeated the referendum mistake in 2008.

The most valid complaint about the mammoth constitution, 448 articles in 450 pages, is that no one could understand it. Millions of copies were distributed, but few bothered to read or discuss it. A sample, Article III-139, shows why:

This subsection shall not apply, so far as any member state is concerned, to activities which in that state are connected, even occasionally, with the exercise of public authority. European laws or framework laws may exclude certain activities from application of this subsection.

Protocol 9, Article 61, limits outsiders who might buy vacation homes on Malta. Constitutions should be clear, brief, and general, outlining the parts of government and civil rights, nothing more. Details should come later, in statutes. This EU constitution seemed calculated to either make people laugh or turn them off.

WHAT EUROPEANS QUARREL ABOUT

Liberal Europe versus Social Europe

As we saw in Britain, France, and Germany, West European countries are welfare states with elaborate and expensive subsidies and regulations to protect citizens from the ups and downs of market forces. This has produced *labor-force rigidities* and high unemployment. Some European thinkers—and not all of them conservatives—recognize that persistent joblessness and anemic economic growth will slowly degrade European living standards and bankrupt several governments. There is simply not enough tax revenue coming in to cover government spending, especially as Europeans rapidly age into retirement. (Notice how America has the same problem but not as urgent.) And Europe's taxes are about 40 percent of GDP compared to America's 27 percent (see page 76).

Some Europeans, probably a minority, recognize the looming economic dangers and urge reforms to cut welfare outlays, taxes, and regulations and increase competition (example: Germany's Angela Merkel). They would like to move Europe in a more U.S. economic direction. Europeans call such

liberal   European and Latin American for unrestrained capitalism (approximately opposite of U.S meaning).

social   European for welfare state ("liberal" in U.S. terms).

measures "**liberal**" or even "ultra-liberal." A majority want to stick with what they call "**social**" protections of welfare and jobs. Many Europeans think that "Anglo-Saxon" (that is, British and American) economic competition is "savage" and "heartless." For them, the EU is bound together by regulation, not competition.

Thus one of the great EU questions is whether Europe should move away from the social model and in a liberal (in the European

Geography

Where Does Europe End and Asia Begin?

The theoretical question of where Europe ends and Asia begins turned real with the collapse of the Communist regimes of East Europe in 1989 and of the Soviet Union in late 1991. How far east does Europe extend? Which countries would be eligible to join the European Union? Central Europe was clearly eligible and joined (along with the Baltic states) in 2004. The Balkans were always marginal to Europe, but Greece was already a member, and Romania and Bulgaria joined in 2007. But what about Turkey, Russia, and the other ex-Soviet republics?

De Gaulle once spoke of Europe "from the Atlantic to the Urals," using the common standard for defining Europe. There is no natural border between Europe and Asia. The Urals are not much of a barrier and do not extend across Central Asia. The Mongols went south of the Urals to conquer Russia in the thirteenth century. On a globe, Europe is just a peninsula of Asia.

Most geographers accept an arbitrary line that runs down the Ural Mountains, then follows the Ural River south into the Caspian Sea to Baku, then eastward along the Caucasus Mountains, across the Black Sea, and through the Turkish Straits. By this definition, most of Russia, Turkey, Georgia, Armenia, Azerbaijan, and Central Asia are not in Europe. There is nothing legally binding about this line. Cyprus, which falls well outside of this line, is the easternmost EU member.

Some urge a cultural definition, namely, that Europe consists of historically Christian lands. Where Christianity ends, they argue, so does Europe. This would shift the boundary to the south of the Caucasus ridge line to include Georgia and Armenia but not Azerbaijan. Many Europeans feel this criterion should be applied to exclude Turkey from EU membership.

At present, Russia has no interest in joining the EU, but Ukraine does. Moscow will not subordinate its sovereignty to Brussels. A proud and nationalistic Russia sees the EU as a rival and possible threat and is interested in nothing more than commercial ties with the EU. Russia sells Europe much of its oil and natural gas. Ukraine, on the other hand, sees EU membership as its path to prosperity and independence from Russia and will likely apply.

Most of Turkey's elites—especially its military—insist that Turkey is in Europe and belongs in the EU, although few Europeans like the idea. Given a chance to vote on Turkey joining the EU, Europeans would overwhelmingly reject it. They fear people of a very different culture and religion swarming into West Europe. Some note that centuries ago Europe pushed back two Muslim invasions, the Moors in Spain and the Ottomans in the Balkans. Every West European country has an anti-immigrant party, all implicitly or explicitly anti-Muslim.

The Muslim ex-Soviet republics—Azerbaijan in the Caucasus and Kazakhstan, Turkmenistan, Uzbekistan, Kyrgyzstan, and Tajikistan in Central Asia—are culturally even less European than Turkey. They are more Middle Eastern as they are mostly Muslim, speak Turkic languages, and for centuries were parts of the Persian Empire. The Caucasian lands of Georgia and Armenia, however, are mostly Christian and are likelier candidates for the EU. But if Europe eventually admits them, could it exclude Azerbaijan? Where to draw Europe's boundary became a major EU political question.

sense) direction. Many French and Dutch voted against the EU constitution in 2005 out of fear that it was too liberal, that is, that it stripped away welfare and job protections. Once used to such programs, citizens fight any trims in them. Americans, too, oppose even small cuts in Social Security or Medicare, which, compared to Europe, are modest programs.

Doubts about the Euro

The EU founded the European Monetary Union (EMU) and its offshoot, the European Central Bank (ECB) and its euro currency. EMU members (Britain is not one) gave up an important element of their sovereignty—control over monetary policy—in favor of a single currency. This is an economic plus but also a straightjacket that soon some regretted. To avoid inflation, the EMU limits members' budget deficits to 3 percent of GDP. Countries like France and Germany, fighting unemployment and paying generous welfare expenditures, find this too low and routinely exceed it. The EMU could theoretically fine them but does not.

The danger and debate is that ignoring the EMU limits could cheapen the euro, while enforcing the limits could persuade countries to drop out of the euro system altogether to regain control over their currency. The EMU and euro could collapse. Britain dropped out of the EMU, rejected the euro, and is doing just fine. By 2007 the euro had actually climbed too high in relation to the dollar, which hurt European exports. Many Europeans would be happy to return to their old currencies.

Europe's Budget Battles

Like a regular country, the EU battles over who gets what. Compared to member states' budgets, the EU's is small, only about 1 percent of combined GDPs, but that is still about $140 billion a year. Europe's big problem is that 40 percent of that goes to the Common Agricultural Program (CAP). French farmers are the biggest recipients, and German and Dutch taxpayers are the biggest payers. Roughly half of West European farmers' incomes are from subsidies (compared to two-thirds for Japanese and one-third for American farmers). Rich farmers get the most. An average European cow gets $2.50 a day in subsidies.

European "liberals" see these subsidies as madness, producing "mountains of butter and lakes of wine" that cannot be sold. They sit in warehouses at taxpayer expense. Accordingly, European liberals would like to cut the CAP and shrink both farm surpluses and the number of farmers. "Social" Europeans, with French farmers in the lead, say, "Don't you dare. The subsidies preserve both our traditions and Europe's food independence from the dreadful U.S. agribusiness and its genetically modified crops."

The British handle the CAP another way. Prime Minister Thatcher, a Euroskeptic, thundered against the CAP because Britain has relatively few farmers and would pay far more than it received. In 1984 Thatcher got her way, and Brussels now rebates several billion a year back to London. (In 2005 Britain contributed some $18 billion to the EU budget but got $6.18 billion back as a rebate.) Some other EU members see this as unfair and wish to cut or end the rebate for Britain. The real problem is the CAP itself, but so far, no one has been able to cap the CAP.

A related problem is how the EU helps poorer members with its *solidarity funds*, EU aid to lift up poor regions. Ireland, Spain, Portugal, and Greece got substantial EU aid and are now no longer poor. (The Irish per cap is now higher than Britain's.) The EU is reluctant to accept very poor countries as new members because they will cost too much, one argument against admitting Turkey. Actually, most EU member countries now fall within a modest 1:2 range in per capita GDPs. Aside from super-rich Luxembourg (per cap around $70,000), the EU's largest countries—Britain, France, Germany, and Italy—are all around $32,000 per cap, only about three times as much as the two new members from the Balkans. (Poorest: Romania at $9,100 per cap, but rising fast.) The EU solidarity fund is a fine, idealistic policy, but it leaves many West European taxpayers resentful that both their euros and their jobs are going to the new, poorer members.

WHAT NEXT?

The failure to ratify the 2004 EU constitution and 2007 Lisbon Treaty did not mean a crisis or collapse. The EU simply rumbled on as it had for years, operating under the rules that had been added in a series of treaties. The EU structure was clumsy, undemocratic, and unintelligible, but it worked. Several pro-Europe observers actually hoped that the 2004 constitution would be rejected, because it was too long and complex and still left the EU undemocratic. After some peevish Irish voters sank the 2007 treaty, the EU continued to work on a reform treaty that would win ratification. Europe was warned: Do not put such complex questions in referendums.

Who will likely join the EU in the future? Here are some approximations:

The Western Balkans—Croatia, Bosnia, Albania, Macedonia, Serbia, Montenegro, and Kosovo—could follow in several years. One limiting factor: Croatia, Bosnia, and Serbia must first surrender those among them accused of war crimes to the Hague tribunal for trial.

Ukraine and Belarus, former Soviet republics, could follow a few years after that. Ukraine is making strides toward democracy; its 2004 Orange Revolution showed that democracy could take root in the ex-Soviet Union. Belarus is Europe's last dictatorship and closely tied to Russia.

Turkey will likely not join the EU anytime soon. Although accession talks between the EU and Turkey began in 2005, the rejection of the EU constitution warned politicians to not let Turkey in. The Turkish issue was put back on permanent hold, where it had been for many years.

Some suggest putting "ever closer union" on indefinite hold and returning to the original concept of Europe as a free-trade area with some added features (such as movement of labor), like the original Common Market. Such a looser arrangement would give little power to Brussels and keep members sovereign. Britain has always favored a looser EU. One of Europe's debates has been "wider or deeper?" Those favoring "wider" wanted the EU to enroll most of Europe but stay structurally loose. Those favoring "deeper" wanted it to become a genuinely federal system. Some critics say the EU was looking for trouble when it tried to do both simultaneously: twelve new members since 2004 and a new constitution at the same time. Those who wish to unify Europe should be warned of seeking too much at once.

KEY TERMS

aggregate (p. 251)

direct democracy (p. 253)

Enlightenment (p. 243)

euro (p. 241)

European Union (p. 241)

Helsinki Final Act (p. 250)

liberal (p. 254)

Maastricht (p. 243)

Mercosur (p. 243)

NAFTA (p. 243)

qualified majority voting
(p. 246)

representative democracy
(p. 253)

Schengen (p. 243)

social (p. 254)

subsidiarity (p. 246)

supranational (p. 243)

utilitarian (p. 249)

FURTHER REFERENCE

Alesina, Alberto, and Francesco Giavazzi. *The Future of Europe: Reform or Decline.* Cambridge, MA: MIT Press, 2006.

Beach, Derek. *The Dynamics of European Integration: Why and When EU Institutions Matter.* New York: Palgrave, 2005.

Bomberg, Elizabeth, John Peterson, and Alexander Stubb, eds. *The European Union: How Does It Work?* 2nd ed. New York: Oxford University Press, 2008.

Dell'Olio, Fiorella. *The Europeanization of Citizenship: Between the Ideology of Nationality, Immigration, and European Identity.* Burlington, VT: Ashgate, 2005.

Dinan, Desmond. *Ever Closer Union: An Introduction to European Integration,* 3rd ed. Boulder, CO: L. Rienner, 2005.

Eichengreen, Barry. *The European Economy since 1945: Coordinated Capitalism and Beyond.* Princeton, NJ: Princeton University Press, 2006.

Hosli, Madeleine O. *The Euro: A Concise Introduction to Europe's Single Currency.* Boulder, CO: L. Rienner, 2005.

Maas, Willem. *Creating European Citizens.* Lanham, MD: Rowman & Littlefield, 2007.

Markovits, Andrei S. *Uncouth Nation: Why Europe Dislikes America.* Princeton, NJ: Princeton University Press, 2007.

McAllister, Richard. *European Union: An Historical and Political Survey,* 2nd ed. New York: Routledge, 2007.

McCormick, John. *The European Superpower.* New York: Palgrave, 2006.

———. *The European Union: Politics and Policies,* 4th ed. Boulder, CO: Westview, 2007.

Menon, Anand. *Europe: The State of the Union.* London: Atlantic Books, 2008.

Morgan, Glyn. *The Idea of a European Superstate: Public Justification and European Integration.* Princeton, NJ: Princeton University Press, 2005.

Norman, Peter. *The Accidental Constitution: The Story of the European Convention,* rev. ed. Brussels: EuroComment, 2005.

Nugent, Neill. *The Government and Politics of the European Union,* 6th ed. Durham, NC: Duke University Press, 2006.

Padoa-Schioppa, Tommaso. *Europe, A Civil Power: Lessons from EU Experience.* New York: Palgrave, 2007.

Pontusson, Jonas. *Inequality and Prosperity: Social Europe vs. Liberal America.* Ithaca, NY: Cornell University Press, 2005.

Rifkin, Jeremy. *The European Dream.* New York: Penguin, 2005.

Chapter 18
Japan

Japanese see themselves as a pure-blooded single tribe, but their ancestors came from other parts of the Pacific Rim, especially from Korea. The Japanese and Korean languages are related, and some scholars suggest that the imperial family is of Korean origin. This finding is controversial, as Japanese look down on Koreans as racial inferiors. Japan and Korea drew much of their culture from the magnificence of classic China, as one can see today in the pictographic writing of Japan and Korea, the architecture, pottery, and much else.

THE IMPACT OF THE PAST

Japan is divided into four main islands, making it hard to unify. Mountainous Japan has little arable land, and much of that devoted to rice, a crop so important it became part of the religion. Early Japanese pushed back the original inhabitants, the *Ainu*, developing a warrior ethos. Japanese were undisturbed on their islands for many centuries, allowing them to selectively borrow from China but alter it. *Confucianism* (see page 381) and *Buddhism* (see page 447) arrived in the sixth century from China but took on Japanese characteristics. Japan absorbed Chinese culture but avoided Chinese takeover.

Japanese called their land, *Nihon* ("sun origin," also pronounced *Nippon*) from the national myth that all Japanese are descended from the Sun Goddess. Marco Polo seems to have recorded the Mongol name *Zipangu*, which among Westerners turned into Japan. In 1274 and 1281, Japan trembled when Mongol Emperor Kublai Khan invaded Japan, but Japanese samurai fought off the Mongols, and both times a "divine wind" (*kamikaze*) wrecked the invasion fleets. The Japanese nobility celebrated themselves as a superior warrior race until 1945.

JAPANESE FEUDALISM

Japan was long dominated by clans and their leaders. According to tradition (still practiced in the **Shinto** faith), Jimmu, a descendant of the sun goddess, founded the Land of the Rising Sun in 660 B.C. Myth aside, by the seventh century A.D. central Japan had largely unified on the Chinese imperial

QUESTIONS TO CONSIDER

1. Why was Japan's feudalism longer and deeper than Europe's?
2. Was the Tokugawa policy of keeping Japan isolated wise?
3. How were the Meiji reforms a logical outcome of Japan's opening by Perry?
4. How does Japan's prime minister differ from other prime ministers?
5. How does Japan's dominant-party system work?
6. Is there a distinct "Japaneseness"? How would you describe it?
7. Between interest groups and government, who bribes whom?
8. What is the "no one in charge" theory? Is it valid?
9. What explains Japan's economic success? What went wrong?

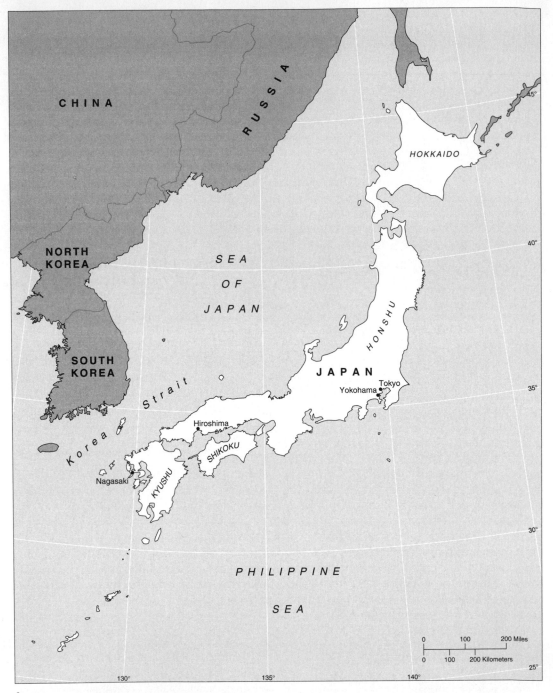

JAPAN

model, bolstered by Confucianism and ruled by a *tenno* (emperor). Under the forms of Chinese centralized rule, however, the clans exercised control and kept figurehead emperors in the palace.

As we discussed in Chapter 2, feudalism grows as central authority breaks down, which occurred in Japan from the ninth to the twelfth centuries and led to seven centuries of feudalism, ending only in the nineteenth century. China overcame feudalism early to become a bureaucratic empire. England overcame feudalism slowly in favor of limited, constitutional government. France overcame feudalism through absolutism. Japan, it has been argued, was feudal so long and deeply that feudal characteristics remain.

The essence of feudalism is power diffused and quarreled over among autonomous lords, each supported by warrior-helpers, whose knightly code—in Japan, *bushido*, the way of the *bushi* (warriors)—stresses obedience and honor. The sure sign of feudalism is castles—the lords needed secure home bases—and Japan has many. Medieval Europe—with its trinity of king, lords, and knights—corresponds to medieval Japan, where they were respectively the *tenno* (starting about 1600 eclipsed by the **shogun**), *daimyo* (regional lords) and *samurai* ("those who serve"). Europe started growing out of feudalism before the fifteenth century, as modernizing monarchs crushed their aristocratic competitors and founded the "strong state" of centralized power and sovereignty. Japan lagged centuries behind.

> **Shinto** Japan's original religion; the worship of nature, of one's ancestors, and of Japan. (See page 259.)
>
> **shogun** Feudal Japanese military ruler.

The European Jolt

The first Europeans to reach Japan, as usual, were Portuguese in 1543, followed by Spaniards in 1587 and Dutch in 1609. The Japanese could not keep them out, and soon European traders and Catholic missionaries made inroads. St. Francis Xavier turned the Jesuits to converting Asia by

Geography

Japan and Britain

Japan and Britain are similar: Both are islands that derived much of their culture from the nearby continent. Why then are they so different? England early became a great industrial seapower, exploring, trading with, and colonizing much of the world. Japan stayed home and did not develop industry beyond the craft level. There were no Japanese fleets or explorations.

They faced different nearby powers. Europe was fragmented into many competing states and rarely a threat to England. Indeed, England played power-balancer on the Continent by injecting its armies into Europe's wars to make sure a unified Europe could never invade England.

Japan faced a unified China that was a threat, as demonstrated by the Mongol invasion attempts of the thirteenth century. Early on, Japan decided isolation was safest and in the ninth century cut most of its contacts with and borrowings from China and turned inward. Unlike European monarchs, Asian monarchs did not engage in competitive expansion, so Japan had no incentive to discover new lands.

Tokugawa   Dynasty of *shoguns* who ruled Japan from 1603 to 1868; also known as the Edo Period.

gaijin   Literally, "outside person"; foreigner. (Japanese suffix "jin" means person, thus Nihonjin and Americajin.)

learned argumentation and better knowledge of astronomy (to impress the imperial court). As many as 150,000 (2 percent of Japan's population) converted by 1582. Japan's rulers feared Christianity was the opening wedge of foreign takeover (which it was in much of the world) and banned it in 1597. Over a few decades, missionaries were excluded and Japanese Catholics slaughtered. In 1635, Japanese were forbidden to travel abroad.

The **Tokugawa** clan established a powerful shogunate in 1603, combining feudalism, military rule, and police state. Spies were everywhere, especially watching the *daimyo*, who had to spend much time, or leave their family, at the palace (as in the France of Louis XIV). The Tokugawa invented the Japanese police state and brought Japan two centuries of peace, prosperity, and isolation. The Tokugawa moved the capital from Kyoto (now a Buddhist cultural site) to Edo (modern Tokyo). Aside from one Dutch trading post allowed on an island in Nagasaki harbor, Japan shut the door to foreigners. The Tokugawa shoguns feared **gaijin** ways and wares were threats to Japanese stability but kept informed of the outside world through Chinese couriers.

The Forced Entry

By the middle of the nineteenth century Japan was a distinctive, prosperous, and highly developed civilization with little Western influence. The wealth of the merchant middle class made the arts flourish. Most Japanese would have preferred to have been left alone.

The United States did business on the China coast, and shipwrecks in the East China Sea washed Western sailors onto Japanese islands. They could be gotten back only with difficulty, through the Dutch trading post. Furthermore, Japan looked ripe for commercial expansion. In 1846, two U.S. warships called at Yokohama (Tokyo's port) to request diplomatic relations but were rebuffed. Then U.S. President Millard Fillmore ordered Commodore Matthew Perry to open Japan. Perry arrived in Yokohama in 1853 with four ships that combined steam power with sails. The Japanese were frightened by these black, fire-belching sea monsters and begged Perry to return next year. After much discussion, Edo decided it could keep the world out no longer, and when Perry returned in 1854, a large Japanese imperial delegation met him and acceded to his demands for diplomatic and trade relations. Soon Europeans followed in Perry's wake, and Japan quickly opened.

GEOGRAPHY

CRUISING THE SEA OF JAPAN

Your aircraft carrier is entering the Sea of Japan from the south, through the Korea Strait. Cruising in a clockwise direction, which countries do you pass to port (left)?

South Korea, North Korea, Russia, and Japan. (It looks like China has a tiny outlet to the sea here, but it does not.)

THE 1868 MEIJI RESTORATION

The long and peaceful Tokugawa period had made the samurai superfluous, but in 1868 some found a new calling: to save Japan by modernizing it quickly, before the West could take it over. With the accession of the new Emperor Mutsuhito, whose era took the name

> **Meiji**   Period of Japan's rapid modernization, starting in 1868.

Meiji, these samurai had the emperor declare a "restoration" of his power (it really was not) and issue a series of "imperial rescripts" in 1868 that ordered the modernization of everything from education and the military to industry and commerce. The Tokugawa were out, but the emperor remained as a nationalistic symbol for rule by samurai clans.

The slogan of the Meiji modernizers: "Rich nation, strong army!" Everything changed, and in a generation Japan went from the Middle Ages to the modern age. The *daimyo* lost their big hereditary estates (but got good deals in the new industries). Feudalism ended, and all Japanese were legally equal. No more could a samurai legally kill someone who disrespected him. (Even today, those of samurai origin are proud of it, but it confers no special advantages.) It was a controlled revolution from above, the only kind Japan has known.

Various daimyo and samurai clans were given monopolies on branches of industry and ordered to develop them. These formed the basis of industrial conglomerates, the *zaibatsu*. Japanese were sent out to bring back the best of the West: British shipbuilding and naval warfare, French commercial law and civil organization, and German medical care, steelmaking, and army organization. Japan quickly copied all. For funds, the peasants were squeezed for taxes.

Some educated Japanese liked democracy, but the Meiji modernizers preferred Bismarck's authoritarianism and copied the political system of newly unified Germany. The 1889 Japanese constitution included a monarch, an elected parliament, and political parties, but underneath, patterns of governance were Japanese and brokered by traditional power holders. It only looked democratic and modern.

Japan's economy grew rapidly. In thirty-four years, from 1885 to 1919, Japan doubled its per capita GDP. Although puny by today's standards, this 2 percent annual growth rate was probably the world's fastest up to that point in time. Japanese products, starting with textiles, charged onto the world market using cheap labor to undercut Western producers. (Notice how China is now doing

COMPARISON

A JAPANESE MODEL OF INDUSTRIALIZATION?

Japan's rapid modernization is sometimes offered as a model for the developing areas to follow. But it was not carried out on the basis of free-market capitalism; it was state-led modernization with much government guidance and funding. And it was not nice or painless; some samurai families got rich while peasants were turned into a downtrodden proletariat.

Worse, its centralization set up Japan for takeover by militarists and later, after World War II, by bureaucrats intent on economic growth regardless of foreign or domestic costs. Now Japan must reform a government-led industrializing machine that has become a hindrance. And Japanese-style modernization would not work in countries with completely different cultures.

the same.) The purpose of Japanese economic growth, however, was less to make Japanese prosperous than to make Japan powerful. Some argue that this impulse still influences Japanese economic policy.

THE PATH TO WAR

With its new Western arms, Japan picked a fight with and beat China in 1895, seizing Taiwan as its prize (and keeping it until 1945). Then it gradually took over Korea—which was even more of a hermit kingdom than Japan had been—and made it a Japanese colony in 1910. If these moves sound wicked, note that the West had earlier taken Asia by force, so why should not Japan do the same?

In 1904, amid growing tensions, Japan attacked, without warning, the Russian fleet on the Manchurian coast. With discipline, enthusiasm, bold officers, and British naval and German army advisors, the Japanese beat the incompetent Russians on land and sea. U.S. opinion favored the Japanese—Teddy Roosevelt called them "plucky little Nips"—because repressive tsarist Russia had a poor reputation in the United States. President Roosevelt personally mediated an end to the war in Portsmouth, New Hampshire, and won a Nobel Peace Prize.

Several *zaibatsu* conglomerates grew into economic giants that bought control of political parties. Japanese politicians, like those of today, took money from private industry. In 1927, even before the Great Depression, the Japanese economy collapsed. The rich *zaibatsu* got richer as the middle class got poorer and peasants starved. Japanese army officers, whose families and soldiers were often just off the farm, resented the economic concentration and crooked politicians. The officer corps, a hotbed of right-wing nationalism and emperor-worship, turned against the democracy and capitalism that bloomed in the 1920s and subverted them.

With no civilian control, the Japanese military ran itself without even informing the cabinet or diplomats. The war minister was a general and the navy minister was an admiral; they got whatever budget they wanted. Japanese armed forces were split by rival cliques—feudalism again—who sometimes fought each other. Emperor Hirohito, largely a figurehead, approved and supported plans to expand his empire. No one was in charge.

In southern Manchuria, the Japanese army built a state within a state aimed at conquest. Any Tokyo politicians who protested were assassinated. By the early 1930s, the army controlled the Tokyo government, and civilian politicians obeyed the military. Japanese learned to say nothing critical, as the dread *Kempeitai,* called the "thought police," kept tabs on everyone. The ideology of the militarists—who supposed that the "Japanese spirit" was invincible—was similar to that of the Nazis, a combination of racism, extreme nationalism, militarism, and a bit of socialism. Both defined their peoples as a biologically superior, warrior race, destined to conquer their parts of the world and dominate inferior peoples. Both were convinced that they needed new lands for their growing populations. Both built societies on military lines into tight, obedient hierarchies. Both offered the working class and farmers some economic help. The difference is the Nazis did it through a party, the Japanese through the army; parties in Japan were unimportant. It was no great surprise when Imperial Japan linked up with Nazi Germany in the 1936 Anti-Comintern Pact and in 1940 joined the Axis. The two had little contact during the war and, fortunately for both Russians and Americans, did not coordinate their military campaigns.

The Japanese propaganda line was "Asia for the Asians." The evil European colonialists were to be kicked out and the region enrolled in what Tokyo called the *Greater East Asia Coprosperity Sphere,* led, of course, by Japan. Some anticolonial Asians went over to the Japanese (Ne Win of

Burma, Sukarno of Indonesia, and Subhas Chandra Bose of India), although the Japanese were worse colonialists and racists than the Europeans. The Japanese governed with a bloody hand, mostly through the *Kempeitai*.

Manchukuo   Japanese puppet state in Manchuria.

THE GREAT PACIFIC WAR

In 1931 the Japanese army in Manchuria blew up some railway tracks at Mukden (the Manchu name, now Shenyang) and claimed the Chinese Nationalist army did it. With this as a pretext, the Japanese army quickly conquered all of Manchuria and set up a puppet state they named **Manchukuo**. The civilian prime minister in Tokyo protested and was assassinated. The Tokyo government was simply not in charge; the army operated on its own. The League of Nations condemned Japan, so Japan walked out of the League. Britain and France, with extensive Asian colonies, did not want to

GEOGRApHY

ANOTHER TALE OF TWO FLAGS

Related to their sun-goddess myth, some Japanese clans used a sun flag at least six centuries ago. With the Meiji modernization, Japan needed a national flag. The head of the powerful Satsuma clan in southern Japan suggested the present flag—*Hinomaru* or rising sun—that was first used in 1860 (by the first diplomatic delegation to the United States). One sinister Japanese flag, with beams radiating out, became a symbol of militaristic expansion. The army version had thicker red rays, the navy version thinner. U.S. occupiers abolished the sun-ray flag, but

the Naval Self-Defense Force resumed using it in 1954.

The national anthem *Kimigayo* ("His Majesty's Reign") was also used by the militarists until 1945. Like the *Hinomaru*, it was never written into postwar law or required at ceremonies. Some nationalistic politicians wanted to do that in the late 1990s, but they were opposed by the leftist teachers, who feared a recrudescence of militarism. The Diet finally made both official and legal in 1999. Japanese students and teachers are now required to face the flag and sing the anthem.

 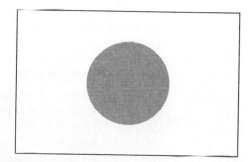

antagonize Japan, so they kept silent. The United States, as an avowed "big brother" to China, protested with words but not with military power, which convinced the Japanese militarists that the Americans were bluffing.

In 1937 the Japanese army began the conquest of all of China. Opposed but wishing to avoid war, the United States in 1940 embargoed scrap steel and oil to Japan, and in 1941 froze Japanese assets in American banks and organized the Flying Tigers. The Japanese military saw these steps as an undeclared war and planned Pearl Harbor. They hoped that by knocking out the U.S. Pacific Fleet they would persuade Washington to leave the Western Pacific to them. This ignored, however, American rage, something the militarists could not comprehend across the cultural gap. The Japanese people were informed of and consulted on nothing.

The war was unusually cruel, what one American historian called "war without mercy." Both Japanese and Americans killed war prisoners and inflicted vast civilian damage. The Japanese fought to death, because surrender meant shame and because they knew they would be killed if they were captured. The nuclear bombing of Hiroshima and Nagasaki in August 1945 tilted Emperor Hirohito to peace, even though some generals wanted to keep fighting. The Japanese language is subtle and avoids blunt statements, so Hirohito went on radio (for the first time ever) to explain to his ruined country why Japan would have to "endure the unendurable" and surrender: "Developments in the war have not necessarily gone as well as Japan might have wished." It was a classic Japanese understatement.

Up from the Ashes

Japanese cities were grey rubble by 1945. Starvation loomed. With no resistance, General Douglas MacArthur and his staff moved into one of the few Tokyo buildings still standing, the Dai-Ichi Bank (later one of the world's largest banks). Emperor Hirohito soon called on MacArthur to express his

Political Culture

Japan's Political Eras

Since the Tokugawa shogunate, Japan's political eras are named for the reigns of each emperor. Indeed, for domestic use only, lunar years in Japan are those of the emperor's reign. Thus 2000 is given as year 12 of the reign of Akihito. Wherever they can, the Japanese do it their way.

Name	Years	Remembered for
Edo Period	1603–1868	Tokugawa shogunate; military feudalism; isolated Japan.
Meiji	1868–1912	Rapid modernization under "restored" emperor; military expansionism begins.
Taisho	1912–1926	Normal but corrupt democracy.
Showa	1926–1989	Militarists take over, lead country to war; postwar economic boom.
Heisei	1989–	Economic slowdown; efforts at reform.

willingness to take blame. MacArthur, speaking as one emperor to another, told him he could keep his throne, but as an ordinary mortal, not as a "living god," something most Japanese already understood. To get Japan on the U.S. side in the Cold War, in 1947 the U.S. occupation began covering up Hirohito's support for the war and blaming General Tojo, the wartime prime minister, who was hanged. Critics claim that MacArthur's "reverse course" of 1947 let Japan avoid coming to grips with its wartime horrors.

In 1946 MacArthur's staff wrote a new constitution in five days to block a Japanese attempt to just lightly revise their prewar constitution. Resembling British institutions, it guaranteed freedom, parliamentary democracy, and peace. Japanese elites did not like the MacArthur Constitution—among other points, it made the emperor merely the symbol of Japan—but grudgingly accepted it when the emperor endorsed it.

The 1947 constitution has not functioned precisely as written, as Japanese power does not flow in neat, Western-type channels. Industry revived, much of it under the supervision of those who had run the war machine. The *zaibatsu* were broken up, but as the Cold War started MacArthur let banks reassemble them under the new name of *keiretsu*, giant industrial-financial combinations with the same names as the *zaibatsu*. MacArthur also let many of the old elites return to political power. Japanese patterns keep reasserting themselves.

THE KEY INSTITUTIONS

Japanese institutions resemble British ones, but they do not function in the same way. The Japanese monarchy, which was constitutionally divine until 1945, for most of history was a figurehead. Some older and more conservative Japanese still see the monarch as divine and will not criticize him, but few young Japanese pay any attention to the monarchy. The two post-war royal marriages were both to commoners, which helped demystify the Imperial Household.

The constitution specifies that the emperor has no "powers related to government." He does ritual and ceremony. Let off the hook by MacArthur, Hirohito for the first time met his subjects face to face and became a symbol of poor little Japanese bravely making do under U.S. occupation. In speeches, Emperor Akihito, son of Hirohito, is vague and idealistic. For a while,

Japan's imperial family: From left, Emperor Akihito, Crown Prince Naruhito, Crown Princess Masako, Empress Michiko. (Japan Information Center)

the Imperial House had no male heirs, the only kind Japanese law permits. Changing the law to allow for an empress stalled in the Diet. Conservatives protested, but most Japanese approved. It was the modern, liberal thing to do, and Japan has had eight empresses. The problem was temporarily solved when a younger brother produced a son in 2006.

THE PRIME MINISTER

Japan's prime ministers have rarely been the real power. A few, including Junichiro Koizumi (2001–2006), were strong, but their powers hinged on their mastery of the fractious Liberal Democratic party and did not carry on to their successors. Following Koizumi, Shinzo Abe (pronounced *Ah-Bay*) lasted only a year, resigning in 2007 after voters gave the (less-powerful) upper house to the opposition Democratic Party of Japan. The LDP then picked a moderate, quiet legislator, Yasuo Fukuda, the 71-year-old son of a former prime minister, but few predicted a long tenure.

Americans often mistake Japanese prime ministers for their British or German counterparts. In trade talks, for example, the Japanese prime minister visits Washington and makes some concessions to the U.S. side, but then nothing changes. The prime minister does not have the power, in the face of major interest groups and in government ministries, to follow through.

PERSONALITIES

FILL IN THE BLANKS: A GENERIC PRIME MINISTER

Japan's prime ministers can change quickly. By the time students read this, there could be a new prime minister. Students may fill in the name of Japan's current prime minister (in pencil) and other details. This exercise is to illustrate that the more things change in Japan, the more they stay the same.

Vowing to free up the Japanese economic system and chart a new course, Prime Minister _____ took office in 200_. He billed himself as a reformer, but _____'s roots are deep in the old system. Born into a political family, he graduated from _____ University and worked briefly as a _____ before he won a Diet seat in _____ Prefecture for the Liberal Democratic party, specifically its _____ faction.

_____ vowed reform, but little came of it. His cabinet is prone to disagreement and breakup. Japan's interests and bureaucrats know how to block reforms.

Print out photo of current Japanese prime minster from *kantei* Web site and lightly tape here. Be prepared to change it.

Japan's economy grows little, and _____ catches the blame. Scandals plague the _____ government, and _____ is rumored to have received "campaign expenses" from a shady _____ company. Initially popular, his plunging ratings suggest he will soon be out.

Japanese prime ministers average only about two-and-a-half years in office. By far the longest-serving prime minister was Eisaku Sato, who served from 1964 to 1972. Junichiro Koizumi did well with his five years, 2001–2006, a time limit the LDP put on its leader, not a government requirement. Ordinary cabinet ministers average about a year and a half in office. The chief limits to their tenures are not votes of confidence or the splintering of coalition cabinets in the manner of the French Third or Fourth Republics. Until 1993, the **Liberal Democrats** (LDP) had a comfortable majority in the House of Representatives and could brush off no-confidence motions.

The problem is the fragmented nature of the Liberal Democrats. The leaders of the LDP's several factions make and unmake prime ministers and ministers in behind-the-scenes deals. Many ministers are simply front-men for their factions. Some allege LDP faction leaders are more powerful than prime ministers. LDP politicians have passed up chances to become prime minister because faction chief was more powerful. Typically, the leader of the dominant LDP faction, called half in jest the "shadow shogun," arranges deals to set up the cabinet and prime minister. Bosses of eight of the LDP's nine factions supported Fukuda for prime minister in 2007. Reformers hope to overcome this feudal arrangement, but it persists.

For ten months the LDP was out of power. In 1993–1994 Japan had a coalition of eight parties, most of them splinters of the LDP, some of which subsequently returned to the LDP. Such coalitions are unstable. Short-term Prime Minister Morihiro Hosokawa had his hands full as the many parties jockeyed for power within the coalition, just as the LDP factions had done. The real weakness of Japanese prime ministers is the parties, either fragmented, as in the case of the LDP, or splintered, as in the case of coalitions.

> **Liberal Democrats** (LDP), Japan's dominant party, a catchall.
>
> **Diet** Name of some parliaments, such as Japan's and Finland's.

THE DIET

The Japanese diet is optimal: light on fat, cholesterol, and calories. The Japanese Diet is marginal: heavy on payoffs, pork, and political squabbling. The 1947 constitution specifies the bicameral **Diet** (legislature) as the "highest organ" of Japanese government. Not strictly true in Europe, it is even less true in Japan. While the lower house selects the prime minister and can oust him on a vote of no-confidence, much of Japan's real decision-making power lies elsewhere, in the powerful ministries.

Japan's lower house, the House of Representatives, has 480 members, 300 elected from single-member districts and 180 on the basis of proportional representation by party lists in eleven regions, a *mixed-member* system (see page 189). The house's term is a maximum of four years. The new Japanese system, which began only with the elections of 1996, resembles the German hybrid system but

The Japanese Diet in Tokyo, a product of the 1920s, was completed in 1936. By then the military ran Japan.

pork barrel   Government projects that narrowly benefit legislators' constituencies.

does not use PR to set the overall number of seats per party (the German system, which does, is *mixed-member proportional*).

As in all parliamentary systems, the lower house can be dissolved early for new elections, which Prime Minister Koizumi did in 2005 (and won a resounding victory). The non-LDP coalition of 1993 rewrote some of the rules that were widely blamed for Japan's endemic political corruption. (See the box on page 284 on reforming Japan's electoral system.)

Japan's lower house has more power than the upper, the House of Councilors, always the case with parliamentary systems. The upper chamber may reject a bill from the lower, but the latter may override with a two-thirds majority. The upper house has no say in electing prime ministers. The House of Councilors has 247 members elected for six-year terms; half are elected every three years. It cannot be dissolved early.

Behind the show of parties, elections, and debates, the larger question of any parliament is whether it actually controls government policy. The career professionals who staff the Tokyo ministries regard most Diet members as clowns, who pass around the **pork barrel** to get reelected but have little interest in running government. The Diet, like Britain's Commons, has a Question Time, but top bureaucrats answer most of the questions, not ministers. Bureaucrats run Japan.

The Parties

Japan is an example of a *dominant-party system*, one with several parties but with one much stronger than any of the others. The big party can theoretically be voted out but seldom is. India and Mexico for many decades had dominant-party systems but grew out of it. For most of Japan's postwar era one party, the LDP, was so strong that some jested Japan was a "one-and-a-half party system." (The much-weaker Socialists were the "half" party.) In the 1990s, some thought the LDP would crack apart into a multiparty system, but the LDP is still the dominant party.

The Liberal Democrats amalgamated several centrist and conservative parties that had been ruling Japan since 1947. With the Cold War, the United States worried that radical Japanese parties, the Communists and Socialists, might turn Japan neutral or pro-Soviet, so the Americans encouraged the mergers that created the LDP.

The Liberal Democrats, although they enjoyed unbroken electoral success and controlled the government until 1993, barely cohered as a party; only the winning of elections and gaining of spoils kept the LDP from breaking up. Some saw it less of a party than an electoral alignment of factions grouped around powerful chiefs, much like samurai clans. Instead of swords, the faction chiefs used money. This feudal arrangement meant that no single faction or chief dominated for long, and no one was interested in or responsible for policy. The LDP is "conservative" not out of ideological convictions but merely because it opposes change. There were no important ideological divisions within the party either, only loyalties to chiefs, some of whom were unsavory holdovers from the World War II militarist government. Asked his political views, one local LDP activist proudly proclaimed, "I am a soldier in the Tanaka faction."

In the early 1990s, the LDP fell into disarray. Dozens of leading LDP politicians stalked out of the LDP to form centrist-reformist parties—Japan Renewal, Japan New Party, and New Party

Harbinger—that constantly reshuffled and renamed themselves into the Democratic, Liberal, and Conservative parties, some of which coalesced into the Democratic Party of Japan (DPJ), which has become the chief opposition party. The DPJ bills itself as free-market in economics but would stop Japanese help for the U.S. Iraq war and improve relations with China and Korea. But the DPJ is incoherent—a mixture of former Liberal Democrats and Socialists. DPJ hopes, dashed by the 2005 elections, were buoyed by its 2007 takeover of the upper house.

The old "half party," the Japan Socialist party (JSP), was formed with the approval of MacArthur's occupation government because it repudiated the militarist regime. The JSP hit an electoral high in 1958 with nearly one-third of the vote but declined because it was doctrinaire and rigid. The JSP, for example, urged neutralism for Japan and gave the Soviet Union and North Korea the benefit of the doubt while criticizing the United States. Renamed the Social Democrat Party of Japan, it joined and ditched the shaky 1993–1994 coalition, then bizarrely joined with its LDP archenemies in a 1994–1996 coalition with Social Democratic leader Murayama as a figurehead prime minister. This coalition alienated Social Democratic voters, and the JSDP now has only 7 of the 136 seats that it had in 1990. Some of its voters went to the new DPJ.

Some less-privileged Japanese turned to the strange Komeito, or Clean Government party, a 1960s offshoot of the Buddhist Soka Gakkai movement, which many Japanese think is warped and fanatic. In coalition, the LDP and Komeito together now have two-thirds of the lower house's seats, enough to override the upper house. A small Communist party wins a few seats in the lower house but was in a quandary when China headed for capitalism. Surveying Japan's messy and changing party system, we can say that no party is strong, not even the LDP, but the opposition parties are too fragmented to unseat the LDP. Half of Japanese say they support no political party.

Japan's Electoral System

Japan's old electoral system was blamed for its weak parties. Elections for the lower chamber were by 130 multimember districts. Instead of European-style proportional representation, Japanese voted for one candidate rather than for one party, and the winners were simply those with the most votes. If there were seven candidates in a four-person district, the four highest vote-getters were elected. Candidates of the same party competed against each other, a system that begged for factionalism and corruption within the LDP. The need for campaign money became desperate and with that came the influence of private donors.

The new coalition elected in 1993 immediately reformed the electoral system. First, they divided Japan into 300 single-member districts with roughly the same number of people to solve the problem of rural overrepresentation. In 1980, it took up to five times as many urban votes as rural votes to elect someone to the Diet. Even today, the gerrymandered districts still give some rural votes twice the weight of urban votes, magnifying the voice of Japan's farmers and letting the LDP win Japan's rural prefectures. The LDP-dominated Diet keeps out imported food and subsidizes inefficient Japanese farmers, giving Japanese consumers the world's highest food prices and angering foreign food exporters, such as the United States.

Now, after the 1993 reforms, 300 districts elect only one member each by simple plurality (not necessarily a majority) of the votes. This was supposed to cut the number of parties in the

Diet, since such systems penalize small parties, but that is not always the case, as small parties that are territorially concentrated may win in a few districts (as we shall see in India). Next, now that candidates from the same party no longer compete against each other, the reform is supposed to overcome the dreadful factionalism within the LDP. Neither reform worked.

The remaining 180 members of the lower house are now elected by proportional representation in eleven regions based on parties. This, too, was supposed to heal party factionalism because candidates from the same party have to run as a team rather than as competitors. This was supposed to give Japan's parties greater ideological coherence. The reformers' end goal: a responsible two-party system with alternation in power, like a real democracy. Years later, Japan's electoral reforms have yet to accomplish this.

Elections for the upper chamber are also similar to the German pattern. Each prefecture has from two to eight councilors based on population, and voters have two ballots; one is for a single-member district with plurality winning. This fills 149 seats; proportional representation at the national level fills another 98 seats. Because they use similar hybrid electoral systems, the distribution of seats in the two Japanese houses resemble each other. A unitary system like Japan really does not need an upper house, especially one that closely matches the lower house.

DEMOCRACY

THE 2005 ELECTIONS: A HYBRID SYSTEM IN ACTION

In the 2005 legislative elections—which Prime Minister Koizumi called two years early—the Liberal Democrats scored a massive victory that gave them over 60 percent of the House of Representative's seats. The table below shows what the Diet's lower chamber looked like with a 67.5 percent turnout.

Is the new mixed-member electoral system accomplishing its goal? The lower house of the Diet is less fragmented than before, and the LDP bounced back from decline to become more dominant than ever. But we should give it more time. If the post-Koizumi LDP returns to its old fractious ways and is unable to reform Japan's economy, voters could turn to the Democrats, who could challenge the LDP and eventually give Japan a "two-plus" party system with alternation in power.

	Single-Member Seats	PR Percent Seats	PR Seats	Total Seats	Change from 2003
Liberal Democrat	219	38.0%	77	296	+54 seats
Democratic party	52	31.0	61	113	−64 seats
Komeito	8	13.0	23	31	−3 seats
Communists	0	7.0	9	9	no change
Social Democrats	1	5.5	6	7	+1 seat
Other parties	20	5.5	4	24	
Total	**300**		**180**	**480**	

THE MINISTRIES

Who, then, holds power in Japan? First, there is no single power center; it is diffused among several centers. Many argue that the 19,000 career bureaucrats at the ministries' executive levels, particularly the Finance Ministry and Ministry of Economy, Trade, and Industry (**METI**)—formerly the famous MITI, the Ministry of International Trade and Industry—are the real powers in Japan. The Ministry of Land, Infrastructure, and Transport (formerly Ministry of Construction) has great clout, too, as it distributes big public-works contracts to benefit the "road tribe," Japan's overlarge construction industry. The four most important ministries—trade, finance, foreign affairs, and police—usually assign top civil servants as secretaries to the prime minister, a further bureaucratic hold on power.

> **METI**   Japan's powerful Ministry of Economy, Trade, and Industry (formerly MITI).

The Japanese cabinet, like most European cabinets, can be easily changed from year to year, with ministries combined, renamed, or instituted. Recent cabinets had the following ministries:

Foreign Affairs	Health, Labor, and Welfare
Justice	Agriculture, Forestry, and Fisheries
Finance	Economy, Trade, and Industry (METI)
Defense	Land, Infrastructure, and Transport
Internal Affairs and Communications	Environment
Education, Culture, Sports, Science, and Technology	Science, Technology, Gender Equality, Food Safety, and Okinawa

In addition, the cabinet included several "ministers of state" for lesser-ranked specialized functions:

Disaster Management	Financial Services
Okinawa and Northern Territories, Science, Technology, Gender Equality, Social Affairs, and Food Safety	Economic and Fiscal Policy
	Regulatory Reform

A minister may get more than one portfolio (as in France). For example, in Abe's cabinet the minister for internal affairs was also charged with privatization of postal services, a hot topic in Japan. Although not a minister, Japan's chief cabinet secretary is second in command after the prime minister and official cabinet spokesman. It can lead to the top; Abe was Koizumi's cabinet secretary. Only in 2007 was Defense made a full cabinet ministry. At least five ministries or agencies deal with economic development. The foreign minister usually doubles as deputy prime minister.

At least half of the ministers must be members of the Diet, and most are members of the lower house. A few are members of the upper house, and occasionally specialists or academics not in the Diet are brought in. The ministers are not necessarily experts in their portfolios (ministerial assignments), which are based more on political criteria than on subject-matter competence. Bureaucrats run the ministries, not ministers.

prefecture   First-order Japanese civil division; like French department.

As in Europe, every party in a coalition has at least one top leader appointed as a minister. The eight-party coalition of 1993, for example, had ministers from eight different parties. Even the small parties got a portfolio, but the parties with the most seats got several. Such distributions of ministries are payoffs used to form and hold a cabinet together. With the LDP controlling a majority of lower-house seats, the LDP governed in coalition with the small Komeito, with most portfolios in LDP hands.

Below the minister, a civil-service vice-minister really runs the ministry. The Japanese vice-ministers, who correspond to the British "permanent secretaries," are more powerful than their nominal bosses, also the case in most of Europe. Reportedly the vice-ministers meet twice weekly to draw up the agenda the cabinet follows the next day. The ministries' top appointed officials—appointed internally on the basis of merit, as defined by the individual ministry, not on the basis of political connections—have years of experience and knowledge; the minister may last only a few months in office. This gives the top civil servants much power and the feeling that they alone run Japan.

Japanese Territorial Organization

Japan is a unitary system that looks a bit like a federal system. It has forty-seven administrative divisions, forty-three of them **prefectures**, after the French *prefect*, the head of a *département*. The other four are special situations: Tokyo, Osaka, and Kyoto are run as large metropolitan districts, and the thinly populated northernmost island of Hokkaido is one big district.

Each Japanese prefecture has an elected governor and unicameral assembly to decide local matters and raise local taxes that cover only about 30 percent of prefectural needs, so the prefectural government is always asking Tokyo for additional revenues. Japanese call this "30 percent autonomy" and wish they had more. The Ministry of Internal Affairs in Tokyo still oversees prefectural matters and can override the local governor. The Japanese situation resembles the modern French territorial structure: unitary, but with certain local-democracy features.

Political Culture

Why Is Wa?

Wa, social harmony, may be the key to Japanese culture. Japanese learn to seek *wa* with each other. Japanese love *beisabaru* but never argue with an umpire. *Wa* is what gives Japan its cooperative group-mindedness. (Notice how the only way to play Pokémon is by cooperation.) Critics charge that *wa* is a device for social control and promotes conformity and obedience. Anyone questioning or criticizing disturbs the domestic peace and tranquility. *Wa* can also induce corporate and government bureaucrats to cover up financial problems rather than face them.

JAPANESE POLITICAL CULTURE

Japan is one of the few non-European countries that modernized while retaining its own culture. One factor may be the *absence* of deep religious values in Japan. Japanese religion, light and flexible, never got in the way of modernization. Japan took on some appearances of Western culture but kept its inner core of Japaneseness (*nihonjinron*, literally, "discourse on the Japanese"). For this reason, many observers see Japan as a unique civilization.

Germany and Japan were defeated in World War II, but missing from the U.S. occupation of Japan was the denazification practiced, however imperfectly, in Germany. Japan had no Nazi-type party to blame or put on trial (just army officers), and MacArthur retained the emperor and Japanese political structures. Japanese bureaucrats and politicians carried over from wartime militarism and quietly resolved not to change Japan too much. Some Germans felt guilty about the Nazi past, but very few Japanese felt guilty over their brutal expansion.

Many Japanese still refuse to believe that Japan did wrong during the war. The way they see it, they were unfairly punished by the hanging of some seven hundred patriotic officers. Bayonet practice on Chinese babies? Never. Germ warfare experiments on American prisoners? No way. Korean and Chinese "comfort ladies"? Not our doing. If you want to see war crimes, say some Japanese, look at Hiroshima and Nagasaki. The Japanese tend to see themselves as poor, downtrodden victims.

Political Culture

THE ROOTS OF NIHONJINRON

Japanese political culture is so distinctive that some Japanese claim their brains are physically different. During the war the militarists touted this racist explanation, but now only a few old people believe it. There are several theories of *nihonjinron*, and it is probably a combination of all.

- *Shintoism* taught that Japan and the Japanese are a wonderful, perfect society superior to others.

- *Buddhism* still teaches the renunciation of desire, enduring pain and difficulties, and being careful and mindful of all persons and things.

- *Confucianism* taught that one is born into a strict hierarchy and must obey authority and defer to superiors with great politeness.

- *Feudalism*, deep and prolonged in Japan, taught all to obey and honor superiors and keep their place but diffused power among several centers. Bowing continues, a remnant of feudalism.

- *Dependency* is inculcated into young Japanese by their parents and teachers. Unlike young Americans, Japanese are not trained for independence but to remain dutiful and submissive to the authority of both the job and the government.

- *Rice-farming* requires sharing water and working in teams that go down the rows at the same speed. Some argue that this makes Japanese cooperative but unoriginal.

- *Crowded* into a small land, Japanese had to develop nice manners and cooperation to make daily life possible. (This would not explain New Yorkers.)

guilt   Deeply internalized feeling of personal responsibility and moral failure.

shame   Feeling of having behaved incorrectly and of having violated group norms.

Only recently have some Japanese officials admitted war guilt—or is it shame?—for World War II. In 1991, Emperor Akihito apologized to Koreans for Japan's colonial occupation (1910–1945). In Beijing in 1992, he told Chinese officials that he "deeply deplored" Japan's long (1937–1945) war in China, which killed, by Beijing's estimate, 35 million Chinese. His father, Hirohito, had stayed silent about World War II. Several prime ministers have apologized, but Japan's signals are mixed. Many Japanese still do not admit the truth and few show remorse. They claim Japan was never aggressive or brutal and had fought only "for self-defense and the independence of Asian countries." A 1995 Diet proposal for a resolution of apology was dropped in the face of a petition signed by five million Japanese and supported by most of the LDP.

Hundreds of Japanese politicians—including prime ministers—visit Tokyo's controversial Yasukuni Shrine. They claim they want to pay respect to Japan's 2.5 million war dead, but the Shinto shrine also honors Japan's militarist past and fourteen Class A war criminals—including wartime chief Tojo—hanged by the Americans. Its attached museum portrays the war as Japan's liberation of Asia from Western imperialists. Fascistic youths in World War II uniforms parade at Yasukuni. LDP chiefs cultivate the important Bereaved Families Association as well as right-wingers and militarists. Beijing claims such gestures show continuing Japanese militarism.

Japan's Education Ministry screens textbooks to promote unity and patriotism. Doubts and war crimes get screened out in favor of mild wording, such as "Japan caused inconvenience to neighboring Asian countries." China and Korea protest deceptive understatement, but many new textbooks stick to the blameless line. Japan only halfheartedly admits war guilt; Germany did a better job and did it decades earlier.

Political Culture

GUILT VERSUS SHAME

Some argue that Japanese, unlike Westerners, are not driven by **guilt** but by the more superficial feeling of **shame**, of not upholding group standards. Guilt is woven into the Judeo-Christian ethos. The idea that God gives you moral choices and judges you is an important component of Western civilization and, according to some, the basis of Western individualism.

Japanese religion—and the Japanese are largely irreligious—has no such basis. Shintoism, a form of animism that includes one's ancestors, now means worshiping Japan. There is no God or code of morality besides serving and obeying. State Shinto was refined into an organized religion by the Meiji modernizers to ensure loyalty and was turned into nationalist militarism. Buddhism, which exists side-by-side with Shintoism, is vague on the existence of God; Lord Buddha was merely enlightened, not divine. Either way, from Shinto or Buddha, few Japanese are on guilt trips.

Instead of guilt, according to this theory, Japanese are motivated by shame. To let down the group is a terrible thing. In World War II, many Japanese preferred death to surrender, which meant shame. (Americans who surrendered were shameless cowards worthy only of harsh treatment.) One Japanese soldier who hid on Guam until 1972 said upon his heroic return, "I have a gun from the emperor and I have brought it back." He added: "I am ashamed that I have come home alive." There are few Japanese criminals, as trial and conviction brings devastating shame to the family. The shame theory helps explain Japanese anti-individualism and the suicides of prominent Japanese, including the crooked agriculture minister in 2007.

The view of themselves as permanent underdogs colors Japanese life. We are, they used to say, confined to a small country with few natural resources and devastated by war. But by 1970, Japan was a rich society with no need for protection for any of its sectors. Psychologically, though, many Japanese, especially older people, act as if they are trapped in wartime and postwar poverty and scarcity. Thus they "make do" with high tariffs, outrageous prices, cramped living quarters, and obedience and loyalty to company and bureaucratic authority.

The Cult of the Group

Americans pride themselves on individualism, Japanese on groupness. We are trained from childhood to "be ourselves" and to attract attention: "Hey, look at me!" Japanese are trained to fit into the group and not attract attention: "It is the nail that sticks up that gets pounded down," goes a Japanese folk adage. Almost like a big family, Japanese feel they communicate with and understand only other Japanese, implying that they have evolved to a higher human level. More plausibly, Japanese groupness is from centuries of isolation and feudalism, which made Japanese obedient. The crime rate is very low. (There are practically no private handguns in Japan.) Students obediently hit the books. Japanese bureaucrats instruct businesspersons on correct strategies, something no American businessman would tolerate.

Unlike American individualists, Japanese try not to attract attention or make a fuss, an attitude called *enryo*. One should always be polite and smile and not sue but should settle disputes quietly. (Japan has fewer lawyers than U.S. law schools produce each year.) One should not go to the doctor; small maladies go away. Japanese medical costs are half of America's, and Japanese have lower infant mortality and live longer. Wow, maybe we should try a little *enryo*.

Political Culture

JAPAN'S CRITICAL CHRISTIANS

Religion strongly influences political culture, and one clear difference is Japan's lack of Christianity. Christians (mostly mainstream Protestant) form less than 1 percent of Japan's population and are not growing much. (The Jesuits in the sixteenth century did better, gaining 2 percent.) Although Christian-related schools and colleges (many with U.S. ties) are numerous and popular, few students are drawn to Christianity. Western-style weddings, complete with marriage chapels and white gowns, are popular but just for show.

Japan's Christians see themselves as an embattled, prophetic minority. They no longer face discrimination, just indifference. They deplore the lack of higher values among Japanese, whom they see caught up in "secular materialism"—the godless getting of money and things. They see Shinto and Buddhism as empty ritual, providing relaxation therapy but no moral grounding. Japanese Christians are willing to face Japan's responsibility and guilt for World War II and to warn that Japan's new emphasis on "patriotism" could be misused.

Christianity always had an uphill struggle in Japan, where it was regarded as a foreign subversion of Japaneseness. Christianity brings with it individualism, guilt, and equality, but Japanese are content in their irreligiosity. In contrast, over a quarter of South Koreans are Christians. Koreans, under the long Japanese oppression, saw churches (many U.S.-sponsored) as a comfort and support for their Koreanness.

meritocracy   Advancement based only on intellectual ability.

But Japanese are shortchanged in civil and legal rights. They rarely sue but settle obediently for the sake of social harmony, almost always in favor of the stronger party, even if their claim is valid. Under police interrogation (some lasting for days, and with no lawyer present), 95 percent of arrested Japanese confess, even the innocent. Recognizing the inequities of the justice system, Japanese universities are expanding their law programs, and Japanese courts will add juries in 2009. Japanese are less obedient and more aware of their rights.

Education for Grinds

The Japanese are strong on education, one of the keys to their success. The Japanese work force is better educated than the American, especially in mathematics, the basis of all high-tech operations. On average, Japanese high-school graduates know more math than American college graduates. Children do their homework—often supervised by "education mamas"—with a determination that leaves French grinds far behind.

Japanese youngsters compete to get into the right schools and universities. As an almost perfect **meritocracy**, all admissions are based on tests; athletic ability or family connections do not help. Many Japanese youngsters take cram courses after school. Young Japanese endure "examination hell" to get into the right high school or university. Those who do poorly on exams may commit suicide out of shame.

Once into college, however, many Japanese students relax and do little work until their junior year, when they take exams that lead to jobs. Few Japanese students do graduate study, so few seek

Comparison

How Would You Do on a Japanese Exam?

This solid-geometry problem is from an entrance examination to Japan's elite Tokyo University. It is aimed at young Japanese in their last year of high school.

A regular pyramid with a height of V and a square base of width *a* rests on a sphere. The base of the pyramid passes through the center of the sphere, and all eight edges of the pyramid touch the surface of the sphere, as is shown in the illustration.

How do you calculate (1) the height of V and (2) the volume that the pyramid and sphere share in common?

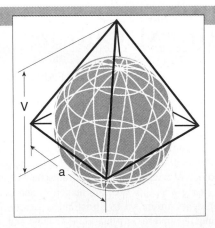

Well, you say, I'm not a math major and should not be expected to know such advanced stuff. But this question is from the exam for *humanities* applicants.

a high grade-point average. Where you studied—Tokyo University (Todai) is the best—rather than grades matter for getting a job.

Few Japanese students care and know about politics, the case in most advanced industrial countries. (See the box on "postmaterialism" on page 201.) Leftist professors influence a few students to criticize the system. With graduation, though, Japanese students get a haircut and new suit and become obedient *sararimen* ("salary men"). Entrepreneurialism is rare; you either go to a big company or you are nothing. Only recently have young Japanese started their own companies.

Japanese education is heavily based on rote learning and multiple-choice exams. Creativity and innovation are not prized; going along with the group is. Debate is taught as part of English-language instruction, implying that only with foreigners does one have disagreements. Fast learners in Japanese classrooms are assigned to help the slow, good both for education and groupness.

Death of a Sarariman

Japanese *sararimen* like to stay with one company, and the company would like to offer lifetime employment. Unemployment appeared only in the late 1990s. Most Japanese employees felt duty-bound to stay with their firm; American-style job-hopping was frowned upon as opportunistic and

Comparison

Destined to Misunderstand?

Viscount Eiichi Shibuzawa (1840–1931), one of the founders of modern Japanese business and an advocate of strong U.S.-Japanese ties, grew exasperated with the difficulties he encountered. Wrote Shibuzawa: "No other countries exist which are as different from each other as the United States and Japan. These two countries seem to have been destined to misunderstand one another."

This shows up in the distinct U.S. and Japanese business cultures. For example, two business seminars are held in New York City, one for twenty-five Japanese executives in America, the other for twenty-five American executives working for Japanese firms in the United States. The Japanese, all males, arrive in dark suits and keep their coats on even though the room is hot. They take exactly the allotted ten minutes for a coffee break. They ask no questions until they get to know each other over lunch. They politely defer to the speakers.

The American group includes eight women. Many of the men immediately take off their coats in the hot room. Chatting during the coffee break lasts more than twenty minutes. The Americans ask many questions, and some dispute the speakers.

These are just a few of the cultural differences between Japanese and American managers. Americans view conflict within the firm as normal; Japanese practice *nemawashi*, patient discussion leading to consensus that all then follow. American managers want quick profits; Japanese want bigger market share and greater efficiency, building for the long run. American firms hire people for specific skills, then downsize them when they are no longer needed. Japanese firms hire for what the person can learn and contribute to improved efficiency and try to not let the employee go. American managers respond to questions quickly and directly, for that indicates frankness. Japanese managers pause before answering and give discreet replies, for that indicates thoughtfulness. It does seem we are destined to misunderstand each other.

disloyal. Corporate downsizing has made Japanese more job-mobile. Japanese work hard; twelve-hour days are common. Some Japanese die of overwork, an illness call *karoshi*. Families have sued the companies that worked the husband to death. (One benefit offered by large firms: burial in the corporate cemetery, so you can be with your group for eternity.)

Japanese work hard and produce much but ask for little. *Sararimen* live in rabbit-hutch apartments and commute for hours in crowded rail cars. The cost of living is among the world's highest, especially for housing. Japan never developed a social safety net or social-security system, so Japanese save for hard times and for retirement. They are bigger savers than Germans, and the capital this made available for investment explains much of Japan's postwar economic growth.

THE "NEW HUMAN RACE"

The generation gap is wide in Japan. Older Japanese are amazed at how younger Japanese have changed and call them the *shin jinrui*, the new human race. Young Japanese are several inches taller than their grandparents, the result of more protein and not kneeling. McDonald's and KFC have become, respectively, Japan's first and second most popular restaurants, bringing a high-fat diet and obesity, previously unknown among Japanese youngsters.

Young Japanese have different attitudes. Working long hours for the sake of the company is no longer desirable; leisure, travel, and spending money are. With jobs scarce and apartments expensive, many young Japanese live with their parents and work only as *freeters*, temporaries. They avoid marriage, have fun, and spend their money on clothes and colorful hairdos. Younger Japanese switch their jobs and their votes and oppose corruption.

Since Perry, Japanese political culture has been a rearguard action to preserve the core of *nihonjinron*. Gradually and grudgingly, Japan accepted *gaijin* ways, but superficially and altered. The Meiji modernizers in effect said: "We have to modernize to prevent the West from taking us over. But we will do it our way." After World War II, Japan in effect said: "We have to become a capitalist democracy. But we will do it our way."

COMPARISON

CHANGING POLITICAL CULTURES IN GERMANY AND JAPAN

Both Germany and Japan long had feudal hierarchies and stressed obedience. Both marched to war under dictators who manipulated traditional-looking symbols. Neither country took to democracy until it was imposed on them after World War II. The devastation of war and lean postwar years taught both to work hard and ask for little. Reliable conservative parties, the CDU and LDP, delivered prosperity, and voters stayed with them. The difference is Germany shed its postwar stability in about a generation; the Japanese are taking two or more generations.

Why is Japan slower? First, Japan's feudalism lasted longer and its obedience patterns were deeper than Germany's. Second, Japan was more isolated even after World War II and its people traveled less than Germans. Third, Japan did not go through the reeducation that West Germany did after the war. Fourth, Japan was a poor country, poorer than most of West Europe, until the 1960s. As Japan got richer and more open to the world, its political culture became less distinctive.

PATTERNS OF INTERACTION

Japanese politics is an **iron triangle** consisting of the Liberal Democratic party, economic interest groups, and the ministries. New prime ministers often vow to break the triangle but have only dented it. The triangle works like this: Liberal Democratic politicians promise most economic interest groups—especially agriculture and the construction industry—to look out for them. In return, the interest groups deliver campaign funds, enabling the LDP to outspend rival parties. (Some LDP politicians also put funds in their own pockets.)

> **iron triangle**   Interlocking of politicians, bureaucrats, and business people to promote the flow of funds among them.

DEMOCRACY

JAPAN'S MAJOR INTEREST GROUPS

Japanese interest groups resemble the French model; that is, they are usually subordinate to bureaucrats and until recently did not dispute the ministry that supervises them. Japanese pluralism is not the same as American pluralism, where interests strive to capture the relevant agency or, failing that, fight it. Here are some top Japanese interest confederations:

- *Keidanren*, Federation of Economic Organizations, the most important business group, speaks for most large corporations and used to work closely with METI to promote exports. Now it is working around ministerial control in favor of deregulation and competition.

- *Shin Rengo*, Japanese Trade Union Confederation, was formed from the 1989 merger of smaller union federations and speaks for eight million members in a moderate and nonideological voice, even though it still has some ties to the Social Democrats.

- *Nissho*, Japan Chamber of Commerce and Industry, with good ties to the LDP, seeks to curb competition, large stores, discounting, and foreign imports.

- *Nokyo*, Central Union of Agricultural Cooperatives, argues for self-sufficiency in food and the exclusion of farm imports with its close friend, the LDP.

The leftist union of Japanese school teachers protests against Japanese rearmament, NATO, and the United States, and for socialism, in a peaceful demonstration across the street from the Diet.

- *Nikkyoso*, Japan Teachers Union, is left wing, pacifist, and critical of government. It is tied to the Social Democrats.

- *Jichiro*, the Prefectural and Local Public Employees Union, is Japan's largest single union and is quite influential. It is also leftist and tied to the Social Democrats.

The ministries and agencies adjudicate the various demands by contracts, loans, regulations, subsidies, and trade protection. The ministries, the commanding corner of the triangle, focus narrowly on their industries and sectors and protect them by controlled markets in which competition is limited or excluded, making the Japanese economy—which looks like a free-market economy—one of the world's most regulated. Although recently reformed a little, some ten thousand bureaucratic regulations govern every aspect of the Japanese economy. The ministries build regulated markets under the control of bureaucrats, a setup reminiscent of the mercantilist system of the French kings. Japanese consumers pay outrageous prices.

Bureaucrats in Command

Japan's ministries came from the militaristic system of the 1930s and 1940s. Munitions, heavy industry, the development of Manchuria, transportation and communications, and many other sectors were under state control and supervision. Indeed, the very founding of the modern Japanese economy during the Meiji Restoration was planned and controlled by the state. Japan has not really known a free-market economy.

After the war, the same bureaucrats who ran Japan's war economy planned its recovery. They did it well with the argument that nothing but Japan's economic growth mattered, and they were the only people who knew how to do it. This is not a "socialist" system, for it kept ownership private and did not redistribute income from rich to poor. It was not directly aimed at living standards but at the growth of the Japanese economy as a whole. Neither is Japan a "statist" system (as in France and Mexico), where the state is the number-one capitalist and owns major industries. Perhaps we should call Japan "guided capitalism."

Comparison

Bureaucratic Elites in France and Japan

The concept of a strong bureaucracy ignoring elected officials is nothing new. France has had such a system for decades. The Japanese bureaucratic elite resembles the French *grand corps*. Both groups are very bright and highly educated and placed into the top executive positions with mandates to modernize and upgrade their economies. Both think that they alone can save their countries and that elected politicians are a nuisance.

The French are trained in a Great School, such as the National Administration School or Polytechnical, whereas the brainiest young Japanese get into Tokyo University, *Todai*, which is publicly funded. Upon graduation, both enter fast tracks to the executive level, and both may retire early into better-paying jobs in private industry. The French bureaucratic elite disdains the views of interest groups, whereas the Japanese listen to the groups but then persuade them to follow the ministry.

A big difference is that French bureaucratic elites cooperate across ministries. The Japanese are soon immersed in their ministries' *sakoku* (closed environment) and ignore other ministries or elected officials. There is no grand plan in the Japanese model, and sometimes ministries work at cross-purposes.

The Japanese bureaucratic method is to leave industry in private hands but to persuade—often over dinner and drinks—the industry to go a certain way. The targets are the areas where Japan can undercut foreign producers and gain a big world-market share. Industries certified as growth leaders got long-term, low-interest loans from banks connected to the important ministries. Those industries not moving down desired paths did not get loans. This is a far more subtle way of steering an economy than Soviet-type socialism. (It also meant, by the 1990s, that many loans were mistakes that ruined Japanese banks. There is a down side to everything.) The Japanese approach was similar to the French "indicative planning" but stronger and more effective because it made the cash flow and utilized the cooperative Japanese setting where business generally obeys government.

scandal Corrupt practice publicized by news media.

walking-around money Politicians' relatively small payments to buy votes.

Finance and METI mostly did a good job. The brightest graduates are promoted rapidly and given major responsibilities while young. Their modest salaries lead some to move into private industry in mid-career (what the Japanese call "descent from heaven" and the French call "putting on the slippers"), and the ministry does not mind, as this broadens its ties with industry (and, with it, the breeding grounds for corruption). Japan recovered quickly after World War II and went on to set economic growth records. But bureaucratic guidance may have distorted the Japanese economy and plunged it into difficulties later.

Foreigners criticized Japan's bureaucracy as too powerful, but Tokyo dismissed that as "Japan-bashing." By the 1990s, however, Tokyo politicians agreed and made reforming the bureaucracies and regulations part of their campaign promises. Yesterday's Japan-bashing became today's conventional wisdom.

It will not be easy; the bureaucrats are used to their power. Fumed one high official of the powerful and conservative Finance Ministry: "We won't accommodate them, I assure you. They will accommodate us." In 2002, the popular and outspoken woman foreign minister, Makiko Tanaka (daughter of a former prime minister), was fired when the ministry's civil servants mutinied over her attempts to impose accountability. Japanese bureaucrats do not like outside control.

Japan's economic downturn of the 1990s showed bureaucrats were unable to reverse the slump; the old formulas no longer worked. Impatient, Keidanren organized its own Competitiveness Committee and made tough recommendations to the government, bypassing METI. Keidanren's message: Fix this creaky economic machine or we move our factories overseas (which is what they were doing anyway). The bureaucracy lost prestige. Todai law students, who used to enter the civil service, turned to private industry. Said one senior: "The bureaucrats have a bad image now—rigid, inflexible, annoying."

Corruption Scandals

Another leg of the "iron triangle," connecting the government to interest groups, is fertile ground for corruption. Japan seems to have a new **scandal** every year, accompanied by officials' resignations and sometimes arrests. Even prime ministers have been brought down. It used to be widely accepted, among both foreign and Japanese observers, that a little corruption was normal in Japan and that most Japanese did not mind it. **Walking-around money** is part of many political systems, and voters expect favors from politicians. But Japanese now criticize corrupt politicians when the amounts are too big, the conflicts of interest too obvious, the methods of donation secretive, or the sources too dirty.

money politics   Lavish use of funds to win elections.

¥   Symbol for yen (and Chinese *yuan*); Japan's currency; in 2008 ¥105 = $1.

structure   Institutions of government such as constitution, laws, and branches.

soft money   In U.S. politics, funds given to parties and other groups rather than to candidates in order to skirt restrictions.

Everyone knows that many public works such as dams, highways, and bridges are unneeded—Japan uses more concrete a year than the United States—but they reward the construction industry, which kicks back a percentage into party or personal coffers. Komeito was founded in the 1950s as the "clean government party" to fight corruption.

Corruption is rooted in Japan's **money politics,** as many candidates do not stress party platform or personality but the nontrivial cash gifts they hand out to constituents, the funds for which they must raise themselves. A typical incumbent spends an estimated ¥120 million (over $1 million) a year but gets an allowance of only ¥20 million. The rest has to be raised somewhere, by the donations of friends, supporters, businesses, and even gangsters.

By the early 1990s, the entire LDP was looking dirty, and some LDP politicians, generally younger and with an eye to the future, began bailing out of the party before it also tarnished them and began forming new parties. In 1993, voters, many now openly fed up with corruption, deserted not only the LDP but the perennial second party, the Social Democrats, who were also tarred with scandal. The immediate reason was both parties' failure to devise and lead the reforms necessary to curb corruption, make voting fair, and break out of the rigid patterns of a state-led export economy that was in difficulty.

The increasing clamor over corruption shows the Japanese voting public is growing more mature and more democratic. What an older generation accepted as normal, a younger generation brands as dirty, dishonorable, and undemocratic. Notice how at this same time Italian and Brazilian politicians were also brought down by the sort of corruption that had been going on for decades. These scandals were good signs, for they showed that people worldwide understand that they are ill-served by corrupt governments.

DEMOCRACY

CAN "MONEY POLITICS" BE BROKEN?

Did Japan's electoral and campaign-funding reforms of 1993 work, or is money politics so deeply rooted in Japanese political culture that legal tinkering cannot end it? It is an old question: Which is more important, **structure** or psychology?

Japan's money politics, alas, continued. Reforms do not necessarily work as planned. The United States has gone through several reforms of campaign financing only to find that both candidates and contributors come up with new ways to beat the system. (Now it is **soft money.**) The underlying problem is the need for campaign funds and the need to please blocs of voters.

Japan, the United States, Britain, France, and Germany have very different electoral systems, but each have recurring scandals related to fund-raising. Why? Because in each system parties and candidates figure out ways to skirt the law. And in each system, some candidates use campaign contributions for personal expenses, which often lead to additional scandals. Notice the underlying similarity: Politicians of all nationalities are addicted to money. In the words of California political boss Jesse Unruh, "Money is the mother's milk of politics."

No One in Charge?

One prominent theory of contemporary Japan is that behind a façade of powerful and orderly government there is no real center of decision-making power, no one in charge. (As hurricane Katrina revealed, the United States is not immune to this accusation.)

Few prime ministers really lead; instead, they hang on to office for perhaps two years until the LDP faction chiefs dump them. The faction chiefs do not really lead either; instead, they simply amass feudal power with which to battle one another. And parliamentarians do little but collect money in order to ensure their reelection. And even the mighty bureaucracies lead only in their narrow subject areas. Japanese government rumbles on, looking efficient, but no one steers it.

The "no one in charge" theory—still controversial—helps to explain the uncoordinated drift of Japan into World War II: The government in Tokyo wanted peace, but the army kept conquering China. The theory also helps to explain the difficulty in getting trade commitments from Tokyo: The prime minister promises to open the Japanese market to American products, but Japanese bureaucrats quietly veto the idea by not implementing policy changes that come from outside their ministry, which has been likened to a feudal fiefdom, without common purpose or leadership.

The "no one in charge" theory also suggests that Japan is institutionally underdeveloped, unable to handle the economic problems of the twenty-first century, including economic distortions that produced a long slump and trade imbalances. The big question for Japan now is whether the LDP is coherent enough to carry out necessary reforms. Previous reform efforts have budged Japan only a little.

DEMOCRACY

Who Bribes Whom?

There are two important flows of money in modern politics. The first is from interest group to political party, implicitly a form of bribery found everywhere, in Europe, America, Japan.

A much bigger money flow, however, is from government to voting bloc, designed to win votes. It, too, is found everywhere and has grown, as all modern governments pay off various groups with spending programs, construction projects, subsidies, and trade protection. This form of bribery is probably a bigger motivator of politicians' choices. Fear of alienating a voter bloc makes cowards out of most politicians. Who dares say no to farmers? Not the Tokyo government and not even the "conservative" Bush administration, which increased farm payments. Mostly governments bribe groups rather than the other way around.

Typically, politicians strive for their immediate advantage (namely, getting reelected) and pay little attention to outcomes (such as war, budget deficits, or inflation). Politicians have to play short-term games and ignore long-term consequences. Those who do not can be voted out. Campaign-law reforms, either in Japan or in America, pay no attention to the more important type of bribery, the "earmarks" (polite term for *pork*) so beloved of both Japanese and U.S. politicians.

NO LOSERS

Related to the "no one in charge" theory is the understanding that no one gets injured by economic change. Although whale meat is now a trivial part of the Japanese diet, Tokyo still defends the right of Japanese whalers to slay the endangered animals. Why? To give into international pressures would put whalers out of business, and in this country no one gets hurt. A single farmer on three acres of eggplants blocks the badly needed expansion of Tokyo's overburdened Narita airport. Why? To expand the airport would put him out of business, and in this country we do not do that.

unit veto   Ability of one component to block laws or changes.

alternation in power   The electoral overturn of one party by another.

The "no losers" impact on Japanese politics is to stifle change. Interest groups such as small retailers have been able to block and delay construction of big department stores and supermarkets. It took years to open Toys "R" Us in Japan; small shopkeepers objected. (It is now Japan's biggest toy retailer.) Japan is slowly modernizing its retail sector, and now most Japanese are happy to shop in large stores.

Informally, Japan has a **unit veto** system, one in which any component, no matter how small, can veto an innovation desired by most. Farmers have especially benefited. Even within the Tokyo area—at 35 million people the world's largest metropolitan area—there are small patches of farmland that the owners will not sell to make way for badly needed apartment houses, and they are supported by laws and lavish subsidies. Japanese consumers lose through the high prices and cramped life they must endure.

DEMOCRACY

CAN JAPANESE POLITICS ALTERNATE?

Maybe Japanese politics can alternate eventually, but not yet. One of the defining features of a democracy is **alternation in power**. If the same party stays in office for decades, the system is probably not a democracy. The ruling party, of course, claims that it is the voters' choice, but its control over the media and ballot boxes makes sure it wins. Few observers counted Mexico, whose Institutional Revolutionary party (PRI) was in power for most of the twentieth century, as a true democracy (see Chapter 30).

Power alternated in Japan briefly, in 1993–1994, but that was an unstable eight-party coalition that fell apart after ten months. (Multiparty coalitions are always difficult to sustain.) Then the LDP, with a Social Democrat as figurehead prime minister, took over again. Will the LDP ever be really ousted and spend a few years in opposition? There are both structural and psychological reasons for the LDP's long tenure. The rural overrepresentation of Japan's electoral system and the unwillingness of Japanese to throw out the party that had brought prosperity explain much of the LDP's longevity. Money politics also favors the LDP. These factors, plus Koizumi's popularity, boosted the LDP in the 2005 election and gave it absolute control of the Diet.

And Japan does not have a good opposition party. The old rigid Socialists were too doctrinaire to challenge the LDP. Now the incoherent Democrats are the lame half party that offers no clear alternative. Until an opposition party can get its act together, Japan's dominant-party system will likely persist.

Reform without Change

France and Germany have been described as "blocked societies" for the way entrenched interests block needed reforms. Typically, such systems rumble on until mounting pressures for change suddenly crack apart the old setup. De Gaulle's 1958 arrival in power exemplified how a blocked society dramatically unblocks. Japan has a similar but perhaps worse problem, for there is no one in charge and no single center of power that can bring about major change. Some observers see Japan as stuck in an institutional paralysis that caused its economy to slow and its status as regional leader to lapse.

For years, Japanese prime ministers have pledged to deregulate the Japanese economy—now they call it *risutora*, "restructure"—but it has been mostly empty talk. Instead of major, sweeping reforms, prime ministers offer minor, almost cosmetic reforms that change little. Many Japanese favor major reforms—Keidanren strongly backs them—hoping to kill as many as four birds with one stone. Namely, by deregulating the strongly regulated Japanese economy, including its barriers to foreign imports, reforms reinvigorate the economy, raise living standards, reduce trade surpluses, and curb the bureaucracy. In Japan, reform is always coming but never arrives.

What Japanese Quarrel About

Like Germany, the Japanese economy soared after World War II but then leveled off and slumped. Over time, the postwar economic advantages enjoyed by the two countries faded. From 1990 to 2005 Japan's GDP grew little. All "economic miracles" tend to undermine themselves, even China's.

The Japanese Economic Miracle

After the war, "made in Japan" suggested a product was junk, but Japan climbed out of the junk stage in the 1950s. In 1960, Japan was the richest country in Asia but still had a per capita GDP of only $380 (around $2,600 in today's dollars), one-eighth the American per capita GDP. By

Geography

Living without Lebensraum

German thinkers of the nineteenth century came up with overly deterministic theories of *geopolitics* such as *Lebensraum* (living space), eagerly embraced by the Nazis and Japanese militarists as justification for their imperial expansion. After their defeat, Germans and Japanese learned that they have never lived so well as when confined to their present crowded countries. If you have the economy, you do not need much land. Prosperity depends not so much on territory as on smart, energetic people and sound economic policy.

Four Tigers   South Korea, Taiwan, Hong Kong, and Singapore.

1990, Japan's per capita was nominally higher than America's. The Korean War brought U.S. military contracts for clothing, footwear, and other items to low-bid Japanese producers. (The Vietnam War was the catalyst for South Korea's industrial takeoff in the late 1960s.) Soon U.S. manufacturers of civilian goods gave Japanese contracts. Quality improved, and costs were a fraction of U.S. costs. In the 1960s, Japanese cars were looked down on, but by the 1970s they were respected for fuel economy and workmanship. Now Toyota is the world's largest (and best-run) car company. A continual pattern has been to underestimate the Japanese product—until it puts you out of business.

As in postwar West Germany, Japanese did not ask for much: a job that put food on the table. In politics most were cautious and voted for moderate conservatives. In 1990, however, Japan's extraordinary economic growth ended with a major recession and unemployment. The collapse of Japan's stock-market and real-estate bubbles left corporations and banks looking poorer and foolish. The LDP started looking incompetent. Younger Japanese, educated and traveled, saw how people in other countries do not live in rabbit hutches and pay exorbitant prices. Many were no longer willing to support the status quo.

THE SECRET OF JAPAN'S SUCCESS

Since the 1960s, when the West realized how fast the Japanese economy was growing, observers have tried to explain the "Japanese model" as a new, different, and better system. Many now suspect there was never a magic formula.

CONFUCIANISM

Several East Asian countries show similar patterns of rapid growth. China (see Chapter 28) and the **Four Tigers** have also grown fast. Culturally, all share a Confucian background that came from China, one that stresses hard work, stability, and obedience. It frowns on high personal consumption; people should save, not spend. Some argue that a Confucian work ethic gave East Asia the functional equivalent of a Protestant work ethic.

PRODUCTIVITY

High productivity and low wages make for rapid growth (see the "productivity" box on page 77). For some decades, Japanese productivity stayed ahead of wages, giving Japan an opening to produce much of the world's advanced consumer electronics. Japanese factories could simply put more high-quality labor into a product, now no longer the case.

EDUCATION

Japan (and the Four Tigers) pay a lot of attention to education, especially K-12. Education is supervised at the national level and compulsory. This gives Japan a highly skilled labor force, one that can read, follow instructions, and do math. (Much of the U.S. labor force cannot.) Interestingly, Japan and its high-growth neighbors pay less attention to college education, finding that much of it contributes little to economic growth.

SAVINGS

Japanese save a lot and consider debt shameful; Americans save little and are almost proud of their debts. Japanese use credit cards far less than Americans and pay off balances monthly. In Japan thrift is an old tradition, and pension plans and social security are weak, so Japanese put aside money. There is practically no welfare. Many economists think that savings alone explains Japan's economic growth. Some now say Japanese save too much; their reluctance to spend kept Japan in recession.

macroeconomy   Big picture of a nation's economy, including GDP size and growth, productivity, interest rates, and inflation.

microeconomy   Close-up picture of individual markets, including product design and pricing, efficiency, and costs.

Savings at one point made Japanese banks the world's biggest with much capital available for investment. Unfortunately, this encouraged businesses to expand until they overexpanded; then banks loaned ever more to these "zombie" companies, piling up bad loans. Japan's banks finally *wrote off* (see page 430) about half of the dud loans and put the banking system back on sounder footing.

STATE SUPERVISION

This is controversial both in Japan and abroad. Is state supervision, going back to the Meiji modernizers and continuing with MITI and the Finance Ministry, a key factor in Japan's rapid growth? Most other fast-growth East Asian economies have some state supervision as well. Hong Kong, however, has none, and China's vigorous free-market sector, based heavily on foreign investment, is essentially unplanned; China's state-owned enterprises lose money.

The value of state planning has not been proved. Some economists say Japan simply got its **macroeconomy** or "fundamentals" right and might have done as well or better without state supervision of the **microeconomy**. Some Japanese firms prospered with no help from a ministry, and some with much help did poorly. (Sony founder Akio Morita publicly disdained government help and got none.) The only way to demonstrate that Japanese economic intervention worked is to have two very similar countries operate under different policies, one with a MITI and the other without, and see which grows faster.

From Bubble to Burst

Japan's economy grew at a world-record average rate of 10 percent a year from 1955 to 1973. But from 1973 to 1991 it grew only 4 percent a year and since then at an average of only 1 percent a year. In 1998 it actually declined. Japanese wages and other costs climbed, and Japanese investment flowed to countries with lower wages and fewer regulations. Investment mistakes were made. MITI prodded and financed Japanese electronics firms to lose vast sums developing the "fifth generation" of computers and high-definition television. MITI encouraged Japan's eleven (11!) car makers to expand until they overexpanded.

Government and banks had pushed the export sectors (cars, electronics) of Japanese industry into high levels of automation, productivity, and efficiency. Other sectors got left behind. Distribution was largely in the hands of expensive and inefficient neighborhood mom-and-pop stores. U.S.-style discounting was denounced in Japan for ruining family shops. Gradually, though, as more Japanese found they could buy Panasonics and Canons cheaper in the United States, foreign retail chains started opening in Japan.

excess liquidity   Too much money floating around.

deflation   Decrease in prices; opposite of inflation.

deficit   Government spends more in a given year than it takes in.

debt   Sum total of government *deficits* over many years.

Agriculture got left behind. The typical small Japanese farm of a few acres was hopelessly inefficient, but the Agricultural Ministry protected Japanese farmers from cheaper imports. This cost Japanese consumers dearly and angered Japan's trading partners. Many Japanese farmers turned to part-time farming anyway, a pattern typical of industrializing countries. The average Japanese farmer is over 60; few youngsters now go into farming. In purely economic terms, they should sell their small holdings, either to more-efficient farmers or to build apartments. There is protected and tax-exempt farmland in and near major cities that should be subject to market forces.

During the 1990s, Japanese grew less satisfied with their economy as the shortcomings of the supervised system became clear. Under bureaucratic guidance, the Japanese economy produced **excess liquidity**, which fueled stock-market and real-estate bubbles, which both burst in 1989. The Tokyo stock exchange lost three-quarters of its peak value and recovered only slowly and partially. Real-estate prices plunged as well, and many Japanese banks and corporations were insolvent or nearly so. Japan suffered from **deflation**, the great plague of the 1930s Depression. Deflation is worse than inflation, as it destroys the value of homes and businesses. Some Japanese who bought apartments around 1990 saw them lose half their worth but still have to pay off the huge mortgages.

To fight the slowdown, Tokyo threw money into the economy—around $1 trillion, mostly in public-works spending—giving Japan the world's biggest **deficits** and national **debt** but producing no economic growth. Tokyo was doing what it had always done—bail out any sector of the economy that is in trouble. But no government can bail out everything forever, and Tokyo trimmed public-works spending from 6 percent of GDP in 2001 to 4 percent in 2005. More cuts are due.

Bailing out firms merely disguises their illnesses and blocks the market's signals that this company must change or fold. Tokyo tried to keep Japan's large banks from collapsing, although based on their assets, several should have. (China's banks face a parallel problem.) Japanese and foreign analysts worry that foolish investments help weak banks and businesses to mask problems but do not solve them. Efforts to cut back Japan's huge subsidies in favor of a free-market economy have to fight Japan's highly organized interest groups.

GEOGRAPHY

RUNNING OUT OF JAPANESE

In 1975, the number of births in Japan started to drop. In 2005 Japan's population began to shrink and could decline below 100 million by mid-century. Japan's colleges worry that the number of eighteen-year-olds, which declined by half since 1974, will not be enough to fill classrooms. Industry worries about sufficient workers. (One solution: Encourage more Japanese women to work; relatively few do.)

The biggest worry is how to support all the Japanese on retirement—and Japanese are the longest-lived folks in the world, seventy-nine years for men and eighty-six for women—with so few workers. Japan's pension system will soon be in the red. Can one Japanese worker support one retiree? Notice that Germany has exactly the same problem, but Japan admits very few foreign workers. Only 1 percent of Japan's population is foreign, and that includes descendants of Chinese and Koreans who have lived in Japan for generations. Japanese discriminate against immigrants—even against Japanese born in Brazil. Japan is a closed society that must learn to open up.

Japan's new age is one of low-cost competitors and open markets. Other lands have taken over several areas that used to be Japanese: steelmaking, shipbuilding, and even consumer electronics. China is taking over much of the world's manufacturing. Japanese should not

trade surplus Exporting more than you import.

despair; it just means Japan has become a mature economy with modest growth rates. And Japan has an excellent foundation for long-term prosperity: a well-educated population, a magnificent high-tech sector, and vast investment capital.

Holding down domestic consumption while accumulating capital resources boosted economic growth. But pursued too long, it overshot the mark and produced serious imbalances. The yen, held too low for too long, suddenly shot from 330 to the dollar to 80 to the dollar at one point in 1995. (The value of the yen is expressed in how many yen per dollar, so when the yen goes "up" it is getting cheaper in relation to the dollar; when the yen goes "down" it is getting more expensive. With the euro, conversely, up means up.) A too-strong yen hurt many Japanese firms that lost foreign sales.

Japan's mammoth **trade surpluses**, especially with the United States, did no earthly good, but for decades MITI was obsessed by them, a sort of latter-day mercantilism. In effect, Japan sold its products too cheaply to Americans and got not enough in return. If the Japanese had simply consumed more—including more imported goods—at an earlier date, they might have avoided the excess liquidity that fueled the stock-market and real-estate bubbles. Too many yen chased investments to the sky; then the bubbles burst.

Should Japan Rearm?

Since World War II, Japan has preached and practiced peace. MacArthur's staff put a "no-war clause" (Article 9) into Japan's new constitution, stating that military forces "will never be maintained." The Korean War in 1950 made some wonder if Japan should stay defenseless and depend on U.S. protection. In the 1950s, Japan began building "Self-Defense Forces" but informally limited defense spending to 1 percent of GDP. It has only some 238,000 under arms, but they are well trained and equipped. As China staked out territorial claims far into the South and East China Seas and North Korea lobbed rockets over Japan as "tests" and built nuclear weapons, the United States and Japan dusted off their defensive alliance.

Japanese leftists argue that their Self-Defense Forces are at odds with both the letter and spirit of the constitution, but most Japanese think them prudent and necessary. Some would end the constitution's pacifist clauses and even acquire a few nuclear weapons to deter attack. A referendum to drop Article 9 could come as early as 2010. The United States also wants Japan to be able to defend itself and take a leadership role in regional security—as Japan did splendidly in Cambodian peacekeeping—and encourages Japan to do more. Japan also sent 550 troops to Iraq for

Hiroshima, Ground Zero: This municipal building partially withstood the first atomic bomb blast and now reminds Japanese of what war does.

noncombat duties, something many Japanese disliked. The Tokyo government thought it would ensure U.S. protection against the growing power of China.

Should Japan expand its Self-Defense Forces? Japan's neighbors used to fear Japanese military power, but with the possibility of China seizing Taiwan and North Korea again invading South Korea, many East Asian countries now see Japan as a strategic partner in a defensive situation. Many Japanese and their neighbors now think that Japan should become a normal country with a credible but not threatening defense capability.

Before Japan can play a major role in East Asian security, it will have to reflect deeply on its World War II atrocities and put them in school textbooks. This is hard, as many LDP politicians, focused on Japanese voters, still portray Japan's aggressions as defensive. Some even say Japanese occupation of Taiwan and Korea was good for those two lands. Amid howls of protest from Taibei and Seoul, they usually resign. Many honor Japanese war dead. Tojo's granddaughter still mourns him as a patriot. In 2007 Prime Minister Abe denied that the wartime Japanese army forced Chinese and Korean women into sexual slavery. Germany has more or less mastered its past, and now Germany's small army participates in European security. Japan could play the same role in East Asia, but first it must face its past.

KEY TERMS

alternation in power (p. 286)
debt (p. 290)
deficit (p. 290)
deflation (p. 290)
Diet (p. 269)
excess liquidity (p. 290)
Four Tigers (p. 288)
gaijin (p. 262)
guilt (p. 276)
iron triangle (p. 281)
Liberal Democrats (p. 269)

macroeconomy (p. 289)
Manchukuo (p. 265)
Meiji (p. 263)
meritocracy (p. 278)
METI (p. 273)
microeconomy (p. 289)
money politics (p. 284)
pork barrel (p. 270)
prefecture (p. 274)
scandal (p. 283)
shame (p. 276)

Shinto (p. 261)
shogun (p. 261)
soft money (p. 284)
structure (p. 284)
Tokugawa (p. 262)
trade surplus (p. 291)
unit veto (p. 286)
walking-around money
  (p. 283)
¥ (p. 284)

FURTHER REFERENCE

Beason, Dick, and Dennis Patterson. *The Japan That Never Was: Explaining the Rise and Decline of a Misunderstood Country.* Albany, NY: SUNY Press, 2004.

Buruma, Ian. *Inventing Japan, 1853–1964.* New York: Modern Library: 2003.

Calichman, Richard, ed. *Contemporary Japanese Thought.* New York: Columbia University Press, 2005.

Carlson, Matthew. *Money Politics in Japan: New Rules, Old Practices.* Boulder, CO: L. Rienner, 2007.

Curtis, Gerald L. *The Logic of Japanese Politics: Leaders, Institutions, and the Limits of Change.* New York: Columbia University Press, 2000.

Feifer, George. *Breaking Open Japan: Commodore Perry, Lord Abe, and American Imperialism in 1853.* New York: HarperCollins, 2006.

Gordon, Andrew. *A Modern History of Japan: From Tokugawa Times to the Present.* New York: Oxford University Press, 2003.

Hayes, Louis D. *Introduction to Japanese Politics,* 5th ed. Armonk, NY: M. E. Sharpe, 2008.

Kingston, Jeff. *Japan's Quiet Revolution: Politics, Economics, and Society.* New York: Routledge, 2004.

Kuroda, Yasumasa. *The Core of Japanese Democracy: Latent Interparty Politics.* New York: Palgrave, 2005.

Martin, Sherry L., and Gill Steel, eds. *Democratic Reform in Japan: Assessing the Impact.* Boulder, CO: L. Rienner, 2008.

Mulgan, Aurelia George. *Power and Pork: A Japanese Political Life.* Canberra: Australian National University Press, 2006.

Nathan, John. *Japan Unbound: A Volatile Nation's Quest for Pride and Purpose.* Boston: Houghton Mifflin, 2004.

Pyle, Kenneth. *Japan Rising: The Resurgence of Japanese Power and Purpose.* New York: Public Affairs, 2007.

Chapter 19

Russia:
The Impact of the Past

Russia is immense, stretching eleven time zones across the northern half of Asia to the Pacific. Looking at a map of Russia, you notice that only a small part of it is in Europe. Perhaps a country as big and ethnically diverse as the Soviet Union was not meant to be. Just holding it together required strong central control backed by force. The very size of Russia may incline it to **tyranny**.

With few natural boundaries, Russia is easy to invade from east or west, although its very size and harsh winters doomed the invasions of Charles XII of Sweden, Napoleon, and Hitler. Winters give Russia a short growing season, making agriculture a chancy business, with crops failing on an average of one year in three. The vast territory that **Siberia** adds to Russia's size is problematic; its weather is hostile to settlement, and its mineral and forest wealth is hard to extract. Most of the Russian population lives in the "European" part, that is, west of the Ural Mountains. Plans to develop Siberia, some of them going back to tsarist days, fall short, and Siberia is now depopulating.

Russia long had difficulty reaching the open sea. The first Russian states were landlocked; only under Peter the Great at the beginning of the eighteenth century did Russians overcome the Swedes to reach the Baltic and the Turks to reach the Black Sea. The North Russian ports ice over in winter, and the Black Sea is controlled by the Turkish Straits, still leaving European Russia without year-round, secure ports. One of the great dreams of tsarists and Communists alike was for warm-water ports under exclusive Russian control.

QUESTIONS TO CONSIDER

1. Does Russia's size make it inherently difficult to govern?
2. What geographic disadvantages has Russia faced over its history?
3. Why does Russia always seem to require modernization from above? Why can it not come from below?
4. How much practice has Russia had with democracy?
5. How does the clash of Westernizers and Slavophiles still echo?
6. Why did Marxism catch on in Russia, where it was not supposed to?
7. How did Lenin alter Marxism?
8. Could the Provisional Government have stayed in power? How?
9. Was Stalin an accident?

The Slavic People

Occupying most of East Europe, the Slavic peoples are the most numerous in Europe and speak languages closer to each other than are the Romance languages (Italian, Spanish, French) of West Europe. A Slovak peasant can converse with any other Slavic peasant—so similar are their vocabularies and syntax.

tyranny   Coercive rule, usually by one person. (See page 295.)

Siberia   From Russian for "north"; that part of Russia east of the Ural Mountains. (See page 295.)

Constantinople   Capital of Byzantium, conquered by Turks in 1453.

Cyrillic   Greek-based alphabet of Eastern Slavic languages.

The way the Slavic languages are written, though, differentiates them. The Western Slavs (Poles, Czechs, Croats, Slovenes, and Slovaks) were Christianized from Rome; hence their alphabet is Latin. The Eastern Slavs (Russians, Ukrainians, Serbs, Bulgarians, and Macedonians) were converted by Eastern Orthodox monks from **Constantinople**, and their languages are written in a variation of the Greek alphabet called **Cyrillic**, after St. Cyril, one of the monks who first converted Slavs.

Their Orthodox Christianity (as opposed to Roman Catholicism) and Cyrillic writing contributed to the Russians' isolation from the rest of Europe. In addition to being at the geographical fringe of

Russia

Europe, Russia was beyond its cultural fringe for centuries. The important ideas that modernized Catholic and Protestant Europe penetrated Russia only later. Rome was a lively fountainhead of thought in West Europe, but the headquarters of the Orthodox faith, Constantinople, under the Turks ceased to provide intellectual guidance for its followers. At the same time West Europe was experiencing the invigoration of the Renaissance, which rippled outward from Catholic Italy, Russia stayed isolated and asleep. It missed most of the Enlightenment.

> **Tatar**   Mongol-origin tribes who ruled Russia for centuries. (*Not* Tartar.)
>
> **tsar**   From "caesar"; Russia's emperor; sometimes spelled old Polish style, *czar*.
>
> **autocracy**   Absolute rule of one person in a centralized state.
>
> **exclave**   Part of country separated from main territory.

A more important factor explaining Russia's isolation and backwardness was its conquest in the thirteenth century by the Mongols, later known as the **Tatars**. The Mongols crushed the first Russian state, centered at Kiev in present-day Ukraine, and enslaved much of the population. For two centuries, while West Europe moved ahead, Russian culture under the barbaric Mongols declined. Some historians believe even after the Tatar yoke was lifted, it still took five centuries for Russia to catch up with the West.

RUSSIAN AUTOCRACY

Under the Tatars, the duchy of Moscow became the most powerful Russian state, first as a tax collector for the Tatars, then as their triumphant enemy. Moscovy's Ivan the Terrible (1530–1584) had himself crowned **tsar** and expanded Russian territory down the Volga to the Caspian Sea and into Siberia. Ivan was both murderous and successful; his brutal use of force set a standard for later rulers. To this day, many Russians think only a strong and ruthless leader can achieve national greatness.

When the Russian nobles (*boyars*) came into conflict with Ivan, his secret police, the *Oprichnina*, exiled or executed them. Since that time, the Russian nobility never played an autonomous role in political life. It was as if the absolutism of France was applied early and completely to a culturally backward country. The result was **autocracy** under the tsar. Unlike West Europe, Russia never experienced the mixed monarchy of autonomous nobles, church, commoners, and

GEOGRAPHY

BOUND RUSSIA

Russia is bounded on the north by the Arctic Ocean;

on the east by the Bering Sea and Sea of Okhotsk;

on the south by North Korea (tiny), China, Mongolia, Kazakhstan, Azerbaijan, Georgia, and the Black Sea;

and on the west by Ukraine, Belarus, Lithuania, Latvia, Estonia, Finland, and Norway.

The Russian **exclave** of Kaliningrad Oblast (region), formerly Königsberg of old East Prussia, is wedged between Poland and Lithuania on the Baltic.

king. Accordingly, Russians had no experience with limited government, checks and balances, or pluralism. As Ivan grew older he became madder. Able to trust no one, he murdered those around him—even his own son—at the least suspicion. By the time he died he had carved out the modern Russian state.

Absolutism or Anarchy?

One of the reasons Russians put up with autocracy—and often admired it—was because they felt that without a firm hand at the top the system would degenerate into anarchy, which happened in the early seventeenth century, the "Time of Troubles." Lacking a strong tsar, unrest, banditry, civil war, and a Polish invasion plagued the land. Russians also willingly served a powerful state. The Russian Orthodox church, which the tsar also headed, became a pillar of autocracy, teaching the faithful to worship the tsar as the "little father" who protected all Russians. The tsar was

Political Culture

"Moscow Is the Third Rome"

The monk Philotheus of Pskov uttered the words "Moscow is the third Rome" after Constantinople fell to the Turks in 1453, indicating that Russia was the last and only center of true Christianity. Rome and Constantinople had failed; now Moscow would guard the faith. Over the centuries, many Russians repeated Philotheus's dictum: "Moscow is the third Rome; a fourth is not to be." After the Bolshevik Revolution, Russia's new rulers felt the same way about world communism; Moscow was its capital and there could be no other. Even today, some Russians still feel that Russia has a holy mission.

St. Basil's cathedral recalls Moscow's former role as a center of Christianity. Russia's tsars were not only heads of state but also heads of the Russian Orthodox Church.

MARXISM COMES TO RUSSIA

According to Marx's theory, backward Russia was far fr[...]
proletarian revolution. There simply was not much of [...]
in agricultural Russia, where industrialization was just b[...]
the late nineteenth century. Marx believed revolution [...]
first in the most industrially advanced countries, such as [...]
Germany. Marxism, though, caught on more strongly in [...]
anywhere else. Marx's works were eagerly seized upon b[...]
Russian intellectuals who badly wanted change but did [...]
theoretical framework for it. Here at last, they believe[...]
found a reason and a means to carry out a revolution.

There were several schools of Marxism in Russia. T[...]
nomic underdevelopment, thought the country would f[...]
it could start on socialism. Marx's deterministic view [...]
stages, first capitalism, then socialism, so the Legal Marx[...]
italism. Another school of Russian Marxism, "Econom[...]
conditions through labor unions resembling West Eur[...]
mellowed into welfarism.

Opposing these two gradualist schools were impass[...]
lution. They argued they could "give history a shove" b[...]
proletariat, gaining power, and then using the state to n[...]
some theoretical changes in Marxism so it fit Russian con[...]
the doctrine of Russian **communism** has been known as [...]

In 1898, after several small groups had discussed M[...]
Social Democratic Labor party was formed. Immediately [...]
the tsarist secret police, many of its leaders went into e[...]
(the Spark), was published in Zurich and smuggled into [...]

In 1903 the small party split over a crucial question [...]
ed a normal party along the lines of the German Socia[...]
membership to enroll the Russian working class. Lenin [...]
lice would make mincemeat out of an open party. Inste[...]
ground party of professional revolutionaries, more a con[...]

Lenin got his way. At the 1903 party congress in Br[...]
Russia), he controlled thirty-three of the fifty-one votes. [...]
total party membership, Lenin proclaimed his faction **Bo**[...]
The *menshevik* (minority) faction at the congress contin[...]
ate line.

CURTAIN RAISER: THE 1905 REVOLUTI[...]

At the beginning of the twentieth century two expanding [...]
Russians were pushing eastward, consolidating their positi[...]
Siberian Railway, the last leg of which ran through Manc[...]

---

both head of state and head of church, a pattern called **caesaropapism**. Russia has been called a "service state" in which all walks of life, from nobles to peasants to priests, served the autocrat. Western concepts such as liberty and individual rights were absent.

During the fifteenth and sixteenth centuries, Russia actually moved backward as previously free peasants became serfs, tied to the land to labor for aristocrats. While West Europe ended serfdom centuries earlier, in Russia the vast majority of the population were poor and ignorant farm laborers.

From time to time these wretched people revolted. Some ran off and joined the Cossacks, bands of mounted freebooters in the border regions between the tsarist and Turkish empires. One Cossack leader, Stenka Razin, immortalized in ballad, led a peasant revolt that seized much of **Ukraine**. In time, the Cossacks turned into semimilitary federations, which the tsars enrolled as effective and ruthless cavalry.

> **caesaropapism** Combining the top civil ruler (caesar) with the top spiritual ruler (pope), as in Russia's tsars.
>
> **Ukraine** From Slavic for "borderland"; region south of Russia, now independent.

FORCED MODERNIZATION

By the time Peter I became tsar in 1682, Russia lagged behind the rest of Europe. Peter, who stood six feet nine inches (206 cm.), forced Russia to modernize and become a major power. Peter personally handled Russia's legislation, diplomacy, war, and technical innovation and was the first tsar to travel in West Europe. Admiring its industries, he ordered them duplicated in Russia. Nearly continually at war, Peter pushed the Swedes back to give Russia an outlet on the Baltic. There he ordered built a magnificent new capital, St. Petersburg (later Leningrad), modeled after Amsterdam, to serve as Russia's window to the West.

Copying the tight Swedish administrative system, Peter divided Russia into provinces, counties, and districts, each supervised by bureaucrats drawn from the nobility. All male nobles had to serve the tsar from age fifteen until death, either as bureaucrats or military officers. Even the bureaucrats were organized on military lines, complete with ranks and uniforms. With Peter, the Russian government apparatus penetrated deep into society. A census determined the number of males available for military conscription, and each community had a quota. Draftees served for life. Taxation squeezed everybody as Peter ordered his officials to "collect money, as much as possible, for money is the artery of war."

When Peter died in 1725, Russia was more modern and Westernized but still behind West Europe. Peter the Great contributed a pattern of forced modernization from the top, pushing a poor, gigantic country forward despite itself. Russia paid dearly. The mass of peasants, heavily taxed, were worse off than ever. The Westernized nobility—forced, for instance, to shave for the first time—was cut off from the hopes and feelings of the peasantry. The pattern continued for a long time.

WESTERNIZERS AND SLAVOPHILES

Napoleon's invasion of Russia and capture of Moscow in 1812 made Russian intellectuals painfully aware of the backwardness of their land. Many sought to bring in Western politics and institutions, including a constitutional monarchy that would limit the autocratic powers of the

tsar. These were called **Westernizers**. Others disli[k]
low and materialistic. The answer to Russia's probl[
Slavic roots and develop institutions and styles dif[
sia will teach the world," was their view. These **Slav**
stressed the spiritual depth and warm humanity o[f
ists who disdained West European culture. In our d[
ject Western materialism in favor of traditional s[
debate still echoes: Liberal reformers are still pro-W[
West nationalists.

FROM FRUSTRATION TO REVOLUTION

Despite calls for far-reaching changes in Russia, [
little progress. All tsars rejected becoming a *cons[
"tsar-liberator," carried out only limited reforms. [

Westernizers Nineteenth-century Russians who wished to copy the West.

Slavophiles Nineteenth-century Russians who wished to develop Russia along native, non-Western lines; also known as "Russophiles."

zemstvo Local parliaments in old Russia.

Narodniki From Russian for "people," *narod*; radical populist agitators of late nineteenth-century Russia.

anarchism Radical ideology seeking to overthrow all conventional forms of government.

cipation, freeing serfs [
in economic bondage [
assemblies called **zer**[
power.

The reforms were [
prove the living cond[
conditions, however, [
likely rather than less [
extensive and genero[
intelligentsia (the edu[
he granted only made [
ted the critics' appeti[
frustrated.

Some intellectua[
1870s thousands of i[
tried "going to the pe[
These **Narodniki** ma[
ants either ignored them or turned them over t[
anarchism and violence, believing that killing the[
deed," a way to arouse the inert Russian masses. O[
(People's Will), after seven attempts killed the ts[
riage in 1881.

Actually, Russia made considerable progress d[
were swept away, industry got up and running (wi[
and German capital), railroads were built, and int[
cial area of political reform—parliaments, parties[
essentially stood still. Political reforms do not m[
ernizes his economy but fails to modernize his pol[
see in Iran.

PERSONALITIES

LENIN, THE GREAT REVOLUTIONARY

Vladimir Lenin

Some claim that Lenin was out for revenge against the tsarist system for hanging his older brother, Alexander, in 1887 for his part in a bomb plot against the tsar. That cannot be proved, but it is clear Lenin was dominated by a cold, contained fury aimed at revolutionary socialism in Russia.

Born in 1870 as Vladimir Ilyich Ulyanov, son of a provincial education official, Lenin was from the intellectual middle class rather than the proletariat in whose name he struggled—a pattern typical of revolutionary socialist leaders. Quickly expelled from university for subversive activity, Lenin was sent into rural exile. With incredible self-discipline, Lenin taught himself and breezed through law exams with top marks.

In the early 1890s Lenin, like many Russian intellectuals, discovered Marx and wrote Marxist analyses of the rapidly growing Russian economy. Recognized as a leading Marxist thinker, Lenin quickly rose to prominence in underground revolutionary circles.

In December 1895, while editing an illegal socialist newspaper, Lenin was arrested and sent to prison for a year followed by three years' exile on the Lena River in Siberia. There he took the name Lenin, the man from the Lena. The solitary hours gave him time to read, learn foreign languages, and write. Released in 1900, Lenin fled to Zurich, Switzerland, where he spent most of the next seventeen years. Until taking power in Russia in 1917, Lenin never held a job.

In Swiss exile Lenin at times worried there would never be a revolution in Russia. The working class was concentrating on higher wages rather than revolution. The Russian Social Democratic Labor party was small, with only a few thousand members in Russia and in exile. Lenin was determined to transform this small party into an effective underground force. Size was not important; organization was everything. His 1902 pamphlet *What Is to Be Done?* demanded a tightly disciplined party of professional revolutionaries, not a conventional social-democratic party open to everybody. Under Lenin the early Communists forged the "organizational weapon": the Party.

But how could proletarian revolution come to preindustrial Russia? In solving this problem, Lenin greatly changed Marxism. Marx theorized that revolution will come in the most advanced countries, where the proletariat was biggest. Lenin said not necessarily: Revolution could come where capitalism is weakest, where it is just starting. **Imperialism** had changed capitalism, Lenin argued, giving it a new lease on life. By exploiting weaker countries, the big imperialist powers were able to bribe their own working class with higher wages and thus keep them quiet. Where capitalism was beginning—as in Russia with heavy foreign investment—was where it could be overthrown. The newly developing countries, such as Russia and Spain, were "capitalism's weakest link," said Lenin.

Lenin also disagreed with Marx's insistence that peasants could never be revolutionary. Marx dismissed country life as "rural idiocy," but Lenin believed that, under certain conditions and leadership, peasants could turn revolutionary and, throwing their weight in with the small working class, provide a massive revolutionary army. (Three decades later, Mao Zedong elaborated on these themes to argue that China, a victim of imperialism, could have a socialist revolution based entirely on the peasantry. Mao completed the train of thought that Lenin started.)

Lenin was not a great theoretician but a brilliant opportunist, switching doctrine to take advantage of situations, like all successful revolutionaries. He was less concerned with pure Marxism than with using it to overthrow the system he hated. Once in power, he practiced the same bloody ruthlessness later associated with Stalin. It is not clear that had Lenin lived he would have been any better than Stalin.

from Korea into Manchuria, which was nominally part of China. The tsar's cabinet, certain they could beat any Asian army and hoping to deflect domestic unrest, thought war with Japan might be a good idea. Said the interior minister: "We need a little victorious war to stem the tide of revolution." Instead, the Japanese fleet launched a surprise attack against the Russians at Port Arthur, then beat the Russians on land and sea.

> **imperialism**   Powerful countries turning other lands into colonies. (See page 302.)
>
> **Duma**   Russia's national parliament.

The Russo-Japanese War revealed the tsarist military as unprepared, inept, and stupid. Weak regimes should not count on a "little victorious war" to paper over domestic unrest; wars make troubles worse. In Russia, rioting and then revolution broke out. Some naval units mutinied. (See Eisenstein's film classic *Battleship Potemkin*.) Workers briefly seized factories in St. Petersburg. It looked like revolution was breaking out.

Tsar Nicholas II gave way and decreed potentially important reforms: freedom of speech, press, and assembly and the democratic election of a **Duma**. Briefly, his 1905 October Manifesto looked as if it would turn autocracy into constitutional monarchy. The tsar and his reactionary advisors backed down on their promises, however. Nicholas, none too bright, refused to yield any of his autocratic powers. Four Dumas were subsequently elected; each was dissolved when it grew too critical. Finally the Duma was turned into an undemocratic debating society without power. The Duma was Russia's last hope for a peaceful transition to democracy. People in modern times need to feel they participate at least in a small way in the affairs of government. Parties, elections, and parliaments may be imperfect means of participation, but they are better than violent revolution. Since the failed Decembrist revolt of 1825, Russian intellectuals had been trying to tell this to the tsar, but he refused to listen.

World War I and Collapse

Communists liked to speak of the Russian Revolution as inevitable, the playing out of historical forces that had to lead to the collapse of imperialism and capitalism. There was nothing inevitable about the October Revolution. Indeed, without World War I, there would have been no revolution in Russia at all, let alone a Bolshevik revolution. Lenin himself, in early 1917, doubted he would live to see a revolution in Russia.

Things were not so terrible in Russia before the war. The Duma struggled to erode tsarist autocracy and in time might have succeeded. Industry grew rapidly. Peasants, freed from old restrictions on land ownership, turned into prosperous and productive small farmers. The war changed everything. Repeating their overconfidence of 1904, the tsarist military marched happily to war against Germany in 1914 with a large but badly equipped and poorly led army. Major offensives ground to a halt before the more effective German forces. The Russian economy fell apart. Troop morale disintegrated, and many deserted. Peasants seized their landlord's estates. The government was paralyzed, but the tsar refused to change anything.

By 1917 the situation was desperate. In March of that year a group of democratic moderates seized power and deposed the tsar. Resembling Western liberals, the people of the Provisional Government hoped to modernize and democratize Russia. The Western powers, including the United States, welcomed them, thinking they would rally Russians to continue the war. The Provisional Government, which by July was headed by Alexander Kerensky, tried to stay in the war, and that was its undoing. If Kerensky had betrayed the Western Allies and made a separate peace with Germany, the moderates might have been able to retain power.

Meanwhile, the German General Staff, looking for a way to knock Russia out of the war, thought it would be clever to send the agitator Lenin into Russia to create havoc. In April 1917 Lenin and his colleagues traveled in a famous "sealed train"—so the Bolshevik bacillus would not infect Germany, where revolutionary discontent was also growing—across Germany, Sweden, and Finland to Petrograd, the World War I name for St. Petersburg (which sounded too German). Without German help and funds, Lenin might never have made it back to Russia.

At Petrograd's Finland Station, Lenin issued his stirring slogan, "Bread, Land, Peace," speaking respectively to workers, peasants, and soldiers. Lenin immediately saw that a "dual authority" was trying to rule Russia. The Provisional Government controlled the army and foreign policy. But in the most important city, Petrograd, a council (*soviet* in Russian) of workers, soldiers, sailors, and revolutionaries ran things. Soon these councils appeared in many Russian cities. The composition of these soviets was mixed, with the Bolsheviks a small minority. Lenin pursued a double strategy: Make the soviets the only effective governing power and make the Bolsheviks the dominant power in the soviets. Lenin's slogan for this: "All Power to the Soviets."

THE REVOLUTION AND CIVIL WAR

The actual seizure of power in October was amazingly easy. In a scene exaggerated by Soviet historians, soldiers and sailors loyal to the Petrograd soviet charged across a big square into the Winter Palace to oust the Provisional Government. But control of Petrograd and Moscow was one thing, control of all gigantic Russia was something else.

PERSONALITIES

KERENSKY: NICE GUYS LOSE

In the late 1950s at UCLA I had an eerie experience: seeing and hearing Alexander Kerensky speak. History lives. Still fit and articulate in his seventies, Kerensky recalled his brief stint (July to November 1917) as head of Russia's Provisional Government. One man in the audience, a Russian emigré, asked angrily why Kerensky did not use his power to have Lenin killed. Kerensky reflected a moment and said, "Sometimes when you have power it's hard to use it."

That was Kerensky's problem. A decent man, he would not have a political opponent murdered. The Western Allies begged him to keep Russia in the war, and he did not have the heart to betray them. What Kerensky lacked in political ruthlessness he may have gained in longevity. Living in New York City, he spent

Alexander Kerensky

his years justifying his brief rule and denouncing both the Bolsheviks and Russian rightists who tried to bring him down. He died in 1970 at age eighty-nine.

The tight organization and discipline of Lenin's Bolsheviks paid off. In a situation of almost total chaos, the best organized win. By a series of shrewd moves, the Bolsheviks were able to dominate the soviets and win converts from deserting soldiers and sailors. Lenin headed the new government and immediately took Russia out of the war, accepting a punitive peace treaty from the Germans at Brest-Litovsk in March 1918. It was a dictated treaty (*Diktat* in German) that enabled the Germans to seize large areas of Russia and redeploy nearly a million troops to the western front.

Feeling betrayed and concerned that allied military supplies would fall into German hands, the Western Allies sent small expeditionary forces into Russia. American troops actually fought the Bolsheviks in North Russia and Siberia in 1918–1919. This started the Soviet propaganda line that the capitalist powers tried to strangle the infant Bolshevik regime in its cradle.

From 1918 to 1920 civil war raged. The White Army, led by reactionary Russian generals and admirals and supplied by the Western Allies, tried to crush the Communists' Red Army. Both sides were ruthless in a life-or-death struggle. Millions of Russians perished from starvation. Expecting their revolution to spread, the Red Army invaded Poland in 1920, hoping to trigger a Europewide socialist upheaval. Instead, the Poles threw back the Red Army and seized parts of Ukraine and Belarus. Lenin and his colleagues saw there would be no world revolution and settled for building the world's first socialist country.

Geography

Another Tale of Two Flags

At the end of 1991 the familiar Communist red flag (with the gold hammer and sickle) came down as the Soviet Union dissolved. Red had been the color of socialist movements (taken from the red shirts of Italian unifier Garibaldi) ever since the nineteenth century, and the Bolsheviks used it in the national flag in late 1917. The old tsarist flag was developed by Peter the Great, who brought the Netherlands tri color back with him from his stay in Dutch shipyards in 1699, but changed the stripes from the original Dutch (from the top: red-white-blue) to white-blue-red, sometimes with an imperial double-headed eagle (from Byzantium) on it. The Provisional Government removed the eagle in 1917; this is what the Russian Federation revived as its flag in 1991.

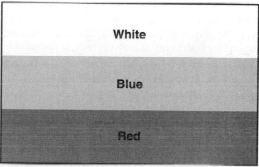

Personalities

Stalin: "One Death Is a Tragedy; a Million Is a Statistic"

The Soviet system was not so much Lenin's as Stalin's. Lenin died in 1924, at the age of fifty-four, before he was able to give definitive form to the system. Exactly who is to blame for the horrors that developed—Lenin or Stalin—is controversial both within and outside Russia. Some still argue that if Lenin had lived, his intelligence and sophistication would have set Russia on the path to "true socialism." Others say that the structure Lenin created—concentrating power first in the party, then in the Central Committee, and finally in his own person—made the abuse of power inevitable.

Stalin aptly illustrates Acton's dictum, "power corrupts." Stalin lived to amass political power and was very good at it. Born Yosif Vissarionovich Djugashvili in 1879, son of a poor shoemaker, Stalin lacked Lenin's intellectual family background and education. Some of Stalin's behavior can be traced to his homeland of Georgia, in the Caucasus, a mountainous land with a warm climate and fiery people given to personal hatred and blood-feuds. In Georgia, "Soso" (his Georgian nickname) is still praised as a local boy who made good.

The young Djugashvili started to study for the Orthodox priesthood but soon turned to revolution and joined the Georgian Marxist underground as an agitator and strike organizer. Repeatedly arrested, jailed, and exiled to Siberia, he always managed to escape. (There is some evidence that he was a double agent for the tsarist police.) Going underground, he took the name Stalin, Russian for "man of steel."

Never a great theoretician, Stalin attracted Lenin's attention as a non-Russian who could write the Bolsheviks' position on the nationalities question. Although he played only a moderate role in the October Revolution, Stalin was named commissar for nationalities in 1918 and then was chosen as the party's first general secretary in 1922. This was Lenin's worst mistake. People thought that the new office would be a clerical job with little power. Lenin and Stalin were never close—although Stalin's historians tried to make it look that way—and toward the end of his life Lenin had an inkling of what Stalin was like. In one of his last messages Lenin urged the party to reject Stalin as "too rude."

It was too late. Using his position as **gensek**, Stalin organized the **CPSU** to his advantage by promoting to key posts only those personally loyal to him, giving him the edge over his rival, Leon Trotsky, organizer of the Red Army and a far more intelligent Marxist. Stalin beat him in party infighting and had him expelled from Russia in 1929 and murdered in Mexico in 1940. Reviled as a deviationist traitor, Trotsky did try to organize an anti-Stalin opposition within the CPSU, a point that fed Stalin's natural **paranoia** and led him to shoot officials on the slightest suspicion of disloyalty.

Stalin, an uncanny manipulator, played one faction against another until, by the late 1920s, he was the Kremlin's undisputed master. Like Peter the Great, Stalin was determined to modernize regardless of human cost. In 1928 he instituted the first Five-Year Plan, beginning the forced industrialization of Russia. Farmers, very much against their will, were herded into collectives and forced to produce for the state, sometimes at gunpoint. Better-off farmers, the so-called *kulaks,* were "liquidated as a class," a euphemism for killed. Economic development was defined as heavy industry, and steel production became the chief goal of the man of steel.

In 1934, during the second Five-Year Plan, Stalin became obsessed with "Trotskyite" disloyalty in party ranks. Thus began Stalin's **purges**: up to one million party comrades killed, some after they confessed to being British spies or Trotskyite "wreckers." People in positions of prominence trembled that they would be next—and many were. Stalin ordered all managers to train two replacements. Stalin even had all his generals shot, a blunder that hurt the Soviet Union in the 1941 German attack. Perhaps another ten million ordinary citizens, arrested on fake charges, also perished, many in Siberian forced-labor camps. In total, Stalin's orders led to the death of over fifteen million people during collectivization and the purges.

Was Stalin mad? There was some Trotskyite opposition to him, but he exaggerated it. It was Plato who first observed that any tyrant, even one who starts sane, must lose his mind in office because he can trust no one. More than a question of personality, Stalin shows what happens when one person assumes total power. The Communists did not like to admit it, but it was their *system* that was at fault more than any particular individual.

During his lifetime, Stalin was deified as history's greatest linguist, art critic, Marxist theoretician, engineer, agronomist, and so forth. His communization of East Europe led to the **Cold War**. By the time he died in 1953—while in the midst of preparing yet another purge—Stalin had turned the Soviet Union into *his* system, and, in basic outlines, the system never did change much. When Mikhail Gorbachev attempted to

Joseph Stalin

seriously reform it, the system collapsed. Today, Stalin's crimes are unmentioned, and he is praised as a symbol of Russian power.

These three St. Petersburg graves of victims of Stalin's Great Purge convey some of the horror of Stalin's "cleansing" of people he thought were unreliable. The family of the victim on the right, by erecting a life-size statue of a man in Bolshevik Young Guard uniform, meant to show that he was a faithful Communist all along.

WAR COMMUNISM AND NEP

During the civil war, the Bolsheviks tried to plunge directly into their utopian system by running the ruined economy by executive fiat. This **war communism**, as it was euphemistically called, was due as much to the demands of a desperate civil war as to visionary schemes. To motivate workers, Lenin ordered: "He who does not work, neither shall he eat" (from 2 Thessalonians 3:10). War communism led immediately to starvation, and only the charity of American grain shipments (supervised by Herbert Hoover) held deaths to a few million.

Lenin realized that Russia was far from ready for pure socialism, so he conducted a planned retreat of state control to the "commanding heights" of heavy industry and let most of the rest of the economy revert into private hands. This period of Lenin's **New Economic Policy** (NEP) brought relative prosperity to Russia; farmers worked their own land, "nepmen" ran small businesses, and life in general relaxed. But the NEP was not moving the Soviet Union, as it was now called, any closer to socialism, and industry grew only slowly. It is likely that Lenin intended the NEP to be only a temporary rest before moving the Soviet Union on toward socialist construction.

That changed when Stalin took full power in the late 1920s. In 1928 he began the first of the government-enforced **Five-Year Plans** that accelerated collectivization and industrialization (see box on pages 306–307). Peasants resisted giving up their fields, farm production dropped, and millions (especially Ukrainians) were deliberately starved to death. In new factories, workers toiled with primitive tools to boost production of **capital goods**. Setting a pattern for all Communist countries, **consumer goods** were neglected, and the standard of living declined. While many admit the forced industrialization of the 1930s was brutal, some argue it gave the Soviet Union the industrial base to arm against the German invasion in 1941.

As it was, the war caused some twenty-seven million Soviet deaths. The Nazis cared nothing for Slavic lives; starvation was their standard treatment for Russian prisoners of war. Faced with extinction, the Soviet Union pulled together. Stalin, like Lenin, recognized the force of Russian nationalism beneath the Communist surface. Reviewing troops marching from Moscow to the front, Stalin mused: "They aren't fighting for communism or for Stalin; they're fighting for Mother Russia." In Russia today, World War II is known as the Great Patriotic War. By the time he died in 1953, Stalin had transformed a backward country into a gigantic empire and major industrial power. He also founded a system that in the long run proved to be inefficient and unreformable and finally collapsed in 1991.

gensek Russian abbreviation for "general secretary"; powerful CPSU chief. (See page 306.)

CPSU Communist Party of the Soviet Union. (See page 306.)

paranoia Unreasonable suspicion of others. (See page 306.)

purge Stalin's "cleansing" of suspicious elements by firing squad. (See page 306.)

Cold War Period of armed tension and competition between the United States and the Soviet Union, approximately 1947–1989. (See page 307.)

war communism Temporary strict socialism in Russia, 1918–1921.

New Economic Policy (NEP), Lenin's economic policy that allowed private activity, 1921–1928.

Five-Year Plans Stalin's forced industrialization of the Soviet Union, starting in 1928.

capital goods Implements used to make other things.

consumer goods Things people use, such as food, clothing, and housing.

KEY TERMS

anarchism (p. 300)

autocracy (p. 297)

Bolshevik (p. 301)

caesaropapism (p. 299)

capital goods (p. 308)

Cold War (p. 308)

communism (p. 301)

Constantinople (p. 296)

consumer goods (p. 308)

CPSU (p. 308)

Cyrillic (p. 296)

Duma (p. 303)

exclave (p. 297)

Five-Year Plans (p. 308)

gensek (p. 308)

imperialism (p. 303)

Narodniki (p. 300)

New Economic Policy
  (p. 308)

paranoia (p. 308)

proletariat (p. 301)

purge (p. 308)

Siberia (p. 296)

Slavophiles (p. 300)

Tatar (p. 297)

tsar (p. 297)

tyranny (p. 296)

Ukraine (p. 299)

war communism (p. 308)

Westernizers (p. 300)

zemstvo (p. 300)

FURTHER REFERENCE

Figes, Orlando. *The Whisperers: Private Life in Stalin's Russia*. New York: Metropolitan Books, 2007.

Fitzpatrick, Sheila. *Everyday Stalinism: Ordinary Life in Extraordinary Times*. New York: Oxford University Press, 1999.

Gilbert, Martin. *The Routledge Atlas of Russian History: From 800 B.C. to the Present Day,* 4th ed. New York: Routledge, 2007.

Gooding, John. *Socialism in Russia: Lenin and His Legacy, 1890–1991*. New York: Palgrave, 2002.

Hosking, Geoffrey. *Russia and the Russians*. Cambridge, MA: Harvard University Press, 2001.

Kort, Michael. *The Soviet Colossus: History and Aftermath,* 7th ed. Armonk, NY: M. E. Sharpe, 2008.

Lewin, Moshe. *The Soviet Century*. London: Verso, 2005.

Lieven, Dominic. *Empire: The Russian Empire and Its Rivals*. New Haven, CT: Yale University Press, 2001.

Madariaga, Isabel de. *Ivan the Terrible*. New Haven, CT: Yale University Press, 2005.

Montefiore, Simon Sebag. *Young Stalin*. New York: Knopf, 2007.

Read, Christopher. *The Making and Breaking of the Soviet System: An Interpretation*. New York: Palgrave, 2001.

Riasanovsky, Nicholas V., and Mark D. Steinberg. *A History of Russia,* 7th ed. New York: Oxford University Press, 2005.

Service, Robert. *Lenin: A Biography*. Cambridge, MA: Harvard University Press, 2001.

———. *Stalin: A Biography*. Cambridge, MA: Harvard University Press, 2005.

———. *Comrades! A History of World Communism*. Cambridge, MA: Harvard University Press, 2007.

Ulam, Adam B. *The Bolsheviks: The Intellectual and Political History of the Triumph of Communism in Russia*. Cambridge, MA: Harvard University Press, 1998.

CENTRAL ECONOMIC PLANNING

The State Planning Committee, **Gosplan**, was the nerve center of the Soviet economic system, attempting to establish how much of what was produced each year and setting longer-term targets for some 350,000 enterprises. Central planning produced both impressive growth and massive dislocations. Under Stalin, it enabled the Soviet Union to industrialize quickly, albeit at terrible human cost. But it also meant chronic shortages of items the Gosplan ignored. One year no toothbrushes were produced in the entire Soviet Union, a Gosplan oversight.

Gosplan   Soviet central economic planning agency.

DEMOCRACY

1991: THE COUP THAT FAILED

In August 1991, as Gorbachev was on vacation in the Crimea, most of his cabinet tried to overthrow him. An eight-man *junta* (Russians used the Spanish loan word) of conservatives, calling themselves the "Emergency Committee," said Gorbachev had taken ill and declared his vice-president acting president.

Some Western experts had been predicting a coup for three years. Gorbachev's reforms, cautious as they were, threatened the Soviet system and the jobs and comforts of the Soviet ruling elite. Gorbachev had been warned repeatedly of their anger. In December 1990 Foreign Minister Eduard Shevardnadze resigned in public protest at what he said was a coming dictatorship.

Gorbachev zig-zagged between promising major reforms and reassuring Party conservatives that he would not reform too much. In 1991 Gorbachev again favored reform and with the leaders of nine of the Soviet republics drafted a new union treaty that would give the republics great autonomy within a market economy. This was the last straw for the conservatives. The day before the treaty was to be signed they staged their coup.

For three days the world held its breath. Would the coup by not-very-bright Kremlin apparatchiks succeed? They seemed to hold the upper hand. Among them were the head of the military, the KGB, and the interior ministry. The following are some of the reasons the coup failed:

- Few supported the coup. Tens of thousands of citizens favoring democracy publicly opposed the coup. Gorbachev was not very popular, but the junta was much worse.

- Boris Yeltsin stood firm. About a mile and a half from the Kremlin is the parliament of the Russian Republic, then presided over by reformist Yeltsin. Yeltsin and his helpers holed up in the building and declared the junta's decrees illegal. A tank column sent to take the building instead sided with Yeltsin and defended it. Thousands of Muscovites came to stand guard and to protest the coup. Yeltsin's toughness galvanized opposition.

- The Soviet armed forces started to split. Many commanders either stood on the sidelines or opposed the junta. Facing a bloody civil war, the junta lost its nerve.

- International pressure opposed the coup. Major countries made it clear that the Soviet economy, desperate for foreign help, would get none. Foreign broadcasts (heard by Gorbachev himself) heartened the anti-junta forces.

A haggard Gorbachev returned to Moscow vowing further reform. The junta was arrested (one committed suicide). The coup attempt actually hastened the end of the Soviet Union. After it, Gorbachev was revealed as an indecisive failure. Yeltsin bumped him out of power and proclaimed an independent Russia. Democracy got a chance.

Soviet leaders claimed that a planned and centrally directed economy was more rational than a Western market economy. Actual results refuted that, but Soviet bureaucrats were reluctant to surrender central planning, an article of faith of "scientific socialism." In Gosplan the hopes, aims, fears, and sometimes caprices of the Soviet system met and struggled. Gosplan, itself quite sensitive to the wishes of the Politburo, determined who got what in the Soviet Union, and whether steel grew at x percent this year and plastics at y percent next. Heavily computerized, Gosplan was the steering wheel of the Soviet economy.

THE NEW SYSTEM

In the months after the failed coup of August 1991, the old Soviet system collapsed, and from the rubble emerged a new system that looks democratic on paper but is not.

NO MORE SOVIET UNION

All of the fifteen Soviet republics took advantage of the turmoil of late 1991 to declare their independence. The Baltic republics especially—Lithuania, Latvia, and Estonia—led the way to full, immediate independence. They expelled Soviet police, issued their own passports and visas, and took control of their borders. The other republics soon followed and now all are independent, some

GEOGRAPHY

THE FIFTEEN EX-SOVIET REPUBLICS

We should learn the names and approximate location of each of the fifteen former Soviet republics; they are now independent countries, but many are under Russian influence. (See the map at the beginning of Chapter 19.) To help you remember the republics, note that there are three groups of three, plus a Central Asia group of five (the five -stans), plus one oddball.

Slavic	Baltic	Caucasian	Central Asian	Romanian-Speaking
Russia	Lithuania[†]	Georgia	Turkmenistan*	Moldova (formerly Moldavia)
Ukraine	Latvia[†]	Armenia	Kazakhstan*	
Belarus	Estonia[†]	Azerbaijan*	Kyrgyzstan*	
			Uzbekistan*	
			Tajikistan*	

[†]not in CIS.
*predominantly Muslim.

more than others. Although Ukraine had been part of tsarist Russia for centuries and was the bread-basket of the Soviet Union, many Ukrainians resented being ruled by Moscow, especially after they read about what Stalin's farm collectivization had done to them—deliberately starved 6 million to death. They voted for independence and, in 2004, for a pro-Western democracy.

Belarus (formerly Belarussia, the area between Russia and Poland), which had never been an independent country or harbored much separatist feeling, voted for independence, too. But Belarus still uses the Russian ruble as currency and gets sweetheart trade deals with Russia. Its army is closely linked to the Russian army. Belarus in reality never cut its Russian ties and is now ranked as Europe's last dictatorship.

DEMOCRACY

1993: THE SECOND COUP THAT FAILED

The 1991 coup attempt was carried out by members of Gorbachev's own executive branch and was stopped by members of the Russian (not Soviet) parliament in its White House some distance from the Kremlin. The October 1993 coup attempt was by a paralyzed parliament that occupied the White House and was crushed by armed forces under President Yeltsin, who was now in the Kremlin.

The trigger of the 1993 attempt was Yeltsin's order to dissolve the Russian parliament and hold new elections. (The old Supreme Soviet disappeared with the USSR at the end of 1991.) The Russian parliament had been elected in 1989 under the old regime, when the CPSU still held sway; accordingly, it was incoherent and incapable of passing a new constitution. Yeltsin could no longer govern with this parliament, and, indeed, it was high time for free and fair parliamentary elections.

But the old parliament did not like being put out of business and called Yeltsin dictatorial. A majority of deputies declared the dissolution unconstitutional and holed up in the White House, hoping that the country and especially the army would side with it. They did not; instead, tanks shelled the White House until it caught fire.

Yeltsin won but he lost. New elections were held in December 1993, but by then so many Russians were

Russian Parliament, the "White House" some distance from the Kremlin, was the scene of two dramatic showdowns. In 1991 Boris Yeltsin stood here and faced down the junta that attempted to oust Gorbachev, but in 1993 it was Yeltsin who ordered the building shelled to break a coup attempt by parliamentarians. The White House was quickly restored and now houses Russia's State Duma.

disillusioned with reforms that brought crime, inflation, and unemployment that they voted in a parliament, now called the State Duma, that was heavily antireformist and anti-Yeltsin. Yeltsin had to dump many reformist ministers.

The scariest problem was the ethnic tension that came out in the republics. Minorities who had lived in peace for generations (probably because the KGB was watching) became the target of nationalist resentment. In the Caucasus, blood flowed. Many politicians at the republic level played the nationalist card, which easily turned into violence. Their messages were simple and effective: Georgia for the Georgians, Uzbekistan for the Uzbeks, Armenia for the Armenians, even Russia for the Russians.

All of the Central Asian republics plus Azerbaijan have a Muslim majority and speak a Turkic language, except the Tajiks who speak a type of Persian (like Iran). There has been Muslim-Christian violence between Azeris and Armenians and in Georgia. Inside the Russian Federation, Muslim Chechnya, brutally crushed by the Russian army, produces murderous terrorists. All together, however, more were killed in ex-Yugoslavia. A big question: In which direction will the ex-Soviet Muslim republics go—toward the modern example of Turkey, to Islamic fundamentalism, or back to an economically and militarily dominant Russia?

A COMMONWEALTH OF INDEPENDENT STATES

Is anything left of the old Soviet federal system? As it officially ceased to exist at the end of 1991, most of its component republics agreed to form a "Commonwealth of Independent States" (CIS), with headquarters in Minsk, Belarus. Conspicuously missing were the three Baltic republics and Georgia. Georgia was later forced, in the middle of a civil war abetted by Moscow, to sign the CIS treaty. No one quite knows what the powers of the CIS are, but most now think it is part of Moscow's plan to regain control over the ex-Soviet republics, in effect, to rebuild the Russia of Peter the Great.

There are valid reasons for some republics retaining ties with giant Russia. First, eight of the twelve CIS member republics are landlocked and need Russia for access to the outside world. Industrially, all are tied to the Russian economy for manufactured goods and energy. Financially, over the decades many of these republics benefited from major Soviet aid.

A NEW CONSTITUTION

Along with voting for a new parliament, in late 1993 Russians also approved a new and completely different constitution, one modeled on de Gaulle's 1958 French constitution.

Semipresidentialism Turned Upside Down   Russia used to follow the French (and Chinese) pattern of a strong president, but in 2008 Putin played with the constitution by making the president weak and the prime minister strong so that Putin could continue as the real power after his two terms. Institutions that can be so remade are weak and fake. French *semipresidentialism* has both an executive president and a prime minister but gives top power to the president. The Russian president is elected for two four-year terms but can repeat after someone else has been president. The president is supposed to set basic policy and name the prime minister and other top officials, and he can veto bills and dissolve parliament. In many areas the president can simply rule by decree and give himself strong emergency powers. There is no vice-president; if the president dies or is incapacitated, the prime minister serves as acting president until elections are held within three months. This happened when Yeltsin suddenly resigned at the end of 1999 and Putin took over.

By prearrangement, after completing his two terms as president in 2008, Putin became prime minister and made clear that power had shifted to that office. The new president, Putin protégé

de facto   In fact, even if not formally admitted.

Dmitri Medvedev, smiled and obeyed Putin. Russia's prime minister is supposed to be the president's chief administrator. The president used to name and fire prime ministers, but they had to be confirmed by the Duma. Putin, who founded and led the largest party, simply told the Duma to make him prime minister. If the Duma should reject the president's nominee for prime minister three times, the president can dissolve the Duma and hold new parliamentary elections.

A Federal System   The federal system is carried over from the old Soviet structure. The country's official name is the Russian Federation; it consists of eighty-nine regions—most of them *republics*—twenty-one of which are predominantly non-Russian. Each region is supposed to be bound by treaty to the Federation, but not all have signed, and they do not all like Moscow's rule. One Caucasian Muslim republic, Chechnya, which had resisted Russian rule since its original tsarist conquest, won temporary **de facto** autonomy but was then shelled into ruin.

PERSONALITIES

PUTIN: THE KGB PRESIDENT

Russian President and then Prime Minister Vladimir Putin came from the KGB bureaucracy and installed fellow KGB officers as Russia's rulers. Putin was a cold, secretive, nationalistic, and popular authoritarian, who boosted his own and Russia's power on the world stage. He tolerated no attempts to build democracy in Russia and turned bitterly hostile toward the United States. While not another Cold War, it was still quite chilly.

In four months during the year 1999, Putin (pronounced POOH-tin) rose from obscurity to powerful president of the Russian Federation, first as acting president and then elected on his own in 2000. In August 1999, Yeltsin named Putin, then forty-six years old, as his fifth prime minister in seventeen months. Many thought that Putin was another temp, but Yeltsin soon designated him as successor. Yeltsin—ill, drunk, and unpopular by that point—resigned at the end of 1999, and Putin constitutionally became acting president.

Putin's rapid rise to power was not accidental; it represented a quiet but thorough KGB coup, one that had been planned for years. Putin graduated law school in 1975 and went right into the KGB, where he

became a lieutenant colonel in spy operations in East Germany. As the Soviet Union collapsed—and the KGB knew precisely how bad the system was—the KGB placed many of its officers into positions throughout the government in order to later reconstitute authoritarian power. Putin went into St. Petersburg's municipal administration and became vice mayor in 1994. In 1996, Yeltsin brought him to the Kremlin to supervise relations among Russia's regions and in 1998 made him head of the FSB. In 1999 Putin was named secretary of the powerful Security Council and then premier, his first substantial exposure to the public. His election to president in 2000 (on the first round) was his first run for any office.

Putin was bright, but his great strength was his background and comrades in the KGB (now FSB), who have *kompromat* on Russia's most powerful people. They knew exactly who was corrupt and who stashed money overseas, including politicians and oligarchs. Putin and dozens of other KGB, military, and other *siloviki* set up an invisible authoritarian system inside the official Russian state. *Siloviki* placed in charge of state-controlled industries also made themselves quite rich.

During the 1990s, local strongmen—"elected," but not democratically—turned republics into corrupt personal fiefdoms. Putin ended that by giving himself the power to appoint republic governors. He further recentralized power in Moscow by creating seven

State Duma	Lower house of Russia's parliament.

new large regions and personally appointing their governors from FSB ranks. Current Russian federalism is no more genuine than the old Soviet federalism: Both give most power to the center. Given the size and unruly nature of many areas and nationalities, Russia needs considerable centralization of power if it is to hold together. Under Yeltsin, Russia was falling apart, so Putin did what he had to do.

A Bicameral Parliament   Russia's bicameral parliament resembles the U.S. Congress but no longer has any power to contradict the Russian presidency. The lower house, the **State Duma** (reviving the old tsarist name), consists of 450 deputies elected for up to four years (but not in sync with presidential elections). The Duma passes bills, approves the budget, and confirms the

Putin's authoritarianism bothers few Russians, who have always rallied to a strong ruler in times of danger and decay, precisely what the Yeltsin years brought. By new laws, threats, demotions, or criminal trials, Putin's people controlled the bureaucracy, media, Duma, regional governors, oligarchs, and private groups. Occasional assassinations, rarely solved, silence persistent critics. Putin's approval rating among Russians was over 75 percent, enough to make any Western leader jealous.

Vladimir Putin

Putin created mass support by renewing the war in Chechnya (see page 361). Chechen bombs in several Russian cities blew up apartment houses and schools and killed hundreds. The Russian people and army wanted revenge. Putin's orders to crush Chechen rebels drew nearly complete support and let him easily win the presidency in 2000 and reelection in 2004. Economic stability and growth, largely from oil and gas exports, made most Russians content. He worked around the constitution's two-term limit by leading his United Russia party to victory in late 2007 parliamentary elections, allowing him, as its head, to become prime minister under a figurehead president. When a president resigns, the prime minister becomes acting president and calls new elections. Putin could repeat what he did in 1999–2000. By whatever institutional means, Putin will remain powerful.

Putin allowed President Bush to portray him as a warm friend, especially after 9/11, but by 2003 he turned hostile over the Iraq war and U.S. help for Russian and Ukrainian democracy. Putin did not object to private industry in some sectors but brought Russia's oil and gas—its major exports—back under Kremlin control. Putin's goals are those of a good KGB officer: restore Russia's power and old borders. Democracy got in the way and was repealed.

president's nominees for top jobs. It can vote no confidence in a cabinet and, along with the upper house, can theoretically override a presidential veto with a two-thirds majority. That is unlikely to happen, as Putin's United Russia party dominates the Duma.

The upper house, the Federation Council, consists of two members named by each of the eighty-nine regional governments of the Russian Federation. Since Putin names the regional governors, he indirectly also picks the regions' deputies for the Federation Council. The Council's duties differ somewhat from the Duma's. Only the Federation Council can change internal boundaries

Democracy

Russia's 2007 Obedient Parliamentary Elections

Russia's December 2007 Duma elections were not really competitive. Putin's control of television, the bureaucracy, and the legal system assured his United Russia party of 64 percent of the votes and a big majority of the Duma's 450 seats. The 2007 elections confirmed the 2003 elections that turned Russia from a fragmented party system into a dominant-party system. Turnout in 2007 was a claimed 64 percent, but many Russians understood the verdict was already decided and did not vote. (Turnout in Chechnya was 99.5 percent, and United Russia won 99.4 percent of the vote there.)

Foreign election monitors were severely restricted, but many Russians called the elections undemocratic because state-controlled television showcased Putin's party and ignored the others. Opposition groups were harassed and arrested. Some parties were banned. Government employees were instructed to vote for United Russia. Putin, to be sure, was genuinely popular for bringing some stability and prosperity to Russia and likely would have won a clean election.

Putin also altered the election rules to favor his United Russia party. In 2004, Russia's mixed-member system filled half the Duma's 450 seats by proportional representation and half from 225 single-member districts, which allowed fifteen independent deputies to win. Putin eliminated the single-member constituencies and made the system straight PR. He also instituted a 7 percent threshold (up from 5 percent) that only four parties passed. Small parties were not permitted to combine forces as electoral alignments, effectively dooming them.

One of Russia's original democratic hopes, the free-market-oriented Yabloko, fell below the 7 percent barrier. Chess master Gary Kasparov's Other Russia alignment of several small parties was not allowed to run. He denounced the election as a farce that was "rigged from the start." Of the four parties in the Duma, three support Putin, giving him 87 percent of the seats. Only the Communists are in opposition.

Party	Orientation	Percent PR Vote	Seats
United Russia	pro-Putin	64.3	315
Communists	socialist	11.6	57
Liberal Democrats	pro-Putin nationalist	8.2	40
Fair Russia	pro-Putin welfare	7.8	38
Agrarian	farming	2.3	0
Yabloko	democratic	1.6	0

and ratify the use of armed forces abroad. It appoints top judges and prosecutors and can remove them. The president controls both houses of parliament, and they pass any law he wants, including laws that give him more power. Putin, of course, now controls the president.

DEMOCRACY

RUSSIA'S 2008 PRESIDENTIAL ELECTIONS

Russian presidential elections, held every four years, are modeled on the French two-round system, minus the democracy. Russia's March 2008 presidential elections unrolled much like the December 2007 parliamentary elections (see box on page 322). Putin told Russians whom to vote for, and they did.

After the parliamentary elections, won by Putin's United Russia party, Putin named a little-noticed helper (with no background in the security services) as United Russia's candidate for the presidency. Dmitri Medvedev, then forty-two, was a close and loyal Putin protégé who followed him from St. Petersburg's municipal administration to the Kremlin in 1999. Among other posts, he was chairman of the board of the state-linked natural-gas giant Gazprom. Like Putin, Medvedev was born in Leningrad (now St. Petersburg) and graduated in law there a decade after Putin. Russian observers described Medvedev as "a creature of Putin" or even "Putin's son" with no power base of his own. Medvedev vowed to faithfully continue Putin's policies.

Putin clearly planned to set himself up to retain power even after he formally left the presidency. Medvedev announced that as president he would name Putin as his prime minister—Putin is the head of Russia's largest party—and Putin modestly said he would accept. Everyone understood that Putin would be the real power, even if on paper President Medvedev ruled. Then, if Putin wished it, Medvedev could step down to make way for another two presidential terms for Putin, allowed under Russia's constitution.

Other 2008 presidential candidates were effectively eliminated. Opposition parties—who did not stand a chance anyway—were kept off the ballot by rigged Kremlin-imposed tricks. Three small parties were allowed to run, but only the Communists offered a weak alternative to United Russia's Medvedev, who won with a big majority on the first round. Russians liked the stability and economic growth Putin had brought and correctly saw Medvedev as a junior Putin. Turnout was an unenthusiastic 64 percent, as many Russians knew the fix was in; 1.35 percent voted for "none of the above," allowed on the Russian ballot. The 2008 results are shown in the table below.

If no one had won a majority—improbable—a runoff would have been held two weeks later between the top two, as was done in 1996. Between the two rounds in 1996, deal-making rounded up majority support for incumbent President Boris Yeltsin. Most of the Russian mass media in 2008, especially television, was owned by corporations tied to the Kremlin and fawned on Medvedev. Voting irregularities were reported, and the 2008 election was not democratic. There was only nominal competition, and competition is the crux of democracy. The outside world was not fooled, but Russians did not mind.

Candidate	Party	Percent
Dmitri Medvedev	United Russia	70
Gennady Zyuganov	Communist	18
Vladimir Zhirinovsky	Liberal Democrat	9
Andrei Bogdanov	Democratic Party of Russia	1

   A Proportional Electoral System   In 2005 Putin ordered the Duma to institute straight *proportional representation* (see page 189) with voting by party list and not for individuals. This replaced the system Yeltsin had instituted, a *mixed-member* system inspired by Germany, with half of the Duma's 450 seats elected by proportional representation (with a 5-percent threshold), and half by single-member districts with plurality win. Under the new PR system, there are no longer any independent candidates because there are no more single-member districts, and the threshold is now 7 percent.

   A Constitutional Court   The constitutional court is borrowed chiefly from the United States but with some French and German features. The Russian Constitutional Court has nineteen judges appointed by the president and confirmed by the upper house. These judges are supposed to be independent and cannot be fired. They may act both on citizens' complaints and on cases submitted by government agencies. The court is supposed to make sure all laws and decrees conform to the constitution. Putin however, put it back under political control so that it does little to promote the rule of law in Russia.

A Party System under Construction

From a one-party system under the Soviets, Russia went to a fragmented system of many weak parties to what is now effectively a dominant-party system (see page 490). Several of Russia's political parties sprang up quickly but were weak, divided, constantly changing, and *personalistic*, like Latin American parties (see page 495). Russia's top parties aimed chiefly at getting their leaders elected. In the 1999 Duma elections, five parties had present or former prime ministers as leaders. Putin invented the United Russia (*Yedinaya Rossiya*) party, his vehicle to win the presidency and prime ministership and dominate the Duma. And not all Russian parties are democratic; some preach chauvinism or a return to communism.

   The party system is perhaps the foundation of political stability in the modern world. Britain is basically a "two-plus" party system, France is a multiparty system, and Germany has turned from a "two-plus" to a multiparty system. Putin marginalized competing parties to make Russia a dominant-party system with no checks or balances on an all-powerful president. Politics in dominant-party systems revolves around struggles, mostly unseen, within the big party for power and spoils, such as control of industries. Russians could theoretically elect a Duma to offset the president, but with the Russian preference for a strong hand at the top and the media back in government hands, this will not soon happen.

Key Terms

apparatchik (p. 312)

bureaucratized (p. 315)

Central Committee (p. 312)

de facto (p. 320)

Gosplan (p. 316)

Gulag (p. 313)

nomenklatura (p. 315)

Politburo (p. 312)

republic (p. 314)

siloviki (p. 313)

State Duma (p. 321)

system change (p. 312)

weak state (p. 312)

Further Reference

Andrews, Josephine T. *When Majorities Fail: The Russian Parliament, 1990–1993*. New York: Cambridge University Press, 2002.

Baker, Peter, and Susan Glasser. *Kremlin Rising: Vladimir Putin's Russia and the End of Revolution*. New York: Scribner, 2005.

Colton, Timothy J., and Stephen Holmes, eds. *The State after Communism: Governance in the New Russia*. Lanham, MD: Rowman & Littlefield, 2006.

Hale, Henry E. *Why Not Parties in Russia? Democracy, Federalism, and the State*. New York: Cambridge University Press, 2005.

Pravda, Alex, ed. *Leading Russia: Putin in Perspective*. New York: Oxford University Press, 2005.

Remington, Thomas F. *Politics in Russia*, 5th ed. New York: Longman, 2008.

Rubenstein, Joshua, and Alexander Gribanov, eds. *The KGB File of Andrei Sakharov*. New Haven, CT: Yale University Press, 2005.

Sakwa, Richard. *Putin: Russia's Choice*, 2nd ed. New York: Routledge, 2007.

———. *The Rise and Fall of the Soviet Union*. New York: Routledge, 2008.

Walker, Edward W. *Dissolution: Sovereignty and the Breakup of the Soviet Union*. Lanham, MD: Rowman & Littlefield, 2003.

White, Stephen. *Russian Politics*. New York: Oxford University Press, 2006.

Chapter 21
Russian
Political Culture

As the Soviet regime declined and collapsed in the late 1980s and early 1990s, the word "democracy" had a positive ring among Russians. It stood for a new beginning, for justice and prosperity, and for joining the Western world. The leading political party was *Demrossiya*, Democratic Russia. Now, after having lived through several years of economic decline, lawlessness, and national weakness, few Russians care about democracy. They want food on the table, order, and stability, and most believe the authoritarian Putin gave it to them. Polls find that only a minority of Russians think democracy is always best, and many say they would vote for Stalin. The school system never educated Russians on the crimes of Stalin, so many think he was just a strong leader. Under orders, Russian schools dropped an honest textbook on Stalin. Germans imperfectly faced their past, Japanese less so, but Russians hardly at all.

Ignoring the crucial factor of political culture, we naively assumed the collapse of the Communist regime would unleash liberal democracy and free-market prosperity. Instead it brought monumental lawlessness and poverty. A handful of **oligarchs** got very rich buying state business (especially oil) at giveaway prices. Mafia gangs were into everything, including the government. Some called the system, half in jest, a **kleptocracy**. The breakdown demonstrated what some scholars long suspected, that under the law-and-order surface of Soviet rule, Russian society was very weak—indeed, it had been made deliberately weak—and could not sustain a free democracy, at least not for some time.

Questions to Consider

1. How can democracy grow in a country where "democracy" brought decay and poverty?
2. Why is democracy harder in Russia than in ex-Communist Central Europe?
3. How can you tell if a system is based on ideology? Was the Soviet system? What empirical indicators could you look for?
4. What is *civil society* and how do you get it? Is it the same as *pluralism*?
5. Has Russia now stabilized, or is it still "Weimar Russia"?
6. What is the difference between immoral business behavior in America and Russia?
7. Why did we think Russia after communism would quickly become like us?

The Russian Difference

Central Europe discarded its Communist regimes in 1989, and within five years Poland, the Czech Republic, and Hungary were functioning democracies with growing, mostly private, market economies. During this period, the Soviet Union, trying to make the same transition, collapsed both economically and politically. Why the difference between Central Europe and Russia?

oligarchy   Rule by a few. (See page 327.)

kleptocracy   Rule by thieves. (See page 327.)

indigenous   Home-grown, rooted in the local soil.

First, there are cultural differences between the mostly Roman Catholic countries of Central Europe and Eastern Orthodox Russia (see box below). Second, the Communists succeeded in capturing Russian *nationalism*, so that a Russian could take a certain pride in communism. For Central Europeans, communism was put and kept in place by Soviet bayonets and was profoundly at odds with **indigenous** nationalism.

Perhaps more basically, communism had been implanted in Central Europe much later (after World War II) than in the Soviet Union (during World War I); it did not have as much time to take hold. Russians had nearly three-quarters of a century of Communist rule (1917–1991), enough for three generations to know only one system. Furthermore, the previous tsarist system had not been democratic either and was just in the early stages of capitalist economic development.

The system Russians were used to provided them with jobs (constitutionally guaranteed) and a low but generally predictable standard of living. An apartment, once you got one, was tacky by Western standards but cost only a few dollars a month. Few Russians worked hard; there was little point to it. Now, suddenly Russians were told their jobs are not guaranteed and that reward is linked to individual achievement.

Geography

Huntington's "Civilizational" Divide in Europe

In an influential but controversial 1993 article in *Foreign Affairs,* Harvard political scientist Samuel P. Huntington argued that with the Cold War over, profound differences of culture were dividing the world into several "civilizations" that have trouble understanding each other. These civilizations mostly follow religious lines: the West European (with a North American branch), the Slavic/Orthodox, Muslim, Hindu, Confucian, Japanese, and Latin American.

In Europe, said Huntington, the key geographic line is still where Eastern Orthodoxy meets the two branches of Western Christianity—Catholicism and Protestantism—a line running south from the Baltic republics (Lithuania is mostly Catholic, Latvia and Estonia mostly Protestant) and along the eastern borders of Poland, Slovakia, Hungary, and Croatia. West European civilization, initially in Protestant countries, led the way to democracy and capitalism. Catholic Europe followed more recently. Poland, the Czech Republic, and Hungary all turned quickly to market systems and democracy after ousting their Communist regimes in 1989.

But notice that Slavic/Orthodox countries such as Russia, Ukraine, Serbia, Bulgaria, and Romania have difficulty in making this transition. Basic assumptions about individual freedom and choice, private property, personal rights, and the rule of law that are widespread in West Europe have not developed in the same way in Slavic/Orthodox Europe. One key point: Orthodox culture is less individualistic, and this helps account for economic behavior.

Economic *shock therapy* (the sudden introduction of a free market) soon brought rapid growth to Poland. Applied in Russia, it simply collapsed the economy: "shock without therapy." Many observers suggest the differences between Poland and Russia are cultural, that Poland has always faced west and Russia not. Huntington's theory does not mean that other civilizations cannot become free-market democracies, just that it may take some time.

The result was psychological disorientation and fear. The economy declined, inflation grew, unemployment increased, and parents worried over how to feed their children. The old legitimacy of Party and leaders collapsed, and nothing took its place. First Gorbachev and then Yeltsin lost their early credibility; they had indecisively zigged and zagged so long on the economy that few saw them as leaders.

---

glasnost   Gorbachev's policy of media openness.

In the vacuum of belief, cynicism and despair reigned. Some Russians rediscovered their Orthodox church, which grew after the Communist collapse but has not kept growing. Few attend Orthodox services (but Catholicism and Protestantism are expanding in Russia). Many Russians believed in nothing and said everything was going wrong. Most are still politically numb and care nothing for democracy. But people have to believe in something; cynicism cannot sustain a society. Western values of a free society, of morality rooted in religion, of civil rights, and of individual achievement in a market economy are talked about by some intellectuals but not widely held. Seven decades of Communist rule stomped them out.

THE MASK OF LEGITIMACY

For decades, the CPSU tried to pound into Soviet skulls the feeling that the regime was legitimate—that is, it had the right to rule—and was leading the country through the difficulties of "building socialism" to the working utopia of communism. It is impossible to say how many really believed this. At various times, many did. Foreigners were treated to performances of marchers, youth delegations, and seemingly frank conversations with officials that were designed to show that Soviets believed in the system. In private, Western journalists sometimes established contacts who told them otherwise: dissident intellectuals, bitter workers, and even Party members who had come to doubt the worth of the system.

When Gorbachev permitted increased freedom of expression in the late 1980s, **glasnost**, torrents of criticism poured out. Freed from fear of the police, the media bitterly criticized the bureaucracy, the Party, and the corruption of both. The mask of Soviet legitimacy slipped away to reveal a system that satisfied few. The trouble was that there was no consensus on what should replace it. The broad masses (Russian: *narod*) generally wanted a cleaned-up socialism that guaranteed everyone a good standard of living. They showed little understanding of democracy or a market system. Many of the better-educated, on the other hand, understood that socialism was defective and should be scrapped in favor of free politics and free economics. Those whose jobs depended on the old system saw change as a threat. And many Russians simply did not know what to think. They had never before been asked for their opinions.

Many Russians have turned to Russian nationalism, a powerful impulse long manipulated by the Communists, and to newly freed Russian Orthodox Christianity. Russian nationalism and the Russian Orthodox faith, however, cannot cement Russia together: Twenty-one ethnic republics are non-Russian, mostly Tatar and Muslim (over 10 percent of Russia's population), which harbor their own nationalism and separatism. No symbols unite all Russians. Some like the new tricolor flag (based on a tsarist design); others want to bring back the red flag with hammer and sickle. National day is no longer November 11 to celebrate the revolution (although thousands, out of nostalgia, still parade) but June 12 to celebrate "Russia Day" when it proclaimed sovereignty in 1990 (for which few parade). Many Russians deplore the breakup of the Soviet Union.

GEOGRAPHY

BOUND SERBIA

Serbia is bounded on the north by Hungary;
on the east by Romania and Bulgaria;
on the south by Macedonia, Kosovo, and Montenegro;
and on the west by Bosnia and Croatia.

In 2003 Yugoslavia, a **rump state**, changed its name to Serbia and Montenegro. The old Yugoslavia of 1918–1941 and 1945–1991 included Slovenia, Croatia, Bosnia, and Macedonia, all of which are now independent. In 2006 Montenegro (Black Mountain) voted in a referendum to depart from the federation. Serbia lost its outlet to the sea and returned to what it was called before World War I. In 1999 Serbia lost control of Kosovo and its largely Albanian population, who in 2008 proclaimed Kosovo independent, which Serbia and Russia did not recognize. With the bounding exercises you have now done, you should be able to locate most countries of Europe. Which European lands have not been named in our bounding exercises?

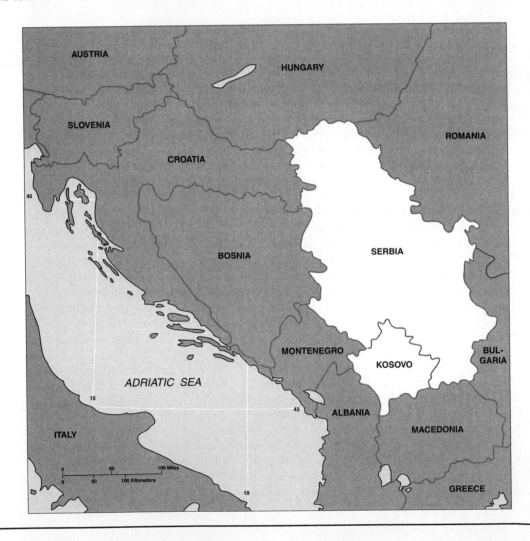

THE ILLUSION OF IDEOLOGY

Some studies of the Soviet Union paid great attention to Marxism-Leninism, the *ideology* of communism. In truth, for many years ideology had counted for little in the Soviet Union; with *glasnost* it disappeared from sight. Much of Soviet "ideology" was little more than Russian national pride masking feelings of inferiority. Marxism, by predicting the collapse of the capitalist West, tried to reassure Russians that they would eventually emerge superior. They were "building socialism," which at a certain point would surpass the United States and turn into a Communist utopia with no social or econom-

> **rump state**   Leftover portions of a country after dismemberment. (See page 330.)
>
> **civil society**   Associations larger than the family, but not part of government, and the pluralistic values that come with them.

ic problems. In earlier decades some Soviets believed it, but American academics went overboard in supposing ideology was the basis of the Soviet system. The Soviet system turned people into opportunists. Young people joined the Party to get into universities, to win job promotions, to become military or civilian officials. Most were cynical and cared nothing for Marxism-Leninism. They were motivated by careers, not ideology.

Marxism is basically a method of analysis, one that stresses social classes and their conflicts. As such, it stayed far livelier in the West, where it faced constant argument and challenge. In the Soviet Union, it atrophied. Applying Marxist analyses to Soviet society was the last thing the *apparat* wanted, as it would have revealed a pampered Party elite lording it over a wretched proletariat. Soviet Marxists thus focused on the West and cranked out the standard clichés, such as the "sharpening of contradictions" and "increasing tempo and magnitude of crises." The West was supposed to collapse any minute. After some decades, few took it seriously. Soviet students took required classes on Marxism-Leninism with the enthusiasm of American students going to compulsory chapel.

The constant mouthing of a dead doctrine created a climate of cynicism, hypocrisy, and opportunism. With the collapse of the Soviet system, Marxism-Leninism collapsed like the house of cards it always was. Marxist ideology was always a defective foundation, but what kind of society can they build with no foundation?

THE REDISCOVERY OF CIVIL SOCIETY

Political scientists since Tocqueville (in his brilliant *Democracy in America* in the 1830s) have held that the crux of democracy is the autonomy of **civil society**. Independent enterprises, churches, associations, clubs, educational institutions, and the media interact with each other and with government to produce democracy. No pluralism, no democracy. The crux of the Soviet system, however, was the stomping out of civil society by the state. Nothing was to be autonomous; everything in society was to be under strict state supervision, in turn supervised by the Party. The Communists had deliberately crushed civil society, and the Soviet collapse left a vacuum in its place. Some happily anticipated that civil society would emerge in post-Communist Russia as it had in Central Europe.

Initially, civil society did emerge in Russia, and within a few years some 450,000 private groups and charities were voicing citizen concerns and demands. In 2005, however, an obedient Duma passed two Putin measures to bring civil society under government control. One law requires all associations to register with the state, effectively banning non-governmental organizations (NGOs), especially foreign-funded foundations that promote democracy and civil rights. Such

socialize   To teach political culture, often informally.

groups encouraged Ukraine's 2005 Orange Revolution, and Putin did not want a replay of it in Russia. Another law set up a "Public Chamber" of 126 distinguished citizens (one-third appointed by Putin), supposedly representatives of civil-society organizations, to monitor government and strengthen democracy. Few were fooled, and many called it a smokescreen to strengthen Putin's power. The crux of civil society is the autonomy of its many groups; place them under state control and they are no longer civil society.

The concept of civil society starts with the understanding that state and society are two different things, although they clearly influence each other. Society over time evolves informal manners, usages, and customs that make living together possible. The "civil" (as in civilized) indicates a reasonable level of trust, politeness, public spirit, and willingness to compromise. A civil society through parents, churches, and schools **socializes** its members to right behavior and "rules of the game" that continue even when the state, through its police and bureaucrats, is not watching.

The state, the formal institutional structures that wield power, cannot substitute for or replace civil society, although the Communists tried. Attempting such a substitution creates a system where people lack basic civility and see no need to play by informal rules of the game. Businessmen cheat and mafia gangs muscle into all sectors of the economy. Politicians attack each other hysterically, immoderately, with no possibility of compromise; they have never learned restraint. Citizens feel little need to obey the law if they can get away with breaking it. Legitimacy is terribly weak.

The West had centuries to build up its civil societies. Philosophers such as Hobbes and Locke explained rationally why civil society is necessary. Churches, often with threats of eternal damnation, inculcated right behavior. The market system generated usages aimed at keeping dealings fair and predictable. Laws and courts enforced this with a system of contracts, both written and unwritten. All of this has been missing in Russia since the 1917 Revolution. Americans tended to take their civil society for granted until corporate misdeeds reminded them that businesses without ethics undermine the whole system. All civil societies need maintenance and reform from time to time when cheats take advantage of the trust that has been built up.

In Russia, unscrupulous cheats are the norm, and Russian corporations do things far worse than Enron or Worldcom. When communism fell, we thought the sudden imposition of democratic institutions and a market economy in Russia would quickly bring a civil society. We now see that without the philosophical, moral, economic, and legal understandings of civil society, Russia turns back to authoritarianism.

Natural Egalitarians?

Marxism-Leninism may have vanished in Russia, but many Russians display a tendency toward extreme equality, a natural socialism. Russians resent differences of wealth or income and enviously try to bring the better-off down to their level. Most Russians hated the new-rich oligarchs and were delighted to see Putin break and jail them. Some observers argue that the Russian peasantry, who for centuries tilled the soil in common and shared the harvest, developed highly egalitarian attitudes, which the Communists nourished. Perhaps so, but attitudes are not genetic; they are learned and can be unlearned, given the right conditions. Until new attitudes are learned, however, the old ones can trip up the best-laid plans of reformers.

Americans also favor equality, but it is "equality of opportunity": Everyone has a chance; the results are up to you. An American who gets ahead is usually applauded for his or her ability and hard work. Most Russians do not understand this kind of equality; they expect "equality of result," with each person collecting the same rewards. Those who get ahead are presumed to have cheated, exploited, or bribed (actually, many have). "The rich are living on our poverty," said one elderly Russian lady. In polls, most Russians say the free market and small state are wrong for Russia; only a few favor them. American values of individual work and achievement lend themselves to capitalism; Russian values until recently have not.

Russian Racism

With *glasnost*, hate-filled racist attitudes latent among the Soviet nationalities came into the open. Under Soviet law, citizens had their nationality stamped in their internal passports, and, contrary to U.S. usage, nationality throughout East Europe and the ex-Soviet Union does not equal

Political Culture

The Philosophical Gap

One of the key differences between us and the Russians is philosophical; namely, we are the children of John Locke and they are not. Although few Americans study the philosopher who is at the root of much of our thinking, most have assimilated what the seventeenth-century English thinker had to say: People are rational and reasonable; they have a natural right to life, liberty, and property. Government is good if it preserves these rights and bad if it infringes on them. If this sounds like the Declaration of Independence, it is; Jefferson was an ardent Lockean, as were most of the Founding Fathers. Ever since, Americans have taken to Locke like a duck takes to water; we love his common-sense emphasis on small government and individuals working for the good of themselves and their families. To Russians, this is not common sense.

Russian thought comes out almost the opposite of Locke and traces back to the geographical dilemma of living on a defenseless plain: Either build a strong state or perish. Plugging into the Russian tradition of a strong state is Jean-Jacques Rousseau (see page 92), the radical eighteenth-century French thinker whose theory of the "general will" rejected Lockean individualism in favor of using state power to "force men to be free." With Locke, people form society, and then society sets up a state, all with an eye to preserving property. With Rousseau, the flow goes the other way: The state, guided by the general will, molds society and then redoes individuals. Marxists added a class-struggle gloss to this; Lenin bought the package and then sold it to the Russian people.

Many Americans thought that once communism was overthrown Russians would rapidly become like us: capitalist entrepreneurs and democrats. This neglected the centuries of philosophical underpinning that is utterly lacking in Russia. If there could be a Peace Corps in Russia, the teaching of the philosophical basis of markets, pluralism, and limited government might be one of its first and most urgent tasks. Without a new philosophical outlook, one taken mostly from the West, the Russians will likely stay trapped in their *statist* frame of mind. (For more on statism, see the India and Mexico chapters.)

citizenship. For example, one can be a Russian citizen of the Komi nationality. This approach is asking for trouble, because it encourages people to demand an independent state. Educated Russians admire the U.S. approach, which prohibits the official identification of citizens by race or national origin.

Political Culture

THE MORAL GAP

America has its share of corporate crooks and cheats, but what would America be like if one could go back over three generations and systematically strip out most moral teachings? What if parents, churches, and schools did not attempt to inculcate a sense of innate right and wrong in young people? What if no one could trust anyone else? The result, I suspect, would be rather like Russia today. This is another area we overlooked in thinking that once communism ended, Russians would quickly become like us.

Russians had ethical training, but it was relativistic, superficial, and based on Marxist theories of social class. That which helps the working class is good, went the litany. The Soviet state helps the working class, so it must be good. The Communist party is totally devoted to the working class, so it must be very good. The state and the Party must therefore be obeyed, respected, and defended. Anyone who goes against them is insane, a wrecker, or a spy. Crime is something that happens only in capitalist countries, where the poor are forced to steal. Private property is inherently wicked, because it has been stolen from the workers who produced it. Under communism, there were no moral absolutes. The Russian Orthodox Church, tightly controlled by the government, confined itself to religious ritual and avoided moral instruction. By contrast, the Polish Catholic Church, for centuries the pillar of Polish civil society, stayed free of state control and critical of communism, always trying to face Poland westward. Religion matters.

Communist rhetoric aside, Soviet citizens soon learned to treat the system with cynicism. With the KGB and its informants everywhere, no one could trust anyone else, and they still do not. With no individual responsibility, stealing, especially from the state, was

okay. After all, it really belonged to no one. Under communism, monstrous rip-offs became standard: Everyone stole and bribed.

When the Soviet Union collapsed, things got worse. Knowing the Party and KGB were watching restrained most Soviets to small rip-offs. Once these external controls vanished, a spirit of "anything goes" was unleashed. Nothing happens without bribes. People who were smart, ruthless, or well-connected grabbed whole industries. Russia was robbed from within by its own bureaucrats. Since Soviets had always been taught that capitalists and *biznesmeny* (long a term of derision, now adopted as a loan word) were crooks and their gains were ill-gotten, many Russians went into business with that image as their norm. The crime rate shot up; only Colombians are more likely to be murdered than Russians. Massive protection rackets, enforced by professional *keelers* (another loan word), were all right because they were just stealing from capitalist thieves.

What escaped both Russians and Americans is that a modern capitalist culture has a considerable moral basis; people have to be able to trust each other. Such a system draws from religious and ethical teachings, legal enforcement, a spirit of trust, and the knowledge that cheating businesses get few repeat customers. It may take a long time to build up this moral consensus. We made the mistake of thinking it would automatically arrive with the free market, which we suppose to be generally self-policing. We have recently discovered that U.S. financial institutions are not self-policing but need some outside controls. For most Russians, a free market means legal cheating. (Some American CEOs think so, too.) For capitalism to work right, both in Russia and America, the moral gap must be filled.

And Russians pigeonhole by nationality. Some are acceptable, others despised. Russians respect the Baltic peoples as European, civilized, and "cultured." On the other hand, Russians speak scathingly of the Muslim peoples of the **Caucasus** and **Central Asia** as lawless and corrupt mafiosi who make too many babies. The theme of the differential birthrate comes up often. Most Russian families nowadays have one child (also the norm in much of West Europe). Muslim families have many children, sometimes eight or more. Some Russians fear that their stagnant numbers will be swamped by a tide of inferior peoples. When bombs blew up apartment houses in 1999, killing close to 300 people, the

---

Caucasus   Mountainous region between Black and Caspian Seas.
Central Asia   Region between Caspian Sea and China.

Political Culture

The Economic Gap

In addition to the philosophical and moral foundations of a civil society, another basic point was overlooked in the eager assumption that Russians would quickly become like us: People have to learn capitalism. A market economy may be something that occurs naturally (whenever buyers and sellers meet), but it is not understood naturally. You have to take courses in market economics and read books and articles about it. Soviet courses covered "bourgeois economics" as part of the history of economic thought but gave it short shrift as a doomed system riven with contradictions, unfairness, and depressions. When their system collapsed, only a few Russian economists had a decent grasp of what makes market economies work.

Especially missing was any appreciation of how money plays an autonomous role in the economy. In Communist countries, there simply was no theory of money. For example, I have tried the following mental experiment on a seminar (at the U.S. Army War College) of U.S., Central European, and Russian colonels, all bright and well-educated. Imagine, I tell them, a miniature country with ten citizens, each of whom works in one hamburger shop. The ten workers make a total of ten hamburgers a day and each is paid $1 a day. Then each buys one hamburger a day with their $1. The government decides to raise the pay of each to $2 a day (by printing an extra ten $1 bills). The output of the workers is still ten hamburgers a day. Within a day or two, what is the price of a hamburger?

Mini-capitalism: A Russian peasant woman sells fruit near Moscow.

The Americans respond quickly and almost instinctively: $2! The East Europeans and Russians do not get it. "You haven't given us enough data," they say. Well, how would you explain it? It is not so simple. Phrases like "supply and demand" by themselves do not explain much. What we accept as basic and self-evident, Russians do not. (By the way, once you can explain the parable, you have a rudimentary theory of money.)

Russian government and the people eagerly blamed alleged Chechen terrorists and supported a new war to crush them. Caucasians and Central Asians who had long run cheap market stalls were expelled. Putin said it was to protect "native Russians" from the Asian "semi-gangs."

The non-Russian nationalities feel little affection or affinity for the Russians. In Central Asia, several republics have made their local language the only official language. Educated Uzbeks, for example, know Russian perfectly, but now they speak only Uzbek as a way of making local Russians feel unwelcome. Many Russians are getting the message and leaving Central Asia. Virtually none have fled from the Baltic republics, however, and some Russians there even support independence. They feel they would be treated fairly by the cultured Balts. They fear the Muslims of the Caucasus and Central Asia.

Antisemitism, deliberately cultivated in tsarist Russia, is back but unofficial and played down in public statements. Russian nationalists and Communists point to the handful of oligarchs of Jewish or partly Jewish origin and see a sinister international conspiracy called "Zionism." Small nationalist parties of skinheads urge violence against Jews, and tens of thousands of Russian Jews have moved to Israel. Most Russians, however, condemn antisemitism, and in 2002 President Putin got the Duma to pass a law against ethnic extremism.

Political Culture

The Legal Gap

Much of Russia is lawless, one characteristic of the weak state. Russian police and courts are chaotic and easily bribed. As in India and Mexico, motorists are used to paying off traffic cops. Law is used selectively: Regime opponents get arrested and convicted, but major assassinations go unsolved, and corrupt officials are untouched. Said one Russian law expert ruefully, "The only lawyer around here is a Kalashnikov," a favorite weapon of *keelers*.

The Soviet legal structure broke down almost completely, and it was deficient to begin with. Soviet law paid minimal attention to property. Any big property (land, factories) automatically belonged to the state, and stealing state property could be harshly punished as a form of treason. The Lockean notion that property is a natural right and basis for human freedom was rejected out of hand. Russians, having been inculcated with the Marxist notion that "all property is theft," have trouble grasping the democratic and capitalist notion that "private property means personal freedom."

Weak or absent in the old Soviet socialist legal code, which Russia inherited, are such basics of the Common Law as ownership, contracts, torts, and bankruptcy. If you set up a business in the United States, Canada, or West Europe, you are reasonably confident your property and earnings will not be taken from you. In Russia, you have no confidence. Not only are business and property laws brand new, there is no legal culture built up over the years that regards these areas as important. One result is that foreigners and Russians alike are reluctant to invest in Russia; many have lost everything.

By way of contrast, Poland adopted its excellent Commercial Code in 1935, borrowed heavily from the Italian. The Polish Communist regime never repealed this code and after the Communists' ouster in 1989, Polish jurists simply dusted it off and put it into practice. Both Poles and foreigners who invest in Poland enjoy legal protections. Result: The Polish economy was for most of the 1990s the fastest growing in Europe. Russia finally passed commercial and criminal codes in 2002, based in part on Western legal concepts.

A Culture of Insecurity

Average Russians are terribly insecure. In the 1990s crime, corruption, and economic decay dominated their lives. Some compared the 1990s to the Time of Troubles in the early seventeenth century. Others used the phrase "Weimar Russia" to suggest a coming fascism. Before Putin took power, most Russians described the situation as "tense," "critical," or "explosive" and expected anarchy. Many feel Putin made things more secure; they liked his increased power and paid no attention to his undemocratic methods. Putin had higher approval ratings than any Western leader.

Ultimately, Russia can become as democratic as Germany or Spain, but not under conditions of chaos. Putin did restore order and was better than Communists, extreme nationalists, and gangsters, but he had no plans for full-fledged democracy.

We now realize that in the early 1990s, when Communist rule cracked and then collapsed, we were expecting too much. We paid insufficient attention to crucial factors of political culture and assumed that capitalism and democracy bring their own political culture with them. They do, but it takes a long time. Thrust onto an unprepared population in the midst of economic decline, democracy and capitalism have not yet taken root in Russia. Spain under Franco was a police state, but strong economic growth made a majority of Spaniards middle class, and in the late 1970s Spain moved easily to democracy. If Putin can do something similar for Russia, he may be remembered favorably.

Democracy

Free Media

One of the basic components of democracy—in addition to competitive elections—is a free press. The easiest way to tell if a country is democratic is to see whether its mass media are controlled or muzzled. If television, radio, newspapers, and magazines routinely criticize the regime and remain in business, you probably have a democracy. The government closing these entities down or taking them over is one of the first signs of authoritarianism. Freedom of information is indispensable to democracies but undermines dictatorships.

As Robert Mugabe consolidated his grip on Zimbabwe, critical newspapers were closed down and critical journalists were jailed or expelled. Mugabe's definition of critical was anyone not supporting his regime and its policies. The struggle for democracy in Iran is inseparable from the struggle of independent publications to stay in business. Most are now closed down. Russia has moved sharply in this direction, with most of the national media, especially television, taken over by government-linked corporations and the rest cowed into "self-censorship," afraid that they will be next. The Kremlin, never stating its intentions, forced the oligarchs to relinquish their television networks and newspapers—which had supported first Yeltsin and then Putin in elections. Moscow also prosecutes Russian writers and journalists for critical views. Some are killed, and their killers are never caught. Although not as bad as in Communist times, all of Russia's national media now praise Putin.

Russia: Paranoid or Normal?

"We could have been contenders," Russians seem to be saying. We once had a great empire that challenged the Americans; suddenly it vanished. Although support of client states around the globe was a net drain on the Soviet economy, many Russians were proud of their empire. Some analysts argue that the feeling of belonging to a mighty empire served to quiet discontent over shortages and poor living conditions. Every time a new client signed up—Cuba, Vietnam, Ethiopia, Angola—Russians could say, "See, we really are the wave of the future." The loss of empire was a psychological letdown for Russians.

Russians used to feel they were the equals—maybe the superiors—of the Americans; now the arrogant Americans sneer at Russia. Indeed, it was they who craftily engineered the fall of the Soviet Empire and the collapse of the Soviet Union. Now they are moving in for the kill: the destruction of Russia. What else could the extension of NATO eastward—by adding Central Europe and the Baltic states—mean? See what they did to our little Slavic brother Serbia. The Americans gave Russia little money and a lot of bad economic advice, making sure our economy collapsed. When we were weak, they cut us off.

Remembering the definition of *paranoia*—unreasonable suspicion of others—observers were distressed at Russia's signs of paranoia. The images carried by many Russians are untrue. The Soviet and later Russian systems collapsed from their own chiefly economic weaknesses; it was not a U.S. plot. Moscow rejected most Western economic urgings and then got angry when Western banks refrained from investing. Foreign support for building democracy in Russia is not a plot to take over Russia. Such a victim mentality contributed to the growth of nationalist authoritarianism.

The September 11, 2001, terrorist strikes on America produced a remarkable (but short-lived) shift in Kremlin policy. Putin declared solidarity and cooperation with America. Presidents Bush and Putin exchanged warm visits. Putin announced that Russia's modernization lay with the West, especially with America, and 9/11 gave him the opportunity to put it into practice. Hostility to America in the Russian Duma, media, and military declined—Putin ordered it so. Since the 2003 Iraq War, Russia again turned frosty to America. Paranoia can be turned up or down by government policy.

One of the leading studies of Nazi Germany blamed its rise on "the politics of cultural despair," a situation where everything seems to have failed, where the bonds of civil society have dissolved and nothing has taken their place. How far can despair go before something snaps? Under Yeltsin, Russia was headed for the abyss; Putin seems to have pulled it back just in time.

There is now political stability—but not democracy—in Russia. Under Putin, the economy grew—based heavily on oil and natural gas exports—and few Russians worried about the choking off of pluralism and democracy. Eventually more Russians are likely to care about democracy. Russians are no more inherently ungovernable or authoritarian than Germans or Spaniards, both of whom grew to democracy after World War II. With some decades of stability and prosperity, Russians can do the same.

Key Terms

Caucasus (p. 335)	glasnost (p. 329)	oligarchy (p. 328)
Central Asia (p. 335)	indigenous (p. 328)	rump state (p. 331)
civil society (p. 331)	kleptocracy (p. 328)	socialize (p. 332)

FurtHer Reference

Alexander, James. *Political Culture in Post-Communist Russia: Formlessness and Recreation in a Traumatic Transition*. New York: St. Martin's, 2000.

Bugajski, Janusz. *Cold Peace: Russia's New Imperialism*. Westport, CT: Praeger, 2004.

Fitzpatrick, Sheila. *Tear Off the Masks! Identity and Imposture in Twentieth-Century Russia*. Princeton, NJ: Princeton University Press, 2007.

Hahn, Gordon M. *Russia's Islamic Threat*. New Haven, CT: Yale University Press, 2007.

Lukin, Alexander. *The Political Culture of the Russian "Democrats."* New York: Oxford University Press, 2000.

Meier, Andrew. *Black Earth: A Journey through Russia after the Fall*. New York: Norton, 2003.

Merridale, Catherine. *Night of Stone: Death and Memory in Russia*. London: Granta, 2000.

Pipes, Richard. *Property and Freedom*. New York: Knopf, 1999.

Politkovskaya, Anna. *A Russian Diary: A Journalist's Final Account of Life, Corruption, and Death in Putin's Russia*. New York: Random House, 2007.

Pridemore, William Alex, ed. *Ruling Russia: Law, Crime, and Justice in a Changing Society*. Lanham, MD: Rowman & Littlefield, 2007.

Rose, Richard, William Mishler, and Neil Munro. *Russia Transformed: Developing Popular Support for a New Regime*. New York: Cambridge University Press, 2006.

Shleifer, Andrei. *A Normal Country: Russia after Communism*. Cambridge, MA: Harvard University Press, 2005.

Smith, Kathleen E. *Mythmaking in the New Russia: Politics and Memory in the Yeltsin Era*. Ithaca, NY: Cornell University Press, 2002.

Volkov, Solomon. *The Magical Chorus*. New York: Knopf, 2008.

Chapter 22

Russia:
Patterns of Interaction

Going back two centuries, Russian politics has been a tug-of-war between reformist and conservative forces. Post-Communist Russian politics reflects, and to some extent continues, Soviet and even earlier Russian patterns. Since tsarist times Russia has been a system that cries out for reform but contains many conservative forces able and happy to block reform. A hundred years ago educated Russians could recognize the problem: How to reform the unreformable system? Many have tried, and ultimately all failed to both reform and preserve the system.

Reformers versus Conservatives

The trouble with Russia is that there are few rules or institutions to regulate and moderate political clashes. Without experience in multiparty competition, a free press, voluntary associations, tolerance, and simple politeness, the new forces freed by the ending of Party control started to play a new game without rules. Their clashes were bound to be chaotic, and they were made worse by insiders who used the unregulated privatization to grab state enterprises cheap.

Earlier editions of this book argued that under the uniform surface of political life in the old Soviet Union existed a permanent struggle between liberals and conservatives, the former for major change toward Western models, the latter for standing pat with the essentially Stalinist system. It is here argued that this conflict continues in the post-Soviet era. In the 1990s, how to build democracy was discussed openly, but now discussions are more subdued, as Putin returned Russia to authoritarianism.

Most of the reformers who rallied to Gorbachev and then to Yeltsin resigned or were dismissed from high office. In many respects they hearkened back to the Russian Westernizers of the nineteenth century who wanted to import Western ways nearly wholesale: a market economy, free democracy, and individualistic philosophy. This led the new reformists to attempt the economic **shock therapy** recommended by Columbia economist Jeffrey Sachs, which earlier worked in Bolivia and Poland. In Russia, such therapy was never fully and correctly applied, and the economy plunged downward (see next chapter).

What we are calling here "conservatives" covers a broad swath from moderates to extremists. What they have in common is their opposition to the thorough restructuring of the Russian economy. Russia may need reforms, some concede, but they must be our reforms tailored to our conditions.

Questions to Consider

1. How are we watching an old problem in Russia?
2. What did Khrushchev attempt to do and why? Why did he fail?
3. What is the difference between totalitarian and authoritarian?
4. What did Gorbachev attempt to do and why? Why did he fail?
5. How would you define *conservative* and *liberal* in the Russian context?
6. Who were Russia's *oligarchs* and what became of them?
7. Why did reforms work in Central Europe but not in Russia?
8. Is *semipresidentialism* inherently unstable? Why?
9. Did Putin build an authoritarian system?

PERSONALITIES

FAILED REFORMERS: NIKITA KHRUSHCHEV

The Soviet Union had petrified under Stalin, and Nikita Khrushchev attempted to revitalize the system and get it moving toward communism again. He was only partly and briefly successful, for much of the Soviet party and bureaucracy resisted him. We now realize Khrushchev was far from the undisputed master of the Kremlin that Stalin was and had to overcome opposition. Like Gorbachev, he failed.

Nikita Khrushchev

Born in 1894 of an ethnic Russian family in Ukraine, Khrushchev joined the Bolsheviks shortly after the revolution and worked his way up through party jobs. A protégé of Stalin, Khrushchev did some of the dictator's dirty work in the 1930s, which earned him a full Politburo membership in 1939. During the war he was a political general on the Ukrainian front. After the war he organized party work in Ukraine and then the Moscow region, and carefully packed the party leadership with his supporters, the key to success in Soviet politics.

Stalin's death in 1953 opened a period of jockeying for power. All the Politburo had feared Stalin and longed for stability and personal security. Accordingly, they immediately had the head of the secret police, Lavrenti Beria (like Stalin, a Georgian) shot, putting the KGB under Party control. The first post-Stalin premier was Georgi Malenkov, who advocated relaxing the Stalin system and producing more consumer goods. But Khrushchev was made party first secretary, a post that was always more powerful, and craftily built a coalition against Malenkov, who in 1955 was demoted to minister for power stations. The Soviet leadership abandoned violent death as a way to run a political system.

To consolidate his power and trounce his enemies within the Party, Khrushchev took a dramatic step: He denounced Stalin to a Party congress. A CPSU that was still Stalinist was immobile, incapable of reform or innovation, and blocking the productive potential of the Soviet Union under a blanket of fear and routine. At the Twentieth Party Congress in February 1956, Khrushchev delivered a stinging, hours-long tirade against the "crimes of Stalin" who, he said, had murdered thousands of Party comrades and top military officers. Stalin had built a **cult of personality** that must never be allowed again.

Communist parties the world over had based themselves on Stalin-worship, and when the speech leaked out, all hell broke loose. A Hungarian uprising was crushed by Soviet tanks; Poland nearly revolted. In the West, longtime Communists resigned from the party. In China, Mao Zedong was horrified at Khrushchev for undermining the Communist camp by denouncing its symbol. Thus began the Sino-Soviet split.

To revitalize the Soviet economy, Khrushchev proposed decentralization. Outvoted in the Politburo, he called a 1957 Central Committee meeting packed with his supporters and backed by the army, which forced his opponents, the "antiparty group," to resign. But CPSU leaders grew irritated at his "harebrained schemes" to boost production (especially of consumer goods), eliminate class differences (everyone would have to work before college, even the elites' children), and outfox Americans by placing missiles in Cuba. They considered him a reckless experimenter and liberalizer, and in October 1964 the Politburo *voted* him out of office, a rare thing in Communist systems. He retired and died in 1971.

The Khrushchev era brought major changes in domestic and foreign policy. A generation of young Party members, including Gorbachev, came of age wanting economic reform. These people, "Khrushchev's children," later staffed the Gorbachev reform effort. Khrushchev was a flamboyant, can-do character, who promised major change. He stressed consumer goods over heavy industry, and this infuriated managers and the military. He permitted publication of anti-Stalin works (such as Solzhenitsyn's *One Day*), then backed off when he saw things getting out of hand. Khrushchev was trying to reform against the interests of the Party *apparatchiki,* the same people who brought down Gorbachev.

Some old-line Party types would go back to a centralized command economy. Like the old Russophiles of the nineteenth century, they reject Western models and would turn inward, to Russia's roots; accordingly, they are nationalistic, some rabidly so.

Liberal and conservative camps are halves of the Russian political spectrum that contains several gradations and combinations. Some worried that two extremes of the political spectrum could form a **red-brown** coalition of old Party supporters plus lunatic nationalists. (Moderate conservatives cluster in the Communist party.) Putin's takeover prevented that, so we should not be too critical of him.

> **shock therapy** Sudden replacement of socialist economy by market economy. (See page 341.)
>
> **cult of personality** Dictator who has himself worshiped. (See page 342.)
>
> **red-brown** A possible combination of Communists and Fascists, the brown standing for Hitler's brownshirts.

Under the label "centrist," another group seeks a middle ground of moderate reforms cushioned by continued state subsidies and ownership. Unfortunately, under Yeltsin this approach led to incredible corruption. Thoroughgoing reformers and democrats, such as the small Yabloko party, are weak because few Russians share their Western-type thinking. One interesting possibility emerged with the 1999 Duma elections. Prime Minister and later President Putin, whose Unity (later United Russia) catchall spanned all political views, indicated he could work with the economic reformers of the Union of Right-Wing Forces. Putin, however, has been cautious about economic reforms. He prefers control.

President versus Parliament

Russia's executive and legislative bodies were at serious odds in the 1990s, and their competing claims led to anger and violence. Now the Duma simply obeys Putin. The initial problem, as noted earlier, was the carryover from Soviet times of a Russian parliament elected under the old rules and under the Communists in 1989. Most members of this parliament stood firm with Yeltsin during the abortive coup of 1991.

But then Yeltsin gathered more power into the office of the presidency. The Russian parliament reacted, claiming Yeltsin was becoming dictatorial. They also disliked seeing their own power and perquisites diminished. Some deputies who had earlier counted themselves as reformers began to discover the negative side of reforms and to slide into the conservative camp. To make clear who was in charge, in 1993 Yeltsin sponsored and won a referendum that endorsed both reform and the power of the presidency. Later that year, he pushed through a new constitution with Gaullist-type presidential powers. The last straw was Yeltsin's dissolution of parliament in order to hold new elections; that produced the parliamentary coup attempt of 1993.

Then parliamentary elections turned into slaps at Yeltsin. Some of the biggest votes were for the Communists and other antireform parties. Yeltsin backed down, jettisoned his main reformers, and made a string of cautious reformers his prime ministers but fired each after a few months.

But is this not just democracy in action? An executive starts showing dictatorial tendencies and implements policies that go farther and faster than citizens want, so the citizens, through their elected representatives in parliament, put on the brakes. That is the way the State Duma liked to see itself, but the problem in Russia is trickier. Without major economic reforms, democracy in Russia does not stand a chance. But such reforms are seldom initiated by purely democratic means because they inflict too much pain, at least temporarily. Major reforms need strong executive leadership; a fragmented parliament cannot do it. If the executive is blocked, the result will likely not be democracy but chaos, and out of chaos grows dictatorship.

Democracy

Defining Democracy

Democracy is not a simple thing or one that automatically grows after *authoritarian* or *totalitarian* regimes have fallen. We were naïve about stable democracy soon coming to Russia and Iraq. Democracy is a complex balancing act, requiring (as we explored in the last chapter) a political culture with the right philosophical, moral, economic, and legal underpinnings. Most definitions of democracy include the following:

Accountability.   Elected officials inevitably face a real possibility of losing reelection. This induces them to adopt Friedrich's *rule of anticipated reactions* (see page 68).

Equality.   One person, one vote. No citizens can be excluded. All may run for office.

Competition.   Several candidates and parties compete in free and fair elections. A one-party system cannot be democratic.

Alternation.   Occasional turnovers in power replace the "in" party with the "out" party.

Representation.   "The room will not hold all," so a few fairly represent the many. The electoral system does this, either by single-member districts (as in the United States and Britain) or proportional representation (as in Germany and Sweden).

Free media.   Only democracies permit the press to criticize the government. This is the quickest check for democracy.

Harvard's Samuel Huntington suggested a "two-turnover test" for stable democracy. Two alternations of government—the "outs" replacing the "ins"—indicate a firmly rooted democracy. Since the Polish Communist regime fell in 1989, Poland has had several turnovers from left to right and back again, indicating stable democracy. Russia has not had a turnover since 1991 and is not soon likely to. No turnovers, no democracy.

Freedom House in New York uses a seven-point scale to annually rank countries on how much they accord citizens political rights and civil liberties. This is basically the same as democracy. FH calls 1 to 2.5 "free," 3 to 5 "partly free," and 5.5 to 7 "not free." Russia slid lower during the Putin years. Some of FH's 2008 findings are shown in the table below.

United States	1.0	free
Canada	1.0	free
Britain	1.0	free
Japan	1.5	free
Brazil	2.0	free
Mexico	2.5	free
India	2.5	free
Turkey	3.0	partly free
Nigeria	4.0	partly free
Russia	5.5	not free
Iran	6.0	not free
China	6.5	not free
Cuba	7.0	not free

The Taming of the Oligarchs

Moscow privatized ("piratized" might be more accurate) the Russian economy in such a way as to make a few people incredibly wealthy. Clever wheeler-dealers, some of them already in management—who understood the value of state-owned firms, chiefly in the oil and natural-gas industries—bought them ultracheap with borrowed money. Most of what they did was legal because there were few laws in these areas. Russia privatized badly.

totalitarianism   Attempts to totally control society, as under Stalin and Hitler.

authoritarianism   Dictatorial rejection of democracy, as Spain under Franco and Chile under Pinochet.

These oligarchs, as they were soon called, either had or quickly developed ties to leading politicians. One of the best-known oligarchs was Boris Berezovsky, a former math professor turned used-car king and then media and oil magnate. Berezovsky's money, newspapers, and TV network helped first Yeltsin and then Putin win election. Putin then had Berezovsky prosecuted and shorn of most of his properties. Berezovsky now lives in Britain, where he has been the target of assassination attempts.

Key Concepts

Totalitarian versus Authoritarian

Since the 1930s, political science has debated the nature of modern dictatorships. Some political scientists developed theories and models of **totalitarianism** to explain Mussolini's Italy, Hitler's Germany, and Stalin's Soviet Union. Carl J. Friedrich and Zbigniew Brzezinski argued that totalitarian dictatorships have these six points in common:

1. An official ideology
2. A single, disciplined party
3. Terroristic police control
4. Party monopoly of the mass media
5. Party control of the armed forces
6. Central direction of the economy

Widely accepted for years, the totalitarian model gradually came under criticism as unrealistic and oversimplified. Far from total, the systems of Mussolini, Hitler, and Stalin were quite messy. Many citizens knew the regimes were frauds; plans were often just improvisations. The dictators like their systems to *look* total. Totalitarianism was an attempt at total control that always fell short.

The word "totalitarianism" fell into disfavor; instead the word **authoritarianism** was used to describe modern dictatorships. It can be quite brutal but does not aim for total control of society. Politics is in the hands of a dictator, such as Spain's Franco or Chile's Pinochet, but wide areas of the economy and cultural life are open. Most or all of the above six points are missing.

Political scientist Jeane J. Kirkpatrick in 1980 argued there are still useful distinctions between the two terms. Authoritarian regimes, more loose and open, can change and reform themselves into democracies. This happened throughout Latin America in the 1980s. Totalitarian systems, especially Communist ones, she argued, cannot reform; they are too rigid. In a way, Kirkpatrick was right. The Communist regimes of East Europe and the Soviet Union never did reform; they collapsed.

Personalities

Failed Reformers: Mikhail Gorbachev

Mikhail Gorbachev

"Life punishes those who delay," said the Soviet president in 1989 as he urged the East German Communist regime to reform before it was too late. The East Berlin regime ignored Gorbachev and collapsed. But Mikhail Sergeyevich Gorbachev did not grasp that he, too, was engaging in delayed and halfway reforms that collapsed the Soviet regime and his own tenure in power.

Amid great hopes Gorbachev assumed the top Soviet political position—Party general secretary—in 1985. The Soviet Union had gradually run down during Brezhnev's eighteen-year reign; growth slumped while cynicism, alcoholism, and corruption grew. Two elderly temporaries, Andropov and Chernenko, followed as the Soviet system atrophied. Gorbachev—age fifty-four, a mere kid in Politburo terms—announced wide-ranging reforms to shake up the Soviet system.

Born into a peasant family in the North Caucasus in 1931, Gorbachev graduated in law from Moscow University in 1955 and returned to his home area for Party work. As Party chief of Stavropol province in 1970, he impressed Brezhnev, who summoned him to Moscow in 1978 to oversee agriculture. (Gorbachev had taken another degree, in agronomy, by correspondence.) Gorbachev by now was under the wing of Andropov, head of the KGB, and Mikhail Suslov, a Politburo kingmaker from Stavropol. Gorbachev was elected to the Party's Central Committee in 1971, to candidate member of the Politburo in 1979, and to full member in 1980. When Andropov took over in 1982, Gorbachev assisted him closely and implemented his tough anticorruption policies.

In 1985 Gorbachev began his reforms as the hero who would turn the Soviet Union into a modern, possibly democratic, system. He announced "new thinking" in foreign policy that led to arms control agreements with the United States and to the freeing of East Europe from the Communist regimes imposed by Stalin after World War II. With these steps, the Cold War ended.

Gorbachev ordered *glasnost* in the Soviet media, which became more pluralist, honest, and critical. Corrupt big shots were fired. Gorbachev also urged *demokratizatzia;* competitive elections were introduced, and a partially elected parliament convened.

Gorbachev first tried to fix the economic system with old remedies: verbal exhortations, anti-alcohol campaigns, "acceleration," and importing foreign technology. After hesitating too long, he ordered **perestroika**, which slowly began to decentralize and liberalize the Soviet economy. Farms and factories made more of their own decisions and kept more of their own profits. Private businesses called "cooperatives" were permitted to grow. But it was too little, too late. By 1989 economic disaster loomed. Economic dislocations lowered Soviet living and dietary standards and angered everyone.

With a freer press, the many nationalities (including Russians) demanded greater autonomy or even independence. Violence between ethnic groups flared. The *apparat* and *nomenklatura* sabotaged economic reforms by hoarding food and raw materials. Some generals and the KGB indicated they would not stand for the growing chaos, which would have soon led to the dismemberment of the Soviet Union, so Gorbachev pulled back from reforms and tightened up in late 1990.

In early 1991 Gorbachev appeared to favor reform again. In opposition, conservative hardliners in his own cabinet—handpicked by Gorbachev—attempted a coup against him in August 1991 (see page 316). The coup failed due to splits in the Soviet armed forces and the stubbornness of Russian President Boris Yeltsin, who then pushed a weakened Gorbachev from office and broke up the Soviet Union by pulling the vast Russian federation out of it.

In part, Gorbachev had himself to blame for the Soviet collapse. He dawdled too long and changed course too many times. He sought to preserve the Party and "socialism" and never did adopt an economic reform plan. Life indeed punished him who delayed.

Russia's oligarchs did not act like the old U.S. "robber barons," who invested and then reinvested to make the economy and jobs grow. Russian oligarchs simply stripped assets from their companies—for example, selling oil abroad—and did not reinvest the money but stashed it in foreign (Swiss, Cayman Islands, Cyprus) banks. They did not like paying taxes or competing in a free market. As they got rich, the Russian economy got poor.

> **perestroika** Russian for "restructuring"; Gorbachev's proposals to reform the Soviet economy. (See page 346.)

Russians, with their penchant for equality, hated the oligarchs and liked how President Putin cracked down on them. Most are in jail or in exile. His *siloviki* targeted some for tax evasion (in a system where everyone cheats on taxes) and forced them to turn over their companies—including oil and gas industries, television networks, and newspapers—to government fronts. Under Putin, most of the big Russian media came under state control, and few dared criticize him.

Several oligarchs, fearing prosecution, fled abroad. One, Mikhail Khodorkovsky, lost his huge (and well-run) Yukos oil firm, allegedly for fraud and not paying taxes but more likely for trying to bring in U.S. partners. He got a show trial and nine years in prison. Putin brought Yukos under state control by having the Kremlin-controlled Rosneft buy it cheap. Like many Russians, he felt that something as important as energy should never have been privatized. Putin also wanted to stop Khodorkovsky from becoming a political rival.

Now smaller, tame insiders, either government officials or those beholden to Putin, are allowed to take over major industries and the media. They kick back money to the Kremlin, and top Russian politicians have become extremely wealthy. The unseen struggle over who gets what industry is an important part of Russian politics. In effect, the oligarch system continues, but without the original oligarchs and now under Kremlin control. Another name for this process is corruption. Western executives call Russia one of the most corrupt countries in the world. (For a ranking of corrupt countries, see page 535). The original oligarchs were egregious, greedy, and sometimes criminal, but their television stations and newspapers gave Russia a brief period of freedom of information.

COMPARISON

SEMIPRESIDENTIALISM IN RUSSIA

Borrowing the French model, which has both an executive president and a premier, Russia borrowed its problems as well. President Yeltsin, in eight years in office, had six prime ministers, some lasting just a few months. An erratic drunk, Yeltsin tried to deflect blame away from himself for Russia's economic collapse and to appease an opposition-dominated Duma. But there were other, deeper causes for the mess.

As we discussed in France, semipresidential systems may be inherently unstable. French semipresidentialism actually worked as written only when *cohabitation* forced the president to share powers with a prime minister.

Most semipresidential systems tilt strongly to a powerful president. Yeltsin would stand for no cut in his presidential power. He really did have dictatorial tendencies. His throwaway prime ministers were a crude attempt at cohabitation that made no one happy and hurt Russia's chances for democracy. One solution: Get rid of this crazy semipresidential system. In effect—without rewriting the constitution—Putin did this by assuming virtually all power. His premiers, like those of de Gaulle, were simply messenger boys. Putin in 2008 became premier himself and made the president his messenger boy. It is still an unstable system.

PERSONALITIES

FAILED REFORMERS: BORIS YELTSIN

Gorbachev was the first *prezident* (they use the loan word) of the Soviet Union. Boris Yeltsin was the first *prezident* of the Russian Federation. As with Gorbachev, both Russians and the world initially hailed Yeltsin as a great reformer who would make a prosperous and peaceful Russia. Both disappointed with halfway, half-hearted reforms that ruined the economy and their approval ratings. Neither were convinced democrats; by background and training both acted like Party big shots. Yeltsin, who resigned the presidency at the end of 1999 and died in 2007, was a gutsy risk taker who put his career and even his life on the line.

Born in 1931 (as was Gorbachev) near Sverdlovsk (now Yekaterinburg) in the southern Urals of a poor peasant family, Yeltsin studied engineering and worked in the housing industry in his hometown. Joining the Party in 1961 at age thirty, Yeltsin was promoted to the Central Committee in 1976. He was noticed as an energetic manager and reformer, and Gorbachev elevated him to head the Moscow Party organization in 1985 and made him a candidate member of the Politburo. A natural populist, Yeltsin, unlike other Soviet leaders, mingled with the people and denounced the privileges of the *nomenklatura*. The common people rallied to him.

Then came a bizarre series of events that, if the Soviet system had not been collapsing, would have led to Yeltsin's permanent banishment if not imprisonment. In a 1987 speech to the Central Committee, Yeltsin attacked Party conservatives by name for dragging their feet on reform. For that, he was relieved of his Party posts and demoted.

But he bounced back. In the first partly competitive election in 1989, he ran on his populist credentials and easily won election to parliament, where he criticized Gorbachev for dawdling on reforms. Shifting his attention to the Russian (as opposed to the Soviet) government, Yeltsin won election to the Russian parliament in 1990. Yeltsin sensed that the

Boris Yeltsin

Soviet Union was doomed, but Russia would survive. In July 1990 Yeltsin resigned from the Party and was now free to be as critical as he wished. As a non-Communist, he won fair elections to become president of the Russian Federation in 1991. This gave him another edge on Gorbachev, who had never been popularly elected to anything.

In the attempted coup of 1991, Yeltsin became a hero, standing firm on a tank in front of the Russian parliament. Mocking Gorbachev as an indecisive weakling, Yeltsin pulled the Russian Federation out of the Soviet Union in late 1991, thus collapsing the entire structure. Conservatives think it was a terrible mistake to break up the Soviet Union.

As president, Yeltsin went from bad to worse. Frequently drunk or ill, Yeltsin and his ministers bungled privatization, the economy tanked, corruption soared, and Russians turned bitterly against him. Consulting with no one, Yeltsin ordered the crushing of breakaway Chechnya (see page 361). Although reelected in 1996 as the lesser of two evils, during his last years in office Yeltsin's public approval rating was under 5 percent. The Duma tried to impeach him but was too divided. One of Yeltsin's favorite stunts was, every few months, to blame his prime ministers for economic failures and replace them. One of the questions of today's Russia is whether a first president other than Yeltsin could have done things differently or better.

THE TWO MAFIAS

The **mafia** (Russians use the loan word *mafiya*) is an important interest group in Russia, for it stands for much more than the criminal un-
derworld. In Russia, the word covers at least two levels of meanings.

mafia   A criminal conspiracy.

At the street level, local strongarm rackets make sure virtually all businesses pay protection money
and make fake deals. *Keelers* enforce things and do contract hits. At a higher level, *siloviki* connected
to and serving the Kremlin are allowed to run major industries. Anyone in their way or who annoys

COMPARISON

THE TIMING OF REFORMS

In addition to the cultural factors we have already discussed, the timing or *sequencing* of reforms can make
a crucial difference to the successful founding of
democracy. The differences in timing between what
happened in Central Europe and what happened in Russia are instructive.

First, in Central Europe (Poland, Czechoslovakia, and
Hungary) a broad anti-Communist movement formed
while the Communists were still in power. By the time
liberal Communists held free elections in 1989 or 1990,
an aware electorate completely voted the Communists
out of power. It was a new broom sweeping clean. The
initial winner was the broad catchall of anti-Communist
forces, the leader of which became either the president
(Walesa of Poland and Havel of Czechoslovakia) or the
prime minister (Antall of Hungary). Later, these
catchalls fell apart, but they had done their job: Communism was out, and democracy and market economies
were established. In a few years these countries joined
NATO and the EU.

In Russia, there was no new broom and the old one
did not sweep clean. There was no nationwide anti-
Communist catchall movement like Solidarity or Civic
Forum. The Communists never allowed that. Instead,
the Communists held semifree elections but did not
allow themselves to be voted out of power. Gorbachev,
who was never elected anything, stayed in office believing he was supervising important reforms.

But Gorbachev still faced major conservative (that is,
Party) forces and continually changed course in the face
of them. Sensing his weakness, Party conservatives attempted to overthrow him. After their defeat, the Party
was finally ousted from office (late 1991) but was still
influential in parliament, industry, and the countryside.
Yeltsin, with no mass movement behind him, attempted serious reform but was still blocked by conservative
forces, some of them remnants of the Party.

If Russia had done it like Central Europe, there would
have been multiparty elections in late 1991 instead of
late 1993. At the earlier date, there might have been
sufficient enthusiasm to elect a proreform majority; by
the latter date, the declining economy had produced
despair and a backlash. This happened in Central Europe as well; in both Poland and Hungary economic
hardship gave electoral wins to their Socialist parties
(ex-Communists). But by then both democracy and the
market economy were established and could not be
rolled back. The Socialists had no intention of dismantling a working market system; instead, they made
minor adjustments in the "social safety net" of Poland
and Hungary.

The desirable sequence, as illustrated by Central Europe: First, form a broad mass movement; second, thoroughly oust the Communists in elections; third,
institute political and economic reforms. The Russians
tried to do it backward.

runaway system   Influential people use their resources to amass more resources.

the regime gets murdered—bankers, reformers, defectors (Alexander Litvinenko, poisoned in London), journalists (including top muckraker Anna Politkovskaya), old people (for their apartments), American businessmen, and Duma members. Most "banks" are simply money-laundering operations.

And no one is brought to justice, indicating the regime either hires the contract killers or orders the police not to interfere. The FSB could solve such cases but does not. Putin controls the FSB. As we shall see in our discussions of the developing areas, the hallmark of the Third World is the penetration of crime into politics. In this respect, Russia has regressed to Third World status.

Russian mafiosi flaunt their new wealth, flashy cars (any make you can name, often stolen), clothes, lady friends, and parties. The average Russian hates those who rapidly enriched themselves as they degraded Russia, and this hatred feeds support for politicians who vow to crack down on them. Thus, lawlessness helped President Putin consolidate his power, although he did little to end it. Russians have long argued that without strict supervision and draconic controls they are the most lawless of peoples. Americans, they say, have internal controls that Russians have not. Historically, freedom in Russia meant chaos and bloody anarchy, and many Russians have welcomed rule by a strong hand, however harsh.

The Army

When a country is in chaos, the army becomes a major player, sometimes injecting itself directly into the political system. The Soviet army played a role in the process of attempted reform; namely, some sectors of the Red Army saw the need for economic changes in order to boost military technology

Key Concepts

Runaway Systems

We earlier (in Chapter 20) referred to Vladimir Putin as authoritarian, a strong ruler who concentrated power in his own hands but preserved democratic forms. Is it likely that Russia and Putin will tend toward greater authoritarianism? The process seems to be already underway.

Yale political scientist Robert Dahl noted that powerful people tend to use their resources (legal, political, economic) to gain more resources. If there are no counterbalancing institutions or strong laws to check them, some amass power without limit: Stalin. Engineers call this a **runaway system**, which keeps concentrating power until it breaks. (Example: The New York Yankees use their resources to buy more top ballplayers, who win more games, which nets the Yankees even

more resources, which enable them to buy . . .) More than unbalanced personalities, this is the product of lawless systems in which any loss of control leads to overthrow. The presidents of Syria or the Congo cannot be nice, easygoing guys. Leaders in such lands must be control freaks; relaxation soon ends in their deaths.

Putin is a test case for the runaway-systems theory. Gradually and skillfully—never revealing his ultimate intentions—he amassed power. Did he reach a point where he had "enough" power, or did he always seek more? One indicator: Did Putin step down in 2008 after his two four-year terms, or did he make himself prime minister with all power in his hands? Did Putin name and supervise a puppet president? Could Putin, after an interval, become president again?

to catch up with the Americans. In 1983 the chief of the Soviet General Staff, Marshal Nikolai Ogarkov, told *New York Times* editor Leslie Gelb that the Soviet military was falling behind technologically. He was later pushed out of command for his outspokenness. "Modern military power is based upon technology," he told Gelb, "and technology is based upon computers," an area where the Americans were well ahead. His conclusion:

> We will never be able to catch up with you in modern arms until we have an economic revolution. And the question is whether we can have an economic revolution without a political revolution.

The price of military backwardness became clear with the quick U.S.-led victory over Soviet-equipped Iraq in early 1991. Late that year, portions of the Soviet army participated in a coup.

The new Russian armed forces are much smaller (nominally 1.2 million members) than the old Soviet armed forces (some 4 million) but still in a wretched condition. Many soldiers and officers have to work off-base. (In comparison, U.S. armed forces total 1.5 million and are superbly fed and led.) Russian armed forces are absurdly top-heavy, with as many officers as enlisted soldiers (U.S. ratio: 1:6). Officers, fearful of losing their jobs and starved for decent housing, are angry. Soldiers go unpaid for months and have to grow much of their own food. Hundreds of conscripts, hazed and starved, commit suicide each year. Most young men ignore the twice-yearly draft calls.

DEMOCRACY

TRANSITIONS TO DEMOCRACY

The spread of democratic regimes in the late twentieth century—what Harvard's Samuel Huntington called democracy's "third wave"—provoked much theorizing and attempts to find common patterns. Some thinkers saw democracy arising after economic growth produced a large, educated middle class (see page 411). Some saw it as going through similar stages—opening, breakthrough, and consolidation—but others saw "multiple paths" to democracy. Several said it needed agreement among elites—a "pacted transition"—to work. Many found that early institutional choices produced "path-dependent development" that deepened democracy with each successful attempt.

By the early twenty-first century, however, doubts arose about "transitology," as it was derisively dubbed. Some theories of transition explained the coming of democracy in one cultural area (such as Latin America) but not others (such as East Asia). Even in the Communist lands of East Europe, the relatively smooth transition to democracy in Central Europe was not duplicated in the Balkans. One size did not fit all. None of the theories fit Russia.

The toughest question asked: "Do all transitions lead to democracy?" Transitologists tended to assume that they did, but this was not always the case. Some countries enjoyed only brief democratic interludes (Peru, Ecuador, Venezuela) but became unstable or quasi-authoritarian. Huntington noted long ago that after every wave of democracy washes in, a reverse wave washes out, as in the rise of the totalitarian dictatorships between the two world wars. Many countries, including Russia, stalled in authoritarianism with democratic trappings.

Theories in political science seldom last more than a generation. They can yield new insights, provided we do not reify them. Theories are only attempts to get a handle on reality; they are not reality itself. Take all theories with a grain of salt. (For more on the dangers of theorizing too much, see the next chapter, page 356.)

Several leading generals either supported the 1991 coup or did not oppose it. Many Soviet higher officers were fired. One, Marshal Sergei Akhromeyev, committed suicide. The Soviet armed forces had been consuming a quarter of the country's gross domestic product, a figure that was cut drastically. The army is still one of the few semistable institutions in Russia and, if Russia's strong presidency ever weakens, could play a direct political role.

When a political system starts falling apart, whatever groups are best organized amid growing chaos are most likely to seize power. This usually means the army. (See the box entitled "The Praetorian Tendency" on page 532.) In some developing countries, military coup is the standard way to change governments. Some believe the Russian army could play such a role, although historically it never has. In 1991 and 1993 the military was divided and most of it hung back, afraid of being used by politicians and of starting a civil war among army units.

The army is surely an interest group within Kremlin politics, and it is an angry one, having suffered several humiliations. Gorbachev tried to limit its size. In 1988 he admitted that the Soviet invasion of Afghanistan had been a mistake and withdrew Soviet forces. In 1989 he gave up East Europe, which the Soviet military defined as a defensive shield. In 1994–1996 Chechen "bandits" beat them; in revenge in 1999 the army began the merciless demolition of Chechnya. Many high officers resent the retreat of Russian power and their shrinking defense budget and manpower. They are also highly nationalistic and see an American plot in the eastward expansion of NATO and U.S. presence in Central Asia. Putin's defense minister, former KGB colleague Sergei Ivanov, wanted to reduce draft calls in favor of a professional and volunteer army like that of the United States.

TRANSITION TO WHAT?

Over the last third of a century, democracy spread, leaving most of the world's nations (over a hundred) democratic to some degree. Starting in the mid-1970s, democracy replaced dictatorships in Portugal, Spain, and Greece, and then in Latin America, East Asia, and finally, in late 1989, in East Europe. Soon academics developed theories to explain the growth of democracy (see box on page 351). Some applied them to the collapse of the Soviet Union and to the new institutions of a democratic Russia. They did not fit.

The collapse of the Soviet system was unique, one of a kind. Much of the old system carried over into the new, stunting the growth of democracy. Culturally, only a minority understood or wished genuine democracy. Economically, Russia collapsed under Yeltsin; people feared chaos and breakup of the federation. Putin was the necessary if authoritarian corrective to this slide. As a friend and supporter of democracy, I am sad to admit this, but if it had not been Putin, it would have been someone worse.

KEY TERMS

authoritarianism (p. 345)	perestroika (p. 347)	shock therapy (p. 343)
cult of personality (p. 343)	red-brown (p. 343)	totalitarianism (p. 345)
mafia (p. 349)	runaway system (p. 350)	

FURTHER REFERENCE

Aron, Leon. *Russia's Revolution: Essays, 1989–2006.* Washington, D.C.: AEI Press, 2007.

Barany, Zoltan. *Democratic Breakdown and the Decline of the Russian Military.* Princeton, NJ: Princeton University Press, 2007.

Beissinger, Mark R. *Nationalist Mobilization and the Collapse of the Soviet State.* New York: Cambridge University Press, 2002.

Breslauer, George W. *Gorbachev and Yeltsin as Leaders.* New York: Cambridge University Press, 2002.

Brown, Archie. *Seven Years That Changed the World: Perestroika in Perspective.* New York: Oxford University Press, 2007.

Desai, Padma. *Conversations on Russia: Reform from Yeltsin to Putin.* New York: Oxford University Press, 2006.

Fursenko, Aleksander, and Timothy Naftali. *Khrushchev's Cold War: The Inside Story of an American Adversary.* New York: Norton, 2006.

Lovell, Stephen. *Destination in Doubt: Russia since 1989.* New York: Palgrave, 2006.

Lynch, Allen C. *How Russia Is Not Ruled: Reflections on Russian Political Development.* New York: Cambridge University Press, 2005.

Satter, David. *Darkness at Dawn: The Rise of the Russian Criminal State.* New Haven, CT: Yale University Press, 2003.

Shevtsova, Lilia. *Russia—Lost in Transition: The Yeltsin and Putin Legacies.* Washington, D.C.: Carnegie Endowment, 2007.

Stoner-Weiss, Kathryn. *Resisting the State: Reform and Retrenchment in Post-Soviet Russia.* New York: Cambridge University Press, 2006.

Taubman, William. *Khrushchev: The Man and His Era.* New York: Norton, 2003.

Wilson, Andrew. *Virtual Politics: Faking Democracy in the Post Soviet World.* New Haven, CT: Yale University Press, 2005.

Chapter 23
What Russians Quarrel About

We are interested in why the Soviet Union collapsed not out of purely historical curiosity but to serve as a warning about what can go wrong again. Whatever happened to the Soviet Union can happen to Russia; the problems and resistance Khrushchev, Gorbachev, and Yeltsin faced, Putin still faces. The question is also part of current Russian politics.

Why the Soviet Union Collapsed

Many Russians, especially strong nationalists, refuse to believe that the Soviet Union collapsed largely because of the inherent economic inefficiency of socialism. They blame sinister forces, especially the Americans, the functional equivalent of the "stab in the back" myth that so harmed Weimar Germany.

The real explanation is that socialist economies—meaning state-owned and centrally planned, "Communist," if you prefer—work poorly. They do not collapse overnight but slowly run down over time. Under certain circumstances, to be sure, centrally planned economies can grow fast, as did the Soviet Union under Stalin's Five-Year Plans in the 1930s. A backward country borrowed capitalist technology and threw all its resources, including labor, into giant projects, chiefly into making steel and then making things from steel. From the 1930s through the 1960s, many observers assumed that the Soviet Union would catch up with and eventually overtake the United States in terms of economic production.

But as the Soviet Union tried to catch up, its economy became more complex and harder to control. Gosplan's **input-output tables** required hundreds of mathematicians to make the thousands of calculations necessary to set the targets of the Soviet economy on a centralized basis. Product quality was poor, as only quantity was calculated and required. Designs, often copied from old Western products, were out of date. Efficiency counted for nothing; there was not even a Russian word for efficiency (the closest was "effective"). Many factories produced things nobody wanted.

The consumer sector, deliberately shortchanged, offered too few products to motivate Soviet workers, who had to wait years for an apartment or a car. Accordingly, workers did not exert themselves but instead chuckled: "They pretend to pay us, and we pretend to work." Many took

QUESTIONS TO CONSIDER

1. What is to blame for Russia's current troubles?
2. Why did political scientists fail to grasp the decay of the Soviet Union?
3. Is it fair to compare Poland's economic *shock therapy* with Russia's?
4. Does Russia now have capitalism? Why or why not?
5. What happened to Russia's economy in 1998? How does it compare to Mexico?
6. What happened in Chechnya? Could similar things occur?
7. What is the *near abroad* and why do Russians want it?
8. What are the difficulties of "middle ways"?

Key Concepts

Lacking Facts, They Theorized

The most stupendous change of the late twentieth century took political scientists by surprise. Why did we political scientists fail to anticipate—notice that I use the word "anticipate" rather than "predict"—the collapse of the Soviet Union? Only a handful of historians and economists sounded warnings. A demographer made the most accurate prediction: Nicholas Eberstadt examined the statistical decline of Soviet health and saw doom years in advance. Political scientists tended to see more of the same, with some reforms.

So why did political scientists miss the signs of impending collapse? There were several mental blocks that we built for ourselves, mostly by reading each others' books and articles, what intelligence officers call "incestuous amplification."

1. *Lousy Empirical Data*. Much of the Soviet system was secret; we had to piece together flimsy indicators and infer how the system worked. We filled the informational vacuum with theory, much of it misleading. In Yugoslavia, by way of contrast, scholars could get accurate data and candid interviews. As early as the 1960s some saw cracks in the Yugoslav federation. Little theory came out of studies of Yugoslavia, as researchers did not need to theorize; they had facts. Lacking facts, Soviet specialists theorized. The moral: We are only as good as our data.

2. *Systems Theory*. Since the 1960s, political scientists had been trained to see all countries as *political systems* that have varying structures but perform the same functions. Whenever the system is thrown off balance, it always corrects itself, by new leaders, parties, or reforms. Systems were thus presumed to be highly durable, possibly immortal. Systems theorists could not imagine system collapse.

3. *Anti-Anticommunism*. The anticommunist hysteria of the early Cold War years, especially McCarthyism, was so primitive that some thinkers gave Communist systems the benefit of the doubt. Specialists tended to accept Communist systems as givens (as did systems theorists) and to conduct detailed studies of how they worked. Anyone who suggested Communist systems were inherently flawed and doomed was read out of the profession as speculative, right wing, and unscholarly.

4. *Undervaluing Economics*. Many Soviet specialists paid little attention to economics; they assumed that politics dominated economics. (Economists assume the opposite.) Few appreciated that a deteriorating economy eventually drags the entire country down with it. Some economists called attention to the Soviet economic decline for years, but political scientists largely ignored the economists.

5. *System Reformability*. Political scientists supposed Soviet problems could be fixed with reforms. (This, too, derives from systems theory.) If the system has an economic or structural problem, it will correct it, was the bland assumption. Eventually, some thought, the Soviet system would reform itself into a social-democratic welfare state. The brittleness of the Soviet system occurred to few.

6. *Fixation on Personalities*. Because reforms are necessary, they will be carried out; they just need the right personality. Ah! Here comes Gorbachev, the man both the United States and the Russian liberals have been waiting for. His reforms will produce a much nicer Soviet Union. In this way, we read into Gorbachev heroic and reformist qualities he never had.

afternoons off to shop for scarce goods; standing in lines took hours each week. These and other factors made Soviets angry with the system. By the early 1970s, the Soviet economy slowed, especially in comparison to the surging economies of West Europe and the Pacific Rim.

> **input-output table**   Spreadsheet for economy of entire nation. (See page 355.)

This by itself, however, was not enough to bring down the system, which could have lumbered on in shabby decay. The real killer was technological backwardness, especially as it impinged on the Soviet military. Computers were transforming Western businesses, research labs, and military systems. The Soviets fell behind in computerization, and the Soviet military knew what that meant: getting beat. (See the words of Marshal Ogarkov on page 351.) Along with U.S. President Ronald Reagan came technological menace: a "Star Wars" shield in space that would make America invulnerable. An important sector of the Soviet military thus turned to economic and technological reform out of the fear of falling behind.

Many thinking Soviet Party people, especially younger ones, knew by the 1980s that economic reforms were necessary and were eager for someone like Gorbachev to lead the way. But by themselves, they could not prevail against the conservative forces of managers and *apparatchiki*, many of whose jobs were at stake. It took, I believe, the high-tech sections of the armed forces to ally themselves with Gorbachev and give the green light to economic reforms in the expectation that these would lead to military technology to equal the Americans.

Oil plays a roller-coaster role in first boosting and then sinking the Soviet/Russian economy. The rapid increase in oil prices in the 1970s meant that Soviet petroleum exports—at that time the USSR was the world's biggest oil producer and exporter—could for a few years pay for Soviet imports of food and technology. When oil prices fell, so did the Soviet Union. Now Russia is again too dependent on oil exports. Current high world oil prices bring Russia incredible earnings and taxes, but on a shaky, one-product basis.

How to Reform?

At no time did Mikhail Gorbachev adopt a thoroughgoing plan for economic reform. His advisors presented him with several plans, each one bolder than the previous one, but he never implemented any of them. He never wanted capitalism; instead, he sought a middle path or "third way" between capitalism and socialism. Gorbachev hesitated and changed his mind more or less annually, one year being for economic reform, the next year being against it. Later he admitted several mistakes. First, he now says, he should have liberalized agriculture, as the Chinese did under Deng (see page 392). Instead, Gorbachev tried a couple of timid steps that he inherited from his mentor, the late Andropov: "intensification" and an anti-alcohol campaign. Both failed.

When it came to real reforms, Gorbachev choked, both out of fear of the consequences and in the face of massive resistance by conservative Soviet forces. Gorbachev finally freed most prices, but he did not privatize industry. The result was far too many rubles chasing too few goods: inflation. Everyone wanted dollars as the ruble dwindled in value. Worried citizens muttered that things could not go on in this manner. It was against this background that Gorbachev's own cabinet plotted a coup in 1991. Before the year ended, the Soviet Union was dissolved, Gorbachev was a private citizen, and Yeltsin was president of the Russian Federation. At last, reform started looking serious, but Yeltsin, too, faced opposition from conservative forces.

From the Rubble of the Ruble

The Russian economy is now growing nicely. With the right policies, growth could have happened much sooner. Gorbachev never restructured the Soviet economy. Yeltsin did not fully restructure the Russian economy. Are we asking for the impossible? Poland initiated a *shock therapy* at the beginning of 1991 and within two years had gone through the worst of its inflation and industrial decline and for several years was the fastest growing economy of Europe.

asset-stripping   Selling off firm's property and raw materials for short-term profit.

public finances   What a government takes in, what it spends, and how it makes up the difference.

Yeltsin's first prime minister (until late 1992) and later finance minister, the dynamic reformer Yegor Gaidar, tried sudden shock therapy as he privatized the large, obsolete industrial enterprises the Communists had built. Terribly inefficient and overstaffed and with no concern for consumer needs, many Soviet plants actually *subtracted* value from the raw materials they processed. But these industries were the wealth and power of the bureaucrats and *apparatchiks* who ran them and gave employment to those who listlessly worked in them. Accordingly, they were able to pressure Moscow to keep the subsidies flowing. In any rational system, they would have been declared bankrupt. But you cannot throw millions of people out of work all at once, protested many Russians.

Privatization in Russia (and some other ex-Communist lands) was carried out badly. A handful of clever operators bought up factories and raw materials cheap and turned themselves into a new class of capitalists. Many of these industries still got government subsidies (such as cheap energy), which allowed the new owners to reap enormous profits as they exported oil, natural gas, and minerals. Much of the profit did not return to Russia, though; it went into foreign banks, a pattern typical of South America. Because this capital was not recycled back into the Russian economy, the rest of the economy declined, making poor people poorer. Capitalism in Russia began as **asset-stripping**, which is no basis for long-term future. Only recently has it begun to work like capitalism elsewhere, with capitalists reinvesting their money inside Russia.

In August 1998 the dysfunctional economy crashed. Some observers saw trouble coming well in advance, in the area of **public finances**. Russia was collecting less than half the taxes it was supposed to. Everyone cheated on taxes. As a result, the budget went dangerously into deficit, so the Yeltsin government simply printed more money. Banks—and anyone in Russia could open a bank—were unregulated and made unsecured

Apartment houses in Russia are prefabricated and small. There is a terrible housing shortage, so flats like these in a Moscow suburb are eagerly sought.

loans to friends. The chief monetary instrument of Russian banks were U.S. $100 bills, some of them counterfeit. Knowing the perils of the Russian economy, Russian oligarchs stashed between $150 billion and $350 billion in **flight capital** offshore. Eventually, this system had to crash. When it did, in 1998, the ruble lost some three-quarters of its value in relation to **hard currencies**. Many banks closed, leaving depositors with nothing. Russia's fledgling stock markets dived. Some industries collapsed. Russia **defaulted** on its loans (biggest losers: German banks, with over $30 billion lent to Russia) and had to beg for new credit. Badly burned, foreign investors fled Russia.

flight capital   Money that the owner sends out of the country for fear of losing it.

hard currency   Noninflating, recognized currencies used in international dealings, such as dollars and euros.

default   Not being able to pay back a loan.

Russians felt angry and betrayed. We had told them that the free market is the path to prosperity, but it brought them only misery. A third now fell below the official (very low) poverty line. Actually, Russia had never fully implemented a functioning market system. Much Western advice was ignored. Most of the $66 billion in Western aid disappeared. There were too many government subsidies and tax breaks and too few rules and regulations that keep a market economy steady. Money, always a weak point with Russians (see page 335), was just something you printed. In the words of one Russian reformer, it was "the most expensive economic education in history."

Before the 1998 collapse, some people got rich fast while many went hungry. Having long been taught by the Communists that material equality is good and just, Russians witnessed the explosive growth of inequality. Some *biznesmeny* and mafiosi (the two words are linked in the Russian mind) enjoyed new wealth while most Russians lived in worse poverty than ever.

Some good emerged from the rubble of the ruble. Fake businesses collapsed, and entrepreneurs started investing their profits in Russia. Russia's economy, helped by high world oil prices, has recently grown by several percent a year. The federal budget is in balance, and inflation eased from 80 percent in 1998 to a few percent. Russia's trade balance, again thanks to oil, has been very positive (in contrast to big U.S. deficits). Putin's reforms of taxes, banks, and land sales, promoted growth. Said Putin in 2002: "Our economy

Traveling Salesmen: These young Russians make a niche in the economy by buying Russian medicines (in the big bags) and selling them in outdoor markets in Sofia, Bulgaria. After a few days at the market, they return home for more, bribing their way across borders. They showed me how to catch a train from Romania to Bulgaria without a ticket: "Just bribe the conductor," they shrugged, "It's a Russian train."

North Caucasus Mountainous region north of Georgia and Azerbaijan, including Chechnya. (See page 361.)

must grow much faster." (Stalin said the same in 1931.) The big test: Will Russia's economy be honest enough to let it join the World Trade Organization, which it very much wants to do?

Two clouds of uncertainty hang over the Russian economy, and Russians live in fear of a major downturn. The first is oil prices, which in 2008 surged past $130 a barrel. But oil prices are volatile and cannot be counted on. The second is Putin's persecution of oligarchs such as Khodorkovsky (see previous chapter), which panicked foreign investors. The entire Russian oil and gas industry is now run by *siloviki*, who both serve the Kremlin and make themselves rich. Seeing Putin bring the energy industries back under state control, most foreign investment stayed away, and it is an important component of economic growth. Russia's economy is not yet stable.

RECOVER THE LOST REPUBLICS?

President Putin described the breakup of the Soviet Union as "the greatest geopolitical catastrophe of the century" and worried that the "epidemic of collapse has spilled over into Russia itself." Most Russians agreed. The non-Russian republics that departed from the Soviet Union in 1991

GEOGRAPHY

YUGOSLAVIA: A MINIATURE SOVIET UNION?

The former multiethnic Balkan federal system of Yugoslavia resembled the ex-Soviet Union. Both countries had a Slavic core nationality: Russians in the Soviet Union and Serbs in Yugoslavia. Serbs and Russians are both Eastern Orthodox Christians and use the Cyrillic alphabet. Both defined themselves as the founders and guarantors of their respective nations. They regarded breakaway republics as traitors to the nation.

The other nationalities resented this overbearing attitude. In each country an advanced northwest (the Baltic republics in the Soviet Union and Slovenia in Yugoslavia) grew tired of being held back by the less-developed core nationality, which economically drained the advanced area. Interestingly, the Baltics and Slovenia declared their independence first.

The second largest nationality in each country was also Slavic but with a distinctive culture and resentments against being bossed by the center; thus, Ukraine and Croatia quickly broke away. In the south, feisty Muslim nationalities demanded greater autonomy and fought neighboring Christian nationalities (the Azeris against the Armenians and the Bosnian Muslims and Kosovar Albanians against the Serbs). In most of the newly independent republics in both the ex-Soviet Union and ex-Yugoslavia, the "new" leaders had been local Communist bosses prior to independence.

A final touch: Russians and Serbs, respectively, formed the bulk of the officer corps of the old Soviet and Yugoslav armies. The top officers were conservative and dedicated to keeping their countries intact. They were not adverse to using force to do so. In 1991, both armies started intervening directly in politics. The key difference is that conservative Communists took over in Belgrade and, with the army's general staff in agreement, attempted to hold Yugoslavia together by force. When that quickly failed, they turned to building a *Greater Serbia* by military conquest, coupled with *ethnic cleansing*. In the ex-Soviet Union, the death toll has not been as large, but it, too, experienced wars in the Caucasus region, which could get worse.

Geography

THE UNRAVELING OF THE NORTH CAUCASUS

Violence flares in Russia's **North Caucasus** despite—or maybe because of—Moscow's bloody efforts to tame it. The poor, angry region is a long-term Russian problem. Like all mountainous regions, it is hard to control and permits small ethnic and religious groups to keep distinct cultures that resist outside rule. The rugged region—home to more than 6 million people, mostly Muslim—is a crazy quilt of ethnic groups, most consolidated into their current borders by Stalin. From west to east they are Karachayevo-Cherkessia, Kabardino-Balkaria, North Ossetia, Ingushetia, Chechnya, and Dagestan. Islamist terrorism and urban shootouts between security forces and rebels are common.

The tsarist army finally subdued the region only in the early nineteenth century. Tolstoy wrote that the conquest created something "stronger than hatred, for [the Chechens] did not regard those Russian dogs as human beings." Emblematic was the tsarist fortress built in 1784: Vladikavkaz (Master of the Caucasus), now the capital of North Ossetia. The locals despised Russian rule, and Russians despised them as bandits. In 1944, Stalin accused several Caucasian nationalities, Chechens among them, of collaborating with the German invaders and brutally exiled entire ethnic groups to Central Asia.

Decades later, a Chechen, Jokar Dudayev, became a general in the Soviet air force. Assigned to an Estonian airbase in the 1980s, Dudayev sympathized with the Estonians, who, like Chechens, hated Russian rule. Dudayev blocked the landing of Soviet troops in early 1991, helping Estonia win independence. He then retired, won an election in Chechnya, and proclaimed its independence as the Soviet Union broke up in late 1991. But Chechnya, unlike Estonia, had never been a "union republic"; it was part of the Russian Federation, and Moscow feared unrest spreading to all the North Caucasus, which is happening. Heavy-handed repression by Russian security forces persuaded many locals to join an Islamic revival.

Yeltsin, in late 1994—with no discussion among military professionals, parliamentary debate, or publicity—gave the order to quickly crush Chechen independence. But the military campaign stalled; the Russian army was pathetic, and Chechens fought boldly and tenaciously. Some 80,000, mostly civilians, were killed, and the capital, Grozny, was shelled into ruin. Most Russians, even military officers, hated the war; partly because of it, Yeltsin's popularity plummeted. Ex-General Alexander Lebed worked out a shaky peace with Chechen fighters in 1996, leaving them an undefined autonomy.

In 1999, Chechen-led Muslim fundamentalists attempted to take over neighboring Dagestan. Moscow retaliated sharply, pursuing the guerrillas back into Chechnya. In Russian cities, several apartment houses were blown up, killing nearly 300. Some charge—at risk to their lives—that it was the work of Russian security police, but Moscow immediately blamed Chechen terrorists and launched a major invasion of Chechnya. This time the Russian army was in much better shape, and the Russian people were behind them. Putin's tough stance made him very popular. Russian soldiers in Chechnya describe it as "without limits" in brutality, corruption, and drug addiction, all of which they bring back with them. Putin declared victory in 2002, but the situation is obviously unstable. Guerrilla warfare, banditry, and terrorism continue and have spread through the North Caucasus. Theatergoers and schoolchildren have been victims. Such attacks enabled Putin to concentrate more power in his hands, and most Russians applauded.

Chechnya's two bloody wars could be just the beginning of the unraveling of the North Caucasus region. In the first war, 1994–1996, Chechen rebels pushed the Russian army out. In the second, 1999–2002, Russians bloodily occupied Chechnya and installed an ex-rebel as puppet chief. News coverage is all but blocked out; those bold enough to report the horrors are mysteriously assassinated. Now Islamism is spreading throughout the region; local Islamists talk of a North Caucasus *caliphate*. Foreign leaders condemn the violence. Putin, angry at U.S. criticism, asked: Just what is the United States doing in Iraq? Fighting terrorism, and so are we. "We showed weakness," he said of the Chechen problem, "and the weak are trampled upon." Stalin could not have said it better.

near abroad   Non-Russian republics of the old Soviet Union.

middle way   Supposed blend of capitalism and socialism; also called "third way."

are what Russians call the **near abroad**. Most of them had been incorporated into the tsarist empire, and many Russians still think of them as belonging to Russia. Some want to restore the Russian empire, especially the Russian army, which still has troops in most of the ex-Soviet republics. For U.S. policy, Moscow's influence in Central Asia was not all bad. Putin helped the U.S. military to use bases in

KEY CONCEPTS

A MIDDLE WAY FOR SOCIALISM?

Confusion surrounds the term *socialism*. Many Russians and East Europeans now tell you they no longer know what the word means. Some people call the welfare states of Scandinavia "socialist" because freely elected Social Democratic governments have gradually introduced elaborate medical, unemployment, educational, housing, and other programs to lift up the lower rungs of society: cradle-to-grave welfare. These Social Democratic parties started out Marxist but all of them shed it. They are all based on large labor-union federations. The aim of these parties is to wipe out poverty without coercion or state ownership.

And here is where Scandinavian *welfarism* differs sharply from Communist-style socialism. The Scandinavian lands have little nationalized industry, and what was nationalized was done so for nonideological reasons (for example, to hold down unemployment). The bulk of the economy is private and capitalist. Swedish managers especially developed a ferocious reputation for efficient, money-making plant operation. Taxes, to be sure, are high, but the economy is otherwise free.

In sum, Scandinavia is not socialist; it is a variation on capitalism called *welfarism*. Note that it was developed after and on top of Scandinavia's capitalist industrial base. First came capitalism, then came welfare. It is doubtful if the order can be reversed or if they can be built simultaneously.

No one has yet found a way to combine capitalism and socialism on a long-term, stable basis. For a while, such a combination sometimes seems to work.

But soon the private sector bumps into the restricted, slow-moving state sector. The private sector needs raw materials, labor, infrastructure, and transportation on a flexible, ever-changing basis. The state sector, still run by a central plan, cannot possibly deliver and has no incentive to. If you allow state enterprises to enter the private-sector market, you gradually desocialize the economy. It gets more efficient but less socialist. Eventually you come to a point where you must either bury the socialist sector as a bad experiment or curb and recontrol the private sector. The mix will not hold steady; you must go one way or the other. China, as we shall see, is caught up in this dilemma.

Putin's ultimate problem—inherited from his predecessors—was that he thought there was a **middle way** between a centrally planned socialist economy and a free-market economy. Reforms, some argue, can blend a market economy with a socialist economy. Some Russians still think that they can reserve the "commanding heights" of heavy industry for the state while permitting small enterprises to operate in a free market. This is what Lenin did with the NEP in the early 1920s, and the NEP was frequently mentioned as a model by Gorbachevites. But the NEP was inherently flawed and was running down in the late 1920s when Stalin dropped it in favor of forced industrialization. Many Russians, including Putin, still suppose they can find a middle way that is uniquely Russian. Experience suggests that middle ways lead to unstable, declining systems with high inflation.

Uzbekistan and Tajikistan to overthrow the Afghan Taliban after 9/11. Until landlocked Central Asia gains access to the outside world through Iran, Afghanistan, and Pakistan, it will remain dependent on Russia for trade and transportation.

In many ex-Soviet republics, the "new" leaders are old Party big shots, and a corrupt and authoritarian elite continues to rule. Not counting the Baltic republics—which have joined both NATO and the EU—Russia had the most progressive and most reform-minded leadership. As bad as Russia was, other republics were worse. A particularly tragic example is Ukraine, potentially rich and European, whose ex-Communist leaders (now out of power) instituted no economic reform program. The result was a hyperinflation that made the Russian economy look good.

One crucial factor in Russian thinking concerns the 25 million ethnic Russians who live in the near abroad. (The term does not refer to the former East European satellites such as Poland and Hungary.) Some Russians in these republics feel threatened. Any outright violence against them, however, provokes the Russian army, which feels that it has a right and duty to come to the rescue. This could someday be used as an excuse to seize all or part of the near abroad.

Recovery of the lost republics could come about by more subtle means as well: economics. As the economies of other republics plunged downward, some turned desperately to Moscow for help.

> **infant mortality rate** Number of live newborns who die in their first year, per thousand; standard measure of nation's health.

GEOGRAPHY

RUNNING OUT OF RUSSIANS

Almost all industrialized countries produce few babies, but Russia is in serious *demographic* decline. In 1989, before the Soviet collapse, an average Soviet woman (many non-Russian) bore 2.17 children. Now an average Russian woman bears only 1.4 children (up from 1.2 a few years before), still among the world's lowest *fertility rates,* which is not the same as the *birth rate,* a different measure (for comparative rates, see page 232). Putin tried to remedy this with financial incentives for women to have more babies.

In Russia, declining health standards raised the **infant mortality rate**, but lately it has improved to around 11 per thousand live births, still worse than West Europe. Expectant mothers were poorly nourished and so were their babies, many of whom suffered protein deficiency. There were isolated reports of children starving to death. Most Russian families have only one child. Meanwhile, the Russian death rate climbed; life expectancy of adult men dropped to fifty-eight years, lower than in many developing countries. Result: Russia's population shrinks by nearly 700,000 a year. In 2006 Putin called demography "Russia's most acute problem today."

HIV/AIDS is growing in Russia. Alcohol consumption (some of it poisonous home-brew) is prodigious, leading to industrial accidents. Russian environmental poisoning, both chemical and nuclear, is among the world's worst, and environmentally caused diseases are common. (Russia's closest rival: China.) Many factories just dump toxic and nuclear wastes into shallow landfills. The air in Russia's industrial cities is dangerous. "To live longer," said one official, "we should breathe less."

geopolitics Influence of geography on politics and use of geography for strategic ends.

Under the banner of the Commonwealth of Independent States, Moscow delivers some aid (for example, a good deal on oil and natural gas) but in return gets trade concessions and general obedience. Moscow successfully used this approach on Belarus—which now uses the Russian ruble as its currency—and briefly cut natural gas to Ukraine to warn it to behave.

A tricky third way appeared in Georgia, which itself is home to many non-Georgian nationalities. The Muslim Abkhazians of western Georgia broke away by force of arms, many of those arms supplied quietly by the Russian army. Georgia had originally refused to join the CIS in 1991 but, faced with military defeat, did so in 1994. Russia still supports Abkhazia with arms and troops against Georgian claims. They call it "peacekeeping," but it is more like a protection racket.

Should we as Americans criticize Russians for wishing to recover the near abroad? What did President Lincoln do when faced with the breakup of the Union? Americans should have a bias toward holding unions together. And has not Europe turned itself into the EU? But Moscow used

GEOGRAPHY

FEAR OF INVASION

Russians are unhappy and fearful that their former Central European satellites (Poland, the Czech Republic, Hungary) joined NATO in 1999 and the former Soviet republics of Lithuania, Latvia, and Estonia joined NATO in 2004, along with Bulgaria, Romania, Slovakia, and Slovenia. NATO, the enemy during the long Cold War, has taken over their former security belt. No Russian likes this, but Putin knows there is little he can do about it now.

Geopolitics has always been important to the Kremlin's rulers. Starting under the tsars but reemphasized by Stalin during and after World War II, it became an article of Kremlin faith that Russia needed East Europe—which Moscow organized as the *Warsaw Pact*—as a defensive shield against attack from the west. There have indeed been many such invasions; the Nazi invasion of 1941 was the most recent. Until Gorbachev, all Soviet civilian and military leaders accepted this argument. To prevent East Europe's departure from the Soviet orbit, Khrushchev crushed the 1956 Hungarian uprising and Brezhnev crushed the 1968 Prague Spring. Both nearly invaded Poland.

But East Europe was a major economic and military drain on the Soviet Union, and it blocked improved relations with the West. By 1989, Gorbachev had decided to no longer support the Communist regimes of East Europe, and the regimes fell. Central Europe quickly became democratic with free markets. Russia's strategic situation actually improved, for the end of the Cold War removed the military threat from the West. NATO, with declining defense budgets and small armies, poses no danger. Costs to Russia, in garrison troops and subsidized trade deals, have been drastically cut. Instead of selling Russian gas and oil at sweetheart prices to their satellites, Russia gets world-market prices for them, and in hard currency. Potentially, Russia is now open for trade with and investment from the West, the ticket to prosperity. Still, many Russian conservatives argue that Gorbachev gave away Russia's defensive shield; a few want it back. The very old fear of invasion from the West played into the hands of demagogic Russian politicians.

economic bribes and threats to recoup the near abroad. Gazprom, 51 percent owned and totally controlled by the government, sold natural gas cheap to those ex-Soviet states that stayed loyal. Those who turned westward paid more than twice as much. In early 2006

> **current-account balance**   A country's exports minus its imports.

Russia demanded a huge price increase in natural gas sent by pipeline to Ukraine and briefly cut off supplies. Moscow said price was the issue, but it was really Ukraine's westward turn with its 2005 democratic revolution. The move underscored Putin's Soviet-era mentality and alarmed Europe, which gets much of its natural gas from Russia.

WhICh WAy RussiA?

Observers of Russia divide into two camps, optimists and pessimists. Pessimists see a botched job. Capitalism has not taken root. At first the oligarchs looted state enterprises and stashed the money abroad; then Putin stole it back from them. The oil and gas industries have returned to state control, much of it owned, respectively, by Rosneft and Gazprom, giant corporations that are tied to the Kremlin, sort of an informal *statism*. Foreign energy companies are pushed out in favor of Rosneft and Gazprom. Corruption and lawlessness link authorities (including the police) and mafias. Many Russians live in worse conditions than ever. No country can take the kind of chaos and decay that the Yeltsin era brought. At that time either Russia was going to collapse or be taken over by an authoritarian. Many expected that authoritarian to be an ex-general, but it was a policeman, Putin.

The optimists argue that most of Russia's economy is private and, after the collapse of 1998, growing nicely. Inflation is dropping, and **current-account balances** are very positive, thanks to high oil prices. The remaining oligarchs have shifted from asset stripping to production and reinvestment, a healthy sign. Privatization was chaotic and crooked, but now owners have a stake in rule of law to keep their gains. Health and economic indicators have improved. Most Russians reject both Communists and extreme nationalists. Putin was a control freak, but he was better than many alternatives one can imagine. A market is now being built in Russia, argue optimists, and in a few years it may lead to democracy. (We will hear similar rosy projections on China's evolution.)

Which way will Russia go? The stakes for us are enormous. We hoped to have a friendly, democratic Russia as a trading partner but now face growing Russian hostility. Many Russians blame America for their decline, and the Kremlin accuses critics of working for foreign interests. True, American economists gave advice that overlooked the lack of cultural and institutional bases for capitalism in Russia. They casually assumed that Russia was a big Poland.

Russia is chilly to the West and openly hostile to Washington—Putin compared U.S. policies to the Third Reich—but this is not yet a new Cold War. Russia is now financially strong but militarily weak, so its chief weapons are oil and natural gas exports, which it hints it could withhold. Moscow's message: "Treat us with respect! And keep out of our internal affairs." Moscow faces some external pressures. To attract foreign investment, Russia needs rule of law. To get major loans it must adhere to international banks' austere limits on budget deficits. With NATO expanded eastward and Russia's military weak, Moscow must be strategically cautious; few fear Russian military action.

Is Russia now a democracy? No. Freedom House (see page 344) demoted Russia from "partly free" to "not free," closer to dictatorship than to democracy. There is little competition, and state control of the mass media skews elections. Protest demonstrations are broken up and their leaders are arrested. Institutions are unbalanced, the executive is too powerful, and the legislature is too weak. Corruption dominates everything. A democratic spirit of tolerance and fair play is absent. Some scholars argue that Russia is comparable to several developing countries in this "in-between" stage. We do not expect instant democracy from them, and neither should we expect it from Russia.

Can Russians eventually govern themselves in a moderate, democratic fashion? I think they can, but it will take many years. There is nothing genetically authoritarian about Russians. In the twentieth century Germans and Spaniards were deemed unfit for responsible self-government, but now they are practicing democracy as well as any Europeans. I believe Russia will eventually turn democratic, in your lifetime if not in mine.

KEY TERMS

asset-stripping (p. 358)

current-account balance (p. 365)

default (p. 359)

flight capital (p. 359)

geopolitics (p. 364)

hard currency (p. 359)

infant mortality rate (p. 363)

input-output table (p. 357)

middle way (p. 362)

near abroad (p. 362)

North Caucasus (p. 360)

public finances (p. 358)

FURTHER REFERENCE

Åslund, Anders. *Russia's Capitalist Revolution: Why Market Reform Succeeded and Democracy Failed.* Washington, D.C.: Peterson Institute, 2007.

Birgerson, Susanne M. *After the Breakup of a Multi-Ethnic Empire: Russia, Successor States, and Eurasian Security.* Westport, CT: Praeger, 2002.

Cox, Michael, ed. *Rethinking the Soviet Collapse: Sovietology, the Death of Communism, and the New Russia.* New York: Pinter, 1998.

Gaidar, Yegor. *Collapse of an Empire: Lessons for Modern Russia.* Washington, D.C.: Brookings, 2007.

Goldman, Marshall I. *Petrostate: Putin, Power, and the New Russia.* New York: Oxford University Press, 2008.

Hughes, James. *Chechnya: From Nationalism to Jihad.* Philadelphia: University of Pennsylvania Press, 2007.

Jack, Andrew. *Inside Putin's Russia: Can There Be Reform without Democracy?* New York: Oxford University Press, 2004.

Kanet, Roger E., ed. *Russia: Re-Emerging Great Power.* New York: Palgrave, 2007.

Kempton, Daniel R., and Terry D. Clark. *Unity or Separation: Center-Periphery Relations in the Former Soviet Union.* Westport, CT: Praeger, 2001.

Meier, Andrew. *Chechnya: To the Heart of a Conflict.* New York: Norton, 2004.

Reddaway, Peter, and Dmitri Glinski. *The Tragedy of Russia's Reforms: Market Bolshevism against Democracy.* Herndon, VA: U.S. Institute of Peace, 2001.

Shlapentokh, Vladimir. *A Normal Totalitarian Society: How the Soviet Union Functioned and How It Collapsed.* Armonk, NY: M. E. Sharpe, 2001.

Trenin, Dmitiri. *Getting Russia Right.* Washington, D.C.: Carnegie Endowment, 2007.

Xenakis, Christopher I. *What Happened to the Soviet Union? How and Why American Sovietologists Were Caught by Surprise.* Westport, CT: Praeger, 2002.

PART II

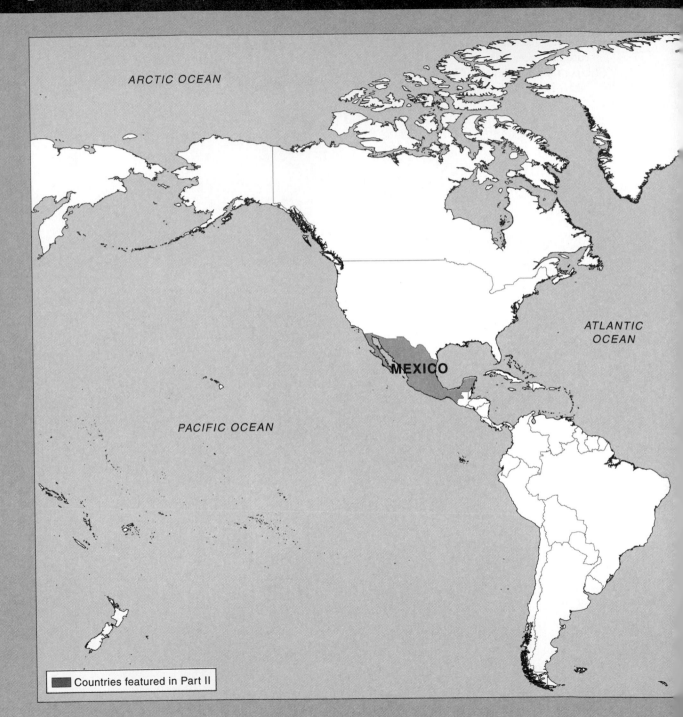

ARCTIC OCEAN

ATLANTIC OCEAN

PACIFIC OCEAN

MEXICO

Countries featured in Part II

The Developing Areas

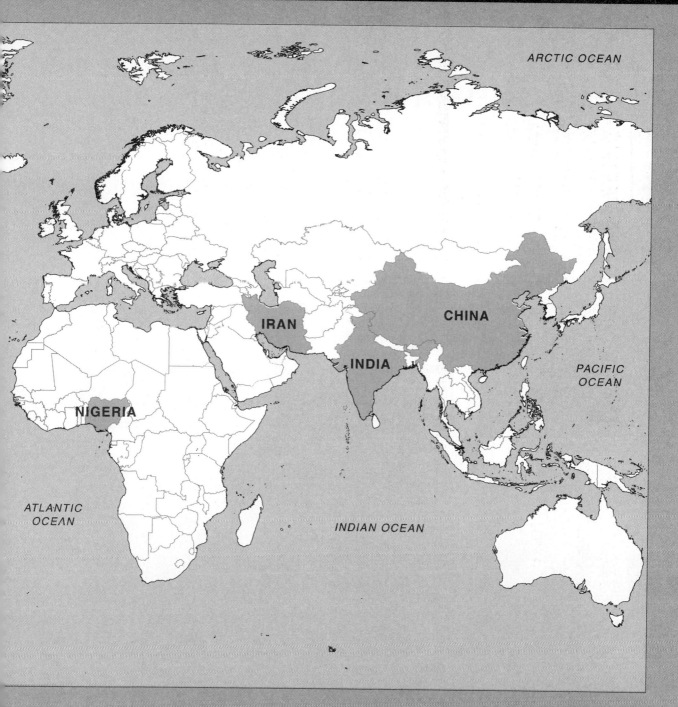

ARCTIC OCEAN

CHINA

IRAN

INDIA

NIGERIA

PACIFIC OCEAN

ATLANTIC OCEAN

INDIAN OCEAN

Chapter 24

China:
The Impact of the Past

China is big—stretching in latitude both further north and further south than the United States (without Hawaii or Alaska)—but only one-third of China's territory is arable, rice in the well-watered south and wheat in the drier north. Lack of surplus grain to feed cattle or hogs made Chinese largely vegetarians. China now has less than half an acre of farmland (and currently shrinking) for each Chinese, and this has long imposed limits on politics, economics, and social thought.

Rice cultivation, for example, uses much water and labor to get major crops (two and even three times a year in South China) from small plots. This labor-intensive farming until recently kept most Chinese tied to the land as peasants and encouraged strong family organization and obedient, cooperative behavior. It also meant that a central authority had to control water canals and determine who got how much water. Irrigation helps explain why Mesopotamia, Egypt, and China produced history's first kingdoms and empires.

Archaeologists find that **civilization** began in ancient Mesopotamia, followed closely by Egypt and then China. During the **Neolithic** age humans began the several-thousand-year transition from hunter-gatherers to settled farmers around 10,000 years ago in Mesopotamia and 8,000 years ago in China. With the **Bronze Age** came the founding of cities around 5,500 years ago in Mesopotamia and 4,000 years ago in China. The shifts occurred first in Mesopotamia (present-day Iraq), scholars believe, because the Middle East was home to more plants and animals that could be domesticated—including wheat and sheep—than anywhere else on the planet. Both the Middle East and China, however, founded civilizations far earlier than Europe, which was just getting out of the ice age.

QUESTIONS TO CONSIDER

1. What are the difficulties with the term *Third World*?
2. What countries did the main European empires rule over?
3. Is Confucianism basically government by political culture?
4. Are *cycles* a general political phenomenon? Why?
5. How did the political development of China differ from that of Europe?
6. Could the United States have uplifted old China?
7. Without the Japanese invasion, could the Nationalists have consolidated their rule?
8. How were the Chinese Nationalists and Communists similar?
9. How did Mao and the Communists beat the Nationalists?

THE BUREAUCRATIC EMPIRE

China, in sharp contrast to Europe, unified and ended feudalism very early. During the Bronze Age, small but rather advanced kingdoms—about as advanced as ancient Greece—appeared along the Yellow River—the Xia around 2000 B.C., the Shang around 1600, and the Zhou around 1045 B.C. Confucius was a public official and philosopher of the late Zhou kingdom. After a period of **Warring States**

GEOGRAPHY

BOUND CHINA

China is bounded on the north by Kazakhstan, Russia, and Mongolia;

on the east by Korea and the Yellow, East China, and South China Seas;

on the south by Vietnam, Laos, Myanmar (formerly Burma), India, Bhutan, and Nepal;

and on the west by Pakistan, Afghanistan (minutely), Tajikistan, and Kyrgyzstan.

By knowing China's boundaries, you can label most of mainland Asia. Only Cambodia, Thailand, and Bangladesh do not border China.

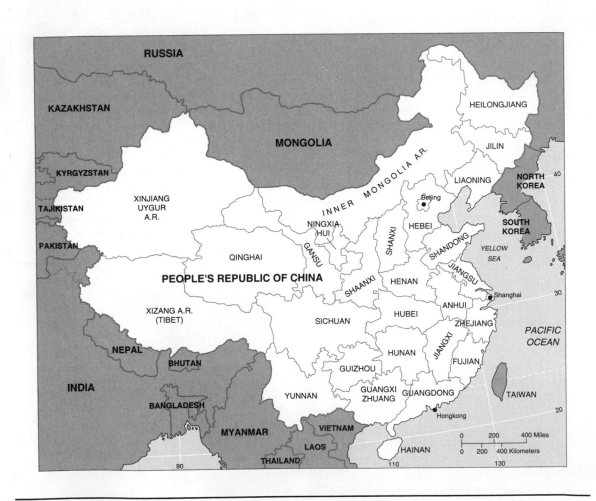

from the fifth century B.C. to 221 B.C., the short-lived Qin dynasty (earlier spelled Ch'in, origin of the Western name for China) established the first unified empire, the **Middle Kingdom** (Zhōngguó, the official and still only name Chinese use). The next dynasty, the Han (206 B.C. to A.D. 220), developed Confucianism into a bureaucratic empire that replaced the old aristocratic families.

Europe, too, had a great empire, Rome, but it collapsed, leading to centuries of feudalism and warring states. During roughly this same time China was a prosperous, mostly unified, highly organized empire, complete with impartial civil-service exams to select the best talent. The resulting **Mandarin** class—schooled in the Confucian classics, which stressed obedience, authority, and hierarchy—was interested in perpetuating the system, not changing it. A gentry class of better-off people served as the literate intermediaries between the Mandarins and the 90 percent of the population that were peasants. The words of one peasant song:

> When the sun rises, I toil;
> When the sun sets, I rest;
> I dig wells for water;
> I till the fields for food;
> What has the Emperor's power to do with me?

civilization   City-based culture with writing, social classes, and complex economic and political organization. (See page 371.)

Neolithic   New Stone Age; beginning of agriculture (See page 371.)

Bronze Age   Beginning of metal-working and cities (See page 371.)

Warring States   China's early period (475–221 B.C.), before unification (See page 371.)

Middle Kingdom   China's traditional and current name for itself, in the middle of the heavens (trans. of Zhōngguo).

Mandarin   High civil servant of imperial China.

Han   Early dynasty, 206 B.C. to A.D. 220, that solidified China's unity and culture. Ethnic meaning: main people of China.

China and Rome invite comparison. Both arose about the same time, the Roman Republic in 509 B.C. and the Qin dynasty in 221 B.C. Both achieved their greatest glory as empires, the Roman from 27 B.C. to A.D. 476, the **Han** from 206 B.C. to A.D. 220 At their peak they were about the same size; Rome covered the Mediterranean basin and much of West Europe, the Han most of present-day China. The two empires knew of each other and traded a little via the Silk Road

GEOGRAPHY

CITIES AND CIVILIZATIONS

The root of "civilization" is the Latin word *civitas*, city, and it is indeed the early cities that created high cultures of art, architecture, writing, money, social classes, and specialized economic functions. Cities arrived only after the domestication of plants and animals, which enabled humans to grow more food than their families needed. Growers traded their food surplus for implements and clothing produced in towns. Food and other production were taxed to support rulers' courts and a professional officer class, who became nobles. Cities, civilization, and taxes were born triplets.

pinyin   Literally, "spell sound"; current system of transliterating Chinese.

through Central Asia. Both achieved a high degree of civilization in terms of art, architecture, administration, commerce, and writing.

There are many contrasts between ancient Rome and China. In the first century A.D. Buddhism arrived in China from India but never

Political Culture

CHINESE WORDS IN ROMAN LETTERS

In contrast to Western alphabetic writing systems, China, starting nearly 4,000 years ago, developed and perfected an ideographic system based on symbolic word-pictures, a system that was copied and modified by Korea, Vietnam, and Japan. Literacy involves memorizing thousands of pictographs, much harder than Western phonetic systems. The pictographs are useful, however, precisely because they do not represent specific sounds. People speaking very different languages—the Wu and Cantonese of South China or even Japanese—can read the same newspaper. This was a great help in unifying China, which is still a country of many different languages. An official did not need to speak the emperor's language in order to understand his written edicts. In the 1950s and 1960s Beijing simplified the pictographs, making them easier to learn and transmit electronically.

Chinese is also tonal, a bit like singing. Standard Chinese has four tones (in addition to no tone). Speak a syllable with the wrong tone and you have said a completely different word, sometimes to comic effect. Chinese sounds are very different and cannot be precisely transliterated into English. One system, the Wade-Giles, devised in the 1860s by two Cambridge dons, was used for more than a century but poorly matched spoken Chinese.

In 1958, Peking—sorry, Beijing—introduced a new phonetic system, **pinyin**, to help Chinese schoolchildren learn to pronounce their own language. Pinyin indicates tones with little accent marks, but it is still a poor guide to spoken Chinese sounds. In 1979 China made pinyin the official standard, and most English-language publications went along with it. On a computer you type in a pinyin word, and instantly a matching Chinese pictograph pops up. You may still see some Wade-Giles spellings in older books. (See table below.)

Wade-Giles	Pinyin
Mao Tse-tung	Mao Zedong
Chou En-lai	Zhou Enlai
Kuomintang	Guomindang
Peking	Beijing
Nanking	Nanjing
Chungking	Chongqing
Shanghai	Shanghai (the same!)
Szechwan	Sichuan
Sinkiang	Xinjiang
Canton	Guangdong
Hong Kong	Xiang Gang
Ch'in	Qin (Q sounds "ch")

established itself as a state religion before it faded. Rome eventually accepted Christianity, which became Europe's unifying culture. Rome kept expanding until it overexpanded. Its legions were superb but too few to hold off barbarians and put down revolts. China did take over the northern parts of Vietnam and Korea for a while but was not keen on expansion. Once it carved out its large Middle Kingdom (in the middle of heaven), it rested content. The Roman economy was based on slaves, China's on peasants, giving China more stability. The Han—who developed paper, silk, the compass, and the rudder—were ahead of Rome in technology.

dynastic cycle   Rise, maturity, and fall of an imperial family.

Mandate of Heaven   Old Chinese expression for legitimacy.

Mongol   Central Asian dynasty, founded by Genghis Khan, that ruled China as the Yuan dynasty in the thirteenth and fourteenth centuries.

Manchu   Last imperial dynasty of China, also known as *Qing*; ruled from 1644 to 1911.

The chief difference is what the two empires left behind. When the Western part of the Roman Empire fell to barbarians in A.D. 476, it fragmented into separate states and stayed that way. After the Han, China, too, suffered periods of fragmentation and chaos, but during their four centuries the Han implanted a culture so deep that later dynasties used it to put China back together. Chinese intellectuals always insisted that China was one country; China broken into separate kingdoms always seemed wrong. China, it has been said, is not a country but a civilization with 4,000 years of cultural continuity.

Dynasties rose and fell every few hundred years in what is called the **dynastic cycle**. As the old dynasty became increasingly incompetent, water systems were not repaired, famine broke out, wars and banditry appeared, and corruption and palace conspiracies grew. As more influential families got their lands exempted from taxation, peasants had to bear heavier and heavier tax burdens until they revolted. In the eyes of the people, it looked as if the emperor had lost the **Mandate of Heaven**, that is, his legitimate right to rule. A conqueror, either Chinese or foreign (**Mongol** or **Manchu**), found it easy to take over a delegitimized empire. By the very fact of his victory, the new ruler seemed to have gained the Mandate of Heaven. Under vigorous new emperors, administration and taxation were restored. After some generations, though, the new dynasty fell prey to the old ills, and Chinese, especially the literate, thought the emperor had lost his heavenly mandate; the cycle was ready to start over.

KEY CONCEPTS

CYCLICAL VERSUS SECULAR CHANGE

China illustrates the two kinds of change that social scientists deal with. Cyclical change is repetitive; certain familiar historical phases follow one another like a pendulum swing. China's dynastic cycles are examples of cyclical change; there is change, but the overall pattern is preserved.

Secular change means a long-term shift that does not revert back to the old pattern. China's population growth, for example, was a secular change that helped break the stability of traditional China. One of the problems faced by historians, economists, and political scientists is whether a change they are examining is secular—a long-term, basic shift—or cyclical—something that comes and goes repeatedly. (Discussions of global warming face the same problem.)

steady-state   A system that preserves itself with little change.

kow-tow   Literally, head to the ground; to prostrate oneself.

Two millennia of empire still mark China today. Not a feudal system like Japan, China unified and centralized early. The defining characteristic of a feudal system is an autonomous aristocracy, which Japan had and China did not. In China, an emperor at the top set the direction and tone, Mandarins carried out Beijing's writ, gentry ran local affairs, and peasants—the overwhelming majority of the population— toiled in the fields.

For centuries China was the world's greatest civilization and biggest economy, far ahead of Europe. By around 1500, however, Europe began surging ahead (for some of the factors, see page 3) while China stagnated. One prominent factor: China was one state when Europe was many states. Europe's monarchs competed with each other for wealth, power, and new territories, whereas huge, unified China faced no competition. Soon expansionist European empires controlled much of the world, including China. Chinese today are well aware that China was a great civilization, one humiliated by the West.

With little new territory to expand into, Chinese society evolved **steady-state** structures aimed at stability and making peasants content with what they had rather than motivating them to pioneer and innovate. Labor-saving devices would render peasants jobless and were not encouraged. China's achievements in science and technology—far ahead of medieval Europe's—remained curiosities instead of contributions to an industrial revolution. Commercial expansion was also discouraged. Instead of a Western mentality of reinvestment, growth, and risk-taking, Chinese merchants sought only a steady-state relationship with peasants and government officials; they depended heavily on government permits, monopolies, and set prices.

China took little interest in anything foreign. The Middle Kingdom was surrounded by barbarians who were walled out or bought off. Chinese culture could uplift the near barbarians (Koreans and Vietnamese), who could then **kow-tow** and pay tribute to the emperor. This was called the *tributary system* and was quite different from the diplomacy developed in Europe. China never held the European concept that other lands were sovereign and should be treated diplomatically as equals. They should simply pay tribute. China's superiority complex poorly equipped it to handle European penetration.

Geography

RAINFALL

A focus on Europe may cause us to overlook one of the most basic physical determinants of a politico-economic system. Rainfall in Europe is generally sufficient and predictable, but in much of the world it is not. There is plenty of land in the world; water for humans and crops is the limiting factor. Over one billion humans do not have clean drinking water, a number that is growing rapidly. Per capita, China has less than a third the water of the global average. With water tables dropping rapidly, many warn that China's water supplies will soon reach dangerous levels. Massive industrial pollution makes matters worse.

Irrigation and conservation can compensate for lack of rain, but they require a high degree of human organization and governmental supervision. This may explain why high civilizations arose early in China and Iran. Large desert or semi-desert areas of our Third World countries—China, India, Mexico, Nigeria, and Iran—limit development.

China was centuries ahead of Europe in naval technology, including the compass and watertight compartments. From 1405 to 1433 the **Mings** sent huge naval expeditions under Admiral Zheng He, a Muslim eunuch (eunuchs were common among court officials) all around the Indian Ocean. Some of Zheng's ships were 400 feet long,

Ming Chinese dynasty between Mongols and Manchus, ruled from 1368 to 1644.

many times bigger than any ship Europeans would build for centuries. If the Chinese fleets had rounded Africa or crossed the Pacific, China would have discovered Europe and the Americas. Would that have mattered? Could we now be speaking Chinese? Probably not, as old China had no thirst for imperial expansion or colonization of distant barbarian lands. Instead, Ming officials decided the expeditions were too expensive and China had everything it needed. For centuries, China remained a stay-at-home country.

The Long Collapse

For some 2,000 years China absorbed invasions, famines, and new dynasties. The old pattern always reasserted itself because it was the most rational way to rule the Middle Kingdom. But as the modern epoch impinged on China, the system could not handle two new factors: population growth and Western penetration. In 1741, China's population was 143 million; just a century later, in 1851, it had become an amazing 432 million, the result of new crops (corn, potatoes, and sweet potatoes from the Americas), internal peace under the Manchu dynasty, some new farmland, and just plain harder work on the part of the peasants. Taxation and administration lagged behind the rapid population growth, which hit as the Manchus were going into the typical decline phase of their dynastic cycle in the nineteenth century.

At about the same time the West penetrated and disoriented China. In a clash of two cultures—Western dynamism and greed versus Chinese stability—China was no match. Over roughly a century, old China went into convulsions and breakdowns, which, some fear, still lurk under the surface.

The first Westerners to reach China were daring Portuguese navigators in their tiny caravels in 1514. Gradually, they and other Europeans gained permission to set up trading ports on the coast. For three centuries the Imperial government disdained the foreigners and their products and tried to keep both to a minimum. In 1793, for example, in response to a British mission to Beijing, the emperor commended King George III for his "respectful spirit of submission" but pointed out that there could be little trade because "our celestial empire possesses all things in prolific abundance."

Geography

Sailing the East China Sea

Now you are on an aircraft carrier entering the East China Sea from the south, the Taiwan Strait. Sailing clockwise in a great circle that includes the Yellow Sea to the north, which countries do you pass on your left?

On your left you pass China, North Korea (steer well away), South Korea, Japan (including its Ryukyu Islands), and Taiwan.

Geography

What Are the Developing Areas?

No one quite knows what to call the mostly poor lands of Asia, Africa, and Latin America, home to five-sixths of the human race. One attempt coined by French writers in the 1950s, *le Tiers Monde* (**Third World**), referred to the majority of humankind that was in neither the Western capitalist First World nor the Communist Second World. It is an awfully broad term that permits few firm generalizations. Critics claim the term "Third World" is pejorative and should be discarded in favor of "developing areas." Now, after the collapse of communism in East Europe and the ex-Soviet Union, there is really no more Second World. Some say the only meaningful dividing line is now "the West and the rest."

The developing areas are mostly poor, but some oil-producing countries are rich, and some of its lands are industrializing fast. It is mostly nonwhite. Almost all of it was once a colony of a European imperial power (see page 514). Most of it is hot and closer to the equator than the rich countries, so some writers call it the Global South. The U.S. State Department and some international banks call it the LDCs (less-developed countries). The ones making fast economic progress are called NICs (newly industrializing countries), with special attention on the BRICs (Brazil, India, China). Business calls them the "emerging markets." Many of them show good and even excellent rates of economic growth.

How to lift up the poor areas is a long and major controversy. Cultural theorists argue that not much can happen until local cultures turn from passivity and fatalism to a modern mentality of change and self-improvement. Once a country has that, it grows on its own with little foreign aid. Without it, aid scores few improvements. Critics argue that good governance and policies can change psychologies and cultures. Sound economic policies have turned previously "passive" peoples into energetic entrepreneurs, as in India.

Liberals generally like foreign-aid programs and easy loans from international banks, but much of this capital is skimmed off by corrupt officials. Some see **micro-credit** as the way to spark economic growth on a free-enterprise basis. Others counter that tiny start-up firms cannot seriously boost economic growth or employ the vast numbers of jobless; major foreign direct investment (FDI) is needed. The growth of many countries is fueled by massive FDI.

Curiously, natural resources such as oil do little to grow the economy. Some of the poorest countries have abundant natural resources, whereas some growth demons have few or no natural resources (examples: Hong Kong, Singapore, and South Korea). **Petrostates**, which concentrate wealth and power into the hands of a few, have also become notorious for thwarting democracy.

One generalization about the developing areas stands up fairly well: They are unstable. The political institutions of almost all of its 120-plus countries are weak. Most lack a single, integrated culture and are pulled apart by region and religion. Most are wracked by tensions that can explode in revolution, coups, and breakaway movements and end in dictatorship. Rule of law is weak or absent. Crime and **corruption** penetrate most Third World political systems. Power holders routinely use their office to get rich. In some countries you cannot tell where politics leaves off and crime begins. Few developing countries have yet made it into the ranks of stable democracies, the characteristic now of all the West. Some developing lands are unstable democracies; **demagogues** gull unsophisticated voters with deceptive promises and turn themselves into dictators, something now happening in Venezuela.

Scholars find an imperfect correlation between economics and democracy. Most countries with per capita GDPs above $8,000 (middle-income countries and higher) are able to found stable democracies that do not revert to authoritarianism. Countries with per capita GDPs below $5,000 have trouble establishing and sustaining democracy; they often revert to authoritarianism. India is an amazing exception to the wealth-democracy link. Pakistan is more typical: unstable elected governments alternating with military rule. Notice how some of the countries discussed here are in this borderline area. Per caps above $8,000 do not guarantee democracy; much depends on the size, education levels, and pluralistic organization of the country's middle class and the cleverness of democratic elites.

But the West, especially the British, pushed on, smelling enormous profits in the China trade. Matters came to a head with the First **Opium War** of 1839 to 1842. Opium smoking was illegal and unknown in China, but for over a century, the British imported more and more opium from the poppy fields of British-held India. The British flouted China's law and popularized opium smoking. When a zealous Imperial official tried to stop the opium trade, Britain went to war, invoking the principle of "free trade" to keep the lucrative commerce open. Britain easily won, but the Chinese still refused to admit that the foreigners were superior. Moaned one Cantonese: "Except for your ships being solid, your gunfire fierce, and your rockets powerful, what good qualities do you have?" For the Chinese, war technology was not as important as moral quality, a view later adopted by Mao Zedong.

The 1842 Treaty of Nanjing (Nanking in Wade-Giles) wrested five **treaty ports** from the Chinese. Britain got Hong Kong as an outright possession. In the treaty ports the foreigners held sway, dominating the commerce and governance of the area, and enjoying **extraterritoriality**, meaning they were not subject to Chinese law but had their own courts, a point deeply resented by both Chinese and Japanese. In the Second Opium War of 1856–1860 an Anglo-French expedition occupied Beijing, burned down the Summer Palace, and forced China to add nine more treaty ports. China called the imperialist land-grabs "unequal treaties."

Around the treaty ports grew **spheres of influence**, understandings among the foreign powers as to who really ran things there. The British, French, Germans, Russians, and Japanese in effect carved up the China coast with their spheres of influence, in which they dominated trade. Foreign powers turned the treaty port of Shanghai into a major and modern trading center. Then and now, Shanghai was China's leading city both in size and commercial importance. China was reduced to semicolonial status.

Third World   Most of Asia, Africa, and Latin America. (See page 378.)

micro-credit   Very small loans to startup businesses. (See page 378.)

petrostate   Country based on oil exports. (See page 378.)

corruption   Use of public office for private gain. (See page 378.)

demagogue   Manipulative politician who wins votes through impossible promises. (See page 378.)

Opium Wars   Nineteenth-century British (and French) campaigns to keep China open to opium imports.

treaty ports   Areas of China coast run by European powers.

extraterritoriality   Privilege of Europeans in colonial situations to have their own laws and courts.

sphere of influence   Semicolonial area under control of major power.

Taiping   Religion-based rebellion in nineteenth-century China.

Boxer   Chinese antiforeigner rebellion in 1900.

From Empire to Republic

Internally, too, the Empire weakened. Rebellions broke out. From 1851 to 1864, the **Taipings**—espousing a mixture of Christianity (picked up from missionaries), Confucianism, and primitive communism—baptized millions in South China and nearly overthrew the Manchu (Qing) dynasty. In 1900, with the backing of some reactionary officials and the empress dowager, the antiforeign **Boxer** movement, based on traditional temple-boxing exercises, killed missionaries and besieged Beijing's Legation Quarter for fifty-five days. What the Chinese call the "Eight Powers Expedition" of British, French, German, Russian, American, Japanese, Austrian, and Italian troops broke through and lifted the siege. The foreigners then demanded indemnities and additional concessions from the tottering Imperial government.

Could the Qing (pronounced "Ching") dynasty have adapted itself to the new Western pressures? The Japanese had; with the 1868 Meiji Restoration (see page 263) they preserved the form

Open Door   U.S. policy of protecting China.

of empire but shifted to modernization and industrialization with spectacular success. Many young Chinese demanded reforms to strengthen China, especially after their humiliating defeat by Japan in 1895. In 1898 the young Emperor Guangxu gathered reformers around him and in the famous Hundred Days issued more than forty edicts, modernizing everything from education to the military. Conservative officials and the old empress dowager would have none of it; they carried out a coup, rescinded the changes, and put the emperor under house arrest for the rest of his short life. (He was probably poisoned.)

A system that cannot reform is increasingly ripe for revolution. Younger people, especially army officers, grew fed up with China's weakness and became militant nationalists. Many Chinese studied in the West and were eager to modernize China. Anarchist, socialist, and Marxist ideas from Europe intrigued Chinese intellectuals. Under an idealistic, Western-trained doctor, Sun Yixian

Political Culture

THE UNITED STATES AND CHINA: THE CHINA TIE

The United States has had long and deep ties to China. Some of Boston's leading families profited early from the China trade (including the sale of Turkish opium). While the British carved up China's coast, we prided ourselves on being above that sort of imperialism (but we did use the British treaty ports). In 1900 Secretary of State Hay issued the **Open Door** notes to stop the dismemberment of China. We saw ourselves as China's "big brother" and were happy to note that Chinese called us their "favorite people," who were only there to help and seized no territory.

American churches sent hundreds of missionaries to China in the nineteenth and early twentieth centuries to make the Chinese Protestant and prosperous. The Boxers killed American missionaries and their converts. Henry Luce, born in China in 1898 the son of a Presbyterian missionary, arrived at Yale speaking Chinese. All his life Luce carried the missionary view that we can and must uplift China by working with the Chinese Nationalists. Luce founded *Time* magazine in 1923 and put Nationalist chief Jiang ten times on its cover. Opinionated and influential, Luce used *Time* to rail against Chinese Communists and U.S. Democrats (he conflated the two).

U.S. support for China had to bring us into war with Japan. When Japan conquered Manchuria in 1931, Secretary of State Stimson issued his *nonrecognition doctrine*. When Japan began its conquest of all of China in 1937, we increasingly embargoed trade with Japan, and this led to Pearl Harbor. China could not be more than a minor theatre of operations for the U.S. war effort. The Japanese occupied the entire China coast, so only a trickle of U.S. supplies could reach Jiang's armies by air and by the Burma Road from India. During the war, U.S. officials attempted to get Chinese Nationalists and Communists to work together against the Japanese, but their alliances were fleeting because the two sides distrusted each other.

When the Communists took over China in late 1949, U.S. Republicans like Luce intoned "Who lost China?" and blamed the Democrats. The "Old China Hands" of U.S. diplomats were purged from the State Department for letting the Communists take over China—they could not have done anything about it—leaving Washington for decades without experts who knew China first-hand. Washington broke all ties with mainland China in 1949 and did not resume them until Nixon's visit in 1972. We fought China in Korea. The twenty-three years of U.S.-Chinese hostility, however, was an aberration in a history of two centuries of good ties.

(Sun Yat-sen in Wade-Giles), disgruntled provincial officials and military commanders overthrew the Manchus in 1911. It was the end of the last dynasty but not the beginning of stability. In the absence of central authority, so-called **warlords** fragmented China from 1916 to 1927.

warlord   Local military chief who runs province.

Confucianism   Chinese philosophy of social and political stability based on family, hierarchy, and manners.

Japan took advantage of China's weakness. Every Japanese land grab generated passionate nationalism in China. In 1894 Japan started a war with China, took Taiwan, and made it a Japanese province from 1895 to 1945. In 1915 Japan issued a far-reaching Twenty-One Demands on China that would have turned it into a

Political Culture

CONFUCIANISM: GOVERNMENT BY RIGHT THINKING

Confucianism is not a religion but a philosophy of governance. It was much more influential than Buddhism in Chinese political culture. The scholar Confucius (551–479 B.C.) advised rulers of the small Zhou kingdom (before China unified) that the key to good, stable government lay in instilling correct, moral behavior in ruled and rulers alike. People can be improved, but they must understand their roles and perform them obediently. Sons must be subservient to fathers, wives to husbands, younger brothers to elder brothers, and subjects to rulers. The ruler sets a moral example. Pure spirit and careful manners create a conservative political culture more effective and durable than mere laws. Japan copied Confucianism from China.

Confucianism emphasized that good government starts with thinking correct thoughts in utter sincerity. If things go wrong, it indicates rulers have been insincere. The system did not depend on Confucianism alone; it also had strong police controls that permitted no dissent. Mao Zedong hated everything old China stood for, but he could not help picking up the Confucian stress on right thinking. Adding a Marxist twist, Mao taught that one was a proletarian not because of blue-collar origin but because one had revolutionary, pure thoughts. Confucius would have been pleased.

Curiously, Confucianism survives more in Japan than in China, often the case of ideologies transplanted from

Statue of Confucius at Beijing Temple.

their country of origin. Japanese are still inculcated with politeness and decorum, of bowing and obedience. Such patterns have disappeared in China, the result of more than a century of revolution and war. Mao Zedong tried to finish off Confucianism with his "destroy the four olds" campaign, part of the Cultural Revolution of the late 1960s. Now Beijing is refurbishing Confucianism as a tool of social control (see page 409). Some propose making it China's official religion.

Nationalist   Chiang Kai-shek's party that unified China in the late 1920s, abbreviated KMT.

mass line   Mao's theory of revolution for China.

Japanese protectorate. Chinese were furious. On May 4, 1919, the Versailles peace conference decided to allow Japan to keep the former German concessions in Shandong Province, the seizure of which had been Japan's tiny contribution to the Allied side in World War I. Beijing students protested and rioted, and anti-Japanese demonstrations broke out in many Chinese cities. The May Fourth Movement that followed was the training ground for young Chinese Nationalists and Communists. In a parallel to the German invasion of Russia in World War I, Japanese incursions into China led to the Communist takeover in 1949. It was foreign invasion rather than mass uprising that brought communism to both Russia and China.

The **Nationalist** party, or Guomindang (in Wade-Giles, Kuomintang, KMT), gradually overcame China's chaos. Formed by Sun Yat-sen shortly after the Manchu's overthrow, the Nationalists were guided by intellectuals (many of them educated in the United States), army officers, and business people. Their greatest strength was in the South, in Guangdong (Canton), especially in the coastal cities where there was the most contact with the West. It was no accident that they made Nanjing their capital; it means "southern capital." (North-South tension still exists in China.)

After Sun died in 1925, General (later Generalissimo) Jiang Jieshi (Chiang Kai-shek) took over the Nationalists, who by 1927 controlled most of China after a series of military expeditions. While many Americans hailed Jiang as the founder and savior of the new China, in reality Nationalist rule

KEY CONCEPTS

MAO AND GUERRILLA WAR

In what became a model for revolutionaries the world over, the Chinese Communists swept to power in 1949 after a decade and a half of guerrilla and civil warfare. During these years, Mao Zedong, often in his Yenan cave, developed and taught what he called the **mass line**. His lessons included the following:

1. Take the countryside and surround the cities. While the enemy is stuck in the cities, able to venture out only in strength, you are mobilizing the masses.

2. Work very closely with the peasants, listen to their complaints, help them (for example, getting rid of a landlord or bringing in the harvest), propagandize them, and recruit them into the army and Party.

3. Do not engage the enemy's main forces but rather probe for his weak spots, harassing him and wearing him out.

4. Do not expect much help from the outside; be self-reliant. For weapons, take the enemies'.

5. Do not worry about the apparently superior numbers and firepower of the enemy and his imperialist allies; their strength is illusory ("paper tigers") because it is not based upon the masses. Willpower and unity with the masses are more important than weaponry.

6. At certain stages guerrilla units come together to form larger units until at last, as the enemy stumbles, your forces become a regular army that takes the entire country.

was weak. The Western-oriented city people who staffed the Nationalists did not reform or develop the rural areas where most Chinese lived, often under the thumb of rapacious landlords. Administration became terribly corrupt. And the Nationalists offered no plausible ideology to rally the big majority of Chinese, who were peasants.

Still, like Kerensky's provisional government in Russia, the Nationalists might have succeeded were it not for war, in this case a Japanese invasion. In 1931 the Japanese army seized Manchuria and in 1937 began the conquest of the rest of China. By 1941 they had taken the entire coast, forcing the Nationalists to move their capital far up the Yangzi River from Nanjing to Chongqing. Jiang's forces preferred fighting Communists to Japanese, while waiting for a U.S. victory to return them to power.

THE COMMUNIST TRIUMPH

One branch of Chinese nationalism, influenced by Marx and the Bolshevik Revolution, decided that communism was the only effective basis for a nationalist revolution. The Chinese Communists have always been first and foremost nationalists, and from its founding in 1921 the Chinese Communist party (CCP) worked with the Nationalists until Jiang, in 1927, decided to exterminate them as a threat. The fight between the KMT and CCP was a struggle between two versions of Chinese nationalism.

Stalin, who knew nothing of China, mistakenly advised the Chinese Communists to base themselves on the small proletariat of the coastal cities, but Mao Zedong rose to leadership of the Party by developing a rural strategy he called the *mass line*. Mao concluded that the real revolutionary potential in China, which had little industry and hence few proletarians, was among the poorest peasants. It was a major revision of Marx, one that Marx would not accept as Marxism. Mao, considered a maverick in the CCP, in 1931 organized peasants in Jiangxi province (Kiangsi in Wade-Giles) into a small Chinese Soviet Republic.

In 1934, with KMT forces surrounding their "Jiangxi redoubt," some 80,000 began their incredible Long March of 5,000 miles (8,000 km) to the relative safety of Yenan (Yan'an in Wade-Giles) far to the north in Shaanxi Province. The march took over a year and led across mountain ranges and rivers amidst hostile forces. Only 6,000 survived. The Long March became the epic of Chinese Communist history. Self-reliant and

Mao Zedong proclaims the founding of the People's Republic of China at Beijing's Tiananmen Square on October 1, 1949.

isolated from the Soviets, the Chinese Communists developed their own strategy for survival, including working with peasants and practicing guerrilla warfare.

China's war against Japan drained and demoralized the Nationalists, but it gave the Communists a chance to seize power. Besides stocks of captured Japanese weapons from the Soviet takeover of Manchuria in 1945, the Chinese Communists got little but bad advice from the Soviets and felt they never owed them much in return. In 1947 full-scale civil war resumed between the KMT and CCP, which the Communists won in late 1949. Mao and the CCP came to power largely on their own, through their peasant and guerrilla strategies, a point that contributed to the later Sino-Soviet split.

After World War II, the Nationalist forces were much larger than the Communists' and had many U.S. arms. Nationalist strength, however, melted away as hyperinflation destroyed the economy, corrupt officers sold their troops' weapons (often to the Communists), and war weariness paralyzed the population. The Nationalists had always neglected the rice roots of political strength: the common peasant. The Communists, by cultivating the peasantry (Mao himself was of peasant origin), won a new Mandate of Heaven. In 1949, the disintegrating Nationalists retreated to the island of Taiwan as the Communists restored Beijing ("northern capital") as the country's capital and proceeded to implement the world's most sweeping revolution. On that occasion, Mao, reflecting his nationalistic sentiments, said: "Our nation will never again be an insulted nation. We have stood up." China today, in its race for respect and prestige, is still putting Mao's words into action.

KEY TERMS

Boxer (p. 379)

Bronze Age (p. 373)

civilization (p. 373)

Confucianism (p. 381)

corruption (p. 379)

demagogue (p. 379)

dynastic cycle (p. 375)

extraterritoriality (p. 379)

Han (p. 373)

kow-tow (p. 376)

Manchu (p. 375)

Mandarin (p. 373)

Mandate of Heaven (p. 375)

mass line (p. 382)

micro-credit (p. 379)

Middle Kingdom (p. 373)

Ming (p. 377)

Mongol (p. 375)

Nationalist (p. 382)

Neolithic (p. 373)

Open Door (p. 380)

Opium Wars (p. 379)

petrostates (p. 379)

pinyin (p. 374)

sphere of influence (p. 379)

steady-state (p. 376)

Taiping (p. 379)

Third World (p. 379)

treaty ports (p. 379)

warlord (p. 381)

Warring States (p. 373)

FURTHER REFERENCE

Antony, Robert J., and Jane Kate Leonard, eds. *Dragons, Tigers, and Dogs: Qing Crisis Management and the Boundaries of State Power in Late Imperial China*. Ithaca, NY: Cornell University Press, 2002.

Fairbank, John King. *China: A New History.* Cambridge, MA: Harvard University Press, 1994.

Gelber, Harry G. *The Dragon and the Foreign Devils: China and the World, 1100 B.C. to the Present.* New York: Walker, 2007.

Hutchings, Graham. *Modern China: A Guide to a Century of Change*. Cambridge, MA: Harvard University Press, 2001.

Morton, W. Scott, and Charlton M. Lewis. *China: Its History and Culture*, 4th ed. New York: McGraw-Hill, 2005.

Mungello, D. E. *The Great Encounter of China and the West, 1500–1800*, 2nd ed. Lanham, MD: Rowman & Littlefield, 2005.

Spence, Jonathan. *Mao Zedong*. New York: Viking, 2000.

———. *The Search for Modern China*, 2nd ed. New York: Norton, 2002.

Terrill, Ross. *China in Our Time*. New York: Simon & Schuster, 1992.

Tuan, Yi-Fu. *A Historical Geography of China*. Piscataway, NJ: Transaction, 2008.

The Soviet Parallel

In a parallel with the Soviet Union/Russia, we must also specify a "before and after" in dealing with political institutions. The break in China was not as sharp as the one that came with the collapse of the Soviet Union in late 1991, but we must remember that Russia has turned part-way back to authoritarianism. China had no comparable interlude of Russia's attempted democracy; it merely shifted into a lighter authoritarianism. The original Communist institutions Mao set up after taking power in 1949 were closely modeled after Stalin's Soviet system. Now they are somewhat changed, and the system as a whole is much looser and freer. Indeed, tourists intent on simply viewing the sights (both ancient and modern) and sampling the cuisine (good and cheap) might not notice they are in a Communist country. Mao's portrait on Tiananmen Square and all paper currency are among the few reminders of his rule.

The institutions of China's government are similar to what the Soviet Union had: interlocking state and Party hierarchies (see Chapter 20). For example, what is supposed to be the top Party body, the National Party Congress, has many of the same members as the top legislative body, the National People's Congress. (The two are easy to confuse. Just remember one is Party, the other state.) Typically, a Chinese leader first climbs into the upper ranks of the Party and then assumes high government jobs as well. In Communist systems generally, position in the Party determines who also gets governing power within the state structure. China's current chief, Hu Jintao, became Party general secretary a few months before being named president.

China, however, adds a Third-World twist to Communist governance: The army has also been quite important, at times intervening directly into politics, as happens in other developing countries. China, like Nigeria (see Chapter 31), has experienced upheaval and chaos, which has led to army participation in politics, the mark of a Third-World country. Typically, the army intervenes not merely to grab power but to save the country from disorder and breakdown. Until China is no longer vulnerable to upheaval, we cannot be sure the army will not intervene again.

As in the old Soviet model, each state and Party level ostensibly elects the one above it. In practice, the Party handpicks delegates to be elected from the lower to the higher congresses. In China, townships elect congresses every two years, which then elect some 2,800 county congresses every three years, which in turn choose provincial and big-city People's Congresses every five years. In the old days of Mao, factories were main base units of political organization; now it is townships. The provincial People's Congresses then elect the unicameral National People's Congress (NPC) of nearly 3,000 delegates—some 70 percent of them government officials—for a five-year term.

As in the old Soviet Union, this parliament is too big to do much at its ten-day annual sessions. Although still carefully controlled, recent NPC sessions have featured motions from the floor, lively debate, contested committee elections, and negative votes—possibly indications that the NPC may turn into a real parliament with some checks on the executive. This would be a major step to democracy, but it would require letting NPC delegates form links with outside groups and other members, whom they could mobilize and represent—in a word, parties. An individual NPC delegate introducing a bill is fine but no substitute for pluralism. Standing alone, the delegate is nothing; with groups behind them they are the building blocks of democracy. A faint beginning could be seen in the growing number of NPC joint motions and bills, each of which requires the signatures of at least thirty delegates. If this were to expand and solidify, the NPC would have the making of parliamentary parties (but not yet mass parties). Long ago such groupings in Britain's House of Commons marked the beginning of parties.

The NPC Standing Committee of about 155 is theoretically supreme, but it, too, does not have much power to oversee the executive branch. The chairman of the Standing Committee is considered China's head of state or president. As is usual in Communist countries, Party General Secretary Hu Jintao became president in 2003. The top of the executive branch is the State Council, a cabinet of approximately forty ministers (specialized in economic

Kremlinology   Noting personnel changes to analyze Communist regimes.

Zhongnanhai   Walled compound for China's top leaders next to Forbidden City in Beijing.

KEY CONCEPTS

INDIRECT ANALYSIS OF AUTHORITARIAN SYSTEMS

Democracies are easier to study than authoritarian systems. In democracies you can get a variety of data, much of it quantified, on public opinion, party positions, election results, legislative votes, and policy shifts. With authoritarian systems you can get only the policy shifts, and they are veiled by obscure wording. It may take a while to figure out what has changed.

During the Cold War, academics and journalists developed indirect techniques to study Soviet politics. Dubbed derisively **Kremlinology,** they focused on who in the Kremlin got promoted, demoted, or executed. By associating these personnel shifts with their positions and statements, observers attempted to infer the direction of Kremlin politics. Stalin's dismissal of Foreign Minister Maxim Litvinov in 1939, for example, and his replacement by Vyacheslav Molotov signaled a major shift in Soviet foreign policy, from trying to gain Western allies to making a deal with Hitler. Even who stood next to whom atop Lenin's tomb could be significant. In 1953, after Stalin's death, Kremlinologists noted that secret-police chief Lavrenti Beria was missing from the reviewing stand. "Maybe he had a cold," scoffed one American editor. Actually, Beria had already been shot as a threat to other Politburo members. In Kremlinology, little things mean a lot.

The equivalent, dubbed "China watching" (much of it from Hong Kong) during the Cold War, applied similar techniques to China. Who is under whose protection? Did Premier Zhou Enlai quietly protect Deng Xiaoping from the ravages of the Cultural Revolution? (It is likely that he did, in order to ensure a pragmatic successor.) Did Deng fire Party General Secretary Zhao Ziyang in 1989? (Clearly he did, because of Zhao's soft line on the Tiananmen demonstrators.) The 2005 Party Congress elevated four new younger men to the Standing Committee, including Xi Jinping, Shanghai's Party boss, and Li Keqiang, Party chief of Liaoning Province. Former Party chief Jiang reportedly favored Xi to take over the presidency when power changes in 2012; current chief Hu favored Li. Apparently a compromise was reached: Xi as president and Li as premier. China watching depends much on hearsay.

Indirect analysis, based on fragmentary evidence, guesswork, and faulty analogies, can lead to mistakes. A bright young Harvard China specialist took at face value an unverified (and probably bogus) report that Mao on his deathbed in 1976 handed Premier Hua Guofeng a note saying, "With you in charge I am at ease." From such dubious indicators, the Harvard professor concluded that Hua was indeed Mao's successor. But behind the scenes Deng Xiaoping still pulled the strings. He gradually sidelined Hua and kicked him out of the Politburo in 1981. The Harvard professor was denied tenure. Don't bet the farm on indirect analysis. Unfortunately, until the politics of the **Zhongnanhai** opens up, indirect analysis is all we have.

Beida   Short name for Beijing University, long China's best (equivalent to Japan's Todai).

Comintern   Short for Communist International; the world's Communist parties under Moscow's control.

branches) and a dozen vice premiers led by a premier, China's head of government, since 2003 Wen Jiabao. China, therefore, has both a president and a premier and superficially resembles the semipresidential system de Gaulle devised in France. In practice, China is more like the Russian system, in which the president (most of the time) is much more powerful than the premier. Most of China's current top leaders graduated in engineering or science and worked in those fields. In terms of education, China's governing elite is now among the world's brainiest and most technocratic, which tends to make them self-assured.

PERSONALITIES

TANDEM POWER: MAO AND ZHOU

For over a quarter of a century, until both died in 1976, power in Beijing was divided between Party Chairman Mao Zedong and Premier Zhou Enlai. This set a Chinese pattern of tandem power that still operates and may now be sufficiently institutionalized (see page 484) to continue into the future.

Both were of rural backgrounds, but Mao was born in 1893 into a peasant family in inland Hunan Province, while Zhou was born in 1898 into a gentry family in coastal Jiangsu Province. Mao's father had worked his way up from poverty to property and was counted as a better-off peasant, exactly the kind Mao ordered tried and executed by the millions in the early 1950s. Mao said his background let him understand China's peasants, but his cold-blooded policies showed no sympathy for them.

Mao went away to school but in late 1911 briefly became a soldier in the revolution against the dying Manchu dynasty. Mao never attended a university but graduated in 1918 from Hunan's teacher-training school. Already a radical nationalist, while there he organized the New People's Study Society, a precursor of the CCP. Mao briefly worked as a library assistant at Beijing University, the famous **Beida**, where he was caught up in the anti-Japanese May Fourth Movement of 1919. In 1921, when Chinese Marxists with **Comintern** help organized the Chinese Communist party (CCP) in Shanghai, Mao was one of its founding members.

Zhou went to a top high school and then to Japan in 1917 to study. Japan, having beaten the Russians

in 1904–1905 (see Chapters 18 and 19), was then an example and magnet for nationalists throughout Asia, including Chinese and Vietnamese. The 1919 May Fourth movement brought an exodus of Chinese students from Japan, and Zhou returned to China. Already a student radical, Zhou was jailed briefly in 1920. Upon release, Zhou went to France in 1920 to study, but with the founding of the CCP he worked at recruiting Chinese students in Europe to join the Communists. Zhou returned to China in 1924 to participate in Sun Yat-sen's Nationalist revolution. Mao had no experience outside of China.

As was often the case with young Chinese early in the twentieth century, Mao and Zhou were passionate Chinese nationalists before they turned to Marxism. Neither of them had much higher education, although both studied, debated, and published in Chinese leftist circles.

Under Moscow's orders, the young Chinese Communist party worked in alliance with the Nationalists. Zhou, for example, was in charge of political education at the Nationalist military academy at Whampoa, where Nationalist Jiang Jieshi was commandant. In 1927, Zhou became CCP military director. As KMT forces approached Shanghai that year, Zhou organized workers to seize the city. But Jiang, who was suspicious that the Communists were disloyal to the Nationalist cause, massacred them by the thousands, and both Mao and Zhou barely escaped with their lives. (Zhou was the model militant Chinese

The formal structure of China's executive may not always correspond to the real distribution of its power. In 1976, after the death of both Party Chairman Mao and Premier Zhou, a relative unknown, Hua Guofeng, was installed in both their offices. On paper, Hua appeared to be the most powerful figure in the land, but an elderly, twice-rehabilitated Party veteran, Deng Xiaoping (see box on page 392), who took the modest title of senior vice-premier in 1977, was in fact more powerful than his nominal boss, Hua. When Deng toured the United States in 1979, he acted like a head of state. Deng's power grew out of his senior standing in the Party and the army. In 1980, he demoted Hua and assumed power himself, still without taking over the job titles, which he left to others. By 1982, Hua was out of the Politburo and out of sight.

revolutionary for French writer André Malraux's novel *Man's Fate*, set in 1927 Shanghai.)

The next decade set the Mao-Zhou relationship. Mao concluded from his work with peasants that they were the means to China's revolution. Zhou initially remained loyal to Stalin's "proletarian line," which argued for a series of worker uprisings in China's coastal cities. Stalin knew little about the world and nothing about China. By 1931, after all uprisings had failed, Zhou changed his mind and joined Mao in his Jiangxi redoubt. From there, the two led the arduous Long March to the north. By the time they arrived in Yenan, Mao was clearly the leader of the CCP, and his "mass line" of basing the revolution on the peasantry prevailed.

Mao dominated mainly by force of intellect. Other CCP leaders respected his ability to theorize in clear, blunt language. Mao became the Party chief and the-oretician but did not supervise the day-to-day tasks of survival, warfare, and diplomacy. These became Zhou's jobs; he was the administrator of the revolution. Never bothering to theorize, Zhou was a master at shaping and controlling bureaucracies, clever compromise, and political survival amid changing lines. Asked for his views on the French Revolution, the cagey Zhou replied, "One should not comment on such a recent event."

There was some tension between the two, but Zhou never showed it. Publicly Zhou dedicated himself to fulfilling Mao's policies, although at times, in the shambles of the Great Leap Forward (1958–1960)

Beijing's Military Museum displays figures of Mao and Zhou at Communist headquarters during the war against Japan.

and the Cultural Revolution (1966–1969), he tried to stabilize things and limit damage. Mao was the abstract thinker, Zhou the pragmatic doer. This made Mao more radical and Zhou more conservative. Mao could spin out his utopian dreams, but Zhou made the bureaucracy, military, and economy function. Zhou's pragmatic views won out; all China's top leaders since 1977 have been Zhou's ideological descendants. Mao's radicalism has disappeared.

PERSONALITIES

THE INVISIBLE PUPPETEER: DENG XIAOPING

Deng Xiaoping

Deng Xiaoping followed a strange path to power. He had been purged from Chinese politics twice before becoming "senior vice-premier" in 1977, a deliberately deceptive title to cover the fact that he was China's undisputed boss. And Deng sought no fame or glory; unlike Mao, he built no personality cult. Deng seldom appeared in public or in the media but governed in the ancient Confucian tradition: quietly, behind the scenes, chiefly by picking top officials. MIT political scientist Lucian Pye called him the "invisible puppeteer." This former protégé of Zhou Enlai—who, like Zhou, was a pragmatic administrator rather than a theorizer—set China on its present course and gave China its current problems.

Deng was born in 1904 into a rural landlord family. Sent to study in France, Deng was recruited there by Zhou Enlai and soon joined the Chinese Communists. As a political commissar and organizer of the People's Liberation Army, Deng forged strong military connections. Rising through major posts after 1949, Deng was named to the top of the Party—the Politburo's Standing Committee—in 1956.

Deng was not as adroit as Zhou and kept getting into political trouble. An outspoken pragmatist, Deng said after the Great Leap: "Private farming is all right as long as it raises production, just as it does not matter whether a cat is black or white as long as it catches mice." During the Cultural Revolution this utterance was used against Deng to show he was a "Capitalist Roader." Although not expelled from the Party, Deng dropped out of sight and lost his official position. His son was crippled by a mob during the Cultural Revolution.

But the little man—Deng was well under five feet tall—bounced back in 1973 when moderates regained control. In 1975, he seemed to be ready to take over; he spoke with visiting U.S. President Ford as one head of state to another. But just a month later Deng was again in disgrace, denounced by the radicals of the **Gang of Four** as anti-Mao. Again, he was stripped of his posts, but an old army buddy gave him sanctuary in an elite military resort. The adaptable Deng bounced back yet again. With the arrest of the Gang of Four in 1976, moderates came back out of the woodwork, among them Deng. In July 1977, he was reappointed to all his old posts. Many Chinese state, Party, and army leaders, badly shaken by the Cultural Revolution, looked to old comrade Deng to restore stability.

In 1978 Deng, then already seventy-four, proclaimed his famous "Four Modernizations" of agriculture, industry, science, and defense. Typical of the veiled language of authoritarian regimes, Deng included permitting "side-occupations," which turned out to mean individuals could work growing, making, and selling things for personal profit. Thus a few words triggered a massive shift, as now city streets are lined with shops and restaurants run by individual entrepreneurs. Deng also urged "adaptation to local conditions," which meant the provinces and localities were freed from lock-step central direction. This was the starting signal for the rapid industrialization of the southern coastal regions.

Deng started China on its present course by splitting economics from politics. He, in effect, offered the Chinese a new deal: Work and get rich in a partly market economy but leave politics to the Communist party. This started China's amazing economic growth. But will not massive economic changes eventually influence politics? How much inequality can China take without unrest? Could provinces go off in their own directions? Apparently Deng never gave much thought to the contradictions he was creating, and they are now China's chief problems.

Deng was no "liberal." He encouraged economic reform but blocked any moves toward democracy, as have his successors. In 1989, Deng brutally crushed the prodemocracy movement in Beijing's Tiananmen Square. Although weak and reclusive in the 1990s, Deng still quietly controlled Beijing's top personnel and main policy lines until he died in 1997 at age ninety-two.

THE PARTY

Like the old Soviet Communist party, the Chinese Communist party (CCP) is constitutionally and in practice the leading political element of the country. With 70 million members, the CCP is large, but relative to China's population it is proportionately smaller than the CPSU was in the Soviet Union. As China's economy decentralized

Gang of Four Mao's ultraradical helpers, arrested in 1976. (See page 392.)

and marketized, the Party began admitting private businesspeople, provided they are patriotic and follow the Party line. Many business people see Party membership as a way to get government permits, loans, and contracts. Perhaps some day these capitalist Communists will introduce pluralistic perspectives into the Party's upper ranks, but so far the Party co-opts (see page 497) them as another device to control the economy and society. CCP leaders no longer wear military-style Mao suits. Instead, in coat and tie (usually red) they look like business executives, which some of them are.

With the economic changes since the late 1970s, the CCP has lost authority and sense of mission. Said one longtime Party member: "What does the Communist party stand for now? Nothing. Stability, maybe. But really no ideals at all." In today's China, lust for money trumps all else. Some Communist officials now use their positions for personal gain; massive corruption has set in. If not revitalized, the CCP could implode, leaving China without a backbone. Such revitalization would have to include, at a minimum, (1) a new, realistic statement of mission, of where the Party wants China to go; and (2) open disagreements among Party factions that media and citizens could discuss publicly. Allowing factions to publicly develop inside the Party could be a major step to eventual democratization, but nothing of the sort has been hinted at.

In organization, the CCP parallels the defunct CPSU. Hierarchies of Party congresses at the local, county, provincial, and national levels feed into corresponding Party committees. At the top is the National Party Congress; composed of some 2,100 delegates and supposed to meet at least once in five years, this congress nominally chooses a Central Committee of about 200 members. Since both bodies are too big to run things, real power is in the hands of a Politburo of about twenty Party chiefs. But this, too, is not the last level. Within the Politburo is a Standing Committee, now with nine members who really decide things. Power in China is highly concentrated.

The CCP's structure used to be a bit different from the classic Soviet model. Instead of a general secretary at its head, the CCP had a Party chairman, Mao's title, which he passed on to the short-term Hua Guofeng. By then, however, the office was robbed of meaning, and Hua was eclipsed by Senior Vice-Premier Deng Xiaoping, who, to be sure, also held important Party and army positions. Under Deng's guidance, the Party abolished the chairmanship—part of a repudiation of Mao's legacy—and upgraded the position of general secretary (*gensek*), so that now the CCP structure more closely matches that of the old CPSU. Since 2002 Hu Jintao has been CCP general secretary.

Generations of Chinese Communist Rulers			Accomplishments
First	Mao and Zhou	1949–1976	Won revolution, brutally communized, destructive upheavals
Second	Deng	1977–1989	Calmed China, allowed private enterprise, crushed Tiananmen
Third	Jiang, Li, Zhu	1989–2002	Foreign investment, rapid growth
Fourth	Hu and Wen	2002–	Calm technocratic rule to promote China's power and prestige

cadre French "framework," used by Asian Communists for local Party leader.

Deng arranged to have his protégé Hu Yaobang named general secretary. Hu, however, proved to be too liberal and unpredictable. He also failed to win approval of the army and was dropped in 1987. His place was taken by another Deng protégé, Zhao Ziyang, who in turn was ousted in 1989 for siding with student demonstrators. Replacing him was the hard-line mayor of Shanghai, Jiang Zemin, who retired as head of the Party in 2002 but retained important positions for a while afterward, just as Deng Xiaoping did. In China, one man no longer rules; a handful of the Party elite does.

China's nervous system is its Party **cadres**. There are 30 million CCP cadres, and whoever controls them controls China. In 1979, Deng Xiaoping began the ticklish job of easing out both the incompetent old guard—whose only qualification, in many cases, was having been on the Long March—and the extreme leftists who wormed their way into the cadre structure during the tumultuous Cultural Revolution. Quietly, Deng brought in younger, better-educated cadres dedicated to his moderate, pragmatic line.

PERSONALITIES

HU IS NEXT, AND WEN

In 1989, when Deng Xiaoping at age eighty-five gave up his last formal post—chairman of the powerful Central Military Commission—he made sure two protégés took over: Party General Secretary Jiang Zemin (who also took on the title of president) and Premier Li Peng. They were, respectively, sixty-three and sixty-one years old, the "third generation" of Beijing's Communist rulers. In 1998, when Li's two five-year terms were up, he was replaced as premier by Zhu Rongji, then seventy.

All three of these leaders kept firm central control of politics while encouraging the growth of a market economy. All silenced troublesome intellectuals. All were graduate engineers—still largely the case today—giving their rule a technocratic bent. None were popular, nor did they seek popularity. None returned to the visions of Mao, but all were cautious about major change. None suggested democracy in China's future. In late 2002, Jiang gave up his Party position, and in 2003 Premier Zhu retired.

China got its "fourth generation" of Communist leaders at the Sixteenth Communist Party conference in late 2002. Succeeding Jiang was Vice President Hu

Hu Jintao

Wen Jiabao

Jintao, then fifty-nine, picked by Deng Xiaoping before he died. An engineer, Hu was typed as an obedient technocrat. He was formally elected China's president by the National People's Congress in March 2003. Jiang tried to stay influential, as chair of the Central Military Commission, but in 2004, at age 78, he reluctantly stepped down, and President Hu became China's military chief, thus completing the triple transfer of power—head of party, of executive, of military. Succeeding Premier Zhu in 2003 was Deputy Premier Wen Jiabao, then sixty. Wen trained as a geologist but is experienced in finance and agriculture; he is reputed to be extremely bright. We do not know who will replace them, or when.

THE ARMY

Until recently, all top figures in the Chinese elite held both high state and high Party offices, as in the old Soviet Union. In China, though, they also held high positions atop the military structure, through the important Central Military Commission, which interlocks with the CCP's Politburo. Mao, Hua, Deng, and Jiang were all chairmen of the Military Commission, as is Hu now. In addition, the CCP Standing Committee usually has a top general.

> **paramilitary**   National police force organized and equipped like a light army, such as the French CRS.

From the beginning, the People's Liberation Army (PLA), earlier known as the Chinese Red Army and Eighth Route Army, has been so intertwined with the CCP that it is hard to separate them. Deng named an active-duty general to the elite Politburo Standing Committee, and several on the Central Committee are PLA. Fighting the Nationalists and the Japanese for at least a decade and a half, the CCP became a combination of Party and army. The pattern continues to this day. Political scientist Robert Tucker called the Chinese system "military communism."

Mao wrote, "Political power grows out of the barrel of a gun," but "the Party commands the gun, and the gun must never be allowed to command the Party." Where the two are nearly merged, however, it is hard to tell who is on top. As the Communists took over China in the 1940s, it was the PLA that first set up their power structures. Until recently, China's executive decision makers all had extensive military experience, often as political commissars in PLA units. Said Zhou Enlai, who had been involved in military affairs since the 1920s: "We are all connected with the army."

When the Cultural Revolution broke out in 1966, as we shall see, the army first facilitated, then dampened, and finally crushed the Red Guards' rampages. By the time the Cultural Revolution sputtered out, the PLA was in de facto control of most provincial governments and most of the Politburo. Several Politburo members are still active military men. At various times during mobilization campaigns, the army is cited as a model for the rest of the country to follow, and heroic individual soldiers are celebrated in the media.

What does PLA influence mean for the governance of China? Armies, as guardians of their countries' security, define whatever is good for them as good for the country. Anyone who undermines their power earns their opposition. During the Cultural Revolution, for example, Defense Minister Lin Biao fanatically supported Mao's program to shake up the Party and state bureaucracy. (The army was not touched.) As the chaos spread, however, military commanders worried that it was sapping China's strength and military preparedness. Lin became increasingly isolated within the military. In 1971 Beijing released the amazing story that Lin had attempted a coup and tried to assassinate Mao. The official story was that Lin fled to the Soviet Union in a plane that crashed. Outside observers accept the attempted-coup story but think that Lin was executed. Mao's bodyguard, the secretive Unit 8341, foiled the Lin plot, making China at that point literally praetorian. Lin's supporters were purged from the military. The PLA thus helped tame Maoist radicalism. China's attempted coup revealed a latent praetorianism that marks it as a Third World country (see Chapter 31 on Nigeria).

China's leaders seem to have decided that the army is not a good way to control domestic unrest. (They are right.) The PLA did not like mowing down students in Tiananmen in 1989. To deal with such situations, Beijing built up the People's Armed Police (PAP), now over 1 million strong. These **paramilitary** police, believed to be under PLA control, are sometimes called internal security forces. In addition, in 2005 riot police and anti-terrorist squads were merged into "special police" in preparation for the 2008 Olympics.

Forbidden City   Emperor's walled palace complex in Beijing.

geomancy   Divinely correct positioning of structures.

Tiananmen   Gate of Heavenly Peace, Beijing's main square.

China's leaders pay special attention to the PLA and are now increasing its budget, but the PLA, with 2.3 million soldiers, is still poor and underequipped. Trying to supplement its meager budget, the PLA went massively into private industry, running some 15,000 businesses. Worried about the PLA's corruption, smuggling, and loss of mission, President Jiang ordered the army to get out of business and get back to soldiering. They complied, indicating that the Party still commands

GEOGRAPHY

HEAVENLY GOVERNMENT: CONCENTRATED AND ISOLATED

The Mongols who founded the Yuan dynasty first made Beijing China's capital in 1267 and it mostly stayed that way. The first two Ming emperors in the fourteenth century set up their capital in Nanjing ("Southern Capital," although it is actually in the middle of China's coast), but the third Ming emperor returned it to Beijing ("Northern Capital"). The southern-facing Nationalists restored Nanjing as their capital from 1928 to 1949, but to escape the Japanese they had to flee far up the Yangzi River to make Chongqing their wartime capital.

The Mings also founded the **Forbidden City** as the divine center of Beijing in the early fifteenth century on a strict north-south axis; the main entrance is the Meridian Gate, so named because it is directly aligned with heaven. **Geomancy** was always important in traditional China. Only the emperor, his family, and a relatively few officials and servants were allowed to enter the walled, 178-acre City, which contains numerous halls and temples. The Forbidden City aimed to show Chinese (and later foreigners) by awe and magnificence that the emperor was the center of the universe. Unfortunately, it was also a huge, costly, extravagant tax drain, which isolated the emperor and absurdly overconcentrated power at a site too far north to be China's original core area, which is to the south, in the Yellow and Yangzi River valleys.

The Communist regime has at great expense elaborately restored the Forbidden City and made it the country's number-one public museum and tourist attraction. It is designed to show how the Communists have returned China to its deserved status at the center of

The Gate of Heavenly Peace to the south of the Forbidden City still bears Mao's portrait, one of the last few public signs of his influence.

heaven. Mao gave his 1949 "China has stood up" speech from the huge Gate of Heavenly Peace overlooking the wide-open **Tiananmen** Square, at the southern end of which sits Mao's mausoleum (officially called a "memorial hall"). Some wonder if the current leaders' isolation and the concentration of power in the adjacent top government offices of the Zhongnanhai spell similar trouble for the Communist regime.

the gun. In general, the PLA has been a conservative force in Chinese politics, for almost axiomatically, an army stands for order and sees disorder as a security problem. In China, when chaos threatens, the army moves.

In 2005 U.S. Defense Secretary Donald Rumsfeld expressed apprehension over China's rapidly growing defense budget, which probably understates actual expenditures. He asked what China is going to use its modernized forces for. The obvious answer is to take Taiwan, either by amphibious invasion across the Formosa Strait or, more likely, by intimidation that will frighten Taiwan into a mainland takeover without military resistance. Recovery of the "renegade province" of Taiwan burns brightly in the PLA, but it is not clear if the PLA sets Taiwan policy or has a deadline in mind. A top PLA general in 2005 warned bluntly of something nasty and nuclear if the United States interferes in the return of Taiwan to China. The PLA is still a major player in Chinese politics.

A Decentralized Unitary System

China, like most countries in the world, is organized on a unitary rather than federal basis, but its provinces and municipalities operate almost like units of a federal system, with what critics claim is too much local autonomy. The problem is an ancient one in China: how to govern a huge country from one capital city. Imperial China did it imperfectly through the Mandarin system. Mao did it

Geography

South versus North China

The way South Chinese see it, they do all the work and make tremendous economic strides while North China, home of the Beijing bureaucrats, just spends their taxes propping up dinosaur industries mostly in the North: "We earn it, they waste it." South Chinese officials proudly show off their instant high-rise cities and industries, implying superiority over North China. Such regional economic resentments are found worldwide—they trouble Italy and ripped apart Yugoslavia—but tend to be especially dangerous in the developing lands, where they can lead to breakaway movements and even civil war. (See the Nigeria chapter for an example of angry tension between the region with oil and the regions without it.)

There is no easy fix for regional economic disparities. If you shrug them off and say that the market will take care of things by automatically drawing capital to low-cost areas, you let wide areas of your country stay poor, weak, and resentful. Even the United States set up the Tennessee Valley Authority to remedy such a disparity.

On the other hand, if you set up a fund—as many countries have done—to develop poorer provinces, the richer provinces (who pay the biggest taxes) resent their extra tax burden. They further argue (often correctly) that investments in backward areas are less efficient than in the already more developed areas, which have the infrastructure and trained people. In the poor area, you have to start from scratch. A government fund can make foolish, costly investments in unsuitable regions—"cathedrals in the desert," as Northern Italians say of their Fund for the South.

China, in the name of regional imbalances, is now extending its industrial zones deep inland, along the Pearl and Yangzi Rivers. Startup and shipping costs are higher than in the southern coastal provinces, but Beijing feels it must be done, and in the long run they are probably right. China cannot have hundreds of millions of its people leaving poor inland provinces and moving to the southern coast. Better to bring jobs to them in their home provinces.

autonomous region   Soviet-style home area for ethnic minority.

Han   The core nationality and main people (93 percent) of China.

through the Communist party and its cadres, but he ruined the coherence and morale of the Party through his periodic upheavals (see Chapter 27). Now, with China dedicated to making money, local Party bosses simply boost the local economy and line their own pockets. They say in effect, "Heck, Beijing wants fast economic growth, and that's what I'm doing." China's unitary system has too little central control to overcome terrible problems of a poisoned environment, health and safety, and corruption. Beijing has laws for all these problems, but they are not enforced locally.

China has twenty-three provinces and four huge cities—Beijing, Chongqing, Shanghai, Tianjin—which count as provinces. In China, a "small" city like Xian, capital of Shaanxi Province, has 8 million people. China has 200 cities with populations of over 1 million. China lists Taiwan as its twenty-third province, something many Taiwanese do not wish to happen. Hong Kong and Macau—taken over from, respectively, Britain in 1997 and Portugal in 1999—are "special administrative regions," allowed to preserve local laws and economic systems (capitalist) for at least fifty years.

China also has five **autonomous regions**, a concept borrowed from Stalin's organization of the Soviet Union, where large nationalities got their own Soviet republics and smaller ones got autonomous regions within those republics. China's purpose here is the same as Stalin's: to give possibly troublesome ethnic groups use of their language and the feeling that they run local affairs. The most troublesome are the 8 million Turkic-speaking Muslim Uygurs of Central Asia in Xinjiang (literally "new frontier," named by the Manchu Qing dynasty). The regime arrests Uygurs of the East Turkestan Islamic Movement as dangerous terrorists with links to al Qaeda.

Tibet has a distinctive Buddhist culture and long ago was independent. First acquired by the Mongols in the thirteenth century as part of their Yuan dynasty, Tibet (Xizang) has been claimed by China ever since. The PLA crushed a major Tibetan independence uprising in the 1950s and a smaller one in 2008. Another potential troublesome area, Inner Mongolia (Nei Mongol), home of nomadic Buddhist herders, covers a huge swath along China's northern border. Stalin set up Outer Mongolia as independent Mongolia, a buffer on Russia's underbelly. China's autonomous regions have been gradually brought under Beijing's control by settling millions of **Han** Chinese in them.

Although a unitary system, Chinese administration is dangerously decentralized. Most national laws are written very generally and provinces are allowed to devise their own laws. Chinese lawyers advising foreign investors must now know the laws and usages of each province (and implicitly, whom to bribe). In China, one law does not fit all. Deng's administrative decentralization opened the gates to massive corruption as local officials seek cash incentives to interpret laws in the needed fashion. In a minor 2003 case about the price of seeds, a young woman judge in Henan Province ruled that national law overrides provincial law. Chinese jurists hoped it would modernize the unprofessional and corrupt court system and lead to judicial autonomy. "It may not be *Marbury v. Madison*," said a Chinese constitutional scholar, "but it is a very important case."

Key Terms

autonomous region (p. 398)	Forbidden City (p. 396)	Kremlinology (p. 389)
Beida (p. 390)	Gang of Four (p. 393)	paramilitary (p. 395)
cadre (p. 394)	geomancy (p. 396)	Tiananmen (p. 396)
Comintern (p. 390)	Han (p. 398)	Zhongnanhai (p. 389)

FURTHER REFERENCE

Ash, Robert, David Shambaugh, and Seiichiro Takagi, eds. *China Watching: Perspectives from Europe, Japan, and the United States.* New York: Routledge, 2006.

Barnouin, Barbara, and Yu Changgen. *Zhou Enlai: A Political Life.* Hong Kong: Chinese University Press, 2007.

Chang, Jung, and Jon Halliday. *Mao: The Unknown Story.* New York: Knopf, 2005.

Dreyer, June Teufel. *China's Political System: Modernization and Tradition,* 6th ed. New York: Longman, 2008.

Gilley, Bruce. *China's Democratic Future: How It Will Happen and Where It Will Lead.* New York: Columbia University Press, 2004.

Gittings, John. *The Changing Face of China: From Mao to Market.* New York: Oxford University Press, 2005.

Gries, Peter Hays, and Stanley Rosen. *State and Society in 21st Century China: Crisis, Contention, Legitimacy.* New York: Routledge, 2004.

Kuhn, Robert Lawrence. *The Man Who Changed China: The Life and Legacy of Jiang Zemin.* New York: Crown, 2005.

Li, Cheng. *China's Leaders: The New Generation.* New York: Rowman & Littlefield, 2001.

Lü, Xiaobo. *Cadres and Corruption: The Organizational Involution of the Chinese Communist Party.* Stanford, CA: Stanford University Press, 2000.

Nathan, Andrew J., and Bruce Gilley. *China's New Rulers: The Secret Files.* New York: New York Review of Books, 2002.

Saich, Tony. *Governance and Politics of China,* 2nd ed. London: Palgrave, 2004.

Chapter 26
Chinese Political Culture

One of the problems of the Third World countries is that few have a consistent political culture that has grown slowly over time. Instead—as we will also see in Mexico and Iran—they have imported and distorted waves of outside ideas that rarely blend into a coherent whole. And each wave of ideas is overthrown, often violently, by the next. We can see, for example, at least three layers in Chinese political culture. They sometimes reinforce and sometimes contradict one another.

Traditional Culture

Mao used to say that his countrymen were "firstly poor, secondly blank," meaning that the Communists could start with a clean slate and create the Chinese citizens they wished. Mao was wrong. Many values deeply ingrained over two-and-a-half millennia of Chinese civilization have carried over into the People's Republic. No one, not even Mao, could wipe them clean. Indeed, even Mao's vision of perfecting human nature by thinking right thoughts is a Confucian notion. Even after a century of upheaval, Chinese are still basically polite and deferential, testimony to the staying power of Confucianism.

When the Communists restored Beijing as the capital in 1949, they were restoring an old symbol, because Jiang's Nationalists had moved the capital to Nanjing (Southern Capital). Many traditionalists felt Beijing (Northern Capital) was the legitimate one. Top government offices and elite living quarters are in the Zhongnanhai, across the street from the old Forbidden City of the emperors. Tiananmen (Gate of Heavenly Peace) Square is still Beijing's parade and demonstration area, much like Red Square is in Moscow.

Another major symbol carried over from China's history is the deeply held conviction that China is one country and must never be divided, first articulated by Confucian intellectuals in reaction to the time of the Warring States. The Qing (Manchu) dynasty annexed Taiwan only in 1683 (to stop Taiwanese pirates and a Dutch takeover), but Chinese still feel strongly it is an eternal part of China and must soon reunify with the motherland. They are not adverse to using force to this end. We feel that Beijing exaggerates the Taiwan question, but it is part of Chinese political culture.

QUESTIONS TO CONSIDER

1. Could any country be culturally "blank," as Mao said?
2. How much of traditional China lingers under the surface?
3. How does the regime now use China's history?
4. Is China now more nationalist or Communist? How can you tell?
5. How do the three layers of China's political culture compare to Iran's?
6. Why does Beijing inflict periodic upheavals on China? What were the big ones?
7. What is *voluntarism* and how did Mao exemplify it?
8. How does China's political culture resemble Russia's?
9. Could nationalism turn aggressive in China?

The Communists' bureaucrats and cadres perform much the same function as the old Mandarins and gentry. Reciting the latest Party line instead of Confucius, the new elites strive to place a huge population under central control and guidance. Their aim now, to be sure, is growth and modernization, but still under a central hand. Mao himself recognized the similarity of old and new when he denounced the bureaucrats as the "new Mandarins" during the Cultural Revolution. Deng Xiaoping governed in the old Confucian style.

Another carryover from Old China: Age confers special qualities of wisdom and leadership in the People's Republic. Mao died at eighty-two and Zhou at seventy-eight, both in office. When he returned to power in 1977, Deng Xiaoping was seventy-three. In his early nineties he was still

GEOGRAPHY

PEASANTS IN THE CITIES

One of the characteristics of the Third World is rapid urbanization. Unemployed or underemployed rural people flock to cities looking for jobs and improved standards of living. The trend is strong in China, where the urban-rural gap is huge. Historically, some 90 percent of Chinese lived in the countryside, and 60 percent—some eight-tenths of a billion people—still do. They are not all peasant farmers; some pursue other rural trades, such as construction and vehicle repair. But in the last quarter-century a quarter-billion rural Chinese have left for the cities (some illegally), making China 40 percent urban, an incredible change with many ramifications.

Back in the village, discontent is no worse than it has always been. Most peasants are wretchedly poor, with some families living on around $1 a day. They can feed themselves, but any medical expense leaves them destitute. There are no health plans in rural China: no money, no treatment. When peasants go to a city to look for work—at 30 yuan ($4.20) a day in pick-and-shovel construction—they often become discontented. They see the vastly better life of the emerging urban middle class—apartments, cars, money to spend—and resent their lowly status. They also resent the regime having spent billions to redo Beijing to impress foreigners for the 2008 Olympics. The games are prestigious but do nothing for them.

There is still a carryover of peasant mentality in the willingness to work hard for one's family and not ask for much. Earthy peasant humor and folkways and frugal personal habits are found not only in villages today but in cities and industries. Many urban and educated Chinese remember growing up poor in a village. Unfortunately, newly arrived peasants in the cities also take a while to learn elementary sanitation and politeness. Spitting on the sidewalks and reckless driving are standard.

Peasants in the cities represent a huge problem for the regime. On the one hand, they know they have to get Chinese out of peasant farming. There is simply not enough land, and ignorant, uneducated peasants do not move China ahead. Unrest is growing in rural China as peasants protest land seizures and local officials who pocket fake taxes. Leading them are often unemployed ex-soldiers. On the other hand, the regime knows its cities cannot absorb hundreds of millions of rural newcomers, even if they are willing to live in shacks. They fear that a large, angry urban underclass might lend their numbers to protests started by students and intellectuals. There are, however, few such contacts across social classes, and the regime aims to keep it that way. China's millions of demobilized soldiers (and even officers) could be the cement that holds them together.

Beijing's current "fourth generation" leaders claim they are fighting rural poverty by spreading rapid industrialization inland, up the great river valleys, and into towns and smaller cities. They are trying to bring jobs to the peasants rather than peasants to the cities. If they can do this, they may succeed in bringing China's rural people up to a level of education and sophistication that could sustain democracy.

politically influential although weak and deaf. Former President Jiang and Prime Minister Zhu still governed in their seventies. Trying to break the tendency to gerontocracy, the Party now does not appoint anyone over seventy to a new position.

NATIONALISM

Overpowering traditional Chinese values is the more recent nationalism that has dominated China's intellectual life for more than a century. Chinese nationalism, like Third World nationalism generally, is the result of a proud and ancient civilization suffering penetration, disorientation, and humiliation at the hands of the West and Japan. This can induce explosive fury and the feeling that the native culture, although temporarily beaten by foreigners, is morally superior and more enduring. In our day, Chinese, Russians, and Iranians still act out their resentment of the West, especially of America. Most of what Beijing does today—from economic growth to space launches to hosting the 2008 Olympics—is out of a sense of nationalism. For the sake of Chinese power, Beijing has even accepted capitalism. Chinese communism is at heart Chinese nationalism.

In Asia, Chinese and Japanese nationalists vowed to beat the West at its own game, building industry and weaponry but placing them at the service of the traditional culture. The Japanese modernizers, starting with the 1868 *Meiji Restoration* (see pages 263–264), were able to carry out their designs; the Chinese are still caught up in this process, which from time to time leaps out in self-destructive campaigns. All of the founding generation of Chinese Communist leaders, including Mao and Zhou, began as young patriots urging their countrymen to revitalize China and stand up to the West and to Japan.

As in the old Soviet Union, the prevailing Chinese attitude is the nationalist drive to catch up with the West. During their good economic-growth years—the mid-1950s and since 1980—Chinese leaders were proud of their rapid progress. The Great Leap Forward and the Cultural Revolution ruined the economy. A pragmatic moderate such as Zhou or Deng always had a powerful argument against such disruptions: They harm growth and weaken China. Basically, this is a nationalist argument and one used by pragmatists today.

Chinese are deeply patriotic, sometimes in an angry way. Anti-U.S. Chinese nationalism is growing. Part is deep and genuine, part is hyped by the regime. Chinese do not like any foreigners pushing them around. Tension with the United States over Taiwan and Tibet and American pressures regarding human rights and copyright violations spark government-approved anti-U.S. campaigns. A popular book (modeled on an earlier Japanese book), *China Can Say No,* portrays a vast conspiracy led by America to keep China down (the same line put out by extreme Russian nationalists). Well, America better watch out, the book says, because China will defend itself. Chinese got angry when U.S. jets mistakenly bombed the Chinese embassy in Belgrade in 1999, a U.S. surveillance plane entered Chinese airspace in 2001, and their Olympic torch runners were harassed in 2008.

Anti-U.S. feelings are nothing compared to anti-Japanese feelings in China. Chinese bitterly remember how the Japanese army butchered Chinese civilians, even babies, during World War II. The 1937 Japanese "Rape of Nanjing"—with an estimated 20,000 female victims—is especially remembered. In 2005 Beijing again sponsored anti-Japanese protests. Emperor Akihito and some Japanese prime ministers, after a delay of several decades, have apologized for Japan's World War II crimes against China, but Japanese textbooks increasingly minimize or fail to mention the crimes, and Tokyo politicians still visit the Yasukuni Shrine, which honors war criminals among Japan's dead soldiers.

Maoism Extreme form of communism, featuring guerrilla warfare and periodic upheavals.

voluntarism Belief that human will can change the world.

Beijing turns on and off anti-U.S., anti-Japanese, or take-over-Taiwan demonstrations to deflect mass discontent, a very old governing technique. These outpourings are partly government-contrived but have strong roots in Chinese nationalism, especially against Japan. But once the protests get rolling, the protesters become too eager and use the demonstrations to vent displeasure at the Communist regime. Then the regime gets frightened and abruptly calls off the protests as "an evil plot to undermine the Communist party" and warns citizens to behave. Especially enthusiastic protesters are jailed. "Look at how worried they are," grinned one Beijing businessman at the 2005 anti-Japan demonstrations. "They lit a spark and set off a wildfire."

MAOISM

China's constitution still proclaims **Maoism**, or Mao Zedong Thought as Beijing calls it, as one of the bases of modern China, but the regime has let it fade to near-extinction. New high-school history books scarcely mention Mao. Maoism draws from both traditional and nationalistic values, despite its claim to be totally new and revolutionary. From traditional China, it takes the Confucian emphasis on thinking right thoughts, based on the idea that consciousness determines existence rather than the reverse: Willpower is more important than weaponry in wars; willpower is more important than technology in building China. The unleashed forces of the masses, guided by Mao Zedong Thought, can conquer anything. This extreme form of **voluntarism** comes from China's past.

From nationalism, Mao took the emphasis on strengthening and rebuilding China so that it could stand up to its old enemies and become a world power. The trouble is that traditional and nationalist values are partly at odds with each other. Traditional values call for China to ignore the West and its technology, but nationalist values call for China to learn and copy from the West. The unresolved conflict of these two streams of thought spells continuing trouble for China.

KEY CONCEPTS

DEFLECTING DISCONTENT

Yale's Harold Lasswell (1902–1978) helped define American political science with his 1936 classic *Politics: Who Gets What*. In that and other works Lasswell claimed that psychology explains much of politics. He argued, among many other points, that a nervous regime will try to deflect discontent away from itself, its problems and shortcomings, and onto allegedly threatening foreign powers; in a word, nationalism.

China's current rulers behave as if they have read Lasswell, cranking up (and then cranking down) anti-U.S. and anti-Japanese campaigns at periodic intervals. Many Chinese are tired of these campaigns and ignore them. The U.S. Congress is not bad at this game either, blaming China for everything from loss of jobs to oil prices. Twenty years earlier, they blamed Japan.

Maoism is an outgrowth of Mao's thoughts on guerrilla warfare (see page 382). According to Maoist doctrine, what the PLA did to beat the Nationalists, China as a whole must do to advance and become a world leader: Work with the masses, be self-reliant, and use more willpower than technology to overcome obstacles. Mao can be seen as a theorist of guerrilla warfare who continued to apply his principles to governance—with catastrophic results.

In the Great Leap Forward from 1958 to 1960, Mao tried guerrilla warfare tactics on the economy, using raw manual labor plus enthusiasm to build earthen dams and backyard blast furnaces. Engineers, experts, and administrators were bypassed. The Soviets warned Mao it would not work and urged him to follow the Soviet model of building the economy by more conventional means; Mao refused. In 1960, unhappy with Mao's radicalism, the Soviets withdrew their numerous foreign-aid technicians, and the Sino-Soviet split became public.

For the Soviet Communists, the revolution was over; the proletariat triumphed in 1917 and moved Russia into the most advanced stage of history. For Mao, the revolution never ends. Mao held that at any stage there are conservative tendencies that block the path to socialism: bureaucratism, elitism, and opportunism. Mao resolved to combat these tendencies by means of "permanent revolution," periodic upheavals to let the force of the masses surge past the conservative bureaucrats.

Socialism and bureaucratism are closely connected—as Max Weber saw long ago—but Mao thought he could break the connection. He saw China settling into the bureaucratic pattern he hated and was determined to reverse it by instituting a permanent revolution. The result was the

Political Culture

BEIJING RULES

Much can be learned from a taxi ride in Beijing. (Under no circumstances drive yourself.) Streets are crowded, sometimes clogged. Drivers dodge, weave, force their way, even drive on the wrong side of the street. They nearly run over bicyclists, pedestrians, and three-wheeled cargo motorcycles. A left turn into oncoming traffic is like a video game. But there are few collisions. Drivers are skilled and miss each other by inches. Car drivers yield only grudgingly to big trucks and buses.

Beijing Rules are basically: "There are no rules." Whatever rules are on the books are not enforced or even understood, so people do whatever they can get away with. In fairness, this lawless culture is standard throughout the Third World. In 2007, poisonous melamine found its way into U.S. pet food. Shrugged a manager of a chemical company that sells melamine: "No law or regulation says 'don't do it,' so everyone's doing it. The laws in China are like that, aren't they?" With close to zero supervision, China produces toxic toothpaste, lead-painted toys, and defective tires. Some mines and factories use child slave labor. Only when subjected to mass outcry do authorities stop covering up and go after wrongdoers.

This "no-rules" rule seems to apply to China's laws, government regulation, diplomacy, corruption, shopping, and fake or hazardous products. No one cares if it is illegal; one does whatever it takes to get ahead in business or traffic. Few pay personal income tax. The Chinese fighter pilot who clipped a U.S. surveillance plane in 2001 (he died) was flying by Beijing Rules. The massive pirating of foreign DVDs and sneaker and handbag labels are Beijing Rules. No accounting and banking standards are Beijing Rules. Beijing Rules exemplify the lack of civil society, of the usages and interactions that over time build up into polite, predictable behavior. Beijing Rules make China colorful but lawless. Eventually, China will have to evolve some rules.

Qin First dynasty to unify China, 221–206 B.C.

Taiwan Large island off China's southern coast, ruled by Nationalists since 1945.

Korean War 1950–1953 conflict involving North and South Korean, U.S., and Chinese forces.

Anti-Japanese War Chinese name for World War II in China, 1937–1945.

Great Proletarian Cultural Revolution from 1966 to 1976, during which young people were encouraged to criticize, harass, and oust all authority except the army. Chaos spread through China, the economy slumped, and the army took over. Shortly after Mao's death, power returned to the bureaucrats; they won and Mao failed.

Mao refused to recognize the unhappy truth that if you want socialism you must accept the big bureaucracy that comes with it. By trying to leap directly into a sort of guerrilla socialism without bureaucrats, Mao nearly wrecked China. On balance, Mao Zedong Thought is inherently inapplicable, and in today's China Mao is quoted little and out of context. Such vague homilies as "Get truth from facts" lets leaders claim they are following Mao even as they repudiate him. Mao's picture is on Tiananmen and *all* paper currency, but he has become a hollow symbol.

Political Culture

HOW CHINA USES ITS PAST

Mao hated old China and denounced it as feudal and reactionary. During the Cultural Revolution he encouraged Red Guards to "destroy the four olds." Zhou Enlai quietly ordered the army to protect important sites from their rampages. Since Mao's death in 1976, the regime has rediscovered—much as Stalin did—the utility of history: The past, artfully interpreted, makes it easier to rule the present. Beijing now uses old China to deliver lessons for today.

In 1974—fortunately after the worst of the Cultural Revolution—a farmer digging a well in the inland Shaanxi Province found the terra-cotta soldiers of **Qin** Shihuang, the emperor who first united China in 221 B.C. Archaeologists unearthed thousands of fragments—there are over 8,000 figures in all—and from them reconstructed hundreds of the life-size soldiers. Each one is different, apparently modeled on strapping individual soldiers of that day. To protect Qin in the afterlife, all were equipped with weapons (looted very early) and drawn up into companies of pikemen, archers, cavalry, and so on. They were originally painted in lifelike colors. Chinese and foreign tourists now swarm to see them at a major pilgrimage site near the city of Xian. The message: China's unity is eternal. You got that, **Taiwan**? (Actually, the pirate sanctuary of Taiwan was taken over by the Qing dynasty only in 1683.)

Likewise Beijing's Military Museum (which has its own subway stop) now devotes much space to an historical review of all China's dynasties, emphasizing that each had to be very strong in the face of peasant uprisings, breakaway provinces, and Mongol or Manchu invasions. No dynasty enjoyed tranquil times; all had to be prepared. If they weakened, they perished. Attempts to undermine or overthrow the emperor were punished by torture and dismemberment. You got that, intellectuals and troublemakers? Also in the Military Museum (but without English captions) is how the heroism of the PLA won the **Korean War**, which China fought to block U.S. aggression. You got that, Americans?

The strongest use of the past in today's China is the **Anti-Japanese War** of 1937–1945. (Remember, World War II began in China earlier than in Europe.) Beijing, in addition to the Military Museum, has a separate Anti-Japanese War Museum that stresses the atrocities the invaders committed. Television series show how China "fought bravely against Japan under the leadership of the Communist party." With communism no longer a usable ideology, the regime hypes hatred of Japan to deflect discontent and hold China together. The regime thunders against Japan getting nuclear weapons or a permanent seat on the UN Security Council, and all Chinese agree. You got that, Tokyo?

CROUCHING ANGER, HIDDEN DISSENT

Protests and demonstrations are increasing in China—among rural people, unemployed rust-belt workers, Tibetans, and Muslim **Uygurs** in **Xinjiang** Province in the west. Security officials admit there are tens of thousands of "mass incidents" every year, some of them ending in police gunfire. Most protests are local and unorganized; most seem to be spontaneous and related to specific grievances, such as evictions, land seizures, pollution, and corrupt officials. Local democracy would let angry people vote out crooked officials, but the regime is cautious about even small-scale democracy. Instead, it crushes protests, jails leaders, and smothers news reports. Brave souls who criticize corruption and incompetence—journalists, lawyers, medical

Uygur   Muslim, Turkic-speaking ethnic group bordering ex-Soviet Central Asia; sometimes spelled *Uighur*.

Xinjiang   China's northwesternmost province, home of *Uygurs*.

Century of Humiliation   China's term for its domination by imperialists from the first Opium War to Communist victory, 1839–1949.

Beijing often invokes its **Century of Humiliation** and sees its every move as erasing the humiliations and restoring China to its rightful place in the world. Mao's mausoleum is perfectly on-axis with the Meridian Gate of the Forbidden City across Tiananmen Square, just where the old geomancers would have sited it. Mao's continuity with the past he hated is now for all Chinese to see. In 2005 Archaeologists unearthed a 4,000-year-old bowl of petrified noodles, proving that China invented pasta. You got that, Italians?

The terra-cotta soldiers of Emperor Qin, who first united China in 221 B.C., remind Chinese of the unity and strength of their country.

Daoism From Dao, "the way"; old Chinese religion originally based on nature; earlier spelled *Taoism*. (See page 409.)

Jesuit Society of Jesus; Catholic religious order once especially active in converting Asians. (See page 409.)

doctors, and academics—are fired, harassed, and arrested. The doctor and editor who first reported the SARS virus were jailed. Workers who try to organize labor unions languish in prison. A nervous regime and Party, afraid that criticisms undermine their rule, deny and cover up problems.

One may find reasoned criticism and intellectual calls for reforms in China's cities, which have always been the sparkplugs of dissent. Although a small minority, the urban educated classes have often taken the lead in changing China. Student protests in Beijing, for example, go back more than a century; Mao himself as a young man participated in the student May Fourth Movement of 1919. Such protests contributed much to the overthrow of the Empire and the rise of first the Nationalists and then the Communists.

During the twentieth century, educated Chinese generally had a cause to believe in. At first it was building a new republic that would not be carved up by foreigners. Then it was in repelling the Japanese invaders. With the Communist takeover, many Chinese idealistically believed that Mao offered them a blueprint for a prosperous, socialist China. After Mao, Deng Xiaoping offered the image of a prosperous, semicapitalist China. After the June 1989 massacre of prodemocracy students in Tiananmen Square, many Chinese fell into despair. For most, Marx, Mao, and Deng have been discredited, and the Party now has nothing to offer except a better job for some.

What then do Chinese have to believe in? Make money, that's all. Chinese now display an almost complete lack of values. Confucian values are erased, bourgeois values never took hold, and Maoist values are discarded. As in Russia after the collapse of communism, China has an "anything goes" mentality in which everyone is out for themselves with no notion of a common good. This is partly the fault of the CCP's power monopoly: It alone is allowed to define the common good, and it fails to do so. Chinese live in a spiritual vacuum, which may be communism's saddest legacy. The regime does not mind the lack of values because it makes Chinese easier to govern. In the long run, though, something will fill the vacuum. We can only guess what it might be.

Missing in China is the *civil society* that is also weak in Russia (see Chapter 21). As Alexis de Tocqueville observed in *Democracy in America,* these are the autonomous associations bigger than the family but smaller than the state—churches, labor unions, business firms, bicycle clubs, voluntary groups—and the habits and usages that come with them. Such associations, the basis of pluralism and a prerequisite of stable democracy, are rising in China, as shown by the voluntary help for victims of the 2008 earthquake.

A huge but unknown number of environmental, farming, business, and homeowner groups form spontaneously in China, but the regime largely ignores them, rejecting their lawsuits and occasionally jailing obstreperous leaders. It takes over and supervises some of the biggest associations, but the key to pluralism is *autonomous* organizations, those outside of state control. (A few business people are co-opted into the CCP.) This has several negative ramifications. No organized group can pressure the regime to clean up China's air and water pollution. Individuals may make occasional environmental statements, and provided they do not push too hard may get away with it. No group can organize an environmental protest—any who try are quickly arrested—or demand elected representatives. No pluralism means no inputting devices from masses to rulers, which can lead to explosive frustration.

Religion, both old (including Christianity) and new, is growing rapidly despite the arrest, imprisonment, and torture of believers. The sudden rise in the 1990s of a new religion, *Falun Gong* (Buddhist Law), illustrates what happens to a spiritual vacuum: Dubious faiths rush in to fill it. Falun Gong

Political Culture

RELIGION IN CHINA

China appears even more irreligious than Japan. Nowadays money seems to be China's main religion. Officially, only 10 percent of Chinese are religious, but survey research suggests that some 30 percent are, two-thirds of them Buddhist or Daoist, China's traditional religions.

Buddhism (see page 447) was less important in China than Confucianism, and it never rooted itself in China as deeply as it did in Tibet, Japan, or Vietnam. **Daoism** survives in the cult of luck, which many Chinese are still obsessed with as the way to win money. Certain numbers, for example, are considered especially lucky and desirable. Muslims, both the Central Asian Uygurs of Xinjiang and the Chinese Hui Muslims in several pockets throughout China, may total 2 percent.

Confucianism—more a system of ethics than a religion—is newly rehabilitated and encouraged because it (1) is a form of Chinese patriotism; (2) offers an ideology now that communism has died; (3) builds the ethics China badly needs; (4) emphasizes order, authority, and obedience; (5) fits the Party's current "harmonious society" line; and (6) could head off the growth of other religions. Beijing has thus rediscovered what many regimes have practiced over the centuries: Religion is important to social and governing stability. Some suggest making Confucianism China's state religion.

Nobody knows how many Chinese are Christians because many Chinese Christians attend "home churches" outside of the few state-supervised churches. An estimated 3 to 6 percent of Chinese are Christians, a number that is believed to be growing. The Communists (and long ago the Boxers) always regarded Christianity as an unwelcome foreign import that missionaries used to subordinate China to the imperialists. Foreign missionary work is prohibited, and the leaders of some home-grown Chinese Protestant sects have been executed.

There has been a Catholic presence in China for centuries. Catholicism was first brought to China, as to Japan, by brilliant **Jesuits**, but the Communists in the 1950s ordered the Catholic Church to break with Rome and become a state-supervised "patriotic" church, which includes a large cathedral in Beijing. There could be as many as 12 million Catholics in China. The regime does not permit Rome to appoint bishops—the argument against foreign influence again—so there can be no ordination of new priests. Ordination of priests by Communist-appointed bishops does not count as Catholic, says Rome. Since 1980 there have been a few cautious contacts between Rome and Beijing, but these are slow to develop for at least two good reasons. The Vatican insists on the right to appoint bishops—which in effect means taking back the church from regime hands—and Beijing is aware of the Catholic Church's role in bringing down Communist regimes in Central Europe.

Some Chinese intellectuals, including a few at the official Academy of Social Sciences, note that Protestant Christianity first appeared in northwest Europe and made it capitalist, rich, and strong (a theory advanced a century ago by German sociologist Max Weber). Accordingly, it might not be a bad thing for China. On this basis, some Chinese intellectuals could be potential converts to Christianity. They, however, have little or no contact with the broad masses of Chinese and are unlikely to link up with underground churches. Christian intellectuals combined with broad masses of believers could produce a major Christian interest group in China, which is why the regime prevents it.

The regime fears any alternative organization that could challenge or ignore the Party. If Beijing permitted it, Christianity could spread rapidly in China, making the missionaries' old dream of a prosperous and democratic Christian China come true. Chinese badly need something to believe in, and Chinese society badly needs the pluralism that comes with churches. Allowing the free exercise of religion would mark a major step toward pluralism and democracy in China.

Tibet Himalayan region of China with distinct language and culture.

Putonghua "Common language" of China, now standard; used to be called Mandarin.

attracted all kinds of Chinese with faith healing and traditional exercises. As we saw in Japan, Buddhism generates offshoots without limit. Beijing understands that religion can bring upheaval—the Taipings and Boxers in the nineteenth century—and in 1999 denounced Falun Gong as a brainwashing cult, outlawed it, and arrested thousands of its followers. This is the reaction of a nervous regime. The chief commandment of Communist regimes: Thou shalt have no autonomous associations outside of Party control. The result is a yet-deeper vacuum where there should be a political culture. Aware of the problem, the regime has rehabilitated Confucius.

Some educated Chinese have rediscovered classic liberalism—the philosophy of freedom and small government of Locke, Adam Smith, and Jefferson—that was popular a century ago among Chinese intellectuals. Now young Chinese returning with American MBAs understand the free markets extolled by Hayek and Friedman. This could challenge the stale Marxism of the regime and lead to democracy, but discussions are low key and among friends. Open advocacy of liberalism could get you in trouble.

Over the decades, Chinese became politically numb. They had to mouth slogans and participate in mass campaigns—one year anti-Confucius, the next anti-capitalist roaders, then anti-Gang of Four, then anti-"spiritual pollution," then anti-"bourgeois liberalization"—without end. Chinese are fed up with this nonsense and mentally tune out. They become apolitical.

GEOGRAPHY

REGION AND LANGUAGE

China illustrates the close connection—and problems—between a country's languages and its regions. All but small countries have regions, often based on language. In some cases, as between Serbs and Albanian-speaking Kosovars, the country splits apart. China is populated mostly by Han Chinese (there are important non-Han minorities in **Tibet**, Xinjiang, and elsewhere), but Han are divided into several languages.

China's rulers have always proclaimed the unity of China, but China is the world's most linguistically complex country with eight main language groups—mutually unintelligible—and hundreds of dialects. The biggest language by far is Mandarin, dialects of which are spoken by 800 million in a broad swath from north to south, but not in the important southern coastal provinces, where 90 million speak some form of the Wu language (including Shanghai) and 70 million speak Cantonese.

China's rulers have always feared that separate languages could lead to breakaway tendencies. Since 1913

under the KMT, the regime has tried to make Mandarin standard and universal. The Communist regime has largely succeeded with the modified Beijing dialect of **Putonghua**, now the language of government and education. Putonghua has been the classroom language starting in elementary school for some time, so now most Chinese who have been educated in the last quarter-century can speak it, sometimes along with the local language. A Shanghai professional, for example, might speak the Shanghai language for daily life but switch to Putonghua to communicate with non-Shanghai Chinese. (In addition, the Shanghai professional is likely to know English, needed for international business.) Unfortunately, some Chinese children get little schooling, and in the countryside local dialects are still used, especially by old people. The new prosperity in China's southern coastal provinces has actually boosted the use of their local dialects. Beijing is not pleased.

The great hope for Chinese students is to go abroad. Many study English and dream of joining the thousands of Chinese students already in the United States, many of whom do not return to China. The regime, aware of this brain drain, now restricts their numbers. Chinese university graduates are supposed to first work five years before they can apply for graduate study overseas. The great prize: a graduate degree, often an MBA, from a prestigious U.S. university. Some high-ranking Chinese get their children into such programs.

bourgeoisie   French for middle class; adjective *bourgeois*.

Qinghua   China's top technological university, in Beijing (still often spelled, in Wade-Giles, *Tsinghua*).

The Chinese way of handling the latest government crackdown on freedom and democracy is called *biaotai*, "to express an attitude." Chinese know how to crank out the current line while concealing their true feelings. This leads to what Chinese call *nei jin, wai song,* "tranquility outside, repression within." Everything looks calm, but only because people know they are being carefully

KEY CONCEPTS

A BOURGEOIS CHINA?

One of the contradictions now troubling China is the fact that a Marxist country is rapidly creating a middle class, precisely the class it claims to staunchly oppose. Anti-bourgeois ideology is woven into Marxism. Even as a student Marx hated the bourgeoisie; he later developed his complex theories to prove that they were doomed. Actually, they were and still are the most successful social class in history. The **bourgeoisie** rose with the modern state and created the modern economy. They brought prosperity, democracy, personal freedom, education, and mass communications. Marxists are loath to admit that middle classes do anything good. They may be a temporary necessity but only in the march to a proletarian paradise.

Now China is creating a new middle class at a record-setting rate by expanding its universities. The regime, itself run by engineers, educates massive numbers of engineers and scientists to push China's economic growth. The portion of young Chinese attending college shot up from 1.4 percent in 1978 to about 20 percent in 2005. (Over 40 percent go to college in the United States.) Students who test well get into one of a dozen prestige universities. China's Harvard is (and for a century has been) Beijing University (*Beida*); its MIT is the nearby **Qinghua**. China has many lesser institutions with lower standards for

admission. A problem for the regime: More students can lead to more student protests.

A major definitional problem appears: What, exactly, makes one middle class? A certain level of income? Of education? Of material possessions? There is no standard definition, at least not one that can be used transnationally. A definition of the Spanish middle class would be useless applied to China. The urban Chinese who dwell in shabby apartments or traditional crowded alleyways (called *hutongs* in Beijing), are poor by our standards but middle-class by Chinese standards. They own televisions and electric fans. What we see as middle class—nice but small apartments with air conditioners (necessary for China's summers)—in China is probably upper-middle class. The few who can afford large, modern housing—most with California-type names—constitute an upper class for China but would be just middle class in America.

The more important question: Does becoming bourgeois make one interested in politics and in favor of democracy? Or can the regime forever feed the material cravings of the middle class and keep it quiet and disorganized? Virtually all industrializing countries show that as middle classes grow they demand responsive political systems and increasingly voice their discontent. They turn from passive to active.

blog   From "Web log"; self-published reviews and comments on the Internet.

Solidarity   Huge Polish labor union that ousted the Communist regime in 1989.

watched. Just below the surface, though, repressed anger waits to erupt. Some of this shows up in the constant flow of nasty rumors about repression, economic incompetence, and the corruption of officials. This has been called a struggle between the Big Lie and Little Whisper: The government tries to fool people with big lies, but the people fight back with little whispers. Chinese, knowing that contacts with foreigners may be monitored, are reluctant to discuss anything political (or religious) with visitors.

Computers and cellphones now provide outlets for and means to organize discontent. China has more than 210 million Internet users, a number sure to increase. Some 30,000 censors supervise China's Net, filtering e-mails for key words such as "democracy," "Tiananmen," and "Taiwan." Chinese students call it the "Great Firewall." The regime jails some **bloggers** for "subverting state power" and closes hundreds of critical sites, but they quickly reopen under new names. "They can keep closing sites, but they never catch up," said one slippery blogger. Cellphones, used by over 350 million Chinese and impossible to monitor, now energize and organize local protesters. A text message, very cheap in China, can reach many, simultaneously and anonymously. (Chinese text message in pinyin.) The digital age may ultimately make dictatorship impossible.

China's elite is frightened, and the system as a whole is unstable. Most Chinese are apolitical, but a fraction dislikes and distrusts the regime. They are more prevalent in the South, which has long resented rule by the North. Many Chinese are frustrated by a Party elite that simply wants to cling to its power and good jobs and hinders China's progress. They know that in the southern coastal zones, where capitalism and foreign investment began, the economy is booming. Why then not just expand free enterprise until it covers all of China? They also know that Taiwanese enjoy five times the per capita income and far more freedom than mainlanders. Some Chinese students speak with shame that they did not have the guts to do what the Romanians did in 1989: stand up to the government's guns and overthrow the regime. In time, Chinese student frustration could boil over again.

In the right situation—for example, a split in Beijing leadership over personnel and policies—China's peasants, workers, and students could make common cause and challenge the regime. Needless to say, the police work hard to prevent a Chinese equivalent of Poland's **Solidarity**. Political repression, of course, solves nothing; it merely postpones the day of reckoning. What happened in East Europe could happen in China.

Proud China

How can a regime handle the several and contradictory impulses of Chinese political culture? Uncontrolled, they could be dangerous. Beijing's answer seems to be to cultivate nationalistic pride. Almost everything the regime does goes toward demonstrating China's greatness. In 2003 China, bursting with pride, sent an astronaut into earth orbit, the third country to do so. China's motive was the same as the earlier U.S. and Soviet space programs: to show the world that it is a great nation. In 2008, Beijing hosted the Olympics, which China used to showcase how modern and powerful it is.

China is quite open about its aim to become once again the leading power in Asia and the second power globally, after the United States. In economics, China has already done this. Will China's policy of national pride ease China through to becoming a normal, prosperous, and respected country? Or could national pride run out of control and turn aggressive and expansionist? This could be the great question of the twenty-first century.

KEY TERMS

Anti-Japanese War (p. 406)

blog (p. 412)

bourgeoisie (p. 411)

Century of Humiliation
  (p. 407)

Daoism (p. 408)

Jesuit (p. 408)

Korean War (p. 406)

Maoism (p. 404)

Putonghua (p. 410)

Qin (p. 406)

Qinghua (p. 411)

Solidarity (p. 412)

Taiwan (p. 406)

Tibet (p. 410)

Uygur (p. 407)

voluntarism (p. 404)

Xinjiang (p. 407)

FURTHER REFERENCE

Bell, Daniel A. *China's New Confucianism: Politics and Everyday Life in a Changing Society.* Princeton, NJ: Princeton University Press, 2008.

Chase, Michael S., and James C. Mulvenon. *You've Got Dissent! Chinese Dissident Use of the Internet and Beijing's Counter-Strategies.* Santa Monica, CA: Rand, 2002.

Chen, Jie. *Popular Political Support in Urban China.* Stanford, CA: Stanford University Press, 2004.

Gifford, Rob. *China Road: A Journey into the Future of a Rising Power.* New York: Random House, 2007.

Goldman, Merle. *From Comrade to Citizen: The Struggle for Political Rights in China.* Cambridge, MA: Harvard University Press, 2005.

Gries, Peter Hays. *China's New Nationalism: Pride, Politics, and Diplomacy.* Berkeley, CA: University of California Press, 2004.

Kang Zhengguo. *Confessions: An Innocent Life in Communist China.* New York: Norton, 2007.

King, Ambrose. *Chinese Society and Politics.* New York: Oxford University Press, 2005.

Leonard, Mark. *What Does China Think?* New York: PublicAffairs, 2008.

Paltiel, Jeremy T. *The Empire's New Clothes: Cultural Particularism and Universal Value in China's Quest for Global Status.* New York: Palgrave, 2007.

Qing, Dai. *Tiananmen Follies: Prison Memoirs and Other Writings.* Norwalk, CT: EastBridge, 2005.

Sang Ye. *China Candid: The People on the People's Republic.* Berkeley, CA: University of California Press, 2006.

Starr, S. Frederick, ed. *Xinjiang: China's Muslim Borderland.* New York: M. E. Sharpe, 2004.

Tang, Wenfang. *Public Opinion and Political Change in China.* Stanford, CA: Stanford University Press, 2005.

Zhao, Suisheng. *A Nation-State by Construction: Dynamics of Modern Chinese Nationalism.* Stanford, CA: Stanford University Press, 2004.

Chapter 27
China:
Patterns of Interaction

Since the Communists came to power in 1949 there have been three major upheavals plus several smaller ones. Among major upheavals are the "agrarian reforms" (that is, execution of landlords and redistribution of land) of the early 1950s, the **Great Leap Forward** from 1958 to 1960, and the **Cultural Revolution** from 1966 to 1976. Smaller upheavals include the brief Hundred Flowers liberalization of 1956, the antirightist campaigns of 1957 and the early 1970s, the crushing of the Gang of Four and their supporters in the late 1970s, and the 1989 repression of alleged "counterrevolutionary rebellion" of prodemocracy students.

Cycles of Upheaval

The big upheavals and most of the smaller ones can be traced to the same underlying problem: Beijing's leaders, having inherited a poor and backward land, want to make China rich, advanced, and socialistic. Mao Zedong Thought taught that everything is possible: China can leap into the modern age and even beyond it. But the old, stubborn, traditional China does not yield; it frustrates the bold plans and tugs the system back toward the previous patterns and problems.

Observers used to label CCP figures as "radicals" or "moderates" according to their willingness to support the upheavals Mao periodically decreed. China's moderates were and still are those high up in the Party, government, or army. Almost axiomatically, anyone who is part of the establishment will not be a radical. Mao was right: Bureaucrats are by nature conservative. China's radicals were drawn largely from those peripheral to power but ambitious for it: students, junior cadres, and some provincial leaders. The old radical-moderate split, however, faded with the death of Mao and was replaced with a right-left split.

One of the prime motivations for radicals, especially during the Cultural Revolution, was the scarcity of job openings in Party, state, army, industrial, and other offices. For the most part, positions in those years were staffed by aging Party comrades who went back to the 1949 liberation or even the Long March. They never retired, and their longevity in office bred impatience and resentment among younger people with ambitions of their own. A further element fueling youthful discontent was the difficulty of getting into a university. Such tensions underlay the radical outburst of the Cultural Revolution. Those who aspired to power enthusiastically attempted to carry out

Mao's designs. Those who held power pretended to go along with it, often by mouthing the correct slogans and self-denunciations. In Mao's words, they "waved the red flag to oppose the red flag." When the campaign burned itself out, the bureaucrats and cadres took over again, and it appeared that the moderates had won.

Chinese Left and Right Politics

With the Maoist demon back in the bottle, a new split between right and left views inside the Party gradually appeared, although few put these labels on themselves, as that would be politically risky. The Chinese left tends to be older people, with secure positions in the Party, army, and bureaucracy, much like Soviet *apparatchiks*. Many are from poor areas that have been left behind. Some academics deplore the major inequality that has developed in China and want to fix it. They note that the constitution still says "socialist," and they want some centralized control over the economy to lift up the vast and impoverished inland provinces with health insurance and free education for all.

The so-called "right" is often younger and includes urban people who favor the free market. They see the inefficiency of central economic control and point to the record-setting economic growth that came with private and foreign enterprises. "All we have to do is expand the market system until it covers the whole Chinese economy,"

Great Leap Forward Mao's failed late 1950s effort to industrialize China overnight. (See page 415.)

Cultural Revolution Mao's late 1960s mad effort to break bureaucracy in China. (See page 415.)

Red Guards Radical Maoist youth who disrupted China during the *Cultural Revolution*. (See page 417.)

KEY CONCEPTS

THE GREAT LEAP FORWARD

In 1958 Mao Zedong launched one of the strangest efforts in the Third World's struggle to move ahead: the Great Leap Forward. Vowing to progress "twenty years in a day" and "catch up with Great Britain in fifteen years," all of China was urged to "walk on two legs" (use all possible means) to industrialize rapidly. Most peasants—then a majority of Chinese—were herded into gigantic communes, some with as many as 100,000 people. Deprived of their private plots, they were ordered to eat in communal dining halls, leave their children in nurseries, and even sleep in large dormitories.

The communes were ordered to participate in engineering and industrial projects. Relying on "labor-intensive" methods to compensate for lack of capital, millions were turned out to move earth with baskets and carry poles to build dams and irrigation works.

Backyard blast furnaces were ordered built so that every commune could produce its own iron.

Within a year the failure was plain for all to see. Even Mao had to admit it; he resigned as president of the PRC but kept his chairmanship of the CCP. Peasants—as in the Soviet Union—failed to produce without private incentives. Labor was wasted in foolish projects. Major food shortages developed, and over 30 million Chinese died of malnutrition. To meet Party quotas, peasants melted down their good tools to produce implements of miserable quality. The communes were phased out, broken first into "production brigades" and then into "production teams," which were in fact the old villages. Private farming was again permitted. Mao lost; old China won.

Key Concepts

The Great Proletarian Cultural Revolution

If the Great Leap Forward was strange, the Great Pro-letarian Cultural Revolution was downright bizarre. In it, an elderly Mao Zedong tried to make his revolution permanent by destroying the very structures his new China had created. Of the many slogans from the Cultural Revolution, "bombard the command post" perhaps best summarizes its character. Mao encouraged young people, who hastily grouped themselves into ragtag outfits called **Red Guards**, to destroy most authority, even the CCP. They did, and Chinese progress was set back years. Some of their slogans, many of them quotes from Mao:

- "Put destruction first, and in the process you have construction."
- "Destroy the four olds—old thought, old culture, old customs, old habits."
- "Once all struggle is grasped, miracles are possible."
- "Bombard the command post." (Attack established leaders if they are unrevolutionary.)
- "So long as it is revolutionary, no action is a crime."
- "Sweep the great renegade of the working class onto the garbage heap!" (Dump the moderate chief of state, Liu Shaoqi.)
- "Cadres step to the side." (Bypass established authorities.)
- "To rebel is justified."

The Cultural Revolution began with a 1965 flap over a Shanghai play some radicals claimed criticized Mao by allegory. Mao turned a small literary debate into a mass criticism that led to the ouster of several Party officials. Then university and high-school students were encouraged to air their grievances against teachers and school administrators. Behind their discontent was a shortage of the kind of jobs the students thought they deserved upon graduation. Some young people saw a chance to cut loose and have fun destroying things.

By the fall of 1966, most schools were closed as their students demonstrated, humiliated officials, wrote wall posters, and traveled to "share revolutionary experiences." China was in chaos. Well over a million victims of the Red Guards were killed or committed suicide. A much larger number were "sent down" to the countryside to work with the peasants and "learn from the people." This included physical abuse and psychological humiliation. Worried officials set up their own Red Guard groups to protect themselves. Different Red Guard factions fought each other.

Even Mao became concerned, and in early 1967 he ordered the army to step in. By the end of 1967 the People's Liberation Army pretty much ran the country. To replace the broken governmental structures, the army set up "revolutionary committees," upon which sat PLA officers, Red Guard leaders, and "repentant" officials. By 1969, the worst was over, although officially the Cultural Revolution did not end until 1976 when Mao died and the ultra-radical Gang of Four (headed by Mao's wife, Jiang Qing) was arrested.

The effects of the Cultural Revolution were all bad. Industry suffered. Education, when it resumed, was without standards, and students were chosen on the basis of political attitudes rather than ability. The more moderate and level-headed officials, whom the Red Guards sought to destroy, laid low and pretended to go along with the Cultural Revolution. When it was over, they reasserted themselves and made sure one of their own was in charge: Deng Xiaoping.

And what became of the Red Guards? Claiming their energy was needed on the farm, the army ordered more than sixteen million young city people to rural communes for agricultural labor and forbade them to return to their cities. By hook or by crook, many of them managed to get back to their homes to try to continue their studies. Some, utterly disillusioned with the way they had been used, turned to petty crime or fled to the British colony of Hong Kong. Some eventually became capitalist millionaires in China's new market economy.

Left and Right in Chinese Politics

Left	Right
selectively quote Mao	forget about Mao
keep Party Communist	admit business people
control media closely	freer media
help the poor	tolerate inequality for sake of growth
don't get too capitalist	largely market economy
oppose foreign influence	open to foreign influence
minimize mass input	expand local elections
take over Taiwan	tolerate Taiwan
ideological	empirical

they say in effect. The inequalities that have developed will also be cured by the market, they argue, as businesses locate to low-wage areas. Some also hint at Western-style political democracy and cultural freedoms.

President Hu and Prime Minister Wen try to balance left and right, with measures to both please poor inland people and the urban coastal middle class, for example, by simultaneously promoting welfare measures and property rights. In the National People's Congress right and left debate such issues. For example, a 2007 law on property rights had to proceed cautiously. No one owns land in China, but city dwellers can get "usage rights" of from forty to seventy years, and farmers can get thirty-year leases. The new law makes these rights more secure, something the left does not like, as it seems to overturn socialism and favor the better off. The urban middle class likes very much the greater security over their apartments and businesses.

As we discussed in connection with the old Soviet Union, ideology is often a mask for self-interest. The people who have the cushy jobs warn that democracy and liberalization mean "abandoning socialism." In analyzing Communist (and many other) systems, take ideology with a grain of salt; follow the jobs. (Think the jobs explanation is an exaggeration? What motivates you?)

The left-right split caused Deng and his successors much grief. They liberalize cautiously, hoping to confine it to the economic sector while still firmly controlling the political sector. But demands keep bubbling up to go farther and faster. In the spring of 1989, tens of thousands of Chinese university students staged giant protests and hunger strikes in favor of democracy. Deng fired his hand-picked and liberal-minded successor, Zhao Ziyang, and had the PLA mow down the students in Tiananmen Square. Several hundred died, and some ten thousand were imprisoned. A chill settled over Chinese life. Conservatives also launched anti-Western campaigns (see box on page 419). The conservatives had one serious drawback: Most were elderly. Time was on the side of the liberalizers, but not without rear-guard conservative actions.

Rule by Engineers

We mentioned *technocrats* in connection with French governing style (and will consider it again in the Mexico chapter), but the term applies much more to China. Of the fourth generation of China's rulers—the nine current members of the Party's Standing Committee, which really rules—

most are graduate engineers. In most of the world, technocrat means a high unelected official who governs by economic and financial skills, often the case in France. In China it means top unelected officials with engineering backgrounds. To be sure, China's engineers often know a good deal about economics, but it is focused on building dams and factories rather than on the bigger questions of where China should go and how to get there. Engineers are more trained in **microeconomics** than in **macroeconomics**.

microeconomics   Close-up picture of individual markets, including product design and pricing, efficiency, and costs.

macroeconomics   Big picture of a nation's economy, including GDP size and growth, productivity, interest rates, and inflation.

What does rule by engineers do for China? They are quite bright, and their emphasis on rationality generally means they minimize ideological considerations, a welcome change for a China that was drenched in and ruined by Maoism. In most cases they will allow the growth of a market economy in China, so long as it builds a richer, stronger China, as they are also very nationalistic. They beam with pride at China's economic growth and the world political clout that comes with it.

But technocrats—whether in France, Mexico, China, or even the United States—have a huge weakness that often dooms their efforts: They expect quick, right answers and pay little or no attention to the human factor and to long-term consequences. They are cool, distant, rational numbers-crunchers. As we discussed in Chapter 10 on France and in Chapter 17 on the European Union, the decisions of distant bureaucrats, even if they are the correct economic decisions of very bright people, rub citizens the wrong way. Thus the French are permanently angry at their own government in Paris and at the EU in Brussels. In 2005 they voted down the new EU constitution. More than a century ago in Mexico, Díaz's *científicos* (an early form of technocrat) thought they were developing Mexico's economy, but they were just making the vast majority of Mexicans poorer and poorer (see page 483).

America has its own painful example of a technocrat in Robert McNamara, Johnson's brilliant secretary of defense (he had a Harvard MBA), who assured us in 1962 that "every quantitative measurement we have shows we're winning the war" in Vietnam. He overlooked the human factor that

Political Culture

ANTI-WESTERN CAMPAIGNS

Every few years China is hit with a campaign aimed at making the Chinese pull away from the Western model of economic and political freedom. The work of conservatives within the CCP, these campaigns warned that decadent Western ideas such as free enterprise, open discussion, and a loosening of Party control would mean the end of socialism in China.

In late 1983, the catchword was "spiritual pollution," meaning that Western styles in clothes, music, and thought were ruining China. Deng, fearing the campaign was being used to block his economic liberalization, called it off after only four months.

In 1986, a somewhat longer campaign against "bourgeois liberalization" appeared, ruling out any discussion of ending the CCP monopoly on power and replacing it with Western-style liberalism. After the 1989 Tiananmen Square massacre, conservatives charged that it was a "counterrevolutionary rebellion" inspired by Western influences, which had to be curbed. We have not seen the last anti-Western campaign.

think tank   Research organization that analyzes problems and advocates policies.

the enemy was willing to take enormous casualties to expel the Americans and unify their country. The human factor did not compute, so he missed it. You begin to see why "technocrat" is often preceded by an unprintable adjective.

China's technocrats operate along similar lines: Numbers matter, people do not. The technocrats argue that at this stage of China's economic takeoff, they are precisely the right people to run things. The quicker they can industrialize China, the sooner they can start spreading the prosperity. No country has industrialized in an even, fair, and balanced way. The beginnings of capital accumulation are rough in any country, characterized by inequality and bad working conditions. That is why labor unions formed in Western countries. China, like all Communist countries, has official unions (under the control of the All-China Federation of Labor Unions), but they do not complain or strike, even over the most wretched and dangerous working conditions. China permits no independent unions and jails anyone who tries to organize one. Unions just get in the way of rapid growth—an old capitalist argument. Even worse, unions (along with churches) would be organizational alternatives that could rally opposition to Communist rule.

Furthermore, China's technocrats could point out, Japan also industrialized on a top-down basis, first with the Meiji modernizers (see pages 263–264) and then after World War II with MITI (see page 273). China should do the same. But beware of analogies between countries; they can be deceiving. Meiji central control of Japan's rapid modernization relied on the brutal suppression of common people and paved the way to Japan's aggressive militarism. (Some see parallels between this and China's current industrialization.) MITI influence after the war—and some say MITI was never really that important—took place in a democratic context with few state enterprises that had to be privatized. One point in common: Both Japanese and Chinese banks lent foolishly and recklessly, and both refused for years to admit that they were insolvent. The Japanese banks, however, are privately held and accountable to shareholders; the Chinese banks are state-owned and little accountable to anyone. The MITI analogy applies poorly to China.

China's current technocrats must be given some credit for trying to correct the imbalances. They recognize that extreme economic unevenness is dangerous, and they are now spreading investment to the north and west of the country to industrialize China's vast interior. There has even been talk of modest welfare programs for the poorest rungs of Chinese society. We will see how clever China's technocrats really are. Will they be smart enough to head off trouble before it gets explosive?

EMERGING PLURALISM?

One difference between the China of Mao and the China of now is the growth of a few different viewpoints. This represents the shift of China from totalitarianism to authoritarianism (see page 345), a hopeful sign. None of the views are really radical, and no one is allowed to organize a pressure group; all operate within the system, and most are Party members. These discussions take place at the elite level in several state-linked **think tanks**, mostly in Beijing and Shanghai (the two cities are sometimes intellectual rivals). They would have to be state-linked; the many private research and advocacy groups one finds in Washington are not allowed in China. The following are some of the views one can encounter among educated Chinese.

PEACEFUL RISE OF CHINA

This school of thought, found heavily in Shanghai university circles, argues that China should keep doing what it has been doing: Take high-tech products developed elsewhere and use China's massive labor advantage to manufacture them so cheaply that China becomes a great economic power. And all this without lifting a hostile finger, hence the name "peaceful rise." Historically, many fast-rising powers have turned aggressive (Germany and Japan), but war is bad and unnecessary for China, argue the peaceful risers. Shanghai has been the epicenter of China's spectacular economic growth, so it is not surprising this view is rooted there. Advocates of this view are sometimes called "liberal internationalists."

Hainan Large island province in the very south of China.

R & D Research and development of new technologies.

neo-cons Short for neoconservatives; originally U.S. liberals who turned to conservative and power-oriented approaches.

Critics in other schools argue that "peaceful rise" makes China sound militarily uncertain of itself and suggests to Taiwan that it could declare independence with impunity. In response, the term "peaceful rise," which first appeared in 2003 at an international forum on **Hainan**, has been diluted to "peaceful development" and "peaceful coexistence." Other problems: If China simply manufactures high-tech products developed in Japan and the United States, it will remain permanently behind more advanced countries. China is now rapidly developing its own **R & D** capacity, but that is something that works best in free societies, not supervised ones. Cheap labor is not necessarily the best kind; China needs better-trained workers and has a serious shortage of skilled managers.

REALISTS

China's realists are sometimes called in jest **neo-cons** because they resemble the tough-minded U.S. intellectuals who did not shy away from the use of military power. Found in Beijing universities, especially Qinghua (see page 411), realists argue that China needs military modernization to contain the threats posed by Japan, Taiwan, and the United States. A weak China will be pushed around, as it was during the Century of Humiliation (see page 407). Chinese realists are not personally hostile toward Americans, provided that we respect them as equals. They may be personally hostile toward Japanese, especially if Japan does not acknowledge its war guilt and give way to Chinese dominance of Asia.

The danger of this view is it parallels the American neo-cons, who now warn in sinister terms of a China threat. Two sides seeing the other as threats means hostility and tension. Likewise some Japanese hard-liners resent being pushed around by China and urge a tighter U.S.-Japanese alliance to offset Chinese power. Mutual fears often precede wars. As Thucydides famously observed about the cause of the Pelopponesian War that devastated Athens in the fifth century B.C.: "War became inevitable with the growth of Athenian power and the fear this caused in Sparta."

MIDDLE GROUND

Between these two views, many Chinese diplomats want to pursue a middle course: peaceful, but with sufficient armed strength. Accordingly, China's military should get major funding increases even as China stresses world cooperation. Taiwan, for example, must be won over with one hand but threatened with invasion by the other. Middle grounders like capitalism and the growth it brings and are delighted to have China buy more foreign firms. It makes China stronger.

Comparison

Equality and Growth

Do big income differentials spur economic growth? Ronald Reagan, George W. Bush, and Margaret Thatcher thought so; under them, incomes in America and Britain grew more unequal. The reasoning: If people can make a lot of money, they will have a greater incentive to work hard and get rich. And rich people invest more. According to this theory, inequality and growth are twins.

Data are not so clear; some may even point in the opposite direction. The data in the table below are from the 2007 United Nations Development Program. Be careful here: Data from the Third World are approximations, so take them with a grain of salt. The first column shows the ratio of the top fifth of incomes to the bottom fifth. The lower this number, the more equal that country is. The second column shows the average annual growth in per capita GDP from 1990 to 2004. Be careful here, too: Countries like Russia, Japan, and Mexico that went through economic downturns score low because this number averages fifteen years. More recently their growth is much better. Causality is another problem: Does inequality spur growth, or does growth create inequality? (Probably the latter.)

China has great income inequality—its top 20 percent rake in almost eleven times what the poorest 20 percent get. China is more unequal than the United States and is a growth demon. That supports the theory. But higher-inequality Mexico and Nigeria score poor growth. Latin America has both some of the sharpest inequality and weakest growth rates.

The theory that inequality accompanies growth is much too simple. There are many factors that make economies grow. Government policies have a lot to do with it. Government—through corruption, high taxes, and state ownership—may discourage private investment. Some cultures have an internalized work ethic or nationalistic pride. Japanese chief executives, who work like maniacs, receive on average only eleven times what their factory workers get; their American counterparts take home a staggering 475 times as much as their workers. Another point: Poor people have no money to save; middle-class people do. The most equal countries on the list, Japan and Germany, are the biggest savers, and savings mean investment, which helped them score rapid growth in earlier decades. Beware of one-cause theories.

	Top/Bottom Fifths Ratio	GDPpc Growth Average 1990–2004
Japan	3.4	0.8%
Germany	4.3	1.5
Russia	4.8	−0.6
India	4.9	4.0
France	5.6	1.7
Britain	7.2	2.2
United States	8.4	1.9
Iran	9.7	−0.1
China	10.7	8.9
Nigeria	12.8	0.8
Mexico	19.3	1.3

Source: UNDP, 2007.

NEW LEFT

Maoism is dead, but there are still some Chinese Marxists—at Qinghua University, for example—who emphasize the equality issue. Differences of wealth were supposed to disappear under socialism, but in China now they are growing rapidly. Chinese incomes by some measures are more unequal than American incomes. For Deng Xiaoping this was not a problem. He observed (correctly) that "some people must get rich first." In China, differences are stark between the urban middle class and people either still in the villages or recently arrived in a city to seek work. You do not have to be a Marxist to see the unfairness in this. China, which still calls itself socialist, treats its workers and poor worse than any capitalist system.

China's New Left would channel funds from rich to poor by government programs funded by higher taxes on the latter. They argue that China should not be so focused on exports but should let poorer Chinese consume more. For example, export tax credits—which allow firms producing for foreign markets to avoid some taxes—should be dropped. The New Left also likes cooperative enterprises that give all members shares rather than capitalist enterprises owned by a few. Their ideal would be a social-democratic welfare state such as Germany (see Chapter 16). The regime is mindful of rural poverty, which it hopes to correct under the name "harmonious society."

INCREMENTAL DEMOCRATS

After Tiananmen in 1989 (see box on page 424), little was said about democracy, but now several Chinese intellectuals quietly suggest steps toward greater mass participation. Without democracy, they fear a rigid system that will eventually collapse. Overthrowing the regime is not the goal, reconnecting the CCP to the masses is. This was always Mao's chief approach, so incremental democrats can invoke Mao's name for essentially non-Maoist purposes. In elections at lower levels—some are already happening—Party members could rededicate themselves to the people instead of using their connections to get rich.

What do we call these several views? Latent pluralism? Some Soviet specialists noted the variety of views that emerged in the late Soviet Union, but they led to collapse rather than reform. The existence of several viewpoints in a few universities or research organizations means little, especially since the regime embraces none of them. What makes *pluralism* (see page 75) is the autonomous interactions of many groups, not just abstract notions of a few elites. If the regime let public groups form to support these and other ideas, then China would have pluralism. There is no sign of this yet.

RICE-ROOTS DEMOCRACY

With the new millennium, scattered across China thousands of village-level competitive elections appeared, like rice shoots just poking out of the soil. Such things cannot happen without Party approval. Some believe it is the work of liberalizers in the Party ever-so-slowly introducing democracy. Others say it comes from the bottom up, from villagers' anger at corrupt local officials who demand arbitrary "taxes." In some villages and townships, the Party candidate loses.

So far, the scope of these elections is limited. Elected village and township chiefs are still controlled by local Party secretaries. But gradually, local Party secretaries are also chosen by more open methods among Party members. Since 1999, a few urban neighborhoods have had direct, competitive elections for minor offices. Some Chinese political scientists predict the level of elections will climb to include

variable   Factor that changes and is related to other factors. (See page 425.)

discontinuity   A break and new direction in the expected course of events. (See page 425.)

analogy   Taking one example as the model for another. (See page 425.)

dysanalogy   Showing that one example is a poor model for another. (See page 425.)

mayors and provincial and eventually even national office. A clever regime could expand democratic elections as a way to defuse anger, but if it does not let democracy go all the way to top national offices it could end up increasing mass anger. There could be other Tiananmens.

There are basically two ways to gradually introduce democracy into China: (1) Let pluralistic groups form in the society at large and voice their views and demands, or (2) let views that are quietly voiced within the CCP establish factions that they then present to the citizenry at large. In a nutshell: Either let it happen inside the Party or outside of it. Best bet for a smooth transition to democracy in China: Let Party factions form first and then go public. Once they have to present divergent views to win votes, the factions will in effect become separate parties but preserve continuity by claiming they are just pursuing "socialism with Chinese characteristics." Gradual change is better than tumultuous change. The regime, however, so far has not allowed either path.

DEMOCRACY

THE TIANANMEN MASSACRE

During the early morning of June 4, 1989, more than 100,000 Chinese troops opened fire on young demonstrators camped out in Beijing's Tiananmen Square, killing hundreds and injuring thousands. (The regime never released figures, so the number of dead is guesswork.) Much of the killing, including tanks crushing protesters and bicyclists shot at random, took place outside the Square, but the horror went down in history as "Tiananmen."

Tiananmen marked the point at which China's Communist chiefs choked over letting China's 1980s experiment with a partially free market economy spill over into political democracy, never the intention of Beijing's rulers. The massacre illustrates the danger of halfway reform: It gets people thinking of democracy.

Trouble began with the death of the liberal ex-Party chief Hu Yaobang in April 1989. Students began mourning him and protesting the current CCP leadership. On April 18, thousands began to occupy the Square. While the regime pondered how to handle the demonstration, the students organized, gave speeches, and built a Goddess of Democracy statue that resembled New York's Statue of Liberty. Around the country, many sympathized with the demonstrators, and criticism of the regime mounted.

If prodemocracy demonstrations had kept going, the regime would have been in trouble. The regime knew

that and struck back. Zhao Ziyang, who succeeded Hu in 1987, went out to talk with the students and took their side. Politburo hardliners immediately ousted Zhao from office. (Zhao was under house arrest until his death in 2005, and his funeral was nearly secret so as not to give mourners another occasion to demonstrate for freedom. Even funerals are touchy events in China.) Deng Xiaoping, still the real power at age eighty-four, ordered the army to crush the demonstrators. "We do not fear spilling blood," he said.

Troops and tanks poured into Beijing. The soldiers, mostly simple country boys, felt little in common with the urban students. In one memorable videotaped confrontation, a lone protester blocked a tank column; when the tanks tried to go around him, he quickly stepped in front of them again. It seemed to symbolize the individualism of democracy standing up to the coercion of dictatorship. Many ordinary Beijingers sided with and helped the students. After the bloodbath, thousands were arrested. The top protest figures received sentences of up to thirteen years, less for those who "repented." Hundreds were held for years without trial. China's elite decided to keep going with economic change but to keep the lid on political change. The ingredients for new upheavals in China are simmering.

COMPARISON

COUNTRY EXPERTS VERSUS COMPARATIVISTS

Should political scientists attempt to predict, to fore-tell what will happen in a given country? The profession is divided. Some argue that there are simply too many **variables**, most of which are hard to define, measure, and weigh. How could one untangle the complex inter-actions of economic growth, regional tensions, ideolo-gy, personalities, and institutions? Everything matters, but we do not know which matters most. Others argue that prediction, or at least anticipation, concentrates the mind on the variables that are relevant. If one vari-able predicts moderately well, we focus on it and ig-nore variables that predict nothing. In doing this, we begin to theorize. If we stay only in the present, de-scribing but refusing to predict, we proclaim that we re-ally do not know much. Predicting, at least approximately, tests whether we have mastered our area of study.

Next we ask which is the best way to predict or an-ticipate. Political scientists who specialize in one coun-try or region immerse themselves in it and accumulate vast data and details about it. They usually know the language and write their dissertations and articles about the area. Many have spent time as researchers in one country and personally know many of its citizens. From talking to them, they are able to delineate the va-rieties of opinions in that country, as we have done briefly in this chapter. Their books and articles are crammed with endnotes, many of them from original-language publications.

Their expertise is impressive, but they are frequently wrong. Many Soviet specialists were unable to detect the collapse of their subject matter (see page 356). They were too optimistic that Gorbachev's reforms would work. And afterward, many Russia specialists confidently portrayed the establishment of democracy in Russia. They were again too optimistic in assuming that ending a dictatorship brings democracy. (Is there a built-in human tendency toward optimism? If so, we must be careful of optimistic analyses of China.) The Soviet/Russia area experts' mistaken predictions sug-gest they were following the wrong variables.

Part of the problem is knowing too much about one country. Specialists often collect masses of details, sup-posing that the data put them "inside" the system and

able to anticipate its evolution. The Kremlinologists and China watchers (see page 389) knew a lot about the Politburo personalities whose rise and fall they charted. Some scholars closely studied city or regional councils or specialized agencies. But such studies as-sumed *unilinear* (see page 84) development and could not anticipate sudden breaks or **discontinuities**. Due to the inherent delays of publishing, some of their de-tailed studies appeared after the Soviet Union had ceased to exist. Soviet specialists got so deeply into the box that they could not think outside of it. We may legitimately fear that China specialists are doing the same. How do we know which details are relevant?

In contrast, comparativists have broader perspec-tives but bring problems of their own. A comparativist might have less language or area expertise but be able to compare and contrast the country under considera-tion with similar cases across a continent or even the globe. They might find, for example, that democratiza-tion in many Latin America countries at about the same time were similar to one another, almost like a conta-gious illness spreading. It does not necessarily follow, however, that this pattern transfers to democratization in Central Europe or the Soviet Union. This was the prob-lem with *transitology* (see page 351). They tried to make an **analogy** between Latin America and Central Europe and then between Central Europe and the Soviet Union. Many, however, failed to note the elements of **dysanalogy** between the cases. The Soviet Union, for example, had nothing remotely resembling Poland's Sol-idarity, and neither does China today.

Comparing is good because it requires its practi-tioners to ask which are the relevant facts and vari-ables we should be studying; in effect, it forces one to theorize and then test these theories against reali-ty. Single-country experts rarely do this. They assume that the accumulation of many facts will point to ob-vious conclusions without having to structure the facts into a theoretical framework that makes sense and works in more than one country. It is the contention of this book that it is better to err on the side of being too broad (comparative politics) than being too narrow (country expertise). Just make sure you have the right analogies.

COERCION IN RESERVE

China's regime retains authority by means of patriotism and performance-based legitimacy. **Coercion** has receded into the background, but everyone knows it is still available. The regime's achievements are impressive and appreciated by average citizens. For a time, that might suffice to keep the regime halfway legitimate. Most Chinese now can speak a common language (*Putonghua*). There has been no famine since 1959–1961 (the Great Leap Forward). Since 1980 a considerable urban middle class has emerged.

Coercive tools are close at hand but needed only occasionally. The Tiananmen area of Beijing is laced with plainclothes police who are trained to instantly pounce on any protest that might form. Any group of three or more that lingers too long in one spot could get spoken to. Security police remember how Falun Gong used e-mails to quietly organize a large and sudden gathering in Tiananmen Square.

coercion   Government by force.

That will not happen again. There is unrest, especially in the countryside, but with no organizational alternatives discontent is unfocused and free-floating. And the regime takes elaborate precautions against the formation of civil society—especially churches and labor unions—that might provide organizational alternatives.

Law can powerfully boost civil society. China claims to have rule of law, but it is selective. Some cases relating to economic efficiency—fraud and corruption—are handled fairly. But cases related to Party control are likely to be smacked down. Lawyers defending church and union organizers risk disbarment and arrest. Some go into hiding. A 1989 law is supposed to give citizens the right to sue state agencies, but only a handful succeed. Western freedoms owe much to courageous lawyers who insisted that even the powerful be bound by rule of law. One hopes that China is slowly moving in this direction.

The 2008 Olympics were a mixed blessing for China. They showcased the modern face of China, but preparations involved displacing tens of thousands of farmers and *hutong* (alleyway) dwellers. By law they were supposed to be compensated but few were. No one owns land in China. The urban underclass resented the costs of preparing for the Olympics. Some critics thought they could use the Olympics to make a statement the whole world would see, like the Mexican student protests on the eve of the 1968 Mexico City Olympics (see page 498). Beijing arrested critics long in advance and banned beggars, poor people, many cars, and smog from the city for the games.

If the authoritarian regime has great powers of coercion, why does it not use some to clean up the corruption that is the Party's most vulnerable point? Corruption—the misuse of major housing, municipal, or retirement funds—already drives Chinese to protests and riots that could spin out of control. Singapore imposed tough rules against corruption (or any form of misbehavior) and now ranks as one of the cleanest countries in the world (see the Transparency International ratings on page 535). Why could not Beijing have a hundred or so of the most corrupt officials tried and speedily executed to get the message out to the thousands of others? (Actually, China already carries out more capital punishment than the rest of the world combined, several thousand a year.) You've got the coercive tools; why not use them?

The only reasonable explanation is that China's top leaders recognize that corruption is so widespread and tolerated that cleaning it up would cost them the support of precisely the Party *cadres* (see page 394) it relies upon to govern. If you shoot all your helpers you will be helpless. Journalists who expose corruption are often beaten and jailed; the regime craves stability. Despite Beijing's promises to crack down on corruption, prosecutions are selective and political, aimed at consolidating the top leaders' power by getting rid of officials who do not hew to central directives. In 2006, for example, Shanghai boss Chen Liangyu was fired from all posts—including the Politburo—for corruption. Many suspect the real reason was that Chen was still close to former President Jiang Zemin, who had built a Shanghai faction, and not loyal enough to current President Hu Jintao.

KEY TERMS

analogy (p. 424)

coercion (p. 426)

Cultural Revolution (p. 416)

discontinuity (p. 424)

dysanalogy (p. 424)

Great Leap Forward (p. 416)

Hainan (p. 421)

macroeconomics (p. 419)

microeconomics (p. 419)

neo-cons (p. 421)

R & D (p. 421)

Red Guards (p. 416)

think tank (p. 420)

variable (p. 424)

FURTHER REFERENCE

Cheek, Timothy. *Living with Reform: China since 1989*. New York: Palgrave, 2006.

Clark, Paul. *The Chinese Cultural Revolution: A History*. New York: Cambridge University Press, 2008.

Dickson, Bruce J. *Red Capitalists in China: The Party, Private Entrepreneurs, and Prospects for Political Change*. New York: Cambridge University Press, 2003.

Ding, Yijiang. *Chinese Democracy after Tiananmen*. Vancouver: University of British Columbia Press, 2001.

Fewsmith, Joseph. *China since Tiananmen: The Politics of Transition*. New York: Cambridge University Press, 2001.

Finkelstein, David M., and Maryanne Kivlehan, eds. *China's Leadership in the 21st Century: The Rise of the Fourth Generation*. Armonk, NY: M. E. Sharpe, 2003.

Gamer, Robert E., ed. *Understanding Contemporary China*, 3rd ed. Boulder, CO: L. Rienner, 2008.

Leib, Ethan J., and Baogang He, eds. *The Search for Deliberative Democracy in China*. New York: Palgrave, 2006.

MacFarquhar, Roderick, and Michael Schoenhals. *Mao's Last Revolution*. Cambridge, MA: Harvard University Press, 2006.

Mann, James. *The China Fantasy: How Our Leaders Explain Away Chinese Repression*. New York: Penguin, 2007.

Moody, Peter. *Conservative Thought in Contemporary China*. Lanham, MD: Lexington Books, 2007.

Naughton, Barry J., and Dali L. Yang, eds. *Holding China Together: Diversity and National Integration in the Post-Deng Era*. New York: Cambridge University Press, 2004.

Perry, Elizabeth J., and Merle Goldman, eds. *Grassroots Political Reform in Contemporary China*. Cambridge, MA: Harvard University Press, 2007.

Shirk, Susan L. *China: Fragile Superpower—How China's Internal Politics Could Derail Its Peaceful Rise*. New York: Oxford University Press, 2007.

Trevaskes, Susan. *Courts and Criminal Justice in Contemporary China*. Lanham, MD: Lexington Books, 2007.

Wang, Chaohua, ed. *One China, Many Paths*. New York: Verso, 2003.

Wang, Hui, and Theodore Huters. *China's New Order: Society, Politics, and Economy in Transition*. Cambridge, MA: Harvard University Press, 2003.

Zheng Bijian. *China's Peaceful Rise: Speeches of Zheng Bijian*. Washington, D.C.: Brookings, 2006.

Chapter 28
What Chinese Quarrel About

China's economy has been roughly doubling every seven years, a spectacular rate. From extreme poverty, China has vaulted to the world's second largest economy (but not per capita). Urban China now shows off its middle-tech industries, modern downtowns, and traffic-clogged streets. And China did this without following the Japanese economic model, which kept out foreign firms and imports and pushed technology and innovation under MITI guidance (see page 273). In contrast, China welcomes foreign investment, technology, and (partial) ownership, and has no equivalent of MITI. China is actually more open and easier to do business with than Japan. All of China's advanced industries are foreign imports. Beijing saw this as the speediest way to industrialize.

QUESTIONS TO CONSIDER

1. What accounts for China's rapid economic growth? Is it like Japan's?
2. What could go wrong with China's rapid growth?
3. What is a *soft landing* in the Chinese context?
4. How does the U.S. economy depend on China (and Japan)?
5. What problems have come with China's economic growth?
6. Is there a middle way between capitalism and socialism?
7. What are second- and third-order effects?
8. Do market systems always lead to democratization?
9. What should the United States do if China takes Taiwan by force?

There are several reasons for China's growth. Unlike Latin America, China has no old dominant class that invests little. Mao had China's old landowners and capitalists executed, so China started capitalism with a clean slate. Unlike Muslim countries, Chinese have no cultural or religious problems with rapid modernization and copying from the West. China had a vast supply of cheap labor plus plentiful capital (much of it foreign) plus a regime that pushed economic growth. Better-paid Chinese workers earn under $2 an hour in wages and benefits, a fraction of U.S. labor costs. General Motors is expanding rapidly in China even as it declines in the United States. With plentiful cash, China has become the second-largest holder of U.S. debt (after Japan).

There are, however, several things that could go wrong with China's economic miracle. No economy—neither Germany's (see Chapter 16) nor Japan's (see Chapter 18)—goes upward forever. Factors limiting China's economy include dependency on imported technology—China invests minimally in R & D—and on the world market staying open for Chinese goods. Pay in China is climbing rapidly due to shortages of *skilled* labor and, more importantly, skilled managers. Employees now easily move to higher-paying jobs, forcing employers to offer higher wages. Two factors predict the upcoming labor shortages: (1) Many of the countryside's surplus labor force have already left for factory jobs, and (2) one-child families. Many countries already have lower wages than China. Much of Chinese investment is politically influenced, incoherent, short-term, and wasted—a mess **masked** by low labor costs. Eventually, bad investments hurt economic growth. A crisis of China's banks and stock markets threatens optimistic projections of growth without pause.

It Only Looks Capitalist

The streets of China's cities are lined with small shops and restaurants and clogged with hawkers and hustlers. ("You want to buy a T-shirt? Special price for you.") It looks like a capitalist boomtown, and, at the micro level, it is indeed one. But virtually all large economic entities are controlled or partially owned by the state and have government or Party officials on their boards of directors with right of veto. Until recently, all of China's large banks were state-owned and are now only partly private. Many "capitalist" firms are actually branches of China's **state-owned enterprises** (SOEs). For example, the Chinese National Overseas Oil Company (CNOOC), which claims to be a commercial operation, is 70 percent owned by China's petroleum ministry. China's market sector produces two-thirds of its GDP, but the state is still in overall control.

mask To cover over a problem.

state-owned enterprises (SOEs), firms still owned by the Chinese government, mostly older and money-losing.

yuan China's currency (symbol ¥), worth 14 U.S. cents in 2008; officially called *renminbi* (RMB, people's money).

insolvent Owes more than it owns.

write off Lender admits that a *nonperforming loan* will never be repaid.

nonperforming loan One that is not being paid back.

Other Communist countries have tried such mixtures. Tito's Yugoslavia and Gorbachev's Soviet Union suggest that such third-way economies are unstable. They tend to turn more and more into market economies until the regime, afraid of losing control, retightens central supervision and discipline. Seeking faster growth, however, after a while the regime loosens controls again. The economy moves in a zig-zag, never finding stability.

Amid incoherence, economic errors grow. Vast sums are invested foolishly, mistakenly, or crookedly. Government control has forced some well-run and rapidly growing firms to make bad business decisions. Peasants fleeing rural unemployment keep labor costs cheap—as low as 30 **yuan** ($4.30) per unskilled worker a day—and lets developers overbuild. Banks lend generously for modern buildings because they impress everyone, especially foreigners. Builders, all aiming for the top of the rental market, constructed too many glitzy high-rise buildings, which became partially occupied money-losers. Shanghai alone has twice as many skyscrapers as New York City. Beijing has the world's biggest shopping mall, but it is nearly empty of customers because it is too expensive and inconveniently located. China's building boom is a bubble that could pop.

After years of bad loans to state-owned enterprises (SOEs), Party officials, and just plain crooks, some of China's banks were technically **insolvent**. Beijing requires banks to lend to SOEs, which rarely repay the loans. With weak (but rising) accounting standards, the banks carry on as if they will be repaid, much like Japan's banks did for years. Massive savings and rapid industrial growth mask the underlying problems. There is no requirement to **write off nonperforming loans**, for that would force many banks and SOEs to admit they are bankrupt. Fears of a Chinese banking crash are widespread.

Virtually all educated professionals, many with U.S. university degrees, understand China's economic imbalances and dislocations, and most say the regime understands them, too. All nine members of the Party's Standing Committee, China's real governing body, are highly educated (most of them engineers). But views on them diverge. Chinese professionals connected to the establishment claim the regime knows what it is doing in bringing the situation under control. "We are well governed by very bright technocrats," is their message. They note that China's leaders avoided the currency and banking crises that swept East Asia in 1997 and 1998, and they will bring China's overheated economy in for a **soft landing**. China's reserves are so huge, some argue, that the government easily injects billions into banks to cover their bad loans (many of them to SOEs). Three of

A Beijing welding shop makes and repairs three-wheeled cycles that clog the streets.

China's biggest banks now sell shares to private investors, and this induces discipline throughout the banking system, as does the new competition from foreign banks. All will be well, regime defenders claim.

Professionals not dependent on state connections, on the other hand, worry that the regime does not know how to cool an overheated and out-of-control economy. Fearful of damaging China's miracle growth and creating unemployment, the regime lets banks and stock markets rumble on to a crash. China's banks, by law, pay very low interest, so savers shift their money to stock markets, producing a speculative frenzy. Chinese stocks, like the economy as a whole, are little regulated and can collapse, as they did in 2005. By 2007, however, share prices were zooming upward again. Some fear a very unsoft landing.

YUAN AND DOLLARS

China's currency situation is not closely parallel to the late 1990s banking problems elsewhere in East Asia, where some countries' currencies were suddenly **devalued**. China's yuan is undervalued but rising. A big and sudden rise, however, could disrupt China's rapid growth of exports. Accordingly, Beijing wants to keep such changes slow. From 1995 to 2005, partly to avoid what was hitting other East Asian currencies, China **pegged** the yuan to the dollar. At the time it was applauded by all, including the United States, as a stabilizing device. For years, one dollar bought a nearly constant 8 yuan (now it's 6.9).

soft landing Gradual calming of destabilizing economic shifts.

devalue To change the worth of a currency downward in relation to other currencies (opposite of *revalue*).

peg To fix one currency at an unchanging rate to another.

revalue   To change the worth of a currency upward in relation to other currencies (opposite of *devalue*).

float   To allow a currency to find its own level based on supply and demand.

Over time, however, America, which imports more and more Chinese goods, complained that the fixed rate was unfair; it kept the yuan too low and allowed China to gain at the expense of U.S. factory jobs. The U.S. Congress thundered that this had to change. Some urged China to **revalue** the yuan 20 to 30 percent. Most economists say an undervalued yuan is not the root of America's trade problems with China (the extremely low U.S. savings rate is the chief culprit). China, due to its low wages (and high savings rate), is just a super competitor, and its inexpensive goods hold down U.S. inflation and lets Americans consume more.

A country with a trade surplus could let its currency **float** to a higher value. The market would in effect revalue the currency. But China, like many countries, wanted to keep the yuan cheap to support its rapid growth of exports. If the yuan got too high, China would lose some of its export advantage. To keep the yuan low and stable, in the 1990s China began buying massive amounts of U.S. Treasury securities (Japan does the same). This has intertwined the Chinese and U.S. economies in strange ways. Rich America is now deeply indebted to poor China. Chinese purchase of U.S. Treasury notes kept our interest rates low and underwrote our real-estate boom. If China were to sell—or simply stop purchasing—U.S. bonds and notes, our interest rates would climb and housing prices would fall. The dollar would weaken around the world. On the other hand, a sudden major Chinese pullout of the U.S. debt market would also decrease the value of China's huge dollar holdings. Would China take a financial hit in order to oppose U.S. policy? In a showdown over Taiwan, it surely would.

In 2005 Beijing gave in a little and switched its peg from the dollar to a basket of currencies that includes dollars, euros, Japanese yen, and South Korean won. The yuan in three years went up 17 percent against the dollar, but much of that was actually due to the weakening of the dollar. Instead of letting the yuan float freely, China carried out a "controlled managed float" in line with its *dirigiste* (see page 143) economy. The move suggested a rolling revaluation of the yuan, which, if done gradually, could correct the yuan-dollar imbalance with harm to neither country. Perhaps China really is governed by brilliant technocrats.

A MARKET ECONOMY FOR CHINA?

Will China become a full market economy? Starting in 1978, the Chinese economy grew at amazing rates. China, like all Communist countries, faced the question of how centralized the economy should be and decided on decentralization while retaining central political control. This, as in other countries that tried it, is an unstable combination.

The earliest changes came in the countryside, where over half of China's population still lives. Collectivized farms were broken up, and families were permitted to go on the "responsibility system," a euphemism for private farming. Peasants lease land from the state for fifteen years or more—still no private owners—and must deliver a certain quota to the state at set prices. Beyond that, they can sell their produce on the free market for the best price they can get. They can choose their own crops and decide how to use fertilizer and farm machinery, which they buy at their own expense. Farm production soared, Chinese ate better, and farmers' incomes went up; some even got rich.

By the 1990s, things were not going so well in the countryside. With substantially all peasants now producing for the market, competition held farm prices and profits down, and farm incomes declined. In many rural areas, order broke down as villagers rioted and attacked local authorities, who extort fake "taxes" from them. In a pattern very typical of the Third World,

COMPARISON

BIG MAC INDEX

Traditional per-capita GDP (GDPpc) figures that use the "market exchange rate" are deceptive because they do not figure in prices in each country. China's GDPpc at exchange rate, for example, is only about $1,800. But exchange rates overvalue or undervalue currencies and change rapidly. To correct for this, economists now calculate GDPpc in *purchasing power parity* (PPP) by measuring what it costs to live in each country. This makes Chinese a lot richer, about $5,000 GDPpc.

PPP is tricky to calculate because economists must evaluate a market basket of goods and services that is the same in each country. New estimates of PPP by the World Bank in 2007 meant that China's and India's economies were 40 percent smaller than was previously thought. A quick and cheeky way to approximate

PPP was devised by the British newsweekly *The Economist:* Compare the price of a Big Mac sandwich at the local McDonald's with its U.S. (big-city) price. Since a Big Mac requires the same ingredients, labor, and overhead wherever it is produced, it is actually a mini-market basket that reflects local costs fairly accurately. A Big Mac that is more expensive than the U.S. price indicates the local currency is overvalued, the case with the euro and the British pound. A cheaper Big Mac indicates the local currency is undervalued, the case in Japan, China, and Russia. The Big Mac Index is a quick way to check currency parities, which can change rapidly as the dollar rises and falls. These Big Macs are big-city prices in mid-2007. India's McDonald's produces tasty veggie-burgers instead of Big Macs, so it is not comparable.

	GDPpc at PPP	Big Mac Price
United States	$46,000	3.41
France	33,800	4.17*
Germany	34,400	4.17*
Britain	35,300	4.01
Canada	38,200	3.68
Mexico	12,300	2.69
Japan	33,800	2.29
Russia	14,600	2.03
China	5,300	1.45

*average of euro-area prices.
Sources: First column CIA, second column *The Economist*.

over 8 million rural Chinese leave every year for work in the cities, a destabilizing tide the regime cannot control. To calm growing rural discontent—and diminish the flow of peasants to the cities—in 2005 Beijing ended millennia-old taxes on harvests and even offered peasants some financial aid. The regime fears that peasant anger could turn into the sort of uprising that has punctuated China's history.

A partly free market was allowed to spread to the cities. Faced with growing unemployment, the regime let individuals open small stores, restaurants, repair shops, and even manufacturing facilities. It was even permissible to hire workers, something Marxists used to call capitalist exploitation. But it worked. The Chinese applied individual hustle to produce and sell more and better products than the indifferent state factories and stores ever could. Hole-in-the-wall "department stores" had customers waiting in line to buy the fashionable clothing and footwear Mao used to scorn. People swarmed to outdoor markets to buy home-produced chairs and sofas. Restaurants grew like weeds.

KEY CONCEPTS

THE TROUBLE WITH MARKETS

The trouble with bringing a market economy into Communist countries—such as Yugoslavia, Hungary, or China—is that it runs out of control and destabilizes. China has seen major increases in the following:

Too-Rapid Growth China's infrastructure cannot keep up with its industrial and urban growth, which creates problems in transportation, energy, water supply, land, housing, you name it. Chinese industry is seriously energy inefficient. Beijing is a traffic and subway jam. The regime tries to fix the immediate problem but does not plan long-term or for efficiency.

Booms China's property and stock-market booms could go bust. From 2005 to 2007 the Shanghai stock exchange index tripled. More than 91 million Chinese play the market, many recklessly (Chinese love gambling). As in Japan twenty years earlier, prices are surging ahead of values, producing a bubble that could easily pop, leaving many Chinese poor and angry. The regime does not know how to cool down the overheated Chinese markets without popping the bubble.

Inflation China in the past has gone through bouts of inflation, the results of rapid growth and economic mismanagement. Some fear a new bout. Now food, energy, and labor costs are climbing. Beijing ordered price freezes in several areas, but these tend to just delay and magnify inflationary pressures.

Inequality Some individuals and provinces get rich; others lag far behind. With FDI, the SEZs of the southern coast got rich fast while inland provinces stayed poor. Skilled and educated urban Chinese became a new middle class, leaving their rural cousins far behind.

Labor Abuses Especially in poor rural areas, many workers, including children, toil in slave-like conditions, deprived of pay, food, sleep, and the freedom to leave. Local governments do little to stop it, figuring that all that really matters is economic growth. Parents desperately search for their kidnapped children in such factories. Faced with low wages and bad working conditions—especially miners—some Chinese workers attempt to form unions; they are jailed. Beijing denies that independent unions even exist. Ironically, a Communist regime that turned anti-labor and pro-capitalist has created the basis of a Marxist revolution.

Starting with the Shenzhen area around Hong Kong, parts of coastal China were declared **Special Economic Zones,** open to private and **foreign direct investment** that was invited to turn China into a modern, market economy. FDI is extremely important in the developing world. Marxists and nationalists hate and fear it as a form of capitalist takeover, but it is the key to rapid economic growth. Possibly a trillion dollars of FDI poured into China (much of it from Taiwan and Hong Kong) to take advantage of low Chinese wages (for unskilled, now 50 cents an hour, but rising), and production soared. These firms compete in a world market to make profits. Because of these firms—which now account for two-thirds of China's economy—since 1978 China's GDP has grown at an amazing average of nearly 10 percent a year to become the world's second largest overall economy (but not per capita) and

Special Economic Zones   Areas originally on China's southern coast where capitalist economic development was encouraged.

foreign direct investment   (FDI), foreign firms setting up operations in other countries.

guanxi   Chinese for connections (do not confuse with Guangxi Province).

Currency Distortion   Beijing fixed the yuan too low in relation to the dollar (¥8 to $1) and revalued it only a little (now about ¥6.9 to $1). Most other countries let their currencies float. The cheap yuan has helped China become the "workshop of the world" but has caused a property bubble and foreign resentment.

Corruption   Corruption grows at the interface of the private and governmental sectors. Economic liberalization multiplies such interfaces as entrepreneurs need permits from government officials, obtained by under-the-table payments. China has become one of the world's most corrupt countries (but not as bad as Russia). Most Chinese business is based on **guanxi**.

Crime   With all of the above factors plus weakened social controls, crime grows, along with campaigns to stop it. Firing squads execute thousands each year. China leads the world by far in capital punishment (Iran is second). Counterfeiting is widespread; banks check U.S. currency, and businesses check larger yuan bills.

Pollution   Focused only on economic growth, China has the world's worst environmental problems. Coal-burning and cars poison the air, chemical dumping poisons ground water and rivers, and diseases spread rapidly. Officials cover up problems and jail environmental and health activists for revealing them. Pollution kills some 750,000 Chinese a year, sparks protests and riots, and slows China's growth.

Poisonous Products   Unregulated Chinese manufacturing ignores safety. In 2007 American pets sickened and died from food containing poisonous melamine, a fake protein put in Chinese wheat gluten. Toys with lead paint were popular on the U.S. market. Chinese cold medicine containing a chemical used in car anti-freeze killed a hundred Panamanians. Toothpaste with the same chemical turned up in the United States. And these problems were discovered only because the products were exported; products for domestic consumption are worse and unnoticed. Beijing's response was to quickly try and execute the head of the Food and Drug Administration.

How to solve these problems? A start is democracy, which permits people to organize interest groups and parties and holds officials accountable.

third biggest exporter (after Germany and America). China's economy was thirty times bigger in 2007 than it had been in 1980. By comparison, one-third of some 100,000 state-owned enterprises (SOEs) lose money and have to be propped up by subsidies and loans that will never be repaid. At least half the SOEs are reckoned to be hopeless. Whether to close them and create unemployment is one of the great questions facing Beijing. The fact that the Standing Committee keeps stalling on this important decision suggests uncertainty and paralysis: They simply do not know what to do.

As modern, high-rise boomtowns sprang up on the coast, some Chinese business people became millionaires, and a substantial middle class formed. Most Chinese liked their taste of the free market, but many cadres did not. If you go all the way to a market system, what do you do with the cadres who make a good living by supervising a controlled economy? They dig in their heels and try to block major change. Deng purged or retired the old guard and replaced them with young technocrats—such as current Party chief Hu and Premier Wen—who pursue capitalist-style economic growth and call it "socialism with Chinese characteristics." Nobody knows what that means.

But market economies produce problems of their own (see box on pages 434–435) and awaken resentments and jealousies. China's leaders fear the economy is careening out of control and have attempted to slow it, aiming for a "soft landing." In the longer term, the system needs democracy, but Beijing vows China will have only one party. What will happen when a

DEMOCRACY

DO MARKETS LEAD TO DEMOCRACY?

Economic liberalization tends to encourage political participation. You cannot reform the economy alone, for economic reform generates demands for political reform, namely, democracy. As political scientist Peter Berger put it: "When market economies are successful over a period of time, pressure for democratization inevitably ensues." A market economy generates a large, educated middle class and interest groups. People start resenting a corrupt government treating them like small children. They want democracy. If the regime is intelligent and flexible, it gradually opens up, usually by permitting a critical press, then opposition parties, and finally free and fair elections.

Taiwan is a textbook example of this transition from authoritarianism to democracy. Some argue that China will follow a similar path, but there are differences. First, Taiwan is small, making it easier to control. Taiwan's elites, many of them educated in the United States, led the way to democracy in the late 1970s. One of their motives: Show the Americans they are a democracy in order to win U.S. support against Beijing's demands to take over Taiwan. Remembering our warning about *dysanalogies*, the Taiwan model does not fit mainland China. China's elite is still firmly Communist, has no desire for democracy, and is not trying to please the Americans. Much of China's economy that looks private is actually still controlled by the state or army. China's leaders are not planning for capitalism; they are planning for Chinese power. China's middle class is rapidly growing, but it is tied to the state, which also blocks the growth of *civil society*, the autonomous groups that underlay pluralist democracy. Calls for democracy are ruthlessly crushed. Do not count on China moving to democracy automatically or peacefully, no matter what its economic growth.

destabilizing economic system escapes the bonds of a dictatorial political system? Think of a bucking bronco (China's economy) throwing its rider (the Party).

A Middle Way for the Middle Kingdom?

The basic supposition of Beijing's recent and current rulers is that there is a middle way between capitalism and communism, between a controlled economy and a free-market economy, between the Soviet model and the American model. (Soviet President Gorbachev entertained similar notions, and you know what happened to him.) By bringing in elements of a market economy while keeping overall control in state hands, they suppose they have found a middle way. Is there one? Not really, and some observers think the Chinese elite quietly admit it among themselves.

When a Communist country introduces a bit of market economics—supply and demand, competing producers, profits, family farming, prices finding their own level—the first few years are usually good. Farm output especially grows, and people eat well. Consumer goods become far more available, and people live and dress better. New industries produce clothing and consumer electronics for the world market. Statistically, growth rates shoot up. It looks like they

Geography

The Hong Kong Example

In 1997 the British colony of Hong Kong reverted back to China. Most of Hong Kong actually consisted of leased territory on the mainland—the source of the colony's water supplies—and the lease was up in 1997. Britain decided to give the whole package back to Beijing. Many prosperous and hardworking Hong Kongers did not want to be part of China (some took their money and fled to Vancouver, Canada). Beijing guaranteed, under the formula "one nation, two systems," that Hong Kong could keep its autonomy for fifty years. In 1999, after 442 years of colonial rule, Portugal turned over nearby Macau to China on the same basis. Hong Kong and Macau are now "special administrative regions" of China with internal autonomy. Beijing's intention, many believed, was to show Taiwan that it could rejoin the mainland and still keep its political and economic system. Few Taiwanese are buying.

Beijing slowly introduced new laws in Hong Kong on "security" and "information" to punish dissent. Beijing court decisions eroded Hong Kong's special status. Critical Hong Kong editors lost their jobs. Corruption grew, as certain cooperative Hong Kongers got special deals. Beijing favors Shanghai as China's financial hub, as it once was before World War II. Prime Minister Zhu—like President Jiang, a former mayor of Shanghai—said in 1999, "Shanghai will be China's New York." Hong Kong will be its "Toronto." (Macau became its Las Vegas.) Hong Kong, one of the world's great financial centers, did more and more business with mainland China and less and less with other Pacific Rim countries. As Hong Kong lost its glitter, Singapore tried to move into its place as the great trading post of the Pacific Rim.

yuppy   Short for "young urban professional."

found the happy balance: a market economy at the *micro* level to produce consumer goods under the benevolent guidance of a state-run economy at the *macro* level (see page 419 for the distinction). Food, clothing, consumer electronics, and much else are produced by private firms, much of them with FDI, but some big industries as well as banking and planning systems are still state-owned and under Party control.

Key Concepts

Second- and Third-Order Effects

China's program to limit population growth shows what can go wrong with coercing society into what the government has decided is desirable. It also illustrates the problem of second- and third-order effects—sometimes called "unforeseen consequences"—namely, how difficult it is to predict the longer-term impacts of a policy.

In the early 1980s China carried out a ferocious program to curb births. Women were ordered to have only one child and were fined and lost benefits if they had more. Many women were forced to have abortions. The first-order consequence, as might be expected, was to bring down China's rate of population increase to under 1 percent a year, similar to Europe but very low for the Third World, much of which grows at 3 percent.

A second-order effect, however, was a large excess of boy over girl babies, both by abortion and female infanticide. About 5 percent of the girls expected to be born from 1979 to 1995 are missing, 10 percent in the 1990s. In 2000, 118 males were born for 100 females. Cheap ultrasound scans permit selective abortions. Like many Third World cultures, Chinese value boys above girls, both to work on the farm and to support the parents in old age. So, if they are allowed only one child, many Chinese strongly prefer a son. This is not the case with educated urban Chinese, who welcome daughters.

Third-order effects flow from the second-order effects. The surplus of males over females mean that millions of Chinese men will never find brides. Further, the drastic restriction in fertility rates—from 2.29 births

per average woman in 1980 to 1.75 in 2007—means that China's retired generation—now much bigger and living much longer, thanks to improved nutrition and health care—will not have nearly enough working Chinese to support it. In 2030 one-fourth of Chinese will be over sixty-five. Chinese speak of "4-2-1": four grandparents and two parents supported by only one child, the logical result of the one-child policy. By 2040 there will be only two working Chinese for every retiree. China, still a poor country, will thus face exactly the same problem as rich Europe. China's State Family Planning Commission, which now emphasizes education and contraception, did not consider the second- and third-order consequences.

How can developing areas handle the serious problem of too-rapid population increases? Economic growth solves the problem without coercion, as Chinese **yuppies** already demonstrate. They have few children (and are happy to have daughters). As the economy grows, more people become urban and middle class and decide for themselves to limit their number of children, as Japanese have done. As more women are educated they postpone marriage in favor of career, a strong trend among Chinese yuppies, who work so long and hard they may not have time for marriage. No rich country has a problem of too many babies (in fact, it is just the opposite), and newly industrializing lands show a dramatic falloff in births. China's demographic debacle is one example of Mao's (and, earlier, Stalin's) thinking that society can be forced into any shape the Party decrees.

But after a few years things start to go wrong. Shortages, distortions, and bottlenecks appear. The private sector keeps bumping into the state sector. Every time it does, there is a "crisis" that can be resolved only by expanding the private sector and shrinking the state sector. After some years of this, there is little socialism left, and this Beijing's rulers do not like.

The Chinese—like the Yugoslavs and Hungarians—found that a little bit of capitalism is like being a little bit pregnant. The choice Communist countries faced was difficult. If they went part of the way to a market economy, they experienced a few years of growth followed by dangerous distortions. If they called off the liberal experiment, they returned to the centralized, Stalinist system that was slowly running down, leaving them further and further behind the capitalist world. If they went all the way to a market system, they admitted they had been wrong all these decades.

Another problem cropped up with the financial problems that hit other East Asian lands in 1997: China's banks also loan recklessly and crookedly; the banking system, until recently entirely state-owned, is fragile. Some loans are under government orders, to prop up money-losing state industries. The central government itself was deeply in debt from subsidizing too much and collecting too little in taxes. With a faulty and foolish financial system, China's growth is threatened. Like America, China has a debt bomb ticking away.

Some observers argue that China's reforms were far cleverer than the Soviet Union's and have a much better chance to succeed. First, China permitted private farming. The Soviet Union was still debating private farming when it collapsed. Then China permitted small businesses. Next, China designated SEZs for foreign investment. Missing in China is the political liberalization that blew up in Gorbachev's face. All Beijing's rulers know how Gorbachev inadvertently collapsed the Soviet Union, and all fear becoming China's Gorbachev, so they tolerate no democracy, competing parties, or free press, precisely the reforms that Gorbachev did first. Did the Chinese do it right, sequencing their reforms so as to build an economic basis for democracy before reforming their political system?

Other observers fear that China could collapse, that its economic reforms without political reforms will blow up. With increasing corruption and inequality (see box on pages 434–435) there is increasing mass unrest. So far, the only successful transitions from communism to free-market capitalism have come in Central Europe—Poland, the Czech Republic, and Hungary—where anticommunists completely threw out the communist regimes. No controlled, middle-way transition has worked.

ENRAGING THE DRAGON

Some Americans feared an aggressive China was buying up the United States, an almost exact replay of the 1980s, when Americans were convinced Japan would soon own us. America seems to need an Asian country to bash. It is more like us selling the United States because we would rather consume than save. The Chinese (and Japanese) do the opposite, and that gives them a lot of money to invest.

Reinforcing a sinister view of China was the 2005 offer by the Chinese National Overseas Oil Company (CNOOC) to buy a U.S. oil company, Unocal, for $18.5 billion. Unocal is not large but owned Asian oilfields that China wants to secure its growing energy needs. CNOOC, however, is a branch of China's petroleum ministry, and that made the offer something different than a purely commercial transaction. Remember, China only looks capitalist; much is still

World Trade Organization (WTO),
120-plus members open themselves to
trade and investment; has
quasi-judicial powers.

state-owned. China is now the world's second largest oil consumer (after the United States) and lines up oil deals worldwide to secure its energy supplies. The U.S. Congress howled in nationalistic anger at the CNOOC bid, much like Mexico or Nigeria do at any mention of foreigners buying their oilfields. CNOOC withdrew its offer, and Chevron bought Unocal. Americans can be economic nationalists, too.

Some observers were bothered by the implications of the failed deal. Were we discriminating against China, creating the very hostility we do not want to happen? How might China react to Congress's economic nationalism? Starting with President Nixon in 1972, we urged China to come out into the world market and make money. China followed our advice and now has a lot of dollars. Why should it not be free to spend them on a U.S. firm—whose main holdings were in Asia anyway? Some worried that America—which continually faults China on trade, currency, and copyright questions—was enraging the Chinese dragon. The road to Pearl Harbor was paved with U.S. trade restrictions on Japan, especially on oil.

China and the World

Several destabilizing forces hit China as its hosting of the 2008 Olympics approached. The easy economic reforms—allowing a capitalist microeconomy—have been done. The really tough parts remain: dangerous government, banking, and state-industry debts; inefficient agriculture and energy usage; and the need to add some 9 million new jobs every year. Any global economic slowdown cuts China's export-led growth. As Japan discovered in the 1990s, exports cannot be the sole basis of an economy.

Another factor will have consequences that are hard to predict. In 2001 China won membership in the **World Trade Organization** (WTO), which it had long sought in order to boost China's exports. But in joining the WTO, China also had to open up its own economy to all manner of foreign investments and companies, including hitherto protected sectors like banking. Many weak Chinese firms will fall. They might include major banks. Imported grains may be cheaper than Chinese rice and wheat.

Membership in the WTO did not calm China's trade relationships with other lands. At the end of 2004 an agreement to regulate the world textile and clothing trade expired, leaving China free to export without limit. China, with plant overcapacity and abundant cheap labor, looked like it would take over the world textile and clothing market, where it already had a major share. (Thought your $5 T-shirt was a bargain? In China they are $1. But careful, a Chinese XL is more like our medium.) Other countries screamed "unfair" and invoked emergency WTO provisions to limit imports from China. China reacted angrily, complaining of unfair treatment of its exports. Such trade lockouts fueled Japanese nationalism before World War II.

The 2008 Beijing Olympics put new strains on China. As noted, preparations displaced and angered many Chinese. Students and dissidents who wanted to use the Olympics to voice demands were arrested months in advance. Warned the *People's Daily*, the official CCP newspaper: "Protecting stability comes before all else." One good point: Beijing could not have a serious showdown over Taiwan until the games were over. The regime would let nothing mar their Olympics. The games themselves made some athletes and tourists unhappy with the heat, humidity, and poisonous air of Beijing in August.

Could China seize Taiwan by force or intimidation? Definitely, and we should decide now how to react. U.S. military intervention could turn into war, even nuclear war. A U.S. trade embargo would not frighten China. China could inflict great economic damage on the United States simply by selling its Treasury notes. China would also take a hit but would not hesitate to do so. Do not underestimate Chinese nationalism.

China has not really been stable in more than a century and could go off the tracks again. China, hard to govern in good times, now has a split and uncertain Party, corrupt local officials, weakening central authority, and growing regional disparities and discontent. Some observers fear Beijing is deflecting discontent outward by promoting an angry nationalism, a common practice of nervous regimes, and this is a very nervous regime.

KEY CONCEPTS

ANTICIPATING CHINA CHANGE

One technique of anticipating change (see box on page 425) is to draw up several scenarios and state which you think are most probable. My list:

1. *No change.* The regime continues doing what it has done since about 1980: steady as she goes with a series of minor reforms backed up by coercion when needed. In the near term this is clearly Beijing's choice, but it may not work much longer, as many problems are coming to a head.

2. *Major reforms.* The technocrats of the Standing Committee see unrest coming and move to head it off by a series of major reforms. No one wants to move too fast and cause system breakdown, as Gorbachev did in the Soviet Union. This scenario is moderately probable.

3. *Panicked reforms.* If unrest grows, the regime could panic and offer hasty and sweeping reforms—even ones leading to democracy—while trying to keep a lid on discontent by coercion. (An analogue to this might be Mexico's "desperate priísmo" discussed on page 494. But remember, be careful with analogies.) It might also attempt to deflect

discontent with nationalism by taking over Taiwan while denouncing U.S. and Japanese pleas not to. Reforms in a panic are often bad reforms, coming too late and revealing regime weakness and fear. This scenario, too, is moderately probable. A hint of it came in 2005 when Beijing ended agricultural taxes, both to mollify peasants and to encourage them to stay on the farm and not leave for the cities.

4. *System change.* Facing massive unrest and a Taiwan crisis, the regime could step down. This would be the Gorbachev scenario and is improbable. In the absence of a Chinese civil society it would also have a chaotic aftermath and would not guarantee a democratic outcome.

5. *Overthrow.* An overthrow is an unlikely scenario because it supposes that Beijing would let discontent get sufficiently organized to challenge the regime in the streets. This could happen only with a drastic slowdown of China's economy that dashed citizen expectations of material improvement. If Beijing lost its performance-based legitimacy it would more likely revert to heavy coercion.

China is already the number-one military power of East Asia, eclipsing Japan. Said former Party chief Jiang: "There will only be two superpowers by around 2020—China and the United States." One of China's priorities is its navy, with which it has claimed and fortified islets far from its shores in the East and South China Seas. This angers other countries in the region—Japan, the Philippines, Malaysia, Indonesia, and Vietnam. And Beijing proclaims the right to seize Taiwan, which it regards as a renegade province, at any time. By a 1979 law, the United States is committed to a peaceful, voluntary reunification. If Beijing applies force or intimidation to Taiwan, how should we react?

Underlying everything is China's deep craving for dignity and respect for what was once the world's greatest civilization but one that was brought low by Western and Japanese imperialists. How China achieves this recognition will be one of the great chapters of twenty-first century history.

KEY TERMS

devalue (p. 431)

float (p. 432)

foreign direct investment
   (p. 435)

guanxi (p. 435)

insolvent (p. 430)

mask (p. 430)

nonperforming loan
   (p. 430)

peg (p. 431)

revalue (p. 432)

soft landing (p. 431)

Special Economic Zones
   (p. 435)

state-owned enterprises
   (p. 430)

World Trade Organization
   (p. 440)

write off (p. 430)

yuan (p. 430)

yuppy (p. 438)

FURTHER REFERENCE

Bergsten, C. Fred, Bates Gill, Nicholas Lardy, and Derek Mitchell. *China: The Balance Sheet; What the World Needs to Know about the Emerging Superpower.* New York: Public Affairs, 2006.

Brown, Kerry. *Struggling Giant: China in the 21st Century.* London: Anthem, 2007.

Brownell, Susan. *Beijing's Games: What the Olympics Mean to China.* Lanham, MD: Rowman & Littlefield, 2008.

Deng, Yong. *China's Struggle for Status: The Realignment of International Relations.* New York: Cambridge University Press, 2008.

Economy, Elizabeth C. *The River Runs Black: The Environmental Challenge to China's Future.* Ithaca, NY: Cornell University Press, 2004.

Fishman, Ted C. *China, Inc.: How the Rise of the Next Superpower Challenges America and the World.* New York: Scribner, 2005.

Gilley, Bruce, and Larry Diamond, eds. *Political Change in China: Comparisons with Taiwan.* Boulder, CO: L. Rienner, 2008.

Greenhalgh, Susan, and Edwin A. Winckler. *Governing China's Population: From Leninist to Neoliberal Biopolitics.* Stanford, CA: Stanford University Press, 2005.

Guo, Sujian, ed. *China's "Peaceful Rise" in the 21st Century: Domestic and International Conditions.* Williston, VT: Ashgate, 2006.

Johnson, Ian. *Wild Grass: Three Stories of Change in Modern China.* New York: Pantheon, 2004.

Kang, David C. *China Rising: Peace, Power, and Order in East Asia.* New York: Columbia University Press, 2007.

Kynge, James. *China Shakes the World: A Titan's Breakneck Rise and Troubled Future—and the Challenge for America.* Boston: Houghton Mifflin, 2006.

Lin Chun. *The Transformation of Chinese Socialism.* Durham, NC: Duke University Press, 2006.

McGregor, James. *One Billion Customers: Lessons from the Front Lines of Doing Business in China.* New York: Free Press, 2005.

Mungello, D. E. *Drowning Girls in China: Female Infanticide in China since 1650.* Lanham, MD: Rowman & Littlefield, 2008.

Peerenboom, Randall. *China Modernizes: Threat to the West or Model for the Rest?* New York: Oxford University Press, 2007.

Terrill, Ross. *The New Chinese Empire: And What It Means for the United States.* New York: Basic Books, 2004.

Tsai, Kellee S. *Capitalism without Democracy: The Private Sector in Contemporary China.* Ithaca, NY: Cornell University Press, 2007.

Wu Chuntao and Che Guido. *Will the Boat Sink the Water? The Life of China's Peasants.* New York: PublicAffairs, 2007.

Chapter 29
India

I ndia is the most complex of our ten countries, arguably the world's most complex. How can a country with such a diverse and mostly poor population of 1.1 billion not only stay together but also function as a democracy? Few poor countries are democracies, but India is the massive exception. And India is enjoying rapid economic growth, forcing the world to pay attention. The big question for the twenty-first century is who will win the Asian economic race, India or China?

THE IMPACT OF THE PAST

India is a very old collection of cultures but a new nation. For much of its history it was not one country. It has great ethnic and regional diversity with at least three main geographical areas: the foothills of the Himalayas in the north, the Indo-Ganges Plain across northern-central India, and the Peninsula of the south, all homes to very different peoples. Long ago India was mostly dense forest; now much of it is densely populated.

As was the case in Mesopotamia, Egypt, and China, India's civilization began along a river. From 2500 to 1600 B.C. the rather advanced Harappan culture flourished in northwest India along the Indus River (which now flows through Pakistan). The name India derives from the Indus River, called the Sindhu in Sanskrit but pronounced Hindu in Persian. Major cities of Hindustan (Persian for land of the Hindus) traded with Mesopotamia. Around 1500 B.C. Aryan immigrants and conquerors pushed in from Central Asia and built kingdoms ruled by *rajans* (Sanskrit for kings, cognate to *reign, regent, roi, rey*) over most of northern India. They made the Ganga (Ganges) a sacred river and a major trade route. With them came the Indo-European language of Sanskrit and four holy books, the Vedas, which form the basis of **Hinduism** and of India's **caste** system. In India, Sanskrit occupies the historical and theological role held by Latin in Europe.

Indian intellectual life flourished. Kautilya in the fourth century B.C. devised a remarkably modern political philosophy. Kautilya, a prime minister and adviser to an Indian monarch,

QUESTIONS TO CONSIDER

1. How did China's, Japan's, and India's unification differ?
2. On balance, was British rule good or bad for India?
3. How was the Indian National Congress unique and important?
4. How do India's institutions blend British and U.S. models?
5. How does help for "scheduled castes" resemble U.S. affirmative action?
6. What was the "Emergency" and how did Indian democracy come out of it?
7. How do India and Pakistan resemble each other? How do they differ?
8. Why does India hold together at all?
9. How does the Congress party resemble the U.S. Democrats and how does the BJP resemble the Republicans?
10. Who will win the Asian economic race, India or China?

GEOGRAPHY

BOUND INDIA

India is bounded on the north by China, Nepal, and Bhutan;

on the east by Bangladesh and Myanmar (formerly Burma);

on the south by the Indian Ocean;

and on the west by Pakistan.

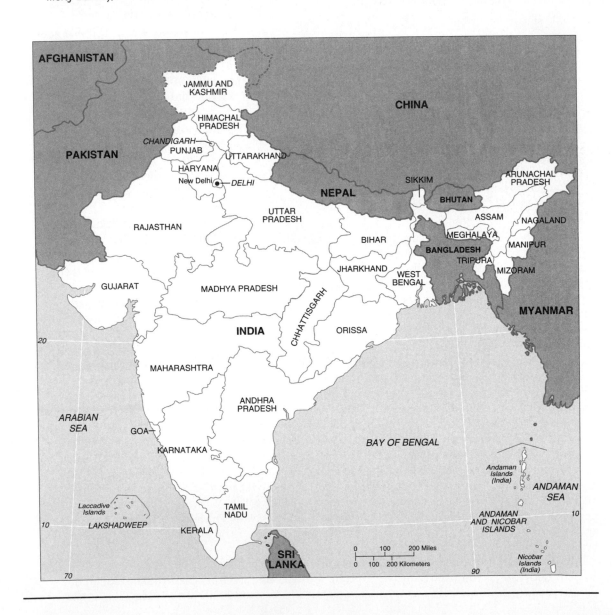

wrote in *Arthasastra* (*The Principles of Material Well-Being*) that prosperity arises from a well-run kingdom. Like Hobbes (see page 27), Kautilya posited a state of nature that meant anarchy. Monarchs arose to protect the land and people against anarchy and to ensure their prosperity. Like Machiavelli, Kautilya advised his prince to operate on the basis of pure expediency, doing whatever it takes to secure his kingdom domestically and against other kingdoms. Kautilya thus could be said to have founded both political economy and the realist school of statecraft. At about the time of Kautilya, Indian mathematicians devised a system of numbers later known as "Arabic numerals" because they were transmitted to the West by Arab traders.

Hinduism Chief religion of India, polytheistic and based on Vedic scriptures, rebirth, and caste. (See page 445.)

caste Rigid, hereditary social stratum or group. (See page 445.)

Buddhism Sixth century B.C. offshoot of Hinduism; seeks enlightenment through meditation and cessation of desire.

In the sixth century B.C., however, northern India was conquered by the Persian Empire, and much Persian culture washed into India. Alexander the Great pushed to the Indus River in 326 B.C. but died before he could conquer India. Several empires and dynasties followed, mostly concentrated in northern India. The Mauryan Empire (326–184 B.C.) united most of India. Its great king Ashoka (273–232 B.C.) was so shocked by the bloodshed of his wars that he embraced **Buddhism** (which originated in India) and turned it into India's dominant faith for a few centuries before it faded to a small minority religion. Buddhism caught on and is still the main faith in Sri Lanka (formerly Ceylon), Mongolia, Tibet, Japan, and Southeast Asia, but not in India. The classic period of India—in some ways like the Han period of China—was the Gupta Empire (A.D. 320–550) of northern India. China unified early and acquired an indelible nationwide Han culture. India mostly stayed fragmented.

COMPARISON

THE UNIQUENESS TRAP

One key question for India (and Japan) is whether it is a country like other countries or hard to compare. Samuel P. Huntington (see page 328) classifies India and Japan as unique, one-of-a-kind civilizations. Many Indian and foreign observers claim India is a society like no other, the complex intermingling of dozens of peoples and religions. Many say the only way to understand India is through its deep spiritual and religious values, which influence its governance today.

It is the view of this book—and indeed probably the basis of comparative politics—that descriptions of a country as totally unique are unwarranted. Granted, Indian and Japanese cultures are different from the European political cultures we discussed earlier. When you compare, though, you discover any country's political patterns can be understood. Much of India can be explained by waves of conquest and fragmentation. Much of Japan can be explained by prolonged feudalism. You find that people everywhere are not so different. For example, both Indian and Japanese politicians take money from interest groups and court voting blocs, just like politicians everywhere. Avoid the uniqueness trap and the related Mystique Mistake, the overly romantic fascination with a supposedly exotic country.

The Arrival of Islam

As we will see in our Iran chapter, Islam spread quickly. In A.D. 711—the same year Arabs conquered Spain—Arabs took the Sindh region of the lower Indus (now in Pakistan), bringing Islam to India for the first time. More substantial numbers of Muslim Turkic tribes from Afghanistan, fighting from horseback with crossbows, arrived around 1000 and set up **sultanates** that rose and fell with new invasions.

The main Muslim conquest was that of the **Mughals** (sometimes spelled *Moguls*), Muslim tribes of Turkic, Persian, and Mongol origin who swept into India from the north in 1526 equipped with artillery. Akbar the Great (1556–1605) expanded and consolidated the Mughal Empire to include most of northern India. An excellent and enlightened emperor, Akbar ordered tolerance of all religions and even held interfaith dialogues. Many of his officials were Hindus. The Mughals used Persian (written in Arabic script) as the administrative language, and it lasted until replaced by English. A Mughal cultural high point is the Persian-influenced Taj Mahal, built by Shah Jahan in the seventeenth century to honor his late wife. The greatest impact of the Mughals, however, was India's Muslim minority of perhaps 25 percent before partition in 1947 (now over 13 percent).

> **sultanate**   Muslim state governed by a *sultan* (holder of power).
>
> **Mughal**   From *Mongol*; Muslim conquerors of India; formed empire.

The British Takeover

As usual in Asia, the first Europeans to arrive were the Portuguese, who rounded Africa in 1488 and explored the Indian Ocean. Vasco da Gama reached India in 1498. One Portuguese colony, Goa, on India's west coast, lasted from 1510 to 1961, when India took it over. The English East India Company was chartered in 1600 to trade in spices, cotton, silk, and sugar through company

Geography

TURBULENT FRONTIERS

UCLA historian John S. Galbraith explained the piecemeal British takeover of India as unplanned but inevitable. London was too distant to run India, and local British governors of the East India Company always faced a "turbulent frontier" at the edge of their holdings: hostile princes, uprisings, and bandit raiders. "Governors continued to try to eliminate the disorderly frontier by annexations, which in turn produced new frontier problems and further expansion," wrote Galbraith in 1960. In this way, the initial British trading posts gradually expanded into coastal colonies, then into whole provinces, and eventually swallowed most of India.

Actually, the turbulent-frontier theory explains much imperial expansion. Lugard in Nigeria had to take over the turbulent north in 1903 (see page 515). The French in the 1830s never intended to take over all of Algeria, just the seaports to stop piracy. But they had to move inland to protect their positions on the coast. The tsars had to take Siberia and Central Asia to protect Russia. In this way, empires tend to expand until they overexpand.

"factories" (actually, warehouses) in coastal enclaves. The Dutch and the French did the same. Mughal emperors and local princes, eager for the foreign goods and money, welcomed the European trade. As in North America, colonization began as money-making enterprises. (For more on colonialism, see page 516.)

maharajah   Sanskrit for "great king"; Hindu prince.

sepoy   Indian soldier in the British Indian Army.

Raj   From Hindi *rule*; British government of India, 1858–1947.

subcontinent   Asia south of the Himalayas (India, Pakistan, and Bangladesh); also called South Asia.

The British under the energetic Robert Clive beat the Mughals in Bengal in 1757 and ousted the French from their small colony of Pondicherry in 1761 (about the same time they ousted the French from Canada). The British takeover of India was piecemeal, though, a province here, a treaty there. Much of India remained legally in the hands of **maharajahs** in their "princely states," under varying degrees of British supervision. A puppet Mughal emperor still reigned in Delhi. Cornwallis, defeated at Yorktown, became governor-general of India and died there in 1805.

By 1818, most of India was under the control, direct or indirect, of the British East India Company and became a captive market for British industry. Many Indians were schooled in English, which became standard for Indian education and administration in 1835, an important measure for the cultural unification of India. Christian missionary schools attempted to convert Indians, with little success.

The East India Company got a major fright with the massive Sepoy or Indian Mutiny of 1857, which Indians call their First War of Indian Independence. It showed that just under the surface Indians deeply resented British rule. The spark was new rifles that had powder and shot packed in paper cartridges. A false rumor spread that these were greased with pig and cow lard. Muslims, who eat no pork, and Hindus, who eat no beef, were outraged because they had to tear open the cartridges with their teeth. The **sepoys** shot their British officers, besieged several cities, and killed English civilians. The East India Company's reaction was so ferocious that London dissolved the Company in 1858 and set up "direct rule" under a governor-general, a system called the **Raj**. The Crown had to take over India to save it from the misrule of a giant corporation, a pattern that also appeared in Dutch, French, and Belgian colonialism. You cannot run countries on a purely commercial basis.

India became the most important and lucrative part of the British Empire. To reach it and other colonies in Asia, Britain (along with France) constructed the Suez Canal, part of the "imperial lifeline" that opened in 1869. Cut off from U.S. cotton during the Civil War, Britain increased India's cotton crop but did not allow Indian industry to make cloth. Instead, Indian cotton fed the mills of Lancashire and was sold back to Indians at high prices. Britain destroyed Indian industry. Restoring Indian cloth production became a symbol of Gandhi's independence movement. Gandhi personally spun his own thread in defiance of the British, and a spinning wheel is in the center of India's flag today.

Indian Independence

British rule, while basically exploitive, also did much to modernize India. The English language allowed educated Indians to speak to each other across the entire **subcontinent** and to voice their discontent. Universities created a new intellectual class of lawyers, journalists, and educators, who soon turned critical of their British masters. The railroad and telegraph stitched together the disparate parts of the country. Before imperialism there was little nationalism. The British, by modernizing India, got themselves invited to leave.

Congress Led India's independence movement and later was the dominant party.

swaraj *Swa* = self, *raj* = rule; Indian independence.

intercommunal Among communities, ethnic groups, or religions.

Muslim League Organization demanding a separate Muslim Pakistan.

In 1885 the Indian National **Congress** (INC) was founded by intellectuals to debate government reforms. It was an elite thing, not radical or aiming for independence. That changed with the return of Gandhi to India, who took over the INC and turned it into a huge, effective mass movement demanding **swaraj**. Indian political stability after independence owes much to age, size, and organization of the Congress, which subsequently turned into a political party that ruled India for many years.

But the Indian independence movement split in three: (1) The mainstream Congress of Gandhi that sought to represent all Indians; (2) a Muslim movement that feared and fought domination by Hindus; and (3) a Hindu nationalist movement that preached exclusivity and hatred of Muslims. In hindsight, there was probably no way India could have achieved independence without releasing the tensions that British colonial rule had built up.

There had long been **intercommunal** tension and sometimes violence between India's Muslims and Hindus. As soon as the INC began agitating for *swaraj* some of India's Muslim minority started to worry. Muslims and Hindus initially cooperated in the INC, but in 1906 the **Muslim League** split off and in 1940 demanded a separate Pakistan for Muslims. Gandhi tried to reassure Muslims that they would be at home in India—150 million still are—but many did not believe it. Exclaimed Muslim League chief Muhammad Ali Jinnah: "Islam is in danger!" The British used the standard line of colonialists everywhere that they alone could keep India together and reasonably calm. Rather blindly, however, they also created much of the tension and did little to prepare India for independence.

Political Culture

INDIA'S POLITICAL ERAS

A bit like Mexico (see next chapter), India has undergone wrenching changes, mostly related to conquest, all of which left behind cultures that imperfectly and gradually melded into a distinctly Indian political culture.

Era	Years	Remembered for
early civilizations	2500–1600 B.C.	Indus Valley culture
Vedic Age	1500–500 B.C.	Migration of Aryan speakers
Mauryan Empire	326–184 B.C.	Ashoka reigns, Buddhism spreads
Gupta Empire	A.D. 320–550	Classic age of Northern India
Islamic India	711–1526	Piecemeal conquest, Delhi sultanates
Mughals	1526–1757	Large Muslim empire, Taj Mahal
British	1757–1947	Colonial rule, ousted by Gandhi and INC
Independent India	1947–present	Nehru, democracy, accelerating growth

In 1925 Hindu nationalists founded the Rashtriya Swayamsevak Sangh (RSS, National Volunteers Union) to make sure **Hindutva** dominated India. Although the RSS for a while worked with Gandhi and the Congress for independence, they, like Jinnah, split from it. An RSS supporter assassinated Gandhi in early 1948, and the organization was briefly banned.

Hindutva	Literally, Hinduness.
satyagraha	Nonviolent protest.
ahimsa	Not injuring any living thing.

Personalities

Gandhi: The Great Soul

Mohandas Gandhi

Mohandas Gandhi (1869–1948) was an unlikely liberator. A slight, bespectacled man often in a homespun loincloth, he exuded a quiet charisma that mobilized millions of Indians to press the British to "Quit India!" Gandhi was called *Mahatma* (great soul in Sanskrit) and *Bapu* (father), as he was indeed the father of modern India.

Son of a prime minister of a small principality in Gujarat (in western India) and a devout Hindu mother, Gandhi showed little intellectual promise early on but did study law in London. His formative experience was as a lawyer and organizer of downtrodden Indians in South Africa from 1893 to 1914, where he felt racism and repression first-hand. There, in 1908, he wrote his most important work, *Hind Swaraj* (Independent India), which the British tried to suppress. Returning to India, Gandhi turned sharply anti-British after the 1919 Amritsar massacre of 400 Indians at a peaceful meeting. In 1921 Gandhi took command of the Indian National Congress and turned it from an elite debating society into a well-organized mass movement that after long struggle persuaded Britain to leave.

Gandhi abjured violence and led the Congress in noncooperation campaigns that ultimately wore down the British. He urged **satyagraha** based on **ahimsa** mixed with Thoreau's civil disobedience. He demanded tolerance for all religions and help for the lowliest, the outcastes. His most famous act was to lead a 250-mile march to the ocean to make salt from seawater to protest the salt tax; 60,000 of his followers were imprisoned. The British saw Gandhi as a ridiculous but irritating figure and jailed him many times. Gandhi disliked industry and cities and offered a vision of an India of villages, where Indians would retain their spirituality. Such rural idylls (see page 497) mean poverty, with farmers starving on tiny plots.

Ultimately, Gandhi succeeded by delegitimizing British colonial rule. Britain was also exhausted after World War II, and India was seething with anger. Besides, how could Britain fight for freedom during the war but deny it to Indians? (Other British colonies such as Nigeria asked the same question.) The Muslim League insisted on a separate Pakistan, and both Hindu and Muslim violence grew. A Hindu fanatic who believed Gandhi was soft on Muslims—he proclaimed them as brother Indians—assassinated him in early 1948. Wishing for precisely the opposite, Gandhi had unleashed terrible violence.

communal Ethnic or religious communities within a nation.

partition Dividing a country among its communities.

In World War II, Japan quickly took Southeast Asia and pushed into eastern India. The British were scared. With only a few British and Anzac troops, they had to rely on Indian soldiers and even officers. (Their best: the Gurkhas, from Nepal.) The Japanese put out the line that they were liberating Asia from the Europeans, and Indians should join them. Some did; a former Gandhi lieutenant, Subhash Chandra Bose, went over to the Japanese in World War II along with thousands of captured Indian soldiers. Britain knew it could not keep India forever.

In 1947 Britain sent Lord Mountbatten, who had commanded Allied forces against the Japanese in Asia, to negotiate independence. The Muslim League, however, insisted on a separate Pakistan, which meant partition, always an unhappy affair (see box below). India's partition

GEOGRAPHY

PARTITION

In colonial situations, the imperial power can sometimes calm **communal** tensions (which it may also have created), but when sovereignty—the key question of who is to be the boss—is up for grabs, deadly conflict can emerge, as it did between Hindus and Muslims in India. In such cases, **partition** may be an unhappy but "least bad" solution, one that seldom leads to peace and stability. India's is not the only sad case of partition.

Ireland, 1922   Britain misruled Ireland for seven centuries, putting down several uprisings and ignoring the Irish Potato Famine of the 1840s. Shaken by the 1916 Easter Rising, Britain agreed to an Irish Free State in 1922, but Northern Ireland, with its Protestant majority, stayed British, and it became the scene of Catholic-Protestant violence (see Chapters 4 and 6).

Palestine, 1948   Britain took Palestine from the Turks in World War I and ruled it under a League of Nations mandate. The Arabs of Palestine rioted against Jewish immigration, which became urgent with the Holocaust. An exhausted Britain threw the question to the UN in 1947, which devised a partition that looked like a checkerboard. The Jews accepted it; the Arabs rejected it. As Britain pulled out in 1948, Israel

proclaimed its independence and has been fighting Arabs ever since.

Cyprus, 1961   Britain took Cyprus from the Turks in 1878, but after World War II the Greek Cypriot majority agitated for *enosis* (union) with Greece. Greek guerrillas harassed the British, who agreed to leave in 1961. The Turkish minority, fearful of Greek massacres, demanded *taksim* (partition). In 1974, Turkey invaded and took the northern third of the island, which stays partitioned to this day.

Bosnia, 1992   After Yugoslav dictator Tito died in 1980, Yugoslavia's "republics" turned to independence (see page 360). Even Bosnian Muslims—a plurality but not a majority of Bosnia—demanded their own country, something that had historically never existed. Amid a terrible three-sided civil war, Serbs and Croats partitioned Bosnia by seizing adjacent portions of it. Bosnia is now effectively a NATO protectorate.

There are no examples of the happy partition of a state with intermingled but hostile peoples. The only argument for it is that trying to hold the country together would be worse. Do not count on partition among Shia, Sunni, and Kurds to solve Iraq's problems.

was a botched job, hasty and unplanned. Borders were drawn arbitrarily without knowledge of local loyalties, and few anticipated massacres or refugees. The predominantly Muslim areas, on the east and the west, went to Pakistan, the rest to India. In the case of a princely state, the maharajah would decide. Muslims did not accept this in **Kashmir**, where the Hindu maharajah decided for India despite a big Muslim Kashmiri majority. The Kashmir quarrel sparked three wars between India and Pakistan.

Kashmir   Valley near Himalayas contested by India and Pakistan.

president's rule   Delhi's ability to take over state governments.

Amid growing violence, India was declared independent at midnight of August 15, 1947. In an early version of ethnic cleansing, over 7 million Muslims fled to newly created Pakistan, while a like number of Hindus and Sikhs fled from Pakistan to India. Altogether, the 1947 partition of India led to 14.5 million refugees and half-a-million deaths. British forces did nothing to stop the violence. Gandhi was horrified at the bloody chaos and soon became a victim himself.

THE KEY INSTITUTIONS

India, like Britain, is a parliamentary system; that is, its cabinet is formed from and staffed by members of parliament. India's constitution defines it as "socialist, secular, and democratic," as its framers, led by Nehru, were caught up in the democratic socialism they had learned as students in Britain. This socialism skewed and retarded Indian economic development but has been partly discarded as India plunged into rapid capitalist growth in the 1990s. Under Gandhi, the Congress movement also insisted on keeping Indian government secular, not tied to any religion. Some Hindu nationalists would like to change that.

Instead of a monarch, however, India has a president who, like Germany's weak president, is largely ceremonial. Like the German president, India's is chosen for five-year terms by an electoral college of both houses of parliament plus state legislatures. Abdul Kalam, a Muslim, was elected in 2002. In 2007 Rajasthan Governor Pratibha Patil was elected with Congress and leftist support to become India's first woman president.

THE PRIME MINISTER

As in Britain, in India power is in the hands of a powerful prime minister. Part of the reason India's prime minister (PM) is so powerful is the imprint its first occupant, the brainy Jawaharlal Nehru, put on the office for its first seventeen years. Nehru, twenty years younger than Gandhi and also British educated, was the day-to-day administrator of India's independence movement under Gandhi and immediately became prime minister in 1947, serving until he died in office in 1964. Nehru devised and built up India's political institutions, with the prime minister in charge overall, giving the office plentiful economic and political powers that have lasted to this day.

The PM may ask the president to invoke **president's rule**, which gives New Delhi the power to take over a state government in an emergency, such as rioting, and run it directly. The prime minister sets the main government policies and can call new general elections whenever he or she likes within a five-year maximum term. To "form a government," the PM must control a majority

Sikh Sixteenth-century offshoot of Hinduism, a minority religion in India concentrated in Punjab; males wear turbans.

balance of payments What a country owes other lands compared to what it can pay.

of seats in the lower house, which sometimes requires a coalition. Like presidents in other parliamentary systems, India's president names as prime minister whomever the largest party in parliament designates. Prime ministers need not be the party chief or a member of the lower house, although they usually are. Current PM is Manmohan Singh, a Congress member of the *upper* house, a first in India's history. The head of the Congress party is now Sonia Gandhi, the Italian-born widow of a son of Indira Gandhi, who chose not to become prime minister after the 2004 elections.

India has a very large cabinet—recently composed of thirty-two ministers—appointed by the prime minister from among the parties supporting the government in parliament. In addition to the usual ministries, India's cabinet has some almost comically specialized ministries, such as railways, chemicals, urban development, rural development, mines, heavy industries, small-scale industries, tribal affairs, textiles, power, minority affairs, petroleum, and water resources. Until the 1990s, India had a government-supervised economy requiring many specialized ministries, and this lingers in present-day India. If India turns all the way to free markets, we can expect many

PERSONALITIES

MANMOHAN SINGH

India's seventeenth and current prime minister was earlier the *technocrat* (see page 110) who set the country on its present course of economic liberalization and rapid growth. A **Sikh**—recognizable by their turbans and uniform family name of Singh (lion)—Manmohan Singh earned an Oxford doctorate in economics and worked for the International Monetary Fund and Reserve Bank of India. He points out that in 1700 India had one of the world's biggest economies but under the British it turned into one of the world's poorest.

Elected to the Rajya Sabha (upper house) for Assam (far from his native Punjab, but in India, as in Britain, this does not matter) in 1991, Singh was immediately named finance minister in the Congress cabinet. India was then in economic difficulty; behind in its **balance of payments**, it did not have enough foreign reserves to meet its obligations. Singh understood the problem well, and much like the PRI technocrats in Mexico and Deng technocrats in China, he opened India to foreign direct investment (see page 435) and reduced business regulation. India's economic growth immediately picked up, and credit went to Singh.

Manmohan Singh

Congress was voted out in 1999 but won the 2004 elections. INC leader Sonia Gandhi declined to become prime minister and nominated Dr. Singh instead. A quiet, unassuming man, Singh was popular as an honest, effective leader who calmed tensions in the Muslim and Sikh minorities. Under Prime Minister Singh, India's economy is growing as never before. As he says repeatedly, "The best cure for poverty is growth."

India's Main Prime Ministers			
Prime Minister	**Party**	**Term**	**Remembered for**
Jawaharlal Nehru	INC	1947–1964	Secularism, statism, neutralism
Indira Gandhi	INC	1966–1977, 1980–1984	Authoritarianism, breaking up Pakistan, Emergency
Morarji Desai	Janata	1977–1979	Repudiation of Indira
Rajiv Gandhi	INC	1984–1989	Computers trigger economic liberalization
Atal Bihari Vajpayee	BJP	1996, 1998–2004	Hindu right, nuclear tests, economic growth
Manmohan Singh	INC	2004–	Calm, faster economic growth

of these ministries to disappear. Titles and responsibilities, as usual in parliamentary systems, are routinely shuffled and renamed.

A Bicameral Parliament

India's parliament is bicameral; the upper chamber represents India's states. Still, as in most bicameral legislatures, the lower house is more powerful. This is the Lok Sabha (People's Assembly), whose 543 elected members serve up to five years, although elections can be called early. All are elected from single-member districts, Anglo-American style, with only a plurality needed to win. The president appoints another two members to represent the small Anglo-Indian community, so the total size of the Lok Sabha is 545. Only the Lok Sabha can initiate money bills.

The Rajya Sabha (Council of States) is the upper house, which can have up to 250 members (up to twelve of them distinguished persons appointed by the president) who serve six years. As in the United States before 1913, they are chosen by their state assemblies, one-third every two years. Each state, depending on population, gets from one to thirty-one representatives. If the two houses cannot agree on legislation, they meet and vote jointly. The greater numbers of the Lok Sabha then give it the upper hand.

A Fragmented Party System

Until 1977 all of India's prime ministers were from the Indian National Congress, making India look, for a while, like a dominant-party system (see the Japan and Mexico chapters). India's Congress party played a role similar to Mexico's PRI: a single large party enrolling many interests that established order and stabilized a potentially tumultuous system for several decades. Never mind that both Congress and PRI became rigid and corrupt; they invented their respective countries and then stood aside. Every developing country should be so lucky as to have an equivalent founding party.

Since 1977, Congress has lost several elections to right-wing parties whose names have changed over the years—from Janata, to Janata Dal, to the current Bharatiya Janata party (BJP,

Indian People's party)—espousing both Hindu nationalism and a free-market economy. (Janata is Hindi for "people's," the same name taken by several European rightist parties.) After some years of center-right rule, Congress was elected again, producing the very desirable *alternation in power* (see page 286), one of the defining characteristics of democracy that keeps rulers on their toes and responsive to voters.

DEMOCRACY

INDIA'S 2004 ELECTIONS

The 2004 general elections in India returned power to the Indian National Congress (INC), which had been an opposition party since 1989. (As in Britain, a "general election" is for all seats, as opposed to a "by-election" for just one seat.) The key motivator in the shift was voters' perception that the BJP-led coalition government had let too many Indians fall behind India's economic growth that benefited relatively few. The Hindu-nationalist BJP also took the blame for failing to stop murderous conflict between Hindus and Muslims, including the 2002 riots in Gujarat that killed over a thousand Muslims, including women who were raped and then burned. Hindu-Muslim tolerance has always been one of Congress's strong points.

Italian-born Sonia Gandhi led the INC but did not become prime minister. Never very political, she became even less so after her husband and mother-in-law were assassinated. She named Dr. Manmohan Singh, a respected economist and member of the Rajya Sabha, as prime minister. With not nearly enough Lok Sabha seats to govern alone, the INC gathered together twelve center, left, and regional parties to form the United Progressive Alliance.

The percentage of the national vote in India is meaningless, as politics in India is regional. Parties may be strong in a few states and weak or nonexistent in others. Many parties are only local. Even the large parties do not contest every seat. The INC, for example, contested 417 seats in thirty-three states, winning 145 seats with 27 percent of the national vote. Indian parties tend to concentrate their efforts where they do best and leave other constituencies to kindred parties they may later be able to form a coalition with. The Communist Party of India (Marxist) contested only sixty-nine seats in nineteen states but won forty-three of them with less than 6 percent of the national vote. U.S. House Speaker Tip O'Neil was famous for his phrase, "All politics is local," and this is especially true for India. The designations in the table below of "Strongest in" and "Caste Base" are only approximate.

Another 200 or so parties also ran, but many won one or no seat. This does not dissuade them; a similar number is expected to run in general elections, which must be held by 2009.

Party	Strongest in	Caste Base	Seats Won
Congress (INC)	most of India	lower and middle	145
BJP	Northern India	middle and upper	138
Communist	Southern India and West Bengal	lower and middle	43
Samajwadi	Uttar Pradesh	lower	36
Rashtriya Janata Dal	Bihar	lower and Muslims	24
Bahujan Samaj	Uttar Pradesh	untouchables	19

But India's party system is far more complex than a simple left-right division. India has gone from a dominant-party system under Congress to a fragmented party system (see page 324). Dozens of Marxist, caste-based, nationalist, regional, and local parties make it impossible for any one party to win a majority of parliamentary seats. This fragmentation is unusual for an FPTP electoral system (see page 45), which tends to produce a two-party, or at least a two-plus, system. In Britain and America it does, but where third parties are territorially concentrated, it can lead to a multiparty system (as it does in a small way in Canada). In India, it does so with a vengeance: The Lok Sabha contains about thirty parties, some with as few as one seat, looking like the results of a proportional-representation electoral system.

The result of this fragmented party system is that in recent decades one of the two large parties—Congress or BJP—has had to form a coalition—arranged among parties before the election—with smaller parties to consolidate a majority of Lok Sabha seats. The current Congress-led coalition of twelve parties rules as the United Progressive Alliance (UPA); the previous BJP-led thirteen-party coalition of 1999–2004 was the National Democratic Alliance.

Indian Federalism

India is federal rather than unitary, but less federal than Canada, Australia, or Germany. India has twenty-eight states with locally elected legislatures and "chief ministers" as executives. Another seven "union territories" have governments named by "the Centre" (New Delhi). Federalism, as we discussed with Germany (see page 181), is especially suitable in large countries or those with great cultural and linguistic diversity. India amply qualifies on both counts. In addition to English, spoken by all educated Indians, and Hindi, which Delhi pushes as the national language, India's constitution recognizes twenty-one languages as legal to conduct government business in.

The provision of president's rule (see page 453)—which has been used more than a hundred times—makes India less federal than other federal systems. It may be invoked if a state government lacks a majority in the state legislature or cannot handle major disturbances. (The closest U.S. analogy is the president's ability to "federalize" the National Guard, as Eisenhower did in 1957 to enforce desegregation in Arkansas.) Indian critics claim president's rule has mostly been used by prime ministers to get rid of political opponents running state governments.

India's Judiciary

An independent judiciary in the Third World, one that can and does nullify laws and executive moves as unconstitutional, is rare. India's judicial system has helped keep India democratic, even during its turn toward authoritarianism under Indira Gandhi in the 1970s (see page 463). India's Supreme Court resembles its U.S. counterpart. Its one chief justice and 25 associate justices are appointed by the president and serve until age 65. Parliamentary consent is not required. Major cases concerning the constitution, including disputes between the states and Delhi, are appealed to India's Supreme Court, which has the final word.

Conflict comes from inserting a basically U.S. institution—judicial review by a Supreme Court—into an otherwise British model of "parliamentary sovereignty." Well, which is supreme

dialect   Mutually intelligible variety
of a language.
Hindi   National language of India.

in India, the court or the parliament? India has had some heated debates about this, usually when the Supreme Court overturns a piece of legislation. India inherited the British common law, and Indian cases are designated by the plaintiff's and/or defendant's names in italics.

INDIAN POLITICAL CULTURE

Similar institutions function quite differently in countries with different political cultures. India is a veritable feast for students of political culture. Its complexity and diversity make one wonder how India can hold together at all, much less get anything done. But these factors may actually support democracy by making pluralism natural and standard. Indians, unlike Russians, did not have to learn about the give and take of diverse opinions and interests. India was born and remains highly pluralistic, and pluralism is the bedrock of democracy, for one group cannot get a hammerlock on politics and institute authoritarian rule, of which India got a taste in the late 1970s.

GEOGRAPHY

INDIA'S LANGUAGES

India has two main language families, many languages, and myriads of local **dialects**. The largest group is the Indo-European languages, spoken by three-fourths of Indians in a broad swath across northern India. Like Persian, they are related to most European languages. Among them are Sanskrit and **Hindi**. Most educated Indians speak English, which was one of the threads that stitched modern India together.

India's constitution, repudiating British colonialism, designated Hindi written in the Devanagari script as the official language of national government but also allowed English to continue in this role. India has eighteen official regional languages, meaning state governments may use them. Hindi (and Pakistan's Urdu, which is similar but written in Arabic script) is unrelated to the Dravidian languages of the south, the second major language family, spoken by nearly a quarter of Indians. Educated southerners preferred English

as the national language, but gradually Hindi has gained ground.

Notice the parallel of India trying to establish Hindi and China trying to establish Mandarin (*Putonghua*) as their national languages. France, Germany, Italy, and many other European lands struggled to establish a common language and pronunciation, a process hastened after World War II by television. The process can also go backward. Serbo-Croatian was the standard language of Yugoslavia for most of the twentieth century, but as it fell apart, Croatian nationalists proclaimed a separate Croat language and Bosnian Muslims a separate Bosnian language. The differences in vocabulary and pronunciation among Serbs, Croats, and Bosniaks are small—they need no interpreters when they meet—but deliberately hyped for political purposes. Language is intensely political.

Most agree that Indians from all walks of life are talkative and argumentative. Everyone has an opinion and shares it. (The opposite: Japanese, who argue little because of cultural tradition and because of a lack of interest in politics.) This has given India a free and lively press of some 300 major newspapers with a combined circulation of 160 million. English-language newspapers such as the respected *Times of India* are popular among the educated and upwardly mobile. Any government attempts to curb the Indian press are howled down, which helps keep India democratic.

> **secularism** In India, treating members of all religions equally.

Religion in India

Some say India is one of the few countries where religion is really alive; for many, faith defines identity. Gandhi was a good Hindu, but Nehru, despite his Brahmin origin, disdained religion. His **secularism**, however, did not dent Indian religiosity. Eighty percent of Indians identify themselves as Hindus. (The Indonesian island of Bali is one of the few places outside of India that is also majority Hindu.) Depending on locale, many Indians pay special homage to one deity—the five main Hindu gods are Shiva, Vishnu, Devi, Ganesh, and Surya—in effect creating denominations within Hinduism.

Over 13 percent of Indians are Muslims, some tracing their origins back centuries to Persian or Mughal invaders, but more to conversion within India. That minority still means some 150 million Muslims, giving India the world's third largest Islamic community (first is Indonesia, second Pakistan). Upon partition in 1947, the majority of India's Muslims did not move to Pakistan. Some have done well in Indian government, science, and business, but on average they are poorer and less literate. Hindu nationalists such as the RSS (see page 451) periodically make Muslims the victims of murderous riots.

Christians and Sikhs account for around 2 percent each, Buddhists less than 1 percent (but growing), Jains less than half a percent. One of the most interesting religious groups is the Parsis, descendants of the Zoroastrians who fled the Arab conquest of Persia (see page 543). Although tiny in number, Parsis are prominent in business and own many of India's largest enterprises (the biggest: Tata, famous for steel, cars, airlines, and information technology). In effect, Parsis form another caste.

Thousands of Castes

Much of Indian politics consists of politicians trying to form caste alliances by promising jobs and affirmative-action programs. No one knows where India's caste system comes from. The conventional story is that it springs from Hinduism, but it may antedate the ancient Vedas, which portrayed four main castes in descending order of moral worth:

Brahmins—priests, teachers, and philosophers.

Kshatriya—warriors and rulers.

Vaisya—farmers and traders.

Sudra—manual laborers.

In addition, there are hundreds of *jatis*, social groups originally based on occupation and family names (Gandhi is "greengrocer"). In theory, one is born into and stays and marries in one's caste. Those outside of these castes are literally "outcastes," called untouchables, *Dalits*, and other names. They, too, subdivide into myriad subgroups, some lower than others. Terribly poor, illiterate, and discriminated against, untouchables are the victims of upper-caste and police brutality. Orthodox Brahmins avoid direct contact with Dalits. By living a moral and religious life, however, an untouchable can be reincarnated into a higher caste in the next life. In reality, there is mobility by stealth, as lower castes change locales and claim they belong to a higher caste.

The caste system also serves this-worldly goals. For the Aryan conquerors, it was an almost perfect device to subjugate and control a large native population. The Aryans could say, "See,

Political Culture

Indian Passivity?

An American who had been on a church project to help poor rural Indians once told me how difficult it was due to Indian passivity. One incident stood out: When his bus got stuck in sand, the upper-caste people stayed seated while the lower-caste went out to push. My friend was furious and ordered everyone out to push. He exploded: "This country needs either a John D. Rockefeller or a Mao Zedong to get it working!" He meant that India needed disciplined coercion—either in capitalist or communist form—to jolt it out of passivity. He chose Mao but perhaps should not have been so pessimistic.

Does India (and the Third World in general) have so much cultural baggage that it cannot escape poverty without coercion? The question is fascinating and important. Cultural theorists blame passivity and fatalism, often rooted in religion, as the key factor. But then how would you explain the excellent economic growth—without coercion—in India in recent years? Indian culture has not changed that much; something else must have changed. The likely factor: Delhi's economic policies.

The difficulty is that you cannot tell whether passivity is the cause or result of a culture. Adverse conditions may give rise to a fatalistic religion rather than the other way around. People who have had no opportunities for centuries will naturally appear passive. You would, too. Change the circumstances, though, and attitudes can quickly follow. In India, government economic policy in the 1990s shifted from statist and anti-market to capitalist and pro-market. Soon Indian entrepreneurs were making fortunes in information technology (IT), manufacturing, and customer support. (Your last call for help with your computer or satellite dish probably went to Mumbai or Bangalore.) It turns out that Indians are as active and materialistic as anyone.

So are previously passive Chinese, Indonesians, Thais, Brazilians, and Botswanans. Lurking under the surface of many "passive" cultures are latent active attitudes waiting for the right economic context in which to emerge, which is why culture is a poor predictor of economic growth. Cultures are durable but not set in concrete. As the late U.S. Senator Daniel Patrick Moynihan said in a 1986 Harvard lecture: "The central conservative truth is that it is culture, not politics, that determines the success of a society. The central liberal truth is that politics can change a culture and save it from itself."

we're up here, and you're down there, so keep your place and obey." (Actually, Plato proposed using much the same myth: Citizens of the Republic would be told they were born with either gold, silver, or iron souls, which determined who should lead and who should follow.) People who believe that the gods have assigned them their status will not complain about poverty or attempt to change it or revolt.

| **reify** To take a theory as reality; to make something more real than it is. |

The British made the caste system worse. By listing caste in Indian censuses starting in the late nineteenth century, they **reified** vague and flexible notions into firm categories. Some see British emphasis of the caste system as a form of the classic "divide and rule" tactic (see the Nigeria chapter) practiced by colonialists everywhere: By keeping them divided, you can more easily rule them.

Political Culture

Anti-Colonial Rage

Many ex-colonial areas harbored resentments against their former masters and the West in general. For this reason much of the Third World was neutralist during the Cold War, siding with neither the United States nor the Soviet Union. India is a good illustration of anti-colonial rage.

Many Indians feel they are twice the victims of conquest and subjugation, first by Muslims, second by British. Hindus and Muslims have lived together in India for a thousand years, mostly in peace but punctuated by occasional outbursts on both sides. The reign of Mughal Akbar the Great in the sixteenth century was a high point of culture and tolerance in India, much like Moorish rule in Spain. The Taj Mahal, India's signature showpiece, is Islamic architecture built for a Muslim ruler.

But underneath, some historians and psychologists claim, Hindus felt shamed and humiliated. They saw their Muslim conquerors as more manly and war-like than Hindus. Under the surface, Hindus raged. Actually, Hindus can be plenty tough; the legendary Gurkhas, Hindus from Nepal, were Britain's best soldiers. The British in the eighteenth century beat the Mughals and lorded it over Muslims and Hindus, humiliating both. Colonialism seems almost psychologically calculated to produce rage among its victims (see Chapter 31, page 516). For what it was like to live in an India with the English on top and the natives—even highly educated ones—on the bottom, read E. M. Forster's classic *A Passage to India*. The novel claimed that colonialism prevented English and Indians of good will from becoming friends. (Many Indians ignore English novels about India, arguing that they were written from the colonialist viewpoint.)

Gandhi calmed and controlled Indian rage, turning it into nonviolent disobedience that finally wore down British ability to govern India. Not all shared Gandhi's nonviolence; some wanted to side with the Japanese or settle scores with Muslims. After independence, India turned a cold shoulder first to Britain and then to the United States, which was seen as the inheritor of Western arrogance. Many Americans favored India's independence (after all, what was 1776?) but were shocked when Indian intellectuals denounced them as the new imperialists. This rage gave India its neutralist foreign policy that tilted toward the Soviet Union. As the colonial era recedes into the past and the Indian economy grows, the resentment has subsided. Many Indians are now rather pro-American.

To escape their wretched status, some outcastes convert to another religion—Islam, Christianity, or Buddhism—that preaches equality of souls. Unfortunately, their old untouchable status follows them into the new faith, and they are still not recognized as equals. There are "Christian Dalits" and "Muslim Dalits," showing the stubborn persistence of cultural patterns. Converting to Buddhism is socially and religiously easier, as it is historically an offshoot of Hinduism. Most outcaste Hindus still believe Hinduism is India's good and natural religion, even if it has penalized them in this lifetime. The caste system, by teaching fatalism, could retard India's economic and political growth.

Gandhi called untouchables *Harijan* ("children of God") and denounced the caste system, but Congress's rule did little to eradicate it. The BJP and Hindu nationalists approve of the caste system because it is part of *Hindutva*. Over time, the importance of caste has faded a bit in urban India, but even there it governs marriage choices. The caste system is still quite strong in the conservative countryside. As a component of religion, the most profound element of any political culture, caste is terribly difficult to cure.

Let us not be too critical of India. Caste systems by other names are found in several countries. Japan's *burakumin*, descended from a feudal outcaste of slaughterers and tanners, are still strongly discriminated against. Much of Latin America is stratified according to how much European blood one has. Until recently, South Africa's *apartheid* system rigidly classified people by race and kept Africans separate and down. And the United States, home of freedom and equality, held blacks to an inferior status—sometimes by Jim Crow laws, sometimes simply by social usage—long after slavery.

PATTERNS OF INTERACTION

Democracy is inherently conservative because it lets influential groups block changes that would hurt their interests. Landlords, businesspeople, and bureaucrats warp policies to favor themselves, either in parliament or in implementation. Nehru, for example, got a land-reform law passed, but landlords, often local Congress party leaders, used it to get more land for themselves. Indeed, every Indian "reform" program to help poor farmers helps mostly rich farmers. In a democracy, one well-placed interest group can subvert the good of the whole. Politicians, wary of offending important groups, hold back from real change, which explains why India changes only slowly and why, in frustration, some supported the authoritarian Indira Gandhi and her "emergency powers" (see box on page 463). A dictatorship can ignore or, as Stalin used to say, "liquidate" recalcitrant groups.

CORRUPTION AND POLITICS

A major impediment to change in India is its vast bureaucracy, which is considered one of the least efficient in the world. Inheriting British colonial administration, Nehru's socialism amplified it with layers of laws to inhibit capitalism, laws that virtually begged for corruption.

Higher-level bureaucrats insist that businesses pay to "facilitate" their applications through the legal maze. (Precisely the same thing happens in Brazil and in many other countries. Solution: Cut the number of laws, regulations, and bureaucrats, like Chile did.) Clerks demand money for official papers that ordinary citizens are entitled to. Funds for subsidized food, schools, or road maintenance "leak" until little is left for the projects themselves. In some cases, officials steal from the starving.

Indians know all about this corruption but assume that it cannot be cured. Instead, many dream of having a government job, not for its mediocre pay but for the chance to take big bribes. Of course, you have to pay a big bribe to get such a job in the first place. The elite Indian Administrative Service has many able, honest people, but they are more than offset by inefficient self-seekers. India consistently rates as one of the most corrupt countries in Transparency International's index (see page 535). Corruption is a permanent political issue, and it is used by

DEMOCRACY

INDIRA'S "EMERGENCY"

One of the most illuminating episodes of Indian democracy was the decidedly undemocratic "Emergency" of Prime Minister Indira Gandhi in 1975–1977, in which she ruled virtually by decree. The interesting point is that most Indians recoiled from her heavy-handed experiment and voted her out. Indian democracy, temporarily abrogated, ultimately worked.

Trouble started with accusations that Indira Gandhi—who was actually Nehru's daughter married to a Gandhi unrelated to the Mahatma—had unfairly used her powers to ensure election of the Congress party in 1971. Although nothing serious was proven, India seethed with protest. Thousands of protesters, including top political figures, were arrested. Indira persuaded President Fakhruddin Ali Ahmed (a Muslim) to declare a "state of emergency" in June 1975. This allowed Indira to use a series of decrees to override civil rights, jail opponents, silence the media, institute massive programs to fight poverty and illiteracy, clear slums, and force vasectomies on thousands of men to control population growth. India started looking a bit like Mao's China. Some, however, said that India needed such centralized power to overcome the institutional and cultural impediments to modernization. A little dictatorship, they argued, can sometimes be a good thing.

Indira's opponents organized a new Janata (People's) party and demanded a general election, which was held in 1977. Janata warned that this was India's last chance to choose between "democracy and dictatorship." In many Third World countries such elections are rigged and lead to dictatorship, but in India they were free and fair. Janata won a majority of Lok Sabha seats, and the INC took a drubbing. Indira and her son Sanjay lost their seats and were arrested on charges that did not stand up in court.

But Indian voters soon grew displeased with Janata's disarray, and in 1980 they voted Congress back in with a chastened Prime Minister Indira Gandhi promising never to pull another "Emergency" again. Indians twice kicked out politicians they did not like. Indian democracy withstood its greatest challenge and came out stronger. Now, corrupt or ineffective state and local governments are booted out by angry voters.

Naxalites   Maoist guerrilla fighters in India.

whatever party is out of power at the moment, and the accusations are almost always true.

Indian parties make the corruption problem worse. Much of Indian politics consists of politicians trying to form caste alliances by promising jobs and affirmative-action programs under the misleading label of "social justice." Instead, the people get a spoils system that spells endemic corruption. Politicians seek not justice or reform but payoffs for their followers and luxurious living for themselves. India has been called a "patronage-based democracy," a corrupt form of democracy. (But notice how most of the presently advanced democracies, including the United States, earlier were also based on patronage.)

India's Fragmented Politics

For many years the Congress party called itself leftist, but now parties much further to its left in effect have shoved it toward the center. Now that Congress has moved away from state ownership of industry—as has Britain's Labour party—it actually has become a centrist or center-left party. Prime Ministers Brown and Singh could be compared: Both promote market economies. The INC is liberal in the sense of upholding secular values in the face of *Hindutva* (see page 451).

To the left of Congress are several Marxist and Communist parties, each accusing the others of revising true Marxism. The largest of these is the Communist Party of India (Marxist); the parenthetical identification of "Marxist" distinguishes it from the other Communist parties that it deems mistaken and misguided. One such party is the violent Communist Party of India (Maoist), the followers of which have been dubbed **Naxalites**. Several left parties—including two Communist parties—ally themselves with Congress in the United Progressive Alliance, which currently rules India.

India's right is also fragmented. The BJP, much like the U.S. Republicans, combines pro-business, anti-affirmative action, and religion. The strands do not fit together in a long-term way. Business wants stability for economic expansion; upper castes want to roll back job "reservations"; and Hindu rightists want to define India as a Hindu country, even if that leads to violence against Muslims.

Its very fragmentation probably prevents India from falling into one-party rule. For the foreseeable future, any one party will not be able to win a majority of Lok Sabha seats, so all governments will have to rely on the support of other parties. If all Hindus voted BJP, India would have an intolerant Hindu-nationalist government in total control of parliament, able to pass any law it wished. But fortunately the BJP limits itself by pitching its message to middle- and upper-caste Hindus in northern India. Lower-caste Hindus are attracted to other parties that promise them a better economic deal. In India, some tell the joke, "you do not cast your vote, you vote your caste." By the same token, Congress now cannot get the votes it once could get because upper-caste voters have switched over to the BJP. India's social fragmentation has prevented its FPTP electoral system (see page 45) from producing a majoritarian (see page 45) parliament. India's complex pluralism has probably saved its democracy, but at the expense of coherence and efficiency.

VIOLENT INDIA

Many think of Indians as nonviolent Gandhians, but India has plenty of violence under the surface that bursts out every few years. Some fear it could rip India apart. For example, in 1984 murderous Sikh secessionists took over the sacred Golden Temple in Amritsar in the Punjab. Indira Gandhi ordered the Indian army to storm the temple, which killed many innocent Sikh pilgrims. Later that year, two of her Sikh bodyguards killed her in revenge. In return, thousands of Sikhs were killed in New Delhi anti-Sikh riots. Indira's son Rajiv was himself killed by a Tamil suicide bomber in 1991.

In 1992 a Hindu mob pulled down the sixteenth-century Babri Mosque in Ayodhya (in Uttar Pradesh in the north of India), claiming Muslims had built it on the site of an ancient Hindu temple to the legendary Lord Ram. The BJP state government of UP, based on the Hindu vote, did not stop them. In 2002 a trainload of Hindu pilgrims returning from Ayodhya rampaged against

COMPARISON

INDIA, MEXICO, AND COLOMBIA

India's Naxalite rural rebels resemble Mexico's Zapatistas (see page 497) and Colombia's FARC (*Fuerzas Armadas Revolucionarias de Colombia*) guerrillas. All are Marxist, armed, and intent on overthrowing their respective governments, which they deem under the thumb of capitalists and imperialists. All three have staked out base areas in remote jungles that make them hard to catch.

India and Colombia encourage ferocious anti-Marxist paramilitaries who are immune to legal restraints. The guerrillas and the paramilitaries both engage in criminal activities. In the Third World, crime and politics overlap. Distant countries with different cultures can produce similar problems. The common factors in India, Mexico, and Colombia are rural poverty, vast inequality, Marxist intellectuals who provide leadership, and peripheral areas bypassed by modernization. Once rooted in jungles and mountains, such movements are hard to crush and can carry on their wars for decades.

Prime Minister Singh called the Naxalites India's greatest security problem, worse than the Pakistan-sponsored Muslim terrorists in Kashmir. Formally the Communist Party of India (Maoist), they are named after the Naxalbari district of West Bengal where they began in 1967. Some 10,000 of their armed fighters try to arouse poor peasants by guerrilla attacks in a "red corridor" down the east side of India. Officials have counted some degree of Naxalism in 170 of India's 602 districts, mostly in rural jungle areas. They kill several hundred people a year, including Indian soldiers and police and the paramilitary Salwa Judum ("Peace Mission") who hunt them, with state encouragement, in Chhattisgarh state.

The Naxalites face the same problem Mao found in China: How can there be a proletarian party when there is scarcely a proletariat? Mao tried to solve it by proclaiming that poor peasants are proletarians, an unmarxist thing to do, but one copied by the Naxalites. Their stated goal is to "liberate India from the clutches of feudalism and imperialism," the same line as that of their Mexican and Colombian counterparts. Few give any of the three movements much chance of winning, but they surely can disrupt.

rupee India's currency (symbol Rs); in 2008 Rs42 = $1.

Muslims at a station. Fire broke out on the train, killing fifty-eight passengers. Angry Hindus, led by the RSS (see page 451), blamed Muslims for the fire. Then Hindu attacks in Gujarat (India's westernmost state, bordering Pakistan and the Arabian Sea) killed between 1,000 and 2,000 Muslims while state officials and police just stood by. Most Indians were shocked that the governing BJP, ideologically tied to the RSS, did nothing to stop the violence. The BJP national government would not declare *president's rule* (see page 453) over the BJP state government in Gujarat. This was one of the reasons for Indians voting out the BJP in 2004.

In 2006 Muslim terrorists bombed seven commuter trains in Mumbai (formerly Bombay), killing 183. There have been other bombings linked to Muslim groups. Until recently, India's nearly 150 million Muslims have been largely quiet, but the 2002 Gujarat pogrom against Muslims turned some into Islamist radicals, who get training and bombs in Pakistan. Indian Muslims are under heavy police surveillance, which makes them even angrier. Complained one: "It has become now very difficult to live as a Muslim in this country." Some Indian Muslims feel trapped in a hostile land. Hindu nationalists created India's Muslim unrest, which threatens massive Hindu-Muslim violence.

India has other areas of violence: Kashmir, the only Indian state with a Muslim majority, has been an insurgency zone since 1990. Some 350,000 Indian soldiers and police patrol Kashmir to repress an estimated one thousand Kashmiri terrorists. The big Indian military presence inflames rather than calms.

The Hill States in the very northeastern part of India, nearly cut off from the rest of India by Bangladesh, are isolated, poor, and populated by ethnic groups and tribes related to Tibetans and Burmese (some of them Christian) who do not feel Indian. Those who wish to break away from India have conducted low-level but nearly permanent guerrilla warfare. Many Naga tribes of Nagaland, bordering Myanmar, have been in rebellion since 1947.

Migration of poor people from other parts of India sparks violence in many areas. Local natives bitterly resent the newcomers for allegedly taking their jobs and crowding them out of their old neighborhoods. Deadly riots break out.

Crime in India is a vast and growing problem, and the police in some states may be a part of it. Backlogged courts and crooked judges make it easy for well-connected criminals to go free. Frustrated, police shoot notorious criminals to save going to trial. They also bash protesters and mistreat suspects, some of them arrested capriciously. Many poor people, innocent of any wrongdoing, die in Indian prisons; better-off people, of course, do not. Few policemen are ever held accountable.

What Indians Quarrel About

Outsiders' perceptions of the "New India" tend to get overblown (as do perceptions of China), marked by phrases like "a booming economy," "gleaming modern buildings," "a dynamic entrepreneurial class," "the world's fastest growth in cell phones," and so on. Led by a huge service sector (see box on the economic sectors on page 467), India's economy has become the fourth largest in the world (and is soon to overtake Japan for third place), and the Indian **rupee** has grown stronger against the U.S. dollar. In 2007 India's Tata Steel bought the big Anglo-Dutch Corus group, which was emblematic of the colonial underdogs now being on top of their former imperialist masters.

KEY CONCEPTS

THE THREE ECONOMIC SECTORS

British economist Colin Clark developed the idea that economies can be divided into three sectors. The "primary" sector is agriculture, which appears with the dawn of civilization. Much later came the "secondary" sector, industry, as factories employed more and farming fewer. With mechanization, one farmer could do the work of many. As an economy modernizes, the primary sector shrinks to single digits and the secondary sector declines, too, but the percentage working in services, the "tertiary" sector, grows. Virtually everyone reading this book is aiming for a career in one service or another: teaching, law, government, finance, IT, and other professions that put no dirt under your fingernails.

One way to tell a country's level of development is by comparing the percent of its workforce in each of the three sectors. A country where most still work the land is less developed than one where most work in factories or services. And where most work in services is a more developed or "mature" economy. Most rich countries have two-thirds or more of their workforce in the tertiary sector and very few in the primary sector.

Some worry that India has jumped over the middle stage, manufacturing, which heretofore has been the basis of economic development. India has many peasant farmers and an unusual number of service workers, especially in IT; it has relatively few factory workers. China shows a more normal progression as its workforce shifts from farming to manufacturing to services. Which path will be more stable and prosperous in the long run?

Percent of Workforce in

	Agriculture	Industry	Services
United States	0.7	23	77
Britain	1.4	18	80
France	4.0	24	72
Germany	3.0	33	64
Russia	11.0	29	60
Japan	5.0	28	68
China	45.0	24	31
India	20.0	19	61
Mexico	18.0	24	58
Nigeria	70.0	10	20
Iran	30.0	25	45

Source: CIA World Factbook.

exponential growth Economy keeps growing faster and faster.

autarchy Economic self-sufficiency, importing and exporting little.

import substitution Policy of excluding foreign goods and producing them domestically; means high tariffs.

Yes, all of the above and more is true, but incomplete. India, like most developing nations, is actually two countries—a small, modern, and prosperous one inside a poor and backward one. India has a new and growing middle class of 100 million to 250 million people, depending on who is counted as middle class. Most Indians, however, are poor, living on $1 a day or less. Most Indians are stuck in the countryside, where many children are nutritionally and educationally stunted. Public services—schools, medical care, water supply, electricity, highways—are spotty. Most urban residents live in illegal or shack dwellings in slums without water or sewers. India's crowded streets are pungent.

India does show **exponential growth**, starting very low but accelerating. Under British colonialism, India's per-capita growth in the first half of the twentieth century averaged zero; that is, slow overall GDP growth was offset by population growth. From 1950 to 1980 its per-cap grew at an average of only 1.3 percent—what economists joked was a "Hindu rate of growth"—less than half what the rest of the developing areas were averaging. During the 1980s, however, this picked up to several percent and now is booming at some 8 percent.

Nehru-Minded Economics

For its first third of a century, India looked like it would stay poor. In 1966 Yale economist Charles Lindblom asked, in *Foreign Affairs*, "Has India an Economic Future?" Lindblom concluded that it did not because of Delhi's anti-growth policies. The socialist/statist shadow of Nehru (India's prime minister from 1947 to 1964) loomed large over India's economy. Nehru, imbued with the socialism that he learned in Britain, aimed for *swadeshi* (self-reliance) or **autarchy**, which Adam Smith saw as a mistake. Nehru promoted **import substitution** (common in Latin America) and money-losing state-owned industries and neglected agriculture. Bureaucracy throttled growth through a jumble of permits. A nightmarish "license *raj*" protected Indian firms from foreign competition and told them what and how much to produce. Strict labor laws still make it almost impossible to fire a worker, so Indian firms hire few workers (note the similarity to West Europe, described on page 152); instead, they outsource to unregulated small suppliers.

During the 1980s, however, this Nehru-minded system began to loosen up; Prime Minister Rajiv Gandhi, along with a new class of young entrepreneurs, took an interest in computers, and information technology took off. The U.S.-funded Green Revolution doubled farm production in the 1970s and 1980s. By 1991, however, India was in economic difficulties and unable to pay what it owed other countries. Dr. Manmohan Singh, a respected economist, was named finance minister in 1991 and immediately opened India to foreign investment and rolled back some controls on business, a sort of Thatcherite "neo-liberalism" (see page 64) that was being introduced in many countries. The subsequent BJP government that took over in 1998 continued and expanded these policies, and India began to boom. Now few Indians oppose economic growth, although some in the Congress party fight to keep state controls, and some on the left want to distribute the economic fruits more equally. How much economic freedom is still a major quarrel in Indian politics.

India was under considerable pressure to open up. Several East Asian economies, especially China, were leaving India far behind with free-market growth. If India did not want foreign investment, plenty of others did, and they would be the winners. No country likes to fall behind; it means poverty, military weakness, and overall ridicule. Now the world respects India.

> **overheat** Too-rapid economic growth characterized by inflation, factories at full capacity, and excessive borrowing.
>
> **sustainable** Can keep going for many years with no major downturns.

COMPARISON

INDIA'S AND CHINA'S ECONOMIES

India's and China's economic development show some similarities but show more differences. Both are booms that run the danger of going bust. Both countries' economies are growing so fast that they threaten to **overheat** and unleash instability, so both try to cool growth—chiefly by raising interest rates a bit. They fear that stock-market bubbles will pop and loans will turn bad. Delhi and Beijing prefer long-term **sustainable** growth to short-term maximum growth. In both India and China, growth is concentrated in certain coastal areas, which are more open to foreign commerce and are home to more sophisticated urban people. Both depend on imported oil, and when oil prices rise they suffer. In both lands an urban middle class is emerging. Both push peasants off the lands they till to make room for factories and push city dwellers out of simple homes to make way for high-rises (but more so in China). Corruption plagues both lands.

The two countries, however, pursue very different development paths. China's path is labor-intensive, using manufacturing with low-cost unskilled labor to export massive amounts of goods. But India's path is capital-intensive, using services such as IT staffed by educated, English-speaking young people. This skews India's growth, however: Only 1 million employees, less than one-quarter of 1 percent of India's workforce, work in IT, and they make India boom. India's millions of unskilled workers produce little and cannot get factory jobs; instead, they do piecemeal, temporary work and are essentially unemployed or underemployed. India employs 7 million in manufacturing; China employs over 100 million. As one Indian put it, "We are a back office and China is a factory."

China's growth exploded decades ago with Special Economic Zones (SEZs) that lure foreign direct investment (FDI) through tax breaks and better infrastructure (see page 435). India, still suspicious of FDI, has been slow in setting up SEZs. China has nearly complete literacy but lags in training a technological and management elite to run its burgeoning economy. India has neglected mass education in favor of training a gifted few in top universities and institutes (see page 471).

Whereas China (like Japan earlier) is an export maniac, India focuses on developing its domestic market. Chinese save much of their income; Indians do not. China uses domestic savings for growth but shortchanges Chinese domestic consumption, so Chinese do not live as well as they could. As a percentage of GDP, 64 percent of India's GDP goes to domestic consumption, as compared to 58 percent of Europe's, 55 percent of Japan's, and 42 percent of China's. Some economists think that India is wise in doing this, as it partially insulates India from the ups and downs of the world export market.

A Secular or Hindu India?

India's constitution specifies that it is secular, but secularism is hard to put into practice. Politicians over the years have bent to the demands of religious groups in order to win their votes, which has resulted in the erosion of secularism and in nasty backlashes from other groups. For example, in the 1985 *Shah Bano* case, a divorced and destitute Muslim woman appealed her claim for alimony to the Indian Supreme Court, which ruled for her under Indian secular law. The Muslim community went into an uproar, claiming that *sharia* (see page 473) must govern family law among Muslims, and *sharia* grants no alimony. Should there be one law for all, or should there be a separate Muslim "personal law"? Prime Minister Rajiv Gandhi pushed through parliament a 1986 law letting Muslims have their way in the matter of divorces. Then the Hindu community was furious, accusing Rajiv of pandering to Muslims for their votes and undermining the secular rule of the Supreme Court. This was one reason that the Hindu-right Janata Dal won the 1989 elections.

The Hindu right constantly tries to redefine India as a Hindu country, much as some U.S. politicians try to define America as a Christian country. RSS *shakhas* (branches) still train hundreds of thousands of uniformed young Hindus in early-morning drills, workouts, and games with an anti-Muslim slant. Bengali poet Rabindranath Tagore, who won the 1913 Nobel Prize for literature, wrote India's national anthem in 1911, the generous *Jana Gana Mana* ("The Minds of All People"), but Hindu nationalists want to change it to the angry and narrow *Bande Mataram* ("Hail Motherland").

It is difficult to tell how many Indians are Hindu nationalists. They are a minority but a substantial one. Votes for the BJP do not measure underlying Hindu nationalism because they include voters who like its free-market policies or dislike something the Congress party has done, such as Indira's Emergency or corruption. Horrors like the 2002 Gujarat pogrom can swing Indians back to Congress. Tension with Pakistan over Kashmir or nuclear weapons can raise nationalist sentiment. We are likely to see Hindu-right governments in the future—that is the nature of alternation in power—but the question is will they pursue militantly anti-Muslim and anti-Pakistan policies?

Quotas and Voters

India's Dalits and lower castes are terribly disadvantaged and have been for centuries. Should they therefore get special treatment—education quotas and job quotas—that expands and lasts indefinitely? Nearly 13 percent of Indians are classified as Dalits; 27 percent are classified as Other Backward Classes; and 10 percent are classified as Advanis (tribal). That makes half of Indians eligible for some form of affirmative action, such as "scheduled" status and "reserved" jobs in the public sector. Dalit political parties demand this as "social justice." One such party, the Bahujan Samaj party (BSP), led a coalition that took a majority of seats in the state legislature of huge and poor Uttar Pradesh (UP) in northern India in 2007, eclipsing both Congress and the BJP. Led by the "Dalit queen," Mayawati (just one name), now UP's chief minister, the electoral upset showed that Indian politics is heavily based on which party can aggregate the most castes.

Upper-caste critics denounced this as affirmative action run amok, resulting in unfairness to better-qualified applicants. Hatred of the lower-caste quotas rallied many upper-caste voters to the BJP. Notice how the Indian situation parallels America's affirmative action, which pushed many white males to the Republicans.

India's Muslim minority gets little from India's rapid economic growth and falls further and further behind Hindus. Their religion does not qualify Muslims for "scheduled" status. If they lag, argue some Hindus, it is because of their rigid religious upbringing and scanty education. Rote memorization of the Koran does not build modern skills. Congress governments are more likely to pay attention to the Muslim gap; BJP claims special efforts for Muslims is just pandering to minorities.

Mass or Elite Education?

India's top universities, such as the Indian Institutes of Technology (IIT), are excellent, but they train only a small elite. Many of India's schools, especially at the elementary level, are terrible: no money, no buildings, no teachers. One in three Indians are illiterate. Education in India is largely a state matter—the case in federal systems generally—and some states either do not have the money or wish to spend it on other things. Public schools in India charge fees that the very poor cannot afford. Indians who can afford it send their children to private schools, but India needs to make all literate and numerate. Note the parallel with the very uneven U.S. education systems among its states.

The brightest Indian students compete to get into one of the several campuses of the world-class IIT, which rival their U.S. counterparts. Some IITians then go on to start businesses either in India or the United States. India graduates over 350,000 engineers a year, the United States 70,000, which explains why many U.S. engineering positions are now staffed by Indians. The mass of poor Indians, however, lag far behind. For these children, college and a good job are rare.

The problem parallels British education and some other countries that educate a small elite superbly while neglecting the needs of the masses. A World Bank study found that the best pay-off is in mass education, K-12, rather than in higher education for a few. India's literacy rate is 60 percent; China's is 90 percent. Much of Indian grade-school education is rote memory, boring, and (depending on which party has ruled the particular state) heavy on *Hindutva*. Many Muslims are too poor to afford school and accept the free education offered by a *madresa* (Muslim school), where boys memorize the Koran and sayings of the Prophet. Most Indians agree that education requires a massive injection of funds and personnel, but India's budget deficit is already too big.

Foreign Policy: Neutral or Aligned?

During the Cold War, India practiced neutralism between East and West and was proud to be a leader of the Nonaligned Movement along with Nasser's Egypt, Tito's Yugoslavia, and Sukarno's Indonesia. Delhi originally proclaimed "Indians and Chinese are brothers" but changed its tune when pushed back by China in a short border war in 1962. India and the Soviet Union grew close while Pakistan and the United States favored each other. With the end of the Cold War, India focused its national interests on securing its borders. It worries that an Islamist takeover of Pakistan and Bangladesh could encourage Muslim extremists inside India. Likewise the Tamil breakaway war in Sri Lanka could embolden Indian Tamils. India aims to become—and may already be—the regional power of the Indian Ocean; its army and navy are not trivial, and it has enough nuclear weapons for what it calls a "minimum deterrent."

For half a century, relations between India and the United States were correct but chilly. Now they are greatly improved but not yet an alliance. Delhi's relations with Beijing are still a little testy. China makes clear that it will be the dominant power in Asia, disquieting some Indian strategic thinkers. China still claims that the Indian state of Arunachal Pradesh (in the extreme northeast of India) is part of China but has made no demands. Islamist terrorism rattles India, promoting a common stand with Washington. India's rapid economic growth, especially in IT, is linked to the U.S. economy. Washington perhaps too eagerly courted India and in 2005 offered India a sweetheart nuclear deal. Washington said in effect, "You can keep your nuclear weapons, but we'll help you with your peaceful nuclear program." The U.S. offer undermined the Nuclear Nonproliferation Treaty by suggesting that other countries could also have two nuclear tracks, one for weapons and one for power generation. India's main Communist party, a member of the Congress-led ruling coalition, warned that the deal made India subservient to U.S. policy and blocked it by threatening to walk out of the coalition and bring it down.

India, worried about China and Pakistan, had been developing nuclear weapons for decades, first testing in 1974. Washington protested for years, but in 1998 India exploded five bombs underground and proclaimed itself a nuclear power. The United States no longer protests, demonstrating that nuclear weapons really do bring respect. India welcomes cooperation with the United States but will not follow American-led crusades, especially in Muslim countries, for that would exacerbate India's own Muslim problem.

India's big problem is still Pakistan, for now both nations have nuclear weapons. India and Pakistan were born hostile, and the Kashmir question has caused three wars—1947–1948, 1965, and 1999—between them. By some accounts, they twice considered using nukes. (A fourth war, in 1971, grew out of the breaking away of Bangladesh from Pakistan.) India accuses Pakistan of supporting Kashmiri terrorists, whose bombings have spread beyond Kashmir. India-Pakistan tensions have lately calmed, as Pakistan knows India is both economically and militarily more powerful. Both sides want to settle the Kashmir issue, although this would not guarantee an end to local terrorism. Diplomats suspect Pakistan would settle for Kashmir's present borders but with a special autonomous status. Top officials and cricket teams exchanged visits, and a rail line across their border reopened. A 2007 bomb attack on this train—possibly by Muslim Kashmiris—actually brought greater antiterrorist cooperation between the two countries. If radical Islamists take over Pakistan (see box on page 473), hostility could quickly resume. India pursues respect and good relations in all directions with no entangling alliances.

THE GREAT ASIA WAGER

In the early 1960s, U.S. Ambassador to New Delhi (and Harvard economist) John Kenneth Galbraith called it "a functioning anarchy." Now observers stress functioning over anarchic. India's GDP grows around 8 percent a year, one of the highest in the world and accelerating. It has lagged a couple of percentage points behind China, which started its economic liberalization earlier (1979) and did it more thoroughly (see Chapter 28). The big question that looms over Asia and the world is who will become the economically dominant power, India or China? This has strategic as well as economic importance.

> **sharia** Muslim religious law based on the Koran.

The early rounds clearly go to China. Chinese are far better fed, clothed, and housed than Indians, as a taxi drive through a Chinese and an Indian city quickly reveal. China's great weakness, however, is that it is politically still a one-party dictatorship, and over the long haul India's

COMPARISON

THE INDIA-PAKISTAN CONTRAST

The sharp differences between India and Pakistan give political scientists a rare chance to examine how similar countries can develop differently. Both were born out of British-ruled India in 1947 but took separate paths. Is it culture or structure that makes the difference? Or some combination of the two?

For more than half of its history, Pakistan has been ruled by generals; India never has been. Pakistan had military coups in 1958, 1977, and 1999. The first brought thirteen years of military rule, the second eleven years, and the third nine years and counting of Pervez Musharraf. In between were elected civilian politicians whom the generals overthrew for egregious corruption. Pakistan alternates between democracy and dictatorship, the *praetorianism* common in the Third World (see page 531). India, perhaps except for Indira's 1975–1977 Emergency (see box on page 463), stayed democratic.

Pakistan's geography was unfavorable; it was founded as two wings separated by a thousand miles of India. In bitter 1971 fighting, East Pakistan, complaining of mistreatment by larger and ethnically distinct West Pakistan, split off to become independent Bangladesh. India, to be sure, is permanently threatened by breakaway movements in its peripheral areas, but none of them has succeeded. Pakistan's economy earlier grew faster than India's but is now slower, with a lower per capita GDP than India's. The high-tech industries developing in India have not developed in Pakistan.

Why the difference? The easiest explanation is Pakistan's Islam. Muslim countries seem to have unusual difficulty modernizing, which some blame on the intertwining of Muslim values, especially **sharia**, with politics. Islam was always intended to be a blueprint for governance, not just a religion. Jinnah himself was rather secular and never intended Pakistan to be an Islamic state; he saw it as a place of refuge for India's Muslims but not explicitly religious. Jinnah, however, unwittingly planted the seeds of Islamism, which blossomed with Pakistani dictator Zia-ul-Haq (1977–1988), who instituted *sharia* as the law of the land in 1984, fanning Islamic fundamentalism. Today, Islamic extremists—still a minority—try to overthrow Musharraf in favor of a Taliban-type Islamist state.

But culture does not explain everything; structures also matter. The Indian National Congress was well organized and *institutionalized* (see page 484) and committed to democracy long before it took power in 1947. The Muslim League was weaker and was unable to turn itself into a durable political party the way Congress did. The beginning of a political system often sets it on its path for generations.

Few expect Pakistani democracy any time soon; some fear it will be overthrown by Islamic fundamentalism. Osama bin Laden has hidden out for years in the tribal areas of northwest Pakistan, along the Afghan border. The Pakistani government, swearing it is fighting terrorism, has not yet caught him. Critics think it does not want to, as that might trigger an Islamist uprising.

democracy may prove more resilient and adaptable. China will eventually reach a point where the Communist party has to give way to democratic forces. Are China's leaders clever enough to engineer a peaceful transition, or will it be traumatic, accompanied by instability and economic disruption? India does not have to transition to democracy; it is already there. What India must overcome is its fragmented and chaotic form of democracy.

KEY TERMS

ahimsa (p. 451)

autarchy (p. 468)

balance of payments (p. 454)

Buddhism (p. 447)

caste (p. 447)

communal (p. 452)

Congress (p. 450)

dialect (p. 458)

exponential growth (p. 468)

Hindi (p. 458)

Hinduism (p. 447)

Hindutva (p. 451)

import substitution (p. 468)

intercommunal (p. 450)

Kashmir (p. 453)

maharajah (p. 449)

Mughal (p. 448)

Muslim League (p. 450)

Naxalites (p. 464)

overheat (p. 469)

partition (p. 452)

president's rule (p. 453)

Raj (p. 449)

reify (p. 461)

rupee (p. 466)

satyagraha (p. 451)

secularism (p. 459)

sepoy (p. 449)

sharia (p. 473)

Sikh (p. 454)

subcontinent (p. 449)

sultanate (p. 448)

sustainable (p. 469)

swaraj (p. 450)

FURTHER REFERENCE

Behera, Navnita Chadha. *Demystifying Kashmir.* Washington, D.C.: Brookings, 2006.

Charlton, Sue Ellen M. *Comparing Asian Politics: India, China, and Japan*, 2nd ed. New York: Public Affairs, 2004.

Dalrymple, William. *The Last Mughal.* New York: Knopf, 2007.

Friedman, Edward, and Bruce Gilley, eds. *Asia's Giants: Comparing China and India.* New York: Palgrave, 2006.

Ganguly, Sumit, and Neil De Votta, eds. *Understanding Contemporary India.* Boulder, CO: L. Rienner, 2003.

Ganguly, Sumit, Larry Diamond, and Marc F. Plattner, eds. *The State of India's Democracy.* Baltimore, MD: Johns Hopkins University Press, 2007.

Guha, Ramachandra. *India after Gandhi: The History of the World's Largest Democracy.* New York: Ecco, 2007.

Kamdar, Mira. *Planet India: How the Fastest-Growing Democracy Is Transforming America and the World.* New York: Scribner, 2007.

Khan, Yasmin. *The Great Partition: The Making of India and Pakistan.* New Haven, CT: Yale University Press, 2007.

Kohli, Atul, ed. *The Success of India's Democracy.* New York: Cambridge University Press, 2001.

Luce, Edward. *In Spite of the Gods: The Rise of Modern India.* New York: Doubleday, 2006.

Menon, Nivedita, and Aditya Nigam. *Power and Contestation: India since 1989.* New York: Palgrave, 2007.

Mishra, Pankaj. *Temptations of the West: How to Be Modern in India, Pakistan, Tibet, and Beyond.* New York: Farrar, Straus and Giroux, 2006.

Mitra, Subrata K. *The Puzzle of India's Governance: Culture, Context, and Comparative Theory.* New York: Routledge, 2005.

Nussbaum, Martha C. *The Clash Within: Democracy, Religious Violence, and India's Future.* Cambridge, MA: Belknap, 2007.

Panagariya, Arvind. *India: The Emerging Giant.* New York: Oxford University Press, 2008.

Rothermund, Dietmar. *India: The Rise of an Asian Giant.* New Haven, CT: Yale University Press, 2008.

SarDesai, D. R. *India: The Definitive History.* Boulder, CO: Westview, 2007.

Sen, Amartya. *The Argumentative Indian: Writings on Indian History, Culture, and Identity.* New York: Farrar, Straus & Giroux, 2005.

Talbot, Strobe. *Engaging India: Diplomacy, Democracy, and the Bomb,* rev. ed. Washington, D.C.: Brookings, 2006.

Chapter 30
Mexico

Roughly 15,000 years ago, hunter-gatherers walked across the Bering Strait from Asia into North America, probably pursuing game. The ice age had lowered the sea level and formed ice bridges across the Strait. In a few millennia these hunter-gatherers spread the length of the Western Hemisphere. Some of them founded civilizations, but several thousand years later than the first civilizations of the Middle East. The domesticated plants and animals that spread from Mesopotamia to Europe and Asia never crossed the Bering Strait. The Americas had few domesticable plants (corn in Mexico and potatoes in Peru) or animals (llamas in Peru), so their civilizations lagged behind Europe's, leaving them easy prey for the greedy Europeans.

QUESTIONS TO CONSIDER

1. What country began the voyages of discovery? Along what route?
2. What civilizations in Mexico preceded the Spanish conquest?
3. How did Mexico's colonial period differ from that of the United States?
4. Why were Calles and Cárdenas so important?
5. In what ways was the PRI reign undemocratic?
6. What ideologies did Mexico import? Do any fit Mexico?
7. Why do elections not equal democracy?
8. What is a *dominant-party system*? Is Mexico still one?
9. Has Mexico become a true democracy? How can you tell?

THE IMPACT OF THE PAST

Several civilizations rose and fell in Mexico long before the Spaniards arrived. The first, the Olmec, flourished around present-day Veracruz a thousand years before Christ and set the pattern for subsequent **Mesoamerican** civilizations. In the first centuries A.D. the Zapotec and Teotihuacán constructed palaces and pyramids that tourists visit today. During the first millennium the Mayas built a high civilization in the Yucatán. From the tenth to twelfth centuries the Toltec held sway in Central Mexico until destroyed by nomadic invaders, the Aztecs among them.

The Aztecs or Mexica, who originated in the northwest of Mexico, pushed into the Valley of Mexico around 1300. They made their capital on an island where they had sighted a prophetic eagle with a snake in its beak, which later became the symbol of Mexico. In 1376 the first Aztec king was crowned. Aztec kings had absolute power and ran their empires through a huge bureaucracy. The Aztecs kept expanding because they needed more land, serfs, and captured warriors to sacrifice to their deities. As a result, subordinate peoples did not love the Aztecs. The Aztec kingdom was complex and highly developed but not terribly old by the time Columbus sailed.

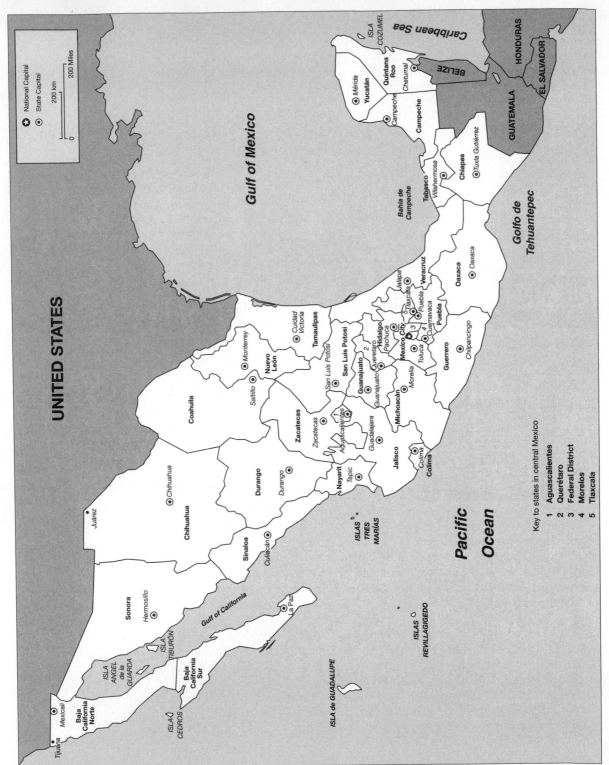

Mexico

NEW SPAIN

Portugal actually started the voyages of discovery, initially aimed at direct access to the wealth (especially spices) of the "Indies" by a route that bypassed the Arab traders and the Moors, whom Spain and Portugal had just expelled. Spain's Ferdinand and Isabella, aware that Portugal was far ahead in opening the Asia trade, accepted Columbus's argument that Spain could reach Asia directly across the Atlantic. (Yes, even then, educated people understood—from the ancient Greeks—that the world was round.) Columbus's 1492 voyage was to be a quick way to catch up with Portugal.

Mesoamerica   Spanish for Middle America; southern Mexico and northern Central America. (See page 477.)

Central America   Countries between Mexico and Colombia.

South America   Continent south of Panama.

Latin America   All countries south of the United States.

Columbus thought that he had nearly reached India, and he called the inhabitants of Hispaniola "Indians." The name stuck, although some now prefer Native Americans, Amerindians, First Nations (Canada), or *indígenas* (Latin America). The Spaniards charged quickly into the New World for "gold, God, and glory," serving respectively the royal treasury, the Catholic church, and the *conquistadores*, who had just won a struggle of nearly eight centuries to expel the Arabs from Spain. The Spaniards regarded the Indians with the same contempt that they held for the Moors. Indian lives meant nothing to them.

The Aztecs had a big population—their capital was probably larger than any European city at that time—and were well organized into a bureaucratic empire. Why could they not send the Spaniards packing? Several factors doomed the Aztecs. First, the Spaniards brought smallpox with them, against which Native Americans had no immunity. Mexico's population plunged from about 20 million at the time of the conquest to barely 1 million by 1600. Only in 1940 did Mexico reach the population it had under the Aztecs. Next, the Spaniards had steel; their swords sliced up the Aztecs (and later the Incas) as steel armor protected them. They also had horses and guns, which the Aztecs had never seen before. Many of the peoples the Aztecs had subjugated aided the Spaniards. Finally, the Aztecs had a legend that the white god Quetzacóatal would return from the east and destroy them.

GEOGRAPHY

BOUND MEXICO

Mexico is bounded on the north by the United States;

on the east by the Gulf of Mexico and the Caribbean;

on the south by Belize and Guatemala;

and on the west by the Pacific.

Geographically, Mexico is considered part of North America. To its south is **Central America**, consisting of Belize, Guatemala, Honduras, El Salvador, Nicaragua, Costa Rica, and Panama. **South America** is south of that. Everything south of the United States, including Mexico, is called **Latin America**.

pre-Columbian   The Americas before Columbus arrived.

creole   Spaniard born in the New World.

cacique   Originally Indian chief; local political boss.

Initially based in Cuba, Spanish ships explored Mexico's coast and brought back news of fabulous wealth in the interior. Partly at his own expense, Hernán Cortés equipped eleven ships and sailed from Havana in late 1518. After founding the city of Veracruz, he pushed inland with a force of 500 Spanish soldiers and several thousand Indians. The Aztec emperor Moctezuma (known to Americans as Montezuma) at first welcomed the Spaniards to his capital of Tenochtitlán, but they soon arrested him, and fighting broke out. Cortés retreated from the city but returned in 1521 after smallpox had killed much of its population. After three weeks of fierce battle, the Spaniards captured and killed the last emperor, Cuauhtémoc. Mexico today celebrates Aztec heroes but no Spanish ones, and many **pre-Columbian** traditions remain in Mexican culture.

On the ruins of Tenochtitlán the Spaniards built a new capital and called it Mexico. Upon the ruins of the main Aztec temple they built a huge cathedral. With little resistance, they soon took over most of Southern Mexico. Rich silver mines moved the Spaniards to expand over Central Mexico, but takeover of Northern Mexico, arid and thinly populated, was not completed until about 1600. North of the present U.S.-Mexican border Spanish occupation was sparse and late—Texas in 1716 and California in 1769—which ultimately led to war with the United States and loss of the vast territories that became the Southwest United States.

To control what they called New Spain, Spain used a Roman institution, *encomiendas*, grants of land and the people who worked on it, to Spanish soldiers and settlers. In the feudal manner, the *encomendero* was the lord and master of Indian serfs. They worked for him, and he looked after their welfare and Christianized them. Actually, the setup was not much different than what the Indians were used to under the Aztecs. The *encomienda* system soon produced a feudal type of social stratification. At the top were those born in Spain, *peninsulares*, who held all administrative positions as well as a social edge over *criollos* (**creoles**). Persons of mixed parentage, *mestizos*, became artisans and foremen, often in competition with poor Spaniards. The Indians worked the land on the *encomiendas* or stayed up in the mountains out of Spanish control.

Geography

MEXICO'S MOUNTAINS

Mexico's geography is distinctive and helped mold its current politics, which is highly regional. Two mountain chains, the Sierra Madre Oriental on the east and Sierra Madre Occidental on the west, connect at Mexico's narrow neck, forming a kind of Y. Between the Y's two arms is the Mesa Central, an upland that includes the Valley of Mexico with its rich volcanic soil and abundant rainfall. Mexico City, at 7,500 feet (a mile and a half), is one of the world's highest capitals.

Like other mountainous areas (Spain, Colombia, and the Caucasus), mountains make a country hard to unify.

With communication slow and difficult, some tribes and ethnic groups live in *patrias chicas* (little countries) outside central control. As the West Virginia motto says, *Montani Semper Liberi* (Mountaineers are always free). Mexico was never well integrated—neither by the Aztecs nor Spaniards—and still retains important regional differences and politics. In remote mountain villages, many still speak Indian languages. Mexico's crumpled geography forced any national government to work through and with **caciques**. Current Mexican voting patterns (and cuisine) are still regional.

THE IMPACT OF THE PAST

The Spanish Habsburgs ran out of heirs; in 1707 a French Bourbon became king. (Spain's present monarch, Juan Carlos, is a Bourbon.) The Spanish Bourbons improved administration by dividing New Spain into twelve *intendencias*, each supervised by a French-style *intendente*, who reported to a central authority. Economic liberalization boosted Mexico's economy, and more Spaniards settled there. Bourbon reforms thus helped wake up Mexico.

> **caudillo** Military chief or strongman, specifically one who takes over the government.

MEXICAN INdEPENdENCE

The late eighteenth century brought new ideas to Spain's and Portugal's Latin American colonies. The Enlightenment and the U.S. and French Revolutions inspired some to seek independence. A parish priest, Miguel Hidalgo, on September 16, 1810, proclaimed Mexico's independence. It got nowhere but is still commemorated as Mexico's Independence Day. Hidalgo led a strange uprising of Indians that presaged the turmoil of the Mexican Revolution a century later. On the one hand, Hidalgo demanded equality of all Mexicans and the redistribution of land to Indians. But he also fought against French-style atheism and for Catholicism. Hidalgo's band ran out of control and massacred Spaniards and creoles. Royalist forces soon captured and executed Hidalgo. Another priest of similar persuasion, José Maria Morelos, in 1814 and 1815 led a widespread guerrilla uprising in Southern Mexico until he, too, was caught and shot. Hidalgo and Morelos are considered revolutionary heroes who founded the populist nationalism still very much alive in Mexican politics. Mexico's states of Hidalgo and Morelos are named after them.

Napoleon's occupation of Spain in 1808 triggered Mexico's independence. Spain's Cortes (parliament) passed the liberal 1812 constitution, which Mexico's conservative elite feared would spread French atheism and liberalism into their realm and threaten their privileged status. To preserve it, they declared independence from Spain in 1821. The impulse to Mexico's independence was conservative, not liberal as in the United States. Mexican independence was an elite thing with no mass participation and no fighting with Spain. Only Brazil's 1822 independence from Portugal was as painless.

BETWEEN MONARChy ANd REpublic

Mexico, like Brazil, began as a conservative monarchy, but that lasted only a year and a half (Brazil's lasted until 1889). Immediately Mexico's elite split into two camps: conservative centralizers and liberal federalists, a split that has never fully healed. For much of the nineteenth century Mexico, like most of Latin America, was led by **caudillos**.

The key figure in the first decades of the Republic of Mexico was Antonio López de Santa Anna, Mexico's off-and-on president, general, and dictator who played both sides of every conflict and continually broke his word. Santa Anna's big problem was Texas. To populate huge, thinly populated Texas, Mexico in 1821 gave American settlers land there, but they soon outnumbered Mexicans. To discourage further American immigrants—who brought slaves with them—Mexico outlawed slavery in 1828. (Texas was later a slave state and joined the Confederacy.)

By 1833 Texas had some 30,000 American settlers who demanded state's rights to govern themselves (and their slaves) within a Mexican federation. Santa Anna rejected the demand, the Republic

positivism   Philosophy, originally French, of applying scientific methods to analyze and improve society.

of Texas declared independence in 1836, and Santa Anna marched north to reclaim it. He took the Alamo but was captured by the Texans. The United States annexed Texas in 1845, but Mexican and U.S. forces soon clashed, leading to the 1846–1848 War with Mexico. The United States, after occupying Mexico City, took the southwest states and paid Mexico $15 million, leaving Mexico permanently humiliated.

Mexico's brief occupation by France (1861–1867) was strange. Mexican conservatives in exile convinced Napoleon III that he could reconstruct a Catholic monarchy in Mexico. The ambitious Napoleon III thought Mexico would be the base for a French-led "Latin America" (the first use of that term). With the U.S. Civil War giving Napoleon III a chance, he used the pretext of Mexico's big European debts to send French troops to install the Austrian Habsburg Maximilian as his puppet emperor of Mexico. The effort found little support in Mexico and collapsed. It cost Paris too much money, and the U.S. Civil War was over. The French left, and Maximilian was shot. The French had supposed that Mexico was more or less like orderly Europe, where rational authority is obeyed. The only remnant of the French in Mexico is the word *mariachi*, from the French hiring musicians for a *mariage*.

The iconic figure of nineteenth-century Mexican politics was Benito Juárez (1806–1872), who was remarkable on several counts. First, he was born of Indian parents (who died when he was three) at a time when all power was in creole hands. Educated in law, Juárez rose in state and national politics and became president in 1858. A classic nineteenth-century liberal, Juárez saw a stagnant Mexico dominated by the old aristocracy and a conservative Catholic Church. He wanted to redistribute their lands and institute a market economy, federalism, and separation of church and state. Juárez did not invent Mexican *anticlericalism* (see page 123) but gave it a powerful boost. Conservatives forced Juárez to spend 1853–1855 in New Orleans, and in the 1860s the French forced him to withdraw to the U.S.-Mexican border, to a city later renamed after him. Although not long in power, Juárez set standards of modesty and honesty that few other Mexican leaders have met.

Porfirio Díaz (1830–1915) followed in Juárez's footsteps but turned himself into a harsh dictator. Like Juárez, Díaz was born in the southern state of Oaxaca (pronounced wha-haw-ka), but of a mestizo family. Díaz studied law, fought the French, but turned against Juárez. Díaz was "elected" president seventeen times between 1877 and 1910 and personally centralized control over all branches of government. With the **positivism** then popular in Latin America, Díaz's top

Political Culture

Poor Mexico!

¡Pobre Mexico! Tan lejos de Dios, tan cerca de los Estados Unidos. "Poor Mexico!" exclaimed President Porfirio Díaz. "So far from God, so close to the United States." He voiced the widespread Mexican view that just sharing a long border with us condemns them to be dominated by the powerful United States. Díaz had seen the U.S. invasion of 1846–1847 that robbed Mexico of its northern half in 1848. The sad exclamation shows Mexican resentment of their rich, well-run neighbor, a sentiment found throughout Latin America.

bureaucrats, *los científicos*, pushed economic growth, but profits and land ownership went to a wealthy few and to foreign investors. Debt forced peasants to sell their land and grow poorer. By 1910 perhaps 95 percent of rural Mexican families were landless and eager to follow Zapata, who preached returning land to them. Díaz's long stay in power, called the Porfiriato, offered Mexicans *pan y palo* (bread and bludgeon), prominent in Mexico's governing philosophy ever since.

THE MEXICAN REVOLUTION

Compared to Mexico's 1910–1920 upheaval, the Russian and Chinese revolutions are clear and easy to understand. They had only two sides; Mexico's had several, and they changed allegiances during the course of it. Mexico's is one of Latin America's few genuine revolutions. Latin America, to be sure, has had scores of military coups and "palace revolutions," but they were among elites. Mexico and much later Cuba and Nicaragua had armies fighting for years to overthrow regimes and replace them with totally different ones. A revolution is seldom caused by just one problem. It takes a series of mutually reinforcing, insoluble problems. Mexico had been storing up its contradictions until they erupted in the Revolution of 1910.

Under the long Porfiriato, discontent increased at the unfairness and cruelty of the Díaz regime. Anarchist and socialist ideas crept in from Europe. Juárista liberals who organized clubs, parties, and newspapers were jailed; many fled to the United States. Government troops crushed labor unrest. Influenced by Russian revolutionary Mikhail Bakunin, in 1906 the Mexican group Regeneration published a manifesto calling for one term for a president, civil rights, public education, land reform, improved pay and working conditions, and ending the power of the Catholic Church. These eventually became the program of the party that ruled Mexico for most of the twentieth century.

The trigger for the Mexican Revolution was Díaz having the obedient Chamber of Deputies "reelect" him once again. Presidential candidate Francisco Madero, from a wealthy family that owned much of Northern Mexico, proclaimed from San Antonio, Texas, that the election was illegal and urged Mexicans to revolt on November 20, 1910, now celebrated as the start of the Revolution. Madero used his own fortune to supply rebels such as Pancho Villa. Díaz's decrepit Federalist army fell back, and Díaz resigned and left for Paris. Mexico's Congress proclaimed Madero the new president. If things had stopped there, Mexico would have had another of its many irregular changes of power.

But Federalist General Victoriano Huerta, encouraged by the U.S. ambassador, had President Madero arrested and shot. Huerta assumed the presidency himself, and full-fledged revolution broke out. Angered by the assassination and believing America could put things right in Mexico, President Woodrow Wilson had the Navy occupy Veracruz in 1914 and sent General Pershing after the bandit and guerrilla chief Pancho Villa in 1916. Wilson announced that America "went down to Mexico to serve mankind," but the effort solidified Mexican opposition to U.S. intervention, and U.S. forces had to fight Mexican guerrillas. (Sound familiar?)

Huerta fell in 1914, but at least four armies then battled for control of the country. Two of them were genuinely revolutionary, that of peasant leader Emiliano Zapata in the south and Pancho Villa in the north. The other two, under moderates Venustiano Carranza and Álvaro Obregón, sought to establish a stable order. The four sometimes collaborated but sometimes fought each other. Zapata was assassinated in 1919, Carranza in 1920, Villa in 1923, and Obregón in 1928. Revolution is a dangerous business. Mexicans still celebrate the revolutionary tradition of Zapata and Villa.

THE REVOLUTION INSTITUTIONALIZED

With the 1917 constitution, Mexican generals and state political bosses started what Peruvian novelist Mario Vargas Llosa called "the perfect dictatorship"—perfect because it looked like a democracy. Others have called it a series of six-year dictatorships because of limits on the presidential term. It was impressive and lasted about as long as Lenin's handiwork in Russia. The system grew out of a deal between Obregón and Calles.

Obregón became president in 1920 and began to implement rural education and land reform, including the granting of **ejidos** to poor villagers. In 1924 he arranged the election of his collaborator, Plutarco Elías Calles, who in turn got Obregón reelected in 1928. But just then a Catholic fanatic assassinated Obregón, part of the bloody 1927–1929 Cristero Rebellion. Calles had implemented the anticlericalism of the 1917 constitution by banning foreign priests and clerical garb. With

---

ejido   Land owned in common by villages.

political institution   Established and durable relationships of power and authority.

institutionalize   To make a political relationship permanent.

KEY CONCEPTS

INSTITUTIONS AND INSTITUTIONALIZATION

Obviously, politics depends on power (see page 4). Power is not necessarily force, which is a subset of power, a coercive one best used sparingly. Reason: If you use a lot of force, people will hate you and be eager for your overthrow. You will build little legitimacy. Political power is temporary unless it is turned into **political institutions**.

Mexico has had plenty of strong leaders who concentrated power, but it vanished when they left office. Then the new leader had to amass power into his hands. Political power must not be too personal. Franco ruled Spain, sometimes by jail and firing squad, from 1939 to his death in 1975. He built what looked like a stable regime, but it was too much based on his one-man rule and quickly unraveled after his death. Dictators rarely **institutionalize** their power. Within two years there was essentially nothing left of the Franco setup.

No country is born with functioning institutions; they have to evolve over time, usually in a series of accommodations among groups. An institution is not just an impressive building—although often they are housed in them to foster respect—but relationships of power that have solidified or congealed into understandings—sometimes written into constitutions or statutes, sometimes just traditions (as in Britain)—about who can do what.

Political scientists speak of Third World governments as "poorly institutionalized," characterized by irregular or extra-legal changes of leaders (such as revolutions and coups) and no clear boundaries as to who can do what. There are no rules; many try to seize power. Long ago, all countries were like that. We admire British government as "well-institutionalized," but centuries ago it suffered conquest, massacre, civil war, a royal beheading, a temporary Commonwealth, and attempts at absolutism. British institutions evolved and did not reach their modern form until the nineteenth century. Go back far enough and Britain resembled Mexico. Thanks to several historical factors, Britain institutionalized out of its tumultuous phase a couple of centuries earlier.

Accordingly, let us not ask too much of countries like Mexico too soon. They are bound to be messy and chaotic. Mexico did not begin political institutionalization until the 1920s, with Calles, and has not yet completed the process. (It will be complete when power alternates democratically among Mexico's parties.) Americans often wonder why Mexico cannot be like us—with democracy and rule of law—but Americans, too, spilled rivers of blood, first for independence, then to hold the country together. And America is no stranger to gangsters, drug traffickers, and crooks in high places.

the cry, "¡Viva Cristo Rey!" (Long live Christ the King), militant Catholics rebelled, and government troops crushed them. Mexico's Church-anticlerical split began to heal only with the election of the conservative and Catholic Vicente Fox in 2000.

corporatism Direct participation of interest groups in politics.

clientelism Government favors to groups for their support.

Calles, still running things from behind the scenes, decided in 1928 on a law making Mexico's presidency a single, nonrenewable six-year term, something Mexicans had wished since Díaz kept reelecting himself. To perpetuate his hold on power, in 1929 Calles organized a coalition of state political bosses, generals, union chiefs, and peasant leaders into the National Revolutionary party (PNR), renamed in 1946 the Institutional Revolutionary party (Partido Revolucionario Institucional, PRI).

The remarkable politician is one who builds lastingly, and Calles did. He founded the political party that brought stability and led Mexican politics for the rest of the twentieth century. It could not, however, last forever. The Calles system masked contradictions and concentrated power in the presidency. From its founding until 2000, PRI never lost national elections (which, to be sure, were less than democratic). Still, considering what much of Latin America went through in the twentieth century—numerous military coups—the "soft authoritarianism" of the Mexican system was not bad.

Calles was basically a conservative, and his PNR made only moderate reforms until the 1934 election of Lázaro Cárdenas, who took Mexico on a radical path by implementing what the Revolution and 1917 constitution had promised. When Calles opposed him, Cárdenas had Calles exiled to California. Cárdenas was of mestizo descent and had little formal education but joined Carranza in the Revolution, becoming a general in 1920. Cárdenas was one of the PNR's founders and its first president, transforming it from a loose coalition to a cohesive and well-organized nationwide party. Upon taking office, President Cárdenas implemented a serious leftist program, including nationalization of U.S.-owned oil industries, which he turned into Petróleos Mexicanos (Pemex). In doing this, Cárdenas connected to an old Latin American pattern, *statism*, that Mexico has been reluctant to shed. Cárdenas carried out massive land redistribution and organized peasants and workers, making their unions constituent groups of the renamed Party of the Mexican Revolution. He left office on schedule, in 1940, but kept a watchful leftist eye on the government until his death to make sure it did not drift under *yanquí* influence. Cárdenas remains a legend of Mexican nationalist radicalism, something that helped his son, Cuauhtémoc Cárdenas, later head of the leftist Party of Democratic Revolution.

Cárdenas also made the party into a corporatist one. **Corporatism**, which brings interest groups directly into parties and parliaments, was riding high at the time. Initially a device of Mussolini's fascism, Brazil's Vargas also adopted corporatism into his New State in 1935. Cárdenas organized the PNR with peasant, labor, military, and "popular" sectors. The last included small businesses, later expanded to include big businesses. He built a large bureaucracy to mediate demands among groups and allocate funds to them, what is called **clientelism**. Initially, they seem to solve the problems of participation, power-sharing, and allocation of resources in chaotic situations. They are, however, not really democratic and over time become rigid and unstable. They are contrived and temporary fixes and leave the system saddled with an overlarge bureaucracy.

THE KEY INSTITUTIONS

The first thing you notice about Mexico's political history is that, prior to 1924, few Mexican presidents either came to power or left office in a regular, legal way. Most were installed and/or ousted on an ad hoc basis by a handful of elites or military coups, sometimes with violence. Mexico has had

constitutionalism Degree to which government limits its powers.	

four constitutions since independence but not much **constitutionalism**. Once in office, Mexico's presidents observed few limits on their powers and tended to construct personalistic dictatorships. This is true of much of the developing areas (and now Russia), where politics consists of strong personalities making their own rules.

That changed—but not completely—with the beginning of the single, six-year presidency in 1928 and the 1929 founding of what became PRI. A contrived stability settled over Mexico for the rest of the century. There were no more upheavals because all the major reins of power—including the military—passed through PRI into the hands of the president. The personality of the president still counted—some, such as Cárdenas, were radical, others conservative—but the system counted more. Mexico was an example of what political scientists call a *clientelistic* system in which most major groups have been *co-opted* (see page 497) into cooperation. They feel they have a stake in the system and minor input into government policy. Peasants get land reforms and ejidos; workers get unions; and bureaucrats get jobs.

The Six-Year Presidency

Latin America generally has modeled its institutions on the U.S. pattern, preferring presidential to parliamentary systems (see page 40). Mexico's presidential system, like that of the United States, combines head of state and chief of government. For most of the twentieth century it was even more

KEY CONCEPTS

CLIENTELISM

How can a society as badly fractured as Mexico's hold together? Why is it not mired down in civil wars, upheavals, and coups (which it was until the 1920s)? Clever political leaders, such as Calles and Cárdenas in Mexico, may be able to calm such situations by making sure that important groups have a share not only of seats in parliament but also of favors, such as development projects, rigged contracts, subsidies, or just plain cash. In a clientelistic situation, the elites of each major group strike a bargain to obtain resources and restrain their followers from violence. Most major groups get something; no one group gets everything. Clientelism is widely practiced in the Third World (heck, maybe in the First as well), as in the Persian Gulf oil sheikdoms and in Nigeria (see next chapter).

Clientelism has at least three problems. First, it may be fake, with only small payouts to labor and agrarian sectors, which PRI kept in line with the traditional *pan y palo*. Second, it may exclude important groups. In Mexico, the Catholic Church got no part of the deal, and big businessmen got little until some were co-opted into PRI during World War II. (The Catholic Church and business are among the groups that brought Vicente Fox to power in 2000.) A third problem is rigidity. The allocation of which group gets how much help and money cannot be frozen; it has to change as society and the economy evolve. Village land held in common and state-owned industries can retard economic growth, but the Mexican groups who benefit from these institutions fight change. Fortunately, Mexico loosened up its system in time to avoid an explosion.

powerful than the U.S. presidency. We must qualify that statement by noting that it was powerful when a PRI president dominated a Congress with a big PRI majority. The 2000 election of Vicente Fox of PAN did not give PAN a majority in the Congress, making Fox much less powerful than his PRI predecessors. Starting in 2000 Mexico tasted the "divided government" that often prevails in the United States, when a president of one party faces a Congress dominated by another. Likewise, the French system devised by de Gaulle made the president very powerful, but these powers shrank when opposition parties won a majority of the National Assembly. Then French presidents had to practice *cohabitation* with prime ministers of opposition parties.

Since 1928 Mexico has not deviated from the single, six-year term devised by calles. Under the long PRI reign, succession was in the hands of the president, who was also party chief. In consultation with past presidents and other PRI leaders, the current president would name his successor, who became the party's nominee for the next election. Once nominated, of course, until 2000 no

COMPARISON

TERM LENGTHS

Some American critics of our two four-year presidential terms say we should consider a single six-year term. The theory here is that presidents are so concerned with reelection that they accomplish little their first term and then do irresponsible things their second term, because they do not have to worry about reelection. It is not clear that term lengths cause anything very specific. Both limited and unlimited terms have lent themselves to mistakes and corruption. The table below shows how our ten countries' terms for chief executives compare.

Remaining too long in office can lead to corruption, but not if chiefs of government must face an informed electorate at regular intervals. Margaret Thatcher served eleven years through three elections until her party dumped her over policy questions and slumping popularity. Term limits in Nigeria, on the other hand, did nothing to curb corruption. A limited term may even encourage officials to grab more sooner. By themselves, term limits do little; it all depends on the institutional and cultural context.

Britain	prime minister	Unlimited terms, each for up to five years (but usually four).
France	president	Unlimited five-year terms.
Germany	chancellor	Unlimited terms, each for up to four years (but sometimes shorter).
Japan	prime minister	Unlimited but usually short.
Russia	president	Two four-year terms but skirted.
China	president	Two five-year terms (but this is recent).
India	prime minister	Unlimited terms, each for up to five years.
Mexico	president	One six-year term.
Nigeria	president	Two four-year terms (barring overthrow).
Iran	president	Two four-year terms (but lifetime Islamist Guide holds real power).

PRI candidate lost, and many won by 90 percent. Presidents would pick their successors—not necessarily well-known persons—with an eye to preserving stability and the power of PRI. The process was called half in jest **dedazo**. It may also have included understandings that the new president would not look into corruption. No choice was absolutely predictable and, once in office, presidents often departed from previous policies. Calles did not know, for example, how far left Cárdenas would veer.

DEMOCRACY

MEXICO'S CLOSE 2006 ELECTION

Mexico's 2006 presidential election, although fraught with peril, showed a real Mexican democracy. Mexicans now could choose among left, right, and center, something PRI had not allowed. The closeness of the election indicated competition, the crux of democracy. It was a dirty campaign, but slinging mud is better than buying votes.

On the left, the populist ex-mayor of Mexico City, Andrés Manuel López Obrador (AMLO) of the PRD, promised money for the poor and curbs on NAFTA (see page 243). On the right, Felipe Calderón of the PAN, which had won in 2000 with Vicente Fox, urged a market economy within NAFTA. He also called López Obrador a radical demagogue like Venezuela's Hugo Chávez. In the center, Roberto Madrazo of the PRI ran third; PRI's old base had collapsed amid corruption. The results are shown in the table below.

Calderón won by less than a quarter-million votes (0.58 percent). López Obrador cried fraud and demanded a total recount. After the Federal Electoral Institute (see page 499) held a partial recount and confirmed the results, Obrador held an alternative swearing-in ceremony and proclaimed himself president. After a while, his supporters tired of his messianic rants and accepted the official results. Many Mexicans breathed a sigh of relief that they had avoided electing a demagogue.

Few demographic factors predicted who voted for Calderón and who for AMLO. The election did not turn on social class or religiosity; ideology was more important. The North, long home to capitalist, market thinking, was more PAN. The South, home to statist/socialist thinking, went PRD. A majority of Mexicans who believe that Mexico is a democracy voted for Calderón; those who believe that it is not went to AMLO. Together the two points—region and perception of democracy—show an underlying radical-conservative ideological polarization.

Calderón took office knowing that most Mexicans voted against him, and he faced a Congress still divided among three parties (see page 492). Calderón—like Fox—did not have a legislative majority, and he tried to build a coalition across party lines.

	Party	Votes	Percent
Felipe Calderón	PAN	15,000,284	35.89
Andrés Manuel López Obrador	PRD	14,756,350	35.31
Roberto Madrazo	PRI	9,301,441	22.26

Mexico's Legislature

Mexico's bicameral Congress (Congreso de la Unión) has been much less important than its presidency. Díaz was famous for putting obedient supporters into the legislature, and PRI did much the same. Legislative elections changed with the 1986 Electoral Reform Law, induced by uproar over PRI's habitual election frauds. Inspired by Germany's *mixed-member* system, Mexico (like Italy) now fills most seats from single-member districts, Anglo-American style, but allocates additional seats based on each party's share of the popular vote, that is, by proportional representation (PR).

Mexico's upper house, the Senate (Cámara de Senadores), now has 128 seats and six-year terms. Ninety-six of the seats are filled from single-member districts, thirty-two by PR. The lower house, the Chamber of Deputies (Cámara de Diputados), now has 500 seats with three-year terms. Three-hundred seats are filled by district voting, 200 by PR in five regions of forty seats each. The 2006 election made PAN the biggest party in both chambers but not a majority party (see table at the top of page 490.)

Personalities

Felipe Calderón

Inaugurated for a single six-year term in late 2006, Felipe de Jesús Calderón Hinojosa was, at age 44, one of Mexico's youngest presidents. He was born in 1962 in Morelia, capital of Michoacán state in Central Mexico, to a father who was one of PAN's founders. Calderón was raised in a middle-class, devoutly Catholic family and remains that way. A quiet, studious youngster, Calderón earned degrees in law and economics, and a master's at Harvard's Kennedy School.

Calderón's real calling was politics. From childhood he worked for PAN in elections and became president of its youth group. He met his wife in the party; she won election as a PAN member of the Chamber of Deputies. Under PRI's long rule, PAN was an underdog party, and Calderón got used to losing. "Felipe knows how to struggle," said a PAN comrade. He waged an uphill battle in PAN primaries in 2005 to become its presidential candidate in 2006, a race he narrowly won.

Calderón, a serious, balding figure, never tried to sell himself on personality but as a calm and rational administrator and reformer. He likes private enterprise and markets, thus going against the statist tendency of most

Felipe Calderón

of twentieth-century Mexico. Rather than battle PRI and PRD figures, including trade unionists, he tries to win them over by compromise. Unlike his predecessor Fox, Calderón is a skilled and patient politician who gently prodded Mexico's congress into more reforms than were thought possible. Mexico had a bigger breakthrough with the quiet Calderón than with the outgoing Fox.

	Senate	Chamber of Deputies
PAN	52 seats	206 seats
PRD	31	127
PRI	35	106

dominant-party system   One party is much stronger than all others and stays in office a long time.

Some smaller parties such as the Greens and Workers parties held a few seats. Calderón's PAN government needs—and sometimes gets—votes from PRI deputies to pass new laws. Radical PRD and establishment PRI do not like each other. Together they could outvote PAN in the Congress and produce the sort of executive-legislative deadlock that hamstrung the Fox *sexenio*. Calderón is more clever than Fox in gaining support from other parties.

Mexico's Ex-Dominant-Party System

We mentioned that Britain is a "two-plus" party system: two big parties and several small ones. Some countries are "one-plus" or **dominant-party systems**, for they are dominated by parties so big that they seldom lose. Japan's Liberal Democrats and Putin's United Russia are examples. Mexico and India, under the long reigns, respectively, of the PRI and Congress party, used to be, but have since experienced electoral alternation.

Comparison of Party Systems		
System	**Example**	**Probable Causes**
two-party	United States	Single-member plurality elections.
two-plus	Britain	Single-member plurality election districts; inherited third party.
multiparty	France	Historical complexity; runoff elections.
two-plus tending to multiparty	Germany	Hybrid single-member and PR elections.
dominant-party	Japan	Postwar consolidation; weak opposition; obedient political culture.
dominant-party	Russia	Personality-based consolidation from fragmented system.
single-party	China	Complete control of Communist party.
fragmented	India	Breakdown of dominant Congress into many state and caste-based parties.
three-party	Mexico	Long PRI dominance eroded.
two-plus tending to dominant	Nigeria	PDP rigs elections.
nonparty	Iran	Formal parties not permitted.

In a dominant-party system, other parties are legal, but the dominant party is so well-organized and has so many resources that challengers seldom have a chance. In some cases, the party founded the country, as the Congress party under Gandhi did in India. The big parties dominate the media and civil service. Voters know the dominant party is corrupt, but some like the stability and prosperity it has brought. Many Japanese voters see the Liberal Democrats in this light. When the dominant party offers neither, as Mexico's PRI discovered, it ceases to be dominant.

populist   Claims to be for common people and against elites.

PRI, founded by Calles in 1929, is Mexico's oldest party. As its name attests, it billed itself as revolutionary and socialist long after it abandoned such policies. PRI presidents such as Cárdenas and Luis Echevarría Álvarez took leftist, especially anti-U.S., stances, but most have been moderate centrists. Calles and Cárdenas designed the party well, with its four sectors and strong patronage network, but as Mexico gained a large middle class, these sectors became less and less important, making PRI out-of-date. Some Mexican commentators call the PRI sector chiefs "dinosaurs." PRI's share of the vote has shrunk, but it still wins in a broad belt across Central Mexico. PRI victories in many state gubernatorial elections did not carry over into the 2006 presidential contest.

PAN was founded in 1939 to oppose PRI on religious grounds. PAN was a Catholic reaction to Calles's anticlericalism. Mexico's church-state relations have been bloody at times, and serious Catholics felt martyred by the PRI government. In the 1980s, the modern business community, which disliked state-owned industries and economic instability, found PAN a useful vehicle for their discontents. The two strands, Catholic and business, coexist uneasily within PAN and could pull it

KEY CONCEPTS

THE DEMAGOGUERY TENDENCY

Conservatives feared that if the **populist** López Obrador of the PRD were elected president in 2006 he would follow radical leftist policies like Venezuela's demagogic Hugo Chávez and bring economic disaster. *Demagogue* has the same root as democrat—*demos*, the people—but demagogues use issues in a manipulative and self-serving way to erase democracy. The populist demagogue or "rabble rouser" whips up poor or frightened masses with promises of jobs, welfare, or law and order, and once in office becomes dictatorial. Classic demagogues include Robespierre (page 95), Hitler (page 174), Perón of Argentina, and Vargas of Brazil.

Demagoguery now tends to appear in poor countries that are only recently democratic, such as much of the Third World today. Desperate people confuse democracy with prosperity, and the populist demagogue helps in this confusion: "The people cry out for bread,

and I shall give them bread!" When the country reaches middle-income levels and has a large, educated middle class, demagoguery fades; few people swallow the populist deceptions.

Latin America has been fertile ground for populist demagoguery. It appears now in Venezuela, where Chávez—a former paratroop officer who earlier attempted a coup—was twice elected president. Chávez's line: Venezuela is rich with oil but has been robbed by the United States, rich Venezuelans, and corrupt officials. Most Venezuelans are below the poverty line and believed him. Chávez's "Bolivarian" revolution (nobody knew what it meant) took over industry and distributed oil wealth to the poor. This was made possible by the big runup in oil prices but is unlikely to last. Mexico's López denied that he was anything like Chávez.

bilateral opposition   Centrist governments undermined from both sides.

apart. PAN makes its best showings in Northern Mexico, where proximity to the United States has contributed to prosperity and a capitalist orientation. PAN, still dominated by Catholic militants, is not nearly as well organized as PRI. Mexicans' votes for PAN did not indicate that they had become conservative Catholics but that they were fed up with PRI. Although many were disappointed with Fox, Felipe Calderón of PAN came from behind in the 2006 elections.

The south of Mexico is the poorest and most radical part of the country. Zapata, a local boy, is remembered. It is here that the PRD makes its best showing. In 2005 the PRD won the governorship of the southern state of Guerrero (and of Baja California Sur). Cuauhtémoc (the Aztec name won him some votes) Cárdenas, son of the oil-nationalizer, might have won the 1988 presidential election if not for PRI rigging. Cárdenas, along with a leftist chunk of PRI, split from PRI in 1988 over its turn to free-market policies. PRI had to split; it had abandoned revolution in favor of business. With some Socialists and Communists, Cárdenas in 1989 formed the leftist PRD, which claims to be true to the ideals of his father, anti-capitalist and anti-United States. With a much weaker organization and base of support than PRI or PAN, PRD too has an uphill struggle. The PRD's Andrés Manuel López Obrador (known as AMLO), the former mayor of Mexico City, was initially the leading presidential contender in 2006. Mildly leftist parties have won elections in Argentina, Brazil, Chile, and Venezuela. Mexico could one day elect a PRD president.

At this point we might call Mexico a "former dominant-party system." The PRI has weakened and now faces **bilateral opposition**, that is, both on its left (PRD) and right (PAN). The key factor in PRI's decline: its corruption and the growth of an educated middle class that no longer stands for it. Mexico is now a three-party system. The United States is no stranger to dominant-party systems: Most U.S. congressional districts reliably return the same party to Congress, sometimes without opposition.

Mexican Federalism

Most countries are unitary systems, but the Western Hemisphere boasts the largest number of the world's federal systems, partly due to the U.S. model and partly to the sprawling geography of many countries. Argentina, Brazil, Canada, and Mexico are federal systems, some more federal than others. Mexico consists of thirty-one states and the Federal District (Distrito Federal, DF, the equivalent of our D.C.) of Mexico City. Each state has a governor elected for a single six-year term but only a unicameral legislature.

In actuality, Mexican federalism concentrates most power in the center, a bit like Soviet federalism, but this is changing. For most of the twentieth century PRI presidents handpicked state governors, who then used the office as a tryout for federal positions. As in the United States, many Mexican presidents first served as governors, including President Fox. The states get much of their revenue from the national government and then dispense it to the municipalities, a food chain that kept subordinate levels of government loyal and obedient. Now the PRD controls six states, the PAN nine states, and PRI sixteen states plus the DF, eroding the former strong connection between national and state governments. The three-party system makes Mexico more federal.

In 2006 violence in Oaxaca tested Mexican federalism. A teachers' strike there grew into a major leftist protest against the unpopular PRI governor. The city's center was barricaded and trashed, ruining the important tourist trade. President Fox hesitated months before sending federal troops to Oaxaca. He saw it as a state affair in which PRI was catching the blame. After plainclothes police and PRI supporters killed several protesters, including a U.S. journalist, Fox sent thousands of federal troops to quell the protests. In response to the repression and the 2006 elections, which they called rigged, a shadowy Marxist guerrilla group rooted in Oaxaca, the Popular Revolutionary Army, bombed pipelines and kidnapped wealthy people. Periodically federal police and troops intervene against drugs, crime, and insurrection at the state level.

> **mercantilism** Originally French theory that a nation's wealth is the gold and silver in its treasury.
>
> **egalitarian** Dedicated to equality.

MEXICAN POLITICAL CULTURE

Mexican political culture—and this is true of much of Latin America—is hard to comprehend because it is a dysfunctional pastiche of several cultures and ideologies: Indian passivity, Spanish greed, Catholic mysticism, populist nationalism, and European anticlericalism, liberalism, anarchism, positivism, and socialism. Unsurprisingly, these many strands never blended. Mexico is regionally, socially, and culturally badly integrated, never forming a coherent whole (see box on page 494). Mexican political culture did not grow slowly and locally over time but was imported in waves, mostly from Europe, none of which sank in enough to create a single Mexican political culture. In comparison, most elements of American political culture blend and reinforce each other: freedom, equality, Protestantism, individualism, pragmatism, materialism, market economics, and rule of law (see box below). The U.S. creeds that did not easily blend—slavery, Catholicism, and welfarist liberalism—formed America's political divides for several generations.

COMPARISON

MEXICO AND AMERICA AS COLONIES

The Spanish colonies of the New World resembled the declining feudal system of Europe. Society was rigidly stratified by birth and race into privileged and lower ranks. The Catholic Church, supervised by Rome, tried to calm Mexico's Indians by both material help and spiritual uplift. Madrid's chief interest in New Spain was the amount of gold and silver it could ship to the royal treasury. For this, Spain set up Mexico (indeed, all of its Latin American holdings) as vast bureaucracies, which plague the region to this day. Latin America was born bureaucratic. Mexico was Spain's richest colony; its gold and silver funded the giant Habsburg military effort in the Thirty Years War. Under the mistaken doctrine of **mercantilism**, Spain reckoned it was rich, but gold and silver produce neither crops nor manufactured goods. Ironically, as Spain stole the vast wealth of the New World it grew poorer. The extractive industries impoverished Mexico, too.

The English colonizers of Virginia and New England arrived a century after the Spaniards did in Mexico. By the early seventeenth century the feudal age was over in England, and the immigrants carried little feudal baggage or bureaucracy. The colonies largely ran themselves. No one expected quick gold or silver, either for themselves or for London. Although the English brought ranks of nobility with them, most settlers were farmers or merchants with an **egalitarian** ethos. They concentrated on agricultural production. Their several varieties of Protestantism—none of which had Catholicism's central control—taught hard work, delayed gratification, equality, and individuality. They pushed the Indians westward but did not turn them into serfs.

Samuel Huntington's controversial book, *Who Are We?*, posits religion as the biggest determinant of political culture. If French, Spanish, or Portuguese Catholics had originally settled the United States, he argues, we would today resemble, respectively, Quebec, Mexico, and Brazil. The fact that we were first settled by Anglo-Protestants has made all the difference.

Mexico's Indian Heritage

Mexico looks Spanish but, many scholars argue, beneath the surface remains very Indian. Indian cultures and languages still survive in isolated villages. Mexico's cuisine is basically Indian. Mexico's spirituality is a blend of pre-Columbian religions and Spanish Catholicism, which was always dipped in

Political Culture

Mexico's Political Eras

Few countries have gone through such radical and bloody changes as Mexico. Most political cultures develop slowly and gradually. Mexico's developed in sudden shifts, each jerked back and forth by the introduction of new cultures and ideas, which never blended into a coherent whole.

The three phases of **priísmo** summarize the thrust of the presidents of each period. The four **sexenios** of the conservative period mark PRI's turning away from the Revolution and from *Cárdenismo,* giving lip service to labor and peasants but favoring business and stability. The three destabilizing *sexenios* mark the oil boom and

government debt plus the 1968 massacre of students in Mexico City and psychological breakdown of President Echevarría. The desperate phase marks the recognition by Presidents de la Madrid, Salinas, and Zedillo that Mexico's economy was in shambles, and the whole system was losing legitimacy. U.S.-trained economic technocrats tried to stabilize it with policies of **austerity** to reign in Mexico's runaway economy, but average Mexicans were hurt by it. Two political assassinations under Salinas turned many Mexicans against PRI. Panismo, barely begun under Fox, still faces an uphill struggle.

Era	Years	Remembered for
Aztec	1325–1521	High civilization, bureaucratic empire, human sacrifice.
New Spain	1521–1821	Colonialist exploitation, Catholicism.
Empire	1821–1823	Conservative independence.
Santa Anna	1830s–1850s	Erratic leadership, lost Texas and U.S. war.
Juárez	1850s–1860s	Equality, federalism, anticlericalism.
Porfiriato	1877–1911	Dictatorship, economic growth, poverty.
Revolution	1910–1920	Complex multisided upheaval.
Maximato	1924–1934	Calles, *el jefe máximo,* founds single six-year term and PNR.
Cárdenismo	1934–1940	Cárdenas makes PRI socialistic and corporatistic; nationalizes oil.
Conservative Priísmo	1940–1964	Favors business and foreign investment; crackdown on leftists.
Destabilizing Priísmo	1964–1982	Oil, overspending, and inflation spur unrest; massacre of students.
Desperate Priísmo	1982–2000	Technocrats calm economy, promote NAFTA, clean up elections; assassinations.
Panismo	2000–	First non-PRI presidents; attempts free-market reforms.

blood. The Indians, of course, were used to blood sacrifice at the hands of the Aztecs and took easily to the blood emphasis of Spanish Catholicism. The Spanish Inquisition, which traveled to Mexico and even to New Mexico, also utilized human sacrifice. Since the Spaniards built their great cathedral on the ruins of the main Aztec temple, it is hard to tell the precise reason why it is a pilgrimage site. Is the impulse purely Christian or an echo of pre-Christian religion?

The Aztecs and earlier Mexican societies were strongly hierarchical. Those at the base, peasants, were taught to defer to their social superiors. Social-class distinctions come with civilization. When the Spanish took over from the Aztecs, Indian peasants were used to subordinate behavior; most accommodated to the forced labor of **haciendas** and silver mines. (In contrast, the Indians of the present-day United States had no cities and were highly egalitarian.) The Spanish, of course, brought their own feudal society with them and imposed it on the Indians.

One important demographic point about Mexico is that its Spanish conquerors were exclusively males; Spanish women did not arrive until much later. (The English settled whole families in America.) Very quickly, a new class of persons appeared in Mexico, mestizos, those of mixed descent. **Mestizaje** was also a cultural and social factor, contributing to Mexican Catholicism and the beginnings of a middle class between the Spaniards (later creoles) and the Indians.

Latin Americans boast, especially to **norteamericanos**, that they are free of racial prejudice. In Latin America, they say, money and manners count for more than skin color in deciding race. A person with the right culture and language is accepted as essentially European. As they say in much of Latin America, "Money lightens" (one's skin color). There is some truth to it, but money and life chances tend to come with racial origin in Latin America. Whites have a much better chance of going to a university, entering a profession, making lots of money, and living in a nice house. Mexicans of Indian descent run a high risk of infant death, malnutrition, poverty, and the lowest jobs or unemployment.

priísmo   Ideology and methods of PRI. (See page 494.)

sexenio   From *seis años*; six-year term of Mexico's presidents. (See page 494.)

austerity   Drastically holding down government expenses. (See page 494.)

hacienda   Large country estate with Spanish owner (*hacendado*) and Indian serfs.

mestizaje   Intermingling of Spanish and Indian.

norteamericanos   "North Americans"; U.S. citizens.

personalismo   Politics by strong, showoff personalities.

machismo   Strutting, exaggerated masculinity.

Political Culture

PERSONALISMO AND MACHISMO

Latin American politicians frequently rely on **personalismo** in politics rather than on parties, ideologies, or laws. Said one Mexican diplomat, "In Mexico we have egos, not institutions." Most Latin Americans like to be perceived as having a strong personality, the men especially as *macho* (male), leading to **machismo**. Latin American leaders traditionally combine personalismo and machismo to gain mass support.

After Cárdenas, Mexican presidents of the PRI era, selected by *dedazo*, did not much utilize these qualities because they did not need them. With the recent arrival of competitive politics, however, personalismo and machismo appeared in Mexico. Vicente Fox and López Obrador ran on their colorful and outspoken personalities (but not Calderón).

Still, Mexico has done a better job historically than the United States at letting at least some nonwhites rise to the top. Juárez, of Indian descent, led Mexico in the mid-nineteenth century. Cárdenas and several other presidents were of mestizo descent. The United States has not yet had a comparable racial breakthrough. Most of Mexico's top leaders, in the economy and politics, to be sure, have been white, a point true of Latin America generally. Because few Mexicans are of purely European descent, all Mexican politicians celebrate the country's Indian heritage. There are no statues of Cortés in Mexico, and the quincentennial of Columbus's 1492 voyage was little noticed.

Imported Ideologies

Latin America is noted for picking up ideas invented elsewhere, warping them, and then trying to apply them where they do not fit. One Latin America expert called the continent a *reliquiario*, a place for keeping old relics of saints, a piece of the true cross, and so on. Now it is a reliquary for old ideas long passé in the rest of the world. This makes Latin American political thought a sort of remainder sale of old ideologies. Following are some notions still or recently alive in Latin America.

Liberalism here means the original, nineteenth-century variety that rejected monarchy and opened society to new forces. The United States, with its large middle class, took naturally to this philosophy of freedom, but Latin America, encumbered by inherited social positions, big bureaucracies, and state-owned industries, did not. No middle class, no liberalism. Juárez and Díaz could not make liberalism work in Mexico. Some Latin American countries have recently turned to economic "neoliberalism" by trying to build free markets.

Positivism, as discussed earlier, proposed that experts should improve society through science. It died out in Europe but caught on in Latin America, especially Brazil, where its motto, "Order and Progress," is in the flag. In Mexico, Díaz's *científicos* typified the positivist spirit, which conflicts with the hands-off philosophy of liberalism.

Democracy

Cautious Democrats

Latin America (except Cuba) turned democratic in the 1980s, but Latins have embraced democracy slowly and cautiously. Like Russians, they expected democracy to bring prosperity; both were slow in coming. Only half of Latin Americans tell pollsters that democracy is always preferable, and a minority still say that an authoritarian government can sometimes be preferable.

Democratic feeling rises and falls with the economy, as most Latins worry about unemployment and poverty. Latin America's economies have been weak lately, and so has democratic support. In a downturn, some say a dictatorship that puts food on the table is not so bad. Many Latin Americans perceive all government, democratic or not, as essentially rigged to favor a few powerful interests. Mexico's numbers are typical: The percent preferring democracy climbed from 53 percent in 1996 to 59 percent in 2005 but fell to 48 percent in 2007. During the same period, however, the percent saying authoritarian rule can be preferable dropped from 23 to 14 percent. Democracy is not yet fully rooted in Latin American political culture, but authoritarianism has been largely uprooted.

Socialism in Europe made sense, as Europe had a lot of industry and a large working class that was amenable to unionization and social-democratic parties, such as Britain's Labour and Germany's Social Democrats. Latin America, however, until recently had little industry and only a small proletariat; it was precapitalist. No working class, no socialism. Governments such as Mexico's and Brazil's invented and coddled unions to make it look like they had a working-class base. Some idealists still see socialism as the answer to Mexico's vast poverty, but they offer no successful examples of it. Chile prospered after it overthrew the Socialist government of Salvador Allende.

quixotic From Don Quixote; romantic, unrealistic efforts to achieve mistaken goals.

co-opt To enroll other groups in your cause, rendering them harmless.

Rural socialism rejects industry in favor of small farms. It proposes returning to a rural idyll of equality and sufficiency based on family farming. Zapata was its hero. It idealizes a past that never existed and cannot be: There is simply not enough land to redistribute to exploding populations. Peasant farming equals poverty. Zapatista guerrillas in Chiapas state in Mexico's south, however, still pursue this **quixotic** vision.

Anarchism is a sort of primitive socialism that argues the end of national government will erase class differences. A small political movement, it appeared in the late nineteenth century in Russia and in Spain, where it became anarcho-syndicalism: no government needed because trade unions will run things. Several Mexican revolutionaries were influenced by anarchism.

Anticlericalism, founded by French writer Voltaire (see page 92), caught on strongly in Spain and then spread to Latin America. Anticlericalists such as Calles claim the Catholic Church has too much political power, favors the rich, and keeps Mexico backward. Few scholars think the Church in Latin America really had much power. Now the shortage of priests has marginalized it, and evangelical Protestantism is growing.

Fascism, founded by Mussolini and copied by Hitler, briefly influenced some Latin American countries, especially those with many German and Italian immigrants. It combines nationalism, corporatism, and fake socialism under a charismatic leader. Vargas's Brazilian New State drew the quip "fascism with sugar." Perón's Argentina was not as sweet and welcomed Nazi war criminals. Cárdenas's nationalism and socialism hinted at national socialism.

Communism, revolutionary Marxist socialism under Moscow's control, was for decades popular among Latin American intellectuals. It proposed to cure the continent's drastic inequality and poverty by the state taking over production and ending U.S. exploitation, a permanent and popular theme. Some of Mexico's leading artists, such as Diego Rivera and David Siqueiros, were Communists. Castro's Cuba and Che's icon drew much support until Latin intellectuals noticed that Cuba is a stagnant tyranny. Although largely defunct, Marxism lingers in *dependency theory* (see box on page 498).

Latin American intellectuals have been so addicted to one ideology after another that they fail to notice the rest of the world has already discarded them. Communism, for example, collapsed in East Europe and the Soviet Union and is meaningless in China but is still alive in Cuba, which will likely be the last Communist country in the world, the reliquary of Marx's bones.

PATTERNS OF INTERACTION

Calles and Cárdenas devised a system of **co-optation** that gave the Mexican government control over groups that might otherwise cause them trouble. They promised peasants and workers a good deal but rarely gave them much. When rural and worker unions got demanding, the government crushed them. The large Mexican Workers Confederation, for example, was under the thumb of

dependency theory   Radical theory that rich countries exploit Third World lands and keep them poor.

PRI through its chief, who served fifty-six years. While professing "socialism," Mexican presidents tolerated no competition from Communists, especially after Stalin had Trotsky assassinated in Mexico in 1940. Even "leftist" presidents such as López Mateos had no trouble arresting Communists and breaking strikes. There was a large element of fakery in PRI governance. Chiefly, they served themselves.

For decades, the Mexican government tried to co-opt students by giving them a nearly free education and then employing them as civil servants. (Saudi Arabia attempted to do the same.) This cannot work forever; there is simply not enough money. Student numbers and discontent grew. Many turned radical and accused PRI of abandoning its commitments to social justice. President Gustavo Díaz Ordaz was obsessed with order and tolerated no criticism. With the 1968 Mexico City Olympics just weeks away, he feared student protests would mar his picture of a modern, happy Mexico. In October at the Plaza of the Three Cultures in Mexico City, police gunned down as

Key Concepts

DEPENDENCY THEORY

During the Cold War, many Latin American intellectuals subscribed to fashionable leftist views that their region's poverty was the result of exploitation by wicked capitalists, especially by *norteamericanos*. After World War II, radicals worked this up into what they called **dependency theory**, a theory that the Third World is economically dependent on the capital, products, and policies of the First World, especially the United States. (Think of U.S. "shark" feeding on Latin American "sardines.") Only by getting out from under the control of U.S. corporations—who dictated what Latin American lands would produce (bananas and coffee) and what they would consume (Chevrolets and Coca-Cola)—would Latin America eliminate poverty. Accordingly, radical regimes such as Cuba, Nicaragua, and currently Venezuela are praiseworthy because they broke their dependency on the Yankees and instituted independent economic development that would benefit their own peoples.

Dependency theory contains several disputes. It is a type of Marxist theory, but some orthodox Marxists disliked it. Marx saw class conflict *within* a country as the key to its economic and political development. Many Latin American critics blame their continent's poverty on its "predatory class structure," in which a few rich families own everything and there is not much of an industrial proletariat. Latin America's problem, in their view, is that it is still saddled with a feudal social structure. Marx had little to say about relations among countries. Lenin made that leap (see page 302) with his claim that the imperialist countries have redone the globe to suit themselves by exploiting their colonial areas. Dependency theory partakes more of Lenin than of Marx. Mexican dependency theorists use Cárdenas as an exemplar of Mexico's efforts to break *dependencia*.

By the 1990s, many dependency theorists came to doubt the theory. Brazilian President Fernando Henrique Cardoso (1995–2002), for example, had been a radical sociologist and promoter of dependency theory, but by the 1980s had abandoned it. A famous Latin American saying: "If you are not a Communist when you're twenty, you have no heart. If you're still a Communist when you're forty, you have no head." Aging wises you up. The demise of Communist regimes in East Europe and the Soviet Union made many wonder if "socialism" really worked. The economic success of Chile, where a military dictator enforced capitalism, made many appreciate market systems and foreign trade. Other Latin American countries restructured their economies in the early 1990s but results were generally unimpressive until 2004. Latin America as a whole has recently enjoyed growth rates of around 5 percent.

many as 300 student protesters. What PRI could not co-opt it crushed. Some mark this as a turning point in PRI rule, the point at which it visibly began to destabilize.

Politics inside PRI

Any party as big as PRI is bound to have factions. The two most relevant are the *políticos* and *técnicos*, politicians and technicians. The *políticos* are populists seeking elected office; they pay heed to mass needs and demands. As such, they pay little heed to economics and are not averse to running up huge

DEMOCRACY

ELECTIONS AND DEMOCRACY

Americans are given to the notion that elections equal democracy. PRI won fourteen presidential elections in a row, illustrating that democracy is more complex than just balloting. As we considered in Russia (Chapter 21), it involves a great deal of philosophical, moral, social, and legal underpinning, and these tend to come with a large middle class. Elections are just the visible parts and can mislead foreign election monitors, who see little more than the physical balloting on election day and miss the longer-term and less-visible problems. Monitors are getting better, though, and in 2004 called Ukraine's elections rigged, forcing a repeat. Few elections in the Third World are completely free and fair. There are several ways to rig them.

Media Dominance The big problem is what happens in the weeks and months before the election. To a considerable extent, he who controls television rules the country, as Putin showed in Russia. A country with one or two government-controlled channels will give much news coverage to the ruling party and little to opposition candidates. Newspapers can suffer distribution problems and shortage of newsprint.

Bribery Poor people are often so desperate for money or jobs that they vote for the party that provides them. Mexico's PRI was notorious for rewarding voters. In the 2000 elections in Yucatán PRI gave voters thousands of washing machines, no doubt to ensure a clean election.

Ballot Security Voting is supposed to be secret, but there are techniques to figure out who voted how. Actually, just telling people you know how they voted is often enough to scare them into compliance. This is especially a problem in unsophisticated rural areas. If a whole village does not vote for the party in power, it may miss out on next year's road-repair hires. Ballot boxes can be stuffed in advance. As they used to say in Chicago: "Vote early and often!"

Ballot Counting Opposition parties may not have enough poll watchers and counters to ensure honest counts. They may be barred from watching. Computers do not necessarily make tabulating votes honest. In the 1988 elections, with Cuauhtémoc Cárdenas mounting a major challenge, Mexico's computers tabulating the vote crashed; when they were back up PRI won with a bare 50.4 percent. Over the sixty previous years PRI had never won less than 70 percent.

Amid major complaints of PRI fraud, especially from PAN and PRD, to its credit the PRI government of Salinas in 1990 abolished the Federal Electoral Commission, widely believed to be crooked. In its place, the Federal Electoral Institute (IFE), autonomous and supervised by representatives of all parties, greatly cleaned up Mexican voting at all levels. Immediately, non-PRI parties started winning more votes. IFE demonstrates that Mexico is getting modern and democratic. Recent problems in U.S. vote counts suggest we could use an IFE.

Geography

Bound Brazil

Brazil is bounded on the north by Venezuela, Guyana, Suriname, and French Guiana;

on the east by the Atlantic Ocean;

on the south by Uruguay, Argentina, and Paraguay;

and on the west by Bolivia, Peru, and Colombia.

Bounding Brazil enables us to locate all South American countries except Chile and Ecuador.

deficits. This pleases the crowd but leads to inflation and outcries from foreign investors and international banks for Mexico to get its economic house in order. Presidents Díaz Ordaz (1964–1970), Echevarría (1970–1976), and López Portillo (1976–1982) typify the *político* approach. They relied too much on Mexico's new oil finds and overspent. Eventually, Mexico's economy crashed.

peso   Spanish for "weight"; Mexico's currency, which fluctuates at around nine U.S. cents.

The *técnicos* (known in much of the world as *technocrats*—see pages 110 and 419) try to fix economic instability. They are more likely to staff appointive positions and worry less about mass demands. Many have studied modern economics in the United States and see a free market and fewer government controls as the path to prosperity. They urge for Mexico what much of the world calls *neoliberalism* (see page 64), the return to Adam Smith's original economic ideas. This confuses Americans, as we call it *conservatism*. For Europeans and Latin Americans, however, Britain's Margaret Thatcher instituted a neoliberal economic program. In Chile under Pinochet, the "Chicago boys" (who studied neo-classical economics at the University of Chicago) put neoliberalism into practice with good results.

Presidents Miguel de la Madrid Hurtado (1982–1988) and Carlos Salinas de Gortari (1988–1994) gave technocrats a chance to stabilize the fiscal chaos wrought by the overspending of their predecessors. Actually, these fiscal technicians in PRI implemented some of the free-market reforms that PAN also sought. But reforms provided insufficient regulation, and Mexico's newly freed banks made bad and even crooked loans. Mexico's financial sector crashed in 1995. The **peso** lost most of its value against the dollar, Mexico's GDP declined by 6.2 percent in 1995 alone, and Mexicans grew poorer. (In 1997, Asian banks folded from exactly the same sort of *crony capitalism*.) The problem is not a lack of bright, well-educated economists. Both PRI and PAN have plenty. The problem is part-way economic reforms that provide freedom without rule of law. These tend to set up wild expansion followed by crashes. Many Mexican groups fight thorough reform, though, and President Fox could accomplish little.

Mexican Catholicism

The real sleeper in Mexican politics has been the Roman Catholic Church. More than 90 percent of Mexicans are professed Catholics, some of them quite serious. Since independence, however, the spirit of the Mexican Republic has been secular. The Church was never happy with Mexico's break from Spain and tilted strongly conservative. It was conservative Mexican Catholics who convinced Napoleon III that France could take Mexico. The republic tilted in an anticlerical direction, which became especially pronounced in the 1910–1920 Revolution. Its leaders saw the Church as a bastion of upper-class conservatism and reaction. The 1917 constitution imposed limits on church lands, educational institutions, and religious orders. Detectives ferreted out secret convents and closed them. Priests had to travel in ordinary clothing, without clerical collar. Calles's anticlericalism provoked the Cristero Rebellion. For much of the twentieth century, the Mexican church was on the defensive.

But the Church never gave up. Through Catholic teachings, lay organizations, schools and universities, and the 1939 founding of PAN, it methodically set the stage for the return of Catholic politics. These are not the politics of a reactionary past but of a modern, business-oriented future. PAN resembles Italy's postwar Christian Democrats, a catchall party that is Catholic but not pietistic.

CRIME AND POLITICS

We have mentioned several Mexican interest groups—labor unions, peasant associations, business, the Catholic Church—but Mexico's most powerful interest group is crime. (Actually, looking at the world as a whole, crime of all sorts is humankind's biggest economic activity.) This is nothing new. Early in human history, the state gave birth to twins—politics, the means of influencing the state, and crime, the means of avoiding the state. Politics and crime know and understand each other quite well, forming an almost symbiotic relationship, one especially clear in a country like Mexico. Politics needs money to win elections and pays little attention to the sources of this money (for example, Japanese Liberal Democratic politicians and *yakuza* gangsters). And crime needs the protection of politics to continue its enterprises (for example, the inability of the Russian police to solve any assassinations). Corruption occurs at the triple interface of the state, politics, and crime. In a weak state, politics, because it is unrestrained, easily turns violent. Crime, because it has little to fear from the state, ignores state power.

---

narcotraficante   Drug trafficker.

Justice has always been weak in Mexico. Pancho Villa blended banditry and revolution. As we noted, starting with Madero in 1914, assassination of top leaders was common. Assassinations continue in our day. Nosy journalists, zealous prosecutors, and aides to Cuauhtémoc Cárdenas have been gunned down. A hit on a rival drug lord in 1993 by mistake killed a Mexican cardinal in his vestments. Mexicans were outraged. Frustrated at police corruption, in 2004 a Mexico City mob lynched two cops. In Mexico, rapists, murderers, and kidnappers are rarely arrested, but police beat innocent people until they confess. Perhaps three-fourths of Mexico's crimes are not reported; people feel it is useless. As in Russia, the inability of police to solve crimes suggests they are in on the deal.

Two killings in 1994 shocked the world and paved the way to PAN's electoral victories. Luis Donaldo Colosio, PRI's own presidential candidate handpicked by President Salinas, was shot dead at

Political Culture

SONGS OF DRUG DEALING

Mexican tradition has long celebrated bandits in folk ballads known as *corridos*. Currently popular are polka-tempo *narcocorridos* that celebrate drug smugglers as romantic daredevils who fight cops and other gangs and die young. Mexicans deplore the drug trade, crime, and insecurity, but, as in most of Latin America, respect for law is not part of the political culture. One Mexican lawyer who worked on judicial reform admitted, "There is no public condemnation of lawbreakers."

Mexicans learn early that the rich and powerful own the police and courts; in defense, the poor learn to evade and ignore the law. It is a logical reaction to an unjust system. Most Mexicans are personally open, honest, and friendly. But they say that obeying a brutal and unfair judicial system is absurd. Everyone knows the police are among the biggest criminals, in the pay of the **narcotraficantes**, who always go free. Police coerce confessions out of suspects, and the courts take that confession as ironclad proof of guilt. Mexican attitudes on law are common throughout the Third World: It is something to be worked around.

an election rally in Tijuana. Who ordered the hit is unclear. PRI party secretary general José Ruiz Massieu was later shot dead. President Salinas's brother Raúl, who got very rich with drug connections during the *sexenio* of his brother, got fifty years for ordering the killing (but was freed in 2005). Massieu's own brother, a deputy attorney general, was assigned to investigate but resigned, accusing PRI bosses of complicity and coverup. President Salinas, who worked his way up as a brilliant U.S.-educated economist, ended his term in disgrace and went into exile in Ireland. In 2004 the youngest Salinas brother, Enrique, suspected of laundering money in France for Raúl, was strangled to death in Mexico City. An interviewer asked Colosio shortly before his death about the Salinas family. He replied, "Have you seen *The Godfather?*"

The killings brought together two trends that had been growing over the years: (1) PRI was stinking more and more, and (2) Mexicans were sufficiently educated to vote out PRI. As the PAN's Felipe Calderón took office, drug cartels began to murder each other over turf. Bodies turned up everywhere, and state governors cried out for federal help. Calderón vowed to break the *narcotraficantes*. Unable to trust the police, who are heavily infiltrated by drug gangs, in 2008 Calderón ordered the Mexican army into open warfare with the heavily armed cartels, much of it in cities on the U.S. border. Hundreds were killed, even top police officials. It will be a long, hard war, as the money in drug smuggling is irresistible to poor Mexicans, including underpaid police officers.

WHAT MEXICANS QUARREL ABOUT

Population and Jobs

Mexico's population exploded from 16 million in 1935 to 34 million in 1960, a growth rate of 2.8 percent a year. The population is now more than triple that but growing at a reasonable 1.15 percent a year. This itself is testimony to the power of economic development to solve the population explosion. Middle-class people turn naturally and with no coercion to small families. Mexico's rate of population increase is not much bigger than the U.S. rate. The difference is that the Mexican rate is held down by emigration while the U.S. rate grows from immigration, much of it from Mexico.

Mexicans do not quarrel about birth rates—Catholic countries seldom do—but they do quarrel about how to create jobs for the millions of unemployed and underemployed. Mexico's institutions and economy cannot keep up with its population growth. The Zapatista dream of land for the poor cannot work because there is not enough land to redistribute. State-owned industries grow too slowly and employ too few. A state-owned oil industry like Pemex needs only a few trained technicians. It generates a lot of money but not a lot of jobs. (The same is true of Nigeria and the Persian Gulf petrostates.)

The gap between rich and poor in Mexico is huge, as it is throughout Latin America. Economists estimate that the top 4 percent of Mexicans own half of Mexico's wealth while 40 percent of Mexicans live below the poverty line, which is not very high. (Brazil has even greater inequality of wealth and incomes.) With no land or jobs, millions of Mexicans stream to the cities, where they live in shanties and eke out a living selling small items or stealing. Some 22 million Mexicans work off the books, in the "informal economy" (black market), and pay no taxes, contributing to Mexico's chronic federal budget deficits. Mexico City, with a population of over 10 million, is one of the biggest cities in the world, and with some of the world's worst air pollution.

Here is a "shantytown" built on a hillside on the outskirts of Mexico City.

Poverty is especially horrible in the interior south of Mexico, precisely where the Zapatista rebellion started in 1994. Although the Mexican army quickly drove the guerrillas from the towns of Chiapas, they still operate in the mountainous jungles of the region, where they are very hard to catch. Their leader, "Subcomandante Marcos," who always wears a ski mask when interviewed, speaks eloquently and accurately about Mexico's history of exploitation and poverty and of PRI's betrayal of its promises to uplift the poor. Marcos, however, has no feasible program of his own. He imbibes the romanticism of the Revolution, as do many Mexicans.

In addition to its obvious injustice, maldistribution of income has several other negative consequences. Some Mexicans go hungry, and many do not earn even the minimum daily wage of $4.50. Poor people have no money to save, which means insufficient capital for investment and growth. Middle-class people save, generating ample capital for investment, as in Germany and Japan. Without domestic capital, Latin American lands must depend on foreign capital, which not everyone likes. (The U.S. middle class also saves little, and the same thing happens: massive inflows of foreign capital, much of it from China and Japan.) The very poor have trouble acquiring the skills needed to lift themselves into the middle class. Schools are inadequate in rural Mexico and in the vast shantytowns around Mexico's cities. The high crime rate frightens away foreign businesses, whose executives are often kidnapped for ransom. Poverty leads to more poverty until it becomes almost endemic. One of the few escape hatches is *el Norte*, sneaking into the United States.

The cures proposed relate to the neoliberal economics mentioned earlier. Populists, leftists, trade unionists, and nationalists—many now clustered in the PRD—want to keep or restore state-owned industries. Privatization of national treasures such as Pemex is deemed a sellout to the foreign capitalists. Mexico's constitution prohibits any private ownership—foreign or domestic—of the country's energy industry. This means lack of investment and shortages; Mexico, which has vast fields of natural gas, must import it from the United States. Young, U.S.-trained economists, on the other hand, recognize that state-owned industries are stagnant, inefficient, corrupt, and employ too few Mexicans. Such people are

gringo From the Spanish for "gibberish"; pejorative for foreigner, specifically *norteamericano*.

Panistas or PRI técnicos. Recent PRI presidents gingerly liberalized Mexico's economy, and Calderón wishes to go much further.

Oil is an unreliable fix for Mexico's economic problems. Indeed, some Arab intellectuals now speak of the "petroleum curse": It skews development away from long-term and balanced growth, employs few, concentrates wealth, and makes the country dependent on the rise and fall of oil prices. (See the Nigeria chapter for further discussion.) When new oilfields were discovered in the south in the 1970s, Presidents Echeverría and López Portillo went crazy with spending. For a while, some Mexicans felt rich, but inflation and the 1995 crash of the peso ended that. Mexico, in effect, followed the path of the oil sheiks in squandering new oil revenues to produce a temporary and unsustainable illusion of wealth. Oil is a kind of drug that induces fantasies of grandeur.

If Pemex is ever privatized and foreign firms allowed to develop Mexico's oil—both very hot political issues—it will mark the coming of Mexican economic maturity. Yes, the **gringos** want your oil, Mexico, but they pay good money for it and bring badly needed technological improvements. The untouchable status of Pemex as a fountain of corruption does no good for Mexico's economy or political culture.

GEOGRAPHY

SHANTYTOWNS

The Third World is characterized by shantytowns, vast tracts of squatter housing that surround most cities, called *barrios coloniales* in Spanish and *favelas* in Portuguese. Many houses are just shacks, but over time some turn into modest homes. Nearly all occupants do not own the land under their dwellings, so they have no legal claim to them and cannot use them as collateral for loans. One Peruvian economist proposes that giving legal title would yield loans and rapid economic growth.

Some inhabitants of Mexico's *colonias* hold regular jobs, others sell things on the street, and some steal. Crime bosses hold sway in the *colonias*. Mexico's crime rates are astronomical. PRI claims to look out for the poor, but urban poor are neither farmers nor, for the most part, organized workers. No one represents them.

If life is so wretched in the *barrios*, why do Mexicans move there? Because it is even worse in the countryside. Moving to a city for many is a step up, for there they have access to more education and health services and may even find a job. If the Mexican economy worked right, more businesses would start up in the *barrios*, taking advantage of the low rent and cheap labor. Historically, cities are the incubators of economic growth, even if they are not pretty.

The NAFTA Question

Globalization has been a buzzword for some years. Whole books are written either praising it or denouncing it. We need to ask at least two questions about **globalization**: (1) Does it really exist? (2) Does it uplift poor countries? Basically, globalization is nothing more than trade, and that has been going on for millennia. World trade increased dramatically with Portugal's and Spain's voyages of discovery and their trade with, respectively, Asia and Latin America. World trade grew quickly with the steamship and the British Empire, "Victorian globalization." Current globalization, aided by instant communication and rapid transport, just accelerates earlier upward trends.

---

globalization   The world becoming one big capitalist market.

But globalization does not really cover the globe. Wide areas—especially the Middle East and Africa—are little involved. Globalization extends in a band across North America and Europe, falls off, and picks up again in Asia. Some developing countries benefit enormously from free trade, namely the "growth dragons" of East Asia. We could nearly cross out "globalization" and put in "Made in China."

Latin America plays a relatively minor role and is not sure about globalization, because so far it has just begun to enjoy its benefits. Some critics cite Latin America's uneven economic growth as proof that globalization either does not work at all or at least does not work in Latin America, where a rigid class structure stifles growth. China zooms along at 10 percent growth a year; only since 2004 has Latin America reached 5 percent. Leftists point out that Latin America's gaps between rich and poor are getting bigger, and this helped produce the leftist electoral victories in Argentina, Brazil, Chile, Bolivia, and Venezuela.

NAFTA (the 1994 North American Free Trade Agreement) was both hailed and feared. American fear-mongers said U.S. jobs would make a "vast sucking sound" as they drained down to Mexico. Nothing of the sort happened; U.S. employment reached record heights in the late 1990s. Canadian and Mexican nationalists feared the U.S. economy would dominate their two countries. Free-market optimists foresaw economic growth for all.

Actually, not much happened, and that is the trouble. Mexican trade with the United States, which had been growing for years before NAFTA, slowed. The Fox administration saw feeble GDP growth and the loss of 2.1 million jobs. The problem was so obvious that few saw it coming: No one can compete with China. No one. What we thought would be produced in Mexico is produced in China, because it is much cheaper. Mexican wages in manufacturing are one-tenth U.S. wages but three times Chinese wages. The globalization paradigm did not ask what would be the effects of free trade when one large producer has incredible advantages over all the others. How many giant, low-cost producers can the world take? Will China's productive capacity snuff out all others? Mexicans might paraphrase Díaz and exclaim, "Poor Mexico! So close to the United States, so far from China."

Much of Mexican politics revolves around NAFTA. The left, including PDR people, want to either scrap the whole thing or seriously modify it. PAN is solidly for it; Vicente Fox, with his Coca-Cola background, exemplified and celebrated globalization as Mexico's way out of poverty. PRI negotiated and ratified NAFTA but has some doubts. It has not produced its expected effects, but home-made Mexican economic instability ruined its first few years. Give it some time, they say, and NAFTA will work. Mexico does not have much time. Its growing population coupled with slow economic growth spells increased poverty and unemployment. To escape them, Mexicans have two poor choices, both related to the United States: illegal immigration and drug smuggling.

DRUGS: A MEXICAN OR U.S. PROBLEM?

Mexico grows marijuana, but most cocaine and heroin come from Colombia, Peru, and Bolivia. Mexico is the most important way-station. Its long border with the United States makes smuggling relatively easy. By air, tunnels, trucks, or "mules," drugs pour into an eager U.S. market. For every kilo found, perhaps twenty or more get through. For several years, drugs on America's streets got cheaper and purer, indicating an excess of supply over demand.

Drugs are both a Mexican and a U.S. problem. For Mexico, drugs have led the penetration of crime into the highest levels of power. Mexico's police, judicial system, and army have all been corrupted by drug money. Even President Salinas had a brother in the drug trade. In 2005 a spy for a drug cartel was found in President Fox's office. One of the characteristics of the weak state is its penetration by crime. In Mexico, crime and politics depend on each other; drug money helps politicians, and politicians help the traffickers, a difficult cycle to break.

The real problem is the lucrative U.S. drug market. If no Americans took illicit drugs, a wide layer of Latin American crime would disappear. But there are drug users

Two U.S. border patrol officers with a sniffing dog walk by cars entering the United States in California.

in every walk of life in America. They might consider that the *narcotraficantes* murder hundreds and harm the stability and growth of several Latin American lands. Drugs finance the decades-long guerrilla war in Colombia. Catching traffickers and checking border crossings has little impact on overall U.S. drug consumption. The profits from feeding the U.S. drug market are so great that many gladly join. In the words of Walt Kelly's Pogo, "We have met the enemy, and he is us."

Illegal or Undocumented?

We call them "illegal immigrants"; Mexicans call them "undocumented workers." An estimated 12 million illegals are in the United States. The Mexican-U.S. border is the only place on earth you can walk from the Third World into the First. For the millions of Mexicans who have made the risky walk, they merely relocated to the northern portion of their republic that the United States seized in 1848. Many die every year, but few worry about breaking the law. The U.S. Border Patrol

remittance	Money sent home.

arrests over 1 million a year and sends them back. Many immediately try again. Probably more than 1 million a year get through.

The problem of the *indocumentados* parallels the drug problem. There is both a push and a pull. Unemployment and poverty push Mexicans to leave, and jobs and the opportunity to give their families a decent life pull. And Americans do hire Mexicans (and others from further south) with little thought to their immigration status. Many businesses, especially in the U.S. Southwest, depend on cheap Mexican labor. "Heck, he gave me a Social Security number," say many employers. (True, but it's probably the same number used by dozens of illegals.) Few U.S. families could afford household help—maids and gardeners—if they had to hire Americans. This, however, depresses the wages of Americans who might otherwise take these jobs.

Again, this is not really a Mexican problem; it's an American problem. The Mexican government, as a humanitarian service, puts out a comic book showing how to survive the dangers and deserts of crossing the border. Mexico wants a better deal from the U.S. administration to accept more immigrants, as either legal or temporary immigrants, and grant amnesty to illegals already here. Americans do not want a flood of Hispanic immigrants, but employers in clothing, manufacturing, meatpacking, and agriculture like the cheap labor and make campaign contributions. Their payoff: U.S. investigators are chronically short-handed in enforcing laws against hiring illegals. Illegal immigration became a hot issue within the U.S. Republican party. One of President Fox's biggest defeats was in not getting President Bush to make legal Mexican immigration easier.

Going to the United States is both an escape valve for Mexican unemployment and source of **remittances** from those already working here, who sent back $24 billion in 2006 (3.3 percent of Mexico's GDP). (India's remittances, mostly from the Persian Gulf, were $23 billion, 3 percent of GDP.) Remittances are the best form of foreign aid; they bypass corrupt officials and go right to families for raising children and starting businesses. The best thing we could do for Mexico's development is to make remittances safe and cheap.

MODERN MEXICO?

Can Mexico be an example of modernization for a continent where it seems that little works right? Compared to most of Latin America, Mexico is a model of growth and prosperity. With the right policies it might become the "Latin tiger," rivaling the growth dragons on the other side of the Pacific.

What is the right policy for growth? The record of the postwar world shows one combination: low wages and good productivity. When labor costs (including taxes, pensions, and hourly wages) lag behind productivity growth you can produce more and earn a share of the world market. Labor costs rise over time. The trick is to keep productivity rising even faster. You do this through more technology and higher worker skills. The models for the combination of low wages and high productivity: postwar Germany and Japan and present-day China. When German and Japanese labor costs became some of the world's highest, their economic growth flattened. Negative examples: postwar Britain and present-day Mexico.

How can you tell if a country's labor costs are too high and its productivity too low? You do not need elaborate economic calculations. Just note whether foreign or domestic businesses invest there. If domestic businesses park their money overseas—*flight capital*, as we saw in Russia—you know there are problems. Other factors that foster a "hostile business climate" include too many regulations, high taxes, state takeovers, strike-happy unions, crime, and corruption. Clean these up, and you can have rapid growth. The late Milton Friedman, winner of a Nobel Prize in economics, long extolled the free market as the basis of economic growth. Asked if he still thought so, he said he now realized it is not; the real basis, he said, is rule of law. He might have been speaking of Mexico.

Key Terms

austerity (p. 495)

bilateral opposition
   (p. 492)

cacique (p. 480)

caudillo (p. 481)

Central America (p. 479)

clientelism (p. 485)

constitutionalism (p. 486)

co-opt (p. 497)

corporatism (p. 485)

creole (p. 480)

dedazo (p. 488)

dependency theory (p. 498)

dominant-party system
   (p. 490)

egalitarian (p. 493)

ejido (p. 484)

globalization (p. 506)

gringo (p. 505)

hacienda (p. 495)

institutionalize (p. 484)

Latin America (p. 479)

machismo (p. 495)

mercantilism (p. 493)

Mesoamerica (p. 479)

mestizaje (p. 495)

narcotraficante (p. 502)

norteamericano (p. 495)

personalismo (p. 495)

peso (p. 501)

political institution (p. 484)

populist (p. 491)

positivism (p. 482)

pre-Columbian (p. 480)

priísmo (p. 495)

quixotic (p. 497)

remittance (p. 508)

sexenio (p. 495)

South America (p. 479)

Further Reference

Ai Camp, Roderic. *Politics in Mexico: The Democratic Consolidation*, 5th ed. New York: Oxford University Press, 2006.

Babb, Sarah. *Managing Mexico: Economists from Nationalism to Neoliberalism*. New York: Routledge, 2001.

Brading, David. *Mexican Phoenix, Our Lady of Guadalupe: Image and Tradition across Five Centuries*. New York: Cambridge University Press, 2001.

Crandall, Russell, Guadalupe Paz, and Riordan Roett, eds. *Mexico's Democracy at Work: Political and Economic Dynamics*. Boulder, CO: L. Rienner, 2005.

Davidow, Jeffrey. *The U.S. and Mexico: The Bear and the Porcupine*. Princeton, NJ: Markus Wiener, 2004.

Dawson, Alexander. *First World Dreams: Mexico since 1989*. New York: Palgrave, 2006.

Eisenstadt, Todd A. *Courting Democracy in Mexico: Party Strategies and Electoral Institutions*. New York: Cambridge University Press, 2004.

Krauze, Enrique. *Mexico: Biography of Power: A History of Modern Mexico, 1810–1996*. New York: HarperCollins, 1997.

Merrell, Floyd. *The Mexicans: A Sense of Culture*. Boulder, CO: Westview, 2003.

Mizrahi, Yemile. *From Martyrdom to Power: The Partido Acción Nacional in Mexico*. Notre Dame, IN: University of Notre Dame Press, 2003.

Needler, Martin C. *Mexican Politics: The Containment of Conflict*, rev. ed. Westport, CT: Greenwood, 1995.

Peeler, John. *Building Democracy in Latin America*, 2nd ed. Boulder, CO: L. Rienner, 2004.

Preston, Julia, and Samuel Dillon. *Opening Mexico: The Making of a Democracy*. New York: Farrar, Strauss & Giroux, 2004.

Shirk, David A. *Mexico's New Politics: The PAN and Democratic Change*. Boulder, CO: L. Rienner, 2005.

Youngers, Coletta A., and Eileen Rosin, eds. *Drugs and Democracy in Latin America: The Impact of U.S. Policy*. Boulder, CO: L. Rienner, 2004.

Chapter 31
Nigeria

Nigeria is important. It has the largest population in Africa—one fifth of Africans south of the Sahara are Nigerians—and is larger than any European country. It produces about one-tenth of the world's oil, making it the sixth biggest oil-exporting country and fifth largest oil supplier to the United States (8.5 percent of U.S. imported oil), so we often treat it as little more than a gas station, like we did the Persian Gulf. Such places do not stay gas stations but turn into zones of chaos and conflict. Nigeria has much influence in Africa and, along with South Africa, has led peacekeeping operations in several African countries. Nigeria is also attempting, for the third time, to establish democracy in a situation that could explode into violence or military coup at any time. Nigerian democracy deserves our support.

QUESTIONS TO CONSIDER

1. What and where are Nigeria's religions and ethnic groups?
2. What were colonialism's effects on Africa?
3. Upon which countries' institutions did Nigeria model its institutions?
4. How does Nigeria illustrate *praetorianism?*
5. What do the Igbo and Biafra illustrate?
6. Does colonialism explain poverty?
7. What did oil do to Nigeria's economic development?
8. Why doesn't fragmented Nigeria just fall apart?
9. Can corruption be measured objectively?
10. Could Nigeria's PDP become like Mexico's PRI?

THE IMPACT OF THE PAST

Nigeria, like Mexico, was home to civilizations long before the coming of the Europeans. The Nok culture, which was adept at grain farming and iron smelting, created an inland kingdom around the time of Christ at the southern end of the trade route from North Africa. Starting in the eleventh century A.D., the Yoruba built a series of city-states in the southwest under a king in the city of Ife. Only the Igbo (also known as Ibo) appear to have been stateless; they lived in egalitarian, self-contained villages in the southeast. There was never a single kingdom of Nigeria.

Islam from the Sudan region arrived in the Sahel of northern Nigeria in the ninth century A.D. and converted the Hausa and Fulani peoples, who are often known as the Hausa-Fulani. The Borno kingdom and later Songhai empire were seats of Islamic learning and culture. Islam also meant that Nigeria would inherit a tragic split between a Muslim north and a largely Christian south, the source of much conflict today.

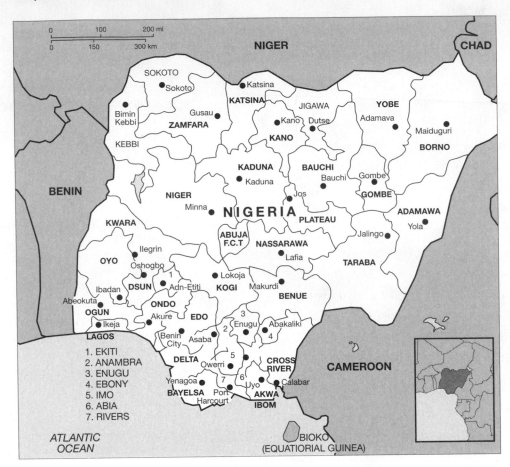

Nigeria

The Coming of the Europeans

Nigeria, like Mexico, was launched by the voyages of discovery. Portuguese navigators, in their effort to round Africa to tap the wealth of Asia, were the first Europeans to reach, in 1471, what was much later called Nigeria. The Portuguese began a pattern later followed by other Europeans. They did not venture far inland—climate and disease made that unpleasant—but set up trading forts along the African coast.

They soon found their chief item of trade: slaves. Slavery had always been practiced in Africa; most were used locally, but some were exported to North Africa. Starting with the Portuguese, local African chiefs, by raiding and kidnapping, delivered slaves to the burgeoning European slave trade on the coast, which became known as the "slave coast." Portugal's colony of Brazil and Spain's colony of Cuba needed labor for their sugarcane fields. England's American colonies needed labor for their cotton and tobacco fields. From the 1530s to the 1850s Portuguese, Spanish, French, English, and later Americans shipped over 3.5 million Africans across the Atlantic, chiefly to Brazil (which took perhaps six times as many as the United States did). Due to this brutal trade, many Americans, Brazilians, and Cubans are of Yoruba or Igbo ancestry.

An Islamic **jihad** from 1804 to 1808 in the northern region was little noticed by Europe but contributed to Nigeria's current difficulties. Islamic scholars, in a familiar pattern, found the Muslim kingdoms there insufficiently pure and demanded their overthrow. That done, they set up what was known as the Sokoto **Caliphate**, a single political system much more powerful than any other in the region, and one motivated by Islamic fundamentalism. In less than a century, it collided with British colonialism.

Scottish explorer Mungo Park, often wracked with fever, surveyed the Niger River from 1795 to 1806 until he drowned while trying to canoe down it. Few ventured after him until quinine was developed for use against malaria in the 1850s. Christian missionaries arrived to convert the Yoruba, Igbo, and others, setting up missionary posts on the coast. Missionaries were often the advance element of imperial expansion, as protecting them soon required a military presence.

Britain's suppression of the slave trade was the first step that led to the establishment of Nigeria. Under pressure from British Christians, Parliament in 1807 outlawed the shipping of slaves (but not slavery itself, which Parliament ended in the British Empire in 1834). To enforce the ban, the Royal Navy stationed a squadron in the Gulf of Guinea. To replace the slave trade, Britain encouraged trade in palm oil, used for soaps and lubricants. An example of "unforeseen consequences," the move stimulated the capture of more slaves, who were needed to produce and transport the palm oil. To suppress this internal trade, Britain first shelled Lagos, the Yorubas' island capital, in 1851 and then annexed it in 1861.

jihad Arabic for "struggle"; also Muslim holy war.

caliphate Islamic dynasty.

desiccation Drying out.

sub-Saharan Africa south of the Sahara.

Sahel Narrow band south of Sahara, arid but not yet desert.

aquifer Underground water-bearing layer.

savanna Tropical grasslands south of Sahel.

Geography

SAHARA, SAHEL, SAVANNA

African geography can be looked at as climate bands running east to west. The northernmost of these bands, the Sahara, is very dry, and the south, close to the equator, is very rainy. The Sahara was not always a desert, but about 5,000 years ago its **desiccation** began, making it difficult to traverse and leaving **sub-Saharan** Africa semi-isolated.

Traders, raiders, and Muslim armies occasionally crossed from North Africa into the **Sahel**, which includes northern Nigeria. With uncertain rainfall, the Sahel can be used for little more than cattle grazing, so human populations are thin. The Sahara has been expanding southward as the Sahel gets drier. Some blame this on global warming, others on ice ages, and still others on growing populations of cattle growers for drawing too much water from its very limited **aquifer**.

South of the Sahel are Africa's vast **savannas**, characterized by hot wet summers and hot dry winters. Much of Nigeria, indeed much of Africa, is savanna. Here rainfall permits farming. Only the south of Nigeria, along the coast of the Gulf of Guinea, has the lush rain forest that some suppose covers most of Africa. Actually, this region of year-round rainfall occupies only the equatorial band of Africa.

Geography

The Geography of Imperialism

We understand much about the developing areas by knowing who their former imperial masters were. Who set up the borders (most of them artificial), languages, legal codes, transportation lines, and styles of governance? Notice how few non-European lands stayed free of imperial rule: Afghanistan, Ethiopia, Japan, Thailand, and Turkey. China and Iran were reduced to semicolonial status. It is easier to enumerate the countries that were never colonies than list those that were.

Much has been written about Europe's imperial impulse. Marxists see it as a race for riches. Lenin (see page 302) theorized that capitalism needs colonial markets to prolong its faltering economies and that World War I was an imperialist competition to gain colonies. This economic theory of imperialism has many holes. Overall, administering and defending colonies cost the imperial powers more than they gained. West Europe's richest countries never had colonies, but its poorest, Portugal, was drained by colonial expenses. Private interests, to be sure, profited from the colonial trade.

Strategists see imperialism as a race for security: "If we don't take it, someone else will." Spain, Britain, France, and others competed for colonies out of fear they would be at a strategic disadvantage if they had none. A "contagion" or "copy-cat factor" was also at work: Colonies brought prestige. Only powers with colonies were respected. This helps explain the U.S. push for colonies in 1898. Roughly, the following is who had what.

Spain, starting with Columbus, had most of Latin America (almost all of it lost in the 1820s) and the Philippines (lost to the United States in 1898). After stealing tons of New World gold and silver, Spain ended up one of Europe's poorest countries.

Portugal's was the first and last colonial empire. In the fifteenth century Portuguese navigators, seeking access to Asia, worked their way down the coast of Africa, setting up colonies as they went. Portugal claimed Brazil in 1500 and held it until independence in 1822. Portugal kept Goa until India took it in 1961; Angola, Mozambique, and Guinea-Bissau in Africa until 1975; East Timor until invaded by Indonesia in 1975; and Macau (near Hong Kong), ceded back to China in 1999.

Britain's was the biggest empire—"The sun never sets on the British Empire"—and included Canada, Australia, New Zealand, India (which then included Pakistan and Bangladesh), Sri Lanka, Burma, Malaya, South Yemen, much of Africa below the Sahara (including Kenya, South Africa, and Nigeria), and Hong Kong, plus temporary rule of Egypt, Palestine, Jordan, and Iraq.

France's was the second-biggest empire. It held Vietnam, Laos, Cambodia, most of North and Equatorial Africa, and bits of the Caribbean and South Pacific. France and Britain gave up their colonies from 1947 to 1964. After France gave independence to its African colonies in the early 1960s, it grew richer.

The Netherlands held the rich Dutch East Indies (now Indonesia) from the seventeenth century to 1949 and South Africa's Cape area in the eighteenth century, plus specks on the Caribbean. Indonesia's instability owes much to Dutch misrule. South Africa's Afrikaners, who long dominated the country, still speak a Dutch-based language, Afrikaans.

Belgium brutally exploited the vast Congo from 1885 to 1960, initially as the personal property of King Leopold. Conditions—described in Joseph Conrad's *Heart of Darkness*—were so horrid that the Belgian government had to take it over.

Germany, a latecomer in 1885, got some leftover pieces of Africa (Tanganyika, Namibia, Cameroon) and half of Samoa but lost them all at the close of World War I.

Italy, another latecomer, took Somalia in 1889, Eritrea in 1890, Libya from the Ottomans in 1912, and Ethiopia in 1935 but lost everything in World War II.

The Ottoman Turkish Empire took the Balkans in the late fourteenth century and held parts of it until the early twentieth. They also took the Middle East in the sixteenth century until they were pushed out by Britain in World War I. Imperialism was not solely a European thing.

Japan took Taiwan in 1895, Korea in 1910, and Manchuria in 1931 but lost them all in 1945.

The United States, let us not forget, had an empire, too. In 1898 America took the Philippines (independent since 1946), Puerto Rico, Hawaii, and Guam, and part of Samoa in 1899.

THE SCRAMBLE FOR AFRICA

The Niger (from the Latin for *black*) River, the greatest river of West Africa, rises far to the west, in Guinea, only 150 miles from the Atlantic, and makes a 2,600-mile semicircle, at first north through Mali, then turning south through Niger and finally Nigeria. During the nineteenth century, trade along the Niger, much of it in cocoa, became more profitable. In response to calls from missionaries, a Scottish captain made monthly steamboat runs up the lower reaches of the Niger.

British businessman George Goldie, the "father of Nigeria," set up the United Africa Company in 1879 and turned it into the chartered Royal Niger Company in 1886, after the Berlin Conference (see box below) had carved up Africa and assigned borders to European imperial powers. The conference stated, however, that no power could claim what it did not occupy, setting off a race to turn vague claims into colonies. This "scramble for Africa" prompted the British to grab Nigeria before the French could.

THE COLONIAL INTERLUDE

In 1894 real British colonialism took shape with the arrival of Fredrick Lugard, one of a remarkable handful of energetic Englishmen who dedicated their lives to the British colonial service and the vision of a British Empire that brought peace and prosperity to the world. To do this, they often used their new Maxim gun on the natives, as Lugard did in many colonial battles around the world. Lugard consolidated the areas of the Yoruba and Igbo—who fought a guerrilla war against him—into two British protectorates and in 1900 moved into the Muslim north with a military force. By 1903

GEOGRAPHY

BOUNDARIES IN AFRICA

The boundaries of Africa are especially artificial. Notice how several of Africa's borders are straight lines, a sure sign that a border is artificial. Many of the ones for Central Africa were drawn up at a conference in Berlin in 1885, the great "carve-up" of Africa to settle overlapping claims of imperial powers. The British envisioned owning a band of Africa running the entire length of the continent, "from Cairo to the Cape." After pushing the Germans out of Tanganyika in World War I, they achieved this. Their competitors, the French, turned a great swath of Africa running east-west across the continent's great bulge into French West Africa and French Equatorial Africa. Portuguese, Germans, and Belgians took smaller pieces of Africa.

The imperialist-imposed, artificial boundaries cut through tribes and forced together unworkable combinations of tribes. A river in Africa is a poor border because typically people of the same tribe live along both banks. In 1963, however, with most of Africa independent, the new Organization of African Unity (renamed African Union in 2002) decided not to change the Berlin borders and even put them in its charter. The new leaders were afraid both of unleashing chaos and of losing their governing jobs. Best to leave these artificial borders alone, they figured. In Africa, the imperialists' land grabs became permanent boundaries.

indirect rule   British colonial governance through native hereditary rulers.

divide and rule   Roman and British imperial ruling method of setting subjects against each other.

colonialism   Gaining and exploitation of overseas territories, chiefly by Europeans; related to *imperialism*.

he had captured Kano and Sokoto to form the Protectorate of Northern Nigeria. In 1914 Sir Frederick (he was knighted) combined Southern and Northern Nigeria into nearly its present form under a governor-general in Lagos. (A piece of the German-ruled Cameroon was added on the east after World War I.) In classic imperialist fashion, Lugard invented Nigeria, and his wife, a journalist, invented the name Nigeria.

Lugard used two British colonialist styles, the twin policies of **indirect rule** and **divide and rule**. With only a few hundred white men the British ran colonies as vast as India by working with and through local chiefs and princes, who were bought off with titles and honors. The French, who practiced a much more direct rule and were reluctant to turn over local responsibilities to natives, needed thousands of Frenchmen to staff their colonies. The British were far more efficient.

Divide and rule is an old technique of the Roman Empire: *divide et impera* in Latin. Its logic: "If you keep them divided you can easily rule them. United they could throw you out." Under this

Key Concepts

Colonialism

Colonialism means several things. From the legal point of view, a colony lacks sovereignty; ultimate lawmaking authority resides in a distant capital. London controlled the laws governing Nigeria, Paris those of Senegal, and Brussels those of the Congo. For the most part, the "natives" were kept politically powerless, as the imperial power deemed them too backward and ignorant. The British in Nigeria and other colonies gave chiefs some local responsibilities.

In economics, **colonialism** involved exploitation by the imperial country. The colonies supplied cheap agricultural and mineral raw materials, which the imperial country manufactured into industrial products that it sold back to the colonies. Marxists argue that colonies were captive markets that were kept poor in order to enrich imperialists. Actually, most colonies cost imperial governments more to administer and defend than they earned. Individual firms, to be sure, often made lush profits in the colonial trade.

Racially, colonies were governed on the basis of skin color on the principle that "the lowest of the Europeans is higher than the highest of the natives." A French policeman directing traffic in Algiers was superior to an Algerian doctor. An English clerk in Calcutta was the social better of an Indian professor. Racism was an important part of colonialism; it psychologically enabled the imperialists to govern millions of unlike peoples who did not want them there. It also contributed to the rage felt by educated subjects, some of whom became leaders of independence movements: "You treat me like dirt in my own country. Well, that will stop!"

In hindsight, colonialism stands condemned as brutal and evil. But it was the unavoidable outcome of the restless, dynamic West encountering the traditional areas of the globe that looked like easy pickings. The imperial powers had no right to conquer and govern others; they simply had guns. Of course, without colonialism there would be no United States. "Colonial" has a nice sound to Americans, connoting hardy settlers, Thanksgiving, and pretty landscapes. It has a bitter ring for most other peoples. Colonialism left a chip on the shoulders of the Third World and helps explain lingering anti-West feelings.

policy colonialist officials emphasized the distinctiveness of cultures, powers, and territories of existing tribes to set them against each other. There were always tribes in Africa, but the Europeans hyped tribalism to facilitate their rule. The often-murderous tribalism found today owes something to colonialist manipulations.

Geography

Bound Guinea

Guinea, a former French colony in West Africa not to be confused with Guyana in South America, is bounded on the north by Guinea-Bissau, Senegal, and Mali; on the east by the Ivory Coast; on the south by Liberia and Sierra Leone; and on the west by the Atlantic Ocean.

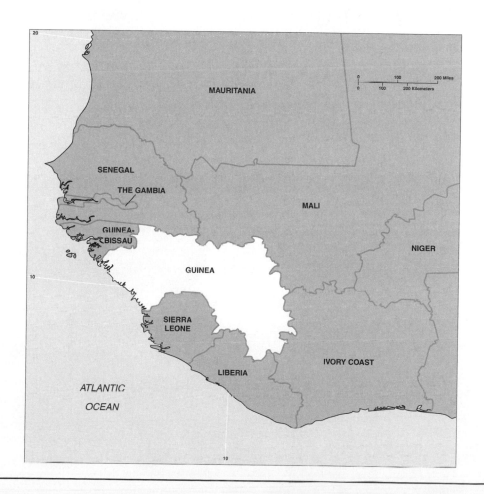

Colonialism, however, is a wasting asset. The more you organize and educate the natives, the more they want to rule themselves. Missionary activity ensured a growing number of educated Africans, some through college level. In the 1920s, especially in the British colonies of Africa,

GEOGRAPHY

BOUND THE DEMOCRATIC REPUBLIC OF CONGO

The Democratic Republic of Congo (formerly Zaire, earlier the Belgian Congo), is bounded on the north by Central African Republic and Sudan;

on the east by Uganda, Rwanda, Burundi, and Tanzania;

on the south by Zambia and Angola;

and on the west by the Atlantic, the Angolan exclave of Cabinda, and (the formerly French) Congo-Brazzaville.

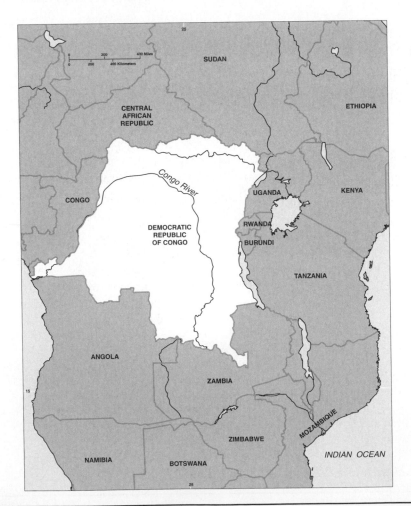

intellectuals developed **pan-Africanism** to liberate the continent from European domination. They argued that without the imperialists to divide them, Africans of all tribes could get along in a united Africa. The British strategy for handling growing political claims from Africans was to cede them local and partial political power in small steps. In 1914 the British established a Nigerian Legislative Council in Lagos and enlarged it with elected members in 1922. It had limited powers and did not include the north. Actually, Britain pursued fairly enlightened colonial policies that may have prevented the worst violence during and after independence. The Belgians, on the other hand, gave the Congolese nothing, trained them for nothing, prepared them for nothing. Result: When Belgium, after some riots, hastily granted the Congo independence in 1960, it erupted into civil war and is still strife-torn.

> **pan-Africanism**   Movement to unite all of Africa.

Independence

World War II weakened the European empires both materially and psychologically. They could no longer afford or justify ruling distant, unlike peoples. Decolonization came first as a trickle and then as a flood: India and Pakistan in 1947; Israel (formerly Palestine) in 1948; Indonesia (the Dutch East Indies) in 1949; Ghana (the Gold Coast) in 1957; then, in 1960, seventeen countries, mostly British and French colonies in Africa. Where there were many European settlers—Algeria, Kenya, and Rhodesia—decolonization was long, hard, and violent, as the settlers tried to keep their privileged status. Where there were few settlers—West Africa in general, including Ghana, Sierra Leone, and Nigeria—decolonization was easy. By the mid-1960s, all of the old African colonies had been liquidated except for Portugal's Angola, Mozambique, and Guinea-Bissau. The first European empire was also the last. In 1975, Lisbon, too, gave way. After white-ruled Rhodesia became black-ruled Zimbabwe in 1980, South Africa was the last white-ruled country in Africa, and this ended in 1994 with the election of a black government under Nelson Mandela. Africa returned to African hands.

Aiming at independence, the first Nigerian political party was founded in 1923. Herbert Macaulay, grandson of a prominent African Christian minister, founded the Nigerian National Democratic party. Macaulay, whom the British fought, is now called the father of Nigerian independence. The Nigerian Youth Movement was founded as a nationwide party in 1934. Macaulay and Nnamdi Azikiwe ("Zik"), a U.S.-educated Igbo, in 1944 brought together more than forty groups to form the National Council of Nigeria and the Cameroons (NCNC). World War II, in which Nigerian soldiers served in the British army, made subject peoples ask what the struggle against fascism meant when they still lived under authoritarian colonial regimes. The British had no good answer. By now many Nigerians were calling for independence.

The British strategy was to give way piecemeal. In 1947 they set up a federal system—the only plausible solution to Nigeria's regional differences—with Northern, Western, and Eastern regions, corresponding, respectively, to the three largest ethnic groups, the Hausa-Fulani, the Yoruba, and the Igbo. (It is now divided into much smaller states.) In 1951 the British set up a national House of Representatives, but it fell apart over the question of who represented what, a harbinger of today's Nigerian fragmentation. In 1954 they made the Nigerian federation self-governing with a Muslim prime minister from the north. Western and Eastern regions got internal self-government, the Eastern under Azikiwe and the NCNC and the Western under Chief Obafemi Awolowo, a lawyer who founded the Action Group, a party for Yoruba. Parties in Africa tend to form along tribal lines.

Nigeria's big problem was clear: how to make the huge Muslim Northern province and the two mostly Christian Southern provinces into one Nigeria. They do not go together easily or naturally. The chief party of the North was the People's Congress, which was always wary that the mostly Christian Eastern and Western peoples and parties would dominate the region. Muslims do not like being ruled by non-Muslims. A parallel happened earlier in India, where in 1906 the Muslim League split off from the Indian National Congress and eventually got a separate Pakistan in 1947.

Britain left Nigeria with a federal constitution and a prime minister that looked pretty good on paper. As in India, the British political position in Nigeria had become impossible to sustain; they had to leave and planned it for years. On October 1, 1960, Britain granted Nigeria independence. It had been a formal colony less than sixty years but had experienced European imperialism for much longer. The imperialists take much blame for Nigeria's troubles. They deranged it with a massive slave trade, took it over at gunpoint, cobbled together an artificial country composed of tribes who disliked each other, and then left. Thus it was not surprising that Nigeria, weak from the start, collapsed into military dictatorships. Nigeria is not unique; it is the story of many nations created by imperialists (example: Iraq).

Political Culture

Nigeria's Political Eras

Even more than Mexico, Nigeria is badly fragmented and lacks a unifying political culture. Consciousness focuses on religions, tribes, and regions. The brief British colonial period had given some Nigerians a modern education and a semblance of unity to Nigeria's elites but was not nearly enough to psychologically unify Nigeria as a nation. Nigeria's elites mostly know each other, but they look out more for their tribes than for Nigeria as a whole, as the tribes are their supporters.

Era	Years	Remembered for
Slave trade	1530–1820	Massive export of humans.
Pre-Colonial	1820–1894	Suppression of slave trade; British explorers and missionaries.
Colonial	1894–1960	By 1914 Lugard consolidates regions into one colony named Nigeria.
Independence	1960–1963	Commonwealth member, falls apart.
First Republic	1963–1966	Becomes republic.
Military rule	1966–1979	Coups, Biafra War.
Second Republic	1979–1983	Presidential system, corrupt civilian rule.
Babangida	1983–1993	Long military dictatorship.
Third Republic	1993	Abortive transition to democracy.
Abacha	1993–1998	Cruel and corrupt military dictatorship.
Fourth Republic	1999–	Another attempt at democracy under Obasanjo.

THE KEY INSTITUTIONS

In the first half-century of independent Nigeria, civilians ruled little more than a third of the time. The other two-thirds of the time were military rule under six different generals, some more brutal and greedy than others. The current period of civilian rule, starting in 1999, is the longest one. We hope it will continue but must be forever mindful that Nigeria is still an unstable country with strong tendencies to fall apart. When breakup threatens, the military takes over.

FROM BRITISH TO U.S. MODEL

The British set up Nigeria on the Westminster model with a prime minister as chief of government, but the 1979 constitution, now somewhat modified, turned Nigeria into a U.S.-style presidential system, and for a good reason. The British system depends on one party winning a majority of seats in Commons, which almost always happens in Britain. But if the legislature is fragmented into many parties, as it was in Nigeria's earlier years, the government must form multiparty coalitions and can "fall" easily on votes of no-confidence.

A U.S.-type presidential system avoids this, as the president can govern with or without majority support in the legislature. Presidents stay until the end of their terms and cannot easily be ousted. Nigeria's president, like the U.S. president, combines head of state with chief of government (see page 33) for a maximum of two four-year terms. Olusegun Obasanjo, the first president of Nigeria's Fourth Republic that emerged after dictator Sani Abacha died, tried to change the constitution so he could have a third term. Parliament was suspicious of his motives and blocked the effort. He left office on schedule in 2007.

NIGERIAN FEDERALISM

Nigerian federalism also resembles the U.S. variety. Nigeria's rulers, some of them military dictators, progressively increased the number of states, from twelve, to nineteen, to thirty-one, to the present thirty-six. Every few years the map of Nigeria is redrawn to calm Nigeria's many ethnic groups, who often feel trapped in a state dominated by another group. When they turn violent, which is often, Nigeria is inclined to carve out a new state for them. It may have worked, as there is less violence between ethnic groups now, but never zero.

In 1991 the military dictator Ibrahim Babangida (1985–1993) moved the capital from the old colonial capital of Lagos on the coast to Abuja, a new capital in the precise center of the country. The move resembled Brazil's shift of capital from Rio de Janeiro to Brasília in 1960 to open up the interior. The purpose of the move in Nigeria was to take the capital out of Yoruba hands and put it in more neutral territory. Abuja is now designated the Federal Capital Territory, rather like the District of Columbia. Like Brasília, Abuja is in the middle of nowhere and has been costly and inefficient.

Nigerian states and their governors have considerable autonomy, but critics complain that Nigerian federalism is less than genuine, because Abuja still controls oil revenues and dispenses them to state governors as bribes to keep them in line. Most governors are reputed to be corrupt. Nigeria's federal government either cannot or will not deliver much in basic services such as road maintenance or schools, so state governments are left with the tasks, which most do poorly. Islamist

sharia   Muslim religious law

groups in the North move into the vacuum by providing many basic services, thereby gaining adherents. Northern Nigeria's states are now under **sharia**, which Muslims claim is the only way to clean up corruption. There is nothing the center can do to stop the use of *sharia* without triggering a major revolt in the North.

Personalities

Umaru Yar'Adua

The good news is that Nigeria's thirteenth president, the quiet and reclusive Umaru Yar'Adua, represents the first transition from one elected president to another. He won the 2007 election in a landslide. The bad news is that the election was badly flawed—critics claim completely rigged—and Yar'Adua took office with little legitimacy. In a move reminiscent of Mexico's *dedazo* (see page 488), Nigeria's previous president, Olusegun Obasanjo, after two terms (eight years) in office, picked the little-known Yar'Adua to succeed him as candidate of the powerful People's Democratic party (PDP). Obasanjo had tried to change the constitution to allow him to serve a third term, but the legislature rejected the move, fearing dictatorship. Some senators had received bribes of up to $400,000 to vote for it.

Yar'Adua was born in 1951 into a prominent Muslim Fulani family in Katsina, in the very north of Nigeria, on the border with what later became Niger. Prior to being elected president in 2007, he had little experience outside Katsina. With a master's degree in chemistry, Yar'Adua taught college before a succession of managerial positions in agriculture and commerce. He had been active in several political parties before joining Obasanjo's PDP. Yar'Adua was elected governor of Katsina state in 1999 and served two full terms to 2007, establishing an uncorrupt reputation, rare for Nigerian governors. During this time, Katsina adopted *sharia*, one of twelve Nigerian states, all northern, to do so. Yar'Adua was always a devout Muslim but was not known as an Islamist.

It is Yar'Adua's reputation as a moderate Muslim that may have persuaded Obasanjo, an evangelical Christian, to pick him as successor. The PDP claims to speak

Umaru Yar'Adua

for all Nigerians but is weaker in the Muslim North, which tends to go to the All Nigeria People's party (ANPP). Yar'Adua could marginalize the ANPP and, hopefully, calm separatist tendencies in the North. For balance, Goodluck Jonathan, governor of Bayelsa state in the very south, part of the oil-rich Niger Delta, was chosen for vice-president. Jonathan had just become governor after his super-corrupt predecessor was impeached. A more cynical explanation is that Obasanjo, who is still the PDP's chairman, picked two weak, unknown figures to be his puppets, whom he could control even out of office.

Yar'Adua invited opposition parties into his government in an attempt to form a government of national unity. Two of his twenty-three ministers are ANPP members. Like most new Nigerian presidents, Yar'Adua proclaimed that eliminating corruption was his top goal. His predecessor promised the same but, according to critics, practiced plenty of corruption. A limiting factor with Yar'Adua is health: a severe kidney problem.

The National Assembly

The U.S. model is again evident in Nigeria's legislative branch, the bicameral National Assembly, which meets in Abuja. The Senate has 109 seats; each of the thirty-six states has three Senate seats plus one for the Federal Capital Territory. The House of Representatives has 360 seats, ten for each state, each representing a single-member district. Both houses are elected for four-year terms at the same time.

The Nigerian setup departs from its U.S. model, because its states get the same ten seats regardless of population. It would be like the United States having two Senates. Nigeria feels it must do this to appease smaller ethnic groups with their own states. Appeasing the smaller groups, however, creates resentment in the more populous states because they are underrepresented. The U.S. solution—a Senate to represent states on the basis of equality and a House to represent districts on the basis of population—strikes us as a good compromise, but we do not have Nigeria's touchy ethnic situation. The danger in Nigeria is *hyperfederalism*, a system that tries too hard to represent ethnic groups. It seems to work for a while but can lead to the country falling apart, as it did in Yugoslavia.

Nigeria's Parties

Nigeria's big Peoples Democratics party (PDP) bills itself as a centrist party, but to a considerable extent it has been the *personalistic* vehicle of former president Obasanjo. The smaller All Nigeria Peoples party (ANPP) gets its strongest following from Northern Muslims; some of its leaders earlier supported the brutal dictatorship of Sani Abacha (1993–1998) and got rich during that time. The Action Congress (AC) party is basically a Yoruba party that does well on its southwest home turf but not so well elsewhere. There are other smaller parties, some of them militant Northern Muslim parties, which win one or two seats in the House.

Nigeria's party system has evolved from many parties—nearly one per tribe—first into a "two-plus" party system and now perhaps into a dominant-party system, a bit like Mexico's PRI. The PDP is a well-funded and well-organized nationwide party and draws votes from all ethnic groups, including many

Locals vote during the countrywide local elections in Lagos, Nigeria.

Muslims. It also ruthlessly rigs elections. The big question: Could the PDP become Nigeria's PRI? Whatever negative things one might say about Mexico's dominant party (see the Mexico chapter), it got Mexico out of *praetorianism* (see page 532) and held it together during times of rapid change and modernization. The PRI analogy may not fit Nigeria, as most Northern Muslims do not support the PDP; some vote for regionalist and Islamist parties. Mexico has troublesome regions, but none with different religions. Nigeria parallels Iraq in its fragmentation. Like Iraq, Nigeria has three major ethnic regions that British imperialists forced into a single artificial state. Suggestions to let Nigeria and Iraq fall apart into their three main components overlook the bloodshed that would accompany such breakups.

NIGERIAN POLITICAL CULTURE

NIGERIAN FRAGMENTATION

Half of Nigerians are Muslim; another 40 percent are Christian, and 10 percent practice indigenous faiths, for example, the Yoruba religion. Nigeria is also ethnically fragmented. Of Nigeria's approximately 250 ethnic groups, these are the largest: 29 percent Hausa-Fulani, 21 percent Yoruba, 18 percent Igbo, and 10 percent Ijaw. In Mexico we spoke of regionalism, but Nigeria's problem is far worse and tends to fragment along religious and regional lines. Eastern, Western, and Northern regions have trouble living together and exist within Nigeria only because the British colonialists set up an artificial country.

The North is especially different—poor, isolated, traditional, and Muslim. It has never liked being ruled by Christians, either British or southern Nigerians. If they had to be in a single country, the northerners always sought to be its rulers. Many especially disliked President Obasanjo for being a born-again Christian who supported the U.S. war on terror. The fundamentalist Islamic Movement of Nigeria has al Qaeda and Iranian ties. U.S. counter-terrorist officials now closely scrutinize Northern Nigeria as a major center of terrorist recruitment and fund-raising.

Islam has been the chief religion in Northern Nigeria for a millennium, and, like Islam elsewhere in Africa, has been spreading south by vigorous proselytizing. African Muslims argue that Islam is the natural religion for Africa because it pays no attention to skin color and has deep roots in Africa, whereas Christianity is a recent arrival brought by Europeans with an implicit racism.

Islam can be rigid and intolerant. Some Nigerian Muslim clerics insist on a strictly religious education of Arabic, memorizing the Koran, and a Muslim dress code, including the *hijab* for women. Those who deviate may be arrested. Muslim preachers insist on Islamic purity, sometimes for all of Nigeria. In the North now a strong fundamentalist movement has made *sharia* state law. This has the potential to rip federal Nigeria apart, because it means states can override national laws. (Note the similarity to the U.S. "nullification" question that preceded the Civil War: Did states have the right to nullify federal laws?) But there is essentially nothing Abuja can do about it. *Sharia* can be harsh, for example, punishing adulterous women (but rarely men) by stoning to death and thieves by chopping their hands off. The penalties, however, apply only to Muslims, not to Christians, producing a bifurcated legal system. A country with two very different legal systems is a house that cannot stand. Some say compromise might be possible—*sharia* for family law in the North, Nigerian secular law for everything else—but Islamists insist that *sharia* is God's law and must not be mixed with other legal systems. (Notice how India has a parallel problem. See page 470.)

Fundamentalist Muslim clerics in the North denounced a World Health Organization project to immunize all children against polio. The clerics preached that it was to sterilize Muslim children. Vaccinations were stopped in three Northern states, and polio cases climbed. Muslims took offense at the 2002 Miss World pageant, which was to be held in Abuja, Nigeria. Riots broke out, and the pageant was hastily relocated to London. The smallest incident can touch off Christian-Muslim riots in Northern Nigeria, and thousands have been killed.

Other regions also present problems. The worst was the bitter Biafra War of 1967–1969, in which the Igbo of Eastern Nigeria attempted to break away with their own country, Biafra. In the Niger Delta, well-armed Ijaw and Itsekiri tribesmen fight government soldiers for control of the oil terminals. The Movement for the Emancipation of the Niger Delta (MEND), demanding compensation for the massive environmental damage the oil industry has caused, sabotages pipelines and kidnaps foreign oil workers, causing oil production to drop by a fifth. Violence in the Delta takes over a thousand lives a year and can explode any time into civil war.

To put things into perspective, though, we might consider what happened in tiny Rwanda, a former Belgian colony east of the Congo. Belgium played classic divide-and-rule by setting up one tribe, the Tutsis, to be aristocratic masters and another tribe, the Hutus, to be underlings. After the Belgians left in 1962, Hutu-Tutsi fighting and massacres became intermittent and exploded in 1994 as Hutu *genocidaires* massacred an estimated 800,000. (See the film *Hotel Rwanda* for a nonfiction glimpse of the horror.) The conflict spilled over into eastern Congo where it took an estimated 1.7 million lives, most from starvation and disease. The combined Rwanda-Congo deaths of 2.5 million is the world's worst since World War II. Nigeria has not had anything that bad, but it could.

DEMOCRACY

ELECTIONS IN NIGERIA

Freedom House doubts Nigeria's democracy and rates it only 4, "partly free," but better than Russia (which earns a 5.5). The 2007 Nigerian elections, for example, were fraudulent and rigged by registration only for favored parties, missing ballots, stuffed boxes, intimidation, and violence. Parties simply hired armed local gangs who killed at least 300 people to make sure that their bosses won. Umaru Yar'Adua of the PDP won with a reported 24,638,063 votes, some two-thirds of voters. But no one—except perhaps PDP officials—believes this number. Runner-up Muhammadu Buhari of the ANPP was far behind with less than one-fifth of the vote. And Atiku Abubakar of the AC got some 7 percent. More than a dozen small parties got a sprinkling of votes.

If the 2007 presidential election was bad, legislative elections were worse. Months later, the Independent National Electoral Commission (which is not at all independent) would not post the results for the House of Representatives and Senate. Whatever numbers INEC issued were made up; everyone laughed at them. To settle the highly suspicious election, the main parties took equal numbers of seats in *both* the House and Senate. The PDP got 76 House seats and 76 Senate seats, the ANPP 27 and 27, and the AD 6 and 6. Phony as this seat count is, remember that the PRI ruled Mexico like this for decades, but eventually Mexico grew into democracy. Perhaps we should get used to rigged elections in a country's early stages of building democracy.

The Igbo and Biafra

Nigeria's prime example of interethnic violence is what happened with the Igbo people of south-eastern Nigeria in the late 1960s. British explorers and colonial officials noted long ago that the Igbo lacked the cities and culture of the Yoruba of the southwest or the Hausa-Fulani of the north. The Igbo, who lived in scattered villages in the rain forest and Niger Delta, seemed rather primitive in comparison. But the Igbo (also spelled Ibo) harbored a competitive and hustling culture that was not noticed until later. Under the British, the Igbo eagerly took to Christianity and to self-advancement through business, education, the civil service, and the military. The Igbo also scattered throughout Nigeria; Igbo merchants dominated much of the commercial life of Northern Nigeria, where they were despised for both their wealth and their religion. Some observers called them the "Jews of Nigeria" because they were hard-working, dispersed, better-off, and of a different faith. The Igbo were the most modern and educated Nigerians but were culturally at odds with more traditional Nigerians.

Independent Nigeria started destabilizing almost immediately; unrest and disorder broke out early and often. In response to the fraudulent elections of October 1965, in January 1966 a group of army officers, mainly Igbo, attempted a coup. Prime Minister Abubakar Tafawa Balewa, a Northern Muslim, was assassinated. General Johnson Aguiyi-Ironsi, an Igbo, took over with a plan to save Nigeria by turning it from a federal to a unitary system. Especially to the Muslims of the North, this looked like an Igbo conspiracy to seize the entire country. In July 1966 another coup, under Colonel Yakubu Gowon, a Christian from a small tribe in the center of Nigeria, the Anga, overthrew Ironsi, who was killed.

Nigeria's ethnic pot boiled over. In October 1966 murderous riots against Igbo merchants and their families in the North killed some 20,000 and sent perhaps a million Igbos streaming back to Igboland. After some futile efforts to hold Nigeria together, a consultative assembly of three Eastern states, knowing that they had Nigeria's oilfields, authorized an Igbo colonel, Odumegwu Ojukwu, to set up a separate country. On May 30, 1967, Ojukwu proclaimed the Republic of Biafra. The federal government also knew where the oil was and therefore had to get back the breakaway area. Much of the Biafra War was about oil. At first the Biafran army did well, almost reaching Lagos, until the Nigerian army under Gowon threw them back. For two painful years, the Biafra fighters held out, improvising munitions within a shrinking perimeter, until they finally collapsed in December 1969. Igbo deaths, mostly from starvation, are estimated at half a million.

Gowon was actually quite magnanimous in victory and brought back the Eastern states into Nigeria as equals within the federation, which he had divided into twelve states. It helped that he was from a small tribe that posed no threat to other ethnic groups. The oil boom that soon followed in the 1970s brought some jobs and a bit of prosperity. Gowon was overthrown by a coup in 1975 by Brigadier Murtala Ramat Mohammed, a Hausa Muslim from the North, who was himself assassinated in 1976. The Biafra War serves as a reminder of just how ethnically fragile Nigeria is and how risky it is to be a Nigerian head of state.

The Trouble with Nigeria

Nigeria has no shortage of intelligent, educated people. Two-thirds of Nigerians are literate, not bad for a still-poor developing country. Nigeria has considerable numbers of college graduates, some from British or U.S. universities. Many of its army officers were trained in British military academies.

Nigeria, in the theory of Samuel Huntington (see pages 328 and 528), is **cleft**, that is, it is split between Islam and Christianity, displaying what he calls "intercivilizational disunity." The two

cleft In Huntington's theory, a country split by two civilizations.

Geography

Bound Niger

Bounding Niger (a former French colony easy to confuse with Nigeria) teaches us more African geography than bounding Nigeria.

Niger is bounded on the north by Algeria and Libya;

on the east by Chad;

on the south by Nigeria (a former British colony), and Benin;

and on the west by Burkina Faso (formerly Upper Volta) and Mali.

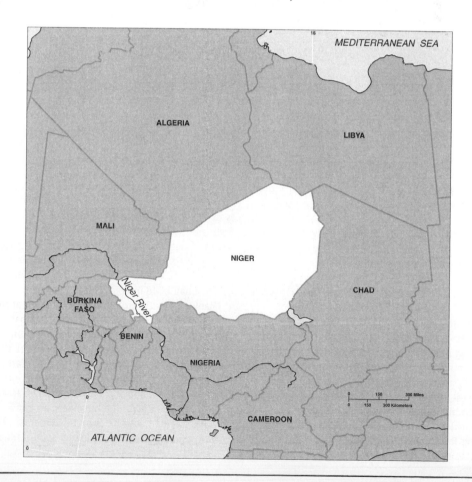

torn   In Huntington's theory, a country with a Westernizing elite but traditional masses.

cross-cutting cleavages   Multiple splits in society that make group loyalties overlap.

cumulative   Reinforcing one another.

civilizations rarely live peacefully within one country. Muslims especially tend to break away from such countries. Upon independence in 1947, Muslim Pakistan split from India, which is a majority Hindu. In Yugoslavia, Muslims in Bosnia and Kosovo refused to be ruled by Serbs. The Muslim Central Asian republics of the Soviet Union separated from it in late 1991. Muslim Turks broke away the north of Cyprus in 1974 from the Christian Greeks who held the reins of government. In a parallel with Nigeria, Christians in the south of Sudan—where oil has been discovered—tried to break away from the Muslims of the north. (Do not confuse "cleft countries" in Huntington's terms with **torn** countries, such as Turkey and Mexico, whose leaders wish to make them modern and Western despite mass reluctance.)

Nigeria is not unique in this regard. Most of the coastal nations of West Africa have a Muslim interior and a Christian coastal region. The reason: Islam came by land from the north and from Sudan; Christianity came by ship from Europe. East Africa, on the other hand, has a Muslim coast and a heavily Christian interior, as in Kenya and Tanzania. Some countries with the two faiths manage to get along tolerably well if they can keep religion in the personal sphere and have adherents of the two faiths dispersed enough to make it hard for either to claim a special area as theirs. The overlap of religion with politics in ethnically specific territories, though, can produce breakaway movements.

KEY CONCEPTS

CROSS-CUTTING CLEAVAGES

One of the puzzles of highly pluralistic or multiethnic societies is why they hold together. Why do they not break down into civil strife? One explanation, offered by the German sociologist Georg Simmel early in the twentieth century, is that successful pluralistic societies develop **cross-cutting cleavages**. They are divided, of course, but they are divided along several axes, not just one. When these divisions, or cleavages, cut across one another, they actually stabilize political life.

In Switzerland, for example, the cleavages of French-speaking or German-speaking, Catholic or Protestant, and working class or middle class give rise to eight possible combinations (for example, German-speaking, Protestant, middle class). But any combination has at least one attribute in common with six of the other seven combinations (for example, French-speaking, Protestant, working class). Because most Swiss have something in common with other Swiss, goes the theory, they moderate their conflicts.

Where cleavages do not cross-cut but instead are **cumulative**, dangerous divisions grow. A horrible case is ex-Yugoslavia, where all Croats are Catholic and all Serbs are Eastern Orthodox. The one cross-cutting cleavage that might have helped hold the country together—working class versus middle class—had been outlawed by the Communists. The several nationalities of Yugoslavia had little in common.

Many of Africa's troubles stem from an absence of cross-cutting cleavages. Tribe counts most, and in Nigeria this is usually reinforced by religion. Nigeria does have some cross-cutting cleavages. Not all Nigerian Muslims, for example, are Hausa-Fulani of the North; some are Yoruba in the Southwest, others are Ijaw in the Delta. Social class may also cut across tribal lines, as when a Yoruba businessman knows he has much in common with an Igbo businessman. Nigeria, indeed all of Africa, needs more such connections across tribal lines.

Political scientists have long celebrated "pluralism" (see page 75) as the basis of modern government and democracy. This is true but only within limits. There must be widespread agreement among groups to not take things too far and to live within certain rules and bounds. Lebanon and Nigeria have plenty of interactions among their many groups, but rules to limit the interactions are weak, so they turn competitive and violent, and the country breaks down. Pluralism without restraint leads to civil war.

Geography

BOUND KENYA

Kenya is bounded on the north by Sudan and Ethiopia;

on the east by Somalia and the Indian Ocean;

on the south by Tanzania;

and on the west by Uganda.

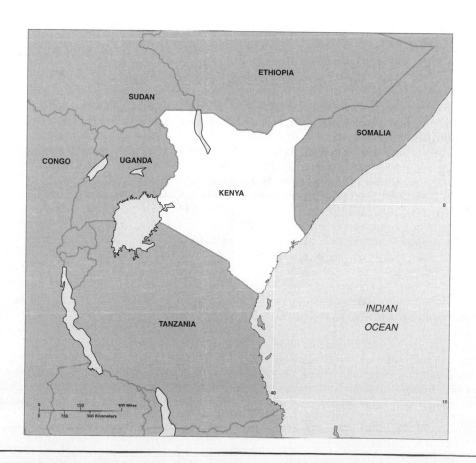

Democrats without Democracy

Most Nigerians want democracy but are bitterly dissatisfied with the present Nigeria government. Amidst corruption, rigged elections, ethnic strife, and poverty, a majority of Nigerians express dissatisfaction with the way democracy works in Nigeria. Two-thirds told a 2007 poll that they ex-pected the next elections would be unfair. Just wanting democracy does not necessarily make it happen. The problem is not that insuf-ficient numbers of Nigerians understand and desire democracy; there are more than enough educated Nigerians who do. If they were not divided by tribe and religion, Nigerians might have achieved stable democracy. The terrible dilemma for Nigerian democrats is that they know that whenever Nigeria attempts democracy—as it is doing now—it can easily fail amidst trib-al and religious animosities, corruption, and military power-grabs. Still, most Nigerians have not given up on democracy.

developmentalism   Early 1960s theory that America could develop Third World lands.

Democracy

The Developmentalist Impulse

In the late 1950s the Cold War refocused from Europe to the Third World. Academics and the U.S. government became fascinated with the developing areas, where the big showdown with communism was to come. Many uni-versities offered "area studies" of Southeast Asia, Africa, Latin America, and every other part of the globe. In a parallel to the academic misperceptions of the Soviet Union (see page 356), political scientists were much too optimistic in supposing the Third World would achieve stable democracy and economic growth. Some developing countries, mainly on the rim of Asia, did achieve both, but few academics predicted these suc-cess stories in advance. As Princeton economist Paul Krugman points out, no one has successfully predicted the next country or region of rapid economic growth; it always surprises us.

The academics' poor predictions grew out of the per-vasive American fear that the Soviets would take over most of the developing areas. Cuba and the 1962 Mis-sile Crisis were frightening warnings. Kennedy's advi-sors wrote urgently that either we develop the newly independent lands or the Communists will. They were in a shaky, vulnerable transition, but U.S. help could guide them through it and put them on the path to free-market democracy. This came to be called **developmentalism**. The Kennedy administration re-sponded with the Agency for International Develop-ment, the Peace Corps, and Vietnam.

The U.S. Agency for International Development (AID), the CIA, and the Ford Foundation funded stud-ies on implementing developmentalist strategies, and academics won grants and built theories to support them. Improving communications was touted as an im-portant technique. But Third World countries developed along the lines of their own internal logic, not ours. Some received lots of U.S. money and advice and bombed. Others received little and prospered. The the-ories underestimated the impact of culture by assuming that all peoples are culturally ready for development. One key topic was almost totally overlooked: corrup-tion. In an echo of the 1960s, new alarms now urge us to democratize the Middle East before radical Islam takes it over. Review the mistaken developmentalism of the 1960s before you sign up.

PATTERNS OF INTERACTION

Mexico is a weak state, characterized by the penetration of crime into politics. Nigeria is even weaker but is not yet a *failed state* (see page 2) such as Somalia or Afghanistan, where national government effectively ceased. Nigeria has a central government and a strong incentive

praetorianism Tendency for military takeovers.

for most of Nigeria's elites to keep the country intact: graft from the lush oil revenues. If Nigeria fell apart, only the Niger Delta would have the oil. This was one of the roots of the Biafra War.

COUNT THE COUPS

Weak states often experience repeated military coups, a condition known as **praetorianism** (see box on page 532). It indicates that the normal institutions of government—parliaments, parties, and presidents—have too little legitimacy and authority to stand up in times of stress. Most coups are easy and involve little fighting, because the government has no mass support. Let us count Nigeria's military coups (see table).

Year	Ousted	Installed
1966 (Jan.)	Balewa (Hausa) killed	Ironsi (Igbo)
1966 (July)	Ironsi killed	Gowon (Anga)
1975	Gowon deposed	Mohammed (Hausa)
1976	Mohammed killed	Obasanjo (Yoruba)
1983	Shagari (Fulani) deposed	Buhari (Hausa)
1985	Buhari deposed	Babangida (Gwari)
1993	Babangida deposed	Abacha (Hausa)

The best of the lot was Obasanjo, who in 1979 turned power over to a civilian government but returned to office as the democratically elected president of Nigeria from 1999 to 2007. The worst was Sani Abacha, a cruel supercrook who, with his family to help him, looted at least $3 billion of Nigerian oil money and stashed it in Swiss, British, and U.S. banks. Oil revenues give a great incentive for Nigerian generals to think about coups. Another cause of Nigeria's coups is apparent: disputes among ethnic groups, a reflection of Nigeria's fractured political culture. Northern Muslims especially bristle at rule by Southern Christians and vice-versa.

Nigeria still seethes with poverty and violence and could experience another coup. Praetorianism tends to become a self-reinfecting illness endemic in the Third World. A country that has had a coup will likely have others. Bolivia has had dozens of coups since independence. Brazil last had a coup in 1964 and was ruled by generals until 1985. Mexico during the nineteenth century was praetorian, but Calles ended it by bringing Mexico's main political forces into one party, the PRI. Nigeria's problem is that it has not yet developed the equivalent of PRI, a dominant nationwide party.

patronage   Giving government jobs to political supporters.

The praetorian tendency raises the question: If these countries slide so easily into military rule, why do they ever slide out? Why does a military dictator ever leave power? The material rewards from control over natural resources could be ample incentives to stay in office forever. The means for keeping power are well known and widely practiced in the Third World: **patronage** and *clientelism* (discussed in the Mexico chapter). Mobutu seized power in a 1965 coup and ruled and robbed the Congo (which he renamed Zaire) until 1997, with the flimsy cover story that he was the only one who could keep the country together. His real strength was the patronage and clientelistic networks he developed. Sani Abacha of Nigeria set up similar networks and died in office of a heart attack in 1998.

But other forces work against permanent military government. Military officers overthrow governments that have little *legitimacy,* but the military regime then has even less legitimacy. The military rulers know they are unpopular. A few heads of military regimes may be genuine patriots and professional soldiers who recognize that military government soon turns rotten. Obasanjo, for example, in 1979 handed power over to a civilian government. The Brazilian generals who seized power in 1964 boasted how they would end inflation and modernize the Brazilian economy. By the 1980s they were embarrassed as their economic miracle stalled; they left power in 1985.

A more persuasive motive for dictators to leave is their recognition that an angry mob or their own officers could overthrow them. Every general who has seized power in a coup knows that there are several colleagues waiting to do the same to him. With no legitimacy to rely on, the dictator may for a time buy support with pieces of graft, but sooner or later those bought off ask, "Why settle for a piece?" Praetorian systems are rife with conspiracies. The dictator may sense when the time has come to flee with his life and his offshore bank accounts.

KEY CONCEPTS

THE PRAETORIAN TENDENCY

As the Roman Empire ossified and crumbled, the emperor's bodyguard, the Praetorian Guard, came to play a powerful role, making and unmaking emperors, some of them their own officers. Political scientists now use praetorianism for a situation where the military feels it must take over the government in order to save the country from chaos.

Praetorianism is not just a problem of power-hungry generals but reflects deep conflict in the whole society. In praetorian societies, it is not only the generals who want to take power, but many other groups as well: Students, labor unions, revolutionaries, and demagogic politicians would like to seize the state machinery. Institutional constraints and balances have broken down; nobody plays by the rules. In such situations of chaos and breakdown, it is the army among the many power contenders that is best equipped to seize power, so praetorianism usually means military takeover, the case in Nigeria.

WHAT NIGERIANS QUARREL ABOUT

Thanks to the big runup in oil prices, Nigeria's GDP growth has been a decent 6 percent a year recently, but much is eaten up by a population growth of 2.4 percent a year (the result of Nigeria's high *fertility rate* of 5.45). Little of the petroleum income goes to investments that give Nigerians jobs and raise their abysmal living standards. Unemployment is high and getting higher. As we discussed in the Mexico chapter, oil wealth is a poor foundation for economic growth. Upon independence in 1960, Nigeria had roughly the same per capita GDP as several East Asian countries. Forty years later, these Asian lands were many times richer than Nigeria.

Political scientists and economists have sought explanations at several levels for this growing gap. They divide into two great camps: explanations from the physical and material world, and explanations from the cultural and psychological realm. The two, of course, are not exclusive; it is likely that one feeds into the other in a continual loop.

The most obvious explanation—that the poor countries have few natural resources—does not hold up. Nigeria and Indonesia have great mineral wealth but are poor. Japan, South Korea, Taiwan, Hong Kong, and Singapore have almost no natural resources and are rich. There may even be an inverse relationship between natural resources and prosperity. Oil may be a curse, its revenues a prize for corruption. With few natural resources, Asian Rimland countries had to get clever, competitive, and productive. It is not natural resources but incentivized humans that really matter.

Another culprit is imperialism, but it does not provide a complete explanation. In some countries there was a great deal of imperialist exploitation; others, where there was not much to exploit, were left largely alone. The imperialists did

Nigerians understand markets, as in this crowded street market in Lagos.

not do nearly enough to get their colonies ready for independence. They should have provided more education and training.

But colonialism does not explain success stories in some ex-colonies. Consider what Hong Kong and Singapore had working against them. Both had been British colonies for more than a century.

534 CHAPTER 31 NIGERIA

strategic variable Factor you can change that makes a big improvement.

policy The specific choices governments make.

transparency Exchanges of money open to public scrutiny. (Opposite: *opacity*.) (See page 535.)

Both are small islands with zero natural resources; they were economically important only for their locations. Both were occupied by the Japanese in World War II. That should predict poverty, but now both are thriving economies at the First World level.

In explaining such apparent anomalies, cultural factors loom large. Some cultures take quickly to economic development, others do not. Those who believe that the future can be formed by one's own activities generally do well. Fatalism, on the other hand, keeps people passive; all is God's will. Cultures that instill discipline and a work ethic can grow rapidly. So far, the winners in this cultural race seem to be the Confucian-influenced lands of East Asia, although few predicted their growth. Indeed, some decades ago scholars attributed Asia's *backwardness* to its Confucian heritage. In the right circumstances, as we discussed in the India chapter (see page 460), a seemingly sleepy culture can wake up and produce an economic miracle. In Nigeria, the Igbo are an example of this; what was latent in their culture became manifest under the British. Do not write off Africa as forever poor. Cultures change.

Some social scientists seek a **strategic variable**, and that is usually in the area of **policy**, a regime's decisions, laws, and programs that may either push or retard growth. Governments have two types of economic policy tools, macroeconomic and microeconomic. Some economists urge governments to get the *macroeconomy* (see page 289), sometimes called "the fundamentals," in order—little public debt, plentiful savings, low inflation, sufficient investment capital—and then stand back and let the market do its stuff. The German "economic miracle" followed this pattern. Third World technocrats—who are now as prominent in Nigeria as they are in Mexico—tend, however, to get into the microeconomy by choosing which industries to foster or phase out. Postwar Japan used considerable microeconomic management (as well as getting its fundamentals right).

Nigeria shows signs of both macro- and microeconomic mismanagement. The president and ministers often propose major reforms, but that means inflicting some of the pain of austerity, at least for the short term. (For the pain of austerity in Mexico, see page 495.) Such reforms could also help clean up corruption. Nigeria's inflation, debt, and unemployment suggest poor choices at the macro level. And the oil industry, in Nigeria as in Mexico, is a constant temptation for microeconomic meddling. Leaving it to market forces would likely produce the best growth. In both countries, that is improbable. Economic rationality often conflicts with political expediency.

The impact of a given policy is hard to judge in advance; you have to see how it works out. Generous public spending (a macroeconomic policy) may keep Nigeria's state governments compliant but unleash inflation, currently around 20 percent a year in Nigeria. Nigeria keeps fuel prices low, because Nigerians demand a special deal on the gasoline they produce. Nigerian subsidies for fuel (a microeconomic policy) mean less to sell on the world market. Nigeria's technocrats understand that the subsidies must be cut, but then you get riots.

THE CORRUPTION FACTOR

Since independence in 1960, Nigerian officials have stolen over $400 billion of the country's oil revenues, and none has been publicly tried for corruption, suggesting that other officials fear what might come out in a trial. Little petroleum money reaches ordinary Nigerians, who stay terribly poor. This is one reason per capita GDP numbers—like all averages—can deceive. Yes, Nigerian oil earns the country a lot, but very few people benefit from the earnings.

COMPARISON

CORRUPTION INTERNATIONAL

Corruption is nearly everywhere, finds Transparency International, a Berlin-based organization that polls business people on their perceptions of having to pay off government officials. TI ranks countries on a ten-point scale, ten being totally clean, one totally corrupt. Some of their 2007 Corruption Perception Index (CPI) findings are shown in the table below.

TI founder Peter Eigen was a World Bank official in charge of loans to East Africa but concluded that so much was skimmed off in graft that the loans did little good. To call attention to the massive problem—and to put pressure on governments for **transparency** in their financial dealings—he formed TI in 1993. A poor TI ranking chastises a corrupt country by scaring away business and aid donors, hopefully pushing it to get clean.

Some scholars doubt the accuracy of the CPI (not to be confused with the U.S. Consumer Price Index), because it is just a compilation of subjective perceptions. These change from year to year—depending on which businessmen are interviewed—and countries often trade positions on the TI rankings even though little in their behavior has actually changed. That weakness is built into TI's methodology, but there is no other way to measure corruption, even approximately. Corruption (along with drugs and crime) does not show up in GDP calculations, and crooked officials do not list "earnings from kickbacks" on their income tax. TI's CPI is the best measure we have. The big question is, will TI's efforts over time increase rule of law and boost economic growth?

Finland	9.4
Singapore	9.3
Canada	8.7
Britain	8.4
Germany	7.8
Japan	7.5
France	7.3
United States	7.2
Chile	7.0
Israel	6.1
Italy	5.2
South Africa	5.1
India	3.5
Mexico	3.5
China	3.5
Iran	2.5
Russia	2.3
Nigeria	2.2
Iraq	1.5

Source: Transparency International

kickback   Payoff to government official for a contract.

Nigeria's Economic and Financial Crimes Commission (EFCC) in 2007 charged 135 officials with corruption. Critics say that the EFCC uses corruption charges as political weapons to make disfavored candidates ineligible for election. President Obasanjo charged his vice-president, Atiku Abubakar, with misusing a $125 million oil fund. Abubakar countered that Obasanjo was out to get him for leaving the PDP and joining the opposition AC, which several did to protest Obasanjo's dictatorial tendencies. The head of the EFCC was booted out in 2008 when he started investigating former state governors, and the EFCC lost credibility. In Nigeria, one cannot tell genuine from political charges of corruption. Chances are, both accuser and accused are corrupt.

The corruption factor trips up the best-laid plans for the developing countries. In addition to the obvious poverty and injustice, it hijacks investment capital into private pockets and away from development. Corruption can be divided into petty and grand. The petty is the small demands for cash—called "dash" or "sweetbread" in West Africa. A friend of mine once flew into Lagos (then the capital of Nigeria) on an assignment for the World Bank. An airport "health officer" stopped him, saying his inoculation record (often required for travel in the tropics) was missing a stamp (it wasn't), but he could fix it for $20. My friend refused, arguing that he was there to help Nigeria. A higher official came and urged him to pay: "You are a rich man, and he is a poor man." My friend finally paid. Such holdups are still standard at Lagos airport and show the logic of petty corruption. Any time you need a stamp, permit, license, or help from the police—even driving or parking a car—in the Third World, be prepared to pay sweetbread, *la mordida*, or *baksheesh*. It is a normal part of daily life. In Nigeria, police set up road blocks and demand 15 cents per car.

Some see petty corruption as an unofficial welfare system to redistribute wealth from the better off to the poor, but it seldom goes to the truly needy and does not spare those with little money. Petty corruption is the demands of underpaid policemen and bureaucrats who are in a position to help or hurt. The historical root of Third World corruption is a less-developed country acquiring a large bureaucracy before it was ready for one. Spain set up Latin America with a giant bureaucracy to supervise its extractive economy, and it has been the source of corruption there ever since. One solution is to pay civil servants more, but developing countries can seldom afford to. Another is to cut the number of regulations and the bureaucrats needed to enforce them. Chile got a lot less corrupt after it did both.

Petty corruption is a minor annoyance compared to grand corruption, the use of official positions to siphon money wholesale—called "eating" in Nigeria. Grand corruption depends on international ties, such as oil contracts and banks that launder money. Petty corruption stays inside the country, but if the money goes into overseas accounts you can be sure it is the grand variety. The governor of oil-rich Bayelsa state stashed millions abroad and was arrested in Britain in 2005 but slipped out disguised as a woman. Back in Nigeria he enjoyed immunity as a governor. Transparency International's CPI (see box on page 535) does not distinguish between the two levels. Theoretically, a country could have grand corruption at the highest levels and still have an honest civil service, and vice versa. But it is unlikely, for one is usually a reflection of the other. If a postal clerk steals your stamps, chances are the minister of communications is stealing much larger amounts. Grand corruption does far more damage than petty corruption, for it eats capital that should go for economic growth, health, and education. It is a major factor in keeping the Third World poor.

Grand corruption is not simply a matter of crooks in government but of foreign businesses willing to pay them—usually by **kickbacks**—for profitable contracts. Many corporations that would never kick back on contracts in their home countries reckon it is normal in the Third World: If they do not pay, a competing firm that does pay will get the contract. There is no quick, simple cure for corruption, which sometimes feels as if it is rooted in the soil. Some countries have developed an ethos of clean administration, but this may take centuries. A nobleman developed the Swedish civil service in the seventeenth century and hired other aristocrats, thereby stamping the Swedish bureaucracy with traditions of honor and service. Looking at the TI rankings (see box on page 535), we might all wish to become Finns or Singaporeans. There is a hopeful sign here, as Singapore is a new country (independent only in 1965) that started poor but cultivated, under draconian penalties, an ethos of clean administration in a part of the world known for the opposite. With enough will at the top, it can be done.

Oil and Democracy

There is an unhappy correlation between petroleum wealth and nondemocratic government. One of the few democratic oil-producing countries is Norway, but it has many other industries and a long history of democracy. Note how the four major oil-producing countries of this book—Russia, Mexico, Nigeria, and Iran—are (or recently were) nondemocratic. Russia attempted democracy but slid

DEMOCRACY

CORPORATE SOCIAL RESPONSIBILITY

A current business buzzword is "corporate social responsibility" (CSR). According to CSR doctrine, large firms must recognize that they owe more than profits to shareholders; they owe fairness and justice to "stakeholders"—their workers, the community, and the environment. Now most corporations' annual reports trumpet their CSR activities, although critics charge they are little more than public relations.

Nigeria offers a good example of CSR—or lack of it—in action. Shell, Chevron, and other oil companies make immense profits from the Niger Delta, but their operations pollute soil and water, leaving local people to sicken and die young. Many fishermen and farmers have lost their livelihood. Poverty feeds rising ethnic tensions in the Delta, where well-armed Ijaw gangs demand "self-determination," that is, control of the oil. The oil companies pay them protection money. Strikes and sabotage are common, and violence, some involving the Nigerian army, takes an estimated thousand lives a year in the Delta. Ken SaroWiwa, a writer and environmental activist from the small Ogoni tribe in the oil region, was hanged in 1995 on trumped-up murder charges. His real crime was calling attention to the ecological damage uncontrolled oil pumping had done to his people. The Nigerian government depends on oil revenues and did not like that kind of criticism.

Most agree that the oil companies have a responsibility, but carrying it out is difficult. The oil companies pay the Nigerian government billions a year in taxes and royalties, but much of it disappears into private pockets; little gets back to the Delta. Trying to practice CSR, the oil companies have also given millions to the Niger Delta Development Commission, but it too is corrupt and inefficient. The companies, aware of the poverty and resentment, also build health clinics in the Delta, but many of them are either empty (because the government will not staff them) or burned down by neighboring tribes who are jealous that they did not get a clinic.

There is no way CSR can deliver help to poor Nigerians; it will always get skimmed. The best thing would be to get the Nigerian government to adopt accountability and transparency standards, but the oil companies have no leverage for this. Said one Chevron executive in Nigeria: "It's very difficult for the private sector to replace government. It's not our role." Some economists argue that corporations should just produce income, out of which come wages and taxes. Stakeholders have real grievances, but they must act through democratic governments to obtain pollution laws, fair wages, public health, and so on. These things need force of law, not corporate generosity. Do not expect CSR to solve vast problems of poverty and corruption.

absolute poverty   Living on $1 a day or less.

micro-loan   Small unsecured loan (of a few hundred dollars) to beginning businesses.

back to authoritarianism. Mexico is coming out of a long period of one-party domination. Nigeria at this moment has an elected government but for two-thirds of its history did not. And Iran overthrew one tyrant but now has worse ones.

What is there about oil that works against democracy? True, it produces vast wealth, but the wealth is terribly concentrated, mostly in government hands, and seldom benefits the whole society. Oil becomes the great prize of politics in that country, for he who controls the oil monopolizes power. One of Putin's main efforts (successful) was to bring back most petroleum production into state hands. The oil industry employs relatively few, and its wealth is squandered in corruption, overlarge bureaucracies, showcase projects, and rewards for supporters of the regime. The oil bonanza lets rulers avoid investing in infrastructure, industry, and other long-term growth mechanisms. The petrostates' impressive incomes have netted them little that can be sustained after the oil runs out. When that happens, the elites will still have their secret overseas bank accounts to live well forever. Their citizens will be poor.

Such is the story of Nigeria, a country with major oil revenues where some three-quarters of the people live in **absolute poverty**. And even with its oil wealth, Nigeria still has an international debt of $30 billion. Some oil was found long ago in the Niger Delta around Port Harcourt, but major oilfields came on line in the 1970s, just as oil prices were quadrupling. Like Iran, Nigeria is a member of OPEC (see page 547), which assigns quotas to member states to keep oil production down and its price up. The good thing about Nigeria here is that it is one of the easiest OPEC members to bribe to get officials to (secretly) produce above Nigeria's quota.

What to do with the oil has thus become one of Nigeria's most difficult political problems: How to make sure oil serves the long-term good of all Nigerians? Most Nigerian oil was produced through joint ventures between foreign firms and the Nigerian National Petroleum Corporation (NNPC), which got most of the revenues. Like Mexico's Pemex, the NNPC was notoriously corrupt. President Yar'Adua broke up the NNPC into five smaller companies to fight corruption and boost efficiency. It is too early to tell if this will work. Some are tempted to nationalize all Nigerian oil production, but that would simply concentrate more wealth and encourage more corruption. Privatizing Nigeria's oil might help, but only if it were total, that is, with oil companies able to buy the oilfields outright. No Nigerian government is likely to sell the fields; that would eliminate the kickbacks that come from leases. The stated reason for rejecting any such sales, as in Mexico, will always be: "What? Sell Nigeria's sacred patrimony to greedy foreign capitalists? Never!" Nationalism cloaks corruption.

One possibility is a joint Nigerian-international board of supervisors (perhaps staffed by Finns and Singaporeans) with power of oversight and audit. Such a board would make Nigeria's oil deals transparent and take them out of government hands. The oil revenues should not go to Nigeria's federal treasury, where they could be disbursed to favored tribes and officials, but into an internationally supervised bank to make loans for infrastructure, education, and founding and expanding valid enterprises. **Micro-loans** have been effective in encouraging thousands of start-up businesses—sometimes just one woman with a sewing machine—at low cost in developing areas. If done well and honestly, oil could give Nigeria a growing economy that would use but not depend on petroleum.

We sometimes forget that there are African success stories. Senegal, Mali, and Botswana are examples of positive development. Effective leadership, sound policies, and the promotion of a national political culture make a difference. Remember, we used to write off Asia as hopeless.

Key Terms

absolute poverty (p. 538)

aquifer (p. 513)

caliphate (p. 513)

cleft country (p. 527)

colonialism (p. 516)

cross-cutting cleavages
  (p. 528)

cumulative (p. 528)

desiccation (p. 513)

developmentalism (p. 530)

divide and rule (p. 516)

indirect rule (p. 516)

jihad (p. 513)

kickback (p. 536)

micro-loan (p. 538)

pan-Africanism (p. 519)

patronage (p. 532)

policy (p. 534)

praetorianism (p. 531)

Sahel (p. 513)

savanna (p. 513)

sharia (p. 522)

strategic variable (p. 534)

sub-Saharan (p. 513)

torn country (p. 528)

transparency (p. 534)

Further Reference

Apter, Andrew H. *The Pan-African Nation: Oil and the Spectacle of Culture in Nigeria.* Chicago, IL: University of Chicago Press, 2005.

Bah, Abu Bakarr. *Breakdowns and Reconstruction: Democracy, the Nation-State, and Ethnicity in Nigeria.* Blue Ridge Summit, PA: Lexington Books, 2005.

Coleman, James S. *Nigeria: Background to Nationalism.* Berkeley, CA: University of California Press, 1963.

Farris, Jacqueline W., and Mohammed Bomoi, eds. *Shehu Musa Yar'Adua: A Biography.* Boulder, CO: L. Rienner, 2004.

Gordon, April A., and Donald L. Gordon, eds. *Understanding Contemporary Africa,* 4th ed. Boulder, CO: L. Rienner, 2006.

Howe, Herbert M. *Ambiguous Order: Military Forces in African States.* Boulder, CO: L. Rienner, 2004.

Larémont, Ricardo René, ed. *Borders, Nationalism, and the African State.* Boulder, CO: L. Rienner, 2005.

Lewis, Peter M. *Growing Apart: Oil, Politics, and Economic Change in Indonesia and Nigeria.* Ann Arbor, MI: University of Michigan Press, 2007.

Moss, Todd J. *African Development: Making Sense of the Issues and Actors.* Boulder, CO: L. Rienner, 2007.

Paden, John N. *Faith and Politics in Nigeria: Nigeria as a Pivotal State in the Muslim World.* Washington, D.C.: U.S. Institute of Peace, 2008.

Rotberg, Robert I., ed. *Crafting the New Nigeria: Confronting the Challenges.* Boulder, CO: L. Rienner, 2004.

Soyinka, Wole. *You Must Set Forth at Dawn.* New York: Random House, 2006.

CHAPTER 32
IRAN

M uch of Iran is an arid plateau around 4,000 feet above sea level. Some areas are rainless desert; some get sufficient rain only for sparse sheep pasture. In this part of the world, irrigation made civilization possible, and whatever disrupted waterworks had devastating consequences. Persia's location made it an important trade route between East and West, one of the links between the Middle East and Asia. Persia thus became a crossroads of civilizations and one of the earliest of the great civilizations.

QUESTIONS TO CONSIDER

1. What has geography contributed to Iran's development?
2. How does Iran differ from Arab countries?
3. What is a *modernizing tyrant*? Why do they fail?
4. What factors brought Iran's Islamic Revolution?
5. How would you explain Iran's dual executive? Who is more powerful?
6. Does modernization always bring secularization?
7. How would you explain the power struggle in Iran?
8. How have America and Iran misunderstood each other?
9. Why is the Persian Gulf region strategic?

THE IMPACT OF THE PAST

The trouble with being a crossroads is that your country becomes a target for conquest. Indo-European-speaking invaders took over Persia about the fifteenth century B.C. and laid the basis for subsequent Persian culture. Their most famous kings: Cyrus and Darius in the sixth century B.C. The invasions never ceased, though: the Greeks under Alexander in the third and fourth centuries B.C., the Arab Islamic conquest in the seventh century A.D., Turkish tribes in the eleventh century, Mongols in the thirteenth century, and many others. The repeated pattern was one of conquest, the founding of a new dynasty, and its falling apart as quarrelsome heirs broke it into petty kingdoms. This fragmentation set up the country for easy conquest again.

Iran, known for most of history as Persia (it was renamed only in 1925), resembles China in that it is heir to an ancient and magnificent civilization that, partly at the hands of outsiders, fell into "the sleep of nations." When it awoke, it was far behind the West, which, like China, Iran views as an adversary. If and how Iran will move into modernity is one of our major questions.

Although it does not look or sound like it, Persian (*Farsi*) is a member of the broad Indo-European family of languages; the neighboring Arabic and Turkic are not. Today, Farsi is the mother tongue of about half of Iranians. Another fifth speak Persian-related languages (such as Kurdish). A quarter speak a Turkic language, and some areas speak Arabic and other tongues. The non-Farsi speakers occupy the Iranian periphery and have at times been discontent with rule by Persians. In Iranian politics today, to be descended from one of the non-Persian minorities is held against politicians.

GEOGRAPHY

BOUND IRAN

Iran is bounded on the north by Armenia, Azerbaijan, the Caspian Sea, and Turkmenistan;

on the east by Afghanistan and Pakistan;

on the south by the Gulf of Oman and the Persian Gulf;

and on the west by Iraq and Turkey.

THE ARAB CONQUEST

Allah's prophet Muhammad died in Arabia in 632, but his religion spread like wildfire. **Islam** means "submission" (to God's will), and this was to be hastened by the sword. Islam arrived soon in Iran by military conquest. The remnant of the Sassanid Empire, already exhausted by centuries of warfare with Byzantium, was easily beaten by the Arabs at Qadisiya in 637 and within two centuries Persia was mostly Muslim. Adherents of the old religion, Zoroastrianism, fled to India where today they are a small, prosperous minority known as Parsis (see page 459).

Islam	Religion founded by Muhammad.
Shia	Minority branch of Islam.
Sunni	Mainstream Islam.

The Arab conquest was a major break with the past. In contrast to the sharp social stratification of Persian tradition, Islam taught that all Muslims were, at least in a spiritual sense, equal. Persia adopted the Arabic script, and many Arab words enriched Persian. Persian culture flowed the other way, too, as the Arabs copied Persian architecture and civil administration. For six centuries, Persia was swallowed up by the Arab empires, but in 1055 the Seljuk Turks invaded from Central Asia and conquered most of the Middle East. As usual, their rule soon fell apart into many small states, easy prey for Genghis Khan, the Mongol "World Conqueror" whose horde thundered in from the east in 1219. One of his descendants who ruled Persia embraced Islam at the end of that century. This is part of a pattern Iranians are proud of: "We may be conquered," they say, "but the conqueror ends up adopting our superior culture and becomes one of us."

The coming of the Safavid dynasty in 1501 boosted development of a distinctly Iranian identity. The Safavids practiced a minority version of Islam called **Shia** (see box on page 544) and decreed it Persia's state religion. Most of their subjects switched from **Sunni** Islam and are Shias to this day. Neighboring Sunni powers immediately attacked Safavid Persia, but this enabled the new regime to consolidate its control and develop an Islam with Persian characteristics.

WESTERN PENETRATION

It is too simple to say Western cultural, economic, and colonial penetration brought down the great Persian empire. Safavid Persia was attacked from several directions, mostly by neighboring Muslim powers: the Ottoman Turks from the west, Uzbeks from the north, and Afghans from the northeast. In fighting the Ottomans, Safavid rulers made common cause with the early Portuguese, Dutch, and English sea traders in the late sixteenth and early seventeenth centuries. As previously in the region's history, the outsiders were able to invade because the local kingdoms had weakened themselves in wars, a pattern that continues in our day.

In 1722, Afghan invaders ended the Safavid dynasty, but no one was able to govern the whole country. After much chaos, in 1795 the Qajar dynasty emerged victorious. Owing to Persian weakness, Britain and Russia became dominant in Persia, the Russians pushing in from the north, the British from India. Although never a colony, Persia, like China, slid into semicolonial status, with much of its political and economic life dependent on imperial designs, something Persians strongly resented. A particularly vexatious example was an 1890 treaty giving British traders a monopoly on tobacco sales in Persia. Muslim clerics led mass hatred of the British tobacco concession, and the treaty was repealed.

Majlis   Arabic for assembly; Iran's parliament.

shah   Persian for king.

At this same time, liberal, Western ideas of government seeped into Persia, some brought, as in China, by Christian missionaries (who made very few Persian converts). The Constitutional Revolution of 1906–1907 (in which an American supporter of the popular struggle was killed) brought Persia's first constitution and first elected parliament, the **Majlis**. The struggles over the tobacco concession and constitution were led by a combination of two forces: liberals who hated the monarchy and wanted Western-type institutions and Muslim clerics who also disliked the monarchy but wanted a stronger role for Islam. This same combination brought down the **Shah** in 1979; now these two strands have turned against each other over the future of Iran.

Notice how at almost exactly the same time—1905 in Russia, 1906 in Persia—corrupt and weak monarchies promised somewhat democratic constitutions in the face of popular uprisings. Both monarchies, dedicated to autocratic power and hating democracy, only pretended to deliver, a prescription for increasing mass discontent. A new shah inherited the throne in 1907 and shut down the Majlis with his Russian-trained Cossack bodyguard unit. Mass protest forced the last Qajar shah to flee to Russia in 1909; he tried to return in 1911 but was forced back even though Russian troops occupied Tehran. The 1907 Anglo-Russian treaty had already cut Persia in two, with a Russian sphere of influence in the north and a British one in the south. During World War I, Persia was nominally neutral, but its strategic location turned into a zone of contention and chaos. Neighboring Turkey allied with Germany, and Russia and Britain allied with each other. Russian, British and German agents tried to tilt Persia their way.

GEOGRAPHY

SUNNI AND SHIA

Over 80 percent of the world's Muslims practice the mainstream branch of Islam, called Sunni (from *sunna*, the word of the Prophet). A minority branch (of 100 million) called Shia is scattered unevenly throughout the Muslim world. The two split early over who was the true successor (*caliph*) of Muhammad. Shias claim the Prophet's cousin and son-in-law Ali has the title, but he was assassinated in 661. Shia means followers or partisans, hence Shias are the followers of Ali. When Ali's son, Hussein, attempted to claim the title, his forces were beaten at Karbala in present-day Iraq (now a Shia shrine) in 680, and Hussein was betrayed and tortured to death. This gave Shia a fixation on martyrdom; some of their holidays feature self-flagellation.

Shia also developed a messianic concept that was lacking in Sunni. Shias in Iran hold that the line of succession passed through a series of twelve *imams* (religious leaders) of whom Ali was the first. The twelfth imam disappeared in 873 but is to return one day to "fill the world with justice." He is referred to as the Hidden Imam and the Expected One.

Shias are no more "fundamentalist" than other Muslims, who also interpret the Koran strictly. Although the origin and basic tenets of the two branches is identical, Sunnis regard Shias as extremist, mystical, and crazy. Some 60 percent of Iraqis are Shia, but only in Iran is Shia the state religion. With their underdog status elsewhere, some Shias rebel (with Iranian money and guidance), as in Lebanon, southern Iraq, and eastern Arabia. Shia imparts a peculiar twist to Iranians, giving them the feeling of being isolated but right, beset by enemies on all sides, and willing to martyr themselves for their cause.

THE FIRST PAHLAVI

As is often the case when a country degenerates into chaos, military officers see themselves as saviors of the nation, the *praetorianism* that we saw in Nigeria. In 1921 an illiterate cavalry officer, Reza Khan, commander of the Cossack brigade, seized power and in 1925 had himself crowned shah, the founder of the short lived (1925–1979) Pahlavi dynasty. The nationalistic Reza took the pre-Islamic surname Pahlavi and told the world to start calling the country by its true name, Iran, from the word *aryan*, indicating the country's Indo-European roots. (Nazi ideologists also loved the word aryan, which they claimed indicated genetic superiority. Indeed, the ancient Persian Zoroastrians preached racial purity.)

> **modernizing tyrant**   Dictator who pushes a country ahead.
>
> **secular**   Nonreligious.
>
> **mosque**   Muslim house of worship.
>
> **Ottoman**   Turkish imperial dynasty, fourteenth to twentieth centuries.

Like Atatürk, Reza Shah was determined to modernize his country (see box below). His achievements were impressive. He molded an effective Iranian army and used it to suppress tribal revolts and unify Iran. He created a modern, European-type civil service and a national bank. He replaced traditional and Islamic courts with civil courts operating under Western codes of justice. In 1935 he founded Iran's first Western-style university. Under state supervision and fueled by oil revenues, Iran's economy grew. Also like Atatürk, Reza Shah ordered his countrymen to adopt Western dress and women to stop wearing the veil. But Reza also kept the press and Majlis closely obedient. Critics and dissidents often died in jail. Reza Shah was a classic **modernizing tyrant**.

World War II put Iran in the same situation as World War I had. It was just too strategic to leave alone; it was a major oil producer and conduit for U.S. supplies to the desperate Soviet Union. As before, the Russians took over in the north and the British (later the Americans) in the south. Both agreed to clear out six months after the war ended. Reza Shah, who tilted toward Germany, in September 1941 was exiled by the British to South Africa, where he died in 1944. Before he left, he abdicated in favor of his son, Muhammad Reza Pahlavi.

COMPARISON

ATATÜRK AND REZA SHAH

During the 1920s, two strong personalities in adjacent Middle Eastern lands attempted to modernize their countries from above: Kemal Atatürk in Turkey and Reza Shah in Iran. Both were nationalistic military officers and Muslims but **secular** in outlook; both wished to separate **mosque** and state.

In economics, both were statists (see page 120) and made the government the number-one investor and owner of major industries. Both pushed education, the improved status of women, and Western clothing. As such, both aroused traditionalist opposition led by Muslim clerics. Both thundered "You will be modern!" but religious forces opposed their reforms, and do to this day.

Their big difference: Atatürk ended the **Ottoman** monarchy and firmly supported a republican form of government in Turkey. He pushed his reforms piecemeal through parliament, which often opposed him. Reza Shah rejected republicanism and parliaments as too messy; he insisted on an authoritarian monarchy as the only way to modernize his unruly country, as did his son. Although Turkey has had plenty of troubles since Atatürk, it has not been ripped apart by revolution. Atatürk built some political institutions; the Pahlavi shahs built none.

containment   U.S. Cold War policy of blocking expansion of communism.

The Americans and British left Iran in 1945; the Soviets did not, and some argue this incident marked the start of the Cold War. Stalin claimed that Azerbaijan, a Soviet *republic* in the Caucasus, was entitled by ethnic right to merge with the Azeris of northern Iran and refused to withdraw Soviet forces. Stalin set up puppet Communist Azeri and Kurdish governments there. In 1946 U.S. President Truman delivered some harsh words, Iran's prime minister promised Stalin an oil deal, and Stalin pulled out. Then the Majlis canceled the oil deal.

The Last Pahlavi

Oil determined much of Iran's twentieth-century history. Oil was the great prize for the British, Hitler, Stalin, and the United States. Who should own and profit from Iran's oil—foreigners, the Iranian government, or Iranians as a whole? Major oil deposits were first discovered in Iran in 1908 and developed under a British concession, the Anglo-Persian (later Anglo-Iranian) Oil Company. Persia got little from the oil deal, and Persians came to hate this rich foreign company in their midst, one that wrote its own rules. Reza Shah ended the lopsided concession in 1932 and forced the AIOC to pay higher royalties.

The AIOC still rankled Iranians, who rallied to the radical nationalist Prime Minister Muhammad Mossadeq in the early 1950s. With support from Iranian nationalists, liberals, and leftists, Mossadeq nationalized AIOC holdings. Amidst growing turmoil and what some feared was a tilt to the Soviet Union, young Shah Muhammad Reza Pahlavi fled the country in 1953. The British urged Washington to do something, and President Eisenhower, as part of U.S. **containment**, had the CIA destabilize the Tehran government. It was easy: The CIA's Kermit Roosevelt arrived with $1 million in a suitcase and rented a pro-Shah mob. Mossadeq was out, the Shah was restored, and the United States won a battle in the Cold War. We thought we were very clever.

Like his father, the Shah became a modernizing tyrant, promoting what he called his "White Revolution" from above (as opposed to a red revolution from below). Under the Shah, Iran had excellent relations with the United States. President Nixon touted the Shah as our pillar of stability in the Persian Gulf. We were his source of technology and military hardware. Some 100,000 Iranian students came to U.S. universities, and 45,000 American businessmen and consultants surged into Iran for lucrative contracts. (This point demonstrates that person-to-person contacts do not always lead to good relations between countries.)

Geography

Cruising the Persian Gulf

The countries bordering the Persian Gulf contain two thirds of the world's proven petroleum reserves. Some of you may do military service in the Gulf, so start learning the geography now. Imagine you are on an aircraft carrier making a clockwise circle around the Gulf. Upon entering the Strait of Hormuz, which countries do you pass to port?

Oman, United Arab Emirates, Qatar, Saudi Arabia, Bahrain (an island), Kuwait, Iraq, and Iran.

The United States was much too close to the Shah, supporting him unstintingly and unquestioningly. The Shah was Western-educated and anti-Communist, and was rapidly modernizing Iran; he was our kind of guy. Iranian unrest and opposition went unnoticed by the U.S. embassy. Elaborate Iranian public relations portrayed Iran in a rosy light in the U.S. media. Under Nixon, U.S. arms makers sold Iran "anything that goes bang." We failed to see that Iran and the Shah were two different things, and that our unqualified backing of the Shah was alienating many Iranians. We ignored how the Shah governed by means of a dreaded secret police, the SAVAK. We failed to call a tyrant a tyrant. Only when the Islamic Revolution broke out did we learn what Iranians really thought about the Shah. We were so obsessed by communism penetrating from the north that we could not imagine a bitter, hostile Islamic revolution coming from within Iran.

OPEC   Cartel of oil-rich countries designed to boost petroleum prices.

mullah   Muslim cleric.

ayatollah   "Sign of God"; top Shia religious leader.

What finally did in the Shah? Too much oil money went to his head. With the 1973 Arab Israeli war, oil producers worldwide got the chance to do what they had long wished: boost the price of oil and take over oil extraction from foreign companies. The Shah, one of the prime movers of the Organization of Petroleum Exporting Countries (**OPEC**), gleefully did both. What Mossadeq attempted, the Shah accomplished. World oil prices quadrupled. Awash with cash, the Shah went mad with vast, expensive schemes. The state administered oil revenues for the greater glory of Iran and its army, not for the Iranian people, creating resentment that hastened the Islamic Revolution. Oil led to turmoil.

The sudden new wealth caused great disruption. The Shah promoted education, but as people became more educated they could see the Shah was a tyrant. Some people got rich fast while most stayed poor. Corruption grew worse than ever. Millions flocked from the countryside to the cities where, rootless and confused, they turned to the only institution they understood, the mosque. In their rush to modernize, the Pahlavis alienated the Muslim clergy. Not only did the Shah undermine the traditional cultural values of Islam, he seized land owned by religious foundations and distributed it to peasants as part of his White Revolution. The **mullahs** also hated the influx of American culture, with its alcohol and sex. Many Iranians saw the Shah's huge military expenditures—at the end, an incredible 17 percent of Iran's GDP—as a waste of money. As Alexis de Tocqueville noted in his study of the French Revolution, economic growth hastens revolution.

One of Iran's religious authorities, **Ayatollah** Khomeini, criticized the Shah and incurred his wrath. He had Khomeini exiled to Iraq in 1964 and then forced him to leave Iraq in 1978. France allowed Khomeini to live in a Paris suburb, from which his recorded messages were telephoned to cassette recorders in Iran to be duplicated and distributed through mosques nationwide. Cheap cassettes bypassed the Shah's control of Iran's media and helped bring him down.

In the late 1970s, matters came to a head. The Shah's overambitious plans had made Iran a debtor nation. Discontent from both secular intellectuals and Islamic clerics bubbled up. And, most dangerous, U.S. President Jimmy Carter made human rights a foreign policy goal. As part of this, the Shah's dictatorship came under U.S. criticism. Shaken, the Shah began to relax his grip, and that is precisely when all hell broke loose. As de Tocqueville observed, the worst time in the life of a bad government is when it begins to mend its ways. Compounding his error, Carter showed his support for the Shah by exchanging visits, proof to Iranians that we were supporting a hated tyrant. In 1977, Carter and the Shah had to retreat into the White House from the lawn to escape the tear gas that drifted over from the anti-Shah protest (mostly by Iranian students) in Lafayette Park.

By late 1978, the Shah, facing huge demonstrations and (unknown to Washington) dying of cancer, was finished. Shooting into the crowds of protesters just made them angrier. The ancient Persian game of chess ends with a checkmate, a corruption of the Farsi *shah mat* ("the king is trapped"). On January 16, 1979, the last Pahlavi left Iran. *Shah mat*.

The Key Institutions

A Theocracy

Two-and-a-half millennia of monarchy ended in Iran with a 1979 referendum, carefully supervised by the Khomeini forces, that introduced the Islamic Republic of Iran and a new constitution. As in most countries, the offices of head of state and head of government are split. But instead of a figurehead monarch (as in Britain) or weak president (as in Germany), Iran now has two heads of state, one its leading religious figure, the other a more standard president. The religious chief is the real power. That makes Iran a **theocracy** and a dysfunctional political system.

---

theocracy Rule by priests.

velayat-e faqih "Guardianship of the Islamic jurist"; theocratic system devised by Khomeini.

canon law Internal laws of the Roman Catholic Church.

Islamist Someone who uses Islam in a political way.

Theocracy is rather rare and tends not to last. Even in ancient times, priests filled supporting rather than executive roles. Russia's tsar, officially head of both church and state, was far over on the state side; he wore military garb, not priestly. Iran (plus Afghanistan and Sudan) attempted a theocratic system. The principle of political power in Iran—in the system devised by Khomeini—is the **velayat-e faqih**. This top Islamic jurist, the *faqih*, serves for life. "Jurist" means a legal scholar steeped in Islamic, specifically Shia, religious law. (The closest Western equivalent is **canon law**. In medieval Europe, canon lawyers were among the leading intellectual and political figures.) Allegedly the *faqih*, also known as the "Spiritual Guide" and "Supreme Leader," can use the Koran and related Islamic commentaries to decide all issues, even those having nothing to do with religion. (An **Islamist** would say everything is connected with religion.)

Khomeini, the first and founding *faqih*, died in 1989. He was nearly all-powerful. Successors are chosen by an Assembly of Experts of eighty-six Muslim clerics elected every eight years, who are supposed to choose from among the purest and most learned Islamic jurists. The man they elect (Islam permits no women religious leaders) is not necessarily an ayatollah, one of the wisest Shia jurists. In 1989 the Experts chose Ali Khamenei, a Hojatollah, the rank just below, but he was immediately promoted to ayatollah. Khamenei, expected to serve for life, lacks Khomeini's (do not confuse the two names) charisma and Islamic authority but is still the real power. He names the heads of all major state and religious organizations and may declare war. He controls the judiciary, armed forces, security police, intelligence agencies, radio, and television. He is much more powerful than Iran's president and blocks any reform efforts.

Iran's Legislature

Iran has a unicameral (one-house) legislature, the Islamic Consultative Assembly (*Majlis*), consisting of 290 deputies elected for four-year terms. Iran uses single-member districts, like Britain and the U.S. Congress. Iran is divided into 265 constituencies, and each Iranian eighteen and older can vote. Additional seats are reserved for non-Muslim deputies: five each for Assyrian Christians, Jews, and Zoroastrians, two for Armenian Christians, none for Baha'is. The Speaker of parliament is a major position. The constitution guarantees MPs immunity from arrest, but the conservative judiciary still jails MPs who call too loudly for reforms.

Electoral balloting is free and fair, but permission to run is totally rigged. The Council of Guardians (see next paragraphs) must approve all candidates, and they disqualify thousands who might be critical. Open liberals are thus discouraged from even trying to run. The low turnout 2008 parliamentary elections gave the Majlis to Ahmadinejad's radicals because no openly liberal candidates were allowed, so not many Iranians bothered to vote.

More powerful than the Majlis is the Council of Guardians, a strange institution combining features of an upper house, a supreme court, an electoral commission, and a religious inquisition. Its twelve members serve six years each, half of them changed every three years. The *faqih* chooses six Islamic clerics; Iran's supreme court (the High Council of Justice) names another six, all Islamic lawyers, who are approved by the Majlis.

The Council examines each Majlis bill to make sure it does not violate Islamic principles. If a majority decides it does, the bill is returned to the Majlis to be corrected. Without Council approval, a bill is in effect vetoed. All bills aiming at reform are blocked in this way. To settle conflicts between the Majlis and the Council, an "Expediency Council" appointed by the Leader, has become like another legislature. In 2005 the Expediency Council—chaired by Rafsanjani, the very man Ahmadinejad had beaten in elections—was given additional powers to oversee the president. Iran's conservative religious establishment does not like the rambunctious Ahmadinejad.

More important, the Council of Guardians examines all candidates for the Majlis and has the power to disqualify them without explanation. The Council scratches a large fraction of Majlis candidates. In 2002 President Khatami and the Majlis tried to take this power away from the Council of Guardians, but the Council vetoed the bills. The Council of Guardians thus makes the Iranian system unreformable.

Emerging Parties?

Parties are legal under Iran's constitution, but the government does not allow them; only individual candidates run. Even Khomeini dissolved his own Islamic Republic party in 1984. Lack of party labels makes Iranian elections less than free, for without them voters cannot clearly discern who stands for what. It is difficult to count how many seats each of the several "tendencies" control; they have to be estimated. In practice, candidates are linked with informal parties and political tendencies called "fronts" or "coalitions." Eventually these may turn into legal parties. Observers see four main political groupings plus many factions and individual viewpoints.

Radicals, the most extreme supporters of the Islamic Revolution—such as President Ahmadinejad (see box on page 550)—adhere to Khomeini's original design for an Islamic republic. They preach a populist line of help for the poor and hatred of the United States. In the 2008 Majlis elections—held French style in two rounds—they ran as the Unified Principlist Front and won 117 out of 290 seats.

Conservatives, calmer and generally older than the radicals, want a nonfanatic Islamic Republic with more economic growth than Ahmadinejad delivered. In 2008 they ran as the Broad Principlists Coalition and won 53 seats. Iran's politics is now largely the struggle between conservatives and radicals, as reformists and liberals are not allowed to play.

Reformists tend to cluster in the educated middle class. They favor privatization of state enterprises, less Islamic supervision of society, elections open to most candidates, fewer powers for the Council of Guardians, and dialogue with the United States. In the late 1990s they held a majority in the Majlis but the Council of Guardians now disqualifies most of their candidates. In 2008 they ran as Reformists and won 46 seats.

PERSONALITIES

MAHMOUD AHMADINEJAD

The surprise winner of Iran's 2005 presidential election was the populist mayor of Tehran, Mahmoud Ahmadinejad, age forty-nine. The radical Ahmadinejad seeks to restore the original Islamist and socialist goals of the 1979 revolution, in which he was a student leader. The expected winner, Ayatollah Ali Akbar Hashemi Rafsanjani, who had earlier been president (1989–1997), promoted a pragmatic and reformist line but was disliked as corrupt and as part of the establishment.

The election was not democratic. The Council of Guardians screened out hundreds of candidates deemed liberal or insufficiently Islamic. Only eight were allowed to run, and one dropped out. Many charged the 2005 balloting was rigged; they were silenced. Two critical newspapers were closed. Iran's religious hard-liners backed Ahmadinejad and ordered the army and the fanatic *Basij* militia to turn out and bring their relatives to vote for Ahmadinejad, who was in the Basij and Pasdaran (Revolutionary Guards, the new Islamist army). Iran elects presidents in a French-style two rounds, the first for the two biggest winners, the second a runoff between them. Rafsanjani edged Ahmadinejad 21–19.5 percent in the first round, but Ahmadinejad won the second round 62–36 percent over Rafsanjani, with a reported (but probably inflated) 60 percent turnout, much lower than the 83 percent turnout in 1997. Many liberal Iranians did not vote in 2005.

Ahmadinejad won chiefly with the vote of poor Iranians, to whom he promised welfare. There was indeed a social-class element to the 2005 election. Rafsanjani ran an aloof campaign based on his religious rank and political experience (he had also been Majlis speaker). He and his relatives had become very wealthy. Ahmadinejad ran as a man of the people who lived modestly and looked after Tehran's poor people during his two years as mayor. Ahmadinejad, the first Iranian president to hold no religious rank, was an engineering professor. Some Iranians may have voted for him just to protest against Iran's corrupt establishment.

Mahmoud Ahmadinejad

Ahmadinejad's victory was, in a way, a mirror image of Muhammad Khatami's, who won in a surprise landslide in 1997. Unknown before the election, Khatami hinted at reform and suddenly became a symbol of change. When no liberals are allowed to run, Iranians turn to any outsider candidate as a form of protest. While in office, Khatami was blocked by Khamenei and the hard-liners and was unable to reform anything. Ironically "conservative" Ahmadinejad was a bigger threat to Iran's establishment than "liberal" Khatami.

Ahmadinejad, fanatic in religion and populist in economics, fired many officials as corrupt. This angered establishment conservatives, who blocked his policies and ministerial nominations and his efforts to redistribute oil revenues to low-income Iranians. Ahmadinejad played the nationalist card by openly defying the West on Iran's "peaceful" nuclear program, which could eventually be used to build nuclear weapons. Many Iranians admired his defiance. He thundered that "Israel must be wiped off the map" and that the Holocaust was a "myth," comments that further isolated Iran from the rest of the world. The mystical Ahmadinejad, who says that the hidden imam will soon appear, has made Ayatollah Khamenei, Iran's Leader, seem moderate and stable in comparison.

Liberals would go farther. Popular among Iranian students, they emphasize democracy and civil rights and want totally free elections. They want to end all social controls imposed by the Islamists. In economics, however, they are a mixed bag, ranging from free marketers to socialists. Knowing the Council of Guardians would reject them, no liberals run for office. Both reformists and liberals know how to keep their mouths shut and do nothing stupid, like having contact with Americans.

Koran   Muslim holy book.

Some of the regime's sharpest critics were leaders of the 1979 revolution who now do not like its authoritarianism and seek separation of mosque and state. They include hundreds of clerics like Grand Ayatollah Hossein Ali Montazeri, one of the most senior figures of Shia Islam, now held in house arrest in the holy city of Qom for denouncing repression and demanding reform. "Either officials change their methods and give freedom to the people, and stop interfering in elections, or the people will rise up with another revolution," he warned.

An Unfree System

Iran could be described as a political system waiting to be free. The potential is there, but important institutional changes would have to be made. First, the power of the Leader would have to be reduced to that of a purely spiritual guide with few or no temporal powers. Next, the Council of Guardians would have to be abolished. If these two things happened, Iran's institutions could quickly turn it into a democracy, with a real executive president, a critical Majlis, multiparty elections, and a free press. Iran has the greatest democratic potential of any Persian Gulf country.

Iranian Political Culture

As in much of the Third World, many Iranians do not want their traditional culture replaced by Western culture. "We want to be modern," say many citizens of the Third World, "but not like you. We'll do it our way, based on our values and our religion." Whether you can be a modern, high-tech society while preserving your old culture is a key question for much of the globe today. Will efforts to combine old and new cultures work or lead to chaos? In some cases, like Japan, it has worked. For Islamic nations, so far it has not. The key factor may be the flexibility and adaptability of the traditional culture, which is very high in the case of Japan. Japan learned to be modern but still distinctly Japanese. Can Muslim countries do the equivalent?

Beneath all the comings and goings of conquerors and kingdoms, Persian society kept its traditions for centuries. As in China, dynastic changes little disturbed the broad majority of the population, poor farmers and shepherds, many of them still tribal in organization. As in much of the Third World, traditional society was actually quite stable and conservative. Islam, the mosque, the mullah, and the **Koran** gave solace and meaning to the lives of most Persians. People were poor but passive.

Then came modernization, mostly under foreign pressure, starting late in the nineteenth century, expanding with the development of petroleum, and accelerating under the two Pahlavi shahs. Iran raises the question of whether you can modernize and still keep your old culture. According

Political Culture

Is Islam Anti-Modern?

Most Middle East experts deny there is anything inherent in Islamic doctrine that keeps Muslim societies from modernizing. Looking at cases, though, one finds no Islamic countries that have fully modernized. Under Atatürk, Turkey made great strides between the two wars, but Islamic militants still try to undo his reforms. In Huntington's terms (see page 528), Turkey is a *torn* country, pulled between Western and Islamic cultures. Recently Malaysia, half of whose people are Muslim, has scored rapid economic progress. Generally, though, Islam coincides with backwardness, at least as we define it. Some Muslim countries are rich but only because oil has brought them outside revenues.

By itself Islam probably does not cause backwardness. The Koran prohibits loaning money at interest, but there are ways to work around that. Islamic civilization was for centuries far ahead of Christian Europe in science, philosophy, medicine, sanitation, architecture, steelmaking, and much more. Translations from the Arabic taught Europe classic Greek thought, especially Aristotle, which helped trigger the Renaissance and Europe's modernization. A millennium ago you would hear Muslims concluding that Christianity was keeping Europe backward.

But Islamic civilization faltered and European civilization modernized. By the sixteenth century, when European merchant ships arrived in the Persian Gulf, the West was ahead of Islam. Why? According to some scholars, early Islam permitted independent interpretations of the Koran (*ijtihad*), but between the ninth and eleventh centuries this was replaced by a single, orthodox interpretation (*taqlid*), and as a result intellectual life atrophied. Islam has never had a reformation.

The Mongol invaders of the thirteenth century massacred the inhabitants of Baghdad and destroyed the region's irrigation systems, something that the Arab empire never recovered from. (The Mongols' impact on Russia was also devastating.) Possibly because of this, Islam turned to mysticism. Instead of an open, flexible, and tolerant faith that was fascinated by learning and science, Islam turned sullen and rigid. When the Portuguese opened up a direct trade route between Europe and Asia, bypassing Islamic middlemen, trade through the Middle East declined sharply and with it the region's economy declined.

Islam has a structural problem in its combination of religion and government, which makes it difficult to split mosque and state. Those who try to do so (such as Atatürk) are resisted. Even today, many Muslims want *sharia* (see page 473) to be the law of the land. This creates hostility between secular modernizers and religious traditionalists, who compete for political power, a destructive tug of war that blocks progress.

A major factor was the domination of European (chiefly British) imperialists starting in the nineteenth century. This created the same resentment we saw in China, the resentment of a proud civilization brought low by unwelcome foreigners: "You push in here with your guns, your railroads, and your commerce and act superior to us. Well, culturally and morally we are superior to you, and eventually we'll kick you out and show you." With this comes hatred of anything Western and therefore opposition to modernity, because accepting modernity means admitting the West is superior. Islam teaches it is superior to all other civilizations and will eventually triumph worldwide. Devout Muslims do not like evidence to the contrary.

If Islamic countries do not discard their cultural antipathy to modernity—which need not be a total imitation of the West—their progress will be slow and often reversed. Millions of Muslims living in the West are modern and still Islamic. Ideas for religious modernization are already afoot in Islam with, ironically, Iranian intellectuals in the lead. Eventually, we could see societies that are both modern and Muslim. One of the best ways to promote this: Educate women.

to what political scientists call *modernization theory*, a number of things happen more or less simultaneously. First, the economy changes, from simple farming to natural-resource extraction to manufacturing and services. Along with this comes urbanization, the movement of people from the country to the cities. At the same time, education levels rise; most people become literate and some go to college. People consume more mass media—at first newspapers, then radio, and finally television—until many are aware of what is going on in their country and in the world. A large middle class emerges and with them interest groups. People now want to participate in politics; they resent being treated like children.

secularization   Cutting back the role of religion in government and daily life.

It was long supposed that **secularization** comes with modernization, and both Atatürk and the Pahlavis had tough showdowns with the mullahs. But Iran's Islamic Revolution and other religious revivals now make us question the inevitability of secularization. Under certain conditions—when things change too fast, when the economy declines and unemployment grows, and modernization repudiates traditional values—people may return to religion with renewed fervor. If their world seems to be falling apart, church or mosque give stability and meaning to life. This is as true of the present day United States as it is of Egypt. In the Muslim world, many intellectuals first passionately embraced modernizing creeds of socialism and nationalism only to despair and return to Islam. (Some intellectuals are now interested in free-market capitalism, which had been unpopular because it was associated with the West.)

The time of modernization is a risky one in the life of a nation. If the old elite understands the changes that are bubbling through their society, they will gradually allow democratization in a way that does not destabilize the system. A corrupt and rigid elite, on the other hand, that is convinced the masses are not ready for democracy (and never will be), block political reforms until there is a tremendous head of steam. Then, no longer able to withstand the pressure, they suddenly give way, chaos breaks out and ends in tyranny. If the old elite had reformed sooner and gradually, they might have lowered the pressure and eased the transition to democracy. South Korea and Taiwan are examples of a favorable transition from dictatorship to democracy. Iran under the Shah is a negative example.

The Shah was arrogant: He alone would uplift Iran. He foresaw no democratic future for Iran and cultivated few sectors of the population to support him. When the end came, few Iranians did support him. Indeed, the Shah scorned democracy in general, viewing it as a chaotic system that got in its own way, a view as old as the ancient Persian attack on Greece. The mighty Persian empire, under one ruler, could surely beat a quarrelsome collection of Greek city states. (Wrong!) The Shah supposed that Iran, under his enlightened despotism, would soon surpass the decadent West. A journalist once asked the Shah why he did not relinquish some of his personal power and become a symbolic monarch, like the king of Sweden. He replied: "I will become like the king of Sweden when Iranians become like Swedes."

The answer to this overly simple view is that, yes, when your people are poor and ignorant, absolute rule is one of your few alternatives. Such a country is far from ready for democracy. But after considerable modernization—which the Shah himself had implemented—Iran became a different country, one characterized by the changes discussed earlier. An educated middle class resents one man rule; the bigger this class, the more resentment builds. By modernizing, the Shah sawed off the tree limb on which he was sitting. He modernized Iran until it no longer wanted him.

ISLAM AS A POLITICAL IDEOLOGY

Ayatollah Khomeini developed an interesting ideology that resonated with many Iranians. Traditionally Shia Islam disdained politics, waiting for the return of the Twelfth Imam to rule (see box on page 544). Khomeini and his followers, departing from this old tradition, decided that while they wait the top Shia religious leaders should also assume political power. Called by some **islamism**, it was not only religious but also social, economic, and nationalistic. The Shah and his regime, said Khomeini, had both abandoned Islam and turned away from economic and social justice. They allowed the rich and corrupt

Islamism   Islam turned into political ideology.

to live in Westernized luxury while most struggled in poverty. They sold out Iran to the Americans, exchanging the people's oil for U.S. weapons. Tens of thousands of Americans lived in Iran, corrupting Iran's youth with their "unclean" morals. By returning to the Koran, as interpreted by the mullahs, Iranians would not only cleanse themselves spiritually but also build a just society of equals. The mighty would be brought low and the poor raised up by welfare benefits administered by mosques and Islamic associations. Like communism, Islamism preaches leveling of class differences, but through the mosque and mullahs rather than through the Party and *apparatchiks*.

Islamism is thus a catchall ideology, offering an answer to most things that made Iranians discontent. It is a potent mix, but can it work? Probably not. Over time, its several strands fall apart, and its factions quarrel. Islamism's chief problem is economics (as we shall consider in greater detail later). As Islamism recedes as a viable ideology, look for the reemergence of other ideologies in Iran.

KEY CONCEPTS

IS "ISLAMIC FUNDAMENTALISM" THE RIGHT NAME?

Some object to the term "Islamic fundamentalism." Coined in the early twentieth century to describe U.S. Bible-belt Protestants, fundamentalism stands for inerrancy of Scripture: The Bible means what it says and is not open to interpretation. But that is the way virtually all Muslims view the Koran, so Muslims are automatically fundamentalists. Some thinkers propose we call it *Islamic integralism* instead, indicating a move to integrate the Koran and sharia with government. Integralism, too, is borrowed, from a Catholic movement early in the twentieth century whose adherents sought to live a Christ-like existence. The Sunni Muslim movement for returning to the pure Islam of the founders is *salafiyya,* which has been around for centuries in several forms. The Wahhabi Islam of Saudi Arabia and al Qaeda are *salafi.*

Some political scientists use the term *political Islam,* indicating it is the political use of religion to gain power. The term *Islamism,* a religion turned into a political ideology, won favor for the simple reason that it is short (not a bad reason).

Democracy and Authority

Many observers think that rule by the mullahs will be overturned. Western diplomats estimate that only a minority of Iranians support the current regime. But can Iranians then establish a stable democracy, or was the Shah right—do Iranians need a strong hand to govern them? There were two impulses behind the 1979 revolution: secularist intellectuals seeking democracy and Islamists seeking theocracy. The secular democrats, always a small minority, threw in with the more numerous Islamists, figuring that they would oust the Shah and then the secularists, being better educated, would lead. But the Islamists, better organized and knowing exactly what they wanted, used the secular democrats and then dumped them (and in some cases shot them). Many secular democrats fled to other countries. Learning too late what was happening to them, some democratic supporters of the Revolution put out the slogan: "In the dawn of freedom, there is no freedom."

But these secular democrats did not disappear; they laid low and went along outwardly with the Islamic Revolution. To have opposed it openly could have earned them the firing squad. Among them are the smartest and best-educated people in Iran, the very people needed to make the economy grow. With Iran's economic decline, many lost their jobs and became private consultants and specialists, working out of their apartments. Tens of thousands emigrate each year, preferring to emigrate to the United States and Canada. Many of them—once they are sure you are not a provocateur for the regime—speak scathingly in private of the oppression and economic foolishness of the mullahs. "I believe in Islam, but not in the regime of the mullahs," said one Iranian.

Political Culture

Are Iranians Religious Fanatics?

Only a minority of Iranians are Muslim fanatics. Not even the supposed Islamic fundamentalists are necessarily fanatic. Many Iranians are perfectly aware that religion is a political tool (more on this in the next section) and are fed up with it. Massive regime propaganda depicts the United States as the "Great Satan," but most Iranians are very friendly to the few Americans who visit. Some have been in the United States or have relatives there; many remember that when Iran was allied with America, Iraq did not dare invade. Iran was the only Muslim country where tens of thousands spontaneously showed sympathy with Americans after 9/11. Do not confuse regime propaganda with the attitudes of ordinary citizens.

Ironically, Iranians pointed to the now defunct Taliban government of neighboring Afghanistan as *salafi* extremists. Far stricter than Iranian Islamists, the Taliban confined women to the home and required all men to grow beards. Why the conflict with Iran? Like most of Afghanistan, the Taliban were Sunni and attacked the Shia minority, some 1.5 million of whom fled to Iran. The Taliban killed Iranian intelligence agents who were aiding Afghan Shias. Dangerous stuff, this religious extremism.

People like these—who voted for Khatami in 1997 and 2001—believe Iranians are capable of democracy. They argue that the anti-Shah revolution was hijacked by the Islamists but that its original impulse was for democracy, not theocracy, and this impulse still remains. Especially now that people have tasted the economic decline, corruption, and general ineptitude of the mullahs, they are ready for democracy. If the regime ever opens up, the secular democrats will go public to demand open elections with all parties eligible. For now, they stay quiet and aim their TV satellite dishes to pick up critical views from the large (800,000) Iranian community in the United States.

Iranian Nationalism

Nationalism, always strong in Iran, is coming back. Some analysts hold that Iran today is more motivated by nationalism than by any religious fervor. Iran, like China, strives to increase its power and prestige. Islam was imposed on Persia by Arab swords, and Iranians to this day harbor folk memories of seventh-century massacres by crude, barbaric invaders. Iranians do not like Arabs and look down on them as culturally inferior and lacking staying power. By adopting Shia, Iranians were and are proud to distinguish themselves from their mostly Sunni neighbors. The Iranian message: "We are actually the best Muslims and should lead the Islamic world." Accordingly, not far under the surface of Iranian thought is Persian nationalism, affirming the greatness of their ancient civilization, which antedates Islam by a millennium.

DEMOCRACY

IRAN'S ANGRY STUDENTS

In the late 1970s, Iranian students, most of them leftists, battled to overturn the old regime. Now Iran's students—whose numbers have exploded to close to two million—again demonstrate for civil rights. Many students are outspoken liberals and push for pluralism, a free press, and free elections. They also worry about the serious lack of jobs for graduates.

Every year hard-line courts—especially the Revolutionary Court—close liberal newspapers and block Web sites. Between 2,000 and 4,000 Iranian editors, writers, professors, public opinion pollsters, student leaders, and politicians are in jail. Some of them fought in the 1979 Revolution and in the long war against Iraq. At least a hundred dissidents were mysteriously killed.

Iran per capita is the world's death-penalty leader. When Ahmadinejad spoke at a Tehran university, students chanted "death to the dictator," which led to an angry regime crackdown on students and professors on many campuses.

Could students and intellectuals one day lead the way to democracy? By themselves, probably not. They are not organized and lack ties to the broad masses of Iranians, few of whom are openly discontent. But if they could organize in combination with other groups, they could destabilize the clericalist regime. In many countries, students have been the spark plugs of revolution.

The Shah especially stressed Persian nationalism in his drive to modernize Iran. The Shah was Muslim and had himself photographed during religious devotion, as during his **hajj**, a pilgrimage required of all Muslims who can afford it once in their lifetime. But the Shah's true spirit was secular and nationalistic: to rebuild the glory of ancient Persia in a modern Iran. If Islam got in the way, it was to be pushed aside. The Shah was relatively tolerant of non-Muslim faiths; Baha'is (a universalistic and liberal offshoot of Islam), Jews, and Christians were unharmed. Since the Islamic Revolution, non-Muslims have been treated harshly, especially the 300,000 Baha'is, Iran's largest minority religion, who are regarded as dangerous **heretics**. For centuries, Iran's sense of its unique Persianness coexisted uneasily with its Islam. The Shah's modernization program brought the two strands into open conflict.

> **hajj** Muslim pilgrimage to Mecca.
> **heretic** Someone who breaks away from a religion.

The Islamic Revolution of 1979 did not totally repudiate the nationalist strand of Iranian thought. It put the stress on the religious side of Persianness, but the long and horrible war with Iraq, from 1980 to 1988, brought out the regime's Persian nationalism. They were fighting not only for their faith but for their country and against Iraq, a savage, upstart Arab country that did not even exist until the British invented it in the 1920s. Iran celebrates two types of holidays, Persian and Muslim. The Persian holidays are all happy, such as New Year (*Noruz*). The Islamic holidays are mostly mournful, such as the day of remembrance of the martyrdom of Hussein at Karbala, during which young Shia men beat themselves until they bleed.

Political Culture

DOES ISLAM DISCRIMINATE AGAINST WOMEN?

Iran is one of the better Muslim countries in the treatment of women. Unlike the Arab kingdoms on the southern shore of the Gulf, Iranian women drive cars, go to school, work outside the home, and participate in politics. But even in Iran there are tough restrictions on dress, contact with males, and travel.

Devout Muslims swear women are deeply honored in their societies, but their place is in the home and nowhere else. Women are kept at a subservient status in most Islamic countries; often they get little education, cannot drive a car, and their testimony is worth half of men's in courts of law. But such discrimination does not always come from the Koran. In some Muslim countries (not Iran), such customs as the seclusion of women, the veil, and female genital mutilation are pre-Islamic and were absorbed by Islam (much as Europeans adopted for Christmas the pagan worship of trees). These non-Koranic imports can therefore be discarded with no harm to the faith, maintain Muslim feminists. Yes, there are such people, and increasingly they are speaking out and organizing. If they succeed, they will greatly modernize their societies. The widespread education of Iranian women predicts social and legal change.

One feminist voice is that of 2003 Nobel Peace Prize winner Shirin Ebadi, a lawyer and regime opponent who defends women's rights and cites the Koran to show Islam should not discriminate against women. Many Iranian women share this view and protest for their rights; some are arrested, tried, and imprisoned. Iran could be the birthplace of Islamic feminism.

Patterns of Interaction

Religion as a Political Tool

Manipulate, use, discard. This is how Khomeini's forces treated those who helped them win the Revolution. Like turbaned Bolsheviks, the Islamists in the late 1970s hijacked the Iranian revolution as it unfolded. First, they captured the growing discontent with the Shah and his regime. By offering themselves as a plausible and effective front organization, they enlisted all manner of anti-Shah groups under their banner—the democratically inclined parties of the National Front, the Iran Freedom Movement, the Marxist (and Soviet-connected) Tudeh party, and Islamic guerrilla movements. They had these groups do their dirty work for them and then got rid of them, sometimes by firing squad. The flowering of democratic, Islamic, secular, and socialist parties that accompanied the Shah's overthrow was crushed within three years. As an example of revolutionary technique, Lenin would have admired their skill and ruthlessness.

In doing all this, the Islamists used their religion much as the Bolsheviks used Marxism, as a tool, a recruiting and mobilizing device, a means of gaining authority and obedience, and a way to seize and consolidate power. This is not to say they were not serious about Islam, but rather that in a revolutionary situation the instrumental uses of their faith predominated over the devotional. If you want to seize state power, you cannot be otherworldly; you must be very shrewd and practical. There is nothing "crazy" about the Islamists who run Iran; they are perfectly capable of calm and rational decisions calculated to benefit themselves. In our eyes, to be sure, some look crazy.

After some time immersed in politics, the power side takes over and the original religious (or ideological) side takes a back seat. As with the Bolsheviks, this soon leads to opportunism and cynicism among the politically involved and ultimately to regime decay. The ruling group turns into a self-serving new class. This is why regimes that base themselves on ideology or religion (Islamism combines both) have finite life spans. After a while, everyone notices the power and greed of the ruling class, and mass disillusion sets in; the regime loses legitimacy. This is happening in Iran. Iran's Islamic revolution will burn out.

An example of this was the seizure of the U.S. embassy in Tehran by student militants in November 1979, which brought American cries of outrage and a complete break in relations. The embassy takeover and holding of fifty-two American officials for 444 days indeed broke every rule in the diplomatic book and seemed to prove that mad fanatics governed Iran.

Looked at more closely, though, the incident was a domestic Iranian power play, cynically manipulated by the Khomeini forces. The ayatollah wished to complete the Islamic Revolution and get rid of the moderate prime minister he had appointed early in 1979, Mehdi Bazargan. The occasion for this political design was the admission of the ailing Shah to the United States for cancer treatment. Khomeini's cadres whipped up mass rage in Iran, claiming that medical help for the Shah proved the United States still supported the ousted regime. Then a group of student militants invaded and took over the U.S. embassy, which had already been reduced to a skeleton staff. No shots were fired; the U.S. Marine guards were ordered not to shoot. The American hostages were treated harshly but none were killed. The militants published classified embassy documents (pieced together from the shredder) purporting to show how dastardly the Americans were. At one stroke, Khomeini got rid of all moderates in the government, prevented U.S. interference (as there had been in 1953), and carried the revolution to a frenzied high point.

The Islamic activists, using anti-American hysteria ("Death to USA!"), consolidated their hold on the country. Humiliated and powerless, Bazargan resigned. Anyone opposed to the embassy takeover was fired or worse. One foreign-ministry official (who had dropped out of Georgetown University to promote revolution) helped some Americans escape via the Canadian embassy. He was tried and shot. Khomeini's followers seemed to enjoy watching President Carter squirm, especially after the aborted U.S. rescue mission in April 1980. Carter's apparent weakness on Iran hurt him in the 1980 election, which he lost to Reagan.

At that point, the holding of U.S. diplomats had exhausted its utility for Khomeini. Knowing Reagan was not averse to military measures, Tehran released the diplomats just as he was inaugurated. The militants who had seized and held the Americans had also served their purpose. Considered unreliable, some were arrested and executed. Others were sent to the front in the war with Iraq, where they died in the fighting. As a historian of the French Revolution observed, the revolution devours its children.

Moderates and Islamists in Iran

Much of Iranian politics takes place in the largely unseen clash between conservative moderates and radical Islamists. You have to look closely for nuances to see the differences between the two. Both are conservative, but in different ways, the former calm and pragmatic, the latter pugnacious and revolutionary. Both are strongly Muslim and support the Islamic revolution, but the conservatives are not interested in spreading it beyond Iran. The conservatives are more open to a free market; the radicals want state controls. In elections no one runs on an opposition platform; direct opposition could be hazardous to your health. Regime change may come from the struggle between Iran's militants and moderates, not from any outside—including U.S.—pressures.

After the 1986 Iran-Contra fiasco, in which White House aides attempted to secretly sell U.S. missiles to Iranian "moderates," the term "Iranian moderate" disappeared from Washington's vocabulary. The U.S. officials fell for a sucker play by Iranian revolutionaries, who set up the deal and then leaked word that the United States was trading with Iran, illegal under U.S. law. The incident embarrassed the United States.

Moderates	Islamists
calm the Islamic revolution	maintain it
shift power to Majlis	preserve power of *faqih*
permit some parties	ban non-Islamic parties
free press	censored press
permit Western women's attire	Islamic attire only (veil)
improve relations with West	keep distant from West
dialogue with America	hate America
open nuclear programs to inspection	continue nuclear programs without inspection
liberalize economy	keep economy statist

Comparison

Is Saudi Arabia Next?

The 9/11 attacks suggested that the Kingdom, as Saudis call their country, is lurching into instability. Fifteen of the nineteen hijackers were Saudis. Al Qaeda terrorists set off bombs in the Kingdom. Islamists such as Osama bin Laden, son of a Saudi billionaire, represent the same kind of forces that overthrew the Shah in Iran. The Saudi regime is almost paralyzed by fear of this. It tries to buy off threats and deflect discontent by funding extremist religious schools (many in Pakistan) and minimizing Islamist recruitment.

The House of Saud conquered the country in the 1920s based on the austere Wahhabi creed of salafi Islam and is highly vulnerable for the same reasons as the Shah of Iran. Saudi Arabia is less democratic than Iran is now, and the legitimacy of the royal family has eroded amidst charges of abandoning Wahhabism in favor of Western pleasures. Of the 5,000 Saudi princes, more than 500 are eligible to become king, an invitation for a succession struggle.

Oil created some very rich Saudis, including the princes, but left many poor Saudis far behind. Earlier, the oil revenues allowed the regime to buy loyalty with subsidies for thousands of Saudis. But oil prices fluctuate, and the population exploded from 7 million in 1980 to 28 million in 2008, cutting per capita Saudi income in half. Forty percent of the population is under fourteen. Cushy jobs no longer await young Saudis; many are unemployed and discontent. Shia Saudis from the oil-producing Eastern Province carry out bombings (with Iranian backing), including American targets.

News from the Kingdom is rigorously censored—nothing negative is allowed—and until 9/11 Washington never criticized "our good friends," the House of Saud. It was the same way we treated the Shah. After 9/11 some Americans called Saudi Arabia a false friend and supplier of money and personnel for Islamist terrorism. Hundreds of young Saudis cross into Iraq for jihad against the Americans and Shia. A succession struggle over the new king could destabilize the Kingdom. It may be too late to do anything to prevent a Saudi revolution. Reforms can hasten revolution, as we saw in Iran. Controlled moves to democracy, such as these, might stabilize the Kingdom.

- Allow some opposition parties. Make sure they are moderate, and let them criticize the regime in a constructive way. Make sure there are several parties (some conservative, some liberal, none radical) to divide public discontent.

- Permit a semifree press along the same lines as parties: limited criticism only.

- Crush and suppress Islamists. Do not ease up on them. These people are out to destroy you, and if they take over they will not be moderate or democratic.

- Hold legislative elections but among parties ranging from conservative to moderate. Gradually, you can let other parties participate.

- Have the new legislature redistribute wealth in the form of heavy taxes on the rich, especially on members of the royal family, who must be seen taking a financial hit. This is to defuse mass anger over the royals' great and unfair wealth.

- Do not automatically follow U.S. policy in the region, as that delegitimizes your regime. Limit any American presence; it is a cultural irritant and natural fodder for Islamic extremists. (Saudi leaders did not support our 2003 invasion of Iraq and had U.S. troops leave. They are not stupid.)

- Crack down on corruption, especially among the highest officials and princes. Show that you mean business here, and that the crackdown will be permanent.

Have we learned anything from Iran? Would any of this work to head off a revolution? Maybe, but it would require the willingness of the House of Saud to cut its own wealth and power, and that is something ruling classes rarely do. But if Saudi Arabia cannot transition to some kind of democracy, revolution and then U.S. military involvement is likely. The Persian Gulf and its oil is one place we do not walk away from.

The term now refers to conservative moderates who favor the Islamic Republic but think the radicals are reckless and dangerous. They are typified by pragmatists like Rafsanjani, who lost to Ahmadinejad in the 2005 presidential race, and diplomatic negotiator Ali Larijani. Iranian conservatives play a cautious game, not directly opposing the Islamist militants, now led by Ahmadinejad. The conservatives quietly exercise their influence in the religious hierarchy surrounding Supreme Leader Khamenei, which curbs some of Ahmadinejad's more impetuous efforts.

The militant Islamists want a truly Islamic republic, one based on religious law and presided over by the *faqih*. Anything else means giving in to Iran's enemies—the West in general, the United States in particular—with eventual loss of Iran's independence, culture, and religion. They block any liberalizing reforms, close newspapers, fire ministers who stray, and put political critics on trial.

The great pillar of the radical Islamists is the Islamic Revolutionary Guards (*Pasdaran*). Originally formed in 1979 to support Khomeini, they took many casualties in the war with Iraq and now, with 125,000 members, are separate from and higher than the regular army, rather like the SS under Hitler. They get the best weapons, run many industries, dominate the defense and intelligence ministries, and supervise Iran's nuclear program. Former Pasdaran hold about a third of Majlis seats and set the agenda. President Ahmadinejad, a Pasdaran in the war with Iraq, placed many in high positions and relies on them. The arrest of fifteen British sailors in 2007 seems to have been a Pasdaran power play to silence conservative pragmatists. Likewise the arrest of visiting Iranian-American academics and a journalist for allegedly trying to overthrow the Tehran regime seems to have been an effort to scuttle U.S.-Iranian talks on Iraq. The Pasdarans' militarization of Iranian politics under Ahmadinejad is dangerous. It stifles any chance for democracy and increases chances for war.

Recent elections have trended against the radicals. Reformists and conservatives beat Ahmadinejad supporters for seats on municipal councils and in the Majlis in 2008. Pragmatic conservative Hashemi Rafsanjani and his supporters easily won control over the Assembly of Experts, which chooses the next supreme leader. Populist Ahmadinejad, who promised to uplift poor Iranians and failed to deliver, could lose reelection in 2009.

On the fringe, both inside and outside the country, are Iranians who want to get rid of the whole Islamic revolution. They stand no chance. A few monarchists would like to restore the son of the last Pahlavi, a young man now living in the West, to the throne, a quixotic venture. The times are against monarchy; every decade there are fewer and fewer ruling (as opposed to figurehead) monarchs.

On the other side, some Marxist-type revolutionaries, the *Mujahedin-e Khalq* (Fighters for the People), who earlier worked with the Islamists to overthrow the Shah now try to overthrow the Islamists. Among them were some of the young militants who seized the U.S. embassy. Subsequently, it is estimated that over 10,000 Mujahedin were executed by the Khomeini forces. Their survivors were sheltered in and sponsored by Saddam Hussein's Iraq, which invaded and massacred Iranians (sometimes with poison gas), during the 1980s, so these Mujahedin have little resonance among Iranians. Even Washington now considers them a crazy cult.

THE REVOLUTION BURNS OUT

Iran illustrates Crane Brinton's classic theory of revolution (see page 94). To review: The Shah's regime loses its legitimacy. Antiregime groups form, rioting breaks out, and the Shah leaves. Initially moderates take power, but the ruthless Khomeini forces soon dump them and drive the revolution to a frenzied high point. But this burns itself out; eventually a *Thermidor*, or calming down, arrives. It was almost as if Iranians had read Brinton and gone through his stages. Every stage, that is, except the last, and even that may have happened without a clear-cut Thermidor. Instead, there may have been a low key, rolling Thermidor marked by Khatami's election in 1997.

No revolution lasts forever. In Iran we can see an effort to become stable and normal, which is opposed by Islamic radicals. But time is probably on the side of the normalizers. Many mullahs have corrupted themselves; some do not go onto the street in clerical garb. Mullahs run the *bonyads*, foundations originally set up to redistribute the wealth of the Shah and his supporters. These *bonyads* now control billions of dollars and much of Iran's industry. They are supposed to be run for the good of all, a sort of Islamic socialism, but in practice they have made their mullahs rich, powerful, and corrupt while their industries are run poorly. As Lord Acton observed (see page 26), power corrupts.

The spirit of Iran's Islamic Revolution lives on in this Tehran cemetery memorial to the fallen of the Iran-Iraq war of 1980–1988. Iranian losses were horrifying—at least half a million killed, many of them boys. Note the women in chadors in the foreground.

Aware of power's tendency to corrupt, many Iranians want the mullahs to return to the mosque and get out of government and the economy. Even some mullahs wish it, as now they see that running a country ruins their reputation and their spiritual mission. Chant Iranian demonstrators: "The mullahs live like kings, while the people are reduced to poverty." Another factor is that now over half of Iranians were born after the Shah and have no personal commitment to the Islamic Revolution. They want jobs and more freedom, and they can vote at age eighteen (recently raised from sixteen).

Will there be a point at which we can say that the Iranian Revolution is finally over? The reestablishment of diplomatic ties between the United States and Iran—something many Iranians want to happen soon—would indicate that point had passed some time earlier. There were hopes of this reestablishment of diplomatic ties during the office of former President Khatami, who mentioned "dialogue" with Americans (but not with Washington) but pulled back when conservative forces objected. Current President Ahmadinejad is bitterly hostile. Other indications would be the mullahs giving up control of the *bonyads* and the *faqih* becoming a figurehead or *dignified* office.

What Iranians Quarrel About

Which Way for Iran's Economy?

Iran has changed rapidly, partly under the Shah and partly under the Islamic Revolution. The countryside has received schools, electricity, health care, and tractors. Infant mortality, a key measure of health

fatwa	Ruling by Islamic jurist.

care, fell from 169 per 1,000 births in 1960 to 38 in 2007. Average life expectancy jumped twenty years, from 50 to 70. Literacy has climbed from less than half to three-fourths. More Iranian women than ever are in schools and universities (segregated from males, of course).

The Iranian economy was hurt by revolution, war, isolation, and mismanagement. Although total oil income has increased, only recently has per capita GDP recovered to pre-1979 levels. Iran depends far too much on the runup in world oil prices. If oil prices fall, Iran is in trouble (as are Russia and Nigeria). There is now growth, but inflation, unemployment, and poverty are considerable. Iran needs some 1.5 million new jobs a year. Pay is low so people hold two and three jobs to make ends meet. Many jobs and business dealings, as in Russia, are off the books. The oil industry, still the pride and basis of the Iranian economy, needs replacement parts and up-to-date technology. Its productivity is miserable. U.S. pressure has kept most oil companies from cooperating with Iran. The *bonyads* are run badly and corruptly, and increasingly Iranians notice this.

By giving all Iranians an expensive welfare floor (including subsidized food and gasoline) while simultaneously damaging Iran's great source of revenue (its petroleum connection with the West), Iran has given itself budget deficits and inflation. Iran has to import some 40 percent of its gasoline at $2 a gallon to sell at 34 cents a gallon because it lacks refining capacity. Motorists, used to cheap gas, rioted in 2007 when the regime started rationing it. Subsidies create costly and dangerous distortions but are very hard to end.

Geography

How Many Iranians?

Islam traditionally frowns on family planning: The more babies the better. After the revolution, Iran's mullahs urged women to produce a generation of Muslim militants; subsidized food helped feed them. Iran's rate of population growth averaged 3.5 percent a year during the 1980s, one of the world's highest. Despite the murderous war with Iraq, since the 1979 Revolution Iran's population doubled from 34 million to 68 million.

By the early 1990s, though, the government, realizing it could not subsidize or employ the vast numbers of young Iranians—two thirds were born after the Revolution—reversed the high-births policy. Amid economic decline, families now can afford fewer children. Clinics offer all manner of contraception free of charge (but not abortions). Women agents go door to door to promote family planning. Food and other family aid decreases after a family has three children. One Muslim cleric even issued a **fatwa** in favor of smaller families. From an average 7 births per woman over her life in 1986, the fertility rate plunged to 1.7 in 2007, lower than in the United States. By 2007, the rate of population growth was down to a low 0.66 percent. The turnaround on births is an indication the revolution is over.

The Islamic Revolution did not dismantle the Shah's *statist* economy. The state still controls 60 percent of Iran's economy (biggest part: the oil industry). The *bonyads* control another 10 to 20 percent. Only about 20 percent of Iran's economy is in private hands. Theoretically, foreigners can invest in Iran, but most are scared off by the many and tangled limits and regulations. Investors must pay numerous bribes. Iran's is not a free-market economy. The big question: Should it become one?

Opposing arguments show up in Majlis debates over economic policy, which have become thinly disguised battles over the future of strict Islamic rule. As we have considered, Islamism is a surrogate socialism; that is, it blends Islamic correctness with collectivist economics. In the minds of many Islamists, socialism is the logical extension of Islam, for Islam preaches equality and leveling of class differences. Thus, they claim, Islam is the true and only path to a just society of equal citizens, where no one is either rich or poor. What the Marxists, Socialists, and Communists talked about, they say, we can deliver.

Most moderates respond that socialism and/or statism is not the way to go, that they just keep Iran poor and backward. The collapse of the Soviet system demonstrates socialism does not work, and the decline of Iran's economy demonstrates statism does not work. Besides, they note, there is no Koranic basis for government control of the economy. It is perfectly feasible to combine free-market capitalism with the alms-giving required of Muslims and achieve social justice. If we keep declining economically, moderates also worry, we will never be able to build a first-class army and so will be vulnerable to hostile outside forces. And if our towering unemployment problem is not solved soon, the whole Islamic revolution could be doomed. The best and quickest way to solve these problems is the free market. State ownership of major industries, especially petroleum, is what the Shah tried, and we certainly do not want to follow in his footsteps. Such are the arguments of Iranian moderates. Notice that outright rejection of the Islamic revolution is not one of their points.

The Veiled Debate on Islam

Iran will always be a Muslim country, but what kind of Islam will it have? A moderate kind that keeps out of most direct political involvement or a militant kind that seeks to guide society by political means? Judging by the Khatami landslides in 1997 and 2001, most opt for the first kind. The 2005 election of Ahmadinejad makes one wonder.

Because the Council of Guardians bars openly liberal candidates, public debate on the religion question is muted. No one risks being branded "anti-Islamic." Still, one can infer that such a debate is taking place. One of the stand-ins for a discussion of Islam in public life is the debate on what kind of clothing is admissible, especially for women. Even for men, though, blue jeans were frowned upon, partly because they represent American culture. Liberals say they do not; jeans are simply a comfortable and international garment with no political connotations.

Before the Islamic revolution, urban and educated Iranian women dressed as fashionably as European women. Then suddenly they could not use makeup and had to wear the veil and *chador*, the single-piece head-to-toe garment designed to cover feminine attractiveness. Devout Muslims, including many women, say this attire is better than Western clothing as it eliminates lust, vanity, and distinctions of wealth. (Notice how some U.S. schools are coming to similar conclusions about school uniforms.) Western clothes and makeup are the first steps toward debauchery and prostitution, they argue.

But in subtle ways urban Iranian women dress in a manner that pushes to the limit of the permissible in public (and in private dress as they wish). The veil and *chador* are no longer mandatory on the street, so long as a woman is dressed very modestly without makeup and with hair and forehead covered by a kerchief. Women still risk Islamic *komitehs* (morals police) stopping them on the street and sending them home or to jail. Young people suspected of having a good time may be beaten by *basij* (militia). These volunteer squads are some of the most obnoxious features of the Islamic regime and have alienated urban and educated Iranians.

Political Culture

The United States and Iran

A culture gap hinders Americans and Iranians from understanding each other. We have not been clever in dealing with the Iranian Revolution. Part religious, part nationalistic, part cultural, and part antityranny, it defied our predictions and efforts to tame it. When we tried to deal with "Iranian moderates" in 1986, we got humiliated. When we tilted toward Iraq in its war against Iran, we supported a bloody dictator (Saddam Hussein) whom we twice fought ourselves. In 1988 a U.S. destroyer mistook an Iranian jetliner for an attacking fighter, shot it down with a missile, and killed all 290 aboard. Iran, and indeed the whole Persian Gulf, is a tar baby: Once you punch it, you get stuck worse and worse.

But if we are calm and clever, things may work out. Ahmadinejad and the radicals are unpopular and could be voted out, leading to improved relations. Many Iranians want contact and dialogue with the United States. In the long term, Iran needs us. We can provide the petroleum technology and other means to modernize the country. U.S. attempts to encourage "regime change" in Iran, however, are counterproductive. American broadcasts, funds, and contacts in support of Iranian critics are the kiss of death, allowing the regime to portray them as traitors and U.S. stooges.

Anthropologists point out that when two Iranian *bazaaris* quarrel, by long tradition they simply shun and ignore each other for some years. Gradually, the quarrel fades and they cautiously reestablish relations with each other. After a while, the quarrel is forgotten. It is a civilized way to handle a quarrel. We might take a leaf from Persian folkway in dealing with Iran.

Iranians do not understand American culture. Americans are in many ways the opposite of Iranians; we are direct, unsubtle, and prone to violence: cowboys. Americans like guns and military solutions, even though most see America as good and trying to do good in the world. We are poorly informed about the Gulf region. Few Americans know as much about Iran as the student who has just read this chapter. To win mass support our presidents use simplified rhetoric—"axis of evil"—and notice only later that it sets back quiet efforts to improve U.S.-Iranian relations (desired by two-thirds of Iranians). Loose talk about knocking out Iran's nuclear facilities makes matters worse, leading to Iranian counterthreats and popular support for the regime.

Iranians must watch their rhetoric, too. Your mass chanting of *Marg bar Amrika!* ("Death to America!") sounds like a direct threat. Do you really want to kill us? Then you'd better stop saying so. After 9/11, we take these things very seriously. The U.S. commitment to making sure the oil of the Persian Gulf flows in a friendly fashion is one point Americans agree on in foreign policy. No amount of bombings can persuade us to abandon this policy. And we can "make your economy scream." Those were Kissinger's words describing what we did to Chile when it came under Marxist rule. (We are probably doing it to you now.)

So stop sponsoring or encouraging terrorism. When a bomb goes off in Beirut, we smell Iranian money funneled through Syria. Do not develop nuclear weapons, which are more likely to provoke than deter the United States. Turn to your own tradition and simply shun America, doing nothing against us. And when you are ready to resume contact and economic growth, let us know in a public way. We understand that you are in a long struggle against an odious theocracy and cannot move prematurely. Eventually, the rule of the mullahs will pass and relations will thaw. We were friends once and can be again. Foolish moves on either side could lead to a war neither wants.

IRAN AS A REGIONAL POWER

Iran makes no secret of its drive to become the Persian Gulf's dominant power. Much of what Iran does internationally is aimed at increasing its power and prestige. "We are rapidly becoming a superpower," said Iranian President Ahmadinejad in 2007. Iran is already the top regional power. Tehran sees itself as the leader of the entire Islamic world and tries to spread its revolutionary influence. Sunnis resent Iran and fear its growing power; they despise Shias. This is the limiting factor in Iran's dream of regional dominance. Indeed, Al Qaeda urges that Shias be killed as heretics.

Iran is the most influential power in Iraq, where Shias have long been a suppressed 60 percent of the population. The Sunni Arabs of central Iraq are only about 20 percent, but they monopolized political power. Many of the main Shia shrines are in southern Iraq, where Khomeini was exiled in 1964. Upon taking power in Tehran, the Khomeini people propagandized Iraqi Shias and urged them to join the Islamic Revolution. This was one of the irritants—but hardly a sufficient excuse—for Iraqi dictator Saddam Hussein to invade Iran in 1980. Now Iranian arms, agents, and money move freely into Iraq, and Tehran encourages the formation of a second Islamic republic. Many Iraqi Shia leaders are closely connected to Iran and heed Tehran's guidance. Iran is the only winner of the Iraq War.

GEOGRAPHY

STRATEGIC WATERWAYS

These are mostly narrow choke points connecting two bodies of water. Hostile control of them causes one or more countries discomfort or fear. Here are the main ones:

Turkish Straits (Dardanelles and Bosporus), connecting the Black and Mediterranean Seas.

Strait of Gibraltar, connecting the Atlantic and the Mediterranean.

Suez Canal, connecting the Mediterranean and Red Seas.

Bab al Mandab, connecting the Red Sea and Indian Ocean.

Strait of Hormuz, connecting the Persian Gulf and Indian Ocean.

English Channel, connecting the Atlantic Ocean and North Sea.

Skagerrak, connecting the Baltic and North Seas.

North Cape, dividing the Atlantic from the Barents Sea.

Cape of Good Hope, where the Atlantic and Indian Oceans meet off the southern tip of Africa.

Strait of Malacca, connecting the Indian Ocean and South China Sea, East Asia's oil lifeline.

Korea (Tsushima) Strait, connecting the East China Sea and Sea of Japan.

Panama Canal, connecting the Atlantic and Pacific Oceans.

You are the captain of a small tanker that has just loaded oil in Kuwait for delivery in Umea, Sweden. Which bodies of water—including seas, oceans, straits, and canals—do you pass through? (Note: Supertankers are too big for Suez; they have to go around Africa. But small tankers still pass through Suez.)

Iran works through its Shia brethren in Iraq, Lebanon, Kuwait, Bahrain, Afghanistan, and Saudi Arabia. Funds, instructions, and explosive devices flow through this connection. Iran, along with Syria, is on the U.S. State Department's list of countries sponsoring terrorism. Iran proclaims its leading role in destroying Israel, which it depicts as a polluter of Islamic holy

GEOGRAPHY

BOUND ISRAEL

Israel is bounded on the north by Lebanon;   on the south by Egypt;

on the east by Syria and Jordan;   and on the west by the Mediterranean Sea.

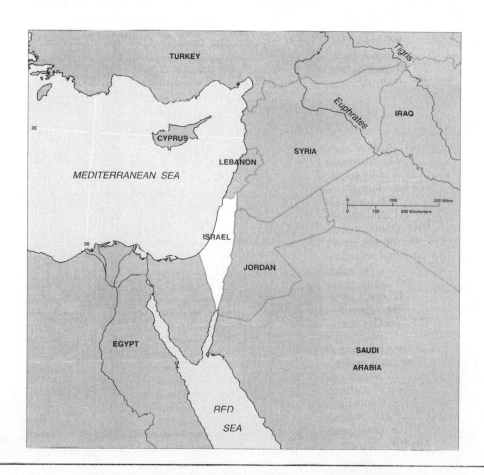

ground (Jerusalem is also sacred to Muslims) and outpost of Western imperialism. Under the Shah, Tehran had good (but informal) relations with Israel and quietly sold it most of its oil. Iran's Islamic revolution totally changed that, and Iran funds Lebanon's *Hezbollah* (Party of God), which provoked a nasty one-month war with Israel the summer of 2006. In this way Iran claims leadership in the struggle against Israel.

Iran isolated itself, creating not only U.S. hostility but angering the Sunni-ruled lands of the Persian Gulf. Iran's stonewalling on its nuclear program alienated Britain, France, and Germany, who had sought a diplomatic solution to ensure that Iran does not build nuclear weapons. Tehran says it seeks only nuclear power generation—in a country with massive oil and natural gas reserves—but no one trusts it. In 2006 the International Atomic Energy Agency (IAEA) referred the matter to the UN, where few supported Iran. Iran's isolation harms its economic growth and requires it to maintain armed forces it cannot afford.

Many Iranians dislike being isolated. They want to avoid conflict and improve relations with the West, even with America, but few dare say so publicly. Meddling in other countries, they argue, brings nothing but trouble and could even lead to war. The radicals, now led by Ahmadinejad, want to keep up the militant foreign policies, no matter what they cost the country. Iran has been both the victim and practitioner of terrorism. Antiregime forces, particularly the nutty Mujahedin-e Khalq, assassinated several Iranian leaders, including one prime minister. Iranian hit squads in Europe took out several regime opponents. Iran's great foreign-policy problem is that by expanding its power and influence it creates enemies.

Do Revolutions End Badly?

Burke (see box on page 27) was right: Revolution brings in its wake tyranny far worse than that of the regime it toppled. Iran is a good example: The Shah was a dictator, but rule of the mullahs is worse. Only in America did revolution lead to the establishment of a just, stable, democracy—and the American revolution was a very special, limited one, aimed more at independence than at revolution. The twentieth century is littered with failed revolutions: fascist, communist, and now Islamist. The few remaining Communist countries that still celebrate and base their legitimacy on an alleged revolution, Cuba and North Korea, are hungry and isolated. Communist China and Vietnam, by partly integrating their economies with world trade, have so far been spared this fate.

Why do revolutions end badly? Several writers have attempted to answer this question. Burke argued that the destruction of all institutional and political structures leaves people confused and ripe for dictatorial rule. François Furet wrote along similar lines that the French Revolution unleashed such chaotic forces that it had to "skid out of control." Crane Brinton wrote that revolutions fall into the hands of their most ruthless element, who then proceed to wreck everything until they are replaced in a Thermidor. And Hannah Arendt wrote that revolution goes astray when revolutionists try to solve the "Social Question" (how to bring down the rich and lift up the poor); to do this they must institute a tyranny. It is interesting to note that all of these writers were, to some extent, conservatives. Radicals and leftists often refuse to admit revolutions end badly; if something goes wrong they tend to blame individuals for "betraying" the revolution.

The unhappy revolution is something that Iranians ponder. Although few want a return of the Pahlavis, many Iranians know that the Islamic Revolution has turned out wrong. At least under the Shah there was economic growth, however unfairly distributed, and modernization. Now there is economic decline and unemployment. Most Iranians live in greater poverty than before. Certain mullahs and their friends, those in charge of the *bonyads*, do well, however. Given a chance, most Iranians would throw these rascals out. The mullahs and their security and judicial forces try to make sure that this never happens. They have some bases of support—more than the Shah had—among the religious and the poor who have benefited from Islamic handouts.

Iran is now caught in a stalemate between moderate and militant forces. Eventually, reform will come to Iran; the status quo is unsustainable. The longer the fanatic Islamists stonewall, the greater the danger of political violence, fueled by millions of angry, unemployed young Iranian males. What can the United States do? U.S. threats just play into the hands of hard-liners, but the right combination of firmness (over Iran's uranium-enrichment efforts) and carrots (trade) could start a dialogue. Time and economic difficulties will calm the Iranian revolution. I am convinced that Iran will one day be free and Iran and the United States will be friends again.

Key Terms

ayatollah (p. 547)

canon law (p. 548)

containment (p. 546)

fatwa (p. 563)

hajj (p. 557)

heretic (p. 557)

Islam (p. 543)

Islamism (p. 554)

Islamist (p. 548)

Koran (p. 551)

Majlis (p. 544)

modernizing tyrant (p. 545)

mosque (p. 545)

mullah (p. 547)

OPEC (p. 547)

Ottoman (p. 545)

secular (p. 545)

secularization (p. 553)

shah (p. 544)

Shia (p. 543)

Sunni (p. 543)

theocracy (p. 548)

velayat-e faqih (p. 548)

Further Reference

Abdo, Genieve, and Jonathan Lyons. *Answering Only to God: Faith and Freedom in Twenty-First Century Iran.* New York: Henry Holt, 2003.

Adelkhah, Faribah. *Being Modern in Iran.* New York: Columbia University Press, 2000.

Alexander, Yonah, and Milton Hoenig. *The New Iranian Leadership: Ahmadinejad, Nuclear Ambition, and the Middle East.* Westport, CT: Praeger, 2007.

Ansari, Ali M. *Confronting Iran: The Failure of American Foreign Policy and the Next Great Crisis in the Middle East.* New York: Basic Books, 2006.

Axworthy, Michael. *Empire of the Mind: A History of Iran.* New York: Basic Books, 2008.

Azimi, Fakhreddin. *The Quest for Democracy in Iran: A Century of Struggle against Authoritarian Rule*. Cambridge, MA: Harvard University Press, 2008.

Beeman, William O. *The "Great Satan" vs. the "Mad Mullahs": How the United States and Iran Demonize Each Other*. Westport, CT: Praeger, 2005.

Crone, Patricia. *God's Rule: Government and Islam*. New York: Columbia University Press, 2004.

Ehteshami, Anoushiravan, and Mahjoob Zweiri. *Iran and the Rise of Its Neoconservatives: The Politics of Tehran's Silent Revolution*. London: I. B. Tauris, 2007.

Jafarzadeh, Alireza. *The Iran Threat: President Ahmadinejad and the Coming Nuclear Crisis*. New York: Palgrave, 2007.

Jahanbegloo, Ramin, ed. *Iran: Between Tradition and Modernity*. Lanham, MD: Lexington, 2004.

Keddie, Nikki R. *Modern Iran: Roots and Results of Revolution*. New Haven, CT: Yale University Press, 2003.

Mackey, Sandra. *The Iranians: Persia, Islam, and the Soul of a Nation*. New York: Dutton, 1996.

Nasr, Vali. *The Shia Revival: How Conflicts within Islam Will Shape the Future*. New York: Norton, 2006.

Sadjadpour, Karim. *Reading Khamenei: The World View of Iran's Most Powerful Leader*. Washington, D.C.: Carnegie Endowment, 2008.

Sedghi, Himdeh. *Women and Politics in Iran: Veiling, Unveiling, and Reveiling*. New York: Cambridge University Press, 2007.

Takeyh, Ray. *Hidden Iran: Paradox and Power in the Islamic Republic*. New York: Times Books, 2006.

Yaghmaian, Behzad. *Social Change in Iran: An Eyewitness Account of Dissent, Defiance, and New Movements for Rights*. Albany, NY: SUNY Press, 2002.

Epilogue

Lessons of Ten Countries

1. States often precede and create nations. Countries are rather artificial things, the product of governments instilling a common culture over many generations. A working, effective government is the crux of nationhood; those without one are *failed states*.

2. The modern state has existed only about half a millennium and is not necessarily the last word in political organization. The emergence of the *European Union* suggests a new entity beyond the nation-state.

3. Most *boundaries* are artificial. Where one country ends and another begins is a political decision, often contested. The expansion and contraction of Germany is an example of how fluid some boundaries can be.

4. Most countries have *core areas*, often where the state began, that are still home to the country's capital. Outside of these core areas, in the *periphery*, regionalism and resentment at being governed by a distant capital often grow. Thus peripheral areas often vote differently than core areas.

5. The past is alive and well in current politics, forming a country's political institutions, culture, and quarrels. The past is especially lively in the resentments of aggrieved people, for example among regions and social groups that feel they have been shortchanged.

6. War can wreck political systems. War, said Marx, is the midwife of revolution. Several of our countries have undergone total system change as a result of war.

7. Economic growth is destabilizing, especially rapid growth. Economic growth and change bring new people into politics, some of them bitterly discontent. Do not think economic growth solves political problems; it often makes them worse. Democracy should follow economic growth to head off systemic upheaval.

8. A system that cannot change to meet new challenges is doomed. Wise rulers make gradual and incremental reforms in order to avoid sudden and radical changes. Rulers who wait to reform until revolution is nigh may actually fuel it by offering concessions. All regimes tend to petrify; the good ones stay flexible.

9. Solid, time-tested *institutions* that people believe in are a bulwark of political stability. No political leader, however clever, has pulled functioning institutions out of a hat. They require time, intelligence, and continual modification.

10. Constitutions rarely work the way they are intended and written. Many factors modify the working of *constitutions*: popular attitudes, usages that change over time, powerful parties and interest groups, and behind-the-scenes deals.

11. Everywhere, *parliaments* are in decline. Some have become little more than ritual, under such tight executive and/or party control that they have lost their autonomy. As governance becomes more complex and technical, power flows to bureaucrats and experts.

12. Everywhere, *bureaucracies* are in the ascendancy. In some systems, the permanent civil service is already the most powerful institution. Bureaucrats tend to see themselves as the indispensable saviors of their countries. No country fully controls its bureaucracies.

13. Multiparty systems tend to be less stable than two-party systems. Much depends on other factors, such as the rules for forming a cabinet or choosing the executive. Reforms can stabilize *multiparty* systems so that their behavior is not much different from two-party systems.

14. Electoral system helps determine *party* system. Single-member districts with a simple plurality required to win tend to produce *two-party systems* because third parties have difficulty surviving in such systems. *Proportional representation* tends to produce many parties.

15. There are no longer purely *federal* or purely *unitary* systems. Instead, the trend is for federations to grant more and more power to the center, while unitary systems set up regional governments and devolve some powers to them.

16. Most cabinets consist of about twenty ministers. By American standards, other cabinets are large and their portfolios rather specialized. In most countries (but not the United States), ministries are added, deleted, combined, or renamed as the prime minister sees fit; the legislature automatically goes along.

17. In some ways, *prime ministers* in parliamentary systems are more powerful than *presidents* in presidential systems. If they have an assured and disciplined majority in parliament, prime ministers can get most of what they want with no deadlock between executive and legislative. Prime ministers who rely on *coalitions*, of course, are weaker.

18. Most people, most of the time, are not much interested in politics. As you go down the socioeconomic ladder, you usually find less interest in political participation. More-educated people participate more. Mass participation in politics tends to be simple and episodic, such as voting every few years.

19. Democracy does not grow everywhere and is not everyone's chief desire. In countries without a history of democratic rule, most people prefer law and order, jobs, and food on the table to democracy. This makes it hard to implant democracy in countries like Russia and Iraq.

20. Political culture is at least as much a reflection of government performance as it is a determinant of the workings of government. *Political culture* can be taught, intentionally or inadvertently, by a regime. Countries with a cynical, untrusting political culture have usually earned it with decades of misrule. By the same token, a democratic regime that does a good job over many years firms up democratic attitudes.

21. Social class is only one factor in establishing political orientations. Often other factors, such as religion and region, are more important. Usually these three—*class*, *religion*, and *region* in varying combinations—explain most of party identification and voting behavior.

22. Religion is important in politics. In Iran, the two merge. More typical are political parties based on religion, as in Nigeria and India, or religiosity (degree of religious feeling), as in France and the United States.

23. Political systems are rarely totally ideological, but neither are they totally pragmatic. Parties and regimes usually talk some *ideology* to justify themselves, but rulers tend to *pragmatism* in making decisions. Ideology as window dressing is a common political device.

24. Every country has its *elites*, the few people with much influence. Depending on the system, party elites, labor elites, business elites, military elites, even religious elites may assume great

importance. Elites pay attention to politics, usually battling for the groups they lead. Elites rather than masses are the true political animals.

25. Elites, especially intellectual elites, create and articulate political ideas (ideologies, reform movements, media commentary), something the masses rarely do. Elite attitudes tend to be more democratic than mass attitudes.

26. Education is the gateway to elite status. Except in revolutionary regimes, most elites now have university educations. Some countries—Britain, France, Japan—have elite universities that produce much of the leadership. Educational opportunity is never totally equal or fair; the middle class usually benefits most from it.

27. Much of politics consists of competition and bargaining among elites. Occasionally elites, in order to gain leverage on competing elites, refer questions to the masses in elections or referendums and call it democracy. Of all the political interactions discussed in this book, notice how relatively few of them involve mass participation.

28. Mass politics is easier to study than elite politics. With *mass politics*—parties, elections, voter alignments, public opinion—political scientists can get accurate, quantified data. Since much of elite politics is out of the public eye, we have to resort to fragmentary anecdotal and journalistic data. This means that some of the most crucial political interactions are hard to discern and even harder to document.

29. Democracy grows when elites open their decisions and deals to public scrutiny and approval. Typically, bargains are struck among elites and then presented to parliament and the public. Much legislative and electoral behavior is in ratifying decisions made earlier among elites.

30. Politicians are endlessly opportunistic. Most will do whatever it takes to get, keep, or enhance their power. To this end, they will change their views and policies. This is not necessarily deplorable, however; it lets democracy work because it makes politicians bend to the popular will.

31. Politicians are addicted to money. They need it for election campaigns and sometimes to enrich themselves. Countries with very different institutions and political cultures have similar scandals over fundraising.

32. Parties are balancing acts. Most parties are invariably composed of different groups, factions, and wings. Some *parties* split apart over personal and ideological differences. To keep the party together, politicians dispense favors, jobs, and promises to faction leaders. This holds for both democratic and authoritarian parties.

33. Once the army has taken power, it will probably do so again. Democracy and reformism are often short-lived phenomena between periods of military rule. Countries can grow out of *praetorianism* with economic growth, increased education, and stable governance.

34. Most of humanity lives in the *Third World*, roughly defined as Asia, Africa, the Middle East, and Latin America. Some are progressing to prosperity and democracy; others, encumbered by institutional, ideological, and cultural rigidity, are not.

35. The Third World is trying to get into the First World. One of the significant issues for the rich world is that of foreign workers—Pakistanis in Britain, Algerians in France, Turks in Germany, Mexicans in America—who come for jobs and then stay. Given the differential rates of birth and economic growth, the trend is increasing and has become a major political issue worldwide.

36. Within developing countries, people are flocking to the cities. Overpopulation and few jobs in the countryside push people to the cities, where many live in *shantytowns*. The Third World already has the globe's biggest cities, most surrounded by shantytowns.

37. Racism can be found nearly everywhere. Most nations deny it, but discrimination based on skin color, religion, or ethnic group is widespread. When searching for *racism*, look to see what a country does, not what it says. Underdog racial and ethnic groups are locked out of economic and political power.

38. Cutting *welfare* benefits and subsidies is extremely difficult; recipients take them as a right and protest angrily. Some conservatives promise to end the welfare state, but they seldom touch the problem. Once a benefit has been extended, it is almost impossible to withdraw it. The most conservatives can do is restrain expansion of the welfare system.

39. Likewise, cutting state sectors of an economy is difficult. Most countries have state ownership, control, or guidance over the economy (the United States relatively little). In countries as diverse as Russia, India, Mexico, Nigeria, and Iran, those who have something to lose oppose ending *statism*. Many governments talk about privatization but delay doing it.

40. Much of what people and politicians quarrel about is economic. Some economists claim that economics is the content of politics. There are important political conflicts that are not directly economic, such as questions of region, religion, and personality. Still, most of the time people argue over who should get what. Study economics.

41. At almost the same time, countries rediscovered the market economy. Most found that statist control retards growth. Markets are now the intellectual trend, but not everyone likes them.

42. Democracy depends a great deal on economic development. Poor countries rarely sustain democracy. Middle-income and richer countries are mostly democracies. The likely reason: Economic growth generates a large, educated, pluralistic, and moderate middle class that insists on political participation.

43. Oil blocks democracy. Regimes that rely on oil exports—such as Russia, Nigeria, and Iran—concentrate great wealth in the hands of rulers who resist reforms, competing parties, and free elections. Oil is a curse.

44. Unemployment is a problem everywhere and one few governments solve. Worldwide, there is a struggle for jobs, ranging from difficult in West Europe to desperate in the developing areas.

45. Many political issues are insoluble. They are the surfacing of long-growing economic and social problems that cannot be "fixed" by any government policy. Time and underlying economic and social change may gradually dissolve the problems. Politics has been overrated as a way to cure problems. Often the best politics can do is keep things stable until time can do its work.

46. Things get more political, not less. As government takes on more tasks, what were previously private transactions become political interactions with all the quarreling that entails. No country ever runs out of political problems. As soon as one is solved, new ones appear, usually over the administration of the problem-solving mechanism.

47. Things do not always get better. Some political systems are unable to handle massive and multiple stresses; therefore, they turn into *weak states*, characterized by crime, corruption, and insecurity.

48. Political movements, parties, ideologies, and regimes are hard to judge by *a priori* criteria. We seldom know how something will work until we see it in practice for a while. We learn what is good and bad by studying results.

49. Whenever you look closely at political phenomena, you find they are more complicated than you first thought. You discover exceptions, nuances, and differentiations that you did

not notice at first. You can modify and sometimes refute generalizations—including the ones offered here—by digging into them more deeply.

50. Ultimately, in studying other countries we are studying ourselves. One of the lessons that should have emerged from this book is that neither our country nor we as citizens are a great deal different from other countries and peoples. When you compare politics, be sure to include your own system.

Glossary

Following are some frequently used words or technical terms from the field of comparative politics. Each is defined here in its political sense. The country where the term originated or is most commonly used is given where appropriate, but often the word is now used worldwide.

absolute decline Growing weaker economically compared to one's own past.

absolute poverty Extremely low income, defined by World Bank as living on under $1 a day.

absolutism Royal dictatorship that bypasses nobles.

affect Individual citizens' feelings of fondness toward political system.

affluence Having plenty of money.

ahimsa Not injuring any living thing.

alienated Psychologically distant and hostile.

Allies World War II anti-Axis military coalition.

alternation in power Overturn of one party by another in elections.

aggregate Items or persons taken together.

anachronism Something from past that does not fit present times.

anarchism Radical ideology seeking to overthrow all conventional forms of government.

analogy Taking one example as the model for another.

ancien régime French for old regime, monarchy that preceded Revolution.

Anglican Church of England, Episcopalian in America.

anglophile Someone who loves England and the English.

anticlerical Favoring getting Roman Catholic church out of politics.

Anti-Japanese War Chinese name for World War II in China, 1937–1945.

antithetical Ideas opposed to one another.

apparatchik "Man of the apparatus"; full-time CPSU functionary.

aristocrat Person of inherited noble rank.

asset-stripping Selling off firm's property and raw materials it controls for short-term profit.

austerity Cutting government expenditures, belt-tightening.

aquifer Underground, water-bearing layer.

autarchy Economic self-sufficiency, importing and exporting little.

authoritarian Nondemocratic or dictatorial politics.

authoritarianism Dictatorial rejection of democracy, as Spain under Franco and Chile under Pinochet.

authority Power of political figure to be obeyed.

Autobahn German express highway, like U.S. interstate.

autocracy Absolute rule of one person in centralized state.

autonomous region Soviet-style home area for ethnic minority.

autonomy Partial independence.

ayatollah (Iran) "Sign of God"; top Shia religious leader.

baccalauréat Exam by which the French finish high school.

backbencher (Britain) Ordinary MP with no executive responsibility.

balance of payments What a country owes other lands compared to what it can pay.

Bastille Old and nearly unused Paris jail, the storming of which started the French Revolution in 1789.

Beida Short name for Beijing University, China's best.

belle époque "Beautiful epoch"; France around 1900.

Berlin airlift U.S.-British supply of West Berlin by air in 1948–1949.

Berlin Republic Reunified Germany, with capital in Berlin.

bilateral opposition Centrist parties or governments being undermined from both sides.

bimodal Two-peaked distribution.

bloc Grouping or alliance.

blog From "Web log"; self-published reviews and comments on the Internet.

blocked society One in which interest groups prevent major, necessary change.

Bolshevik "Majority" in Russian; early name for Soviet Communist party.

Bonn Republic West Germany 1949–1990, with capital in Bonn.

bounce-back effect Tendency of trends and values to reverse.

bound To name bordering countries.

Bourbon French dynasty before the French Revolution.

bourgeois Pronounced "boozh-wah"; middle class.

bourgeoisie French for middle class; adjective *bourgeois*

Boxer Major Chinese antiforeigner rebellion in 1900.

Bronze Age Beginning of metal-working and cities.

Buddhism Asian religion that seeks enlightenment through meditation and cessation of desire.

Bundesrat Literally, federal council; upper chamber of German parliament that represents states.

Bundestag Lower house of German parliament.

bureaucratized Heavily controlled by civil servants.

burghers Originally, town dwellers; by extension middle class; French *bourgeoisie*.

by-election Midterm election for vacant seat in Parliament.

cacique Originally Indian chief; local political boss.

cadre French "framework"; used by Asian Communists for local Party leader.

caesaropapism Combining top civil ruler (caesar) with top spiritual ruler (pope), as in Russia's tsars.

caliphate Islamic dynasty.

canon law Internal laws of Roman Catholic Church.

capital goods Implements used to make other things.

carpetbagger In U.S. usage, outsider attempting to run in different constituency.

Cartesian After French philosopher René Descartes, philosophical analysis based on pure reason without empirical reference.

caste Hereditary social stratum or group.

catchall Parties that welcome all and offer little ideology.

Caucasus Mountainous region between Black and Caspian Seas.

caudillo Military chief or strongman, specifically one who takes over government.

causality Proving that one thing causes another.

Celts Pre-Roman inhabitants of Europe.

censure Condemnation of executive by legislative vote.

center Politically moderate or middle-of-the-road, neither left nor right. In federal systems, powers of nation's capital.

center-peaked Distribution with most people in middle, a bell-shaped curve.

center-periphery tension   Resentment of outlying areas at rule by nation's capital.

center-seeking   Parties trying to win big vote in center by moderate programs.

Central America   Countries between Mexico and Colombia.

Central Asia   Region between Caspian Sea and China.

Central Committee   Large, next-to-top governing body of most Communist parties.

central office   London headquarters of British political party.

Century of Humiliation   China's term for its domination by imperialists from the first Opium War to the Communist victory, 1839–1949.

chancellor   German prime minister.

charisma   Pronounced "kar-isma"; Greek for gift; political drawing power.

chauvinism   After Napoleonic soldier named Chauvin; fervent, prideful nationalism.

civility   Keeping reasonably good manners in politics.

civilization   City-based culture with writing, social classes, and complex economic and political organization.

civil society   Humans after becoming civilized. Modern usage: associations larger than family but not part of government.

class voting   Tendency of a given class to vote for the party that claims to represent its interests.

cleft country   In Huntington's theory, a country split by two civilizations.

clientelism   Government favors to groups for their support.

coalition   Multiparty alliance to form government.

coercion   Government by force.

cohabitation   French president forced to name premier of opposing party.

Cold War   Period of armed tension and competition between the United States and the Soviet Union, approximately 1947–1989.

colonialism   Gaining and exploitation of overseas territories, chiefly by Europeans.

Comecon   Trading organization of Communist countries, now defunct.

Comintern   Communist International, world's Communist parties under Moscow's control.

Common Agricultural Program   EU program to subsidize farmers; biggest single part of EU budget.

Common Law   System of judge-made law developed in England.

Commons   (Britain) Lower, popularly elected, and more important house of Parliament.

commonwealth   A *republic*.

communal   Ethnic or religious communities within a nation.

communism   Economic theories of Marx combined with organization of Lenin.

compartmentalization   Mentally separating and isolating problems.

Confederation of British Industry   Leading British business association.

Confucianism   Chinese philosophy of social and political stability based on family, hierarchy, and perfection of manners.

Congress   Led India's independence movement and later was dominant party.

consensus   Agreement among all constituent groups.

conservatism   Ideology aimed at preserving existing institutions and usages.

consociation   Sharing of political power at executive level, giving all major parties cabinet positions.

Constantinople   Capital of Byzantium, conquered by turks in 1453.

constituency   District or population that elects legislator.

constitution   Written organization of a country's institutions.

constitutionalism   Degree to which government limits its powers.

constitutional monarchy   One whose powers are limited.

constructed   Deliberately created but widely accepted as natural.

constructive no-confidence   Requires parliament to vote in new cabinet when it ousts current one.

consumer goods   Things people use, such as food, clothing, and housing.

consumption   Buying things.

containment   U.S. policy throughout the Cold War of blocking the expansion of communism.

Continent, the   British term for the continent of Europe, implying that they are not part of it.

co-opt   To enroll other groups in your cause, rendering them harmless.

core   Region where state originated.

corporatism   Representation by branch of industry, device of Mussolini.

Cortes   Spain's parliament.

corruption   Use of public office for private gain.

counterculture   Rejection of conventional values, as in 1960s.

courtier   Person who hangs around royal court.

CPSU   Communist Party of Soviet Union.

Creole   Spaniard born in the New World.

cross-cutting cleavages   Multiple splits in society that make group loyalties overlap.

Crown   Powers of British government.

CRS   Republican Security Companies, French riot police.

culmination   Logical outcome or end.

cult of personality   Dictator who has himself worshiped.

Cultural Revolution   Mao's late 1960s mad effort to break bureaucracy in China.

cumulative   Reinforcing one another.

current-account balance   A country's exports minus its imports.

cynical   Untrusting; belief that political system is wrong and corrupt.

Cyrillic   Greek-based alphabet of Eastern Slavic languages.

daimyo   Feudal Japanese regional lords.

Daoism   From Dao, "the way"; old Chinese religion originally based on nature; earlier spelled Taoism.

deadlock   U.S. tendency for executive and legislature, especially when of opposing parties, to block each other.

dealignment   Voters losing identification with any party.

debt   Sum total of government *deficits* over many years.

decentralization   Diffusion of administrative power from nation's capital to regions, localities, or economic units.

decolonization   Granting of independence to colonies.

dedazo   From *dedo*, finger; tapped for high office.

de facto   In practice although not officially stated.

default   Not being able to pay back loan.

deferential   Accepting the leadership of social superiors.

deficit   Government spends more in a given year than it takes in.

deflation   Overall decrease in prices, opposite of inflation.

deindustrialization   Decline of heavy industry.

demagogue   Manipulative politician who wins votes through impossible promises.

democracy   Political system of mass participation, competitive elections, and human and civil rights.

demography   Study of population growth.

denazification   Purging Nazi officials from public life.

département   Department; French first-order civil division, equivalent to British county.

dependency theory   Radical theory that rich countries keep poor countries poor by siphoning off their wealth.

deputy   Member of French and many other parliaments.

deregulation   Cutting governmental rules on industry.

desiccation   Drying out.

deutsche Mark   German currency from 1948 to 2002.

devalue   To change the worth of a currency downward in relation to other currencies (opposite of *revalue*).

developmentalism   Early 1960s theory that the United States could develop Third World lands.

devolution   Central government turning some powers over to regions.

dialect   Mutually intelligible variety of a language.

Diet   Name of some parliaments, such as Japan's and Finland's.

dignified In Bagehot's terms, symbolic or decorative offices.

diplomatic recognition State announcing official contact with other state.

direct democracy One in which citizens vote on many issues, bypassing elected representatives.

dirigiste Bureaucrats directing industry, closely connected to French *statism*.

discontinuity A break and new direction in the expected course of events.

divide and rule Roman and British imperial ruling method of setting subjects against each other.

division Vote in House of Commons.

Dolchstoss German for "stab in the back."

dominant-party system One in which one party is much stronger than all the others and stays in office for a very long time.

dries In Thatcher's usage, Tories who shared her *neoliberal* vision.

Duma Russia's national parliament.

dynastic cycle (China) Rise, maturity, and fall of an imperial family.

dysanalogy Showing that one example is a poor model for another.

eclectic Drawn from variety of sources.

Ecole Nationale d'Administration (ENA), France's school for top bureaucrats.

efficient In Bagehot's terms, working, political offices.

egalitarian Dedicated to equality.

Eire Republic of Ireland.

ejido Land owned in common by Mexican villages.

electoral franchise Right to vote.

elites Those few people with great influence.

Elysée Presidential palace in Paris, equivalent to U.S. White House.

emigration Moving out of your native country.

Enlightenment Eighteenth-century philosophical movement advocating reason and tolerance.

entitlement Spending programs that citizens are automatically entitled to, such as Social Security.

entrepreneurial Starting your own business.

Establishment Term used half in jest, supposed monopoly of the clubby social elite in British politics.

Estates-General Old, unused French parliament.

ethnicity Cultural characteristics differentiating one group from another.

euro (symbol: €) Currency for most of West Europe since 2002; in 2008 €1 = $1.55.

Eurocommunism Move in 1970s by Italian Communists away from Stalinism and toward democracy.

European Central Bank Supervises interest rates, money supply, and inflation in the euro area.

European Union (EU), federation of most West European states; began in 1957 as the *Common Market*.

Euroenthusiast Likes the EU and wishes to strengthen it.

Euroskeptic Does not wish to strengthen the EU at the expense of national sovereignty.

Events of May Euphemism for riots and upheaval of May 1968 in France.

excess liquidity Too much money floating around.

Exchequer Britain's treasury ministry.

exclave Part of country separated from main territory.

exponential growth Keeps growing faster and faster.

extraterritoriality Privilege of Europeans in colonial situations to have separate laws and courts.

extreme multipartism Too many parties in the parliament.

failed state Collapse of sovereignty, essentially no national governing power.

fatwa Ruling by Islamic jurist.

Federal Constitutional Court Germany's top court, equivalent to U.S. Supreme Court.

federalism System in which component areas have considerable autonomy.

Federal Republic of Germany Originally West Germany, now all of Germany.

fertility rate How many children the average woman bears.

feudalism Political system of power dispersed and balanced between king and nobles.

fiefdom Land granted by king to noble in exchange for support.

Fifth Republic French regime devised by de Gaulle, 1958 to present.

Final Solution Nazi program to exterminate Jews.

first-order civil division Main units countries are divided into, such as departments in France.

Five-Year Plans Stalin's forced industrialization of Soviet Union starting in 1928.

flash party One that quickly rises and falls.

flight capital Money owner sends out of country in fear of losing it.

float To allow a currency to find its own level based on supply and demand.

Forbidden City Emperor's walled palace complex in Beijing.

foreign direct investment Foreign firms setting up operations in other countries.

Fourth Republic 1946–1958 French regime.

Four Tigers South Korea, Taiwan, Hong Kong, and Singapore.

FPTP "First past the post"; brief way of saying "single-member districts with plurality win."

francophobe Someone who dislikes France and the French.

Free French De Gaulle's World War II government in exile.

French Revolution 1789 popular ouster of monarchy.

fusion of powers Combination of executive and legislative as in parliamentary systems; opposite of U.S. separation of powers.

gaijin Japanese for foreigner.

Gang of Four Mao's ultraradical helpers, arrested in 1976.

Gastarbeiter "Guest workers"; temporary labor allowed into Germany.

GDP Gross Domestic Product; sum total of goods and services produced in a country in one year.

general election British for nationwide vote for MPs.

generalization Finding of repeated examples and patterns.

general will Rousseau's theory of what whole community wants.

genocide Murder of an entire people.

geomancy Divinely correct positioning of structures.

gensek Russian abbreviation for "general secretary"; powerful CPSU head.

geopolitics Influence of geography on politics and use of geography for strategic ends.

glasnost Gorbachev's policy of media openness.

Gleichschaltung Nazi control of Germany's economy.

globalization World becoming one big capitalist market.

Good Friday agreement 1998 pact to share power in Northern Ireland.

Gosplan Soviet central economic planning agency.

government A particular cabinet, what Americans call "the administration."

grand coalition Coalition of two or more large parties who previously opposed each other.

grande école French for "great school"; elite, specialized institution of higher education.

Grands Corps Top bureaucrats of France.

Great Leap Forward 1958–1960 failed Chinese effort at overnight industrialization.

Greens In Europe, environmentalist parties.

gringo From the Spanish for "gibberish"; foreigner, specifically *norteamericano* (pejorative).

Grundgesetz Basic Law; Germany's constitution.

guanxi Chinese for connections.

guilt Deeply internalized feeling of personal responsibility and moral failure.

Gulag Soviet central prisons administration.

Habsburg Leading Catholic dynasty that once held Austria-Hungary, Spain, Latin America, and Netherlands.

hacienda Large country estate with Spanish owner and Indian serfs.

Hainan Large island province in the very south of China.

hajj Muslim pilgrimage to Mecca.

Han   The core nationality and main people of China.

hard currency   Noninflating, recognized currencies used in international dealings, such as dollars and euros.

heckling   Interrupting a speaker.

hegemony   Being the top or commanding power.

Helsinki Final Act   1975 agreement to make Europe's borders permanent.

heretic   Someone who breaks away from a religion.

Hindi   National language of India.

Hinduism   Chief religion of India; polytheistic and based on Vedic scriptures, rebirth, and caste.

Hindutva   Literally, Hinduness.

Holocaust   Nazi genocide of Europe's Jews during World War II.

home rule   Giving region some autonomy to govern itself.

hooliganism   Violent and destructive behavior.

Huguenots   French Protestants.

human capital   Education, skills, and enthusiasm of nation's work force.

hyperinflation   Very rapid inflation, more than 50 percent a month.

hypermarché   French for "hypermarket"; store that sells everything.

ideal-typical   Distilling social characteristics into one example.

ideology   Belief system to improve society.

immigration   Resettling into new country.

immobilisme   Inability of government to solve big problems.

imperialism   Powerful countries turning other lands into colonies.

import substitution   Policy of excluding foreign goods and producing them domestically; means high tariffs.

indicative planning   (France) Governmental economic research and suggestions for business expansion.

indigenous   Home-grown, rooted in the local soil.

indirect rule   British colonial governance through native hereditary rulers.

Indochina War   First Vietnam war, 1946–1954, between the French and Communist Viet Minh.

infant mortality rate   Number of live newborns who die in their first year, per thousand; the standard measure of a nation's health.

inflation   Systematic rise of almost all prices.

informal economy   Under-the-table transactions to avoid taxes and regulations.

input-output table   Spreadsheet for the economy of an entire nation.

insolvent   Owes more than it owns.

Inspection   Short for General Finance Inspection, very top of French bureaucracy, with powers to investigate all branches.

institution   Established rules and relationships of power.

institutionalize   To make a political relationship permanent.

intendants   French provincial administrators, answerable only to Paris; early version of *prefects*.

intercommunal   Among communities, ethnic groups, or religions.

interested member   MP known to represent interest group.

interest group   Association aimed at getting favorable policies.

interior ministry   In Europe, department in charge of local administration and national police.

Irish Republican Army   Anti-British terrorists who seek unification of all Ireland.

iron triangle   Interlocking of politicians, bureaucrats, and business people to promote flow of funds among them.

Islam   Religion founded by Muhammad.

Islamism   Islam turned into political ideology.

Islamist   Someone who uses Islam in political way.

Jesuit   Society of Jesus; Catholic religious order once especially active in converting Asians.

jihad   Muslim holy war.

jihadi   From *jihad*; Muslim holy warrior.

junior minister   MP with executive responsibilities below that of cabinet rank.

Junker Pronounced "yoon care"; Prussian nobility.

junta Pronounced Spanish-style, "khun-ta"; group that pulls military coup.

jus sanguinis Latin for "right of blood"; citizenship based on descent.

jus soli Latin for "right of soil"; citizenship given to those born in the country.

Kaiser German for Caesar; emperor.

Kashmir Valley near Himalayas contested by India and Pakistan.

kickback Payoff to government official for a contract.

kleptocracy Rule by thieves.

knighthood Lowest rank of nobility, in Britain carries title of "Sir."

Koran Muslim holy book.

Korean War 1950–1953 conflict involving North and South Korean, U.S., and Chinese forces.

kow-tow (China) Literally, head to ground; to prostrate oneself.

Kremlinology Noting personnel changes to analyze Communist regimes.

Kulturkampf Culture struggle, specifically Bismarck's struggle with the Catholic Church.

labor-force rigidities Unwillingness of workers to take or change jobs.

Land (plural *Länder*), Germany's first-order civil division, equivalent to U.S. state.

landlocked Country with no seacoast.

Landtag German state legislature.

Latin America All countries south of the United States.

Law Lords Britain's top judges, members of Lords.

Lebensraum German for "living space" for entire nation.

legitimacy Mass perception that regime's rule is rightful.

Levellers Radicals during English Civil War who argued for equality and "one man, one vote."

liberal European and Latin American for unrestrained capitalism. (Note: approximately opposite of U.S. meaning.)

liberal democracy System that combines tolerance and freedoms (liberalism) with mass participation (democracy).

Liberal Democrats LDP, Japan's dominant party, a catchall.

life peers Distinguished Britons named to House of Lords for their lifetimes only, does not pass on to children.

Lords (Britain) Upper, originally aristocratic house of Parliament; less important than Commons.

lycée French academic high school.

Maastricht 1992 treaty setting up the EU.

machismo Strutting, exaggerated masculinity.

Machtpolitik Power politics.

macroeconomics Big picture of nation's economy, including GDP and its growth, productivity, interest rates, and inflation.

mafia Criminal conspiracy.

Maginot Line Supposedly unbreachable French defenses facing Germany before World War II.

Magna Carta 1215 agreement to preserve rights of English nobles.

maharajah Sanskrit for "great king"; Hindu prince.

Majlis Arabic for assembly; Iran's parliament.

majoritarian Electoral system that encourages dominance of one party in parliament, as in Britain and the United States.

Malthusian View that population growth outstrips food.

Manchu Last imperial dynasty of China, also known as *Qing*; ruled from the seventeenth century to 1911.

Manchukuo Japanese puppet state set up in Manchuria.

Mandarin High civil servant of imperial China.

Mandate of Heaven Old Chinese expression for legitimacy.

Maoism Extreme form of communism, featuring guerrilla warfare and periodic upheavals.

Marseillaise French national anthem.

Marshall Plan Massive U.S. financial aid for European recovery.

Marxist Follower of socialist theories of Karl Marx.

mask   To cover over a problem.

mass   Most of citizenry; everyone who is not *elite*.

mass line   Mao's theory of revolution for China.

Medef   French business association

Meiji   Period starting in 1868 of Japan's rapid modernization.

mercantilism   Theory that nation's wealth is its gold and silver, to be amassed by government controls on economy.

Mercosur   "Southern market"; free-trade area covering southern part of South America.

meritocracy   Advancement based only on intellectual ability.

Mesoamerica   Spanish for Middle America; Southern Mexico and northern central America.

mestizaje   Intermingling of Spanish and Indian.

METI   Japan's powerful Ministry of Economy, Trade, and Industry (formerly MITI).

Metternichian   Contrived conservative system to restore pre-Napoleon European monarchy and stability.

microeconomics   Closeup picture of individual markets, including product design and pricing, efficiency, and costs.

micro-credit   Very small loans to startup businesses.

micro-loan   Small unsecured loan to beginning businesses.

middle class   That of professionals or those paid salaries, typically educated beyond secondary school.

Middle Kingdom   China's traditional name for itself.

middle way   Supposed blend of capitalism and socialism; also called "third way."

Midi   French for "noon"; South of France.

Ming   Han Chinese dynasty between Mongols and Manchus, ruled 1368–1644.

minister   Head of major department (ministry) of government.

Mitbestimmung   German for "codetermination"; union members participating in company decisions.

Mitteleuropa   German for Central Europe.

mixed-member   Electoral system that combines single-member districts with proportional representation.

mixed monarchy   King balanced by nobles.

Modell Deutschland   German economic model.

modernizing tyrant   Dictator who pushes country ahead.

monetarism   Friedman's theory that rate of growth of money supply governs much economic development.

money politics   Lavish use of funds to win elections.

Mongol   Central Asian dynasty, founded by Genghis Khan, that ruled China in the thirteenth and fourteenth centuries.

monocolor   In parliamentary systems, cabinet composed of just one party.

mosque   Muslim house of worship.

MP   Member of Parliament.

Mughal   From *Mongol*; Muslim conquerors of India; formed empire.

mullah   Muslim cleric.

multiculturalism   Preservation of diverse languages and traditions within one country.

multinational   Country composed of several peoples with distinct national feelings.

Muslim   Follower of Islam, also adjective of *Islam*.

Muslim League   Organization demanding separate Muslim Pakistan.

NAFTA   1994 North American Free Trade Agreement among the United States, Canada, and Mexico.

Narodniki   From Russian "people," *narod*; radical populist agitators of the late nineteenth century.

narcotraficante   Drug trafficker.

nation   Cultural element of country; people psychologically bound to one another.

National Assembly   France's parliament.

National Front   French anti-immigrant party.

nationalism   Belief in greatness and unity of one's country and hatred of rule by foreigners.

Nationalist   Chiang Kai-shek's party that unified China in late 1920s, abbreviated KMT.

Naxalites   Maoist guerrilla fighters in India.

near abroad   Non-Russian republics of old Soviet Union.

Neo-cons   Short for neo-conservatives

neo-Gaullist   Chirac's revival of Gaullist party, Rally for the Republic (RPR).

neoliberalism   Revival of free-market economics.

Neolithic   New Stone Age; the beginning of agriculture.

NEP   Lenin's New Economic Policy that allowed private activity, 1921–1928.

New Labour   Tony Blair's name for his very moderate Labour party.

nomenklatura   Lists of sensitive positions and people eligible to fill them, the Soviet elite.

nonaggression pact   Treaty to not attack each other, specifically 1939 treaty between Hitler and Stalin.

nonperforming loan   One that is not being paid back.

Normans   Vikings who settled in and gave their name to Normandy, France.

norte americano   North Americans; U.S. citizens.

North Caucasus   Mountainous region north of Georgia and Azerbaijan; includes Chechnya.

objective   Judged by observable criteria.

old boy   Someone you knew at boarding school.

oligarchy   Rule by a few.

omnipotent   All-powerful.

OPEC   Cartel of oil-rich countries designed to boost petroleum prices.

Open Door   U.S. policy of protecting China.

Opium War   1839–1842 British-Chinese war to enable Britain to sell opium to the Chinese.

opportunist   Unprincipled person out for self.

opposition   In parliamentary systems, parties in parliament that are not in cabinet.

Orangemen   After King William of Orange (symbol of Netherlands royal house), Northern Irish Protestants.

Ossi   Nickname for East German.

Ostpolitik   Literally, "east policy"; Brandt's building relations with East Europe, including East Germany.

Ottoman   Turkish imperial dynasty, fourteenth to twentieth centuries.

output affect   Attachment to system based on its providing material abundance.

overheat   Too-rapid economic growth characterized by inflation, factories at full capacity, and excessive borrowing.

Oxbridge   Slang for Oxford and Cambridge universities.

Palais Bourbon   Paris building of French National Assembly.

Pan-Africanism   Movement to unite all of Africa.

paramilitary   National police force organized and equipped like a light army.

paranoia   Unreasonable suspicion of others, not same as fearful.

parliament   National assembly that considers and passes laws. When capitalized, Britain's legislature, specifically its lower chamber, *Commons*.

Parliamentarians   Supporters of Parliament in English Civil War.

Paris Commune   Takeover of Paris government by citizens during the German siege of 1870–1871.

particularism   Region's sense of its difference.

partition   Dividing a country based on its communities.

party identification   Psychological attachment of voter to particular political party.

party image   Way the electorate perceives a given party.

party list   Party's ranking of its candidates in PR elections; voters pick one list as their ballot.

passé   Outmoded, receded into past.

patrie   French for fatherland.

patronage   Using one's political office to hire supporters.

peerage   British Lord or Lady, higher than *knighthood*.

peg   To fix one currency at an unchanging rate to another.

per capita   GDP divided by population, giving an approximate level of well-being.

periphery   Nation's outlying regions.

perestroika   Russian for "restructuring"; Gorbachev's proposals to reform the Soviet economy.

permanent secretary Highest British civil servant who runs ministry, nominally under a minister.

personalismo Politics by strong, show-off personalities.

peso Spanish for "weight"; Mexico's currency, which fluctuates at around ten U.S. cents.

petit bourgeois Small shopkeeper.

petrostate Country based on oil exports.

pinyin Current system of transliterating Chinese.

plebiscite *Referendum,* mass vote for issue rather than for candidate.

pluralism Autonomous interaction of social groups with each other and government.

pluralistic stagnation Thesis of Beer that interest groups out of control produce policy log jam.

plurality Largest quantity, even if it is less than a majority.

polarized pluralism Sick multiparty system that produces two extremist blocs with little in center.

policy The specific choices government makes.

Politburo "Political bureau"; small, top governing body of most Communist parties.

political culture Values and attitudes of citizens in regard to politics and society.

political generation Theory that age groups are marked by the great events of their young adulthood.

political geography How territory and politics influence each other.

political institution Established and durable relationships of power and authority.

Popular Front Coalition government of all leftist and liberal parties in France and Spain in 1930s.

populist Claims to be for common people and against elites.

pork barrel Government projects that narrowly benefit legislators' constituencies.

portfolio Minister's assigned ministry.

Positivism Philosophy of applying scientific method to social problems and gradually improving society.

postmaterialism Theory that modern culture has moved beyond getting and spending.

power Ability of A to get B to do what A wants.

praetorianism Tendency for military takeovers.

pragmatic Without ideological considerations; based on practicality.

precedent Legal reasoning based on previous cases.

pre-Columbian The Americas before Columbus arrived.

prefect French *préfet;* administrator of department.

prefecture First-order Japanese civil division, like French department.

premier French for prime minister.

president Elected head of state, not necessarily powerful.

president's rule Delhi's ability to take over state governments.

prime minister Chief of government in parliamentary systems.

priísmo Ideology and methods of PRI.

privatistic Tending to purely private and family concerns.

privatization Selling state-owned industry to private interests.

production Making things.

productivity Efficiency with which things are produced.

proletariat Marx's term for class of industrial workers.

proportional representation Electoral system that assigns parliamentary seats in proportion to party vote.

protectionism Keeping out imports with tariffs and regulations in order to aid domestic producers.

protective tariff Tax on imported goods to prevent them from undercutting domestic products.

protest vote Ballot cast against existing regime.

Prussia Powerful North German state, Berlin its capital.

public finances What government takes in, what it spends, and how it makes up the difference.

public school In Britain, private, boarding school, equivalent to U.S. prep school.

purge   Stalin's "cleansing" of suspicious elements by firing squad.

Putonghua   "Common language" of China, now standard; used to be called Mandarin.

Qin   First dynasty to unify China, 221–206 B.C.

Qinghua   China's top technological university, in Beijing.

qualified majority voting   Complex voting procedure in EU Council of Ministers that weighs votes by member countries' population.

quarrels   As used here, important, long-term political issues.

quasi-federal   Halfway federal

Question Hour   Time reserved in British Commons for MPs to question members of the cabinet.

quixotic   From Don Quixote; romantic, unrealistic efforts to achieve mistaken goals.

R & D   Research and development of new technologies.

Raj   From Hindi *rule*; British government of India, 1858–1947.

reactionary   Seeking to go back to old ways, extremely conservative.

Realpolitik   Politics of realism.

recession   Economy going downward.

Rechtsstaat   Literally, state of laws; state based on written rules and rights.

red-brown   Possible combination of Communists and Fascists, brown standing for Hitler's brownshirts.

Red Guards   Radical Maoist youth who disrupted China during *Cultural Revolution*.

redistribution   Taxing better off to help worse off.

referendum   Mass vote on issue rather than on candidates, same as *plebiscite*.

Reform Acts   Series of laws expanding British electoral franchise.

regierungsfähig   German for "able to form a government"; party that has matured and shown itself capable of ruling.

regional nationalism   Particularist and separatist movements in some peripheral areas.

regressive tax   Tax that is lighter on the rich than on the poor.

Reich   German for empire.

Reichstag   Pre-Hitler German parliament; its building now houses *Bundestag*.

reify   From Latin *res*, thing; to take theory as reality.

Reign of Terror   Robespierre's 1793–1794 rule by guillotine.

relative decline   Failing to keep up economically with other nations.

remittance   Money sent home.

reparations   Paying back for war damages.

representative democracy   One in which citizens do not rule directly but through elected and accountable representatives.

republic   Country not headed by monarch. Also civil division of Communist federal systems and now of Russia.

republican   In its original sense, favoring getting rid of monarchy.

Résistance   Underground French anti-German movement of World War II.

revalue   To change the worth of a currency upward in relation to other currencies (opposite of *devalue*).

revisionism   Rethinking of ideology or reinterpretation of history.

revolution   Sudden and complete overthrow of regime.

Rhodes scholarship   Founded by South African millionaire, enables top English-speaking students to attend Oxford.

romanticism   Hearkening to ideal world or mythical past.

Royalists   Supporters of king in English Civil War.

rule of anticipated reactions   Friedrich's theory that politicians plan moves in anticipation of how the public will react.

rump state   Leftover portions of country after dismemberment.

runaway system   Influential people use their powers to amass more power.

rupee   India's currency (symbol Rs). In 2008 Rs42 = $1.

Russification   Making non-Russian nationalities learn Russian.

safe seat   Constituency where voting has long favored given party.

Sahel   Narrow band South of Sahara, arid but not yet desert.

satyagraha   Nonviolent protest.

Savanna   Tropical grasslands south of *Sahel*.

scandal   Corrupt practice publicized by news media.

Schengen   1990 treaty ending passport controls in most of west Europe.

seat   Membership in legislature.

secular   Long-term, irreversible trends; also nonreligious.

secularism   In India, treating members of all religions equally.

secularization   Cutting back role of religion in government and daily life.

select committee   Specialized committee of Commons focusing on a ministry.

semipresidential   System with features of both presidential and parliamentary systems.

sepoy   Indian soldier in the British Indian Army.

sexenio   From *seis años*; six-year term of Mexico's presidents.

shame   Feeling of incorrect behavior and violation of group norms.

shah   Persian for king.

sharia   Muslim religious law.

Shia   Minority branch of Islam.

Shinto   Japan's original religion; the worship of nature, of one's ancestors, and of Japan.

shock therapy   Sudden replacement of socialist economy with free-market one.

shogun   Feudal Japanese military chief who ruled in name of emperor.

Sikh   Sixteenth-century offshoot of Hinduism, a minority religion in India concentrated in Punjab; males wear turbans.

siloviki   "Strong men"; security officials who now control Russia.

single-member district   Sends one representative to parliament.

skinheads   Racist youth group, begun in England, with shaved heads and quasi-military attire.

Slavophiles   Nineteenth-century Russians who wished to develop Russia along native, non-Western lines.

sleaze factor   Public perception of politicians on the take.

snap election   One called on short notice, ahead of schedule.

social   European for welfare state ("liberal" in U.S. terms).

social class   Layer or section of population of similar income and status.

social costs   Taxes for medical, unemployment, and pension benefits.

socialize   To teach political culture, often informally.

social mobility   Movement of individuals from one class to another, usually upward.

soft landing   Gradual calming of destabilizing economic shifts.

soft money   In U.S. politics, funds given to parties and other groups rather than to candidates in order to skirt restrictions.

Solidarity   Huge Polish labor union that ousted Communist regime in 1989.

South America   Continent south of Panama.

sovereignty   Last word in law in a given territory; boss on your own turf.

Sozialmarkt   "Social market"; Germany's postwar capitalism aimed at reconstruction and welfare floor.

SPD   German Social Democratic party.

Special Economic Zones   Areas originally on China's southern coast where capitalist economic development was encouraged.

sphere of influence   Semicolonial area under control of major power.

stalemate   Politically stuck among competing groups.

Stalinist   Brutal central control over Communist party.

state   Institutional or governmental element of country.

state-owned enterprises   Firms owned by Chinese government.

State Duma   Lower house of Russia's parliament.

state of nature   Humans before civilization.

statism Idea that strong government should run major industries.

statute Ordinary law, usually for a specific problem.

steady-state System that preserves itself with little change.

strategic variable Factors you can change that make a big improvement.

structure Institutions of government such as constitution, laws, and branches.

structured access Permanent openness of bureaucracy to interest-group demands.

subcontinent Asia south of the Himalayas (India, Pakistan, and Bangladesh), also called South Asia.

subject Originally, subject of the Crown; now another term for British citizen.

subjective Judged by feeling or intuition.

Sub-Saharan Africa south of Sahara.

subsidiarity Letting smaller government units decide most questions (equivalent to U.S. Tenth Amendment, "reserved to the states").

subsidy Government financial help to private individual or business.

sultanate Muslim state governed by a *sultan* (holder of power).

Sunni Mainstream branch of Islam.

supranational Organizations that group together several countries; literally, "above national."

sustainable Can keep going for many years with no major downturns.

swaraj *swa* = self, *raj* = rule; Indian independence.

swing Those voters who change party from one election to the next.

symbol Political artifact that stirs mass emotions.

system affect Attachment to system for its own sake.

system change Displacement of one set of political institutions by another.

Taiping Major religion-based rebellion in nineteenth-century China.

Taiwan Large island off China's southern coast, ruled by Nationalists since 1945.

Tatar Mongol-origin tribes who ruled Russia for centuries.

technocrat Official, usually unelected, who governs by virtue of economic and financial skills.

Thatcherite Free-market, anti-welfarist ideology of former British Prime Minister Margaret Thatcher.

theocracy Rule by priests.

theory Firm generalizations supported by evidence.

Thermidor Month when Robespierre fell, calming down after revolutionary high.

think tank Research organization that analyzes problems and advocates policies.

Third Estate Largest chamber of *Estates-General*, representing commoners.

Third Republic France's democratic regime from 1871 to 1940.

Third World Most of Asia, Africa, and Latin America.

Thirty Years War 1618–1648 Habsburg attempt to conquer and Catholicize Europe.

threshold clause Minimum percent party must win to gain any seats.

Tiananmen Literally, "Gate of Heavenly Peace"; main square in central Beijing, site of 1989 massacre.

Tibet Himalayan region of China with distinct language and culture.

Tokugawa Dynasty of *shoguns* who ruled Japan from 1600 to 1868.

Tories Faction of British Parliament that became the Conservative party; now their nickname.

torn country In Huntington's theory, one with a Westernizing elite but traditional masses.

totalitarianism Political system that attempts total control of society, as under Stalin and Hitler.

Trades Union Congress TUC, British labor federation equivalent to U.S. AFL-CIO.

trade surplus Exporting more than you import.

traditional Tory Moderate or centrist Conservative, not follower of Thatcher.

transparency Making public political and economic information.

Treasury British ministry that supervises economic policy and funding of other ministries.

treaty ports   Areas of China coast run by European powers.

Trotskyist   Follower of Marxist but anti-Stalin theories of Leon Trotsky.

Tsar   From "caesar"; Russia's emperor. Sometimes spelled *Czar*.

turnout   Percentage of those eligible who vote in given election.

tutelle   French for tutelage; bureaucratic guidance.

"two-plus" party system   Two big parties and several small ones.

tyrannical   Coercive rule, usually by one person.

Ukraine   From Slavic for "borderland"; region south of Russia, now independent.

underclass   Permanently disadvantaged people.

unilinear   Progressing evenly and always upward.

unimodal   Single-peaked distribution.

unitary   System in which power is centralized in capital and component areas have little or no autonomy.

unit labor costs   What it costs to manufacture same item in different countries.

unit veto   Ability of one component to block laws or changes.

utilitarian   Promotes material payoffs; "useful."

Uygur   Muslim, Turkic-speaking ethnic group bordering ex-Soviet Central Asia; sometimes spelled *Uighur*.

value-added tax   Large, hidden national sales taxes used throughout Europe.

variable   Factor that changes and is related to other factors.

Vatican   Headquarters of Roman Catholic church.

velayat-e faqih   (Iran) "Guardianship of the religious jurist"; theocratic system devised by Khomeini.

Vergangenheitsbewältigung   Literally, "mastery of the past"; coming to grips with Germany's Nazi past.

Versailles   Palace and estate on outskirts of Paris built by Louis XIV.

Versailles Treaty   1919 treaty ending World War I.

Vichy   Nazi puppet regime that ran France during World War II.

volatile   Rises and falls quickly.

Volksgeist   German for "spirit of the people"; has racist connotations.

voluntarism   Belief that human will can change world.

vote of no confidence   Parliamentary vote to oust cabinet.

wage restraint   Unions holding back on compensation demands.

walking-around money   Relatively small payments by politicians to buy votes.

war communism   Temporary strict socialism in Russia, 1918–1921.

warlord   In 1920s China, general who ran province.

Warring States   China's early period (475–221 B.C.), before unification.

Warsaw Pact   Soviet-led alliance of Communist countries, now defunct.

weak state   One unable to govern effectively; corrupt and crime-ridden.

Weimar Republic   1919–1933 democratic German republic.

welfare state   Political system that redistributes wealth from the rich to the poor, standard in West Europe.

Weltanschauung   German for "world view"; parties offering firm, narrow ideologies.

Wessi   Nickname for West German.

Westernizers   Nineteenth-century Russians who wished to copy the West.

Westphalia   Treaty ending the Thirty Years War.

wets   In Thatcher's usage, Tories too timid to apply her militant neoliberalism.

Westminster   British Parliament building.

whig democracy   Democracy with limited participation, typical of democracy's initial phases.

Whigs   Faction of British Parliament that became Liberal party.

whip   Parliamentary party leader who makes sure members obey party in voting.

Whitehall   Main British government offices.

Wirtschaftswunder   German for "economic miracle."

working class   That of those paid hourly wage, typically less affluent and educated.

World Trade Organization   120-plus members open selves to trade and investment; has quasi-judicial powers.

write off   Lender admits that a *nonperforming loan* will never be repaid.

xenophobia   Fear and hatred of foreigners.

Xinjiang   China's northwesternmost province, home of *Uygurs*.

¥   Western symbol for yen, Japan's currency, and for yuan, China's currency.

yuan   China's currency, worth 14 U.S. cents; officially called *renminbi* (RMB, people's money).

yuppy   Short for "young urban professional."

zemtsvo   Local parliaments in old Russia.

Zhongnanhai   Walled compound for China's top leaders next to the Forbidden City in Beijing.

Zionism   Jewish nationalist movement, founded Israel.

Photo Credits

Index